NEW YORK CITY HISTORY

Bob Swacker

Request for permission to reprint material from this book should be directed to info@disruptionbooks.com.

Distributed by Disruption Books

For ordering information or special discounts for bulk purchases, please contact Disruption Books at info@disruptionbooks.com.

First Edition

ISBN 978-1-63331-024-7

CONTENTS

DUTCH COLONIAL PERIOD 1625-1664

ENGLISH COLONIAL PERIOD (1664-1783)

19TH CENTURY NEW YORK CITY

20TH CENTURY NEW YORK CITY

• Dutch Colonial Period (1625-1664)

CHAPTER ONE
Henry Hudson

Henry Hudson was not looking for land when he sailed to North America. He had read reports and heard stories about land exploration during the century since Columbus' first voyage in 1492 voyage. Hudson was seeking a water passage through the land that would enable ships to pass from the North Atlantic Ocean through North America to the North Pacific Ocean. The elusive route was called the Northwest Passage. Though an Englishman by birth, Hudson was working for the Dutch when he visited our harbor in 1609.

Other explorers had passed through nearly a century earlier. Giovanni da Verrazzano, an Italian seafarer sailing for France, visited the harbor in 1524. A Portuguese captain of African descent, Esteban Gomez, sailing for Spain, entered the harbor and sailed up the river in 1525.

While Hudson's main goal was exploring the large river that he found flowing south into the bay, he explored the harbor area in small boats for ten days. He was impressed with the deep harbor, secondary rivers and coves, the plentiful marine life, and richly forested land. He sailed up what he described as the Great River of the North and also the Great River of the Mountains (Catskill Mountains) for ninety miles, close to where Fort Orange (Albany) was later built, but turned around as the river became increasingly shallow, narrow, and less salty. It was not the trans-oceanic Northwest Passage for which he was searching.

Native people came out to greet the *Half Moon*, Hudson's brightly colored blue, green, white, yellow, and red ship. It was ornamented with a carved red lion on its bow (front) and on its stern (rear) was painted a white half moon on a blue background. Hanging lanterns rocked and flags fluttered everywhere.

The Indians had fresh fruit, meat, tobacco, and pelts of small animals to offer the visitors. Beaver, mink, and otter skins were valuable because Europeans liked hats, coats, and coat collars made of furs. The Indians were willing to trade them to the Dutch for knives, hatchets, and pots and pans. Technologically, the Indians were using stone tools as they did not know how to make metal but found it very desirable for their daily life.

News of Hudson's report set off a wave of excitement in the Netherlands where traders and merchants were eager to enter the fur trade from the region described by Hudson. The beaver became so important to the economy that when the English took over in 1664 they included two beavers on the city seal.

Dutch captain Adriaen Block sailed to the area four times. He stayed on Manhattan for a year between 1613 and 1614 while he and his crew constructed a new ship after his original vessel was destroyed by fire. While here, he thoroughly explored the nearby waterways. He named Long Island, and gave the dangerous passage in the upper East River a colorful name: Hell Gate. Block Island (a part of Rhode Island) is named for him.

Henry Hudson had led two earlier voyages to seek a short cut to Asia. In 1607, sailing in the *Hopewell*, he sought a passage through the North Pole to Japan and China, but turned back somewhere between Svalbard (now Norway) and Novaya Zemalya (now Russia) in the icy Barents Sea. In 1608 he again sailed the Hopewell north and reached Novaya Zemalya before returning. New York City remembers Henry Hudson for the 1609 trip on the *Half Moon* when he explored our harbor and sailed up the Great River to search for the elusive passage to the Pacific.

His last voyage was on the ship *Discovery* in 1610. He departed in April trying a route that went far to the northwest. There he found a broad sea passage (Hudson Strait) and an enormous bay (Hudson Bay) and began exploring it. On November 10th he was in the lower part called James Bay when the *Discovery* was frozen in the water close to shore. Some stayed on the ship and others constructed a primitive longhouse. The crew spent a bitter cold winter there until the ice broke in middle of June 1611.

Hudson had found no river that led west. Had he kept looking he would have discovered that the Arctic Ocean led to the Pacific Ocean. But that would have been impractical because it froze in the winter and contained icebergs in the summer. Hungry and frightened, Hudson's crew mutinied in the bay because they feared staying a second winter while their captain kept searching all summer for the elusive passage. They put Hudson, his son John, the ship's carpenter Philip Staffe, and six other men into a *shallop* (a small open boat with a sail) and left them while the large ship sailed back to Great Britain.

The rest of the story is largely unknown. On the *Discovery's* return trip native people attacked the mutineers while the crew searched for food on land near the mouth of the Hudson Strait. All but nine were killed and others starved to death before reaching Britain. Five years after they returned six were tried for mutiny. They were examined but there are no records to show if they were actually tried, found guilty, and hanged.

What became of Hudson and the other seven in the shallop? The mutineers had given the carpenter his toolbox and provided the group with an iron cooking pot, a sack of wheat flour, and a blunderbuss with some pellets and powder. We can speculate that they died very quickly at sea or that they landed on shore and managed to survive through the summer or for many years.

Henry Hudson, like all the others who tried, failed to find the passage to the Pacific Ocean. Much later, President Theodore Roosevelt, a New Yorker who grew up on East 20th Street in Manhattan, sponsored a project to dig a canal through the narrowest part of the Central American isthmus. The Panama Canal, completed in 1914, accomplished what nature had not provided: a passage between the two great oceans through the Americas.

New Yorkers and other North Americans have honored Henry Hudson in many ways. The Great River of the North (or the Mountains) is called the Hudson River and the roadway along its east side in Manhattan is the Henry Hudson Parkway. The Hudson Line of the Metro-North commuter railroad goes from Grand Central Terminal in Manhattan to Poughkeepsie. There is a 16-foot tall statue of Hudson on top of a 100-foot column in Henry Hudson Park in Spuyten Duyvil (The Bronx), a Hudson Street in Greenwich Village (Manhattan), a Hudson Avenue in Fort Greene (Brooklyn), a Hudson Street in Stapleton (Staten Island), and a Hudson Walk in Breezy Point (Queens). Hudson Bay, the huge body of water in Canada where he was finally set adrift, is named for him.

Notations:

Verrazzano

Giovanni da Verrazzano (1485-1528) was born in Italy but explored for France. In 1524 he led an expedition that navigated along the coast between what is now North Carolina and Cape Breton, Canada. Verrazzano was the first European to record entering New York Harbor. He found the area ***hospitable and attractive*** but did not stay long; in fact he thought the Inner Harbor was a lake and named it Santa Margarita to honor the sister of Francis I, King of France. *La Dauphine*, his ship, anchored in the narrows that separates Brooklyn and Staten Island. Over time, the Narrows was called the Verrazzano Narrows. The Verrazano Narrows Bridge opened in 1964 and the spelling of his name was changed. The Triborough Bridge and Tunnel Authority dropped one z. Robert Moses, chairman of the government agency that owns the suspension bridge, deleted the z to make it easier to pronounce Verrazzano's Italian name. But don't we do just fine pronouncing *pizza*?

Spuyten Duyvil, a Creek and a Neighborhood

Spuyten Duyvil, the neighborhood where the immense statue of Henry Hudson is located, is south of Riverdale in the Bronx. It took its colorful name from a Dutch saying, *spuit den duyvil* (in spite of the devil), which early settlers gave to the narrow body of water with dangerous tides, a strait that connected the Hudson River with the Harlem River. Henry Hudson once sheltered the Half Moon there during a storm. The Spuyten Duyvil Creek twisted and turned until 1895 when engineers dynamited through rock to straighten out the passageway for construction of the Harlem River Ship Canal. Blasting left the northern tip of Manhattan, called Marble Hill because of an old stone quarry, as an island. Within twenty years the old creek at the northern part of Marble Hill was filled in and the neighborhood, still a political part of Manhattan, became geographically attached to the Bronx. The name Spuyten Duyvil was used for the portion of the natural creek that remained as well as for the ship canal. If you live in Marble Hill, you live in Manhattan, though you have to cross the Spuyten Duyvil Creek to get to the rest of it.

CHAPTER 2
Original Inhabitants: Sorting Out the Lenape, Munsee, Delaware, Algonquian

The identity of the American Indians who inhabited the metropolitan area often appears more complicated than it is because a variety of names have been used to refer to the same people. Native Americans in the land that became New York City and its surrounding area were the Lenape, sometimes called Munsee. They spoke a dialect of the Algonquian (Algonkian or Algonquin) language, in which *len* means human and *apé* means person. The Lenape were the same people as the Delaware Indians. The Delaware were Lenape people living to the west in lands on either side of the Delaware River. (Delaware is not an Indian word, but rather a corruption of the name of English baron, Thomas West, Lord de la Warr, who received a royal charter for the colony in 1610.)

Many of the Lenape lived in a region they called *Lenapehoking* (land of the Lenape), which encompassed the coastal region drained by the lower Hudson, Raritan, and Delaware Rivers. Today that would be New York City, Nassau County, southern New York State, New Jersey, eastern Pennsylvania, and eastern Delaware. They were subdivided into three tribes named for their totems, or ancestral emblems: *Minsi* (Wolf), *Unami* (Turtle), and *Unalachto* (Turkey). When the Dutch used the term Munsee, they were referring to the *Minsi* tribe. Tribal subgroups in the Lenape nation had different clan names: *Canarsie* (coastal Brooklyn), *Gowanus* (west Brooklyn), *Sapokanikan* (Greenwich Village), *Raritan* (Staten Island and Perth Amboy), *Rechgawawanches* (Inwood and Riverdale), *Hackensack* (New Jersey side of the Hudson River), *Siwanoy* (Astoria and Flushing), *Maspeth* (western Queens), *Rockaway* (southern Queens), and *Wiechquaesgecks* (northern Manhattan and the Bronx). No matter which term for a tribe or a subgroup was used, they were all Lenape Indians.

Manhattan was not the name of a tribal subgroup, but an Algonquian word adopted by the Dutch for the island where they built New Amsterdam. In earliest maps and records it shows up as *Manhates* or *Manahatta*. It may have meant either island or hunting place.

The Dutch considered the Indians savages or wild men, and some had neither the intellectual curiosity nor sociological inclination to learn very much about them. Johannes Michaelius, the first *dominie* (minister) of the Dutch Reformed Church took a dim view of the Indians. He bellowed that they were *entirely savage and wild, strangers to all decency, yea, uncivil and stupid as garden poles, proficient in all wickedness and godlessness; devilish men who serve nobody but the devil.* The Lenape, were woodland Indians very similar in lifestyle to Native Americans all along the East Coast. The Dutch settlers saw the Lenape as either a means to an end or an impediment to colonization. The Europeans wanted to trade their products with the Indians for furs. If the Indians stood in the way of Dutch money making activities, they would be driven from the area.

Most Dutch colonists wrote only scattered and brief comments in letters and reports about the Indians. Many of the Dutch lacked interest in learning about the Lenape language or culture. In 16th century New Spain (Mexico) and the Caribbean, the Spanish had Bartolomé de las Casas, a Roman Catholic priest with both a conscience and a sense of inquiry, who wrote *The Tears of the Indians*, which contained careful descriptions of the Native Americans and reports on the excesses of the *conquistadors*. The Dutch had no one as well known as de las Casas. Historians are left with much sketchy and biased information about the First Americans of New York City.

There were exceptions. Recent scholarship by Russell Shorto, author of *The Island at the Center of the World*, has shown that some Dutch trappers working independently or for large estates along the upper Hudson River Valley had a good working relationship with the Indians. They learned the Algonquian and Mahican languages and even maintained friendships. But bigotry was the rule, not the exception.

Prejudiced attitudes toward the natives were not limited to

17th century Europeans. At the beginning of his *History of the City of New York*, which was published in 1853, historian David T. Valentine, described New York's first inhabitants. *Their appearance, customs, and manners were so far distinct from those of other nations known to the civilized world, and their individual character had so little in common with the more restrained and law-abiding European, that they were, in the first stages of their acquaintance with the whites, classed by the latter among those wild and lawless races known as savages, who, it was supposed, had few, if any, of the affections and higher emotions of humanity, but rather were bound, by some mysterious link, to the lower and baser passions of the animal creation.*

There are a few things that can be gleaned about the Indians, particularly housing, lineage, division of labor, weapons, food, clothing, travel, trade and *wampum* exchange. Lenape lived in long houses where extended families shared the same hearth and accommodations. Bent saplings covered with tree bark, grasses, and clay provided insulation from the cold. The Lenape bands usually had two homes: a winter campsite in the craggy hills of central Brooklyn, Staten Island, or Queens, or in the northern ridges of Manhattan and the Bronx. Summer campsites were along the coast where seafood and berries were readily available.

The Lenape traced their lineage through their mothers and their clan names (turkey, wolf, turtle) referred to their matrilineal ancestry. There was division of labor according to gender, which was not so much different from the European pattern, except that the Lenape women did the farming. Hunting was the primary task of the men. Warfare was another important part of a male's life. Many of the skills learned and practiced in hunting were applied to battle. Their weapons included arrows, spears, hatchets, knives, and clubs.

Food was gathered, hunted, and fished, but rarely planted. The Indians collected and ate oysters, clams, scallops, mussels, whelk, crabs, and lobsters. Shellfish could be plucked from the water by hand, an easy task usually given to children. The proof of the Lenape's enormous shellfish consumption is found at shell dumping sites near their settlements. It is difficult to know what kind of fish they caught, but sturgeon, striped bass, shad, herring, and eel were found in great quantities in the harbor and rivers.

Whales, porpoises, and seals also filled the waterways. Gathering wild fruit, berries, nuts, roots, and leaves was a summer activity. The area was rich in apples, cherries, and pears. Deer, rabbit, and squirrels were hunted for meat and their skins used for winter clothing. There is scant evidence that the *Three Sisters* (corn, beans, and squash) were extensively cultivated.

Giovanni da Verrazzano, who sailed into the harbor in 1524, a century before the Dutch founded New Amsterdam, wrote a clear description of Lenape clothing. Verrazzano wrote that the Indians were *dressed out with the feathers of birds of various colors.* He described two men he thought to be *kings,* who came aboard the *Dauphine,* his ship flying under the flag of France: *The oldest had a deer's skin around his body, artificially wrought in damask figures, his head was without covering, his hair was tied back in various knots; around his neck he wore a large chain ornamented with many stones of different colors. The young man was similar in his general appearance.* Henry Hudson, who sailed through the waterways in the *Half Moon* mapping the area in 1609, described them similarly: *They are clothed in mantles of feathers and robes of fur, the women clothed in hemp, red copper tobacco pipes, and other things of copper they did wear about their necks.* Bear grease was a valued cosmetic to keep away mosquitoes in the summer and prevent chapping in the winter.

Without draft animals, Lenape travel was limited to walking and canoeing. Their dug-out canoes were made by charring and scraping the interior of large logs. While labor intensive, it produced sturdy boats to ply the waterways. They traded with other coastal tribes and, by their own efforts and through intermediaries, with the Mohawk, Mahican, and Pequot.

The Indians periodically used *wampum* as a medium of exchange. White wampum was tube-shaped beads made from the center of a whelk shell. Purple wampum was from the purple spots on *quahogs* (hard-shell clams). Purple wampum was more valuable because it was less abundant in nature. Wampum beads were strung on individual strings of animal sinew (tendons) or embedded in belts, often in a design. The Indians did not use wampum as currency in itself, but as a good-faith accompaniment to a trade. Europeans traded in wampum and used it as an alternate currency in the 17th century.

The Lenape were in large part a Neolithic (Stone Age) people who were almost completely limited to stone tools and were enormously impressed with iron and steel objects, especially knives, axes, hoes, and cooking pots. They were also willing to trade items they had for woolen blankets, cotton cloth, and the trinkets and gewgaws (colorful ribbons, beads, buttons, clips), which the Dutch brought for trade. They desired Dutch guns. Some Indians quickly developed an insatiable appetite for alcohol, which Native Americans had never produced. The clash of two cultures was disastrous for the Indians who lost their land to the Europeans and lacked the technology to fight back successfully. The Dutch broke all bi-lateral peace treaties. It seemed the Dutch colonists held all the cards and the Lenape none of them.

Disease and warfare annihilated the Lenape. Measles, influenza, typhus, diphtheria, bubonic plague, and smallpox were European diseases for which the Indians lacked antibodies. The Dutch in New Amsterdam believed that the affliction, which ravaged the Indians was the Hand of God reaching out to help them colonize North America. Warfare was a calamity for the Lenape. Between 1643 and 1645, the period called Kieft's War, when the most violent armed clashes occurred; at least sixteen hundred Lenape were killed.

The diaspora (dispersal) of the Indians was almost finished within one generation. By 1664 when the English captured the Dutch colony, the territory of the five boroughs was in the hands of Europeans. The English alliance with the Iroquois pitted both groups against the last remnants of the coastal Algonquian-speaking Indians. Most fled far to the west to escape the English and their Iroquois allies. (Those who fled eastward were folded into the Shinnecock and Matinecock tribes of Long Island.)

Lenape settled in several places on their way to the Great Plains, Northern Wisconsin, and Canada. By the time they stopped migrating, most of the Lenape bands had merged with other tribes. Except for Monsey, New York, most of the villages and towns which took their names from the Lenape-Munsee-Delaware Indian nation are far to the west: Muncy, Pennsylvania; Delaware, Ohio; Muncie, Indiana; Muncie, Illinois; Lenapah, Oklahoma; Munceytown, Ontario. There is nothing in New York City named for the

Lenape, only a few of their tribal sub-groups.

Most Lenape have lost their separate cultural identity, though some of their descendants are presently identifiable living in Oklahoma, Wisconsin, and Ontario. A few dwell among the Shawnee and Miami tribes in Oklahoma, and as the Stockbridge Munsee with the Oneida in Stockbridge, Wisconsin, and as the Moraviantown band of Munsee close to Thamesville, Ontario, and as the Munsee Delaware Nation in Munsey, Ontario.

By tradition, the last Lenape in New York City was Jim de Wilt who died in 1803 in Canarsie, Brooklyn. (The name *de Wilt* means wild in Dutch.) By then, the other Lenapes had succumbed to disease or fled the area.

CHAPTER 3
Dutch West India Company

The reason the Dutch came to the New World was to prey on Spanish shipping, earn a place for their United Provinces of the Netherlands as a European superpower, and make a handsome profit exploiting the resources of the land and sea. To that end they organized joint-stock companies that would explore, plant colonies, administer order, and exploit whatever resources were discovered. The companies were subsidized by the United Provinces, a confederation of seven states with some characteristics of a republic. The subsidies came in the form of financial, legal, and military backing for the companies.

When Henry Hudson explored the area in 1609 he did so under the authority of the Dutch *East* India Company, which is the company that handled trade with Java (in Indonesia), Goa (in India), Japan, and China. Hudson was sent to find a passage through North America so the Dutch company could more easily reach its trading partners and colonies in the Eastern Hemisphere. That quest failed to turn up a passageway and the Dutch realized they needed to organize a new company for the Western Hemisphere.

Between 1614 and 1617 the United New Netherland Company, was chartered to explore and settle the North American coast between the Connecticut River and the Delaware River. The company staffed a small trading post far up the Hudson River at a place they called Fort Orange (Albany) but no settlements were attempted.

The States-General organized the Dutch West India Company in 1621. The States-General was the representative assembly of the seven sovereign states composing the United Provinces. Ultimately the company controlled several colonies: Curaçao, Bonaire, Aruba, St. Maarten, Dutch Guiana (Suriname), Bahia (northeast Brazil), and New Netherland. The Dutch West India Company had been the brainchild of William Usselincx, a merchant from Antwerp, who had fled north to Holland to escape religious persecution from the Spanish who controlled Antwerp and the surrounding area. Usselincx was a Protestant and the Spanish were Roman Catholics. At the time, religion was a great motivator in politics and commerce.

During the 16th and 17th centuries Europe was torn by religious wars, and national or dynastic wars, which had religious components. Spain possessed the entire Netherlands until the seven predominantly Protestant northern provinces formed the Union of Utrecht in 1579 and declared their independence from Spain in 1581. Warfare between the United Provinces and Spain continued for the next three decades. During that time Spain lashed out aggressively against Protestant England in 1588 with the unsuccessful Spanish Armada (*armada católica*).

In 1609 a truce was called between the United Provinces and Spain. The Spanish kept the ten southern provinces including the cities of Antwerp, Brussels, and Ghent, but the seven northern provinces including the cities of Amsterdam, Utrecht, and the Hague remained independent. Most of the Protestant minority in the south fled to the north leaving the Spanish Netherlands (Belgium since 1830) increasingly Catholic while the north became increasingly Protestant.

Many of the investors in the Dutch West India Company, like William Usselinx, were refugees from the southern ten provinces. Likewise, most of the thirty families to initially settle New Amsterdam were Protestant Walloons from the Spanish Netherlands. (Walloons came from the southern French-speaking part of the Spanish Netherlands. The Dutch-speaking people from the north of the Spanish Netherlands were known as Flemish.)

It was under the aegis of the Dutch West India Company that its first director-general, or governor-general, Cornelius Jacobsen Mey (1624-1625) landed a party of settlers on Governors Island in 1624. The Algonquian-speaking Lenape Indians called the island *Pagganck*. The Dutch named it *Nooten Eylandt* because of the presence of nut trees, presumably chestnuts and acorns. Sometime after the English capture of New Netherland in 1664, the name was Anglicized to *Nutten* Island and following the American Revolution it was called Governors Island.

In 1624 the little island in the inner bay served as a safe place to reconnoiter while the pioneers prepared to establish a permanent settlement in Manhattan. They moved to the southern tip of Manhattan in 1625 and built a village, which they named New Amsterdam.

The Dutch West India Company made most of its profit from frequent European wars, or to be more precise, government sanctioned piracy. The Spanish had expropriated enormous amounts of gold and silver from the Aztecs and Incas, and continued to operate Native American mines. Their mining operation at Potosí (in today's Bolivia) was the richest source of silver in the world, producing more than half of the global output in 1600. (The population of Potosí in 1600 was 160,000, roughly the size of London or Paris.) Dutch West India Company ships preyed on Spanish galleons hauling their treasures home. They also robbed the Spanish of slaves and plantation products.

Little money was made from the New Netherland colony because the costs of administering and garrisoning were large compared with the output of the small number of settlers attracted to life in the New World. Some income did accrue from the fur trade, production of naval stores (especially masts for ships), and fishing. The Dutch may be credited, however, with choosing a particularly attractive and ultimately lucrative location to build a town.

CHAPTER 4
First European Settlers on Governors Island

The Dutch desired to settle on the island of Manhattan though they made a temporary settlement on one of the harbor's three small islands for the first year. The island is just a half-mile off the coast of Manhattan's southern tip. It attracted the first wave of Dutch and Walloon settlers in 1624 because it offered natural protection from the Indians and was a safe place for their cattle and other livestock to graze. It served as a secure headquarters while they prepared to establish a permanent settlement in Manhattan.

The island is actually closer by half to Brooklyn than Manhattan. The Red Hook section of Brooklyn lies just across the narrow Buttermilk Channel from Governors Island. In 1698, during the English period, the provincial assembly set the island aside for the use of the royal governors while the colonial capital was in New York City. Lord Cornbury, an English governor, completed a Georgian-style mansion on the island in 1708.

The Dutch settlers in 1624 were people from the United Provinces, or the Dutch Republic, of which Holland was a province. The country is now known as the Netherlands. Walloons were not Dutch, they were French-speaking people from Walloonia, provinces now in southern Belgium. The Walloons who came to *Nooten Eylandt* were Protestants living in the Spanish Netherlands, a territory of Spain, which was a Roman Catholic country. Some Walloons relocated to the Dutch Republic where the majority of people were Protestants. Possessing no land, a few ambitious Walloon families were willing to face the dangers of ocean travel and uncertainties in the New World to become settlers.

Of the thirty-two families who arrived on Nooten Eylandt in May 1624, most were Walloons. In fact, the first provincial seal of New Netherland was a crown over a shield bearing a beaver, encircled with the Latin words *Sigilum Novi Belgii* (Seal of New

Belgium). There is a stone shaft in the northeast corner of the Battery in Manhattan honoring the Walloon settlers. The monument was presented to the City of New York by the Belgian government in 1924, which was the 300th anniversary of the landing of the Walloon settlers. Very little is known about the first families who came to New Amsterdam. None became prominent and they were quickly joined and vastly outnumbered by other settlers from the Netherlands and elsewhere.

New Netherland was not a political colony *per se*, but a company colony protected by the Dutch military. The corporation was the Dutch West India Company, which had existed since 1614, a decade before it sent settlers to permanently occupy its lands. Governors of New Netherland were really directors-general (or governors-general) of the Dutch West India Company. There were seven such governors before the English captured New Netherland in 1664 and renamed it New York.

In 1625 the colonists left Nutten Island for Manhattan and established the town of New Amsterdam. Land ownership was an unknown concept to the Lenape Indians, but the Dutch hurriedly *bought* all the surrounding land in Manhattan and beyond from the Indians. To the Dutch such property transactions were legal and permanent.

Governors Island, the first place the Dutch purchased from the Lenape, went on to have a colorful military history beginning during the American Revolution. After the American loss at the Battle of Long Island (in Brooklyn) in 1776, Governors Island was held briefly by the troops of General Israel Putnam. British Admiral Richard Howe soon recaptured the island for the British. When the British evacuated in 1783 New York State resumed ownership. The New York State Legislature turned the island over to the federal government in 1800. State and federal officials cooperated in building two major defenses on the island. Fort Jay and Castle Williams were quickly constructed as part of a series of fortifications to protect New York Harbor. Though war with Great Britain commenced in 1812, New York Harbor was not attacked. Over the years, Governors Island served as a recruitment center, an administrative headquarters, and a prison for Confederate officers during the Civil War.

Beginning in 1901, landfill from the Interboro Rapid Transit (IRT) excavations was dumped off the southern end of the island. Rock and sand from the Brooklyn-Battery Tunnel (1940-1950) was also deposited at the southern rim of the island. (The tunnel's large octagonal ventilator was built just off the island's north end.) The landfill nearly doubled the island's size, from 90 acres to 172 acres. In 1909, aviator Wilbur Wright used the level, treeless southern end of Governors Island to take off on the first flight over water, a brief trip which included a loop around the Statue of Liberty and ended with a safe landing at the edge of Riverside Park near Grant's Tomb.

Governors Island continued to be used for a variety of military purposes. During the First World War it was a supply depot for soldiers sailing for Europe, a pilot training center, and a coastal defense center. The United States Army used it for a regional headquarters during the Second World War. The most recent military tenant was the United States Coast Guard, which received the island from the United States Army in 1966 and used it for its east coast regional headquarters. At its height, 3,500 Coast Guard personnel and dependents lived on Governors Island. As a cost-cutting measure, the Coast Guard withdrew in 1997 leaving the pear-shaped island uninhabited. Governors Island had been the oldest continuously functioning United States military installation.

Even before the Coast Guard vacated, President Bill Clinton offered to sell the island back to New York City for $1 in 1995 if the city and state came up with a land-use plan, which included public access. (The island had never actually belonged to the city.) Nothing happened until President George W. Bush reiterated the offer in 2002. Governor George Pataki and Mayor Michael Bloomberg accepted the 2002 offer. They suggested a new City University of New York (C.U.N.Y.) campus specializing in teacher training and the sciences. Ample dormitory space, classrooms, and some laboratories already exist. At the end of January 2003, a $1 check was written by the State of New York to the United States Government and after 203 years Governors Island passed back to state ownership. A twelve member Governors Island Preservation and Education Corporation was appointed, six by the governor and six by the mayor, to manage most of the island. The north portion of the island, which is designated a National Historic Landmark, twenty-two acres encompassing Fort Jay, Castle Williams, and seven houses, will remain under the oversight of the National Parks Service. In 2012 a creative plan for a mixture of historical, cultural, and recreational space was approved for the southern part of Governors Island. It opened to the public in 2014.

Notation:

Directors-General of the Dutch West India Company

Cornelius Jacobsen Mey............................1624-1625
William Verhulst...1625-1626
Peter Minuit..1626-1632
Sebastian Jansen Krol.................................1632-1633
Wouter van Twiller.....................................1633-1638
William Kieft... 1638-1647
Peter Stuyvesant...1647-1664

CHAPTER 5
Buying Manhattan: Two Concepts of Property

Europeans and Native Americans had very different views of their relationship with the land. Europeans came from countries where individuals could own land, whether or not they used it. Many European noblemen and urban businessmen were absentee landlords. The Indians had a concept of possession, but not ownership. Free use of the land was a cherished economic principle to the woodland Indians. They believed that individuals, families, and tribes could possess land while they used it for hunting, gathering, fishing, farming, and building villages. Indian religious beliefs stressed stewardship of the land, and treated landforms as important spiritual entities, removed from possible private appropriation by individuals. If they left the land to migrate elsewhere, newcomers were free to occupy it.

In 1625, Dutch colonists left their temporary quarters on Nutten Island (Governors Island) for Manhattan and began building the town of New Amsterdam. Soon after, the colonists began *buying* land from the Lenape tribes. In 1626, Governor-General Peter Minuit *bought* Manhattan Island from some *sachems* (chiefs). Presumably the sachems represented at least one Lenape band, and received 60 guilders ($24) worth of beads, cloth, and trinkets. (Shorakopock Rock in Inwood Hill Park, in the northwest corner of Manhattan, is the legendary site of the famous real estate deception.) Subsequent governors and individual colonists bought land from the Indians in surrounding areas.

Staten Island was *bought* by Dutch *patroon* Michael Paauw from local Lenapes in 1630 during the governorship of Peter Minuit for a treasure chest of kettles, axes, hoes, and awls. He never succeeded in establishing his patroonship (estate). In fact, between 1630 and 1661 the Dutch bought Staten Island five different times. Dutch Governor-General Wouter van Twiller, had bought Governors Island from the Indians in 1637 for some axes, nails, and colored beads. He also bought Randall's Island, Ward's Island, and Roosevelt Island in the East River. He purchased two hundred acres from the Sapokanikan band of Lenapes in the southwest part of what later became Greenwich Village to build a Dutch West India Company tobacco farm. (A colorful mosaic in the Christopher Street Subway Station features Wouter van Twiller. It distorts the truth and paints a rosy picture of Dutch-Indian real estate deals by describing van Twiller simply as a *land developer*.)

The idea of buying and selling land was an example of a serious culture clash between the two sides. Ownership of land was an unknown concept to the Lenape Indians. Adriaen Van der Donck, general agent and *schout* (sheriff and public prosecutor) for the wealthy Dutch patroon Kiliaen Van Rensselaer, wrote in *A Description of New Netherland*, that *wind, stream, bush, field, sea, beach, and riverside are open to everyone of every nation with which the Indians are not embroiled in open conflict.* To the Europeans the ownership of land mattered enormously. They would not invest time, effort, and capital into developing farms, houses, and businesses on land they did not own.

In addition, the Europeans had no respect for the subsistence agriculture practiced by the Indians. To them it seemed the Indians constituted a lower order of civilization (they were usually referred to as *savages*) and were not capable of fully using and exploiting the land. The Europeans believed the Bible supported their position. Genesis I:26 reads: *And God said, Let us make man in our image, after our likeness: and let them have dominion over the fish of the sea, and over the fowl of the air, and over the cattle, and over all the earth, and over every creeping thing that creepeth upon the Earth.* The European model for agriculture was the intense cultivation of farmland in Netherland, Spanish Netherland (Belgium), France, and England.

To add to the confusion, neither side could understand the other's language. The Lenape may have understood the Dutch payments as gifts. Regardless of Indian ignorance of European property law, and Dutch ignorance of Lenape land custom, the sales were legal and permanent as far as the Dutch were concerned.

Land ownership was not settled by sales, which the Indians

did not accept. Lenape bands launched raids against the settlers to persuade them to leave. The retaliatory assaults by the Dutch, who possessed guns, caused many Indians to flee. But the greatest ally for the Europeans was their disease pool from which most Indians had little immunity. They died by the thousands and by the end of the 17th century their deaths left all the land in the hands of the Europeans.

Notation:

European Concepts of Property:

While it is now generally understood that Native Americans did not buy and sell land, including the Algonquian-speaking Lenape Indians in New York, land ownership among Europeans is not so well understood. Some, perhaps all, early European societies did not initially recognize individual land ownership. Customs varied considerably throughout European history, but at an early point in some regions, and a much later time in other places, European concepts of land ownership, stewardship of the land, and the mystique of forests and waterways may not have been so different from what the Dutch encountered among the Lenape Indians.

The Greeks practiced individual property ownership and the Romans carried the notion that an individual could buy and sell land with people anywhere in the European continent. The Germanic and Slavic tribes, initially forest hunters and plains herders, viewed land as beyond individual ownership.

The Germanic concept of land ownership differed radically from that established by Roman law. Germanic agriculture, first described by Roman writer Tacitus, allowed for temporary possession for individual use without bestowing permanent property rights. Roman law treated forests, fields, rivers, and lakes as capital, which could be fully owned and exploited, but the Germanic concept held that all land was *sacred ground* to the nation as a whole. The Germanic concept of land ownership extended over forests, rivers, lakes, and for an unknown period of time, farmland.

Franz Heske, a forest expert and historian, described how early Germans could use land individually although it could not be *the object of arbitrary action by an individual.* He offered a Romantic explanation for *Gemeinschaft* (community) applied to the land. *The whole race conquered it; the whole race defended it with its life-blood; and the whole race stood back of the peasant and enabled him to till the soil in peace.* Heske drove home the point with regard to the woodlands. *The forest owner, like every other owner of German soil, is only a trustee for the people.*

Common land ownership was also the economic basis for Slavic social structure. Because Russian and Eastern European forests were vast and no labor was appropriated to them, they were used by nearby villagers though ownership was theoretically vested in the whole people and control that was usually exercised by the nobility.

German historian August Freiherr von Haxthausen, documenting his extensive travels through Russia in 1843, found that the family and common land ownership were the basis for Slavic social structure. *The forests and pasture land always remain undivided.* Haxthausen observed that it was neither the family nor the village which held forests and untilled land but *the entire nation,* with the tsar acting as steward.

This practice of holding cultivated land in common and viewing forest land as belonging to the whole people prompted 20th century Russian philosopher Nikolai Berdyaev to characterize Russians as still possessing a unique ***community spirit***. Berdyaev wrote: *If the word socialism is not taken in its doctrinaire sense, one might say that socialism is deeply rooted in the Russian nature. There is already an expression of this truth in the fact that the Russian people did not recognize the Roman conception of property.*

Forests and the mysterious atmosphere they evoke have been central to the mystique of Russia from earliest times. Pre-Christian animists believed in the supernatural power of wood sprites and honored them as they also propitiated river, lake, and home sprites. Olga Semyonova Tian-Shanskaia, an ethnographer at the turn of the 20th century, saw tree sprites as part of a pre-Christian pantheon of forces including spirits of the earth, water, house, barn, and even steam bath. Historian George Vernadsky documented the worship of trees in the Kievan period. He explained how some practices continued until the last century. *After Russia's conversion to Christianity tree worship was forbidden by the clergy but the habit of decorating trees at the time of folk festivals held in the woods was kept in some remote parts of Russia even as late as the nineteenth century.* Anthropologist and religious writer Sonia E. Howe's research showed that in the later pre-Christian period when early Russians added anthropomorphic gods to their religious world, Perun, associated with thunder and lightning, was worshipped *in the forests under gigantic oaks, where nature rules supreme, and where the trunks of the trees form the pillars of temples not made with hands.*

Some of the customs surrounding land and ideas about religion, which were held by the Lenape had once been embraced by at least some of the Europeans. Neither side knew the customs of the other, and if they had, it probably would have had no impact on their separate worldviews. This was a conflict bound to end disastrously for the Native Americans.

CHAPTER 6
Fur Trade

Henry Hudson explored New York Harbor and surrounding waterways in 1609, and reported that the area was rich in fur-bearing animals. Within a year, Dutch merchants sailed across the Atlantic Ocean and began trading with the Indians in order to bring the valuable furs back to Amsterdam. Once the Dutch West India Company organized the commercial colony of New Netherland and sent thirty families who started New Amsterdam on Manhattan Island in 1625, the fur trade was well under way. The next year ships were taking thousands of pelts back to Europe on each voyage.

For the Dutch the fur trade was a source of quick profits with the Indians doing most of the work. Indians hunted and trapped near the tributary streams flowing into the Hudson and Delaware Rivers. Some of the trade was direct between the Dutch and the inland Indians, but the coastal Indians often served as middlemen for the furs or a source of wampum.

What did the trade entail? The Native Americans had little the Europeans wanted except pelts of small animals. Beaver, otter, mink, and muskrat skins were worth a great deal to the European traders because of the demand at home for soft, fashionable, warm winter clothing. The Dutch would barter metal products, glazed pottery, combs, ribbons, buttons, glass beads, cloth, and liquor to coastal Indians for wampum, and then trade wampum with Indians further up the rivers for animal pelts. Wampum was also used among the Dutch in New Netherland and the English in New England as legal tender (money) along with Dutch guilders and English sterling. Eventually most of the fur trade was direct between upstream Indians and the Dutch and wampum became less important.

The Native American lifestyle was rapidly changed by the introduction of so many new products in such a short time. Old skills of weaving, handicrafts, farming, fishing, and hunting were devalued while trade and trapping became prestigious and lucrative occupations. The strong effect of alcohol on Indians was disastrous. Contact with Europeans also introduced numerous fatal diseases to the Indians, especially smallpox, from which they had little natural immunity. Within fifty years fewer than ten percent of the area's original inhabitants survived.

Before the east coast of North America was opened for animal pelt exports to Western Europe their chief source had been Russia. The growing American trade soon gained dominance. Beavers led all others in the number killed and turned into furs, but large numbers of otter, mink, and muskrat were also hunted. A much smaller number of wildcat, deer, and bear ended up as clothing in Europe.

Beavers are large rodents who are energetic woodland builders. They gnaw at trees, toppling them into streams and build dams to create small shallow lakes. Beavers make their wood-mound island homes in the lakes out of logs, sticks, and mud. For safety, the entrance is always under water. The colonists wanted the beavers because their thick, smooth furs could be fashioned into hats, coats, coat collars, stoles, scarves, robes, and blankets. Beaver oil was sold as an ointment cure for all sorts of illnesses.

The beaver became so important to the colonial economy that the Dutch included the beaver on their city seal. When the English took over in 1664 they also included two beavers on their newly designed city seal. Four of the five boroughs have streets named for the Beaver: Beaver Street in Manhattan's financial district; Beaver Road in Jamaica, Queens; Beaver Street in Bushwick, Brooklyn; and Beaver Street in Charleston, Staten Island. The Astor Place Station on the I.R.T. subway (#6 local train) has colorful decorative glazed tile emblem panels of beavers. Each portrays the animal standing on its hind legs gnawing on a tree. The subway station beavers are a testament to the importance of the beaver skin trade and an indication for Astor Place, named for the wealthiest fur trader in New York's history, John Jacob Astor.

By 1793, Astor, a recent German immigrant, had made a fortune from furs. He became the city's first millionaire. But the fur pelts were no longer from upstate New York; they came from the Great Lakes region, Rocky Mountains, Pacific Northwest, and

Canada. The eastern sources of furs had been completely depleted. Nonetheless, the Erie Canal, which opened in 1825, made it easier for New York City fur dealers to obtain furs from western sources and stay in business.

The fur trade was not always stable. There were some interruptions in the local beaver trade caused by wars, devalued wampum, hostility of the Iroquois, periodic changes in European fashion during times when people cared less about fur, and finally the relentless hunting of the beaver which led to its effective extinction in upstate New York in the 19th century. (Beavers were later successfully reintroduced as a protected species into the ecosystem from the surviving western beaver stock and are now off the protected list.)

Even without a regional source of furs, New York City has remained the capital of the American fur industry. German furriers established the Lower East Side as the fur district in the 1830s. Eastern European Jews from Russia and Poland continued the fur business later in the century. In the 1920s the fur district migrated to the west side of Manhattan, mostly along 7th Avenue between 23rd and 34th Streets. Today the business in dominated by immigrants from Korea and Greece.

Late in the 19th century the fur market became domestic. American fur-bearing animals were being trapped or farm-raised for American customers. By the end of the 20th century the United States imported furs from Asia and South America. In recent years the live fur trade has been hurt by consumer acceptance of synthetic furs and anti-fur sentiment popularized by animal rights activists. A 21st century example of beaver fur as clothing was President George W. Bush's cowboy hat. The $2,500 size 7 1/2 hat was made from beige-dyed beaver skins in 2002 in Colorado. It was decorated with a 14-carat gold buckle.

CHAPTER 7
Fate of the Indians: The Effect of Disease Pools

It is a myth that Europeans discovered and populated an almost empty land in the years after Columbus crossed the Atlantic in 1492. The heroic story of Europeans building cities and farms in the empty wilderness was appealing to the settlers and their descendants. The reality is that the area now constituting the United States was home to at least six million Indians divided into different cultural and linguistic groups. Thousands of Native Americans made their homes in villages in what ultimately became Greater New York. What is true about their differences is that the Indians had a much less sophisticated civilization lacking the technological and writing skills that the Europeans possessed. The Eastern Woodland cultures were the first Native Americans to meet and confront Europeans and so they were the first to be cut down by unfamiliar disease pools.

We can imagine that before the establishment of New Amsterdam in 1625 the first encounters between local Indians and ships bearing explorers, traders, and fishermen from the Netherlands, England, and France must have caused great enthusiasm among the native population. The impressive size of the brightly painted European sailing vessels, the exploding sounds of muskets and cannon, the introduction of metal tools, and the odd appearance of the bearded foreigners must have been striking.

The Native Americans in the land that became New York City and its surrounding area were the Lenape, woodland Indians who spoke a dialect of the Algonquian language. In spite of initial hopefulness, the Indians quickly learned that death and destruction mysteriously accompanied the Europeans. A diabolic host of Old World diseases in several widespread epidemics ravaged the vulnerable Indian population often wiping out entire villages. Viruses and bacteria accompanied trade transactions and spread from person to person in the Lenape communities. Neither Europeans nor Indians understood the medical science behind the phenomenon. Probably ninety percent of the Indians succumbed to the newly introduced illnesses. Those who survived were left weak and frightened.

Measles, influenza, typhus, diphtheria, bubonic plague, and smallpox traveled with the Europeans. They were new diseases in the Western Hemisphere and the Indians had no immunity to the foreign pathogens. The infectious diseases were an unintentional result of the contact between the two cultures.

The Indians were not alone in suffering from smallpox. Europeans and Africans also contracted smallpox. They became ill, some died, and some were scarred for life with pockmarks all over their bodies. But the inhabitants of the Eastern Hemisphere had built up considerable immunity to the diseases that had been sweeping through Europe, Africa, and Asia for centuries. A smallpox epidemic during the American Revolution (1776-1783) killed 130,000 European Americans out of a population of about three million in the thirteen colonies. (By contrast, a far lower number of white Americans died in the Revolutionary War: 4,000.)

The Indians received no sympathy from the settlers. Some were pleased to see the *Hand of God* at work removing the original inhabitants. The settlers had a low opinion of the Native Americans who they frequently described as savage, thievish, lazy, and wild. The Dutch commonly called the Indians *wilden* (wild people). To the Europeans, the Indians served a positive function only when they provided furs for trade and game for food. In terms of power, the contact between the two cultures was usually one-sided. The Europeans were clearly dominant and the Indians must have profoundly regretted their arrival. Even the memory of the contact is uneven. We have biased reports from the Dutch complaining about the Indians, but as the Indians never developed writing, their response can only be imagined.

Warfare also took a toll on the Indians. Most conflicts started when Indians trespassed on Dutch farms and helped themselves to produce, or when out of frustration the Indians attacked isolated farms. The response was swift and deadly. Governors William Kieft and Peter Stuyvesant ordered several expeditions against

Indian villages. Between 1643 and 1645, during the Indian War, sometimes called Kieft's War, 1,600 Indians were slain.

We can presume a general demoralization of the Indian population as their lives were shattered within a generation. By the time the English took over New Amsterdam and renamed it New York (1664) virtually no Indian presence was left in the area. European newcomers had encroached on their ancestral lands and taken over the governing authority of the region, which changed their lifestyle by the introduction of new values, tools, animals, and foods. Liquor and guns also changed native culture. Disease, however, was the greatest challenge and it effectively removed entire tribal populations from the seacoast within four decades.

CHAPTER 8
Forest Products & City Trees

Before the Europeans came to this region it was covered with forests of oak, chestnut, hemlock, and tulip trees. Systematic harvesting of forests was too efficient and today only four city forests with old-growth trees remain.

Forest products were one of the enticements that brought European settlers here. The production of naval stores (wood tar, pitch, and turpentine) was a big business. Those forest by-products were used to caulk the seams of wooden ships. The publishing industry grew in New York partly because of its proximity to sources of wood pulp for paper. Lumber (smoothed boards) was used for housing and farm building construction, and for building ship hulls and masts. The five counties that ultimately became the five boroughs of New York City produced enormous amounts of lumber for housing and the woodworking trades.

By the end of the 18th century German woodworkers dominated the woodworking trades, though Scandinavians and other groups were also involved in turning trees into furniture and cabinets. The early German and Scandinavian presence in Astoria, Long Island City, Maspeth, Greenpoint, Williamsburg, and Bushwick was often associated with woodworking companies that liked to locate near forests in Brooklyn and Queens and easy transportation to the wooded areas of Long Island.

The piano industry used lumber to construct quality instruments. Steinway & Sons Piano Company in northeast Astoria (Steinway), and the former Sohmer Piano Company in northwest Astoria (Hallets Cove), became the two largest piano manufacturers. Steinway still produces 2,500 pianos each year.

There are many furniture makers and cabinetmakers currently operating in Astoria, Long Island City, the Lower East Side of Manhattan, and in Greenpoint and Williamsburg. Most of the wooden water tanks above New York buildings are constructed in Williamsburg. Many recent Polish immigrants have gone into the furniture crafting business. These industries use wood brought from other locations. New York City ceased to provide lumber in the mid 19th century.

The area occupied by the city is no longer forested, and trees are not seen as crops to be harvested, but as treasures to be guarded. Today, two million of New York City's 2.5 million trees are found in parks. Most of the other half million line the streets providing shade and breaking up the harshness of the city's cement, asphalt, and brick landscape.

Many of the most commonly found trees in the city are imports. Some native trees --- oak, maple, hemlock, and tulip trees --- still exist throughout the city. Many new varieties, which are better able to withstand the hazards of urban life, have been planted. London plane trees are predominant in Brooklyn. Their shedding bark, which is unusual in the world of trees, gives their trunks a dappled look and makes them easy to spot. Early in the 20th century they were planted in great numbers along streets and in parks. Their broad five-pointed leaf is the insignia for the N.Y.C. Department of Parks.

Honey locusts, a native variety, eclipse all other trees in Manhattan. They are known for their tiny, delicate leaves and long, brown seedpods. The Norway maples hold first place in the Bronx, Queens, and Staten Island. They have typical five-pointed maple-style leaves similar to the one found on Canada's flag. Norway maples produce a pair of winged-seeds, which delights small children who stick them on their noses. The Bradford Callery Pear is a new favorite in Manhattan. They have an abundance of rounded leaves and grow quickly. In spring they produces clusters of tiny white flowers. These European imports, and the native honey locusts, work well because they are highly tolerant of drought and pollution.

Beside the most common native trees and the popular European imports there are many other varieties from home and abroad to be found in the city. Botanists count over one hundred species in Central Park. The sycamore, buttonwood, pin oak, black oak, sugar maple, beech, birch, sweet gum, elm, ginkgo, and ailanthus are all found in the city.

The ginkgo, brought here from China, is a living fossil from dinosaur days. It has two noticeable characteristics: fan-shaped leaves with two lobes, and seeds from the female trees that give off a terrible odor as they rot on the ground.

A 1943 novel by Betty Smith immortalized the ailanthus, another import from China, which grows almost anywhere it can find a patch of dirt. An ailanthus can sprout out of cracks in walls and from roof gutters. A sapling can grow ten feet per year. They are very hard to kill; when chopped down, new shoots arise from the roots. Detractors call them weed-trees.

Williamsburg, Brooklyn was the setting for Smith's A Tree Grows in Brooklyn. It portrayed a poor, gritty Williamsburg from 1902 to 1919 filled with competing and colluding ethnic enclaves. The sturdy ailanthus was romantically called the Tree of Heaven after its Latin name, Ailanthus altissima. No matter where its seed fell, it made a tree, which struggled to reach the sky. It grew in boarded-up lots and out of neglected rubbish heaps and it was the only tree that grew out of cement. It grew lushly, but only in the tenement districts. The ailanthus was a metaphor to explain how immigrants struggled and survived in harsh surroundings.

Old-growth forests may still be found in the city. They have been preserved as parks. Inwood Hill Park in the northwestern tip of Manhattan, a 40-acre section of the New York Botanical Garden in the Bronx, and Van Cortlandt Park's Northwest Forest at the northern edge of the Bronx, are old-growth forests. Staten Island's sprawling Greenbelt has some old-growth trees in it. Old-growth forests have never been cut and some of the trees are over three hundred years old. New York's old-growth forests pale in comparison to the 2,000 year-old redwood and sequoia trees in Northern California, or Methusalah, a bristlecone pine in California's Inyo National Forest estimated to be 4,600 years old.

There are severe problems facing city trees. Many are water-starved and salt-choked. The lucky ones live in parks and backyards. The trees squeezed between the streets and sidewalks are assaulted by pollution throughout the year, salt during snowy winters, and careless truck drivers ripping off limbs.

Sidewalks and streets often strangle the tree right to its trunk and keep it from its natural source of water, which is open ground. Many city trees are dehydrated because water finds its way to the roots of curbside trees, but seldom enough.

Salt and salt-based products are spread on the city's streets and sidewalks to melt slippery spots. The salt poisons trees. It also leaches into the areas where curbside trees draw their water and competes with the trees by absorbing water. Dog urine does similar damage. Before the late 1950s, the city, individual homeowners, and landlords spread sand and cinders from coal-burning furnaces to give traction on ice. It was dirty, but harmless to trees.

Diseases have killed many of New York City's trees. Dutch Elm Disease (1930s-1960s), a potent fungus, attacked millions of beautiful American elm trees all across the country. It destroyed most American elms in the city. Among the fortunate few to survive are those in Manhattan's Riverside Park, along Riverside Drive between West 80th and 116th Streets, and along Central Park's mall, south of the bandshell between East 67th and 70th Streets. American elms are noted for fullness and abundant foliage that turns bright yellow in autumn.

Asian longhorned beetles arrived in wooden shipping crates from China in 1996 and have caused an arboreal infestation. They are destroying hundreds of maple, elm, horse chestnut, poplar, willow, and birch trees. Brooklyn and Manhattan have been hardest hit. Greenpoint was the first hot spot for the ravage. Two thousand trees have been chopped down since 1996 to prevent the spread by destroying the food the beetles eat. The pests, which bore deep, dime-size holes in the trunks, have spread from Greenpoint to Williamsburg, the Lower East Side, the East Side, and Central Park. Bayside, Queens has also experienced infestation. Oak trees, which are resistant to the beetles, have been replanted along the streets and backyards to replace destroyed trees.

Keeping the city green is an ongoing task for the Department of Parks. There are few sights more ugly than a treeless street, especially when the sun beats down in July and August. Healthy trees benefit all New Yorkers.

CHAPTER 9
Climate & Weather

New York is an ocean city with a temperate or moderate continental climate. The Atlantic dominates many aspects of the city's atmospheric conditions. The temperature is moderate because New York City is located at the edge of the North American continent at the Atlantic Ocean. The city is almost surrounded by the ocean, watery fingers of the ocean (Long Island Sound, East River, Harlem River, Arthur Kill, Newtown Creek, the Harbor), and the broad mouth of the Hudson River. There are 580 miles of shoreline in New York City. It is instructive to remember that its 42-degree north latitude puts New York City on a similar plane with Madrid, Spain and Naples, Italy.

The predominant air and wind currents also affect climate. Westerly winds blow cold or hot air across the United States. That includes both the high-level Jet Stream and lower wind patterns. It means that New York City often gets the weather that places to the west, northwest, or southwest had the previous day or so.

The ocean currents, which affect New Yorkers in all seasons, originate in the tropical Caribbean Sea and the Gulf of Mexico. They warm the air above them as they converge and flow on their way across the North Atlantic toward the Arctic Sea north of Norway, Finland, and Russia. They are called the Gulf Stream and the North Atlantic Current. Tropical currents heat all locations on the East Coast, but New York City is kept warmer than most cities because it has waterways conveying the warm water throughout the city.

Despite the term *moderate,* and unlike Madrid and Naples, the climate in New York City can be bitter cold in the winter due to humidity and icy winds, though it can also be mild with little snow. The coldest day recorded in the city was February 9, 1934 when the temperature stood at -15 °F. Cold winters are caused by the frigid Arctic air mass moving southeast from Canada.

Hot and humid summers make the city usually resemble an

oven with the cement, brick, and asphalt surfaces radiating the sun's heat. The hottest day in New York City was July 9, 1936 when the temperature rose to +106 °F. New York has four distinct seasons, each of equal duration. The most pleasant may be spring and fall, during which the extremes of winter and summer are absent.

Climate and weather are related. Climate is the general condition of the atmosphere (temperature, precipitation, and wind) averaged over many years. Weather is the specific characteristic of the atmosphere at a given moment or a specific day. The key components of weather deserve individual treatment. Beside temperature, the precipitation, wind, and periodic abnormalities (hurricanes, tornadoes, earthquakes) affect the city.

Rainfall is remarkably even throughout all twelve months. Average precipitation ranges from 4.5 inches in November to 3.3 inches in February. Of course there are exceptions. On October 8, 1903, 11 inches of rain fell during the city's biggest rainstorm. The source of much of the humid air that causes rain is natural evaporation from large bodies of water. The Atlantic Ocean, and to a lesser extent, the Great Lakes, contribute greatly to the humid air in New York City.

Snowfall is both delightful and potentially dangerous. Average New York City snow accumulation measured in inches at Central Park's Belvedere Castle is 5.5 in December, 7.6 in January, 8.5 in February, and 5.0 in March. When a heavy snowfall is propelled by wind, the result is a blizzard, which is a violent windstorm accompanied by a heavy, prolonged snowfall.

The blizzard of 1888 came unexpectedly late and did an enormous amount of damage. It was the result of two converging winter storms, a *nor'easter* packed with humidity coming up the East Coast and an Arctic blast from the Midwest. It snowed from March 12-14, and deposited 21 inches of snow and in some places left drifts ten feet high. Approximately two hundred people died as a result of heart attacks, exposure to the cold, and traffic accidents. Telegraph lines fell, shop signs and awnings collapsed, and the transportation system, which was entirely surface-level or elevated, came to a halt. Snow removal was very slow because it was done by hand with shovels and carted away in horse-drawn wagons. Two important municipal decisions were reached after the disaster. All telegraph lines (and later telephone and electrical lines) had to be buried underground, and the city committed itself to build a subway system.

Some subsequent blizzards have blanketed the city with a covering of snow the same amount, or more than in 1888, but the effect has been dulled by a largely underground subway system, modern snowplows affixed to Sanitation Department trucks, salt spreaders, and a communication system unfazed by the snow.

There were two powerful blizzards in mid-20th century New York. The blizzard of March 7-8, 1941 left 18.1 inches of snow and the blizzard of December 26-27, 1947 deposited 26.4 inches of snow. More recently, the January 7, 1996 blizzard left 20.2 inches of snow on the ground, and the February 17-18, 2003 blizzard deposited 19.8 inches of snow. New York City now uses 2,700 sanitation workers, 1,600 snowplows, 350 salt spreaders, and budgets money for 300,000 tons of rock salt for snowstorms and blizzards. It costs the city about $1 million for every inch of snow to clear the 6,000 miles of streets throughout the five boroughs. As unforgettable as blizzards are, none has compared in severity with the 1888 blizzard.

Every year the city is hit by *nor'easters*, a colorful word reflecting its nautical origins. Nor'easters are storms, often packing 50-75 mile winds, which begin over the Atlantic off North Carolina near Cape Hatteras. The storms, several hundred miles across, are formed by the convergence of warm air from the Caribbean and cold air from Canada. They travel northward along the East Coast with their winds spiraling counter-clockwise, hence the name nor'easter.

Hurricanes begin off the Atlantic Coast of West Africa, swirl through the Caribbean, and often make their way up the Atlantic Coast. Most hurricanes either turn inland and lose their wallop before ever getting close to the city, or go out to sea where they eventually lose their strength. In August and September, the *hurricane season*, New Yorkers watch the news for hurricanes 1,500 miles to the south because they know that there is always a possibility that one will strike New York City.

Since 1950, the United States Weather Service has anthropomorphized hurricanes by giving them names. Hurricane Diane

(1955), Agnes (1972), Gloria (1985), Bob (1991), and Edouard (1996) have come close to New York. Storm tides can double or triple the usual high tide when a hurricane is in the vicinity. Storm tides erode beaches, flood coastal areas, and back up storm sewers.

The Hurricane of 1938 cut across Long Island, sliced Block Island (off the coast of Rhode Island) in two for several hours, and then veered off into central New England. That was close, and many New Yorkers experienced electrical power outages, flooded basements, broken windows, ripped roof shingles, and uprooted trees. New York City received a direct hit from Hurricane Sandy on October 29, 2012. The storm surge occurred during high tide and flooded streets, tunnels, and subway lines. Power was cut off for days in several sections of the city. Sustained damage was suffered in coastal areas of Brooklyn, Queens, Staten Island, and Manhattan, especially in the Rockaways and the Lower East Side.

Tornadoes usually stay away from water, so while they are common summer occurrences in New Jersey and upstate New York, they rarely release their fury on the city. Nonetheless, between 1975 and 2012, eight medium-sized tornadoes touched ground in the five boroughs. New York City experiences at least two-dozen thunderstorms each year, caused by hot, humid summers. Negative energy on the ground connects with positive energy in colder storm clouds yielding lightning. Bolts of lighting regularly strike skyscraper pinnacles but the electrical energy is conducted harmlessly into the ground.

New York City experiences several earthquakes each year though to most people they are usually imperceptible. The city rests on the North American plate, which, like all tectonic plates, moves, but this area of the United States is not filled with faults, as is the West Coast, so the earthquakes are minor. As is the case with hurricanes and tornadoes, nature is unpredictable and generalizations need to be tempered by the sober realization that natural disasters can occur anywhere.

CHAPTER 10
New Amsterdam's Defenses: Wall, Fort, & Battery

The first settlers in the various communities of New Netherland were understandably insecure. They feared Indian attacks, wild animals, and assaults by other European countries. The best defense for New Amsterdam was the area's natural barriers provided by the inner bay (harbor) and the Hudson and East Rivers. When New Amsterdam's wall was built it needed only to stretch across the north side of the town between the two rivers. The remainder of New Amsterdam was bordered and protected by the rivers and bay.

On the other hand, when New Amsterdam was conquered by the English in 1664 and taken back as New Orange by the Dutch in 1673, it was in each case an overwhelming naval force sailing right up to the land, which overcame the town's paltry defenses. No shots were fired in each instance when the town changed hands. (New Orange was awarded by treaty back to the English in 1674.)

The difference between European and Indian maritime threats to New Amsterdam was the size of the enemy's ships. While large European frigates with canons were an overwhelming threat to the settlement, Indian canoes were not.

In 1639, the Dutch attacked a village of Lenape Indians near Pavonia, a settlement across the Hudson in today's New Jersey. Dutch forces sent by Governor-General William Kieft killed eighty Indians and burned their village and crops. In an attack on a Lenape village at Corlear's Hook (just south of the eastern end of Grand Street in today's Manhattan), Kieft's men killed fifty Indians. Yet the town did not feel threatened enough to build a wall. Other cities and towns along the Atlantic seaboard built fortifications. Only Philadelphia did not need a wall, because William Penn's Quaker philosophy yielded good relations with the Indians. Pennsylvania colonists never attacked the Indians nor bought their land without mutual consent and a fair price. (Trust that the powerful English Navy would protect Philadelphia from French, Dutch, or Spanish attack also dissuaded the Quakers from building a wall.)

The New Amsterdam wall came into existence in response to rumors in 1653 that New Englanders, always a threat to the Dutch colony, were preparing to mount an attack on New Amsterdam. The attack never happened, but Governor-General Peter Stuyvesant ordered construction of the wall. It was funded by a tax on the wealthiest citizens, and donations of supplies and labor. Slaves owned by the Dutch West India Company did much of the physical work.

It was a frontier wall, not a thick stone and brick wall like those found in European cities. New Amsterdam's wall was made of wood planks placed vertically. It appears to have been only ten feet in height. Sometime before the town fell to the English, the wall was strengthened by the addition of several stone bastions each mounted with a canon. There were two gates, one at Broadway and one at Pearl Street, then the closest road to the East River. The water gate near the East River was for the convenience of carts bringing in agricultural goods delivered to the ferry dock from the village of Breukelen. The dock was about two hundred yards north of the wall, approximately at today's Fulton Street.

The wall was never used. The English began tearing it down in 1699 and the space became a street. (In 1865 the New York Stock Exchange moved to the corner of Broad Street and Wall Street, giving Wall Street an association with stock trading.) In 1745, fearing a possible French attack from the north, a second wall was built. But, as New York City had grown, the new wall was constructed several blocks north, approximately across Chambers Street between the Hudson and East Rivers. The wall was a few feet higher than the Dutch wall, with a dry trench running along its north side. Like the first wall, the second wall was never used.

The Battery and Fort Amsterdam were part of the same defensive system located at the south end of Manhattan. The Battery, now a park southwest of Bowling Green, is named for fortifications which have always dominated the southern tip of the island. The Battery was a long low wall fortified with cannons built just a few feet west and south of the fort. Today it would run about three blocks long just inside Battery Park, a few feet west of State Street, from Battery Place to where State Street turns east to merge into Water Street. At the time, that was where Manhattan ended and the harbor began.

Fort Amsterdam, built in 1625 to protect New Amsterdam, housed four gun batteries and was built of logs, mud, and stone. It was located where the western wall of the United States Custom House now stands, and a few feet west into the park. The fort and battery complex contained the governor's residence, a windmill, barracks, and a Protestant (Dutch Reformed) church. From the fort, Governor Peter Stuyvesant reluctantly surrendered the town to the English in 1664. The fort was reconstructed and renamed Fort James (later Fort George). The new American government demolished it in 1788, and its remnants, along with other landfill and garbage, were dumped into the harbor to extend Manhattan Island southward.

Notations:

Castle Clinton

The circular fort near the harbor and about one hundred yards west of the Custom House is called Castle Clinton. It was not part of the colonial fortification system. Castle Clinton was built by the United States federal government in 1811 on an islet thirty yards offshore to defend the harbor. The fort was named for George Clinton, the first American governor of New York State, and vice president under Thomas Jefferson and James Madison. A 200-foot long wooden causeway connected the fort to Manhattan. In 1823 the fort was demilitarized and given to the city; more landfill was added to envelop the fort as part of Manhattan. The squat rough-faced brownstone fort was outfitted with a roof and renamed Castle Garden. P. T. Barnum and others regularly leased it as an entertainment center. The highlight was the American debut of the *Swedish Nightingale*, Jenny Lind, who sang to packed audiences in 1850. Between 1855 and 1890 it became the main east coast immigration center and from 1896 until 1941 it was the New York City Aquarium. Presently called Castle Clinton again, its center houses a small bookstore and postcard kiosk and a ticket booth for ferries going to Ellis Island and Liberty Island.

European City Walls

Most city walls in Europe were torn down in the 18th and 19th centuries when powerful artillery made them obsolete and their narrow gates impeded traffic. There are some exceptions and partial exceptions. Rome has several intact segments of its ancient walls. At the *Porta Maggiore* (Major Gate) in the Lateran neighborhood, two arches large enough for cars and trolleys to pass through, remain in very good condition. The double gates were originally part of a new aqueduct built by Emperor Claudius in AD 52. Subsequently the city walls were extended and merged with the aqueduct, so the top of the wall carried water from the Apennine Mountains. The city walls of Dubrovnik, on the Dalmatian coast of Croatia, are in excellent condition and encircle the old part of the town. Visitors may walk along the top and look down on the Adriatic Sea. Sections of the massive land wall (Wall of Theodosius II) in Constantinople (now Istanbul, Turkey) are still standing. The wall stretched from the Golden Horn to the Sea of Marmara. The main gate and sections of the medieval wall in Prague, capital of the Czech Republic, is intact. The crenellated walls of Moscow's medieval fortress, the *kreml* (kremlin), finished in 1495, are undiminished by time. Only about one hundred yards of the Moscow's medieval wall, built in 1530, stands alone in a parking lot in the Kitai Gorod neighborhood a few blocks northeast of the kremlin.

CHAPTER 11
Schools

Early colonial education revolved around individual teachers or tutors, not schools. The schoolmasters who took in children charged tuition and taught rudimentary subjects usually limited to reading, writing, arithmetic, and bookkeeping. Dutch schoolmasters, who taught classes in their homes, kept strict discipline. There was no established curriculum or concept of diplomas or graduation. Each teacher set his own curriculum and children were withdrawn when their parents thought they had learned enough, or in rare cases when they intended to pursue further education in the Netherlands.

The Dutch Reformed Church opened classes for those too poor to pay tuition. Collegiate School, which commenced operations in 1628, is the oldest independent school in the United States. In the English period the Anglican (Episcopal) Church also founded schools. Trinity School, established in 1709, is an example. Numerous small private academies developed during the 18th century. Columbia Grammar and Preparatory School, opened in 1764, still survives. Friends Seminary in Manhattan was established in 1784, the year following the British evacuation.

Private foundations organized *charity schools* and free lending libraries to promote literacy. They included several schools managed by the Free School Society and the Manumission Society's African Free School. Sunday Schools organized by the New York Sunday-School Union Society instructed poor students on Sunday afternoons in basic literacy and arithmetic.

Despite the hit-or-miss educational methods in early New York, it appears that most residents during the colonial period could read and write. Their literacy may be a testament to the expectations of the Protestant faith which expected its members to be able to read the Bible, and to the ability of parents to pass on whatever reading and writing skills they possessed to their offspring.

After the American Revolution a common feeling emerged that the state government should mandate some form of free and public education. The Regents of the University of the State of New York was created in 1784 when George Clinton was governor. Its task was to oversee King's College (later Columbia University), various private academies, and to establish and fund public education. Education began to be funded by the state in 1795 when funds were distributed directly to charity schools operated by churches or private philanthropists.

Erasmus Hall, at Flatbush and Church Avenues in Brooklyn, was chartered in 1787 as a private school for Dutch farm children. Later it was transformed into a public school and was the first institution to be chartered as a high school by the State of New York. The original structure still exists inside a quadrangle formed by four large buildings added between 1905 and 1939.

In 1801, New York State began to subsidize the Free School Society with public funds. The goal was to pay the costs of educating all children in New York, though it was done by state grants to private agencies, notably Protestant-dominated societies. Roman Catholic Archbishop John Hughes opposed the Public School Society, successor to the Free School Society, for referring to Catholics as *Papists*, teaching anti-Catholic history and literature, and reading from the King James (Protestant) version of the Bible. He demanded state tax money for *parochial* (church sponsored) schools. His request refused, he proceeded to establish a separate Roman Catholic school system.

By 1839 the Public School Society ran 86 schools with taxpayer funds while the seven Catholic schools received no state support. In 1841, reacting to the refusal of both Democratic and Whig political parties to change the school funding arrangement, Archbishop Hughes called a meeting in Carroll Hall and formed a Catholic political party to put forward a slate of candidates for the State Assembly. Not a single candidate running on the Catholic ticket (Carroll Hall slate) won, but it split the Democratic vote and three Whigs from the city were elected. Tammany Hall, the Democratic political organization, was alarmed and successfully sought a compromise with Hughes. In 1842 the New York State Legislature passed, and Governor William H. Seward signed, the

Maclay law setting up a new Board of Education in New York City, which prohibited the teaching of any specific religious doctrine. Eleven years later the Public School Society dissolved and donated its property to the new public school system. The Catholic schools did not disband.

The 19th century growth of public education meant that lower middle class and working class children would be assured a rudimentary education. The children of the wealthy and the upper middle class went to private schools (academies) or paid tutors. The vast majority of New Yorkers could not afford any type of private education. Charity schools and religious schools educated some children but the task of providing a general education to all children was so large that only the government could manage it.

Part of the reason that the idea of universal public education gained popularity was that many saw it as a way to combat poverty and tame unruly youths. As more immigrants entered New York the schools served to Americanize the newcomers teaching them the English language and American ways. A problem that remained unsolved until the adoption of the Compulsory School Act in 1874 was that many of the immigrant children did not register and attend school. Some needed to work to help support their families and others preferred to be on the streets. By consolidation of all five boroughs in 1898, the school-age population had grown to more than 500,000 and New York City scrambled to build more schools. At the turn-of-the-century some children were turned away for lack of space. Many schools resorted to half-day sessions so the students could receive at least part of the standard curriculum.

Compulsory education at first meant only eight years of *grammar school*. While a few high schools existed they were reserved for a small number of students who had to apply and earn acceptance. New York State was the last state in the United States to include high school in its compulsory education. However, New York was in the vanguard of offering vocational and adult education courses.

The 20th century witnessed the peak of public educational success in the city. Increasingly, immigrants were willing to take advantage of formal schooling as an avenue of upward social and economic mobility. The city built schools with modern, well-stocked science laboratories and facilities for physical education sometimes including swimming pools. In tenement neighborhoods residents felt great pride in the public schools.

The teaching staff, while never adequately paid, was highly qualified and dedicated to their career. Pay increased and working conditions improved long after the formation of the New York City Teachers Union in 1916, the forerunner of the United Federation of Teachers. Salaries did not appreciably improve until the 1960s. Interested parents organized the United Parents Association in 1921 to support the schools and protect their interests as parents.

City College, formed in 1926, has played an important role in New York City's educational system by offering affordable college education to those without the money or the correct social and ethnic pedigree to gain acceptance to private colleges. Hunter College, also a city-owned college, was originally a *normal school* for women (teacher training institute) and prepared many of the public school teachers. Hunter College School, grades 7-12, was the *lab school* for Hunter College where new methods were tried and where *practice teaching* was concentrated. Later, City College, Hunter College, Brooklyn College, and others were folded into the City University of New York. C.U.N.Y now has eleven four-year colleges, six community colleges, and graduate, technical, law, and medical schools.

Some extraordinarily selective schools, primarily Hunter College High School, Stuyvesant High School, Bronx High School of Science, and Brooklyn Tech High School attracted talented young people and were models for other schools to emulate. They also had the effect of keeping families without the means to send their children to private schools within the public school system and dissuading them from moving to the suburbs where better-funded schools were widely perceived as superior to most city schools.

For those parents with thick wallets private schools offered an alternative to the public system. Private independent schools increased in number during the 19th and 20th century though by 2012 they were attended by fewer than thirty thousand of the city's 1.1 million children. Most of the private independent schools, which are very expensive, are located in Manhattan with a few in Brooklyn and the Riverdale section of the Bronx. Noted examples include the Dwight School (1880), the Brearley School (1884), the Browning School (1888), the Spence School (1892), the Calhoun School (1896), the Chapin School (1901), Nightingale-Bamford School (1906), Birch Wathen Lenox School (1916), the Dalton School (1919), Elizabeth Irwin School (1921), Lycée Française (1935), the United Nations Independent School (1947), and Trevor Day School (1993) in Manhattan.

Brooklyn schools include Packer Collegiate Institute (1845), Polytechnic Preparatory Country Day School (1854), Brooklyn Friends School (1867), and Saint Ann's School (1965). The Riverdale neighborhood of the Bronx has Horace Mann School (1887), Riverdale Country School (1907), and the Fieldston School (1878). Staten Island Academy opened in 1884 in Todt Hill. The high school division of an independent private school is often known as an upper school.

There are many Roman Catholic schools in New York City. They are the product of the aggressive organizing effort of Archbishop John Hughes beginning in the 1840s. High-end Catholic secondary day schools include Fordham Preparatory School (1841), Convent of the Sacred Heart (1881), Loyola School (1900), Regis School (1914), and Marymount School (1926). Others include Aquinas School (1923) and Cardinal Spellman School (1959) in the Bronx, Xavier School (1847) and St. Jean Baptiste School (1929) in Manhattan, Bishop Ford School (1962) in Brooklyn, Holy Cross School (1955) in Queens, and Monsignor Farrell School (1961) in Staten Island.

There are many Jewish schools in New York City. *Yeshivas* are Orthodox Jewish schools, which teach high school age boys. Most classes focus on religious curricula with minimum attention given to secular subjects. The schools may be operated by synagogues, Hasidic sects, or as proprietary schools by individual rabbis. Generally Orthodox Jews establish separate schools for boys and girls, though there are exceptions such as Yeshiva of Flatbush. Traditional yeshivas, mostly in Brooklyn, include Bnos Yisroel, Rambam Yeshiva, Lubavitch United Yeshiva, Bais Yaakov of Gur, Bnos Zion of Bobov, and the Novominsker Yeshiva. Reformed, Conservative, and Modern Orthodox Jewish day schools, which teach secular subjects in great detail, including the Ramaz School (1937) and Solomon Schechter School (1993).

Lutherans, Greek Orthodox Christians, and Russian Orthodox Christians also operate high schools in New York City. In the last two decades of the 20th century a few Muslim, Hindu, and Buddhist elementary schools have opened. Most are newly organized and located in Brooklyn and Queens. In years to come, there will undoubtedly be religious high schools serving these communities.

One of the reasons private independent schools (non-religious) and parochial schools (religious) exist is to foster religious, ethnic, and class affinity. Another is to offer parents the choice of avoiding some of the public school system's difficulties. Education problems in New York City became serious in the 1960s and 1970s when the tax base plummeted, societal informality and anti-authoritarian sentiments fostered student unrest, and racial tensions seethed. The drug culture and increased violence, especially in the 1970s, had a strong negative impact on the whole system. The Board of Education, mired in paper-pushing bureaucracy, remained unattached and ineffective, concentrated in their maze-like Brooklyn headquarters at 110 Livingston Street and 65 Court Street. Many veteran teachers gave up and relocated to the suburbs or took early retirement. Inexperienced idealists who could not manage their classrooms often replaced experienced teachers.

It would be difficult to over-estimate the ill effects and demoralization caused by the racial turmoil within the public school system itself that began in 1968 in the Oceanhill-Brownsville section of eastern Brooklyn. Oceanhill-Brownsville was the epicenter of an acrimonious battle between parents and teachers for control of the schools. The struggle pitted black parents against white, often Jewish, teachers and principals. The discord moved rapidly from educational issues to racial grievances and racial and religious stereotyping.

African-Americans raised the call for *community control*, fearing their children's education had been taken out of their hands by the largely white school bureaucracy. A pilot community control program was instituted in Oceanhill-Brownsville and the teachers responded angrily. The next two years was filled with strikes, boycotts, marches, and demonstrations. Community control was finally victorious and in 1970 the New York State Legislature passed the *School Decentralization Act* that set up a new layer of bureaucracy on the neighborhood level that would be controlled by parents through public elections.

An elected community school board that hired a district superintendent and staff operated each new district. The city's 32 community school districts functioned with mixed reviews over the next 33 years. While in some cases parents had easier access to the schools, many of the districts were riddled with corruption and cronyism, and often served as another unneeded level of bureaucracy. Fewer than 10 percent of the eligible residents voted in school elections and there was no noticeable improvement in the schools.

The community school districts were shut down and replaced by 10 new instructional divisions in 2003. For example, instructional division 3 headquarters on Sutphin Boulevard in Queens replaced former community school districts 25, 26, 28, and 29. The new instructional divisions intend to serve the schools more than the interests of the parents. Offices and skeletal staffs remain at the newly re-configured community district level to support advisory parent panels. The 32 panels each have 11 members: 9 parents elected by local PTA members, 2 community members appointed by borough presidents, and a non-voting student member. A separate 33rd citywide advisory parent panel oversees special education programs. Twelve hundred new parent coordinators were chosen by principals to act as full-time liaisons between school administrators and parents. *Ombudsmen* (advocates), who were parent activists, were paid regular salaries for their work involving other parents in the schools.

Lingering problems relating to attendance, discipline, dropout rates, and the level of scholarship have been exacerbated by a strain on the budget caused by the United States Supreme Court ruling to provide bilingual education and the Congressional mandate to provide special education and handicapped education. New York City also has the task of educating thousands of non-English speakers. Many schools suffer from large class sizes, a shortage of appropriate books and basic supplies, and a staff attrition rate that reaches 50 percent after five years of teaching.

There are some promising notes regarding the public schools. Teacher salaries increased modestly in the new millennium, violence decreased, and math and reading scores inched up. The creation of almost 200 smaller high schools in the past two decades has offered students and parents more choices in curriculum and philosophy, and has created a more intimate environment for learning. Based on the educational philosophy of Theodore Sizer at Brown University, New York City has embraced the idea of ultimately decommissioning the large education mills, which often had 3,000-5,000 students, and superseding them with high schools enrolling fewer than 500 students. In 2003, the New York State Court of Appeal, ruled that the city had been short-changed on its share of state education aid from Albany, and that the city schools were entitled to more funds.

Progress in a huge system with 60,000 teachers and 1,100,000 students comes slowly. The replacement of the Board of Education with the Department of Education in 2002 may augur well for the system. For many years the Board of Education in New York City, which is one enormous school district, was unlike most of the 16,400 school districts in the United States because its seven members were unelected. The borough presidents appointed five; the mayor appointed two others. As a result the school board members, or the chancellor they selected, were not directly responsible to the voters. The Board of Education has been abolished. The chancellor of the new Department of Education is appointed directly by the mayor and has a cabinet-level position with its executive offices in the Tweed Court House located behind City Hall. Now the buck stops at the mayor's desk. Half of the city's $68 billion yearly budget goes to education and parents and taxpayers have the right to accountability from the public school system.

Notations:

Dutch Teachers

A bronze tablet on the northwest corner of New York University's Main Building, Washington Square East and Waverly Place, reads: *In honor of the Seven Public School Teachers who taught under Dutch rule on Manhattan Island: Adam Roelandsen, Jan Cornelissen,*

Jan Stevensen, William Vestens, Jan de la Montagne, Harmanus Van Hoboken, Evert Pietersen, 1633-1674. They were public school teachers only in the sense that they accepted children of the general public, but only those who could pay tuition. The end-date reads 1674, ten years after Dutch rule ceased, because some of the Dutch instructors continued to teach during the first decade of British hegemony.

Restoration Schoolhouses

Richmondtown Restoration in Staten Island and Old Beth Page Village in nearby Suffolk County are village restoration projects that include old schoolhouses. The combination house and school of the *voorlezer* (schoolmaster appointed by the Dutch Reformed Church) in Richmondtown dates from 1695. The Old Beth Page one-room schoolhouse dates from the middle of the 19th century.

CHAPTER 12
Children's Games

Children's games have been the product of free time, space, and style. Creative imagination and inventive adaptation have helped. In colonial days everything was labor-intensive. Children did not have a lot of free time since they were busy helping their parents with chores. Fetching buckets of water, preparing firewood, feeding the animals in the backyard, and walking the cow to and from the town common each day were boys' tasks. Girls were expected to aid in washing clothes, help with food preparation, watch the infants, and sweep the floor. Special skills needed to be learned: cooking and sewing for girls, woodworking for boys. When boys were eight or ten they were often sent to a neighbor's house to be apprenticed to learn a different trade than the one practiced by their father, especially if there was an older brother who would inherit the father's business. An apprentice was a boy who worked for a master craftsman to learn skills so he could someday become an expert craftsman himself.

Nonetheless, there was always time for recreation. No one had lawns as we know them, and there were not any parks, so if a trip to the country or the riverside was not planned, it meant that games were played in the street. Activities moved inside during bad weather. House games, usually in the winter, included hide-and-seek, cat's cradle, backgammon, checkers, and card games. Outdoor games were a lot more active.

Many of the games children played resembled those of today. Some games have gone out of style but most survived. Rules changed over the centuries and names (and jingles) changed even more frequently. The main elements of play always included some skill, some chance, and, of course a sense of entertainment.

Jumping rope, hopscotch, shooting marbles, and *hooping* could be done solo. (Hooping entailed pushing a wood hoop along the cobblestone streets.) Other games, like crack the whip, stoop ball, and blind man's buff (not bluff) needed groups. In congested

New Amsterdam or New York it was rarely difficult to get a crowd of children together.

A very old New York City game was *chuck-farthing*, shooting the most *pence* (pennies) into a small hole in the ground to win the pot. Kite-flying was popular. The children first had to make their own kites. Another old game was mock military maneuvers and drills based on 18th century straight-line formations. Leap-frog, jumping contests, various races, and badminton were all popular activities.

Cricket, which we now associate with England, was a sport that was well known here during colonial days. An old jingle proclaimed:

This lesson observe
When you play at Cricket,
Catch All fairly out,
Or bowl down the Wicket.

There were a lot of ball games played in New York City. Many are familiar today, though football and basketball were not around 150 years ago. Stool-ball was a combination handball, baseball, and musical chairs using stools or a single bench:

The Ball once struck with Art and Care,
And drove impetuous through the Air,
Swift round his Course the Gamester flies,
Or his Stool's taken by Surprise.

The game of Fives (meaning five fingers on your hand) was what we would call handball. You can see people playing this rigorous sport at handball courts in Coney Island, Pelham Bay Park, Cunningham Park, Alley Pond Park, and South Beach Park.

With what great Force the little Ball
Rebounds, when struck against the Wall!
See how intent each Gamester stands;
Mark well his Eyes, his Feet, his Hands!

Base-Ball in one form or another was played in New York City since at least 1767.

The Ball once struck off,
Away flies the Boy
To the next destin'd Post,
And then Home with Joy.

A dancing ritual, most likely supervised by teachers, was dancing around the May-Pole:

Compose a num'rous jovial Ring,
To welcome in the cheerful Spring.

When children found a level spot they sometimes tried a game some of their fathers played, nine-pins, a kind of outdoor bowling. It was one of the few games they played that needed much equipment. American author Washington Irving described the mysterious game of fairy nine-pins in colonial New York in *The Legend of Sleepy Hollow.* Adults paid money to bowl at a private court at Bowling Green in English colonial days.

Old style lawn bowling is still done at a place called Bowling on the Green in Manhattan's Central Park northwest of the Sheep Meadow. It is very formal; participants dress in white from head to toe. *Bocce,* an informal Italian variation, is played in several parks including Carroll Park and Marine Park in Brooklyn, and South Beach Park in Staten Island. Of course, modern bowling on varnished wood alleys with machine-set pins is available in numerous indoor commercial bowling lanes.

Some outdoor activities gravitated to the *stoop* (a Dutch word). The stepped-porch leading up to the front door of a brownstone, row house, or tenement always served as bleacher seats for everything that happened on the block. Stoop ball can be played against it, and it proved the best spot for dominoes and card games if you didn't mind people looking over your shoulder. Mostly the stoop was for hanging out, gossiping, and people watching. Sometimes the most devoted stoop-sitters were called *mayors of the block.* Front stoops were also where sweethearts sat and where smokers and insomniacs went at night.

Children still play on the stoop and in the street. But the tremendous increase in traffic makes it very dangerous and unwise. The city's parks and playgrounds help make up for the loss of street games.

Many contemporary games have moved indoors. Most New Yorkers have larger living spaces now than in the past. Board games and cards achieved a niche of indoor popularity. Electronic activities have been powerful inducements to get kids off the street. So, too, is centralized heating in the winter and air-conditioning in the summer. In temperature-controlled rooms, young people can put in hours of screen time often isolated from children in the real world.

CHAPTER 13
Public Spaces in New Amsterdam: Town Common & Bowling Green

In a very small town bordered on three sides by water there was not much need for public spaces. If people wanted to amble through the countryside, they could walk a few blocks north into rural Manhattan, or row across one of the rivers. What public spaces existed also had a commercial or military rationale. The first public market was set up along the east wall of Fort Amsterdam and was used only on market days. On other days the space was kept clear for military security.

The Town Common, a triangle north of Broadway and Park Row, was a few blocks outside the wall. The placement of the common grazing area beyond the wall by the Dutch shows they did not usually live in fear of Indian attacks. Many early families kept a cow; a child would be appointed to take it to the common, or green, to graze during the day. At night the cow would be returned to its shed or barn behind the house in town.

The Town Common eventually became a park when the present Georgian-style City Hall was constructed there in 1812. After the city consolidation in 1898 it became the center of the unified government of all five boroughs.

City Hall Park remained an open space with walkways, benches, and no fences. The Old Post Office cluttered the south end of it when it was built in 1875. It was restored to a larger park after the post office was demolished in 1939, this time with low rails built around its perimeter. Reconstructed again in 2000 for $30 million, the park has been saddled with the overdone appearance of Napoleon III's style of imperial elegance, egregiously conflicting with the Georgian simplicity of City Hall. A shoulder-high fence tipped with dart-shaped gold spikes and a fountain made of oversized black ironwork with superfluous flaring gas lamps are uninviting and clutter the space. The reconstruction seems more interested in crowd control and imperial grandeur than restoration or renovation. Intimidating fences, gates, and guard posts installed after 2001 have cut off public access to City Hall.

Facing City Hall on its west is a Nathan Hale statue, forged in 1890 to honor the popular hero of the American Revolution. Hale, a young Yale graduate and a schoolteacher, enlisted in Washington's army and served briefly as a spy until he was caught and hanged by the British at age 21. His parting words have been memorized by generations of school children: *I only regret that I have but one life to lose for my country.* The statue with a noose around its neck implies that Hale was hanged in the Common, though recent scholarship places the execution far uptown, either near today's Grand Central Terminal or Hunter College.

Across Park Row, once the center for the city's numerous daily newspapers is a bronze statue of Benjamin Franklin, cast in 1872. Franklin, the patron of printers and editors, is holding a copy of his *Pennsylvania Gazette.* The public space in front of the former New York Times Building (41 Park Row) was once called Printing-House Square, but is now known as Pace University Plaza. An imperiously seated Horace Greeley, editor of the former *New York Tribune,* is found to the east of City Hall.

The Dutch used the small open space at the south end of Broadway at Battery Place as a cattle and fodder market. The Hay Market was important for townspeople who kept horses, cows, and other livestock. In 1733, the English colonial government rebuilt the half-acre public space for lawn bowling. Bowling Green was a private concession leased to operators for the token yearly fee of one peppercorn.

The British authorities erected a gilded lead equestrian statue of George III in 1770, which was pulled down by American patriots in 1776 and melted for bullets after the first public reading in New York of the Declaration of Independence. When Washington left office in 1797, a simple polychrome wood statue was erected to honor him at the spot where the king's likeness had stood. The folk image of the first president was standing, left hand on hip, and unlike the king, not riding a steed. In 1819, Bowling Green became a private park for use by owners of townhouses which had been built around it. About 1850 it was transformed into a public park and was restored to its English colonial appearance. The iron fence is original though the royalist crown finials were broken off in 1776.

A large bronze statue of a bull (representing financial market optimism) was installed at the north end in 1989. It was entitled *Charging Bull* by its sculptor Arturo DiModica. In a case of wishful economics there was no bear in sight until 2002, and then again in 2008. In 2002 the City of Berlin donated a life-size standing bear, the symbol of the German capital. The upright bear is called *Buddy Bear*. It is painted with various American symbols, and has been placed at the south end of Bowling Green.

By the 21st century, New York City's population of eight million had several large public parks, a national park (Gateway), promenades, and hundreds of small parks and playgrounds. Some of the larger parks include Central Park, Riverside Park, Fort Tryon Park, Inwood Hill Park, Van Cortlandt Park, Pelham Bay Park, Ferry Point Park, Prospect Park, Marine Park, Astoria Park, Alley Pond Park, Cunningham Park, Jacob Riis Park, Flushing Meadows Park, LaTourette Park, Great Kills Park, Clove Lakes Park, Willow Brook Park, and Wolf's Pond Park. Since the 1980s the city has been slowly developing its extensive shoreline to gain more public space.

CHAPTER 14
Rivers: East & West

New York is a port city and there are waterways everywhere. Four of the five boroughs are islands: Manhattan and Staten Island are each separate islands, Brooklyn and Queens occupy the western end of Long Island, only the Bronx is on the mainland of North America.

It was the waterways, which attracted the European settlers. Giovanni da Verrazzano, an Italian explorer sailing for King Francis I of France, visited the harbor in 1524, and called it a large lake which he christened Lake Santa Margarita, the saint's name of the king's sister. The following year, a black Portuguese captain, Estéban Gómez, sailed into the harbor and up the Hudson River, which he called Deer River. Henry Hudson, an Englishman sailing for the Dutch, carefully explored the harbor and river, which bears his name in 1609. In 1614, Adrian Block explored the Hudson River, East River, and Long Island Sound. Henry Hudson, who sailed all the way to the site of Albany, was trying to find a passage to the Pacific Ocean. Though he failed, he enthusiastically described the river he alternatively called the Great River of the North and the Great River of the Mountains.

Some of New York's river terminology needs explanation. Henry Hudson called the river ultimately named for him the *Great River of the North* to distinguish it from the Great River of the South (Delaware River). When he called it the *Great River of the Mountains* he was referring to the Catskill Mountains, along its west bank. North River was used all through the Dutch and English colonial periods. The Algonquian-speaking Lenape Indians called it the *Muheakunnuk (river that flows both ways)*, which it does twice each day at high tide when salt water rushes upstream. During the Atlantic Ocean's low tide, fresh water flows to the sea.

The source of the Hudson River is Lake Tear of the Clouds in the Adirondack Mountains on the slope of Mount Marcy, New York State's highest point (5,344 feet). The river continues, fed by more than one hundred tributaries, 310 miles to the inner harbor of New York City. It is a true river, except at its southern sixty miles during high tide when it becomes an *estuary* or a *fjord*.

Estuary, from the Latin word æstus (tide), is the lower course of a river where its current meets the ocean tides. *Fjord* is a Norwegian word for a long, narrow, river valley cut by glaciers during the last ice age. The lower segment of the Hudson River is both an estuary and a fjord.

The East River, which borders Manhattan on the east, is not a river at all. The wide churning body of water, which sometimes flows north and other times south, is a *strait*. A strait is a natural waterway that connects two larger bodies of water, in this case two parts of the Atlantic Ocean: New York Harbor and Long Island Sound. Dutch and English colonists discovered very early that the East River had no source, as a true river must. But the name stuck, so despite its incorrect label, everyone calls it the East River.

Beside the two very large rivers, the harbor, the Verrazzano Narrows, and Long Island Sound, there are smaller rivers. Some like the East River are straits. They include the Harlem River and Spuyten Duyvil Creek, which separate Manhattan and the Bronx, and the Arthur Kill and Kill Van Kull, which divide Staten Island from New Jersey.

There are some degraded rivers that have been mostly filled in such as the Newtown Creek, which separates northern Brooklyn from western Queens, Flushing Creek and Alley River (in Alley Pond Park), which were once significant in Queens. The Gowanus Creek was Brooklyn's only interior waterway but has been so corseted that it has become a canal.

Jamaica Bay, between Brooklyn and the Rockaway peninsula of Queens is a saltwater lagoon. Bushwick Inlet in Greenpoint, Wallabout Bay and Navy Yard Basin west of Williamsburg, Erie Basin and Gowanus Bay south of Red Hook, and Gravesend Bay and Sheepshead Bay indent the waterfront of Brooklyn, but are all segments of the Atlantic Ocean.

Three small rivers which all begin on the mainland are still true rivers. The Bronx, Westchester, and Hutchinson Rivers flow southward through the Bronx into the East River. Once thoroughly polluted, they are being cleaned of debris and pollutants.

Though the East River is as salty as the ocean, it can still freeze, and did freeze several times in the city's history. In 1867 the river froze and disrupted ferry service for weeks. Many commuters were unwilling to brave the jagged ice and stayed home from work. Stores and restaurants ran out of supplies and commerce was seriously harmed in communities on both sides of the river. Later that year the state legislature set up the New York Bridge Company to investigate the possibilities of erecting a bridge between lower Manhattan and Brooklyn. In 1870 construction began on the Brooklyn Bridge, which opened in 1883.

The Hudson River froze over on January 25, 1821. Thousands of people on both sides walked out and some intrepid individuals crossed over. Quick-thinking entrepreneurs set up portable taverns on the ice to sell alcoholic drinks.

River pollution in New York City was severe throughout most of the 20th century. Until the early 1970s the city dumped ninety percent of its raw sewage completely untreated into the waterways. By 1930 the city was dumping 1.3 billion gallons of raw sewage into New York Harbor daily. Between 1937 and 1987 fourteen Sewage Treatment plants were constructed to treat 1.6 billion gallons of sewage each day. Dumping raw sewage into the waterways finally ended in 1992.

Pollution in the Hudson River was a combination of raw sewage discharged by river towns and New York City along with serious industrial pollutants, notably mercury and *polychlorinated biphenyls* (PCBs), both especially harmful to humans and aquatic life. PCBs accumulate in the fat of fish and can cause cancer and birth defects. While the Hudson River's health has dramatically improved since the 1980s, there are still problems and some restrictions. Commercial fishing for striped bass north of the George Washington Bridge is prohibited. Sport fishermen may keep one striped bass per day in the river north of the bridge, though the New York State Health Department recommends eating no more than one portion of striped bass each month for males, none for women of childbearing age, and none for children. Dredging of the Hudson River for PCB-contaminated mud and gravel by the Environmental Protection Agency began in 2006.

Traditionally, in the days before pollution, the Hudson River was known as an attractive river for sailing and canoeing, and as a rich treasure trove for anglers, where they fished for sturgeon, striped bass, shad, and herring. The Hudson and other New York waterways are slowly recapturing their recreational heritage.

Notations:

Clearwater

The Hudson River Sloop Clearwater, Inc. is an environmental group initially organized by folk singer Pete Seeger operating a 106-foot sloop, which sails up and down the Hudson River offering educational programs to draw attention to the area's aquatic environment. The boat, which uses a dock in Poughkeepsie, New York as its base, symbolizes the decades-long effort to clean up the fouled river. Since 1969, environmentalists aboard the *Clearwater* have taught students how to sail, conduct research on the Hudson's plant and animal life, investigate the many causes of river contamination, inform the public about the dangers of pollution, and foster policies to fully restore the Hudson River and its tributaries to good health.

Hudson River as Setting for the *Hudson River School* and Early American Novels and Short Stories

The Romantic landscape painting tradition called the *Hudson River School* dates from approximately 1820 to 1870. Thomas Cole, Asher B. Durand, Frederick E. Church, Albert Bierstadt and others glorified natural scenery by presenting a robust, enchanting countryside often located in the Catskills, Adirondacks, or along the Hudson. They painted in rich colors with careful attention to details. Frequent inclusion of storms and wild animals added a dimension exploring the mystery of nature and spiritualism. This was American art, which highlighted what was unique and exotic about our country's rustic scenery, distinguishing it from European landscape motifs. The Brooklyn Museum and the Albany Institute of History and Art hold extensive collections of Hudson River School paintings.

The Hudson River Valley was also the setting for popular books by early American writers James Fennimore Cooper and

Washington Irving. Cooper wrote *Leatherstocking Tales* (1823-1841), a set of five novels, featuring Natty Bumpo, a rugged hunter and woodsman triumphing over both the *savage* Indians and the *over-civilized* Europeans. The best known of his set is *The Last of the Mohicans*. Irving is best known for his humorous short stories, *Rip van Wrinkle* (1819), and *The Legend of Sleepy Hollow* (1820). Rip van Winkle was an amiable, henpecked husband, who escaped his nagging wife by taking a walk in the mountains. He met a group of phantoms from Henry Hudson's crew, drank gin with them, and fell asleep for twenty years. When he woke, almost no one remembered him and his wife died from a stroke while scolding an itinerant peddler. In *The Legend of Sleepy Hollow*, Ichabod Crane, an awkward schoolmaster, courts Katrina Van Tassel, daughter of a prosperous Dutch farmer, but falls for the Headless Horseman trick of his rival, Brom Van Brunt. The frightened schoolteacher fled town and Brom married Katrina.

CHAPTER 15
Canals & Docking Facilities

The city's site was chosen for its advantageous harbor and rivers, so canals and docking facilities were very important until late in the 20th century. A dock, alternatively called a pier, wharf, or *quay* (pronounced *key*), is a platform, reinforced by pillars or posts, extending into the water to facilitate loading and unloading cargo from ships. Canals had the inverse function. In areas of soft ground, or where a creek existed, the land was dug out and turned into a short waterway that ships or barges off-loaded from ships could enter and use one or both sides for loading and unloading freight.

The main canal in New Amsterdam began just east of the southern tip of Manhattan and went north about four and one-half blocks. It had narrow lanes on either side to serve as service roads. The canal was called the *Heere Gracht* (Gentlemen's Canal), and, when it was covered up in 1676, became Broad Street. A one-half block side spur to the west, called *Bevers Gracht* (Beaver Canal), when filled in became Beaver Street. There were bridges over the canal at Bridge, Stone, and Beaver Streets. The bridges connected the east and west sections of town but prevented ships larger than barges and small boats propelled by oars from entering.

Canal Street was never a canal. It was constructed over an open drainage ditch with wood planks on its sides that drained the 40-acre Collect Pond where Foley Square is now located. The drainage canal went west, channeling water from the Collect Pond into the Hudson River. The pond, fouled by tanneries, breweries, and slaughterhouses along its shore, was filled in between 1803 and 1813, and the Collect Pond Canal, which became Canal Street, was covered up shortly thereafter.

Newtown Creek was turned into a canal to facilitate barge traffic to and from farms and factories. In colonial times the waterway was used to transport agricultural products on small barges and skiffs from riverside farms to Manhattan. As industries developed along Newtown Creek it became the repository for sludge and acids from manufacturers in Greenpoint and Long Island City. Constantly dredged and widened, the channel now resembles a fetid canal rather than a creek.

The shellfish-rich Gowanus Creek was once a pleasant waterway fed by numerous streams and rivulets draining west central Brooklyn. The Indians, Dutch, and English used it as a source of bi-valves; it was especially noted for succulent oysters. The Gowanus Creek was transformed in several steps between 1840 and 1884 into a shipping canal as Brooklyn grew and industry took precedence over ecology. Eventually it became a loathsome, 1.8-mile waterway with no clearly identifiable source other than run-off rain from the streets. The stagnant water gave off putrid smells though it served the commercial interests of coal, oil, paint, ink, brick, cement, stone, plaster, paper, and wrought-iron manufacturers. A flushing tunnel was built under DeGraw Street from Buttermilk Channel to the north end of the canal in 1911. A pump flushed seawater from the harbor into the canal to clean out some of the pollutants. The pump and fan mechanism broke after the Second World War and were not replaced until 1999. Since then there has been some improvement in the Gowanus Canal. The odor is less offensive and a few fish, eels, and ducks are using it. An occasional kayak or canoe can be seen exploring the waters, and a few pleasure craft are tied up along its sides.

Among the other rivers and creeks transformed into canals are the Arthur Kill and Kill Van Kull west of Staten Island, Flushing Creek and Alley River (in Alley Pond Park) in Queens, Bushwick Inlet (once Bushwick Creek) in Greenpoint, Brooklyn, and Wallabout Bay (once fed by Wallabout Creek) in Williamsburg, Brooklyn.

The Dutch constructed primitive docks soon after settlement in 1625. Deep water near the shore, rivers generally ice-free in the winter, and broad spaces to maneuver ships, made the harbor, East River, and Hudson River attractive places to build docking facilities. Permanent piers were constructed along the East River to the northeast and southwest of the Heere Gracht. Later canal and pier combinations called *slips* were built along the East River and known as Fish Market Slip, Coenties Slip, Old Slip Market,

Meat Market Slip, Fly Market Slip, Lions Slip, and Beekman's Slip. A slip is a sheltered area, in most cases a short canal, between two piers.

Warehouses were built next to the wharves to hold cargo until it could be sold. The first warehouses were along Pearl Street near Whitehall and the Heere Gracht. (Pearl Street got its name because its surface was covered with crushed oyster shells.) Some of the most common products traded in New Amsterdam were animal furs and skins, Virginia tobacco, whale oil, Caribbean sugar, grain, vegetables, timber, dried fish, and liquor (wine, port, gin, rum, corn whiskey), ceramic tiles, and ceramic smoking-pipes. New York City became an *entrepôt* center as well as a major importer and exporter of goods. An entrepôt is a place where products are stored and redistributed to other ports.

Shipping changed markedly during the 19th century as sailing vessels gave way to steamships powered initially by wood and coal and later by oil. Eventually, steamships became so large they needed to turn off their engines soon after they passed the Verrazzano Narrows so they would not crash into piers while attempting to dock. Tugboats, small powerful crafts with enormous engines, towed or pushed larger vessels to guide the freighters and ocean liners into their berths. Since the decline of shipping there are very few tugboats left, though a tugboat festival is held at the end of summer to remember their role in the city's maritime history.

Each Sunday before Labor Day, a *Tugboat Challenge* is held in the Hudson River off Pier 86 at West 46th Street starting at noon. About a dozen boats participate, one outfitted to look like *Theodore Tugboat*, from the PBS children's show. The muscular harbor workhorses, some with 4,000 horsepower engines, evoke nostalgia for the former swirl of activity in New York City's harbor. Activities include a parade of tugboats, tugboat race from 79th Street Boat Basin south to the U.S.S. Intrepid Museum, nose-to-nose tugboat pushing contest (like an Upstate New York tractor-pull), and for the crew, a spinach-eating contest and a line-throwing contest. Prizes are awarded for Best Looking Tug, Best Vintage Tug, Best Dressed Crew, Best Tatoo, and Best Mascot (Past mascot winners have been a dog, rabbit, iguana, duck, ferret, lobster, and a fish in a bowl).

New York City became the world's busiest port by cargo tonnage in 1901 and remained so until shortly after the Second World War. (In 2012 Shanghai was the world's busiest port.) The East River and Hudson River were lined with docks and warehouses. During the war, the enormous Bush Terminal Warehouses were built on the Brooklyn waterfront between 39th and 66th Streets in the north part of Bay Ridge now called Sunset Park.

During the first half of the 20th century the main competitor for shipping by sea was the railroads. Increasingly, airplanes carried cargo in the 1950s. It was a new form of transportation, and trucks, a method made feasible by the construction of the Interstate Highway System between 1956 and 1991.

Containerization further changed shipping. Products were placed in crates and put in large containers, which were loaded and unloaded by huge gantry cranes. Many containers could be moved as trailers by trucks. The number of dockworkers (longshoremen or stevedores) was drastically reduced. Container terminals still exist in Red Hook and Bush Terminal, but most shipping has left New York City and moved to other ports. The high cost of labor and the crowded roads drove away business. Even the Fulton Fish Market now gets one hundred percent of its fish flown in to Kennedy Airport or trucked in from other port cities.

CHAPTER 16
Peter Stuyvesant & the Earlier Dutch Governors

Peter Stuyvesant (1592-1672), the last governor-general of New Netherland, is best known of the seven Dutch leaders who ruled the colony before it was conquered by the English in 1664. It is not surprising that we remember Stuyvesant. He was an ambitious, tireless administrator, though also an irascible, arrogant dictator, intolerant and dismissive of anyone with whom he disagreed. Peter Stuyvesant had a colorful military career in the Caribbean. Stuyvesant had ruled New Netherland for seventeen years when Colonel Richard Nicolls appeared in the inner harbor with an English squadron of four frigates. The colony surrendered and became New York. Today, of all former Dutch leaders, it is Stuyvesant's name that is attached to public places in New York City: Stuyvesant Square, Stuyvesant Street, and Stuyvesant High School.

A review of the first six governors-general will help place Peter Stuyvesant in perspective. The title, governor-general (alternatively director-general) meant that each of these men was employed as a local leader by the Dutch West India Company, a corporation with headquarters in Amsterdam, the Netherlands. The goal of the corporation was to conquer land and exploit resources in the New World in order to make profits for its stockholders in the Netherlands. Each of the colonies --- Curaçao, Bonaire, Aruba, St. Maarten, Dutch Guiana (Suriname), Bahia (Brazil), and New Netherland --- had a governor-general. The private corporation administered the colonies with military and legal backing from the Dutch government. It was the responsibility of the governor-general to make laws, rule the colony, encourage fur trapping, agriculture, lumbering, fishing, and trade. Ultimately they expected to produce a profit.

Cornelius Jacobsen Mey (1624-1625), the first governor-general, led a small group of Dutch and Walloon settlers in 1624 to

Governors Island because it offered natural protection from the Indians and was a safe place for their cattle and other livestock to graze. It served as a site from which to reconnoiter while the settlers prepared to establish a permanent settlement in Manhattan the next year.

Mey was ordered to branch out in a frenzy of activity even though he had very few settlers and even fewer soldiers. Nonetheless, he established a tiny fort up the North River (Hudson River) at Fort Orange (Albany), fortified High Island (Burlington Island) in the South River (Delaware River), and established a trading post near the mouth of the Connecticut River.

William Verhulst (1625-1626) also kept his job only one year. He was asked to increase the fur trade, expand Dutch West India Company farms (though not private farms), and expand Dutch control in to the watershed of the Delaware River. Little is known of Verhulst's brief tenure though the New Netherland Council removed him just a year after he assumed directorship of the colony. There is reason to believe he was accused of neglecting his duties while busy embezzling company furs. In 1626 New Amsterdam was very small. It had about thirty log cabins, a fort, a windmill for grinding grain, and a church. Thousands of beaver and mink pelts, otter skins, and wildcat hides brought the Dutch West India Company a small income from the outpost.

When Peter Minuit (1626-1632) was appointed governor-general, about 200 settlers lived in the colony, and many were scattered at outpost along the Hudson River. Minuit is credited with securing Manhattan from the Indians. Shorakopock Rock, now in Inwood Hill Park, is one of the two legendary sites of the 1626 real estate swindle when Minuit *bought* Manhattan Island from some sachems, who were supposedly representing the Lenape Indians, for 60 guilders ($24) worth of beads, cloth, and trinkets. A small boulder marks the place in Inwood Hill Park where many believe Minuit laid the legal groundwork for dispossessing the Indians of their land. Shorakopock Rock is at the end of a pathway 100 yards from the salt marsh up from the bank of Spuyten Duyvil Creek leading toward the woods. Like Verhulst, Minuit also came under suspicion of thievery and was relieved of his duties. He got revenge by working for Sweden and in 1638 established New Sweden as a colony along the Delaware River on land claimed by the Netherlands.

There is little known about Sebastian Jansen Krol (1632-1633), who filled in as the next governor-general. He had been a Dutch Reformed clergyman, a *comforter of the sick,* which was a rank of parish employee just below the minister. Krol had also been an agent for Kiliaen Van Rensselaer, proprictor of a million-acre *patroonship* centered at Fort Orange. The estate, called Renseelaerwyck had been purchased from the Mahican Indians. The small portion of Renseelaerwyck that was developed contained grazing lands for cattle, a tannery, lumber mill, gristmill, and brewery.

Governor-General Wouter van Twiller (1633-1638) had been a clerk in the office of the Dutch West India Company. He was a nephew of Kiliaen Van Rensselaer. As leader of New Netherlands van Twiller rebuilt the fort to make it sturdier and struggled to enlarge the territory of New Netherland through purchasing land from the Indians. He *bought* Governors Island, which the Dutch were already using, from the Indians in 1637 for some axes, nails, and colored beads. He also bought Randall's Island and Ward's Island in the East River. He purchased two hundred acres from the Sapokanikan band of Lenapes in the southwest part of what later became Greenwich Village for a company tobacco farm. Regardless of Indian understanding of European property law, the sales were legal and permanent as far as the Dutch were concerned.

Van Twiller expanded Dutch control on Long Island Sound and the Connecticut River Valley by settling a few families at the mouth of the river, trading with the Algonquian-speaking Pequot and Mohegan Indians, and ultimately buying the Connecticut Valley from the Pequots in 1633 for metal tools, cloth, and alcohol. But the Dutch did not have enough immigrants to settle in Connecticut and after the Puritans fanned out from Boston they began settling the Connecticut River Valley. The Dutch soon lost what little control they had. Van Twiller was recalled in 1638 after complaints over his disputes with some of New Netherlands' leading residents.

It is unclear how the next governor-general managed to get his appointment. Willem Kieft (1638-1647) had been unpopular in the Netherlands. He was accused of embezzling money raised to ransom Christian captives taken hostage by the Turks. In New Amsterdam he threw himself into his work with great zeal. He sponsored the building of a new brick church and governor's mansion inside Fort Amsterdam, and in town he ordered construction of an inn to accommodate visitors. He encouraged Englishmen dissatisfied with Puritan rule in New England to settle in Long Island. Kieft also rushed headlong into a series of Indian Wars. He had his men attack on several occasions, which poisoned already tense relations with the native population.

Many of the Lenapes had fled the area or died of European. They also realized that Dutch land purchases were not just symbolic gestures of friendship and peace, but had dispossessed them of some of their best hunting and fishing grounds. A flood of European products had destroyed their native crafts, and the insatiable Dutch appetite for furs disrupted traditional Indian occupations and social roles. Their society was in disarray.

The slow series of wars was precipitated in 1639 when Kieft tried to collect taxes from Indians in the surrounding areas to help the Dutch maintain their fort and wall. He also issued new rules prohibiting the sale of firearms to them. When word came that the Raritan Indians had killed some pigs in Staten Island, a squadron of soldiers was sent to punish the offenders. The Dutch tortured the chief's brother but never identified any perpetrators. The Indians protested that it had been white thieves who took and butchered the pigs and blamed it on the Indians. Another punitive expedition resulted in more Indian deaths.

Shortly thereafter, the Dutch attacked Indians near Pavonia, a settlement across the Hudson in today's New Jersey. Dutch forces killed eighty Indians and burned their villages and crops. In an attack on an Indian village at Corlear's Hook (just south of the eastern end of Grand Street in today's Manhattan), Kieft's men killed fifty Indians. It was at this point that Kieft ordered construction of a wall to protect New Amsterdam from the enraged natives.

Warfare took a great toll on the Indians. Most conflicts started when Indians trespassed on Dutch farms and helped themselves to produce, or when out of frustration the Indians attacked isolated farms. The response was swift and deadly. Governor Willem Kieft ordered several expeditions against Indian villages. Between

1640 and 1645, during the Indian War (or *Kieft's War*) 1,600 Indians were slain.

The wars also took a toll on the Dutch farmers, especially those in Brooklyn, Queens, Staten Island, and New Jersey. Spread out and defenseless, most abandoned their homesteads and fled to New Amsterdam. Some gave up altogether and left the colony. The Indian War was disruptive to commerce since much of the fur-gathering had been done by Indians.

Kieft was recalled to the Netherlands by the Dutch West India Company but died in a shipwreck during a storm off the coast of England. At the end of Kieft's tenure New Amsterdam had grown to about 1,500 inhabitants and was attracting settlers from many European countries. Kieft had written that eighteen languages could be heard on the streets of multi-ethnic New Amsterdam.

Peter Stuyvesant (1647-1664), the most colorful Dutch ruler, was born the son of a Dutch Reformed minister in Friesland, on the north coast of the Netherlands. He entered military service in 1625 and was governor-general of Curaçao from 1634 to 1644. He led a naval battle to capture the Portuguese island of St. Martin and was severely wounded by a canon ball. Stuyvesant returned to the Netherlands where his right leg was amputated. Thereafter he wore a wooden peg decorated by bands of silver fastened to the wood by silver nails and was sometimes called Old Silvernails or Pegleg Pete. In 1647 he was named governor-general of New Netherlands and relocated to New Amsterdam. He is credited with bringing order to the sloppy bookkeeping of the Dutch West India Company, and establishing rules of cleanliness in New Amsterdam.

His accomplishments include banishing animals from the town streets to corrals, pens, and coops, clearing the main canal of rubbish, banning log chimneys, appointing two fire wardens and establishing a volunteer fire company, instituting a night watchman, and repairing Fort Amsterdam and the town wall. In 1658 Stuyvesant succeeded in planting a new settlement at the northeast corner of Manhattan. The small village of Nieuw Haarlem anchored Dutch presence at the north end of the island. Stuyvesant also prohibited the sale of liquor and guns to the Indians.

Stuyvesant was soon presented with a Swedish threat to

Dutch hegemony. New Sweden was a small colony spread along both sides of the Delaware River, land that the Netherlands had claimed. The Dutch were hesitant to attack New Sweden because of the legacy of Swedish King Gustavus II Adolphus as a key Protestant monarch of northern Europe, though his successor and daughter, Christina, a child when he died, had become theologically undependable as an adult, eventually converting to Catholicism. (The Swedes and Dutch were not exactly co-religionists; the Swedes were Lutheran Protestants and the Dutch were Calvinist Protestants.) Perhaps a more important factor to the Dutch West India Company was that some of the investors in the Swedish settlement were Dutch.

At any rate, as the population of New Sweden approached four hundred, the Swedes took a larger share of the regions' furs, and Swedish governor Johann Printz spread rumors among the Indians that the Dutch intended to exterminate Native Americans, Stuyvesant decided to move against the interlopers.

In 1651 Stuyvesant built Fort Casimir at Newcastle on the Delaware River, to guard land that the Dutch claimed from encroaching Swedish settlers. The Swedes captured the fort in 1654 and renamed it Fort Trinity, but Stuyvesant led a force of seven hundred soldiers to retake it the next year. The new Swedish governor Johan Rising surrendered and New Sweden ended without a shot being fired, foreshadowing what would happen to New Netherlands nine years later.

Like his predecessor Kieft, Stuyvesant vigorously put down Indian uprisings in 1655, 1659, and 1663. Most were along the Hudson River and involved the Hackensack Indians near Manhattan or the Esopus Indians up river near Kingston. The common denominator was the Indian response to being pushed off their lands. Some wars and skirmishes, like the Peach War in 1655, had to do with cultural misunderstandings. In the Peach War a Dutch settler murdered an Indian woman who picked a peach from a tree he claimed belonged to him.

Stuyvesant's long rule provides numerous examples of his arbitrary style of work and his intolerance, usually based on his inability to appreciate any religion except his own. A group of English settlers in Flushing fought back against him in a famous case involving religious liberty.

Several English families had entered Flushing Bay from New England in 1654, after securing permission from Stuyvesant to settle in the colony of New Netherlands though not in the town of New Amsterdam. New England's Puritan leadership had been too intolerant for these Englishmen and women. The pioneers from New England developed land that had been purchased from Algonquian speaking Lenape Indians. They called it Vlissingen, in a gesture of appreciation to the New Netherlands authorities, after a Dutch port town.

Reacting to their shared background of suffering Puritan intolerance, the English in Flushing were magnanimous and allowed Quaker missionaries in their settlement. When Stuyvesant learned of the Quaker presence, he reneged on his assurance of religious freedom for the village, and his council promulgated a law banning Quaker activity. In those early years Quakers often proselytized by verbally disrupting services in other Protestant churches, so they were often unpopular among other Protestant Christians.

After Henry Townshend was convicted and fined for being a Quaker, thirty-one residents signed a 1657 petition, known as the *Flushing Remonstrance*, which declared their freedom of religion. Stuyvesant rejected the document and persecution continued. John Bowne, a farmer, was arrested, imprisoned and fined in 1662 for allowing Quakers to meet in his house. Not a Quaker himself, but married to one, he took the fight to the directors of the Dutch West India Company in Amsterdam. They sustained Bowne's argument and ordered Stuyvesant to allow all varieties of Protestant worship and to tolerate Quakers as long as they did not disrupt services.

Stuyvesant outlawed all public devotions inside the walls of New Amsterdam except for the Reformed Church, the official state religion of the Netherlands and its colonies. Residents holding other Protestant beliefs had to worship privately in their homes. Upon death their bodies had to be buried outside the wall. He also banned Roman Catholics and Jews from living anywhere in New Netherland. In 1654 twenty-three Sephardic Jews from Recifé, Brazil arrived in New Amsterdam. Stuyvesant imprisoned the Jews. He refused to allow them to settle in the colony. The Dutch West

India Company ultimately overturned the decision. The corporation had some Jewish investors, and the refugees were allowed to remain, though without a synagogue.

By 1664 there were about eight thousand Europeans and their slaves living in New Netherlands, and perhaps two thousand residents of New Amsterdam. Probably no more than half were Dutch. There were English, Scots, Germans, Swedes, Danes, French and Walloon Huguenots (Protestants from the traditionally Roman Catholic lands of France and what is now southern Belgium). There were also African slaves.

New Netherland was disintegrating as a Dutch colony because Dutch citizens chose not to immigrate to the New World in appreciable numbers. Some lived too well in the Netherlands to risk everything on the frontier of North America. Others were unwilling to go to a mercantile colony where a single company controlled all economic and political decisions. Some wealthy Dutch families tried to establish *patroonships* along the Hudson River. The lord of the *patroon* (estate) owned a vast tract of land and sought workers by bringing poor people across the Atlantic to work as indentured servants under harsh conditions similar to the European *feudal* and *manorial* system. But the frontier was enormous and many of the indentured servants escaped into the wilderness and started their own pioneer farms.

The English colonies, on the other hand, were more entrepreneurial and rewarded the hard work and risk of individuals by limiting the role of government and corporate monopolies. The building block of most English settlements was the self-sufficient *yeoman* farmer. The consequence for New Netherland of its inability to cater to the hopes and dreams of immigrants was that English settlers, and people from other European countries, chose to go to New England, Pennsylvania, or other English colonies. Foreign nationals who lived in New Netherland made up half the population and had no allegiance to either the Netherlands or the Dutch West India Company.

England, which owned the colonies north and south of New Netherland, was increasingly eager to capture the Dutch colony in order to control the entire Atlantic coast and its trade. James, Duke of York, the brother of King Charles II, was to receive New

Netherland as a proprietary estate if it could be conquered. James sent Colonel Richard Nicolls with four frigates and two thousand soldiers to take the colony.

Nicolls offered Stuyvesant and the inhabitants of New Netherland exceptionally generous terms. The governor-general wanted to fight but New Amsterdam's leading citizens, including the minister and Stuyvesant's son, signed a petition calling on him to accept the English terms and turn the colony over to Colonel Richard Nicolls who became the first English governor of New York.

Peter Stuyvesant was recalled to the Netherlands after the English victory and became a scapegoat. He was accused of incompetence and cowardice. Stuyvesant vigorously defended his actions in a written statement to the States-General, the Parliament of the Dutch Republic. He accused the Dutch West India Company of shortsightedness and stupidity.

Stuyvesant returned to New York in 1667 and retired with his family and slaves to his country estate, known as the *bouwerie* (meaning farm in Dutch). It was located off the main rural road running north on Manhattan's east side, approximately along the route of today's Bowery and 4th Avenue. Stuyvesant was not fond of the crowded conditions that he felt characterized New Amsterdam. He had built his country house as a working farm, a convenient two-mile ride north from the town wall, though far enough away to afford some isolation. He chose a tract of land that stretched from the marshes along the East River to the Bowery. Using today's street grid, Stuyvesant's estate stretched from the East River to 4th Avenue and from East 5th Street to East 20th Street. For almost two centuries the Stuyvesant holdings remained farmland and were held by the family though some of the fields were leased to others. His manor house burned down in 1778.

A seldom-noticed plaque marks the spot at the northeast corner of 3rd Avenue and 10th Street where a pear tree stood which the governor-general brought back as a sapling from the Netherlands and planted on return from his temporary recall. He intended it to be his memorial: *By which my name may be remembered.* The old fruit tree survived more than two centuries and died shortly before the Holland Society of New York erected the quaint plaque in 1890.

Peter Stuyvesant enjoyed a quiet retirement. Nicolls met often at the bouwerie with him to seek advice and discuss events of the day. They became close friends. After Peter Stuyvesant's death in 1672, he was buried on his farm under a small wooden Dutch Reformed chapel, now the site of a much larger stone church, Saint Mark's-in-the-Bowery (Episcopal), completed in 1799 on Stuyvesant Street, then the dirt pathway that led from the Bowery to the governor-general's farm. The plaque affixed to the lower part of the church's schist basement wall indicates Stuyvesant's approximate burial site. (His stone bust in the east yard near the portico, carved in 1915, should not be taken as an indication of his precise place of rest.)

Notation:

Dutch Connection with the New York City Flag

The New York City flag is a conscious effort to reach back to the Dutch period and bypass the symbolism of English colonialism. (It is not unique in that regard. Only in Hawaii is the *Union Jack* used on a state or city flag.) The color orange refers to the Dutch monarchical House of Orange, enthroned as *stadtholder*, which was a position of pre-eminence for royalty within the Dutch *Republic* during New Netherland's existence from 1625 to 1664. The flag's seal in the central white bar is decorated with beavers and barrels arranged around a windmill on a shield flanked by figures of an Indian with a hunting bow and a Dutchman with a plumb line. Above the ensemble perches a benign-looking eagle and the date 1625 is inscribed below. This was not the seal used in Dutch colonial times (there was a separate seal for each of the succeeding seven Dutch governors-general), but evolved to its present form after the American Revolution. Its latest alteration came in 1974 when City Council President Paul O'Dwyer, born in Ireland and no friend to England, shepherded a bill through the City Council to change the date on the bottom from 1664, the beginning of English rule, back to 1625 when the Dutch established the village of New Amsterdam in their colony of New Netherland.

CHAPTER 17
Flushing Remonstrance

Though it was settled in the Dutch colonial period, Flushing's founding families were English. They chose flat, wooded land just east of a narrow inlet of the East River, close to where it meets Long Island Sound, to build a settlement. Later the inlet was named Flushing Bay. They sailed from New England in 1654, after having secured permission from Dutch Governor Peter Stuyvesant to remain in the colony of New Netherlands but not in the town of New Amsterdam. Stuyvesant had agreed and issued the Patent of Flushing in 1645 and promised *liberty of conscience* as well as land to the English.

The English settlers developed land that had been purchased from Algonquian speaking Indians and named it Vlissingen, after a Dutch port town. Locating close to the water guaranteed them access to trade and provided some semblance of safety from the unknown surroundings. Living twenty miles from the Dutch authorities in New Amsterdam promised to provide a considerable degree of political independence for the new village.

The English had not been particularly welcome because the Dutch, already sandwiched between larger English colonies in New England and Pennsylvania, feared becoming a minority in their own colony. Stuyvesant's grudging tolerance shifted to hostility when Flushing began to attract English Quakers (Society of Friends) in 1657.

The governor, actually the *director-general* of the mercantile colony, had a poor track record regarding religion. Upon becoming governor in 1647 he forbade all public worship except for the Reformed Church, the official state religion of the Netherlands. Stuyvesant imprisoned twenty-three Sephardic Jews from Recifé, Brazil when they arrived in New Amsterdam in 1654. Governor Stuyvesant refused to allow them to settle in the colony. His ally, the Reformed Church pastor Johannes Megapolensis, wrote to the company directors in support of his boss: *For as we have here Pa-*

pists, Mennonites, and Lutherans among the Dutch; also many Puritans or Independents, and many atheists and various other servants of Baal among the English under the Government, who conceal themselves under the name of Christians; it would create a still greater confusion, if the obstinate and immovable Jews came to settle here. The Dutch West India Company, Stuyvesant's employer, overturned his decision. The Dutch West India Company, which had Jewish investors, allowed the refugees from Brazil to remain.

With Quaker missionaries active in his colony Stuyvesant reneged on his earlier assurance of religious freedom for the village, and his council promulgated a law banning Quaker religious activity and even forbade hosting Quakers in Dutch or English homes. George Fox had organized the Society of Friends in 1650 in England. They had split off from the Puritans and rejected most Christian doctrines including the Trinity. They put tremendous emphasis on the belief that within each person could be found an inward light of God. Quakers believed in peace and would not fight in wars. They refused to take off their hats or kneel before kings or other notables. They constructed simple prayer houses, called meeting houses, with pews or chairs usually arranged to face each other on all four sides. Quakers had no clergy and all people, women included, were welcome to speak at their meetings. Their popularity, never high, was severely damaged by their zeal. At the time, Quakers often proselytized by going into other Protestant churches and disrupting their religious services.

In 1657, Henry Townshend was the first to be convicted and fined for violating the Anti-Quaker law. Thirty-one residents signed a petition, known as the Flushing Remonstrance, rejecting Peter Stuyvesant's law and declaring their freedom of religion. The document was called a *remonstrance* from the word *remonstrate*, to speak out or protest. It contained a combination of religious and political reasoning with some flattery directed toward the United Provinces (Dutch Netherlands). It said, in part: *The law of love, peace and liberty in the states extending to Jews, Turks and Egyptians, as they are considered sons of Adam, which is the glory of the outward state of Holland, soe love, peace and liberty, extending to all in Christ Jesus, condemns hatred, war and bondage. And because our Saviour sayeth it is impossible but that offences will come, but woe unto him by whom they cometh, our desire is not to offend one of his little ones, in whatsoever form, name or title hee appears in, whether Presbyterian, Independent, Baptist or Quaker, but shall be glad to see anything of God in any of them, desiring to doe unto all men as we desire all men should doe unto us, which is the true law both of Church and State; for our Saviour sayeth this is the law and the prophets.*

The Flushing Remonstrance was rejected and suppression continued. Another English settler, John Bowne, was arrested, imprisoned and fined in 1662 for allowing Quakers to meet in his house. On appeal, the Dutch West India Company in Amsterdam ordered Stuyvesant to allow all Protestant worship in the colony.

Quakers prospered in Flushing and built a meetinghouse in the village center in 1694. The old wooden building, still used by the Flushing Society of Friends, is on Northern Boulevard near Main Street and is the oldest house of worship in New York State. The second generation of Quakers rejected the fanaticism of the early converts though they retained the simplicity and serenity advocated by Fox. They continued their hostility to war and later became leaders in the movement to abolish slavery. (Their major colony was Pennsylvania, which was founded by William Penn.)

The Flushing Remonstrance showed bravery on the part of the signers. Religious liberty was important to many Americans and the people of Flushing took it seriously. John Bowne became a local hero and all New Yorkers are better off because of his efforts to expand freedom of religion.

CHAPTER 18
Colonel Richard Nicolls Takes New Amsterdam for England

England owned colonies north and south of New Netherland and was intent on capturing the Dutch colony, controlling the Atlantic seacoast, and dominating its trade. James, Duke of York, the younger brother of King Charles II, was promised New Netherland if he could conquer it. James engaged Colonel Richard Nicolls for the assignment. Nicolls was supplied with four frigates, medium-sized war ships, and two thousand soldiers to defeat the Dutch and occupy the colony. On the way to New Amsterdam, Nicolls stopped in Boston to obtain supplies and pick up Governor John Winthrop of Massachusetts.

Nicolls planned his attack on New Amsterdam methodically, hoping to check the Dutch and seize their colony without a fight. With his four ships anchored off the shore of Manhattan, he had a letter delivered by Winthrop to Stuyvesant promising that residents of New Netherland could keep their property, religion, and language if they surrendered. A gathering of townspeople requested to see the letter.

Stuyvesant at first had hidden the letter and then tore it up in front of the crowd. One of the residents picked up the pieces, put it back together and read the favorable English offer of surrender. While Stuyvesant resolved to resist the English, the town residents, Dutch and non-Dutch alike, recognized a good deal and preferred surrender to a battle they had slim chance of winning.

Militarily, Nicolls had divided his forces by landing some soldiers at the English town of Gravesend and marched them north through Flatbush to take the Dutch village of Breukelen on the East River. Another group of soldiers took Staten Island. Then the four vessels sailed through the narrows into the bay, very near the Battery, and aimed their sixty-two cannons on Fort Amsterdam. Stuyvesant, who had twenty cannons but little gunpowder and few willing soldiers, was on the ramparts poised to resist but he stood alone. Dominie Johannes Megapolensis, the Dutch Reformed minister, and ninety-three of the leading citizens in town, including Stuyvesant's 17-year old son Balthazar, signed a petition urging him to surrender.

Realizing the inevitability of defeat, Stuyvesant accepted the petition, and six appointed negotiators from each side met at the governor-general's farm and drafted the *Articles of Capitulation*. The articles took effect on September 8, 1664. The English flag was raised, the small Dutch garrison marched to the wharf to board a ship for home, and Nicolls announced that the colony and the town would be renamed New York in honor of his royal benefactor. Colonel Richard Nicolls became the first English governor of New York.

Nicolls' served as English governor for four years and guided the transference of power from the Dutch West India Company, which had controlled economic and political activity in the colony, to the English system of commerce and government. The company was abolished and a limited variety of free trade within New York was allowed to flourish. Few mourned the restrictive rules and general monopoly of the Dutch West India Company after it was disestablished. Nicolls set up local governments with limited white male suffrage with further restrictions based on property ownership. Colonial governors appointed mayors but a board of aldermen (city council) was elected. (Thomas Willett was the first mayor.)

Stuyvesant was recalled to the Netherlands for an upbraiding by the Dutch West India Company, which had just lost their entire investment. They accused him of lying about the preparedness of the town, general incompetence, and cowardice. He responded by defending his actions as governor-general and explained that he had no choice in the surrender. Further, he accused the directors of the Dutch West India Company of failing to send enough soldiers and supplies to defend the town adequately.

Rather than remain in the Netherlands, in 1667 Peter Stuyvesant returned to Manhattan, his home of seventeen years. He retired to the *bouwerie*, his farm, located two miles north of the town and enjoyed a quiet retirement with his family while managing his farm. His successor, New York Governor Richard Nicolls, regularly rode out to the bouwerie to discuss political events and economic policy with Stuyvesant. Despite having been on opposite sides in 1664, they shared many common experiences and became close friends. Nicolls was recalled to England in 1668. Stuyvesant died at home in 1672. Nicolls was killed when a Dutch cannonball hit him during the Third Anglo-Dutch War the same year.

CHAPTER 19
New Orange Interregnum

The colony changed hands in 1672 and 1673 because as a European outpost it was caught up as a pawn in international rivalries among European countries. The leading position of Spain and Portugal as colonial powers was already diminishing in the late 17th century. France, England, and the Netherlands were competing and colluding to replace them as superpowers. As part of this struggle the Third Anglo-Dutch War began in 1672. French forces led by Louis XIV were allied with the English under Charles II against William II of Orange, the Dutch *stadtholder* of Zeeland, and the Captain-General and Admiral-General of the United Provinces. These were position created for House of Orange royalty within the republic, consisting of Holland, Zeeland, Friesland, Gelderland, Utrecht, Groningen, and Overijssel.

A Dutch naval force was sent to the Caribbean and then up the North American coast to disrupt English and French shipping routes by confiscating slaves, tobacco, sugar, and rum, and harassing their colonial possessions. When they got to the edge of New York's outer harbor the fleet under the command of Admiral Cornelius Evertsen dropped anchor and met secretly with local Dutch loyalists eager to have Dutch rule reestablished.

Learning that Fort James, which had been Fort Amsterdam under the Dutch, was poorly fortified and that Governor Francis Lovelace was out of town, Admiral Evertsen decided to attack on August 8, 1673. Aided by Dutch saboteurs who disabled some of the English canons, Evertsen brought his ships through the inner harbor and dropped anchor in the Hudson River just north of the fort. When the English commander ignored his request to surrender, Evertsen bombarded the fort and landed a party of several hundred Dutch soldiers under the command of Captain Anthony Colve. They were joined by some of the local Dutch residents as they advanced on Fort James, which surrendered without a shot. Admiral Evertsen renamed the colony New Netherland and the town New Orange in honor of Prince William of Orange. Colve was appointed governor-general.

For the five months that New York was New Orange, the Dutch population was pleased to restore Dutch forms of local government and law, the Dutch language, and reestablish the Dutch Reformed Church. Special jubilation was noted in the five overwhelmingly Dutch towns of western Long Island, later to become Kings County: Brooklyn, Bushwyck, Flatbush, Flatlands, and New Utrecht.

Colonel Francis Lovelace, the former English governor who had been in Connecticut, came back to town and was arrested by the Dutch. They sent him to England where he was accused of incompetence and briefly incarcerated in the Tower of London.

Exhausted by years of war and more concerned over the threat posed by France than England, the Netherlands sued for peace with the English. (The French were occupying four of the seven provinces of the Netherlands.) The Treaty of Westminster, which was signed on February 19, 1674, ended hostilities between the English and the Dutch. The city of New Orange and province of New Netherland were awarded to England, and were named New York for the second time.

English institutions were reestablished in the province and city of New York. The King Charles II appointed Major Edmund Andros as the new governor. The Dutch inhabitants were treated with leniency though many had supported the overthrow of English rule. They were able to keep their property and in many ways continued to live in a parallel society. Many Dutch families spoke Dutch at home, socialized, worshipped, and married within their ethnic group. Dutch families, many years later called *knickerbockers* by author Washington Irving, remained an important segment of upper class establishment for the next three centuries. Many place names in New York City come from early knickerbocker families: Bayard, Beekman, Lefferts, Roosevelt, Stuyvesant, Van Cortlandt, Van Rensselaer, Van Wyck, Vanderbilt, Varick, Wyckoff.

In an interesting twist of monarchical politics, religion, and intrigue among royal families, the son of the Dutch prince who fought against England eventually became king of England. Prince William III of Orange, born eight days after his father died of smallpox in 1650, became joint-sovereign (co-ruler) with his wife Mary, daughter of King James II of England, in 1689. William and Mary landed fifteen thousand Dutch troops near Plymouth, England, which was enough to send the king packing, though not before he tossed the Great Seal of England into the Thames River for spite. The revolution was bloodless. James II was allowed to escape to France. Supporters of William and Mary, pleased to secure a dependably Protestant royal family and give a little more power to the Parliament, called this coup d'etât the *Glorious Revolution*. Parliament passed a Bill of Rights, which protected commoners from some of the more flagrant abuses of royal power. England was becoming a constitutional monarchy.

CHAPTER 20
Architecture of the Dutch Period

It was predictable that the Dutch and Flemish settlers sought to recreate the familiar architecture of their hometowns in Europe. Other colonists did the same. The Pilgrims and Puritans in Massachusetts as well as the settlers in Virginia, all from places in England, constructed mud and wattle buildings made with wooden beam frames and woven sticks, reeds, and branches packed with mud or clay for the walls. The Swedes in New Sweden along the lower Delaware River built log cabins. So what did the Dutch build in New Amsterdam?

Houses in town and country differed, though not at first. Initially, most houses in New Amsterdam and the rural parts of New Netherland were similar. Houses were built of fieldstones held together by cement. The stones could be gathered from almost anywhere. Thick squared wood beams rested on the heavy stone walls and held up the roof. Steep-pitched roofs kept snow off in the winter and provided room for an upstairs sleeping loft. The eaves (lower ends of the roof) were flared out, sometimes so broadly they needed a row of slender columns to hold them up. The roof was covered with split-wood shingles. Windows always had wood shutters and did not usually have glass, which was expensive. Front and back doors were divided *Dutch* doors with top and bottom halves opening independently. Fireplaces were on the side walls and were enormous medieval-style jambless areas. Each had a single hearthstone, tile backing, and overhanging mantel with no *jambs* (sides). A short cloth skirt around the mantel helped coax the smoke up the chimney. The non-gable side of the house faced the street. Usually a house had two equally sized rooms, kitchen and parlor. That style house predominated in countryside, but was replaced in New Amsterdam by a taller, more substantial model.

In the latter part of the Dutch colonial period (1625-1664) town houses began to resemble those in cities in the Netherlands.

They were built of brick, usually stood three or floor stories high with the narrow gable side facing the street, and had a distinct step-gable roof. A hoisting bracket, the end of the main roof beam that extended three feet out in the front, was fitted with a hook and was used to hoist furniture or storage supplies in and out of the upper floors through windows. Roofs in New Amsterdam were half-barrel tiles made of red clay. A Dutch townhouse was usually raised off the ground, which meant steps were needed to get to the first floor. They called it a *stoop*.

An interesting adornment on later Dutch houses in the countryside was the *gambrel* roof which extends up in three segments: the gently sloping flared portion at the bottom, a highly pitched mid-section, and then a separate top portion pitched less steeply toward the center. The point was to give the attic more space and turn it into a proper second story.

Lenape Indians lived in villages scattered through the area during the Dutch period. Each Indian band, or sub-group, had two sets of dwellings: one tucked into the interior hills for winter, and the other located near the sea or rivers in the summer. The communal longhouse predominated in the more substantial settlements. Construction was of bent saplings, woven with sticks, and covered with bark and grass matting. Half-barrel style roofs were used. Smoke holes were left open at the top. Thatched partitions separated individual family areas. A fence made of wood stakes placed close together usually surrounded a cluster of longhouses. Seaside homes were often *wigwams*: (roundhouses) made of bent saplings covered with grass mats.

Examples of Dutch houses are very rare in New York City. None exists in the center of New Amsterdam, presently a forest of skyscraper in the Wall Street Financial District. But there is one remaining Dutch farmhouse in Manhattan: the Dyckman House (1661) at Broadway and 204th Street in Inwood. Brooklyn also has one Dutch farmhouse: the Pieter Claesen Wyckoff House (1652) at Clarendon Road and Ralph Avenue in East Flatbush. The Queens farmhouse of John Bowne (1661) is from the Dutch period, but since Flushing's settlers were English, the architecture is slightly different. It is located on Bowne Street and 37th Avenue in Flusing Each of these three farmhouses is now a museum.

• English Colonial Period

(1664-1783)

CHAPTER 21
Fraunces Tavern

Fraunces Tavern is located at the corner Pearl and Broad Streets at the southern end of Manhattan's Wall Street Financial District. It was built as a large private dwelling in the center of New York City's most attractive residential neighborhood, the area southeast of Bowling Green. Pearl Street glistened with the crushed oyster shells that provided its name.

The merchant Stephen DeLancey constructed the house in 1719. It was transformed into an inn, called the Queen's Head, or Queen Charlotte, by Samuel Fraunces, after he purchased it in 1762. Most of the patrons referred to it by its owner's name, and called it Fraunces Tavern. He had a reputation for supervising a kitchen that produced fine food. The restaurant even had a take-out component, and customers could send a servant or slave to order food to be delivered to their homes. There were five bedrooms on the third floor of the inn for overnight guests. Fraunces had immigrated to New York from the West Indies. Though he was a slave owner and traveled in elite circles, some historians believe he may have had one black grandparent. In numerous documents of the time he was called Black Sam, though in the 1790 census Fraunces is listed as *free, white, head of household.*

Fraunces was part owner of several other taverns and a *pleasure garden* (an outdoor café with entertainment) in New York City, and an inn in Philadelphia. He was forced to remain in Loyalist-controlled New York City during the Revolution and serve the Redcoats, though he also spied on them, and for his efforts received a $2,000 grant by the new American government. Following the Treaty of Paris, the tavern dropped its royalist name, which honored Queen Charlotte, wife of George III. In 1785, Fraunces sold the establishment to George Powers, a butcher from Brooklyn. Fraunces managed his other businesses until 1789, the year the national capital was placed in New York and George Washington resided in the city. Samuel Fraunces served as Washington's chief steward, supervising the staff and preparation of meals at Washington's two temporary presidential residences, the first one a town house on Cherry Street and the second a town house on Broadway. From 1790 until 1794 Fraunces was Washington's chief steward in Philadelphia, the second capital of the United States.

Fraunces Tavern was a focal point for patriots in the years leading to the American Revolution. The Sons of Liberty and the Committee of Correspondence regularly held their meetings at Fraunces Tavern. General George Washington bid an emotional farewell to his officers in 1783 in the Long Room, a dining room on the second floor: *With a heart full of love and gratitude, I now take leave of you. I most devoutly wish that your latter days may be as prosperous and happy as your former ones have been glorious and honorable.*

In 1785, the government of the Thirteen Colonies, which was organized under the Articles of Confederation, moved some offices into the building. The very limited national government had a congress but no president and lacked power to compel the thirteen independent components to act in unison. By 1787 leaders throughout the colonies realized their mistake and began working on the Constitution in Philadelphia, which produced a new government called the United States of America.

In 1789, the new republic elected former Revolutionary War General George Washington its first president and chose New York City as its temporary capital. New York's City Hall, located four blocks north from Fraunces Tavern at the corner of Broad and Wall Streets, was given to the new national government by the City Council as the headquarters its government. (A new City Hall, which is still in use, was finished in 1811.)

Federal Hall was the new name given to the three-story old City Hall. The French architect Pierre Charles L'Enfant remodeled it in 1788, so it could be used for Washington's presidential office, the Senate and House of Representatives, and the Supreme Court. (In 1791, L'Enfant was commissioned to design the street grid and some of the buildings for the new capital, Federal City, later called Washington, D.C.)

Before Federal Hall was completely ready, Fraunces Tavern temporarily housed the Departments of Foreign Affairs (State), War (Defense), and the Treasury. After those departments relocated to Federal Hall, Fraunces Tavern reverted to its former status as an inn, though a busy one since the capitol building was only four blocks away.

The next several decades were not kind to Fraunces Tavern. As the city grew and many businesses moved northward, it became a run-down waterfront bar and pool hall. In 1904 the Sons of the Revolution purchased the red and yellow brick building and remodeled the interior, which over the years had been altered several times. The Sons of the Revolution is a fraternal organization open to any man with ancestors who fought with the patriots in the American Revolution. (The Daughters of the American Revolution is a similar organization with membership open to women.)

The plans developed by the Sons of the Revolution, however well intended, were based mostly on romantic conjecture. There were no floor plans of what the original building looked like. Fraunces Tavern reopened in 1907 as a restaurant and bar with a museum upstairs. There are two large works of art, which help transport visitors to the 18th century. A faded oil painting in the back dining room portrays New York City in 1717 when its population was only about six thousand. The bar, decorated with muskets and swords, holds a very large though less than convincing scene from the Battle of Long Island (1776). More interesting and completely authentic are the framed documents hanging on the walls associated with Washington, Jefferson, and Hancock.

The museum is located on the second and third floors. The second floor has a rebuilt Long Room and a period room named for Governor George Clinton. The rooms are furnished with items from the late English colonial period. The third floor includes a lecture hall, wall hangings, and numerous exhibition cases. Displays include political and legal documents, books, paintings, lithographs, maps, muskets, swords, cannonballs, household items, military uniforms, flags, tobacco pipes, commemorative pitchers, mugs, and plates. The Fraunces Tavern Museum is located at 54 Pearl Street, corner of Broad Street. It is open to the public and tours may be arranged.

The new Fraunces Tavern was America's original historical theme restaurant. Through several incarnations beginning in 1907, Fraunces Tavern served what was generally perceived as colonial

American fare in an 18th century atmosphere. The colonial-style *bill of fare* included corned beef hash, roast beef, ham pasty (cubed ham in a puff pastry), braised rabbit, venison medallions, duck stuffed with cornbread, pheasant, rack of lamb with mint sauce, flounder baked in a puff pastry, Yorkshire pudding, clam chowder, fish chowder, and oyster stew. Desserts offered were pies, cobblers, and trifle. Drinks included gin, rum, bourbon, sour mash, ale, port, and sherry. Though restaurant critics regularly poked fun at the food for being old-fashioned and unsophisticated, the experience of eating in the place where the Founding Fathers gathered has been attractive to many people.

In its latest incarnation, the menu is *nouvelle cuisine* or New American. Fraunces Tavern reopened in 2002 with a menu including sesame-seared tuna, steak *tartar*, shrimp in peanut sauce, lobster, mesculun salad, and other choices *not* enjoyed in the colonial period. Clam chowder is still available, but other examples of early American cuisine are offered only as periodic specials.

The reason 18th century New Yorkers did not eat some of the foods now served at Fraunces Tavern vary depending on the dish. Raw fish or meat would have repulsed diners of the time, sesame crust and mesculun salad was unknown, peanut sauce had not yet been developed, and shrimp was from sources that were too far away. Lobster (along with monkfish and skate) was considered junk-fish and fed to slaves, indentured servants, and prisoners.

CHAPTER 22
Trans-Atlantic Shipping and the Slave Trade

Dutch trade patterns were relatively uncomplicated. They involved finished products, especially metal, ceramic, cloth, liquor, and gunpowder from the Netherlands, exchanged with products from Goa (India), Java and the Molucca Islands (Indonesia) and the Dutch colonies in the New World: Curaçao, Bonaire, Aruba, St. Maarten, and Dutch Guiana (Suriname) in the Caribbean, Bahia (northeast Brazil), and New Netherland, which stretched from the Connecticut to the Delaware Rivers.

The Dutch West India Company, organized in 1621 by the government, controlled the colonies and their trade. The system was neither efficient nor profitable because of the high costs of administering and protecting the colonies. Few Dutch people were willing to be settlers and live under the control of the company.

Trade depended on the cooperation of the Native Americans, who were often hostile, and who had little the Europeans desired except furs from small animals. Beaver, otter, mink, and muskrat hides led the list of export items from the docks at New Amsterdam. *Naval stores* (masts for ships, wood tar, pitch, and turpentine), lumber (smoothed boards), salted and dried fish (mostly cod), and grain rounded out the trade items. Dutch ships brought rice, sugar, and spices to New Amsterdam from the other colonies, all located in the tropics.

During the English period, a semblance of free trade developed, which made the Atlantic maritime trade considerably more profitable. Long Island farms exported grain to the less fertile New England colonies across Long Island Sound. Some agricultural products were sold to English importers, but most went to the Caribbean colonies owned by England: Jamaica, Trinidad, Granada, Antigua, Barbados, Bermuda, the Bahamas, and British Honduras (Belize). With little arable land on each Caribbean island, plantation owners wanted to concentrate on sugar, their most profitable crop. Ships from the Caribbean brought slave-produced sugar to refineries in New York, and would return with grain, vegetables, fruit, pork, beef, and cheese.

Colonial commerce is often presented as the *triangle trade*, which, while it has some truth, is an over-simplification and ignores the pivotal role of shrewd sea captains in making financial judgments and business deals. The triangle trade paradigm, in the English case, portrayed rum from the North American colonies shipped to West Africa to be exchanged for slaves who were transported to the British West Indies, and exchanged for raw sugar and molasses, which was sent to the Thirteen Colonies in North America.

In reality the trade during the English period was much more complicated and individualistic depending on the entrepreneurial skill of each sea captain, who, as buyer and seller, took into consideration cost and profit margins, as well as wind and sea current patterns. Very often ships traveled beyond the triangle destinations to Great Britain or Ireland to sell goods, or to British African ports to buy and sells goods that had nothing to do with the slave trade. In the later colonial period a few ships ventured as far as India and China in quest of profitable exchange.

After independence, a large part of early American trade involved Asia. The China trade captured the imagination of many investors and ship captains. The strategy involved loading a ship with American products, sailing to China, reaping a profit from the sale of American goods, and investing part of the profit buying items to bring back to the United States to sell. The furs and hides of beaver, mink, fox, rabbit, raccoon, muskrat, buffalo, deer, otter, sea otter, and seal, as well as grains, cotton, and *ginseng* were traded in China for Chinese products. American ships had to navigate the dangerous, stormy waters of Cape Horn in order to reach New York City.

They brought home tea, silk, carpets, ivory, jade, porcelain, and *cloisonné*. Some American merchants, including John Jacob Astor, bolstered their trading power by buying opium off the coast of China, either from English privateers or Chinese pirates, and sold it in Canton or Shanghai.

Trading opium was not the only despicable commerce that attracted ship owners, captains, and investors. The trans-Atlantic slave trade is unparalleled in colonial-era barbarity. Plantation and mine owners in South America and the Caribbean felt the *need* for slaves in the 16th century. Free Europeans refused to cross the ocean and labor in silver mines in Peru or toil in sugar and rice fields in the Caribbean and Brazil. The owners wanted a dependable source of labor, which could be forced to work. Enslaved Indians died from diseases, mostly smallpox, or slipped away into familiar territory.

Africa was first used as a source for slaves even before Columbus first arrived in America in 1492. The Portuguese captured Ceuta, in present-day Morocco, in 1415, and used it as a trading post to obtain gold and slaves from the interior of the continent. The Portuguese used the slaves in Portugal until they established Bahia, their colony on the coast of South America. Later in the century they founded El Mina, Bissau, São Tomé, Luanda, Delagoa Bay, Sofala, Mozambique, Zanzibar, and Mombasa, fortresses and colonies for the slave trade in the modern African countries of Guinea-Bissau, Ghana, São Tomé and Principe, Angola, Mozambique, Tanzania, and Kenya.

The European slave trade was made possible by unscrupulous African middlemen, often rulers, who captured people in the interior of the continent, marched them to the coast where they were sold to white slave traffickers, and held in prisons until the arrival of the next slave ship. Slavery existed in Africa, with Africans enslaving other Africans, before the arrival of the Europeans, just as it existed in all the other continents until recent times. It was the Europeans, however, who profited most from the system because it provided slave-owners with a cheap labor force for centuries.

The *middle passage* is the term denoting the slaves' traumatic cross-Atlantic journey to the New World. Slaves suffered terrible conditions chained in the holds of ships and an estimated twenty percent died on the voyage. Their bodies were unceremoniously thrown overboard. Estimates of how many Africans were enslaved vary widely. The answer is probably between ten and twenty million people. The slave trade enriched the callous and greedy slave owners, especially plantation proprietors, caused long-term misery and deprivation to the slaves, and significantly altered demographics in both Africa and the Americas.

The Netherlands had become a powerful maritime country by 1600 when at least ten thousand commercial ships sailed under the Dutch flag. By the 1630s the Dutch had displaced the Portuguese as the principal slave trading country. In 1626 the Dutch West India Company brought the first African slaves to New Amsterdam to work on its farms, buildings, and fortifications. Individual Dutch residents also bought slaves. Because the slave system in 17th century New Netherland did not consume vast numbers of Africans as it did in the Caribbean and Brazil, slaves were rarely brought to the colony directly from Africa. They often came in small groups from purloined Spanish and Portuguese vessels, or were bought in other Dutch colonies: the Dutch Antilles in the Caribbean (Curaçao, Aruba, Bonaire), St. Maarten, or Dutch Brazil (Recifé and Belém).

In the English colony of New York trafficking in slaves became a very big business. Some of the slave companies supplying the southern colonies had headquarters and investors in New York City. Slave sales and auctions were held publicly, often in front of the Merchants' Coffee House. Slavery was open and few 18th century white New Yorkers objected to it. Slaves in rural counties in New York were used for farm work. Slaves in the city labored as dockworkers, warehousemen, porters, road builders, as well as skilled tradesmen, and a smaller percentage worked as servants in middle and upper class homes. In 1664, one-fifth of New York City's population was black, and Brooklyn 's black population reached one-quarter. Most black New Yorkers in the 17th and 18th centuries were slaves. The percentage of slaves in New York City declined to about fifteen percent after the American Revolution. European immigrants progressively outnumbered slaves.

The official end of the trans-Atlantic slave trade came in 1807 when Britain abolished the slave trade and declared it a capital crime. The next year the United States Congress joined in abolishing the international slave trade, although allowing it within the United States. Pleased, President Thomas Jefferson wrote to Congress: *I congratulate you, fellow citizens, on the approach of the period at which you may interpose your authority constitutionally to withdraw the citizens of the United States from all further participation in those violations of human rights which have been so long continued on the unoffending inhabitants of Africa.*

The motivation for ending international slave trafficking was anything but altruistic. In 1791, slaves in Saint Dominigue, the French half of the Caribbean island Hispaniola, exploded in revolt. Despite French and British military intervention and the capture of leader Toussaint L'Ouverture, the slaves gained independence in 1804. It was the first successful slave revolt in history. Terrified that slave insurrections would spread from one country to another, the British and Americans decided to end the international slave trade.

Because slave trading was profitable, some ship captains continued to buy, transport, and sell slaves. A case in point involved an illegal Spanish slave ship, the *Amistad,* sailing from Cuba in 1839. A slave mutiny led by Sengbe Pieh, an African recently captured in Sierra Leone and given the slave name Joseph Cinque, caused the ship to end up docked in Connecticut. A contentious legal question arose: should the Africans remain in Connecticut as free blacks, or should they be sent to Cuba where they would be returned to slavery. In 1841 the United States Supreme Court found in favor of the Africans and they were released. Former President John Quincy Adams had argued their case. Slavery was finally abolished in New York State in 1827 though it continued in the South until the end of the Civil War in 1865.

New York City's position in international trade was magnified greatly by an internal development project, the Erie Canal, completed in 1825. While the city had a superb harbor it needed more to export, and a greater population to produce export goods and consume imported products. Wheat, corn, apples, potatoes, cheese, corn whiskey, furs, hay, live hogs, hams, finished lumber, and coal were brought to the city by the canal from the Great Lakes region and Upstate New York. The Erie Canal provided products to trade along the Atlantic coast, Europe, and the Caribbean. Migrants and immigrants streamed into the city seeking employment and the population rose from 124,000 in 1820 to 814,000 in 1860.

Early 19th century industries included wool and cotton mills, chemical plants, saw mills and lumber yards, furniture factories, ceramic and terra-cotta works, iron foundries, metal factories, glassware companies, shoe factories, chewing tobacco producers, glue factories, distilleries, breweries, and food processing plants. Later 19th century industries included the production of refined oil, natural gas, ready-to-wear garments, paints, dyes, cut and polished marble and granite, pharmaceuticals, industrial chemicals, refined sugar, drain pipes, cooking ware, plumbing supplies, flowerpots, porcelain, glassware, processed spices, printers' ink, newspapers, magazines, and books.

The era of heavy industry in New York City ended in the years after the First World War. Factories and mills sought cheaper land, proximity to raw materials, and lower labor costs in other parts of the United States, and ultimately in foreign countries. Today, even light industry hangs on perilously. The city and its workforce have entered a post-industrial phase. Service industries, especially financial services, and the tourist and hospitality industry (hotels and restaurants), are the dominant engines of the local economy.

Shipbuilding was an industry that spanned the centuries. It began, after a fashion, with Dutch explorer Adriaen Block in January 1613, a dozen years before New Amsterdam was founded. Block's ship, the *Tijger* (*Tiger*), burned while it was tied up in the Hudson River toward the tip of Manhattan. Block had two more ships, the *Fortuyn (Fortune)* and the *Nachtegael (Nightingale)*, though the latter was seized by its mutinous crew and sailed off. That winter, Block's remaining crew and some helpful Lenape Indians built a very small ship, the *Onrust* (*Restlessness*) and with the *Fortuyn* explored and mapped the Hudson River and Long Island Sound. The *Fortuyn* and the *Onrust* would be too small to carry the remaining crew and acquired furs back to Amsterdam. Fortunately, two Dutch ships arrived unexpectedly in spring 1614 and took Block's crew back to the Netherlands. The charred remains of the *Tijger* were found and photographed in 1916 during excavations for the Cortlandt Street Subway Station of the Interboro Rapid Transit system, which was obliterated on September 11, 2001.

Early commercial shipyards in the colonial era were small and generally situated on the Manhattan shore of the East River near Corlear's Hook at the far eastern end of the island near Grand

Street. Hulls were constructed on wood frames and braces on the riverbank and slid into the water when finished. Robert Fulton's steamship, the *Clermont*, was built in 1807 at the yard of Charles Browne, an eminent shipwright, at Corlear's Hook. Local shipyards began producing naval vessels in 1790 and the New York Navy Yard (later called Brooklyn Navy Yard) opened specifically for that purpose in 1806. The ironclad *Monitor* was built at the Continental Iron Works in Greenpoint in 1862.

In the late 19th century more sophisticated shipyards were built with *dry docks*, basin enclosures where ships can be constructed. When the vessel was completed the basin was slowly flooded to let the new ship proceed into the river. Dry dock shipyards were constructed across the river in Brooklyn, notably at Wallabout Bay (Brooklyn Navy Yard), Bushwick Creek, Newtown Creek, and Gowanus Bay. Shipyards also opened in Flushing Bay, Queens, in Tottenville and along the Kill Van Kull, Staten Island, and in the Bronx at City Island.

Steam-powered *packet ships* (passenger vessels with scheduled service) began to cross the Atlantic between New York and European ports in 1838. The clipper ships operated only from 1843 until 1860 when they were replace by steamships. Over one hundred docks protruded into the Hudson and East Rivers. Passenger ships used many of the docks. By the 1860s there was at least one trans-Atlantic departure each day, and between 1900 and 1950 the Port of New York was the busiest commercial port in the world. At that time there were 150,000 longshoremen in the city.

The number of dockworkers swelled with the increase in maritime business. The International Longshoremen's Association (I.L.A.), which was organized in 1938, represented most of them in collective bargaining. Unions had existed since before the Civil War, but the I.L.A. was a tightly controlled, patronage-laden union, which secured high wages and benefits for its members but was ultimately undone in New York City by the decline of the entire industry.

A colorful aspect of the I.L.A. was the way their representatives (not the company's) chose extra men to supplement a work gang. Hiring was done at a shape-up at the foot of the pier. Union stewards would choose the men in a process noted for kickbacks and ethnic favoritism. The novel, *Last Exit to Brooklyn*, by Hubert Selby, Jr., and the 1989 film by the same name, depict Red Hook and its rough longshoremen in 1952. Matty Rich's bleak 1991 film, *Straight Out of Brooklyn*, also presents a debased and violent waterfront subculture. Novels and films inevitably portrayed the brawling, raw side of life among dockworkers.

Shipbuilding in the 20th century was predominantly military. In the Second World War the Brooklyn Navy Yard and the Bethlehem Navy Yard in Staten Island produced destroyers, battleships, cruisers, and aircraft carriers. City Island shipyards produced yachts through most of the century except during the World Wars when their facilities were re-tooled to manufacture smaller naval craft. By the 21st century only the Brooklyn Navy Yard remained active in shipbuilding, but at about one-tenth its former capacity, and since 1966 as a private shipyard in an industrial park, no longer affiliated with the United States Department of Defense.

Shipping in the Port of New York declined precipitously in the closing four decades of the 20th century. Air transport and overland trucking often proved more competitive than shipping by sea. What little maritime business remains in the 21st century is confined to several wharves in Carroll Gardens and Red Hook, Brooklyn where giant gantry cranes load and unload standard-sized steel containers measuring forty feet in length. Few employees are needed for the highly automated and downsized industry and the rough stevedore (longshoreman) culture of the waterfront has ended.

Notation:

***Amazing Grace* by John Newton**

John Newton composed *Amazing Grace*, the instantly recognizable Protestant hymn that has achieved special gospel music status and popularity in the United States. Newton, an English sea captain, composed the hymn sometime in the 1770s. It was first published in 1779 under the title *Faith's Review and Expectation*. The music may have been adapted from either an African melody or an American folk song known as *Loving Lambs*.

Newton, born in London in 1725, went to sea at age eleven

and began working on slave ships in 1745. He ultimately became captain of an independent slaver, an occupation he continued until he retired from the business. *During the entire time I was engaged in the slave trade, I never had the least scruple to its lawfulness. I was upon the whole satisfied with my employment, usually very profitable, though to me it did not prove so, the Lord seeing that a large increase of wealth would not be good for me. However, I considered myself a sort of jailer and I was sometimes shocked with an employment that was perpetually connected with chains, bolts, and shackles. In this view I had often prayed that the Lord, in His own time would place me in a more humane calling, and where I might have more frequent fellowship with His people and ordinances.*

There is a general misconception regarding the story of John Newton's conversion from non-believer to devout Christian. The conversion, which he called his *Great Deliverance*, took place in 1748 when his ship safely survived a ferocious storm in the Atlantic Ocean. Contrary to common belief, Newton did not give up the slave trade but continued slaving until 1775. While generally uncomfortable with his occupation, the only change he made regarding slave trading after his conversion experience was that he treated his captives more humanely.

Newton's metamorphosis was purely a religious experience. He began to study Hebrew and Greek, the original languages of the Bible, sought out the leaders of early Methodism, John Wesley and George Whitefield, preached, and wrote several hymns.

In a 1774 letter he wrote: *How wonderful is the patience of God toward sinful men.* Like Reformation leader Martin Luther, Newton believed in *salvation by grace alone*. He wrote and preached on that issue very often. *Salvation is wholly of grace, not only undeserved by us until God is pleased to awaken us to a sense of our need of it. And then we find everything prepared that our wants require or our wished conceive, yea, that He has done exceedingly beyond what we could either ask or think.* Newton's conversion was not from his dishonorable occupation but from his irreligious attitude.

Text of *Amazing Grace*:

Amazing grace!

how sweet the sound,
That saved a wretch like me!
I once was lost, but now am found,
Was blind, but now I see.

'Twas grace that taught my heart to fear,
And grace my fears relieved;
How precious did that grace appear
The hour I first believed!

Thro' man-y dangers, toils and snares,
I have al-read-y come;
'Tis grace hath bro't me safe thus far,
And grace will lead me home.

When we've been there ten thousand years,
Bright shin-ing as the sun,
We've no less days to sing God's praise
Than when we first be-gun.

CHAPTER 23
Farming

Farming did not completely disappear from the five boroughs until November 2003 when the city's last farm, a two-acre patch of land in Fresh Meadows, Queens was sold to a developer for $4.3 million. In earlier centuries agriculture was an important part of the economy of the five boroughs.

Native Americans practiced limited agriculture in the area focusing on corn, beans, and squash, which they called the *three sisters*. Women in Native American society did the farming. With a small population and enormous resources in the forests (hunting), meadows (gathering), and waterways (fishing), the Lenape Indians had little incentive to increase crop production.

Some Dutch settlers began farming immediately. They brought livestock, which the Indians did not possess, from Europe, and soon established farming settlements in the surrounding counties. The Dutch introduced the production of grains: wheat, rye, barley, and oats. They borrowed corn cultivation from their Lenape neighbors and also used raised hillocks in which to plant vegetables following the native practice. Agriculture caused friction between the Dutch and Indians. Often Dutch livestock, which usually grazed and rooted around in the open, trampled Indian gardens causing arguments and fights.

At first the European farmers planted traditional grains because two of their basic foods, bread and gruel, were made from cereal crops. As meat eaters, they also raised cows, pigs, sheep, ducks, pigeons, and chickens. As New York City's population grew it made less sense to grow such crops and the farmers responded by changing their focus. Grain and livestock could be imported from counties further away. Cattle and sheep from outlying areas were herded to the riverside, ferried live to Manhattan where they were kept at slaughterhouses, or in the yard behind a butcher shop, and slaughtered as needed. Pigs, ducks, and sheep had to be moved by carts. In the days before refrigeration butchers kept small corrals of live animals behind their shops.

New York area farmers realized that the most profitable crops for them would be highly perishable items like fruit, vegetables, and dairy products, though they never completely gave up on livestock and grain. Farmers could take the perishable goods across the rivers and sell them in the open markets. Apple, pear, plum, and peach orchards soon dotted upper Manhattan and the outer boroughs. Vegetables included beans, beets, onions, cabbage, tomatoes, and potatoes. Dairy cattle produced milk for the city and a thriving cheese and butter industry began. Delmonico's, a well-known Wall Street area restaurant, which has existed in one form or another since 1827, built part of its reputation by proudly advertising its fresh dairy products, fruit, and vegetables supplied daily from its rural Brooklyn farm.

Garden farming, which is what this type of agriculture is called, is labor intensive. A relatively small farm can yield a great deal of agricultural produce if there is sufficient labor. The Dutch began importing African slaves by way of the Caribbean and Brazil. The first slaves were eleven African men imported in 1626 and three African women brought over in 1628. Soon a substantial percentage of the rural population of Brooklyn and Queens was slaves. They did all types of farm work: cutting firewood, thatching roofs, building fences, mowing hay, plowing fields, planting, weeding, harvesting, milking cows, and butchering animals.

By the English take-over in 1664, slaves composed twenty percent of the colony's population. At the time of the first United States Census in 1790, there were 2,369 slaves in Manhattan, 2,309 in Queens, 1,432 in Brooklyn, 759 in Staten Island, and 1,419 in Westchester County, the lower portion of which eventually became the Bronx. Except in New York City (the lower part of Manhattan) where slaves toiled as dockworkers, road builders, carters, and domestic servants, most slaves in the area of the five boroughs were farm laborers. Slavery was finally outlawed throughout New York in 1827, but the prohibition did not go into effect fully until 1841.

In the English period, New York's farms exported some of their goods to towns in the less fertile New England colonies across

Long Island Sound. The big purchasers, however, were the Caribbean colonies. The world was developing a sweet tooth and New York was no different. Ships from the Caribbean brought slave-produced sugar to refineries along the East River to be turned into table sugar. The empty ships would load up on grain, vegetables, fruit, pork, beef, and cheese from area farms for the return voyage.

As New York City grew it became increasingly hard to farm. Houses crowded next to fields and made transportation and manure removal difficult. As transportation developed, area farmers had to compete with larger, more efficient farms elsewhere. But land speculation was the main cause of the decline of farming. Rising land values tempted many farmers to sell out and let their farms be subdivided for housing. Some enterprising farmers, like Hezekiah Pierrepont in Brooklyn Heights, divided and sold the land themselves.

In 1900 there were still two thousand farms in the five boroughs. By 1930 only two hundred were left. Manhattan's last farm was the Bendetto farm, Broadway and 213th Street in Inwood, which ceased operating in 1930. The last pair of working oxen toiled at the LaTourette farm in Staten Island into the first decade of the 20th century. Two waves of real estate speculation, one in the 1910s and the other in the 1960s when the Verrazano Bridge was built, converted most Staten Island farmland to lots for housing.

Brooklyn's last farms were in Bay Ridge, Flatbush, Bensonhurst, Sheepshead Bay, Brownsville, and New Lots. None is left though Brooklyn does retain a striking monument to early agriculture. The oldest house in the five boroughs, and all New York State, is the Pieter Claesen Wyckoff Farmhouse. The oldest part, just one room with an upstairs sleeping loft, and an enormous medieval European style hearth, is dated 1652, just twenty-seven years after the Dutch settled New Amsterdam. It was part of a 66-acre farm abutting Jamaica Bay. Wyckoff's descendants occupied the house until 1902, donated to the city in 1969, and carefully restored and turned into a museum by New York City and the Wyckoff House Foundation in 1982.

The Bronx, which had numerous farms specializing in wheat and livestock, as well as orchards and vegetable farms, especially in Mott Haven, West Farms, and Belmont, became urbanized quickly after the introduction of railroads, and farmers sold their land for residential development.

Queens retained two types of specialty farming well into the 20th century. Cut flowers (especially tulips, carnations, and roses) were raised in Floral Park for New York City florist shops. Astoria had several farms specializing in Chinese varieties of vegetables rarely available at most greengrocers and sold mostly in Chinatown: *baicai* (cabbage), *xiao baicai* (white cabbage), *gai lan* (broccoli), *jiucai* (flowering chives), *qiezi* (eggplant), *luobo* (radish), *ku gua* (bitter melon), *dong gua* (winter melon), *you caixin* (flowering greens), and *lian ou* (lotus root). Asian vegetables are now raised in garden farms in New Jersey, or transported by truck from California and Florida.

Toward the end of the city's agricultural life, some farms converted their operations into nurseries where in greenhouses and small fields owners raised tree saplings, decorative shrubs, flowers, and houseplants. A few of those remain though they have little resemblance to farms.

Notations:

Last Farm in New York City

The John Klein Farm, just two acres, was sold to a developer for $4.3 million in November 2003. Originally the Klein farm had been two hundred acres. In 1890 there were 2,800 working farms in the five counties that united in 1898 to form New York City. The city's last farm was at 194-15 73rd Avenue in Fresh Meadows, Queens between the Long Island Expressway and Union Turnpike, next to the playground of P.S. 26. Because the large farmhouse in front blocked the view, many people never noticed it. Produce from the John Klein Farm, mostly sweet corn, eggplants, carrots, beets, scallions, peppers, and arugula, was sold from a large wooden stand that the proprietor opened for business each year in mid-July.

Queens County Farm Museum

The Queens County Farm Museum in Floral Park is on a 47-

acre parcel of land, which passed to government ownership in 1926. The farm dates from 1697 and had been a 101-acre farm in the past. The farmhouse was built in 1772, and expanded in 1856. The restored broad plank floors, beamed ceilings, overhanging eaves, and hand-split shingles represent what it looked like after the 1856 enlargement. The museum comprises the farmhouse, outbuildings (barns, wagon shed, chicken coop, potting shed, and greenhouses), the orchard, and the fields. Programs include workshops on apple pressing, honey collection, sheep shearing, chicken egg hatching, greenhouse planting, quilting, colonial cooking, and barnyard life. The museum is 73-50 Little Neck Parkway in Floral Park, Queens between Grand Central Parkway and Union Turnpike.

CHAPTER 24
Slavery in New York & Slave Revolts

The Dutch West India Company was unable to entice many Dutch settlers to move across the ocean and face the uncertainties of life in the New World. Facing a labor shortage they turned to slavery and enslaved American Indians and Africans. Because the Dutch needed to trade with local Indians they usually sought Indian slaves from tribes who lived at a distance from New Amsterdam. Enslaving Indians continued through most of the colonial period though it had two serious drawbacks apart from its moral bankruptcy. Indians could escape and often find their way back to their tribal land, and many Indians succumbed to the European diseases.

The first African slaves were brought to New Amsterdam in 1626 by the Dutch West India Company to work on its farms, buildings, and fortifications. Slaves constructed many of the public projects. Later, the company encouraged individual Dutch residents to import slaves. Transient slavers, not dealers operating in New Amsterdam, carried on most of the slave trade during the Dutch period. That changed in the English colony when trafficking in slaves became a big business in New York City.

Most of the slaves in New Netherland came from hijacked Spanish and Portuguese ships, or were purchased from the Dutch colonial possessions in the Dutch Antilles (Caribbean islands of Curaçao, Aruba, Bonaire), St. Maarten, or Dutch Brazil (Recifé and Belém).

The business of buying and selling slaves was exceptionally profitable though dangerous since pirates and *privateers* (government sanctioned pirates) plied the Atlantic searching for slave ships to hijack. Slave auctions were held at several public markets. The institution of slavery was open for everyone to see, though few of the whites had any qualms about it.

During the Dutch period a few slaves purchased or were granted their freedom. Some became farmers or tradesmen. They were at liberty to own slaves themselves or hold white indentured servants. Free blacks could travel, own property, learn to read and write, and join the militia, though they were obliged to carry papers to prove their status and faced the threat of re-enslavement if they could not prove that white people had freed them.

Because the Dutch saw slavery as an expedient, they developed a strange policy, which created results very different than found in the English, French, or Spanish colonies. The Dutch West India Company initiated a policy of *half-freedom,* which freed the affected slaves until they were needed. The half-free slaves had to pay the company a yearly tribute of grain and livestock in return for a pass stipulating their half-free status. They could farm, practice a trade, work as a laborer, or open a shop, but when the company needed their services, usually on the construction of public works, they had to leave their private pursuits and work without pay. The policy freed the company from having to house, clothe, or feed their slaves when they were not needed.

Children of half-free slaves remained fully owned by the company though they were never sold and separated from their families. Half-freedom clouded and confused the line separating the free from the enslaved. The policy has no philosophical consistency and was instituted merely to solve the problem of supporting slaves at times when their labor was unneeded. Half-slavery was abolished when the colony changed hands from the Netherlands to England.

By the English takeover in 1664, New York City was approximately one-fifth black, and Brooklyn 's black population was about one-quarter. Most of the black New Yoerkers were slaves. In Brooklyn and Queens, where Dutch farmers predominated in most towns, the figure was higher, probably because fewer immigrants (willing to do rigorous work for low pay) settled in those areas, and because agriculture, especially vegetable, dairy, and orchard farming, was labor-intensive. English towns in Brooklyn and Queens (Gravesend and Flushing) had fewer slaves. The reason is that those areas were Quaker strongholds and the Quakers opposed slavery.

New York became the largest slave importing and auctioning center in the English colonial period. Slaves came from Jamaica and Barbados, or directly from Africa. Some matters worsened for slaves under English rule. The half-free status was eliminated, and legal acceptance of black marriage and family units ended.

Punishment of slaves was left to the discretion of the owners, with some exceptions. The law prohibited murder and mutilation, while floggings and other forms of brutal physical punishment were allowed. The English sought to compel slaves to absolute obedience to their masters. Gatherings by three or more slaves were prohibited, and even slave burials, were regulated by laws. Fearful of the effect of African customs, and always concerned about slave revolts, the English government prohibited night funerals (common in parts of West Africa), and burials with more than twelve participants.

New York experienced two slave insurrections. In 1712 a slave revolt broke out in Manhattan, eight whites were killed, and some farm buildings at the outskirts of town were burned. Twenty-five defendants were convicted and received the death penalty. They were burned alive. Another revolt occurred in 1741, which lasted intermittently for several months. The governor's mansion, Fort George, and several houses and stores were burned. After accusations and confessions in court, thirteen blacks were burned at the stake, sixteen were hanged, and seventy-two were deported. Two white men and two white women were also executed as accomplices.

When blacks escaped from their owners in New York, some fled to Canada. To make that route more difficult, the state legislature in 1705 ordered the death penalty for any slave caught more than forty miles north of Albany. Others sought refuge with Indian tribes, especially the Shinecocks and Minisinks in eastern Long Island, and the Senecas and Onondagas in Upstate New York.

Most slaveholders were artisans, builders, shopkeepers, or farmers. Few owned more than six slaves, but many families owned one or two slaves. As the city increasingly attracted immigrants from Europe, slaves competed with new arrivals, mostly from England and Germany. The immigrants complained bitterly that their wages were depressed because they were forced into competition with people who received almost nothing for their labor. The increase in free and mobile labor made slavery less competitive economically. When the labor of a free worker was unneeded, he was laid off or fired, but slave owners had to keep housing and feeding their slaves. The competition drove a wedge between the two poorest and least powerful groups of New Yorkers: immigrants and slaves. The rivalry and antagonism was not ended by the full emancipation of New York State's slaves in 1827. The fear of competition from freed slaves during the Civil War was one of the main reasons why predominately Irish mobs indiscriminately turned on blacks during the Draft Riots in 1863.

The Society for the Propagation of the Gospel in Foreign Parts, a Protestant Christian missionary group, organized in England by Episcopal churchmen and prominent government leaders, had an unsettling effect on New York slaveholders and others. In the 18th century the society offered *catechism* classes (religious education) to slaves as well as unchurched whites. In 1760 the society opened a school for black children in New York City where reading, writing, and mathematics were offered in addition to religious education. Slave owners and other whites did not want slave children educated. Nor did they want religious education offered, because, while some Bible stories show the characters owning slaves (Abraham), others are stories about liberation (Moses). Further, English law prohibited the enslavement of Christians. The legal status of slavery could be threatened if black slaves could successfully claim to be Christians.

The Quakers had meetings (churches) in Manhattan, Brooklyn, Queens, and eastern Long Island. While never numerous, the Quakers were prominent in public debate and opinion leaders in their communities. Most Quakers had always opposed slavery and by 1770 the New York area meetings passed resolutions condemning slavery. Quakers were active in setting up schools for emancipated blacks and, in the 19th century, operating way stations in the Underground Railroad.

At the time of the American Revolution, when most national leaders waffled on slavery and were willing to compromise their principles for the sake of national unity, some prominent New Yorkers were staunch opponents of slavery. John Jay, Aaron Burr,

Gouverneur Morris, and Alexander Hamilton were principled in their condemnation of involuntary servitude.

In 1785, two years after the conclusion of the American Revolution, the New York Manumission Society was formed to promote its objective to end slavery in the state. John Jay and Alexander Hamilton each served as president. Other prominent New Yorkers active in the society were Hector St. John de Crèvecœur, Philip Schuyler, and Melancton Smith. New York City's mayor, James Duane, and New York State's Governor, George Clinton, were involved. Some of the society's members owned slaves, including John Jay, but were willing to give them up once the institution of slavery was ended.

Hector St. John de Crèvecœur was a French immigrant to upstate New York who loved the freedom he found in America. He wrote *Letters of An American Farmer*, and posed the question: *What is an American?* He filled his book replying to his rhetorical question with answers like this: *The American is a new man, who acts upon new principles; he must therefore entertain new ideas and form new opinions. And: We have no princes, for whom we toil, starve, and bleed. We are the most perfect society now existing in the world. Here man is free as he ought to be.* The effusive love for his new country and its freedom led de Crèvecœur to demand the same rights for blacks. Many New Yorkers agreed.

Since the Founding Fathers dropped the ball on the abolition of slavery in 1789, the Protestant clergy took up the issue throughout the northern states. New England led the national campaign against slavery, though Massachusetts, Vermont, New Hampshire, Rhode Island, and Connecticut had only outlawed slavery in 1783.

New Englanders led the private abolitionist societies and were leading spokesmen in the Protestant churches against slavery. Eventually the dispute over slavery caused a split in the two largest Protestant denominations, the Baptists and Methodists. Baptists formed two separate groups, the Northern Baptist Convention, which opposed slavery, and the Southern Baptist Convention, which supported it. The Methodist Church split into the Methodist Episcopal Church in the north and the Methodist Protestant Church in the south.

John Hughes, New York's Roman Catholic Archbishop, took

a complicated stand, undoubtedly affected by his personal background and the experiences of Irish immigrants who made up the bulk of the Diocese of New York. As a young Irish immigrant, Hughes landed in Baltimore, briefly worked on a plantation as a slave overseer, and moved to Pennsylvania where he earned a living as a day laborer and gardener. He enrolled at Mount St. Mary's Seminary in rural Maryland in 1819 where Hughes earned his room, board, and tuition as gardener and overseer for the seminary's slaves.

Despite having been slave overseer, Hughes disapproved of slavery. The problem was that he opposed both slavery *and* abolitionism. Pope Gregory XVI had condemned slavery in 1838. But Hughes believed that whites had done blacks a favor by bringing them to America, even in chains. He also voiced concern as to what would happen to the four million American slaves if freed throughout the nation.

Hughes' arguments betray serious ambivalence about his commitment to freedom for blacks. He also had an intense aversion to the abolitionists who he considered inauthentic. Usually Protestant, most abolitionists were fervently anti-Catholic and had questioned the patriotism of Roman Catholics. Hughes also sympathized with Irish day laborers and domestics who faced competition from blacks.

During the Draft Riots in 1863 Hughes was asked by city officials to quiet the rioters. He hesitated since during nativist attacks on Catholic churches the police had stood aside. Now the shoe was on the other foot and the mayor was asking him to ease a dangerous situation. Ultimately, he agreed to speak to the rioters and ask them to cease their destruction.

The Gradual Manumission Act of 1799 was a compromise, which gave no relief to any slaves for at least a quarter century. It freed slaves who were born after that year upon reaching age 28 for males and age 25 for females. Finally, the Act of 1817 freed most slaves throughout New York State. It mandated that every slave born before July 4, 1799 was to be free on July 4, 1827. The law permitted one exception, mostly to aid Southerner cotton merchants doing business in New York City. It allowed non-residents to enter New York State with their slaves for as long as nine months until the year 1841. On July 4, 1827, Governor Daniel D. Tompkins signed legislation officially ending slavery. For almost a century, blacks in New York State celebrated Manumission Day with festivities and church services. It was marked on July 5th so that it would not compete with the observance of Independence Day.

After the emancipation of New York State's slaves, Henry Ward Beecher, a Brooklyn clergyman originally from Connecticut, assumed a position of highly visible leadership among abolitionists. Beecher was a Congregationalist minister from a famous New England family. He was the son of Lyman Beecher, a well-known theologian, and brother of Harriet Beecher Stowe, author of *Uncle Tom's Cabin*. Henry Ward Beecher was minister of Plymouth Church of the Pilgrims in Brooklyn Heights from 1847 until 1887. Plymouth Church, located on Orange Street, was one of the most influential houses of worship in Kings County. Its nationally known pastor, a spellbinding orator who was well connected with opinion leaders throughout the country, played host to many guest lecturers including Frederick Douglass. Three times Abraham Lincoln attended Beecher's sermons. Beecher used the church as a station on the Underground Railroad, and held mock slave auctions to raise money for abolitionist work as well as to publicize the horrors of slavery. During the Bloody Kansas wars between pro-slavery and anti-slavery forces in the 1850s, he shipped rifles to the anti-slavery settlers in boxes marked *Bibles*. They were known as *Beecher's Bibles*. When the Civil War began, Beecher led his congregation in raising money to equip and support a volunteer regiment.

Before the abolition of slavery, free blacks lived in several *Little Africas*, on the city's periphery, being pushed out of settlements as soon as whites wanted to encroach. Free black communities developed around the Collect Pond in the Dutch period. By the end of the 18th century there were Little Africas in the southwest section of Greenwich Village and what would later be called SoHo, Hell's Kitchen, and Columbus Circle. Seneca Village (8th Avenue at 82nd Street in Central Park) was a mixed community of free blacks, Irish, and Germans. Their town, with three churches and one cemetery, was destroyed to make room for the construction of Central Park. In north central Brooklyn, Weeksville was a rural community where free blacks gravitated to farm and pursue mechanical trades. Four modest houses from Weeksville remain intact on Hunterfly Road, in Weeksville, on the border of Bedford-Stuyvesant and Crown Heights.

CHAPTER 25
Fish Market

Together, the five boroughs of New York City have 580 miles of coastline. For centuries local waters have furnished people with an abundance of seafood. Oysters, an important source of protein, may have been the first seafood gathered by the ancestors of the Lenape Indians. Seven thousand year-old archaeological sites have yielded mounds of oyster shells. Oysters were easy to gather along the shore and they could be eaten fresh, smoked, or dried.

Excavated sites show that local Indians also consumed great quantities of clams, scallops, and crabs. Wampum, their currency, was made from the shells of whelk or quahog clams. Most clans like the Canarsie in Brooklyn, had two settlements: a permanent collection of longhouses nestled in the protective interior hills and a summer settlement at the sea for collecting shellfish and perhaps enjoying the ocean breezes.

Both colonial rulers, Dutch and English, came from countries with high rates of fish consumption. It was an important business in the colonies from the start and remains a big business today. Early fishing boats plied local waters and the Grand Banks of Newfoundland. They came back into port when they had filled their hulls with fish. The big difference today is that any port will do to unload fish because it gets trucked or flown to regional markets such as the Fulton Fish Market.

New York City was never a large whaling port, though in the first half of the 19th century there were several whalers operating from the city's docks. Larger whaling ports existed on nearby eastern Long Island and the Connecticut shore.

In 1831 fish dealers began concentrating along the East River at the foot of Fulton Street. A permanent building was constructed to house their stalls in 1869. It quickly became the largest fish market in the United States. It had two advantages: New York City was the largest consumer market for fish in the country, and the Fulton Fish Market was located along the edge of the East River close to the harbor and ocean.

Fish were unloaded from the ships to the docks with ease and sold to owners of fish stores and restaurants. Once electricity became available an enormous amount of ice was used for cooling the fish. Handcarts delivered containers of ice cubes throughout the workday, which by necessity has always been at night. Buyers needed to start their day with fish on hand so the task of supply needed to take place throughout the night. The market began business about 2:00 AM and by 7:00 AM the activity was over for the day.

The romantic notion of chefs going out to personally pick the day's special is pretty much fiction. Many restaurants and small fish stores hire professional buyers to do their shopping for them and to spot good financial deals and the best looking fish.

Nearby, the South Street Seaport, an urban shopping mall, took advantage of the Fulton Fish Market's fame in the 1970s. The commercial centers are Pier 17, and two stately rows of houses on Fulton Street and Water Street, which have mixed architectural heritage, Federal style and Georgian. Beyond the shopping possibilities, and the early morning trip to the fish market, the South Street Seaport Museum was an attraction.

An interesting note is that the whole area of the Fulton Fish Market and the South Street Seaport was once part of the East River. The eastern three blocks of Lower Manhattan were filled with excavated rock and debris. Pearl Street was along the East River's original shore. Water Street, Front Street, and South Street are manmade intrusions into the river.

The fish offered for sale has not always been the same. Taste is a constantly changing variable with fish. Lobsters, monkfish, and skate were considered trash-fish or junk-fish by the colonists. Today, lobster with drawn butter, monkfish with fennel sauce, and pan-seared monkfish are served in the best restaurants. In general, the mild tasting fleshy varieties of white fish were popular among the settlers: cod, haddock, halibut, flounder, striped bass, and shad. Later bluefish, mackerel, and tuna joined the list. Shrimp, which come from the Gulf of Mexico, the Caribbean, and South Pacific arrived in large numbers made possible because of refrigeration and air transport.

Squid, octopus, anchovies, sardines, and eels became popular when immigrants from the Mediterranean basin and Asia came to New York. Shellfish were always appreciated for appetizers, soups, and entrees. That has remained consistent with present taste except that lobster and shrimp have joined the ranks of cherished shellfish: crabs, scallops, mussels, periwinkles, and clams.

The enormous oyster and clam beds in Raritan Bay and Long Island Sound, the two main sources, were finally depleted by the late 19th century. Local fish --- striped bass, shad, and flounder --- almost disappeared. Over fishing, industrial waste, and raw sewage poisoned the waters of New York City. Hot dogs and pretzels replaced oysters and clams as fast food served from vendors' pushcarts. The Fulton Fish Market adjusted by serving as a buying and selling center for fish and shellfish brought in by ships plying waters throughout the North Atlantic and the Caribbean.

Though still the largest commercial fish market in the United States, fishing vessels stopped directly unloading their goods at the Fulton Fish Market by 1980. All fish and shellfish now arrive by truck or from airplane to truck to the market.

Since 2005, trucks no longer arrive at Fulton Street in Manhattan, but rather unload their crates of fish at the new Hunts Point facility next to the New York City Terminal Produce Cooperative Market handling fruit and vegetables. The new fish facility is called the New Fulton Fish Market Cooperative. It is no longer outdoors and dependent on ice, but its enclosed stalls and lockers use electric refrigeration to keep the fish and seafood either cool or frozen. It is also much less accessible to the public.

Consumption of fish in the United States steadily increased after the Second World War. By the 1980s fresh ocean fish was available throughout the interior of the United States. The possibility of buying fresh fish and the growing interest in low fat diets significantly increased its demand.

Many newly popular species are for sale: pompano, red snapper, mahi mahi, tilefish, swordfish, and shark. In addition, farm-raised fish (aquaculture) have joined their free-range cousins. They include salmon, trout, and catfish. The Fulton Fish Market is purely an *entrepôt* (repackaging) center, similar to the Hunts Point Produce Market in the Bronx.

CHAPTER 26
Pushcart Peddlers

Pushcart peddling was simple and served the manufacturer, vendor, and customer. The vendor bought the goods wholesale, then took them out to the street to sell, sometimes paying for them up front, other times returning the next day with the cash. Poorer vendors rented their 4 x 8 foot pushcarts. In the 1880s and 1890s the rent was a dime a day, which rose to a quarter by the 1920s. At the turn of the last century about two-thirds of the vendors were Jewish and most of the others were Italian. Vendors have always been drawn from the most recent immigrant groups.

Peddling was a difficult job. Concerning early 20th century pushcart peddling, Yiddish author Abraham Cahan has the protagonist of his novel *The Rise of David Levinsky*, complain: *I rented a push-cart and tried to sell remnants of dress-goods, linen, and oil cloth. This turned out somewhat better than basket peddling; but I was one of the common herd in this branch of the business as well...I hated the constant chase and scramble for bargains and I hated to yell and scream to create a demand for my wares by the sheer force of my lungs. Many an illiterate dolt easily outshouted me and thus dampened what little interest I had mustered.*

Food vendors proliferated from the earliest days in New York City. Many people looked to the street for bargains and convenience. Dutch-era pushcarts sold fish, shellfish, fruit, corn, as well as animal hides and pelts. Food is still often sold from pushcarts. Some offer a single variety of food, usually with an ethnic connection, for example Jewish kosher deli-style, Vietnamese, or Puerto Rican food pushcarts. Some specialize in tropical fruit drinks: an array of fruit, or sometimes just one kind, all papayas or only bananas. Pushcarts may offer a selection of candy or honey-roasted nuts. At Christmas the charcoal heated pretzel and chestnut stands come out in the shopping districts. In the summer, it is cold treats.

Delicioso Coco Helado has one hundred ten pushcart vendors mostly in the South Bronx, Spanish Harlem, Washington Heights,

Corona, Sunset Park, and the Lower East Side. Vendors scoop tropical flavored (mango, passion fruit, coconut, tamarind, pineapple, cherry) ices into paper cups. Others, called *piragua* or *frio-frio* vendors, use a large block of ice that they scrape to fill a cup full of ice flakes to be covered with sweet syrups. Some regional and national brands, like Häagen Dazs, Breyers, Frozfruit, and Good Humor, are also sold from carts.

As food admixture took place, most vendors began to offer a variety of cuisines. A single vendor may now offer pretzels (German), kosher franks and knishes (Jewish), and halal shish kebab (Arab or Turkish).

What are today's possibilities for lunch from a vendor? In addition to a hot dog, giant pretzel, or knish, you could have shish kebab, souvlaki, falafel, eggroll, roast pork bao, fajita, taco, or empanada. Most vendors sell more than one item.

Goods otherwise bought in clothing stores have traditionally been sold on the street as well. Year round you may find racks of dresses, as well as underwear, hats, socks, and neckties. In the summer T-shirts and sunglasses take precedence. In the winter scarves, gloves, and earmuffs crowd the carts and tables. Jewelry items, especially watches, necklaces, earrings, and wallets can also be found on the street.

Commodities usually found in stores selling houseware, hardware, or music turn up with the vendor: adhesive tape, hooks, hangers, DVDs, and batteries. Toys, houseplants, books, folding umbrellas, toiletries, and carved wooden animals can be bought without stepping into a shop. New Yorkers appreciate the fact that when they are caught in the rain, a street vendor selling inexpensive umbrellas always appears.

Pushcarts and shopkeepers always had an adversarial relationship in New York City. Prices were cheaper when merchandise came from a pushcart because the vendor paid no rent. That, of course, was the problem for the storeowners who either owned their building and paid property taxes, or leased their shop and paid rent. The point of view of the itinerant vendor was that he lacked the money to start a store, and until he could, he felt he had a free-market right to sell goods on the street.

Most pushcart vendors occupied a marginal place in the economy, making little money. Others were able to convert their businesses into stores. An example was Guss' Pickles, seller of coleslaw, pickled tomatoes, and pickled cucumbers, which originally operated out of a pushcart, then from a storefront on Essex Street and later on Orchard Street in the Lower East Side until it closed in 2010. The goods swam in large barrels of brine while waiting to be scooped out. (Guss' was called Posner's Pickles in the 1988 film *Crossing Delancey.*)

During the Great Depression, pushcarts flooded city streets and merchants stepped up their campaign against their mobile competitors, often using a health argument, which claimed pushcart food was unsanitary. Mayor Fiorello LaGuardia became the point person for storeowners and led a campaign against street peddling in 1938. He accepted the shopkeepers' argument that peddling was unfair competition. He also thought food vendors were unsanitary and that all vendors were eyesores. He persuaded the City Council to ban pushcarts and had large indoor Retail Markets constructed where vendors could rent space to sell their wares. Vendors paid $4 per week for space, much more expensive than their former rent. It left the street vendors unhappy but they had to comply with the new law. The only advantages for them was that the Retail Markets got them out from the winter cold and summer heat, and they had rest rooms. Most pushcart operators went out of business because with no mobility, they earned less profit, and could not afford the rent.

Several bleak institutional *civic moderne* buildings, built with funds from the New Deal's Works Progress Administration (WPA), are the fruit of the drive by Mayor LaGuardia and Robert Moses to get pushcarts and itinerant peddlers off the street and into sanitary indoor spaces. The white sterile-looking interiors of the minimalist Art Deco buildings are clean and light, though not very busy. The Arthur Avenue Retail Market in the Belmont neighborhood of the Bronx and the Essex Street Retail Market on the Lower East Side are the only remnants of LaGuardia's capitulation to the shopkeepers that are lively and thriving. As time went on, anti-pushcart laws were less often enforced, and new vendors appeared on the streets that did not want to be corralled into a Retail Market.

Rules do exist for street vendors. Both food vendors and general-merchandise vendors need licenses, which they buy from the city, to sell goods legally. Some are allowed to occupy a certain location for years. Others may wander the streets looking for customers. All food vendors are periodically inspected by the Health Department.

The only new type of vending outdoors is really very old: the farmers market, or greenmarket. From the 1930s until the 1980s many Americans became convinced that buying food from vendors was dirty and unhealthy. Instead, they patronized grocery stores. People got over that stereotype when they began to value freshness and enjoyed meeting the people who actually raised the produce they were eating. Farmers markets gained new popularity. They are now found in scores of New York neighborhoods. Noted examples include Union Square (Manhattan), St. George (Staten Island), and Brooklyn's Grand Army Plaza and Borough Hall. Most of them operate two days per week. There are eighty markets in New York City visited by 250,000 customers each week.

Farmers rise before dawn, quickly pick their fruits and vegetables, and drive to their spot at a market. They are willing to get up early to make the trip because they earn the full price of their produce since there are no middlemen to take part of their profits. They pay the city a modest fee for the spaces where they park their trucks. Farmers come from Upstate New York, Long Island, Connecticut, New Jersey, and Pennsylvania just like in early New York when farmers brought their wagons from nearby rural areas to Astoria, Williamsburg, Brooklyn Heights, St. George, and Hoboken, New Jersey and took ferries to markets in Manhattan.

A city regulation states that greenmarket farmers may only sell what they raise or make. Some offer fruit and vegetables, cheese and other milk products, poultry, regional fish, apple cider, cherry juice, herbs, and flowers. Some farmers sell bottles of wine from grapes in their vineyards. Late summer is the best season because the farmers markets are flooded with fresh sweet corn and sun-ripened tomatoes.

In the 21st century, pushcarts occupy a place midway between established shops and selling out of a knapsack (a basket in the 19th century), a card table, or a cloth placed on the sidewalk. All of these forms still exist, and many New Yorkers depend on street vendors to buy cheap food, umbrellas, batteries, and baseball hats.

Shopkeepers still dislike pushcart vendors who take up sidewalk space in front of retail stores. Shopkeepers' complaints sometimes get fast action from City Hall. Police are sent out to check if the vendor has a right to be in a certain location. Still, while licensing restrictions keep the number of pushcarts low and forbid them from setting up at certain busy intersections, the Mayor and City Council know that pushcarts offer New Yorkers products at inexpensive prices. Vending is also an important entry-level job for many new immigrants. Anyhow, what would New Yorkers do without the ubiquitous early morning coffee vendor who also sells egg sandwiches, muffins and bagels?

CHAPTER 27
Governor Cornbury: A Case of Political Dirty Tricks?

Lord Cornbury (later Viscount Cornbury) whose given name was Edward Hyde, was a first cousin of Queen Anne of England. His royal connections got him appointed governor of New York from 1702 until 1708. He ruled autocratically and ineptly, took bribes, embezzled public money, and ignored the rights of the people. When the Colonial Assembly disagreed with him, he dissolved the gathering and sent them home. Governor Cornbury also ran up personal debts, which he failed to repay. His enemies were legion.

During his tenure as governor it was widely gossiped that he regularly dressed in women's clothing. It was spread about that he wore a woman's wig and gown to government meetings, formal dances, and even to his wife's funeral. Some said he used the excuse that he was dressing up the way his cousin Queen Anne dressed. Some of these rumors were printed and circulated as leaflets. An oil painting by an unidentified artist depicting Governor Cornbury dressed as a woman hangs in the New-York Historical Society on Manhattan's Upper West Side. In the 18th century rumors of cross-dressing would be very damaging to a politician's reputation. A suspicious thing is that no one actually claimed to have personally seen the governor attired in women's garments. Further unsubstantiated claims were made that the governor had some kind of an ear fetish.

The Provincial Assembly of New York unanimously condemned Lord Cornbury, though not for cross-dressing, and in 1708, he was recalled to England on charges of corruption. Once in England he was arrested for bad debts. New Yorkers universally detested him as a corrupt, irresponsible, and arrogant politician. Many said he cross-dressed, though no one seems to have seen it. Clearly the portrayal of Governor Cornbury as a transvestite was an attempt to discredit him. In the 20th and 21st century such political tactics are called *dirty tricks*. Beyond the obvious prejudice involved in the Cornbury case, it appears that there was adequate genuine cause to jeopardize his reputation without stooping to fantasy. It also shows the long history of political slander, and of prejudice against anyone who steps over the line of publicly acceptable behavior in any way related to sex.

CHAPTER 28
Naming Streets

In Manhattan most of the streets and avenues have numbers. In Brooklyn and Queens there are some numbered grids of streets as well. The Bronx and Staten Island do not use numbers for names. Numbering streets is a modern method of making it easier to locate places in large cities. Numbers are impersonal and not as interesting as names, and they do not have stories to tell. Fortunately, despite the numbering systems, there are plenty of streets with names. Each has a story though some are more interesting than others.

We have many words for street. Street comes from the Old English word *straet*, which in turn come from the German *strasse*. Though the Germans probably got it from the Latin word *strata*. Avenue is a French word derived from the Latin *advenire*, meaning to approach. Road is Middle English for *rood*, meaning riding. Street, avenue, and road all mean the same thing in modern English.

Lane is a bit different as it suggests a narrow passage. Mews, court, or alley, refer to a small street behind a block of buildings. Though court can also be an area enclosed on three sides. Place is Old French for open space derived from the Latin word *platea*, meaning broad street. Plaza means the same as place. A square is a four-sided space bordered by buildings.

Boulevard actually has military roots. It is derived from *bolwerc*, which is Middle Dutch for bulwark, and *boloart*, Old French for a rampart converted to a promenade. We use this grand term to mean a broad street usually with a tree-lined median. Parkway is a modern American term for either a landscaped highway or a broad street with a planted median.

The list continues. Terrace, from the Latin term *terra*, meaning earth, describes a street built on a raised earthen platform. Drive, from *drifan*, Old English for driven, suggests being moved along on a roadway. Way comes from the Old English (or modern German) word *weg*, or the Latin word via, meaning a road or path.

In New York City, the words for streets have been applied without adherence to exact meanings. Most have been used interchangeably. The exceptions are boulevards and parkways, which describe large roadways, and lane, mews, court, or alley which suggest very small passages.

How did streets get their distinctive names? Farmers named the roadways on their land, especially the ones leading to their farmhouses. Developers who bought tracts of land, put in streets, and built rows of houses named the streets. They commonly chose the names of trees or flowers. Sometimes they chose the first names of their family members the way a tractor-trailer driver might paint the names of his wife and kids on the cab he drives. Citizens often agitated for a street to be named (or re-named) for a favorite politician, war hero, or local religious or ethnic leader. The City Council makes those decisions. The derivation of most New York City street names is known. There are a few, however, whose origins have never been discovered.

Signs telling street names and house numbers were not common until the early 19th century. They were needed by the Post Office and other delivery services. Most of the early signs were chiseled into the stone of corner houses. Some are still there. By the end of the 19th century freestanding street signs clearly labeling the streets appeared on every corner.

Staten Island, one of the two boroughs without numbered streets, has plenty of names. Tompkins Avenue in Tompkinsville was named by real estate developer Daniel D. Tompkins to honor himself. He had been governor of New York State (1807-1813) and vice-president of the United States during the administration of James Monroe (1817-1825). Tompkins initiated the first regularly scheduled steam ferry between Staten Island and Manhattan. He also owned a wide swath of land from 2nd Avenue to the East River in Manhattan, once part of the Stuyvesant estate. Tompkins Square Park is named for the politician and developer.

Huguenot Avenue was named for a settlement of French Huguenots (Calvinist Protestants from France) who chose to relocate in Staten Island. Some notable New Yorkers were Huguenots or had Huguenot ancestry: Dutch colonial governor Peter Minuit, the Bayard, Leisler, de Lancey, and Delanoy families (the Delanoy family were ancestors of President Franklin Delano Roosevelt's mother), to name a few.

Snug Harbor Road was named for Sailor's Snug Harbor, a retirement home, which opened in 1831. It provided for *aged, decrepit, and worn-out sailors* and was funded by founder Robert Richard Randall, a wealthy merchant. The retirement facility moved to North Carolina in 1975 and the following year the buildings on Richmond Terrace became the site of the Snug Harbor Cultural Center. The complex of twenty-six Greek Revival buildings on an eighty acre site just one and a half miles from the ferry includes galleries, museums, studios, concert spaces, and gardens. It constitutes Staten Island's premier cultural center.

Hylan Boulevard was named in honor of a Brooklynite who became mayor of New York City. John Francis Hylan, a lawyer and judge, was elected mayor in 1917 and served until 1925.

The story of Billop Avenue in Tottenville is long. It was named for British naval officer Christopher Billopp whose descendants dropped a p in the surname. On a hill overlooking Raritan Bay sits the family's stone house, which experienced a few hours of fame on September 11, 1776, and thereafter was called Conference House.

According to local Staten Island legend, Christopher Billopp, the original owner of the house, was responsible for Staten Island being part of New York. When the British captured New Amsterdam from the Dutch in 1664, two colonies claimed Staten Island. Lord Berkeley and Lord Carteret, royal proprietors of New Jersey, claimed the large hilly island barely separated from New Jersey by the narrow strait called the Arthur Kill. (*Kill* means stream in Dutch.) The governor of New York also claimed it. To settle the matter, the Duke of York (brother of the King of England), sponsored a unique competition: the island would go to whichever colony whose resident could circle the island in a boat within twenty-four hours. Christopher Billopp, a former sea captain, won for New York.

Billopp had been granted 932 acres at the south end of Staten Island in 1675. Later he increased his landholdings to 1,600 acres. In 1709 he began ferry service from his land in Staten Island across the Arthur Kill to Perth Amboy, New Jersey. The Tottenville area was once called Billopp's Point.

Brooklyn was originally composed of six towns, five Dutch and one English. As they began to grow together, five separate systems of street numbering and one of alphabet lettering (Flatbush to Sheepshead Bay) were put in place to fill in the gaps. Williamsburg, Flatbush to East Flatbush, Park Slope to Sunset Park to Bay Ridge, Bath Beach, and Coney Island each have separate numerical street grids. Nonetheless, most Brooklyn streets have names.

Pierrepont Street in Brooklyn Heights was the private dirt driveway that ran from Fulton Street to the home of Hezekiah Pierrepont, who subdivided his property in 1816. Pierrepont was on the cutting edge of the suburban movement because he was providing 25 x 100 foot lots for commuters whose jobs were in downtown Manhattan. To get to and from work they had to walk to the Fulton Ferry.

Cadman Plaza West is a segment of Fulton Street that makes the west flank of a long skinny park with two names, Cadman Plaza Park and Columbus Park. The park and the street were named for radio preacher and pastor of the Methodist Metropolitan Temple, and later the Central Congregational Church, Samuel Parkes Cadman. The Sunday afternoon NBC radio show, which Cadman hosted popularize liberal Protestant ideas about Biblical scholarship.

Roebling Street in Williamsburg was named in honor of John Augustus Roebling, the architect of the Brooklyn Bridge. Construction on the bridge began in 1870 and was completed in 1883. Roebling died from blood poisoning caused by an accident before work commenced. His son, Washington Augustus Roebling, also a civil engineer, took charge of the construction of the Brooklyn Bridge. He suffered a debilitating case of the bends in 1872 after descending deep below the East River and remained bedridden. His wife, Emily Warren Roebling, who was not an engineer, relayed messages from his sickbed to the construction site.

Union Street runs east to west from the harbor to East New York Avenue toward the eastern end of Brooklyn. It opens into the Grand Army Plaza and is briefly interrupted by Prospect Park, the Main Branch of the Brooklyn Public Library, and the Brooklyn Museum. Union Street was named to salute the Union (the United States, or the North) in the Civil War. Grand Army Plaza is named for the Grand Army of the Republic, or the Northern army. The centerpiece of the oval plaza is an elaborate triumphal arch adorned on top with a bronze chariot group pulled by four horses.

Flatbush Avenue goes from the East River across Brooklyn to Jamaica Bay. It took its name from the town of Flatbush, which is the English way of pronouncing the Dutch word *vlackebos* (wooded plain). The center of the Dutch town was the intersection of Flatbush and Church Avenues. One corner is occupied by the Flatbush Reformed Dutch Church (1798) and surrounding cemetery.

Eastern Parkway, a grand boulevard with trees on two median strips and service roads, was built along an east-west axis on the top of the glacial moraine in north central Brooklyn. When Frederick Law Olmsted and Calvert Vaux, landscape architects of Central Park and Prospect Park, designed it in 1866, it was the first six-lane roadway in the United States. Like Ocean Parkway, which runs between Parkside Avenue (near Prospect Park) and the Atlantic Ocean, these grand showcase boulevards attracted wealthy homeowners. Eastern Parkway opened in 1874.

Mermaid, Neptune, and Surf Avenues in Coney Island, evoke the idea of the ocean. The 19th century developers of several competing amusement parks thought that maritime names would help draw customers.

Queens streets were mostly named by developers for their relatives, or for trees, flowers, and romantic names calculated to attract home-buyers. Examples would include British baronial names: Aberdeen, Asquith, Cambridge, Chelsea, Hampton, Irving, Langston, Putnam, Radcliff, Roxbury, Standish, Suffolk, and Thornton. Romantic names evoking nature are also common: Bayfield, Bridgewater, Cedarlawn, Daisy, Forest, Garden, Glenwood, Highland, Linden, Myrtle. Pinegrove, Ridgedale, Seaside, and Woodhaven. Utopia Parkway is the ultimate in positive thinking by real estate boosters.

Jackie Robinson Parkway (formerly Interboro Parkway) is a curving four-lane road running through Forest Park and a group of several cemeteries (Catholic, Protestant, and Jewish) near the border with Brooklyn. It was named for a courageous symbol of racial openness, Jackie Robinson, who integrated major league baseball when he played at Ebbets Field for the Brooklyn Dodgers in 1947.

Steinway Street is located in Steinway, a neighborhood between Astoria and LaGuardia Airport. It was built by the piano manufacturing company, Steinway and Sons, to serve as the main street for the 400-acre company town they established for their employees.

Astoria Boulevard is, in a sense, a sad story of failed *sycophancy* (servile flattery). It was the main east-west street for a new town developed by promoter Stephen A. Halsey, a fur merchant, who got the state legislature to change the name of the small, pre-existing village, Hallett's Cove, to Astoria in 1839. Halsey hoped that flattering America's largest fur trader, John Jacob Astor, would encourage him to invest in the area. Astor never did.

Hunter's Point Avenue was the main road leading east from Hunter's Point, a small community south of Long Island City, which was named for George Hunter who inherited the land in 1817. It has nothing to do with hunting.

Douglaston Street, which runs north to south through the Douglaston neighborhood was named for George Douglas, who purchased the land in 1835. It is just east of Alley Creek and Alley Pond Park and south of Little Neck Bay. The peninsula (neck) was known as Little Madman's Neck in the 17th century.

The Bronx has a number of interesting street names. Belmont Avenue is a small residential street, which passes through Belmont, a well-known neighborhood west of the Bronx Zoo and south of Fordham University. Originally the area was part of a large estate called Fordham Manor. When the manor was divided, the area went to Jacob Lorillard and was called Belmont, meaning beautiful mountain in French. The neighborhood is known for Italian shops and restaurants along Arthur Avenue, which runs parallel with Belmont Avenue. *Dion and the Belmonts*, a 1960s recording group, projected the name nationally.

Fordham Road, along with Fordham neighborhood, Fordham University, and Fordham Preparatory School, takes its name from the large estate of Dutch settler John Archer. He named it *Fordham*, an Anglo-Saxon term for *hamlet by the fording place*. To *ford* is to cross a river or stream when there is no bridge.

Tremont Avenue runs across the central Bronx through the Tremont neighborhood. It took its name from the settlement, formerly known as Upper Morrisania, until Tremont caught on in the 1850s. The French name refers to three mountains in the area: Mount Eden, Mount Hope, and Fairmount.

Gun Hill Road has an evocative name referring to the American Revolution when patriots dragged cannon to the area from the Battery in Manhattan's southern tip, when the island fell to the British.

Kingsbridge Avenue was an Indian path and colonial trail from Manhattan to the Bronx at a narrow point in the Spuyten Duyvil Creek. The first bridge constructed from Manhattan to anywhere was built there in 1693 and called King's Bridge to honor William III of England. Where the bridge was built is no longer water since the construction of the Harlem River Ship Canal, completed in 1895, cut off the northern loop of the Spuyten Duyvil Creek and left Marble Hill connected to the Bronx by a dry riverbed which was soon filled in to raise the level of the land for construction of houses.

The Grand Concourse, officially the Grand Boulevard and Concourse when it opened, is a central north-south artery of the Bronx. It runs between 138th Street and Mosholu Parkway, past the Bronx Borough Hall and near Yankee Stadium. The wide boulevard has two tree-lined dividers and service roads. It was built to provide an elegant civic center for the Bronx.

Manhattan's streets with names include some, which are obviously descriptive: Bridge, Beaver, Canal, Wall, Hudson, Spring, Broad, and Broadway. But some that seem obvious are not.

Gold Street has nothing to do with gold. It was named for the color of ripened wheat grown around Golden Hill. Pearl Street was wishful thinking. The street was surfaced with crushed oyster shells, not pearls. Pine Street (formerly King Street) and Spruce Street (previously George Street), were renamed after the American Revolution to erase the connection with British royalty. Neither pine nor spruce graced the area but they were convenient replacement names. Mulberry Street did pass through a grove of mulberry trees and Orchard Street went through an orchard.

The Bowery was the main road north from New Amsterdam, at the southern tip of Manhattan. It ran through farmlands and a lane leading from it, now Stuyvesant Street, went to Peter Stuyvesant's farm. The word Bowery comes from the Dutch *bowerij*, meaning farm.

Stuyvesant Street, in the East Village, is Manhattan's only street that follows an east-west axis; all the other pseudo east-west streets from the 1811 grid were laid out to follow the positioning of the island, which is closer to northeast to southwest.

John Jacob Astor named Lafayette Street, through land he owned, to honor the Marquis de Lafayette, George Washington's young military assistant from France. Marie Joseph Paul Yves Roch Gilbert Du Motier, Marquis de Lafayette (his full title) volunteered to help Washington because he believed in republican principles though he was a nobleman. He also sought adventure and was able to avenge the death of his father who had died fighting the British. Lafayette was wildly popular in the United States and throngs came out to see him when, as an older man he revisited New York City and other parts of the United States from 1824 to 1825.

Irving Place, near Union Square and Gramercy Park, was named for author Washington Irving. He had been a diplomat in Great Britain, ambassador to Spain and author of two biographies, *The Life of George Washington* and *The Life and Voyages of Christopher Columbus*. Irving was the first American to win international literary fame. He wrote about America, usually New York, and produced a large volume, *A History of New-York*, which focused on old Dutch and English families and their culture. His short stories were always written as told to him by the fictitious Dietrich Knickerbocker, as was *A History of New-York*. Knickerbocker became a term referring to the descendants of the Dutch colonists. The best remembered stories in the collection are *Rip van Winkle* and *The Legend of Sleepy Hollow*.

Taras Shevchenko Place, a short block along side St. George Ukrainian Catholic Church in the East Village, was named for Ukraine's most famous national poet and novelist. The Byzantine-style Roman Catholic church's congregation formerly referred to themselves as Ruthenians (borderland of Slovakia and Ukraine) but a name change went with a new church building in 1977.

St. Nicholas Avenue was named for the 4th century Christian bishop of the seaside town of Myra in the Roman province of Lycia, Asia Minor (now Demre, Turkey). Nicholas of Myra was known for doing good deeds for children, and he evolved in New York City, by way of the Netherlands, into the figure of Santa Claus. Real estate developers in Washington Heights wanted to foster an Old New York sentiment and chose the name St. Nicholas for an important street.

North Moore Street in TriBeCa honors Episcopal Bishop Benjamin Moore, rector of Trinity Church. Moore's son, Clement Clark Moore, was author of a tremendously popular poem, *A Visit from St. Nicholas,* which was originally composed for his own children as he rode home on a sleigh to his farm in Chelsea from the Wall Street area one evening in 1822. The next year the poem was published in the *Troy Sentinel,* an upstate newspaper. Soon it was circulated widely and regularly throughout the city and the country and was known popularly as *The Night Before Christmas*. The poem helped define a new vision of St. Nicholas. The *North* was added to differentiate the street from Moore Street in the Financial District near the Staten Island Ferry Terminal.

The Moore Street near the Ferry Terminal is a spelling error. It should be *Moor* Street to designate one of the places where ships moored, or tied-up at the docks.

Another confusing label belongs to two roadways named the same but for very different people. Tiny York Street in TriBeCa honors James, Duke of York, who received the charter to govern the newly captured province of New Netherlands and town of New Amsterdam from his older brother, King Charles II. Later he ascended England's throne as James II, but was deposed during the Glorious Revolution in 1689. The city and state were named for the Duke of York.

York Avenue, on the Upper East Side, or Yorkville, is the northern extension of Avenue A. In 1928 it was renamed to honor an American hero in the First World War, Sergeant Alvin York.

Cooper Street in Inwood was named to honor author James Fenimore Cooper who wrote the *Leather-stocking Tales*, a series of five romantic novels, which includes *The Last of the Mohicans*. His novels presented vivid pictures of frontier life in New York State.

Cooper Square, next to Astor Place in the East Village, was named for Peter Cooper, an inventor, engineer, and industrialist who built the first working steam locomotive, the *Tom Thumb*. Cooper owned steel mills, wire factories, and a glue factory. The wealthy entrepreneur established and endowed Cooper Union, an art, architecture, design, and engineering college, so that to this day it is tuition-free. Cooper Union's Great Hall is where Abraham Lincoln delivered the speech that gained him support of east coast Republicans as he sought his party's 1860 presidential nomination. The speech was enormously important. Lincoln took a definitive stand against slavery in his remarks, which had an immediate appeal since many of the Abolitionist Republicans in attendance were veterans of the struggle against slavery in New York State, which had ended with the discontinuance of slavery nineteen years earlier in 1841. Overlooking his square a statue of Peter Cooper sits regally in a chair on a pedestal shielded by a covering of granite and flanked by two columns.

There are more cases that almost seem designed to befuddle. Jones Street, a narrow one-block lane in Greenwich Village was named for physician Gardiner Jones.

Great Jones Street, a particularly wide two-block street in NoHo was named for lawyer Samuel Jones. The adjective refers to the width of the street, not a comparison of any of the two men's attributes.

Luis Muños Marin Boulevard, the eastern portion of 116th Street, in East Harlem was named was a three-term governor of Puerto Rico. He is credited with bringing business investment to the island and improving the education system.

Juan Pablo Duarte Boulevard is a thirty-block stretch of St. Nicholas Avenue in Washington Heights. He was a leader of an early 19th century revolt by people in the Dominican Republic against domination by Haiti.

Lenox Avenue, co-named Malcolm X Boulevard (6th Avenue) received its first non-numbered name in honor of James Lenox, a collector of books and art, and founder of the Lenox Library, which, in 1895 merged with the Astor Library and Tilden Trust (a bequest of books owned by Samuel J. Tilden) to form the New York Public Library. The second non-numbered name honors Malcolm X, the Black Muslim leader who was assassinated in 1965 shortly after he left the Nation of Islam (Black Muslims), made a pilgrimage to Mecca, and became an orthodox Sunni Muslim. Unlike 6th Avenue, which was co-named Avenue of the Americas in 1945, but is rarely used by New Yorkers, the names Lenox Avenue and Malcolm X Boulevard are both used to refer to 6th Avenue north of Central Park.

Adam Clayton Powell Jr. Boulevard (7th Avenue) was renamed in 1974 to honor a Harlem community leader who was concurrently pastor of the Abyssinian Baptist Church and an eleven term United States Congressman. He was an outspoken fighter for Civil Rights and well known across the nation.

Frederick Douglass Boulevard (8th Avenue), in Harlem, was named for the enormously influential anti-slavery crusader, author, and speaker. He had escaped slavery in Maryland and later made powerful speeches in the north giving dramatic performances about the horrors of the slave system. He was editor of *North Star*, an abolitionist newspaper published in Rochester, New York. During the Civil War he met with President Lincoln on several occasions.

Lexington Avenue, between 3rd Avenue and Park Avenue (4th Avenue), was named for the Revolutionary War battle in Lexington, Massachusetts. Lexington Avenue was not part of the original 1811 grid plan but was laid out in 1832 in response to calls for two additional north-south arteries on Manhattan's East Side. Madison Avenue, likewise, was added to the grid in 1836 and named for our country's fourth president.

Park Avenue (4th Avenue), between Lexington and Madison Avenues, had a narrow middle strip granted to the New York and Harlem Railroad for trains: first horse-drawn, later steam locomotives. The name change in 1888 from 4th Avenue to Park Avenue was optimistic. But in the 1913 a large trench was excavated between 42nd Street and 96th Street for railroad tracks and the top was covered over in the 1920s. A median with flowers was added and it finally looked park-like. Metro North trains now use the railroad tunnel on their way to and from Grand Central Terminal at 42nd Street.

Cathedral Parkway, a portion of West 110th Street, in Morningside Heights on the Upper West Side, forms the southern border of the largest cathedral in the world. Cathedral comes from the Greek word *kathedra*, meaning chair or throne of the bishop. The Cathedral of Saint John the Divine (Episcopal), facing Amsterdam Avenue, is surpassed in size only by two other large Christian churches, Our Lady of Yamoussoukro in the Ivory Coast, and the Basilica of Saint Peter in the Vatican, neither of which is a cathedral. (While the Pope is the Bishop of Rome, the cathedral of the Diocese of Rome is Saint John Lateran, not Saint Peter's.) Saint John the Divine is two hundred yards long and the Statue of Liberty could fit in the center of the cathedral. It is twice the size of Saint Patrick's Cathedral on 5th Avenue, the seat of the city's Roman Catholic archbishop.

CHAPTER 29
Market Squares

The first outdoor market in New Amsterdam was along the east wall of the fort. Lenape Indians, and colonial fishermen and farmers brought farm produce, fish, and furs to sell to the townspeople. Later, weekly market days and seasonal fairs were established. The purpose of a market was to directly bring together the seller and buyer.

Another early market was located just northeast of Fort Amsterdam where Bowling Green now stands. The Dutch used Bowling Green, the small triangular open space at Lower Broadway and Battery Place as a cattle and fodder market. Called the Hay Market, it was set aside specifically for buying and selling livestock and hay. In 1733, the English colonial government rebuilt and privatized the half-acre public space for lawn bowling.

Following European custom, separate markets were used for categories of items for sale. In 1658 the first public meat market was instituted. There was a market for dairy products, and one for grain, fruit, and vegetables. Fish and shellfish were sold directly from ships docked along the town's East River wharves. As the town grew into a city more stores opened and wealthier people shopped indoors. Even so, there were outdoor components to many stores. A butcher shop, for example, would keep animals penned in the yard behind the shop. When an order came in, the butcher would slaughter the animal for the customer who was obliged to buy the entire animal, or share the meat with other customers.

Some of the city's parks began as public markets. By the English colonial period, Greenwich Village developed as a small community two miles north of New York City. Washington Square, now at the southern foot of 5th Avenue, was a market as well as a Potter's Field and a place for public hangings, until it was landscaped and established as a park in 1828. Many of the 2,086 victims of the 1798 yellow fever epidemic had been hastily buried there. Both Minetta Creek, which meandered through the square and the burial ground, received shabby treatment by the growing city and were covered up and left unmarked.

Washington Square Park became a sought-after residential area once its marketing function ended. From 1832-1839 a set of elegant town houses was built on the north side of the park. Many have survived. They now serve as offices and classrooms of New York University. The park, the row houses, and the Washington Arch, completed in 1895, have attracted numerous painters: Ferdinand Lungren, John Sloan, Edward Hopper, Jessie Tarbox Beals, Ben Shahn, and Red Grooms. Henry James's 1881 novel, *Washington Square,* was set a half century earlier amidst the self-important social caste which dominated the row. Much of what James portrayed can still be seen. *The ideal of quiet and genteel retirement, in 1835, was found in Washington Square, where the Doctor built himself a handsome, modern, wide-fronted house, with a big balcony before the drawing-room windows, and a flight of white marble steps ascending to a portal which was also faced with white marble. This structure, and many of its neighbors, which it exactly resembled, were supposed, forty years ago, to embody the last results of architectural science, and they remain to this day very solid and honorable dwellings. In front of them was the square, containing a considerable quantity of inexpensive vegetation, enclosed by a wooden paling, which increased its rural and accessible appearance; and round the corner was the more august precinct of the Fifth Avenue, taking its origin at this point with a spacious and confident air which already marked it for high destinies.*

Tompkins Square, a quadrant bounded by Avenues A and B, and 7th and 10th Streets, was initially an empty space used as a market by Long Island farmers coming from Williamsburg and Greenpoint. Daniel D. Tompkins owned the land. He had been governor of New York State (1807-1813) and vice-president of the United States during the administration of James Monroe (1817-1825). A major landowner and developer, Tompkins owned the land from 2nd Avenue to the East River and the park is named for him.

As Tompkins Square evolved from a square into a park it became a natural meeting place for new Americans. The encounters were not always friendly; ethnic and block turf wars were often played out there.

Tompkins Square Park became the rallying point for the 19th century labor movement. In January 1874 it was the site of the first labor demonstration in New York City, which was organized by the International Workingmen's Association (or First International), a group with headquarters in London set up by Karl Marx. The police attacked the workers and the *Tompkins Square Riot* ensued. By the 1920s Union Square usurped the role of Tompkins Square as the labor movement's main rallying place.

In the 1960s Tompkins Square Park became a center of radical activities: rallies against the War in Vietnam, marijuana smoke-ins, and concerts by The Fugs, Country Joe and the Fish, and the Grateful Dead. From 1988 until 1991 it was the scene of violent confrontations between police and squatters who had constructed shacks in the park. The struggle pitted the remnants of the hippie subculture, youthful anarchists, and some of their neighborhood allies against the first wave of upper middle class *gentrification*. The favored anti-gentrification and anti-yuppie graffiti was an up-ended martini glass with a slash through it and the inclusion of the ominous date 1933, the year Hitler assumed power in Germany. The N.Y.P.D. and the yuppies won. The squatters were removed, the park was closed and renovated, and by the time it re-opened in 1993 yuppies were moving into the East Village, driving up rents, and opening wine bars and Tuscan restaurants.

Union Square was not a market square, but a transportation hub for streetcars and trolleys. Contrary to popular perception, Union Square did not receive its name from the Union Army during the Civil War, or from labor unions, which regularly rallied there. The origin of its name is purely geographic. Union Square was named for the *union* of Broadway and Park Avenue South.

As transportation developed and retail outlets increased, grocery stores, butchers, green grocers and other purveyors of food put most outdoor markets out of business. Health Department regulations and the Department of Markets (set up in 1917) confined wholesale food to specific markets. In Manhattan, fish was sold at the Fulton Fish Market, and meat at the Gansevoort Market. In Brooklyn, meat was sold at the Atlantic Avenue Market. In the Bronx, produce was confined to the Hunts Point Market.

There were some multi-product *jobbers markets* where wholesalers sold various products, notably Wallabout Market in Williamsburg, Brooklyn, and Washington Street Market west of the Financial District in Manhattan. Mayor Fiorello La Guardia herded retail pushcarts, including many that sold food, into Retail Markets in 1938.

Supermarkets achieved dominance after the Second World War. There were local chains and national chains with stores in the five boroughs. Each had several departments (meat, dairy, produce, baked goods, deli) and many New Yorkers did most of their shopping in the relatively large stores.

Greenmarkets revived retail sales of food in some parks, which had been market squares. It came out of the environmental movement and the general dissatisfaction with the low quality offered in supermarkets, especially produce. Modern distribution of produce has guaranteed a wide variety of fruits and vegetables available throughout the year, but they are often picked before fully ripened, treated with preservatives, partially frozen, and generally degraded by the long trip to the grocery store shelf from farms in Florida, California, Texas, Mexico, and Central America.

The first greenmarket was set up in 1976 at 59th Street and Second Avenue in Manhattan. Only area farmers are allowed booths or truck space and they may only sell what they raise or make. Like New Amsterdam's markets, they are confined to specific days. At Union Square, Manhattan the market exists on Fridays, Saturdays, Mondays, and Wednesdays, in Poe Park, the Bronx on Tuesdays, in Borough Hall, Brooklyn on Tuesdays, in St. George, Staten Island on Saturdays, and in Tompkins Square, Manhattan on Sundays.

The greenmarket scene is an interesting throw back to an earlier day. Lively conversation and bantering between buyers and sellers punctuates the atmosphere where city and country meet over tables offering freshly harvested onions, garlic, scallions, cucumbers, squash, sweet corn, new potatoes, and a variety of berries. Some farmers also bring in baked goods: pies, cakes, brownies, and breads. Fishermen bring in fresh fish and shellfish, vineyard owners sell wine, apiarists sell honey, dairy farmers offer cheese and butter, and livestock farmers bring in meat. Most farmers drive in from Long Island, New Jersey, Pennsylvania, and upstate New York. Everyone but the supermarkets wins: the farmers receive one hundred percent of the profit from their sales (minus the nominal rental fee), and the customers obtain fresh products directly from the growers.

CHAPTER 30
Cemeteries, Tombstone Designs, & Potter's Fields

Early gravesites in the colonial city were scattered around the island. Neither the churches nor the government established cemeteries. Farmers used space at the edge of their fields for family burial plots. Town people buried the dead at the end of the town in open, unused places or at the edge of the town common. The ridge along Broadway was a favored spot for burials. One stone in Trinity Graveyard, which marks the burial spot of five-year-old Richard Churcher who died in 1681, is the oldest gravestone in the five boroughs. It predates the first Trinity Church that was constructed nearby on the same ridge in 1698. In this case, the burial came before the church and the graveyard.

The first New Yorkers were buried in shrouds or in wooden caskets. Materials used to mark graves included wood, slate, and marble. Wood planks with painted or chiseled names and dates did not last long. Carving was amateur at first, often rough and uneven, but was later professionalized.

Most of the early cemeteries of New Amsterdam and New York have disappeared. Houses or roads were built over them. It is hard for us to imagine destroying a cemetery to put through streets or build housing, but there were no laws preventing it in early New York.

In the Dutch period and for much of the English period only white Protestants could be buried inside the Wall. Blacks and Jews established their own burial locations. A small section of the second Jewish cemetery, called the Jews' Burying Ground, can be found on St. James Place just off Chatham Square in Chinatown. A few tombstones are left. This is the second of four small Jewish cemeteries outside the Wall operated by the Spanish and Portuguese Congregation Shearith Israel, formed in 1654 by Sephardic Jewish immigrants from Recifé, Brazil. Jews were denied permission to build a synagogue until 1729 or to build a cemetery within the walled city. (The first cemetery has disappeared. The other two surviving cemeteries are in Greenwich Village and in Chelsea.)

The Negro Burial Ground is located at Duane and Elk Streets. This burial ground outside the Wall was for free and enslaved Blacks, Indians, white paupers, and prisoners. No stones remain. A small corner of the land has been preserved with a memorial. A large black granite sculpture in the center of nearby Foley Square, *Triumph of the Human Spirit,* memorializes all enslaved Africans and celebrates their will to survive. Special mention is made on the dedication plaque to those interred in the Negro Burial Ground. (Inspiration came for the striking monument from the tall West African *Chi Wara* headdresses.)

Washington Square, once a large Potter's Field, a burial place for the poor, has no markers or memorials. It was turned into a park in 1828. New York City still has a Potter's Field on 45-acre Hart's Island. About 2,700 unclaimed bodies each year make the one-way trip to interment in tarpaper-lined pine boxes placed in long common trenches by convicts from Riker's Island Prison. The bodies are collected at the morgues in the five boroughs, driven over the City Island Bridge to City Island and then transported by ferry to Hart's Island.

The trenches, dug by a backhoe, are stacked three high, two across with coffins. About half of Hart's Island's dead are infants or stillborns, placed in tiny coffins, stacked five high and twenty across in separate trenches. There is a third trench where organs and limbs from hospital operations, wrapped in black plastic bags, are buried. The public cemetery for paupers, all in unmarked graves, was opened in 1869 and holds the remains of at least one million people. The city-owned island is administered by the New York City Department of Corrections and closed to the public. In the 21st century there has been some pressure to transfer Hart Island's administration to the Parks Department and open it up to periodic public tours.

Two Anglican (Episcopal) burial grounds five blocks from each other in the oldest part of Manhattan have survived. Some unique folk-art designs are found in Trinity and Saint Paul's cemeteries on lower Broadway. These striking folk-art gravestones represent the belief system of the time and the simple colonial artistic tastes of many 17th and 18th century Americans. The thin, flat slate stones with rounded tops featuring skeletal or cherubic faces surrounded by a halo of feathery wings barely survived the colonial period, giving way to a more stylish European form by 1770.

The two graveyards have scores of headstones, which, like the designs commonly found in New England and eastern Long Island, show a religious shift written in stone. The most striking symbol is the winged death's head. Today's cemetery visitors shrink back in astonishment at stones decorated by a skull or skull and crossbones. In the United States there is no medieval tradition to compare it with and it paints some early Protestants as a very gloomy group. The art form was useful as a teaching tool and an obvious public warning to prepare to meet God at the Final Judgment. It came from medieval European traditions (Roman Catholic) and achieved special force in the stark simplicity of Puritan New England from which it spread among some New Yorkers. The winged death's heads or winged angel's heads were meant as public statements and teaching tools about the nature of God and the expectations of humans. Winged death's heads reflect fear of the stern God of Judgment Day and winged angel's heads, usually carved after the Great Awakening of the 1730s, display an optimistic belief in a benevolent God of Love.

Sometimes the burial markers had other symbols around their borders like an hourglass, scythe, coffin, pick and shovel, or a standing or reclining skeleton. The idea of death as both inevitable and indiscriminate was a cornerstone of conservative Protestant theology.

Crosses and statues were not used because they symbolized Roman Catholicism to the Protestants. Quakers in Brooklyn and Queens used no gravestone decorations for fear of producing a *graven image* and violating the second commandment. Not all the colonial Americans of the northeast were conservative religiously, and a few monuments have no religious markings. They merely state the names and dates of birth and death, or carry a simple Latin inscription such as *memento mori* (in memory of the dead) or *fugit hora* (time flies). A few are occupation-related and show a carved ship, military insignia, or a coat of arms.

The religious revival of the 1730s and 1740s heightened a sense of piety and altered popular beliefs. Theologically, there was less emphasis on a fearful Day of Judgment and more on forgiveness and the redemption of the soul. God was seen more as a loving creator and benefactor than a strict magistrate.

American funeral art reflected the altered theology; soul and cherub symbols replaced the fearful skull on the tops of grave markers. Sometimes a crown of heavenly righteousness hovered over the winged cherub's head. Some stones have the crown resembling a tulip and feature a border of flowers. Clearly the Great Awakening softened the stern ideas toward death and salvation, and cemetery artwork reflected it.

The innocent charm of colonial funerary art died out after only a century of prominence. Between 1770 and 1800 the Romantic and Neo-Classical motifs popular in London and Paris dominated cemeteries throughout the United States and edged out the winged cherub's heads. The complicated process reflected a growth of American secularism, a turning away from symbols of the colonial past, and enthusiasm for the new art forms of the Romantic movement on one hand and the Neo-Classical movement on the other.

In the early 19th century American cemetery art was already using sorrowful Romantic images of weeping angels, wreaths and garlands of fruit and flowers, and angels with trumpets. Urns of Egyptian revival, willows of Gothic revival, and columns of Classical revival also gained popularity. Green-Wood Cemetery in Brooklyn is the best place to see this later Romantic tradition.

Two cemeteries around the corner from each other in the East Village show another experiment of burial. The New York Marble Cemetery, 2nd Avenue between East 2nd and 3rd Streets is a tantalizing treasure, but difficult to get inside, or even to see. Established in 1831 as a private non-sectarian cemetery it served as a burial place primarily for Protestants from English Episcopalian, as well as Dutch and German Reformed denominations. It is only open to the public about once a year. Built as an innovative concept that never caught on elsewhere makes this a truly exceptional cemetery. It is in the center of a square (not rectangular) block with a high brick wall surrounding it. Imbedded in the wall are marble markers denoting the interred that are buried in 156 individual crypts below the plain grassy area. A solid black metal gate on 2nd Avenue is the only access, but it is locked and offers little possibility to see inside. (Consult www.marblecemetery.org for dates and times of the periodic public opening.)

The New York City Marble Cemetery, 52-74 East 2nd Street midway between 1st and 2nd Avenues was established in 1832, a year later than its neighbor around the corner. This cemetery, built by the same corporation, has its entire south side exposed through a cast iron fence to the public view. Underground crypts hold the coffins but tombstone are allowed and many are interspersed in the well-kept yard. One eye-catching stone marks the interment site of New York patrician Preserved Fish (pronounced Preservéd) who must have had enough respect for his parents, or fear of them, never to have changed his name --- unless he actually liked it!

Notation:

Thoughts on the Etymology of Potter's Field

The etymology of potter's field may come from Ancient Greece or Ancient Israel. Originally the New Testament was written in Greek and the Ancient Greek word for potter is *kerameos*. The potters' area of Athens was called kerameos, location of an ancient cemetery, probably taken from the very early Greek (not Hebrew) custom of interring the dead in large pots.

The term Potter's Field comes from the Christian Bible (New Testament book of Matthew 27:6-7). The text explains what was done with the body of Judas after he had hanged himself following his betrayal of Jesus for thirty pieces of silver. *And the chief priests took the silver pieces and said, "It is not lawful to put them into the treasury because they are the price of blood." And they took counsel and bought with them the potter's field, to bury strangers in.* Another translation puts it this way: *The chief priests picked up the coins and said, "This is blood money, and it is against our Law to put it in the Temple treasury." After reaching an agreement about it, they used the money to buy Potter's Field, as a cemetery for foreigners.*

The intent of the Book of Matthew was to show that the Jewish Bible (Old Testament) foretold the story of Jesus as messiah. Matthew was referring to Zechariah 11:13, which relates a story about two shepherds and foretells the breakup of the Kingdoms of Judah and Israel: *And I took the 30 pieces of silver and cast them into the House of the Lord for the potter.* The New Testament Book of Acts also mentions the 30 pieces of silver. Acts 1:19 reads: *And it became known to all those dwelling in Jerusalem; so that field is called in their own language, Akel Dama, that is, Field of Blood.* Blood and the potter's field were set apart as unclean or isolated in Biblical references.

Tracing the Biblical use of the term still does not answer why it was a potter's field and not, say, the field of a carpenter or a weaver. A possibility is that potters in Jerusalem had to locate outside the city walls so the smoke from their kilns would not mingle with smoke from the sacrifices made at the Holy Temple.

CHAPTER 31
Buttonwood Agreement & the Stock Exchange

New Amsterdam was organized and colonized by a joint-stock enterprise, the Dutch West India Company, which was chartered in 1621 by the States-General, the representative assembly of the seven sovereign states constituting the United Provinces, or the Netherlands. The company had been the innovation of William Usselincx, an Antwerp merchant, who was forced to flee north to Holland to escape religious suppression by the Spanish who controlled Antwerp and the surrounding region. Usselincx was a Protestant and the Spanish were Roman Catholics. Religion was the midwife of many political and commercial decisions in the 17th century. The Dutch West India Company existed to make a profit for its investors, a small group of Dutch citizens. The joint-stock company, which pioneered the colony, was a limited partnership, which means its stock was restricted to the original investors. New Amsterdam under the Dutch and New York under the English were commercial colonies.

Public corporations, where stock purchase was open to any investor, flourished in England in the 18th century and caught on in North America, especially in money-minded New York. Risk-taking people could be found in abundance in the Thirteen Colonies because life in the New World attracted the adventurous.

Few colonists, however, had capital to invest after putting money into improvements on their farms, workshops, and stores. Those with investment capital usually bought European securities. Even in Philadelphia, Boston, and New York, the main business centers, there was no organized trading until after the American Revolution. In general, what is necessary for a stock market to function is a public eager to buy and sell, brokers and dealers to facilitate trading, places to carry out the trades, and public joint-stock companies inviting investments. As the 18th century progressed these factors increasingly came into play. By 1791 public auctions were held at coffee houses, usually the Tontine Coffee House on Wall Street, where citizens could bid on and buy or sell stocks and bonds. (Tontine means *pledge* in French.) Much of the trading was on bank stocks. James Madison visited the Tontine Coffee House in 1791 and wrote to Thomas Jefferson complaining that: *The coffee house is an eternal buzz with the gamblers.*

Because the trading was completely unregulated there was considerable uncertainty about the safety of investments, and many New Yorkers were reluctant to invest their money in stocks and bonds. That was particularly true after the Panic of 1792, when a speculative wave of bank stock purchases engulfed the moneyed men as well as many middle class New Yorkers. In March, fear that the buying frenzy was out of control drove buyers to sell and a serious recession occurred as the whole lending and borrowing mechanism collapsed. The Panic of 1792 had been caused by a plot orchestrated by William Duer, former assistant secretary of the United States Treasury, who, with a group of unethical investors, had hoped to run up prices of stocks in five banks and then quickly sell their stock at top price. Ultimately, Duer's scheme failed and he was unable to repay the $750,000 he had borrowed to buy the stock. Duer was arrested and sent to debtor's prison. In contemporary lingo Duer's plan would be called *pump and dump*.

The problem that remained after the panic was how to separate crooks from respectable investors. Sometimes the line between the two has been thin, but the *Buttonwood Agreement* hoped to begin to sort it out. In 1792 a group of twenty-two merchants, brokers, and auctioneers met under a buttonwood tree in front of the Tontine Coffee House and worked out a simple agreement on procedures for buying and selling shares in companies. A few months later the twenty-two signers left the coffee house and opened a Stock Exchange Office at 22 Wall Street.

What the signatories really accomplished was setting up a system of scheduled private auctions three times each week at 1:00 P.M. and 7:00 P.M. where brokers who signed the agreement could buy and sell stocks through auctions. They pledged to charge all non-signers a commission of at least one quarter of one percent. By removing the public from an active role in the auctions, the compact ended the adversarial relation between brokers and auctioneers and assured commissions to all signers. The public could only participate in the process through brokers.

The Buttonwood Agreement evolved into the framework for the development of the *New York Stock & Exchange Board*. In 1817, twenty-eight brokers organized a new trading center to attract more companies to list with them. By 1820 the New York Stock & Exchange Board had thirty-nine brokers who met daily to buy and sell shares. Participation was limited to members who bought or sold for their own accounts or on behalf of customers who paid them a fixed commission. Membership was made salable through auction in 1868, and the next year the exchange had 1,060 members. The going price for a seat on the exchange reached $4,000. In 2005, a seat sold for a record $4 million. There are 1,366 seats on the New York Stock Exchange.

The laws of the United States support the concept of private property and freedom of contracts. While some American opinion leaders such as Jefferson, Madison, and Monroe worried that the values of the American farmer and craftsman, especially self-reliance and the work ethic, would be overshadowed by stock speculators and bankers, others saw investment capital as an engine for growth and prosperity. Farmers themselves, while rarely possessing much money for stock investment, were continually engaging in small-scale land speculation. A frequent pattern was to clear land and develop a farm, sell it at a profit, and move farther west to repeat the process.

While in theory anyone could contact a broker and put in an order to buy stock, the reality was tempered by the price per share, which many companies set at $1,000, even in the early 20th century. In the early 19th century $1,000 was a year's wage for a tradesman and half a year's earnings for a lawyer. A high par value on stock kept the masses out of the stock market.

The Federal Reserve System, often referred to as the *Fed*, is often called the *lender of last resort*. It was established in 1913 during the administration of Woodrow Wilson. Its tasks include conducting national monetary policy, regulating banks, maintaining the general stability of the financial system, and providing services to member institutions. One of the services is to store gold deposits. The Federal Reserve Bank of New York holds more than forty percent of the world's gold, much of it for foreign countries, in its underground vaults at 33 Liberty Street in Manhattan.

The Federal Reserve System was established to dominate and curb a group of powerful New York bankers. According to a series of Congressional investigations by the Pujo Committee in 1912 and 1913, J.P. Morgan and John D. Rockefeller had achieved a near monopoly in important sectors of American business by effectively controlling hundreds of banks, insurance companies, and major corporations. They achieved dominance through a complex system of interlocking directorates. The Federal Reserve Act of 1913 went into effect in 1914 and founded twelve regional banks, which all national banks were obligated to join. Setting the *discount rate,* which is the interest the Fed charges its member banks for loans, is now a key function of the Federal Reserve Board, the seven-member board of directors of the Federal Reserve System who are appointed by the president of the United States.

The Stock Exchange also instituted reforms. It set certain rules for business behavior and personal etiquette by brokers and regulated their commissions. Some of the rules regulated trading practices, methods of payment, and interest rates. Nonetheless there was still deep-seated suspicion by the public that the stock market was rigged. Much later, in reaction to the Stock Market Crash in 1929, President Franklin D. Roosevelt sponsored a series of federal laws regulating the New York Stock Exchange and the banking industry. They included the Truth in Securities Act and the Glass-Steagall Act in 1933 (now repealed by Bill Clinton and Congress), the establishment of the Securities and Exchange Commission in 1934, and the Banking Act of 1935. The new laws were intended to curb manipulation of the market and protect the investments of Americans who had lost confidence in the financial services sector of the economy.

Initially, just fifteen companies were listed with the New York Stock & Exchange Board. The number of companies, which listed their stocks and bonds to be bought and sold, increased steadily. In 2003 there were nearly 3,000 firms listed with a global market capitalization of approximately $17 trillion. Companies listed on the *Big Board,* as the New York Stock Exchange is sometimes called, achieved an enhanced level of prestige as well as accessibility to the public.

The volume of trades on the NYSE has increased greatly over the years. In 1824 it reached 3,500 shares per day and by 1835 the volume rose to 14,000. In 1867 stock tickers were introduced which opened the exchange to investors throughout the country. Because of the rapid industrialization of the United States, the increase in population, and the ease of investing, the number of shares rose rapidly in the following century. In 1886 daily trades reached 1.2 million shares. The Stock Market Crash, which ushered in the Great Depression, saw 16,410,000 shares traded on October 29, 1929. In 1982 the market reached 132 million shares, and the record was set on July 24, 2002 when 2,810,000,000 shares were traded. In 2001 the NYSE began quoting share prices in decimals instead of eighths of a dollar, a practice that dated to the frequent use in the United States of Spanish-minted *Pieces of Eight*.

Some political and economic changes in the early years of the republic caused private investment in companies to grow enormously. The United States doubled in size and a tremendous amount of new land was opened for settlement by the Louisiana Purchase in 1803. The War of 1812 stimulated United States government spending on the military, the Erie Canal connected New York City to upstate New York and the whole Great Lakes region in 1825, railroads encouraged commerce everywhere beginning in the 1830s, and technological inventions fed the expansion of the Industrial Revolution.

In 1863 the New York Stock & Exchange Board built lavish new headquarters at 8 Broad Street just south of Wall Street and shortened its name to the New York Stock Exchange. In 1903 the NYSE building was replaced by a richly decorated gray Roman Revival building. The enormous trading floor had several oval trading posts where trades were recorded. In 1982 the trading posts were removed and replaced by large banks of computer screens. The balcony of the trading floor was open to visitors until the attack on the World Trade Center in 2001.

CHAPTER 32
John Peter Zenger's Trial

The trial of John Peter Zenger was a benchmark in the long road toward establishing freedom of the press in the English colonies. Zenger (1697-1746) was an ambitious German from the Rhineland Palatinate who had immigrated to New York City at age ten. After serving an apprenticeship for master printer William Bradford, he opened his own print shop in 1726, and founded a newspaper in 1733. As editor of *The New-York Weekly Journal*, Zenger satirized and attacked the power and greed of Governor William Cosby, an appointee of the king. Zenger's attacks on Cosby cited the governor's corruption, election fraud, pandering to the rich, and incompetence. *The New-York Weekly Journal* printed parodies, satires, rhymes, caricatures, and even mock advertisements insulting the governor and his officers.

Cosby reacted in November 1734 by instructing his officers to confiscate copies of the newspaper and arrest Zenger on charges of *seditious libel*. The young editor was kept in jail because the judge, Chief Justice James Delancy, a royal appointee and an ally of Governor Cosby set bail prohibitively high.

Delancy disbarred each New York lawyer Zenger hired, forcing Zenger to hire Andrew Hamilton of Philadelphia to defend him. Philadelphia was the largest city in the Thirteen Colonies at the time and its lawyers were imputed to be the sharpest, Hamilton among the best. (By the 19th century the term *Philadelphia lawyer* was commonly used to describe a high priced, proficient attorney.)

The trial finally began in August 1735 in the courtroom of the second New York City Hall, built in 1699, at the corner of Wall and Nassau Streets. Zenger had been detained for nine months in a basement jail cell awaiting trial.

Defense lawyer Andrew Hamilton admitted his client had printed the bold attacks on New York's governor, but argued that the facts were true, so they could not be declared libelous. *Libel* is to write slander that maligns a person untruthfully. *Sedition* is to incite rebellion against the government. Hamilton ended his summation by calling John Peter Zenger's news stories and editorials completely justified. He told the jury: *The question before the court --- and you, gentlemen of the jury --- is not of small or private concern. It is not the cause of a poor printer, nor of New York alone, which you are now trying. No! It may in its consequences affect every freeman that lives under a British government on the main of America. It is the best cause. It is the cause of liberty! And I make no doubt but your upright conduct this day will not only entitle you to the love and esteem of your fellow citizens, but every man who prefers freedom to a life of slavery will bless and honor you, as men who have baffled the attempt of tyranny, and by an impartial and uncorrupt verdict have laid a noble foundation for securing to ourselves, our posterity, and our neighbors, that to which nature and the laws of our country have given us a right --- the liberty both of exposing and opposing arbitrary power --- in these parts of the world, at least--- by speaking and writing truth!*

The jury was instructed by Chief Justice Delancy to ignore the question of whether the printed criticisms were truthful. He told the twelve jurors that printing seditious words was enough to convict the defendant of seditious libel. The jury returned from their deliberations after only several minutes. They acquitted Zenger and great applause erupted in the courtroom. The jury had *nullified* the law and rejected the judge's instructions.

The John Peter Zenger case was immediately heralded, not because it established a legal precedent for freedom of the press, rather it showed that tyrannical government was unpopular with the public and served to warn government leaders that juries might well respond to similar prosecutions with continued nullification.

Freedom of the press remained a contentious issue throughout the British colonial period. After the American Revolution freedom of the press became a crucial bulwark of the new American republic. A written guarantee of freedom of the press was added to the United States Constitution in 1791 as part of Article I of the First Amendment. *Congress shall make no law respecting an establishment of religion, or prohibiting the free exercise thereof; or abridging the freedom of speech, or of the press; or the right of the people to peaceably assemble, and to petition the Government for a redress of grievances.*

Notation:

Federal Hall (formerly U.S. Subtreasury Building, originally U.S. Custom House)

This building, now called Federal Hall, is not the second New York City Hall, but its *site* at 28 Wall Street at the corner of Nassau Street. It is also the site where George Washington was inaugurated President from its second floor balcony in 1789. The original edifice had been the second New York City Hall, built in 1699, and remodeled in 1788 by Pierre Charles L'Enfant, who later laid out the street grid of Washington, D.C. (The first City Hall, called *Stadt Huys* by the Dutch, was in a tavern on Pearl Street facing Coenties Slip.) In British colonial days, John Peter Zenger's famous libel trial was held here in 1735, and the Continental Congress met here in 1785. The old building was demolished and a new Greek Revival structure was constructed on the site in 1842. A gargantuan statue of Washington was erected in 1883. The present City Hall, New York City's third, is a Georgian style building with ornate French Renaissance details constructed in 1812. It houses the office of the mayor, the 51-member City Council Chamber, and a large hearing room that was formerly the chamber of the now defunct *upper house* of the New York City government called the Board of Estimate. City Hall is located in City Hall Park, formerly the Town Common, north of Broadway and Park Row.

CHAPTER 33
Surfacing the Streets

Main roads in New Amsterdam usually followed Indian trails, which in turn, had probably followed deer paths. The goal for deer, Indians, and Dutch alike was to get from one place to another directly without encountering too many ponds, lakes, streams, hills, or cliffs. Initially, colonial Dutch and English roads, like Indian trails, were made of soil packed down by traffic. In larger settlements, like New Amsterdam, gravel was sometimes placed on the streets. Pearl Street, along the East River waterfront, took its name because it regularly received a layer of crushed oyster shells. The greatest problem with country roads and village streets was that the surfaces became mud after each rain.

Eventually cobblestones, granite blocks, and asphalt were used to cover the streets and prevent potholes and the formation of mud puddles. The process of finding an affordable solution took many years.

For more than a century complaints mounted over the conditions of the streets. The city council created the Highway Department in 1764 to maintain roads. The obstacle to solve was general surface unevenness; potholes became mud holes after rain. Litter and horse manure remain unaddressed. In the early years *grading* the road surface back to uniformity was time-consuming because it was done by hand with workmen using shovels and rakes.

The earliest answer to the rough road surfaces was covering the streets with cobblestones, a labor-intensive job that was expensive for the city. Cobblestones are just rounded stones usually obtained along rocky beaches. Often they were used as *ballast* in ships, weights to stabilize the vessel when it was sailing empty or carrying a light load. For example, small ships from Maine regularly brought dry goods to New York City as well as barrels of light bird down for pillows and comforters. The loads were light so the ships also carried tons of beach stones from New England's rocky shore as stabilizing ballast.

Cobblestones solved the general problem of keeping down mud and water puddles, but they were bumpy and made walking or wagon and carriage driving over city streets a jarring experience. Cobblestones could not be a satisfactory long-term solution to the problem.

Finally the Department of Public Works relied on the *Belgian method* of laying granite blocks tightly against each other on a level bed of sand. This method was far superior to cobblestones because the resulting surface was flat. The rectangular blocks, twice the size of a brick, covered hundreds of streets. They still form the foundation over which subsequent layers of asphalt have been spread. Chiseling granite into uniform blocks at a quarry, shipping them to New York City, and painstakingly placing them on the road bed was labor-intensive and cost the city a great deal of money. Today, the *Belgian blocks* can often be seen wherever asphalt has been worn away. Some streets, notably in Manhattan's SoHo neighborhood, have been purposefully stripped of asphalt to restore the antique look given by granite blocks.

Macadam, or asphalt, has been a popular material used for road surfaces. The successful road covering mixes two common ingredients. It is a pavement of one or more layers of compacted crushed stones mixed with tar or other petroleum byproducts. It was named after road surface developer John L McAdam (1756-1836).

Macadamizing the streets began in the 1870s when the Department of Public Works hired thousands of men to spread crushed stone over the streets and cover the stone surface with tar which was packed down manually to create a relatively hard surface.

Concrete was rarely used in New York City because it was expensive to install and more difficult to break up and replace when water mains running under the streets had to be repaired. Concrete is a building or surfacing material made of *cement* (mortar) mixed with gravel and usually reinforced with iron rods or netting. Cement is a thick soupy mixture of lime (calcium oxide), sand, and water. The lime comes from pulverized limestone (a shaly sedimentary rock). In colonial days the lime was usually made from the shells of clams or oysters that had been burned and crushed. Today concrete is widely used for sidewalks.

Streets in New York City take a beating from the weight of constant traffic, extreme changes in weather between hot summers and cold winters, salt spread to control ice, and incessant digging. The streets are regularly opened up for repair of water mains, sewer pipes, electric cables, steam pipes, gas pipes, telephone cables, and subways tunnels. Asphalt has proved to be the best surface covering for city streets because it holds up against the elements and allows excavation for repair of underground mains, pipes, and cables.

CHAPTER 34
Brickmaking

Bricks have been the primary building material from the early years of the Dutch settlement. At first bricks served as a complement to the more dominant use of wood. But the Dutch, who had few forest products in the Netherlands, were experienced brickmakers and preferred bricks as a building material for aesthetic reasons and also as a fire retardant.

Bricks were used for fireplaces and chimneys even if the rest of the house was constructed of wood. *Cisterns* for collecting rainwater from the roof, and *privies* (outhouses) were found in each urban backyard. Because they were permanent structures in the ground they were lined with bricks or stones, but *dry-laid*, that is, without mortar.

For a fireplace or house walls, it was important to hold the bricks together, so mortar, or cement, was used. Mortar is a thick soupy mixture of lime (calcium oxide), sand, and water. Sometimes finely cut horsehair or straw was added to the mortar. Placed in between the bricks, the mortar dries and hardens by chemical action and holds the bricks in place.

During the Dutch period, all bricks made or used in the colony had to be a standard size. The bricks were laid in patterns, usually the English bond or the Flemish bond system, which gave added strength and provided a decorative face. English bonding alternated rows of bricks set as *stretchers* (sides showing) and *headers* (ends showing). Flemish bonding alternated stretchers and headers in each row.

The color of bricks is dependent on the source of clay and what elements have been dissolved in it. Yellow and red were the dominant brick colors used in New Amsterdam. Various shades of red are still the most common colors in present-day New York City. Clay is a firm-grained natural substance (hydrated silicates), which is malleable when moist. Archaeologists have found that the clay used for bricks in the city had many places of origin.

Clay pits were found in all five boroughs, but the best known were several clay pits sites in southwestern Staten Island between Port Socony and Charleston near the Arthur Kill. The largest operation in the area was B. Kreisher and Sons. In 1854 Balthazar Kreischer opened his first brick factory and quickly dominated the market. Large industrial ovens (kilns) baked the clay until hardened. Clay Pit Ponds State Park Preserve, on Nielsen Avenue off the intersection of Arthur Kill Road and Sharrotts Road, now occupies the site. Now numerous walking paths for hikers and birders crisscross the 250 acres of woodland, wetland, sandy barren, and meadow habitats.

Clay was also used in the large ceramic and porcelain industries that developed in New Amsterdam. This was a skill inherited from the Netherlands. Ceramics and porcelain are made by heating clay at high temperatures to achieve a heat resistant and waterproof substance. Glazed with colorful designs, the clay ultimately became cooking pots, serving vessels, cups, plates, doorknobs, keyhole covers, nameplates, and decorative fireplace tiles. In the early 19th century, Greenpoint, Brooklyn emerged as a center of porcelain manufacturing.

Terra-cotta (*cooked earth* in Italian) is baked clay, either glazed or unglazed, used for lightweight pottery, shingles, and decorative elements in buildings. In the late 19th and early 20th centuries terra-cotta blocks were used to ornament roof cornices, window lintels, door pediments, and exterior brick walls of houses, offices, and tenements. The Flatiron Building (1903) and the Woolworth building (1913) as well as ordinary Lower East Side tenements used terra-cotta to add color and design to their wall surfaces. It can be easily molded into intricate shapes and designs and looks like sculptured stone. B. Kreisher and Sons in Charleston, Staten Island and the New York Architectural Terra Cotta Company in Long Island City, Queens were leaders in the field.

Very few new office buildings in New York City are built with bricks anymore. Steel and glass dominate the construction of office towers. Houses and apartments are still constructed with bricks, an old building product and technology that remains useful.

<u>Notation</u>:

Rubblework Masonry

Bricks were more expensive to use than stones for building purposes. Stones could be gathered all over the landscape of rocky Manhattan. So *rubblework masonry* was often used for farmhouses, house foundations, barns, root cellars, well houses, and some city houses. Sometimes the front of a house would be constructed of bricks but the back and side walls would be made of rubblework masonry, which is made of gathered fieldstones, usually Manhattan *schist*, which is coarse grained, gray-black metamorphic rock composed of flaky layers of mica, held together with mortar.

CHAPTER 35
Theater & Music

New York City is the theatrical capital of the United States. But New Amsterdam was founded and ruled by Dutch merchants who came from a Calvinist heritage that eschewed theatrical productions. Their purpose was to build a colony and make money. The English, who possessed New York after 1664, had a vibrant theatrical heritage, though not during the Republican interlude and Cromwell years. The ruling Puritans closed down England's theaters between 1648 and 1660. There was no documented theatrical activity in the colony of New York during the 17th century.

Even in the late 18th and 19th centuries many observant Presbyterians, Baptists, Congregationalists, and Methodists opposed theatrical performances. As the city attracted Roman Catholic immigrants from Germany, Ireland, and Italy, and Jewish immigrants from Eastern Europe, acceptance of staged entertainment grew. In the 20th century the city was sufficiently secular to make theater attractive to most people.

The first regularly operating theater in New York City opened in 1732 and was called the New Theater. It was a warehouse at the corner of Maiden Lane and Pearl Street. Rip Van Dam, the proprietor, had a stage built at one end and enough benches installed to seat three hundred people. Most of the performances at that time, when New York's population numbered fewer than 9,000 people, were simple English skits.

In 1800, the Park Theater, located on Park Row just east of Broadway, was the only playhouse operating. New York City's taverns and coffee houses usually had public rooms large enough to host traveling musicians and dramatic performances, so the paucity of theaters did not reflect a lack of performance venues.

The new country needed a distinctly American theater and eventually it evolved. The product, whether it was sophisticated or silly, often included music, lavish costumes, and extravagant stage sets. Live entertainment in the city was always of two types:

high culture and low culture. The lines between more thoughtful amusement and flippant or raucous entertainment were often blurred.

Minstrel shows, a contemptible form of entertainment, were popularized partly by the efforts of P.T. Barnum. The white singers and dancers would paint their faces black, dress in excessively colorful costumes, put on skits, and sing denigrating and racist songs to the accompaniment of a banjo. *Old Zip Coon* and *Jimmy Crack Corn* were favorites. The point was to show blacks as fun-loving, lazy, ignorant slaves to the delight of the prejudiced lower class white audiences.

In 1841, Barnum bought Scudder's American Museum, a failing exhibition hall for oddities. After the purchase, Barnum dropped the name Scudder's. The imposing building was in Lower Manhattan on the corner of Broadway and Ann Street across the street from Saint Paul's Chapel. He offered a combination of scientific exhibits, outlandish hoaxes, and live musical entertainment that ranged from minstrel shows to classical music. At the time, New York City's theater district was centered around the corner on Ann Street.

Most theaters were never far from Broadway. They clustered around Broadway and City Hall in the early years of the republic, and by the Civil War many theaters were found along the *Great White Way* from Chambers to 8th Street. Astor Place was surrounded with theaters and opera houses by 1850. Theater life there proved a tinderbox for one of the worst riots in New York City's history. On the surface, the Astor Place Riot pitted the supporters of American actor, Edwin Forrest, against the followers of English actor, William C. Macready. Forrest's partisans interrupted Macready's performance at the Italian Opera House in May 1849, fights erupted and the streets were filled with brawling rioters. The police and the state militia fired on the crowd when they refused to disperse. Twenty-two died and forty-eight were wounded. The underlying causes were the raw ethnic and class tensions between the Irish and the Yankees in the rapidly growing city.

Moving progressively uptown, the next centers of the theater world were the areas around Union Square, then Madison Square, and finally extending on either side of Broadway from 6th to 8th Avenues and from 38th to 54th Streets. The lower class theaters and performance saloons were located along the southern part of the Bowery. The fare they offered included minstrel shows, bawdy singing, and an occasional Wild West show. In the backyards of the performance saloons the patrons were entertained by bear-baiting, rat-fights, cock-fights, and dog-fights, all accompanied by intense gambling.

Popular theater, which took on the name *Broadway* arguably began at Niblo's Garden, an entertainment hall that could seat three thousand with adjacent hotel, saloon, and beer garden at the corner of Broadway and Prince Street. The blockbuster musical, *The Black Crook*, opened there in 1866 and ran for four hundred seventy-five performances. It started a tradition of staged extravaganzas featuring splendid scenery, flamboyant costumes, orchestras, and actors who talked, sang, and danced. The goal of musical comedy was to entertain, not to offer serious issues for the audience to ponder.

From 1878 to 1884, Ned Harrigan and Tony Hart wrote and produced several musical comedies featuring the everyday life of New York's immigrants and lower classes. The characters, situations, and music were distinctly American and helped form the Broadway genre. *The Mulligan Guard Picnic*, *The Mulligan Guard Ball*, and *Cordelia's Aspirations* were wildly popular with New York's lower and middle classes.

In the latter 20th century Irving Berlin, Cole Porter, Richard Rodgers, Oscar Hammerstein, Meredith Wilson, Stephen Sondheim, Andrew Lloyd Webber and others provided a steady steam of popular shows that filled theater seats and brought in tourist dollars. Many have been long-lasting spectaculars. With 7,500 performances, *Cats* was the longest-running Broadway musical.

Popular musicals were not the only shows in the city. Serious drama, American fare as well as Shakespeare and other European plays, also had a following. Serious plays by Eugene O'Neill, Tennessee Williams, Edward Albee, Arthur Miller, Lillian Hellman, and Stephen Sondheim had significant audience support.

Avant-garde drama in small theaters was called the Little Theater movement in the 1920s and 1930s. After the Second World

War it was known as Off Broadway. Some of the best-known Off Broadway venues are the New York Public Theater, the Roundabout Theater, and the Jean Cocteau Repertory. Off Broadway and Off Off Broadway are the names given to serious drama staged in small theaters often in Greenwich Village, Chelsea, or Hell's Kitchen. Off-Off-Broadway Theater Row is on East 4th Street between 2nd Avenue and the Bowery. Scores of experimental theater groups in various incarnations have thrived on that block for fifty years. The theaters are intimate and the tickets are inexpensive. They provide thespians opportunity to act in serious plays, often experimental, performances.

Plays in New York can run for years or close after a single week. An Off-Broadway production, *The Fantasticks*, a whimsical musical tale about young love, ran at the Sullivan Street Playhouse in Greenwich Village from 1960 to 2002 for a total of 17,162 performances. Its producers, who boasted it was the world's longest-running musical production, finally closed it because of increasing costs and declining attendance.

Known for a string of long running shows such as *Little Shop of Horrors*, *Eric Bogosian's One Man Acts*, and *Stomp*, the Orpheum, a small theater where everyone gets a good seat, has long been a neighborhood favorite for avant-garde fare. In the first half of the 19th century the stretch of 2nd Avenue between East Houston and 14th Streets was called the Jewish Rialto, and in its earlier years the Orpheum was a Yiddish theater that often featured vaudeville shows.

Vaudeville gained popularity in the 1880s and remained significant until it was pushed aside as mass entertainment by sound motion pictures in the 1930s. Developed as a distinct theatrical form by Tony Pastor it was America's most popular form of theater at the time. New York City was the center of vaudeville and musicians from Tin Pan Alley, the area around Union Square, provided much of the sheet music. Vaudeville had broad appeal that cut across lines of class and ethnicity, but not race. Vaudeville became an outlet to mainstream American culture for ethnic humor, especially Irish and Jewish humor. The Bronx and Brooklyn also had thriving vaudeville theaters by the 1920s.

African-Americans had theaters in New York City since at

least 1821. The African Grove Theater was located in a black retreat complex along Broadway near Duane Street. Successor theaters serving the black community were located at Bleecker and Mercer Street (Little Africa), and at Prince and Mercer Streets. The Apollo Theater on 125th Street in Harlem, built in 1914, has featured stage shows, vaudeville, jazz orchestras, singers, and cabaret revues. *Show Time at the Apollo,* a Wednesday night amateur hour, is broadcast on cable television.

Who attends Broadway performances? According to a 2005 survey from *Live Broadway* six out of ten audience members are tourists from other states or foreign countries, twenty-three percent come from the suburbs, and only seventeen percent are city residents. Musicals are especially popular with out-of-towners. No matter what the theatrical fare, seeing *the Broadway show* punctuates everyday life for many New Yorkers and is an essential part of most vacations to the city. New Yorkers and tourists alike scour *The New York Times* Theater Directory on the Internet to find out what is playing on and off Broadway.

Music performances of all types have been popular in the city for the past two centuries. The earliest symphonic productions were background music for church services or dinner parties. Romanticism elevated the status of music in the late 18th century and sometimes separated it completely from religion and banquets. Concert halls began to be constructed and people would attend just to listen to music. Live music in dance halls served as popular entertainment for working class people.

The New York Philharmonic was organized in 1842 and has offered a season of symphonies each year. It has performed in several concert halls including a long tenure in Carnegie Hall. In 1962 the New York Philharmonic left Carnegie Hall for Avery Fisher Hall in Lincoln Center. Among its music directors and conductors are many illustrious names including Arturo Toscanini (1928-1936) and Leonard Bernstein (1958-1969). The Mostly Mozart Festival Orchestra has entertained music lovers since 1966.

Concerts by individual and group artists have been crowd pleasers since P.T. Barnum sponsored a series of performances by Jenny Lind, the *Swedish Nightingale,* at Castle Garden at the Battery in 1850. Recent venues have sometimes included stadiums, arenas, and parks. Most concerts are held in music halls or clubs.

Jazz concerts, usually in clubs or bars, are popular with Americans and foreigners. While early venues were in Harlem, most are now in Greenwich Village, Williamsburg, or Park Slope. The Blue Note, Iridium, and the Village Vanguard are familiar names to jazz aficionados.

The *Christmas Show* at Radio City Music Hall in Rockefeller Center is an extravaganza of music and dance each December. The Rockettes, a high-kicking chorus line, delight audiences who come to hear popular seasonal music.

Italian opera was introduced in 1825, long before an Italian ethnic presence developed. When Italians began to arrive late in the century several small opera houses were established to entertain the Italian community. German opera halls, theaters, and venues for orchestras and chorale societies date from the 1840s. But lowbrow German entertainment was also found, especially in German language minstrel shows.

In 1854 the lavish Academy of Music was constructed on 14th Street and Irving Place giving wealthy citizens a place to hear opera and symphony productions, and see staged productions. The Academy of Music remained the premier opera house until the Metropolitan Opera House was built in 1883 at Broadway and 39th Street. The new Metropolitan Opera House at Lincoln Center replaced the old Met in 1966. Classical ballet, a form of formal dance, is an art form in itself, but its movements follow the music of the orchestra. Current ballet companies include the New York City Ballet (formed in 1948), American Ballet Theater (1939), Ballet Hispanico (1970).

Theater and music are important to New York City's identity. The entertainment possibilities are great and locals as well as tourists search for performances that they hope will be enjoyable. Attending a show or a concert can be uplifting and is often used to mark special events.

CHAPTER 36
Early Immigration & Religious Pluralism

Two important truths about early immigration and religious pluralism are that there were many immigrants from a variety of countries and that they were profoundly divided by religion. Though New Netherland was a Dutch colony sponsored by the Dutch West India Company, Walloon settlers populated the town of New Amsterdam. The Walloons were Flemish-speaking Protestant refugees from the Spanish Netherlands. Soon a significant number of settlers arrived from elsewhere in Western Europe: French Huguenots, Germans, Scandinavians, English, Welsh, Scots, and Scots-Irish. The Scots-Irish were Protestants from Northern Ireland (Ulster) whose ancestors were primarily Scottish Presbyterians who had been enticed to colonize Northern Ireland for the English. Also in New Amsterdam were African slaves who came by way of the Caribbean or South America, and Iberian Jews who came by way of Brazil. Soon after 1664 the Dutch became a minority in their former colony and an ethnic bifurcation developed between the *Natives* and the *Others*.

The identity of the Natives, who often loathed new immigrants, was English, or other Protestant groups from Great Britain, though they were often people whose English, Welsh, Scots, or Scots-Irish backgrounds were mixed. Some had mixed backgrounds with Dutch, German, French Huguenot (Protestant), or Scandinavian ancestors. By the early 19th century many of the Natives in the city had come from rural New England, upstate New York, and Pennsylvania. They migrated into the city in search of jobs, especially in the boom years after 1825 following the opening of the Erie Canal.

The Dutch Reformed Church was a strict branch of Protestant Calvinism and the official state church of the initial colony that did not allow other Protestant denominations to construct church buildings. Worship by Presbyterians, Lutherans, Episcopalians, and Jews was confined to private homes. The official religion of Colonial New York under the English was the Anglican Church, which allowed other Protestant groups to build churches. The Sephardic Jews of Spanish and Portuguese descent erected a synagogue in 1730 on Mill Street. Laws against Roman Catholics were inflexible and priests were not allowed in the colony until the 18th century. It was not until 1786 that Roman Catholics received permission for the first parish to construct a church, St. Peter's, on the corner of Barclay and Church Streets.

Only 25,000 Roman Catholics lived in all the Thirteen Colonies at the time of the American Revolution out of a population of about three million. There were only a few hundred Catholics in New York City. The Protestant majority disliked and mistrusted the Catholic Church. The earliest Catholics were English, French, and Spanish. Later, when French Canadians, south Germans, and Irish Catholics arrived prejudice against Catholics, especially Irish Catholics, increased and was aggravated by ethnic antagonism.

Protestant ranks were strengthened in the early 19th century by a considerable influx of Baptists, Methodists, Congregationalists, Lutherans, and Quakers. Each November 5th, Guy Fawke's Day, also called Pope's Day, was celebrated by militantly anti-Catholic Protestants who, after being fortified by alcohol and fiery speeches, paraded with straw effigies of the Pope and St. Patrick. By evening large bonfires consumed the effigies. (Guy Fawkes's Day was an English holiday celebrating the unsuccessful Catholic attempt to blow up Parliament in 1605.)

Some Natives formed gangs and others formed the Know Nothing Party, or other anti-foreign fraternal organizations. The Know Nothing Party, formally the American Party, sought to stop Catholic immigration and bar Catholics from voting or holding public office. One of their popular fraternal groups was the Orangemen, who sponsored a yearly anti-Catholic parade. The building that held Lamartine Hall, the Orangemen's headquarters, is still extant at 383 - 8th Avenue at the corner of 29th Street. Their 1871 parade backfired when Catholics attacked the Protestant Orangemen and both sides used guns to inflict damage. Fifty people were killed along 8th Avenue between 23rd and 25th Streets on

July 12th.

Time and a generally open immigration policy until after the First World War changed the religious composition of the city. By 1900 the Roman Catholic Church had become the largest single Christian denomination in the United States. There were more Protestants living in the U.S., but no single denomination of Protestants (out of 550 groups) outnumbered Catholics. Southern Baptists were the second largest Christian denomination. In the early 21st century the Catholic Church is spiritual home to at least 65 million people in a national population of 310 million and has an organizational structure of 18,500 parishes with 11,000 parochial schools, 250 colleges, and 750 hospitals and other health facilities. Catholic Charities is the largest private organization to help the poor in the United States.

The Catholic Church is also a national church in that it has congregants in every part of the country. Its major concentrations are in southern New England and the Middle Atlantic states, the industrial cities of the Great Lakes region, parts of the South (Louisiana, Texas, Florida), the Southwest, and California.

New York City's Catholic population achieved majority status by 1870 when just over half the city's 942,000 residents were Catholics. Throughout the 20th century the city has had a Catholic majority, though certain shifts have occurred. Irish, Italians Poles, and south Germans, traditionally Catholic, have left the city for the suburbs and elsewhere following the Second World War, but many of the newcomers, especially Puerto Ricans, Dominicans, Cubans, and Mexicans have been Catholic. Others, of course, Eastern Europeans, American and West Indian blacks, Middle Easterners, Filipinos, Indians, and Chinese, have been either Protestant, Eastern Orthodox, Jewish, Muslim, Hindu, or Buddhist.

The drama of religious pluralism has been the story of how a Protestant country and city became a mosaic of scores of ethnicities and religious traditions. Clashes between groups in the 19th century were often violent. The first two-thirds of the 20th century was marked by peaceful coexistence but often ghettoization in terms of residence, work, school, and cultural and social interaction. Since the Civil Rights Act (1964) outlawed discrimination, and a feeling of inclusion and shared interest in each other gained maturity, some of the segregation has diminished, especially regarding the workplace and cultural events. Still, much of the housing and many of the schools, and restaurants in the city remain segregated. A notable difference is that for most groups religion is less of an impediment to integration than race.

CHAPTER 37
Staten Island's Conference House & the American Revolution

On September 11, 1776, just as the American Revolution was beginning, three noted Americans met with Admiral Lord Richard Howe to see if the two sides could resolve their issues and stop the fighting. Howe, who commanded the large British naval fleet anchored off Staten Island in the Outer Harbor, had been authorized to act as a peace envoy. He had suggested the meeting by letter delivered to the Congress meeting in Philadelphia. Most representatives were suspicious and skeptical, especially John Adams, but on the strong urging of Edward Rutledge the Congress chose three members, including Adams and Rutledge, to meet with Howe.

Benjamin Franklin, John Adams, and Edward Rutledge represented the Americans and traveled through New Jersey toward Staten Island. It was ironic that New Jersey's royal governor was William Franklin, the estranged loyalist son of Benjamin Franklin. He had been captured by the Americans at the start of the war and sent to a prison in Connecticut.

It took two days for Franklin, Adams, and Rutledge to reach Perth Amboy where the Americans were met by a British naval barge to take them to Staten Island. Franklin and Rutledge, each with a servant, had traveled in separate carriages. Adams and his servant rode horses. After a day of bumpy, dusty roads in hot weather they spent the night in New Brunswick at a crowded inn. The moody Adams was especially agitated that he had to share a room with the talkative Franklin. They argued over whether the windows should be opened or closed. Adams lost and had to listen to Franklin's long lecture on the benefits of fresh air at night.

Christopher Billop, a British loyalist who often entertained Redcoat officers in his home in Staten Island arranged details of the conference. Billop's great grandfather, who had the same name, built the house. Billop and Howe put the Americans at ease and provided them with a sumptuous lunch of ham, tongue, and mutton. Conference House had been decorated with moss sprinkled over the wood floors, and walls and windows trimmed with green tree branches.

The American representatives suspected that the war would prove bloody and long. Great Britain was the world's superpower at the time and the Americans had little but courage and determination on their side. They had low expectations that the meeting with Howe would gain the colonies independence but followed the directive of Congress to discuss the issue in good faith.

The afternoon conference, just two months after the Declaration of Independence had been signed in Philadelphia, took place amidst hard feelings. Many Americans felt the only way to secure the full rights of Englishmen was to become independent of England. Many British believed the Americans were ungrateful for the military protection they had been receiving to protect them from French and Indian attacks. Just after the Declaration of Independence was read aloud on July 9th at City Hall, a group of zealous Americans marched to Bowling Green and pulled down the recently erected equestrian statue of King George III. They took the metal statue to Connecticut where it was melted down to make bullets for their muskets.

The conference went nowhere. The two sides never progressed beyond their opening demands. Howe offered amnesty to any American who swore allegiance to George III, King of England. He had no authority to offer any other concessions. Rutledge suggested to Howe the advantages to Britain of recognizing American independence, forming an alliance, and carrying on profitable trade. But Howe had not been authorized to negotiate.

Five weeks earlier, Franklin had written to Howe: *Long did I endeavor, with unfeigned and unwearied Zeal, to preserve from breaking that fine and noble China Vase, the British Empire; for I knew, that, being once broken, the Separate parts could not retain even their Shares of the Strength and Value that existed in the Whole, and that a perfect Reunion of those Parts could scarce ever be hoped for.* It is not known if Benjamin Franklin repeated those thoughts at Conference House. They sound as much like a veiled threat as a peace proposal.

The meeting adjourned as a failure, the Americans crossed

the Arthur Kill by ferry and made their way back to Philadelphia. The American Revolution continued from 1776 until 1783 when the two sides signed the Treaty of Paris and the British withdrew from the colonies.

The war that Franklin, Adams, and Rutledge were hoping to avoid would be costly. That was shown during the Battle of Long Island (which took place in Brooklyn) just two weeks earlier on August 27th. General George Washington's nine thousand troops retreated from an overwhelming British and Hessian force of thirty-five thousand commanded by General Sir William Howe, the brother of Admiral Lord Richard Howe. In that series of battles roughly twelve hundred Americans died and fifteen hundred were wounded, missing, or captured. The British reported sixty dead and three hundred wounded or missing. All told, approximately four thousand Americans died fighting for independence.

About 100,000 loyalists were expelled to British-owned Canada or other British colonies. Many fled voluntarily. More than seven thousand left New York Harbor in just one day, April 26, 1783. In some locations loyalists were tarred and feathered, a painful torture, and a few were murdered. During and after the American Revolution, prominent loyalists had their houses, farms, and businesses confiscated and auctioned off by the new state governments.

The conference showed the sadness felt by many on both sides. About eighty percent of all white Americans, and almost all the leaders of the American Revolution, had English ancestry. It seemed tragic for a war to break out among kinsmen. But, the British would not accept the political and economic freedoms the Americans sought and the war proceeded for seven years.

Conference House, where the meeting took place, had just one day of fame, though the history of the house itself is interesting. Built in 1680, the elegant two-story fieldstone house, called Bentley Manor before the 1776 conference, has a beautiful sloping lawn that goes to the edge of the water where the Arthur Kill meets the Raritan Bay section of the Outer Harbor. It is located at the foot of Hylan Boulevard in Tottenville, the southern point of Staten Island.

Billop had been granted 932 acres at the south end of Staten

Island in 1675. Later he increased his landholdings to 1,600 acres. In 1709 he began ferry service from his land in Staten Island across the Arthur Kill to Perth Amboy, New Jersey. (The Tottenville area was once called Billop's Point. Billop Avenue in Tottenville is named for him.)

The house was confiscated from the Billop family by the State of New York at the end of the Revolution as punishment for the Billops siding with the British. It was turned into apartments and then a hotel. The house gradually fell into disrepair and was eventually abandoned as any kind of residence. In the early 20th century it was used as a factory making rat poison. It was deserted in 1918 when an explosion in a nearby gunpowder factory blew out its windows. The building was left unprotected until restoration began in 1926.

Conference House opened as a museum in 1937 with the rooms furnished in 18th century furniture. Of special interest is the vaulted root cellar, large basement kitchen with a floor of glazed bricks made in Holland, and the exposed hand-hewn beams throughout the building.

Notation:

Benjamin and William Franklin Unable to Make Up

The American Revolution broke the family ties between patriot Benjamin Franklin and loyalist William Franklin, his illegitimate son whom he raised. Each had strong feelings and tried in person and by letter to convince the other to change his mind. William had been appointed royal governor of New Jersey but was arrested and taken to an American prison in Connecticut. Governor William Livingston, a patriot, replaced him. A prisoner exchange in 1778 freed William and he sailed to London after spending some time in loyalist controlled New York City. He had been kept in solitary confinement for two hundred fifty days, his wife had died while he was gone, and his forty thousand acres of property in several colonies was being confiscated. At the war's end he chose to stay in England.

Meanwhile, Benjamin Franklin was in Paris as the American ambassador. The son attempted reconciliation. In 1784 William wrote: *Ever since the termination of the unhappy contest between Great Britain and America, I have been anxious to write to you and to endeavor to revive that affectionate intercourse and connection which, till commencement of the late troubles, had been the pride and happiness of my life.* Benjamin answered with similar sentiments but then opened up the issue of politics: *Indeed, nothing has ever hurt me so much and affected me with such keen sensibilities as to find myself deserted in my old age by my only son; and not only deserted, but to find him taking up arms against me in a cause wherein my good fame, fortune, and life were all at stake. Then he added: This is a disagreeable subject: I drop it.* Benjamin was busy with work and pleasure in Paris and in no hurry to see his son: *I will be glad to see you when convenient, but would not have you come here at present.*

In 1785 Benjamin Franklin sailed from France to London. The reunion was frosty and he hounded William about money he owed him. Most of the time the father dined and socialized with old friends. When he left for the United States he did not even offer a final good-bye. In 1790 Benjamin Franklin died at age 84. He left nothing to his son and his Will contained a nasty remark directed at him: *The part he acted against me in the late war, which is of public notoriety, will account for my leaving him no more of an estate he endeavored to deprive me of.*

CHAPTER 38
Battle of Long Island (in Brooklyn)

Brooklyn played an important role in the history of the American Revolution as the scene of the Battle of Long Island, a 12-hour series of military clashes fought on August 27, 1776. In the first large conflict of the struggle for independence, a British and Hessian force of thirty-five thousand led by General Sir William Howe, which had disembarked at Gravesend Bay five days earlier, marched toward the glacial moraine in north central Brooklyn where they fought with General George Washington's nine thousand soldiers. The combat came five months after Howe had been forced to evacuate Boston and seven weeks after the Declaration if Independence was issued.

The American field generals serving under Washington, John Sullivan and Israel Putnam, were determined to hold Valley Grove Pass on the old Flatbush Road (now inside Prospect Park) and Bedford Pass, at Bedford Avenue and Montgomery Street. The British divided their forces and marched their west flank up Gowanus Road (approximately 4th Avenue), their Hessian mercenary center moved up Flatbush Road (Flatbush Avenue), and their right flank went far to the east on Kings Highway up to the moraine, through Jamaica Pass (in Queens), and then turned west along Jamaica Road (approximately Fulton Street) outflanking the two passes fortified by the Americans. The British Gowanus Road column held the Old Stone House and environs to block an American retreat west.

The main battle involved the British using their Jamaica Road column and the Hessian Flatbush Road column to simultaneously cut off the Americans at Bedford Pass, while mounting a pincer attack on American positions at Battle Grove Pass. Outmaneuvered, the American forces retreated from both positions in disarray. A series of ferocious firefights between American and British-Hessian forces took place in the fields and wooded glens west of the Lefferts House, now Prospect Park. The Americans withdrew across Gowanus Creek and its swampy tributaries to reconnoiter in Brooklyn Heights before evacuating across the East River to Manhattan.

The American retreat was made possible by the heroic actions of the Maryland Regiment led by Lord William Alexander Stirling. The four hundred brave men of the Maryland Regiment charged the Old Stone House six times (briefly taking it twice), a suicidal diversion which allowed the bulk of Washington's troops to escape. Of the four hundred Maryland soldiers, two hundred fifty-six were killed and all but ten of the remainder were captured. Washington watched the entire battle from a small hill where Atlantic Avenue and Court Street intersect. He reportedly exclaimed: *Good God! What brave fellows this day I must lose.* Today the Old Stone House stands rebuilt in the playground at Byrne Park, 5th Avenue between 3rd and 4th Streets.

The excitement that accompanied the first year of the American Revolution seemed quickly extinguished in Brooklyn. The Battle of Long Island yielded the slaughter of more than twelve hundred patriots (seven hundred more died captive on British prison ships anchored in the East River), a high percentage of the four thousand American battle deaths in the entire war. The enormity of the American losses caused Washington to change his strategy and adopt a form of guerrilla warfare rather than try to hold territory against English forces, the most powerful in the world. The disastrous result for the Continental Army meant evacuation from Brooklyn and subsequent withdrawal from Washington Heights, its last foothold in Manhattan. The metropolitan area remained in British hands until the War of Independence ended in 1783. The clash was called the Battle of Long Island because all the territory on Long Island except a handful of villages was commonly called by its collective geographic name.

Two weeks later, on September 11, 1776, Benjamin Franklin, John Adams, and Edward Rutledge, were sent by the Continental Congress, which was then meeting in Philadelphia, to negotiate with Admiral Lord Richard Howe, brother of General Sir William Howe, in hope of preventing further bloodshed. The meeting, which was held in Staten Island, adjourned as a failure, and the Americans returned to Philadelphia.

Today, there are several places where those with imagination can get a sense of the Battle of Long Island: Gravesend Bay, the Lefferts House and Battle Grove Pass in Prospect Park, the Old Stone House, the corner of Atlantic Avenue and Court Street, and the Brooklyn Heights Promenade, the location where Washington gathered his soldiers before evacuating them across the East River to Manhattan, which was not yet under the grips of the British army.

Battle Hill, farmland, which later became Green-Wood Cemetery, is a magnificent place to view the terrain where the skirmishes of the Battle of Brooklyn took place. It is Brooklyn's highest point, two hundred twenty feet above sea level, and each side wanted the location for reconnaissance. It was the scene of a brief encounter on August 27, 1776 between units from the left flank of the British invasion force-marching up Gowanus Road (4th Avenue) and an exploratory party of Americans from the Maryland Regiment commanded by Lord Stirling. The skirmish ended quickly with the Americans retreating in front of the much larger British force.

Battle Hill can be reached by walking along Battle Avenue from the main gate of Green-Wood Cemetery, 5th Avenue and 25th Street, past the Vann Ness - Parsons pyramid, and past Fern Avenue (the overlook above the south terminus of 7th Avenue) to the intersection of Battle Avenue and Border Avenue. Battle Hill is made up of cemetery sections G and H, with crosswalks named Battle Path and Liberty Path. The vantage point offers spectacular views in all directions, especially when the leaves have fallen from the trees.

The largest monument on Battle Hill is an elaborate *Civil War Memorial.* A few steps to the north stands the *Altar to Liberty,* alternatively called the *Revolutionary War Memorial.* It is a statue of Minerva (Athena) next to a low Roman altar. The Goddess of War (as well as Wisdom) faces west and looks directly at *Liberty Enlightening the World* (the Statue of Liberty) on Liberty Island in the New York Harbor. Minerva wears a helmet and armor. Her breastplate is adorned with the snake-haired head of Medusa, a gift to her from Perseus for display. Minerva and Mercury (Hermes) had helped Perseus kill Medusa, a repulsive and terrifying Gorgon.

(It was common to use Greek and Roman mythology as political metaphors in the Republic's first century when everyone was familiar with the stories.)

CHAPTER 39
American Revolution in New York City

New York City has the dubious distinction of having remained in the hands of the British for almost the entire Revolutionary War. Redcoats occupied the city on September 15, 1776, just ten weeks after the Declaration of Independence was signed in Philadelphia, and held it until the Treaty of Paris was successfully negotiated in 1783.

New York City had never been the Cradle of the Revolution. That honor belongs to Boston where Samuel Adams, John Adams, Paul Revere, John Hancock, James Otis and others provided the conceptual framework for independence as well as the inspiration and organizational leadership to encourage colonialists to think of themselves as Americans and fight for separation from England.

The Sons of Liberty and the Committees of Correspondence originated in Boston under the influence of Sam Adams. The Sons of Liberty also organized in New York where they made speeches, held rallies, organized parades, erected liberty poles as symbols of independence, led boycotts against British products, and sometimes attacked British officials, especially tax collectors. The Committees of Correspondence was a slow-moving but effective communications network. Members would write to their friends and relatives throughout the thirteen colonies posing cogent arguments for independence, and, in turn, ask the recipients to write several more letters. Both groups were active in New York City, especially among the *mechanics*, the 18th century term for artisans and skilled workers. The Sons of Liberty held their meetings at Fraunces Tavern at the corner of Broad and Pearl Streets.

Many New Yorkers were also moved by the words of New Englander Thomas Paine in *Common Sense*, a widely distributed pamphlet, which argued that monarchy was a poor form of government, England would continue to harm the colonial economy with arbitrary taxes, and that it was foolish for a small island three thousand miles across the Atlantic Ocean to rule a continent. (The city honors Thomas Paine today with a small park named for him in Foley Square.)

Many New Yorkers were passionate about independence and ultimately became well known politicians: Philip Livingston, George Clinton (who later became New York State's first governor), John Jay, and Alexander Hamilton. Less well known were the three fiery leaders of the Sons of Liberty: John Lamb, Alexander McDougall, and Isaac Sears.

The causes of the American Revolution were evident years before the hostilities began. Any number of incidents can be considered a precipitant of the war. The Declaration of Independence, on July 4, 1776, came half a dozen years after the occurrence of one of the best known of the sudden, attention-riveting events, the Boston Massacre.

In 1765 the British imposed the Quartering Act on the American colonists. Three years later they sent troops to Boston and forced some households to quarter them. Boston families had to accept the capricious quartering of British soldiers in their homes. The Americans were forced to make room for them, and provide bedding and food. Citizens often taunted the soldiers, called them *lobsterbacks* (because of their red coats) and other choice names.

In March 1770 a confrontation between some redcoats and young Bostonians erupted outside a tavern across from the State House. The Americans pitched snowballs and stones at the soldiers. Initially the British tried to hold their fire but eventually unleashed a volley into the crowd. Five Americans were shot dead and seven were wounded. Sam Adams coined the term *Boston Massacre* and lithographers Paul Revere and Henry Pelham quickly made printing plates showing a somewhat sensationalized street battle that were used to print pamphlets distributed throughout the colonies. The dead became political martyrs and were buried with great honor at the Old Granary Cemetery, three blocks away. Among them was Crispus Attucks, the first black American to die in the prelude to war.

The Stamp Act was imposed on the colonists in 1765. Americans were supposed to buy paper stamps from British tax agents to affix on a whole list of items: books, court documents, writing paper, and playing cards. The Americans resisted and raised the cry: ***No taxation without representation!*** Some patriots reacted violently and tarred and feathered British tax collectors. The Stamp Act was repealed, but the British wanted to raise money to help defray the cost of garrisoning the colonies, and they also wanted to show their authority.

The Townshend Acts, passed in 1767, were a series of taxes sponsored in the British Parliament by the Chancellor of the Exchequer (Minister of Finance), Charles Townshend. They taxed lead, paper, glass, cloth, paint, lead, and tea. In the face of strong resistance they were also repealed, in 1770, except for the tax on tea. Arguments over the tax led to a riot on Manhattan's Nassau Street.

Sam Adams and his supporters stepped up their agitation against the tax on tea. In 1773 a group of them clownishly dressed as American Indians, as a tongue-in-cheek way to deflect detection, gathered at Boston's Old South Church, marched to the docks, and climbed aboard a British vessel carrying crates of tea. They used hatchets to break open the containers and dumped the contents into Boston Harbor. The *Boston Tea Party* enraged the British. Lord North, the British prime minister closed the harbor to collectively punish the people of Boston, who could then neither import nor export goods by sea. In March, General Sir William Howe had been forced by the unruly Boston public to evacuate Boston and his soldiers stayed aboard naval ships anchored in the harbor.

In April 1775 the British suspected that the *minutemen* in Massachusetts, a group of patriots pledged to be ready to fight in a minute, were storing guns and ammunition in Lexington and Concord. They disembarked their ships and marched out to disarm the rebels. Paul Revere, William Dawes, and Dr. Samuel Prescott rode ahead of them warning the minutemen of the approaching column of redcoats. At the town common in Lexington eight Americans were killed in an open field face-off. The British went to Concord, met only sporadic resistance, and never found the cache of weapons. On their way back to Boston the British column was attacked from behind and the sides by Americans using trees, stone fences, and boulders for cover. The minutemen had quickly changed their tactics. British casualties were high and it helped convince General Howe to eventually quit Boston and use New York for his military operational center.

In New York, patriots organized a private election to choose a Committee of One Hundred in April 1776 that in turn would select delegates to send to the Second Continental Congress and prepare for war. Colonial Governor William Tryon held an official election to the New York Colonial Assembly to steal the thunder from the revolutionary group. Tryon's new Assembly never convened and the governor escaped to a British frigate moored in the harbor.

Stories about the lanterns in Boston's Old North Church (*one if by land, two if by sea*) and the *Midnight Ride of Paul Revere* (the poem was written by Henry Wadsworth Longfellow a century later), and the Battle of Lexington and Concord energized patriots. The actions, however, were precursors to the Revolutionary War. Events were rapidly thrusting the colonies toward open, sustained hostilities with England. On May 10, 1776 the Second Continental Congress convened in Philadelphia. The same day Benedict Arnold and Ethan Allen led revolutionary soldiers (*Green Mountain Boys* from Vermont and others) to capture Fort Ticonderoga at the south end of Lake Champlain.

On June 15 Washington was appointed to lead the Continental Army. The Battle of Bunker and Breed's Hill on June 17th pitched Boston's revolutionaries against General Howe's soldiers in Charlestown, just across the Charles River from Boston. The Americans lost, but the British paid a very high price in casualties for their victory. On July 3rd Washington took command of seventeen thousand soldiers west of Boston. Realizing that they could not expect to capture and hold Boston, the British made plans to sail to New York, secure it, and use it as the center for their war operations. The Declaration of Independence was signed on July 4, 1776, and on August 23rd George III declared the thirteen American colonies to be in rebellion.

One reason the British opted for New York City was that its hinterland, especially western Long Island (Kings and Queens counties) and Staten Island was heavily Loyalist. Many Dutch farmers were very conservative and did not trust rapid change or the revolutionary ideas and leadership that had emerged from New York City, Boston, Philadelphia, or Virginia.

The Battle of Long Island was fought in Brooklyn on August 27, 1776. It was the first large conflict of the Revolutionary War. A British and Hessian force of thirty-five thousand decisively defeated Washington's nine thousand soldiers. The battle was fought four months after Howe had been forced to evacuate Boston and seven weeks after the Declaration if Independence was issued.

The Continental Army retreated from Brooklyn at nighttime across the East River and camped in and around New York City. Two weeks later, on September 15th General Howe entered the city as Washington retreated to the northwest corner of Manhattan, now known as Washington Heights, Inwood, and Marble Hill. The cliffs and rugged ledges along the two parallel ridges of Manhattan schist began their long association with Washington's name during the American Revolution. Five days after the patriot army left the city, a fire broke out and burned one-quarter of New York. Called the Great Revolutionary War Fire, it consumed more than one thousand buildings. No evidence has ever been offered to link Washington's troops to the arson, though the British suspected it.

As Washington's army retreated from the city, other well-known patriots also fled, either to join the Continental Army or to relocate with friends and relatives. Augustus Van Cortlandt was the city clerk of New York where he owned a large town house. Fleeing the British, he removed important municipal documents and placed them among the caskets in the underground Van Cortlandt Family Burial Vault on a hill at his country estate. The British never found the documents and never captured Augustus Van Cortlandt. (Vault Hill, three hundred yards north of the Van Cortlandt House Museum is now part of Van Cortlandt Park in the Bronx. The weed-choked vault site is bordered on three sides by a high stonewall and on the fourth by iron bars with an open gate. There are no tombstones or inscriptions in the enclosure to hint at the burials below or the historic significance of the site.)

After fleeing from New York City, Washington's troops had regrouped in Manhattan's northwest corner stretching from Inwood to Washington Heights. The northern tip of Manhattan was important to both sides during the war and the Americans built four small temporary fortifications in Washington Heights and one in Inwood to hold their positions.

Washington's men hastily constructed the fortifications to protect themselves from Howe. The four redoubts in the area were each built on steeply elevated ground. Fort Washington was constructed amidst the high rocks in what is now Bennett Park, Fort Tryon was located on a hill in the southern portion of Fort Tryon Park, Fort George was built on Fort George Hill, south of the eastern end of Dyckman Street between St. Nicholas and Fort George Avenues, and Cock-Hill Fort was constructed on a bluff overlooking Broadway at West 212th Street.

While there are no longer any indications of Fort Washington (Bennett Park) that are recognizable on its rocky promontory, a granite plaque on the eastern retaining wall tells the story of the Continental Army's brief defense of the elevated position. It was lost when twenty thousand Hessian mercenaries and British Redcoats attacked in November 1776. The British captured two thousand eight hundred Americans that day. (Another marker imbedded into a rock outcropping on the top of the hill marks it as the highest natural point in Manhattan: two hundred sixty-five feet above sea level.)

Fort Tryon (now in Fort Tryon Park) occupied a high ridge south of where the Cloisters is now located. The fortification fell to Hessian mercenaries and redcoats just after the fall of Fort Washington. The name the Americans gave their fort is unknown. But when the British captured it they renamed it Fort Tryon in honor of William Tryon, the colonial governor of New York. The designation was never changed. (The south entrance to the park is named Corbin Plaza, to honor Margaret Corbin, a female soldier supporting the American cause, who helped defend the American battlement. She was wounded, captured, eventually released, and in old age received only a *half-pension* from the new American government because she was a woman.)

Washington was forced to leave behind in New York thousands of his soldiers captured by the British and held in appalling conditions on eleven prison ships moored in Wallabout Bay (now the Navy Yard) in Brooklyn. At least eleven thousand five hundred perished from malnutrition, disease, exposure, and brutal treatment, and their bodies unceremoniously thrown overboard. A tall Doric column with a bronze brazier (which once held an eternal flame) commemorating the *prison ship martyrs* was built in the center of Fort Greene Park in 1908.

Washington's forces withdrew from Manhattan in two units. One group went north, clashing with the British in White Plains, then crossed the Hudson River at Peekskill. They were joined in New Jersey by the remainder of Washington's army that had crossed from Washington Heights to Fort Lee. From there they retreated toward Valley Forge, Pennsylvania. On the way west, Washington doubled back across the Delaware River on Christmas night, in 1776, to scatter a force of Hessian and English soldiers at Trenton, and shortly thereafter at Princeton.

After a difficult beginning the American army passed a harsh winter in Valley Forge by practicing military drills and battle tactics led by Prussian Baron Friedrich von Steuben. Washington reflected on the series of early defeats, altered his strategy, and the Continental Army regrouped to carry on the war.

British colonial civilian government did not return to New York City after 1776. While Governor Tryon, who had briefly fled, returned to his post, he remained a figurehead and General Howe and other military authorities ruled the city by proclamation and enforced orders with their soldiers. No dissent was tolerated and suspected spies were given summary trials and executed.

The occupying British forces commandeered numerous houses and buildings in Manhattan to use as military headquarters and places to quarter their officers. The British were impressed with the location of the Dyckman Farmhouse. The house is perched on a hill just a few yards from Broadway (at 204th Street) and close to the northern tip of the island. The British used it as their northern Manhattan military headquarters. (It is the only extant 18th century farmhouse on the island, and was built by descendants of Jan Dyckman who emigrated from Germany to Dutch New Amsterdam in 1661. The house was substantially rebuilt after being largely destroyed by British forces when they withdrew.)

The Morris-Jumel Mansion (on West 160th Street just east of the point where Amsterdam and St. Nicholas Avenues merge), a sumptuous Federal-Georgian residence, was abandoned by its owner, Colonel Roger Morris, a Loyalist who fled to England at the beginning of the war. General George Washington briefly used it as his headquarters after he retreated to the area following the American defeat in the Battle of Long Island. British General Sir Henry Clinton moved in after Washington retreated across the Hudson. Built about 1765, it is the oldest surviving mansion in Manhattan. Situated on what is now called Sugar Hill, the mansion had an expansive view in all directions.

Lower Manhattan where the City of New York was located was held by the British and cut off from much of its usual trade with the mainland, though overall commerce increased due to the large maritime shipments of supplies sent to the city from England and other British colonies.

Once the Americans and their French allies defeated the British at the Battle of Yorktown, the parliament and king decided the war was not worth pursuing and commenced peace talks in Paris. Even after the war was over, the British dragged their feet leaving New York City. They finally evacuated, along with thousands of their Loyalist supporters on November 25, 1783, seven weeks after the Treaty of Paris was signed on September 3rd. The British completed their withdrawal at 1:00 P.M. and one hour later General Washington reentered New York City. Several days of parades, bonfires, and banquets marked the occasion. On December 4th Washington bid farewell to his officers at an emotional banquet at Fraunces Tavern. Subsequently known as *Evacuation Day*, November 25th became a local holiday celebrated by boisterous parades and speeches, patriotic and anti-British, until 1917 when the United States alliance with the British in the First World War made anti-British sentiments appear unseemly. (Evacuation Day also conflicted with Thanksgiving, a holiday unknown outside New England in 1783, but which assumed greater importance throughout the United States during the late 19th century.)

The war had a great effect on the city's population. It dropped from about twenty-two thousand in early 1776 to five thousand following the Battle of Brooklyn and the Great Revolutionary War Fire. It rose to thirty-one thousand between 1777 and 1783, when the English used New York City as their colonial military headquarters and many Loyalists fled their homes upstate and in other colonies and gathered in the city for protection. Once the English soldiers and civilian Loyalists evacuated in 1783, the population temporarily fell to eleven thousand but quickly expanded so that it reached thirty-three thousand in 1790 and sixty thousand in 1800.

Notation:

Morris-Jumel Mansion, 1765 Jumel Terrace at West 160th Street

After the Revolution the mansion was confiscated from the self-exiled Roger Morris by the new American government in 1783. It became a popular tavern called Calumet Hall until it was purchased in 1810 by Stephen Jumel, a wealthy French wine merchant, whose widow Eliza married Aaron Burr. The marriage ended in six months but during that time Burr lived there with Eliza. Burr had been United States vice president during Thomas Jefferson's presidency, and had killed Alexander Hamilton in a duel in 1804. Eliza became increasingly eccentric and reclusive in her later years. The house was purchased from subsequent owners by New York City in 1903 and opened as a museum.

In his *New York City Ghost Stories*, Charles J. Adams III, chronicler of phantom phenomena, describes the history of sightings of Eliza Jumel. She ostensibly appears in a white dress making rapping sounds on windows, walls, and metal pails. It was reported that in 1964 an apparition of Madame Jumel harshly scolded four obstreperous schoolchildren on a class visit.

CHAPTER 40
Nathan Hale

This Revolutionary War patriot was born in Coventry, Connecticut in 1755, graduated from Yale College, and taught school for one year. He joined the Continental Army in 1775. General George Washington commanded the revolutionary army that had been established by the Continental Congress, which was the coordinating organization of the revolution, in order to overthrow British rule in the thirteen colonies.

Nathan Hale joined Knowlton's Rangers, a brigade of soldiers operating in Connecticut. When asked, Hale volunteered to be a spy for Washington. His mission was to take a boat to Long Island, buy a horse and get to Manhattan. He was to find out the number of British soldiers, ships, and cannon, and their places of deployment. Such military information would help Washington plan how and where to engage the British in battle.

Nathan Hale decided to pose as a teacher, which was easy for him since he had been a teacher. He wore what was the typical teacher style of the day for men: brown wool *knickers*, brown wool *frockcoat*, and white linen shirt. Knickers were full breeches gathered and tightened just below the knees, and a frockcoat was a knee length dress coat. Dressed as a schoolteacher, Hale took a ferry across the East River, and slipped into New York City without notice. He spent a few days walking around town taking notice of British military strength.

The Americans had lost the Battle of Long Island on August 27th and the British moved in to New York City on September 15th. Fire broke out in many buildings in New York City on Friday, September 20, 1776. The arsonists were never found. But it was presumably started by patriotic Americans who felt it better to lose New York City to flames than to let it fall into the hands of the British. About one-quarter of the city burned. That night the British arrested scores of Americans who they thought might support independence for the colonies.

Nathan Hale was arrested and searched. Notes written in Latin detailing British military positions were found in his boots. (Most successful espionage is much more sophisticated.) He was accused of spying for the patriots and given a perfunctory trial by General Sir William Howe, the brother of Admiral Lord Richard Howe.

The prisoner was led to a spot under a sturdy tree. A noose was made out of a length of rope. Hale asked for a minister and a Bible but his requests were denied. After slipping the noose around his neck he was asked if he had any last statement. Nathan Hale paraphrased lines from Addison's play *Cato,* a theater production in which he had acted at Yale: *I only regret that I have but one life to lose for my country.*

The 21-year-old was hanged and buried nearby. Nathan Hale did not become an instant martyr. His story of dedication and patriotism was not widely told for half a century. Eventually he entered history books as a hero of the American Revolution. A heroic-style bronze statue of him, forged in 1890, stands in City Hall Park as an example of dedication and courage. The statue with a noose around its neck implies that Hale was hanged in the Common, though recent scholarship places the execution far uptown, either near today's Grand Central Terminal or Hunter College.

CHAPTER 41
Architecture of the English Period

During the English colonial period many farmhouses continued to be built in the Dutch style. Sharply pitched roofs proved well adapted for New York's snowy winters and the extended, columned eaves afforded a shady rest place in the hot summers. An example of a Dutch-style farmhouse built in the English period is the Lefferts Homestead (1783) in Prospect Park, Brooklyn.

Manor houses, or mansions in the country, were a new phenomenon during English rule. A few wealthy landowners built substantial homes and some still exist. Christopher Billopp, a British naval captain built Conference House (1680), at the southern point of Staten Island (now Tottenville) with government help to establish a firm British presence in the area which was mostly inhabited by Lenape Indians and Dutch farmers. The large two-story house overlooking Raritan Bay was built of native fieldstone. The Van Cortlandt House (1749) at Van Cortlandt Park in the Bronx is the oldest house in the borough. It also is made of fieldstone and has a third floor lined with pitched-roof dormers.

The big difference between architecture in the Dutch and English periods was in the construction and style of townhouses. English townhouses were larger and dropped some Dutch details like the step-style roof, hoisting bracket, and divided doors. They kept the *stoop*, and the word for it. The English sometimes put an immense fireplace with two, three, or four openings in the center of the house so the heat and light radiated outward. Bricks were a more common building material than fieldstone though wood was also used.

The style that developed in the 18th century was called Georgian, after the first three Hanoverian monarchs of England: George I, George II, and George III. The Georgian form took its inspiration from Ancient Roman and Greek principles of symmetry and balanced proportion. For example, if there were two windows to the left of the front door, there would need to be two windows on the right. Inside the larger houses more rooms were designed for specific purposes: dining room, parlor, library, bedrooms. In larger houses the structure was built higher off the ground and a semi-basement was added to become the kitchen and laundry room. (New Yorkers now call that floor the *garden* floor.)

Indoors, white lime plaster was generally used to cover the walls. Molds were used to make decorative plaster features such as central ceiling medallions and elaborate pre-cast cornices were placed up near the ceiling.

Along the edges of the house *quoins* were inserted into the brickwork. *Quoins* were cornerstones usually made of blocks of white limestone, larger than the bricks, which ran up the sides in an alternating pattern of long and short. The point was to decorate the four corners of a house. (Quoins have been used well into the 20th century especially on New York apartment buildings.)

Windows in the Georgian period were *sash-windows,* which opened and closed by sliding up or down. Windowpanes separated by *muntins* (narrow wood frame pieces) were divided into twelve or twenty-four sections called *six-over-six* or *twelve-over-twelve* style windows. *Louvred* shutters predominated. Carved cornices above windows were rare in the Georgian period though *pediments* (triangular gables) began to decorate the area above front doors. A pediment that was used above a front door was usually flanked by decorative *pilasters,* which are flattened non-structural columns.

Examples of English colonial houses are no longer numerous in New York City, but there are some fine examples. Conference House (1680), in Tottenville, Staten Island, Van Cortlandt House (1749), in Van Cortlandt Park, Bronx, and Kingsland Homestead, (1785), in Flushing, Queens are now museums. Fraunces Tavern, at the corner of Pearl Street and Broad Street in downtown Manhattan has been almost totally rebuilt in the Georgian style though no one knows what it looked like in 1719 when it was initially built.

The Friends (Quaker) Meeting House (1694) on Northern Boulevard in Flushing, Queens, and St. Paul's Chapel (1764-1796), on Broadway near City Hall, marked opposite ends of the English period and strikingly different architectural visions. The Friends Meeting House is a plain two story wood frame structure with a sharply pitched four-sided hip-roof, wood shingles, and long covered porch facing away from the street toward a small Quaker cemetery. It has a dark medieval look. Inside the church, the pews, which face each other from four directions, are made of unstained wood.

St. Paul's Chapel was built of Manhattan fieldstone (mica-schist) and brownstone. Inside, it has an ornately carved wood altar and a highly raised, covered hexagonal pulpit. Elaborate chandeliers light the nave, which is filled with pews in family boxes. On the side a separate throne-like, armchair (originally canopied) was reserved for President George Washington, who attended St. Paul's during the year the national capital was located in New York City. Interestingly, St. Paul's was built to face west, at that time only one hundred yards from the Hudson River, so that is where the tall steeple was placed, though the back, facing Broadway, ultimately became the main entrance and was later given a colonnaded portico. In effect, the church has two fronts. A cemetery surrounds St. Paul's.

• 19th Century New York City

CHAPTER 42
New York City: National Capital for One Year

There was a great deal of political confusion in New York and the other twelve colonies during the years of the American Revolution about their ultimate organization and relationship with one another. The uncertainty continued for the next decade. A state constitution had been adopted in Kingston, New York in 1777, but because the Redcoats controlled New York City for the entire length of the war, the constitution could not be put into effect everywhere. The state legislature met in several different upstate towns during the Revolution. After the British evacuated in 1783, New Yorkers throughout the state began to actively transform the Colony of New York into the State of New York. In 1785 the state capital was placed in New York City where it remained until its removal in 1796 to more centrally located Albany.

Political decision-making was diffuse and perplexing on the national level as well. The Continental Congress, which met sporadically from 1774 to 1781, was a wartime alliance, which evolved into a national government. Once all Thirteen Colonies ratified the Articles of Confederation in 1781, the Continental Congress ceased operating, though many of its members became delegates to its successor, the Confederation Congress. Under the Articles of Confederation the national government had no home base, though it often met in Philadelphia, until 1785 when it set up its headquarters in New York City.

In 1785, the Confederation's national government, began to move into Fraunces Tavern and by 1789, when it was supplanted by the United States government established by the Constitution, the second and third floors of the tavern housed the Departments of Foreign Affairs (State), War (Defense), and the Treasury. The Confederation government was a weak compromise between differing views of delegates representing the newly independent

Thirteen States. Each state was jealous of its own sovereignty. It was not an effective government and it left its thirteen participants weak and disunited. It had no president and no supreme court. It did have a legislative body, a one-chamber Congress of the Confederation, and a few administrative departments.

A much stronger national government was needed for defense, trade, banking and the courts. Under the Articles of Confederation there was no uniform procedure for solving jurisdictional disputes between the states. The states acted as individual countries and established tariffs on goods crossing their borders. Without a uniform currency each state set up its own rules. New York State allowed the state, county, and town governments, as well as banks, companies, and individuals to mint coins and print banknotes. It is estimated that during the Articles of Confederation, New York State was swamped with three hundred different currencies. Unable to trust the value of money, citizens relied on currency from abroad, mostly the British pound.

A Constitutional Convention was called in Philadelphia to remedy the situation and met in the Pennsylvania State House (later called Independence Hall) throughout the hot summer months of 1787. A much more comprehensive document resulted, and the government of the new republic went into effect in 1789. Alexander Hamilton signed for New York, though ratification was needed by New York's legislature.

The delegates to New York State's legislature had argued over the merits of the new United States Constitution and finally on July 26, 1788 became the eleventh state to sign the document. Political disagreements continued during the deliberations surrounding the selection of the first president. New Yorkers never agreed on a method of choosing presidential electors, and did not cast electoral ballots, so New York missed the first presidential election that chose George Washington.

At his Mount Vernon estate Washington was informed on April 14, 1789 that he had been elected president. Two days later he left Virginia and headed for New York City, which had been chosen as the interim capital of the United States. After a nine-day procession by carriage, with many gala celebrations along the way, Washington's entourage crossed the Hudson River in a barge festooned in red, white, and blue bunting, and entered the city on April 23rd. He made his way by carriage to the spacious home of Samuel Osgood, who rented it to the president for 900 British pounds per year. New Yorkers called Osgood's home *the palace*. It was located at 3 Cherry Street, near the East River under what is now the Brooklyn Bridge. (Finding the house too far from the center of town, Washington moved a few months later to the McComb House, a four-story townhouse at 39 Broadway, just north of Bowling Green.)

On Thursday, April 30th crowds gathered around Federal Hall at the corner of Wall and Broad Streets for the republic's first presidential inauguration. Many of the city's thirty three thousand residents turned out for the event. They were joined by thousands of guests arriving by boat, carriage, and horse. Washington was escorted from the Osgood mansion to Federal Hall by a delegation of senators. His clothing caused a second glance by most who were near enough to see him. Rather than dress in a colorful silk jacket and trousers as he usually did, Washington chose to wear a suit of brown homespun broadcloth (homemade cotton). The plain look was intended to set a pattern discouraging excessive pomp. Many of Washington's choices, whether symbolic or substantive, had to be original because the United States was the first republic in a world of monarchies.

Nonetheless, the occasion was less than completely populist, and after leaving his carriage Washington entered the ornately adorned Senate chamber where members of the Senate and House of Representatives had gathered. Vice President John Adams formally presented Washington to the Congress before being escorted to the second floor balcony of Federal Hall. There Chancellor Robert R. Livingston, wearing a judge's black robe, administered the oath of office. *I do solemnly swear that I will faithfully execute the office of the President of the United States and will, to the best of my ability, preserve, protect, and defend the Constitution of the United States.* Robert Otis, Secretary of the Senate, held a Bible, on loan from the Masonic Lodge of New York City, for the ritual. Washington leaned down, kissed the Bible, and as he stood up added: *So help me, God.* Livingston called out a cheer: *Long live George Washington, President of the United States!*

Washington delivered his inaugural address to the assembled citizens from the second floor balcony and then walked seven blocks to St. Paul's Chapel to pray. St. Paul's, an Episcopal church, and part of Trinity Church parish, is the oldest church in Manhattan. Located on Broadway between Fulton Street and Vesey Street, it was completed in 1766. President Washington attended church at St. Paul's where a special throne-like canopied armchair was built for him. (Trinity Church had not yet been rebuilt from the 1776 fire that had reduced it to ashes.)

Federal Hall, built in 1699, had been the second City Hall for New York. The mayor and city council gave the building to the new national government. A new city hall for New York was built in the town common and completed in 1811. (The first city hall, called *Stadt Huys* by the Dutch, was above a tavern on Pearl Street facing Coenties Slip.)

Pierre Charles L'Enfant, a Frenchman, remodeled Federal Hall in 1788. He later achieved eminence by designing the street grid of Washington, D.C. Even before it became the capitol building of the United States, Federal Hall was well known. In 1735, during British colonial days, John Peter Zenger's celebrated trial for seditious libel was held there, and the Continental Congress met there in 1785. Sadly, the historic building was demolished and a new Greek Revival structure, the U.S. Custom House, was constructed on the site in 1842. A gargantuan statue of Washington was erected on its front stairs in 1883.

New York City accommodated the national government generously, though southerners were unhappy. They wanted the capital moved further south. In 1790 the capital was relocated to Philadelphia where it remained for a decade. The Philadelphia city government and the Pennsylvania state government moved out of three important adjoining buildings in Philadelphia. The State House (Pennsylvania state capitol) became the presidential office, both Houses of Congress used the County Courthouse, and the City Hall was readied for the Supreme Court. (A new city hall for Philadelphia was constructed a few blocks away and the Pennsylvania state capital moved west to Harrisburg.)

In 1800, during the presidency of John Adams, a new national capital was established even further south. Located on the banks of the Potomac River, it was first called the Federal District, then the District of Columbia, and finally Washington, D.C. Its 100-square mile territory was ceded to the national government: seventy by Maryland and thirty by Virginia. Eventually, Virginia, irked that no national government buildings had been constructed on its side of the Potomac River, asked for and received the return of its thirty square miles. The irony of that decision is that in 1942 the largest national building in the country, the Pentagon, was constructed in Arlington, Virginia, which had been part of the thirty square miles of land.

While New York City was national capital for only one year, its population soared and it became the economic and cultural capital of the country. In 1783, at the end of the American Revolution, New York City's population was eleven thousand. Philadelphia, Boston, and Charleston, South Carolina each had more people. By 1800 New York's population reached sixty thousand and by 1850, it grew to 600,000. In 2014 the population of New York City reached 8,400,000 making it the largest city in the United States.

Notation:

Terminology for the Two Levels of Government in the United States

There are two levels of government recognized in the United States Constitution: the national government and the state governments. All local governments (cities, towns, villages, counties) exist at the pleasure of the states and are regulated by the state legislatures. The system is called the *federal system* because the state governments and the national government share certain powers, which are enumerated in the Constitution. The terminology that can be confusing is that while we call the state governments *state governments*, we call the national government the *federal government*.

CHAPTER 43
Castle Clinton

After independence, the United States remained deeply suspicious of all three powerful European countries: Great Britain, France, and Spain. To protect New York City from possible enemy naval attacks, forts were built at the Verrazzano Narrows, Governors Island, Bedloe's Island, and in Manhattan at Corlear's Hook and the Battery.

Castle Clinton, the circular fort at the Battery, is about one hundred yards west of the Custom House at Bowling Green. The squat, rough-faced brownstone block fort was built by the U.S. federal government between 1808 and 1811 on a rocky islet thirty yards offshore. Twenty-eight gun mountings were included in the design. The fort was connected to Manhattan by a 200-foot long wooden causeway.

Initially called West Battery, it received the name Castle Clinton, for Governor George Clinton in 1815. Its purpose, as with other forts guarding the harbor, was to defend access to the city. The Verrazzano Narrows had Fort Wadsworth and Fort Hamilton, Fort Jay and Castle Williams were on Governors Island, Bedloe's Island (Liberty Island) was dominated by Fort Wood. Corlear's Hook Fort was built in the place where Manhattan bulges into the East River. These forts were placed throughout the harbor area to make an enemy landing or bombardment of New York City very difficult.

None of the forts ever saw military action and after the War of 1812 and the Napoleonic Wars, the federal government sought to decommission Castle Clinton. In 1823 the fort was demilitarized and given to the city. More landfill was added at the edge of Battery Park to join the former fort with Manhattan.

Castle Clinton was remodeled to hold a large auditorium, outfitted with a two-tiered conical roof and renamed Castle Garden in 1824. The city leased it to entrepreneurs who staged popular events on its stage. P.T. Barnum rented Castle Clinton for the debut of Jenny Lind, dubbed the *Swedish Nightingale,* who sang to packed audiences in 1850. The balloonist or æronaut Charles Durant used Castle Clinton for his celebrated flight, which took him thirty miles.

Between 1855 and 1890, Castle Clinton became the Emigrant Landing Depot, the largest east coast immigration center. Almost eight million newcomers passed the cursory inspection and became legal residents. Immigrant centers, or as they were called at the time, *emigrant* centers, were operated by the states. Uneven application of the laws and corruption caused the federal government to take control of the process in 1890. Two years later Ellis Island became the federal immigration center for the New York port.

Castle Clinton was transformed again and from 1896 until 1941 it served as the New York City Aquarium. Robert Moses forced it to close and move to a new facility at Coney Island. The autocratic commissioner of highways and parks wanted to demolish the old fort and use the space for a bridge to connect Manhattan and Brooklyn. The bridge idea was ultimately rejected in favor of the Brooklyn-Battery Tunnel.

In 1946 the fort was listed as a National Historic Monument but spent three decades closed off by a cyclone fence while it slowly deteriorated. Reborn in 1980 as Castle Clinton again, its center, which is now open to the sky, houses a small National Parks Service shop for books and postcards and a ticket booth where visitors can buy tickets for ferries going to Ellis Island and Liberty Island. Castle Clinton has served the city well in its various incarnations, but this underused old fort needs a more meaningful role on the waterfront.

CHAPTER 44
Washington Irving

Washington Irving was born in Manhattan in 1783. It was the year the British soldiers evacuated New York and Irving was named in honor of General George Washington. The last of eleven children, Irving was taken care of financially by his older brothers because they wanted to give him ample opportunity to use his literary talents. He made friends in New York's emerging literary circle and soon was a regular at taverns where intellectuals gathered. Irving had become a man-about-town. His friends and he published *Salmagundi,* a literary magazine where many of his stories first appeared. (Salmagundi was a whimsical name for a spicy hash.)

After achieving some success as a writer by middle age, Irving moved to a house in the country near Tarrytown in Westchester County. He visited Manhattan often, usually staying with a nephew near Gramercy Park. Irving Place, which is Lexington Avenue south of Gramercy Park, was subsequently named for the author, and Washington Irving High School is located on Irving Place.

Washington Irving was mildly involved in politics and served as a diplomat in Great Britain and ambassador to Spain. Political figures were the subjects of two of his books. He authored two political biographies, *The Life of George Washington* and *The Life and Voyages of Christopher Columbus.* Though he never wrote on economics, he did coin the phrase *the Almighty Dollar.*

Irving was the first American to win international literary fame. He wrote about America, usually New York, and produced a large volume, *A History of New-York,* which focused on old Dutch and English families and their culture. Clever in gently mocking the established families of the city, Irving used informality, extravagant speech, and outrageous tall tales to paint a picture of colonial culture. He developed a uniquely American style, which was different from the formal, self-confident sanctity of European observers. On the other hand, his history was only involved with cultural and business elites. Irving's New York ignored slavery, poverty, poor housing, pollution, and other problems of society.

A History of New-York and his short stories were written as told to him by the fictitious character, Dedrich Knickerbocker. The term *knickerbockers* became the designation referring to descendants of Dutch colonists. In clothing, *knickerbockers* for men and boys were full breeches gathered and tightened just below the knees, and *knickers* were long bloomers worn as underwear by women and girls. John Jacob Astor commissioned the elegant Knickerbocker Hotel at 42nd Street and Broadway in 1902. (It is now an office building.) The New York Knicks is a basketball team. The term Knickerbockers can now be used to refer to any New Yorker.

Irving is best remembered for his short stories. In *Rip van Wrinkle*, a good-natured, henpecked husband, with an *insuperable aversion to all kinds of profitable labor*, left his town, widely believed to be Palenville, and went for a walk in the Mountains with his dog Wolf, to escape his scolding wife. He met a group mysterious little men in a mountain hollow. We later learn they were Henry Hudson's crewmen (or their ghosts) from his 1609 voyage up the Hudson River. *On a level spot in the center was a company of odd-looking personages playing at nine-pins.* Rip drank gin from a flagon (large drinking vessel) with them and fell asleep. When he awakened it was twenty years later, and at first the townsfolk failed to recognize him. Among other things he had missed the American Revolution. When he visited the inn, the painting of King George III was missing, replaced with a new portrait. *The red coat was changed for one of blue and buff, a sword was stuck in the hand instead of a scepter, the head was decorated with a cocked hat, and underneath was painted in large characters, GEORGE WASHINGTON.*

Eventually he met his daughter who took him into her household. Hesitatingly, he inquired: *Where's your mother?* The answer injects welcome finality to this misogynous tale. *Oh, she too had died but a short time since; she broke a blood vessel in a fit of passion at a New-England peddler.* The story ends in a new American myth about the Dutch inhabitants of the Catskill Mountains. *Even to this day they never hear a thunder storm of a summer afternoon, about the Katskill, but they say Hendrick Hudson and his crew are at their game of nine-pins; and it is a common wish of all henpecked husbands in the neighborhood, when life hangs heavy on their hands, that they might have a quieting draught out of Rip Van Wink's flagon.*

The Legend of Sleepy Hollow tells of Ichabod Crane, a gawky schoolmaster, who met up with the Headless Horseman. Set near Tarrytown, close to the Tappan Zee in Westchester County, Irving wrote striking descriptions of his main characters. *The cognomen of Crane was not inapplicable to his person. He was tall, but exceedingly lank, with narrow shoulders, long arms and legs, hands that dangled a mile out of his sleeves, feet that might have served for shovels, and his whole frame most loosely hung together. His head was small, and flat at top, with huge ears, large green glassy eyes, and a long snipe nose, so that it might have been mistaken for a weathercock perched upon his spindle neck, to tell which way the wind blew.* Ichabod was courting Katrina Van Tassel, daughter of a wealthy Dutch farmer. His competitor for Katrina's affections was local bully Brom Van Brunt. Coming home from a party at the Van Tassel homestead, after being rejected by Katrina, Ichabod rode home quickly on Gunpowder, his borrowed horse. Out of the dark appeared the Headless Horseman. The race was on. Just before Ichabod got to a bridge over a stream --- superstition holds that a spirit cannot cross water --- he was knocked to the ground by the ghostly rider's head. *Just then he saw the goblin rising in his stirrups, and in the very act of hurling his head at him. Ichabod endeavoured to dodge the horrible missile, but too late. It encountered his cranium with a tremendous crash---he was tumbled headlong into the dust, and Gunpowder, the black steed, and the goblin rider, passed by like a whirlwind.* The Headless Horseman disappeared and so did the schoolteacher. Brom married Katrina, and rumor has it that the head that downed poor Ichabod was a pumpkin hurled at him by one of Brom's friends.

Washington Irving was a New York literary pioneer and remained America's most famous writer until his death. His satires were biting and humorous for their time. Two centuries later *Rip van Winkle* and *The Legend of Sleepy Hollow* still delight listeners. Washington Irving died in 1859.

CHAPTER 45
Fires

Periodically all cities are damaged by fires, and New York City has had many conflagrations. There were relatively few widespread fires in the 17th century because houses and buildings were unattached and most were built of bricks or fieldstone. As the city grew, contractors often chose to construct buildings of wood and to build them next to each other to save money by economizing on building materials and land.

One of the positive accomplishments of Dutch West India Company Director-General Peter Stuyvesant was a broad edict *banning log chimneys, appointing two fire wardens and establishing a volunteer fire company, instituting a night watchman,* as well as banishing animals within the town to corrals, pens, and coops, clearing the main canal of rubbish, and repairing Fort Amsterdam and the town wall. *Old Silvernails* knew that there were reasonable precautions, which, if taken, would reduce the risk of fire to the city.

As New York City expanded and wood buildings covered entire lots, fires spread rapidly and whole blocks were in danger of being consumed by flames. English colonists had a heightened sensitivity to fires after the devastation caused by the Great London Fire of 1666 destroyed thirteen thousand houses and eight-nine churches. Most fires were started accidentally, but some were arson. The Revolutionary War Fire of 1776 wiped out the western portion of the city. George Washington's Continental Army retreated from Brooklyn at nighttime across the East River and camped in and around New York City. Two weeks later, on September 15th, General Howe entered the city as Washington retreated to the northwest corner of Manhattan, now called Washington Heights, Inwood, and Marble Hill. As the patriot army left the city, a fire broke out and burned one-quarter of New York. Called the Great Revolutionary War Fire, and widely believed to be arson, it consumed more than one thousand buildings including Trinity Church (Episcopal), which had been built in 1698. (The present Gothic structure completed in 1846 is the third Trinity Church built on the site.)

There were several fires in the early years of the republic. Fifty houses surrounding Front Street were destroyed in the First Coffee House Fire in 1796, and in 1804 forty more houses burned in the Second Coffee House Fire, which swept through the vicinity of Wall and Pearl Streets. The Great Fire of 1811 consumed one hundred two houses and killed one fireman in the area around Chatham Square. Ninety houses were destroyed by fire in 1833 in nearby Greenwich Village near the intersection of Greenwich and Hudson Streets.

The Great Fire of 1835 destroyed seven hundred buildings on many blocks in the city's south central section, which was its commercial center. The crowded blocks between Wall Street and Coenties Slip, and Broad Street and South Street, were consumed. The fire began at 9:00 P.M. on December 17th, a cold and windy night, which greatly increased the difficulty of fighting the flames. The East River shoreline was frozen as were most of the backyard wells and cisterns. When sources of water were found some of the small fire hoses froze when water was pumped through them.

Firefighting was primitive and had changed little since the days of *bucket brigades*. Fire engines in 1835 were simple pumps placed on hand-drawn carts. While some of the fire carts were elaborately ornamented with decorative lanterns, bells, and identification shields, their effectiveness was limited. Members of volunteers fire companies would pull the wheeled hand-pumped contraptions to a source of water, place one end of the hose in the water, then two teams of six men would begin pumping which would draw water through the hose so it could be aimed at the fire. At least sixty strokes per minute was needed to maintain a steady flow of water though the amount of water that could be pumped was rarely enough to save a burning building.

One firefighting strategy that worked was to tear down buildings in a fire's path to prevent it from spreading across narrow streets. Two buildings facing Exchange Place were blown up during the Great Fire of 1835 to prevent it from crossing west on Broad

Street.

Fire companies from Greenwich Village, Brooklyn, Jersey City, and Newark helped the fire companies in New York City, but it took hours for most of them to reach the scene. The movement of firefighters and police was impeded by employees of stores and warehouses in the area who rushed to empty their buildings of goods and move the stock a few blocks away where, under guard, it would be safe from flames and looters. About fifty-two acres of the city (seventeen blocks) burned in 1835, destroying about seven hundred buildings. Thousands were left without jobs, and most of the city's fire insurance companies were rendered insolvent.

An investigation later determined the cause to have been caused by the explosion of a gas pipe at a building on Merchant Street, and no individual or company was blamed for the conflagration. The area was quickly rebuilt and in the affected area the street pattern was simplified and the streets were widened.

The electorate authorized a referendum in April 1836, and the government initiated the Croton Aqueduct System to supply clean water to the city for drinking and for hydrants to use against fires. The Croton System was finished in 1842 and a great celebration on July 4th honored the project that included Croton Lake, a reservoir in Westchester County, an aqueduct over High Bridge from the Bronx to Manhattan, a receiving reservoir between 79th and 86th Streets (now in Central Park), a fanciful Egyptian-style holding reservoir where the 42nd Street library and Bryant Park are now located, and forty-one miles of cast-iron pipes protected by bricks to transport the water to the city.

New York City experienced other large-scale fires. The Great Fire of 1845 destroyed several square blocks of offices and warehouses in the southeast section of the city and consumed three hundred buildings. Fires were set throughout Manhattan during the Draft Riots in 1863 and forty-three buildings were destroyed.

To assist the work of fire carts, a fireboat was introduced in 1800, though it was only a simple barge fitted with a 12-man hand pump with a hose which, once put over the side, could find an unlimited supply of salt water. Fireboats were useful for combating ship, pier, and dockside warehouse fires.

Two civic improvements also helped early fire fighting. The

systematic numbering of houses and the posting of street signs in 1793 made it possible to give exact locations for fires. The Commissioners' Plan, or the Randel Plan, in 1811 aimed to prevent street chaos in Manhattan by creating a uniform grid plan. The purpose was to make straight streets with a uniform width from Houston Street north to 193rd Street in Washington Heights, excluding Greenwich Village. Twelve numbered avenues would run north and south. The plan, which created a grid of more than twenty-one hundred rectangular blocks, was to allow rapid vehicular movement on the broad streets and avenues and to lessen the possibility of fires leaping across streets to engulf entire sections of the city.

In the 1840s horses were hitched to fire carts, which sped the response time considerably. In 1858 steam-powered pumps were introduced. In the two decades before and after the Civil War a series of fire towers, often quite decorative, was built where fire wardens could scan the neighborhood for signs of a fire. Each was equipped with a bell to alert nearby fire companies. The Jefferson Market Courthouse (now the Jefferson Market Branch of the New York Public Library), 6th Avenue at West 10th Street, was built in 1877 to incorporate a pre-existing red brick fire tower. (The upper portion of the tower is embellished with a clock facing each direction, corner gargoyles, and a crowning weather vane.) An original cast-iron fire watchtower can still be found on the rocky hill in the center of Marcus Garvey Memorial Park (alternatively Mount Morris Park), in Harlem.

A major unintended consequence caused by the downtown fires was that while the affected areas were being rebuilt, companies, shops, and residences moved uptown never to return to former locations. Beside the devastation caused by fires, old buildings downtown did not last long because the constantly escalating cost of real estate in the most congested parts of the city fostered constant reconstructing. In crowded sections it always seemed financially sound to build more densely whenever possible. The successive buildings got progressively higher as the old buildings were destroyed. Few downtown buildings survived the twin threats posed by fires and the constant process of tearing down and rebuilding. Survivors include Fraunces Tavern, the Shrine of St. Elizabeth Ann Bayley Seton and its Rectory (Roman Catholic), and St. Paul's Chapel (Episcopal).

As time went on, firefighters became more effective at containing fires and fewer buildings were destroyed in each blaze, though some fires killed many people at a single location. In December 1876 the Brooklyn Theater Fire began during a performance. The death toll was two hundred ninety-five people, with one hundred three bodies later interred in a mass grave in Green-Wood near the front gate on 5th Avenue and 25th Street.

One block east of Washington Square Park, at the corner of Washington Place and Greene Street, is the site of the March 25, 1911 Triangle Shirtwaist Factory Fire. The conflagration killed one hundred forty-six people, mostly young Jewish and Italian women who worked in a garment factory with locked exit doors and clogged stairways. The tragedy spurred legislation to regulate factory conditions with regard to fire. (A plaque marks the site at 19 Washington Place, originally the Asch Building, now known as the Brown Building of New York University.)

Not including the World Trade Center tragedy in 2001, which was partly a fire but mostly a collapse of both towers caused by airplane suicide attacks, the last two devastating fires were each in social clubs in the Bronx: 1973 with twenty-five dead, and 1990 with eighty-seven people killed.

The Fire Department of the City of New York was established in 1778. The small volunteer staff had a rough start and was often accused of drunkenness and disorganization. The FDNY existed alongside numerous private fire companies, many were affiliated with criminal gangs or political clubs, especially between 1825 and the Civil War. William Marcy Tweed, later Boss Tweed, organized the American Engine Company in 1848 and used it as a base to gain power in Tammany Hall and city government. Rivalries between volunteer fire units often impeded firefighting. A scene showing fisticuffs between fire companies while a house burns appears in *The Gangs of New York* (2003). Nonetheless, the volunteer fire companies were popular especially with the working class.

By 1800 there were about six hundred public (paid) and private (volunteer) firefighters in the city. Their numbers increased rapidly as the city grew during the Civil War. In 1865 the FDNY and forty thousand volunteer firefighters were disbanded by the

New York State Legislature, which folded their equipment into a state-operated Metropolitan Fire Department. Eight hundred full-time, professional firefighters were hired. The new department was organized into fire houses, each with a separate identifying number. Fire houses held engine companies to drown fires and ladder companies to search and rescue. In 1870 the MFD was replaced by the second incarnation of a city-run FDNY. The department's numbers rose to a height of 14,855 in 1970.

Today the FDNY handles all fires in New York City, though some isolated neighborhoods, such as the island community of Broad Channel, Queens, have a volunteer fire department. Broad Channel is located in Jamaica Bay. The Broad Channel Volunteer Fire Department and Ambulance Corps exists to bolster fire prevention and for social reasons in an uniquely separate community where the closest FDNY stations are across the causeway in Howard Beach or across the bridge in Far Rockaway.

Firefighting is a bedrock community service in modern New York City. The FDNY is a large, efficient force spread through the five boroughs. It uses the most advanced equipment and strategy to contain and extinguish fires. Its goal is to save lives first, and then to protect property in a city with over eight million people living in a three hundred twenty-two square mile area. The roughly eleven thousand firefighters (fewer than one percent were women in 2014) are represented in collective bargaining with the City of New York by the Uniformed Firefighters Association, which was organized as a labor union in 1917. (The New York City Fire Museum is located in a former firehouse at 278 Spring Street in Manhattan.)

Notation:

FDNY Fireboats and Helicopters

Powerful diesel powered fireboats were introduced by the FDNY in the 1920s. They numbered ten from 1945 until 1975 when, because of a drastic reduction in harbor activity and a severe budget crisis, their number was reduced to five. The largest fireboats can deliver twenty thousand gallons of water per minute. The FDNY began depending on the police department's helicopters after the Second World War for aerial surveillance of large fires.

CHAPTER 46
Pestilence

There were many rapacious killers among the diseases that periodically swept through New York. Epidemics moved round the city with frightening speed, killed many residents, and often caused serious side effects for survivors. The rapid spread of pestilence in New York City was well known in the regional hinterland from rumor and newspaper articles. It was an impediment to migrants from upstate New York and New England before the Industrial Revolution. By the 19th century, the lure of good jobs and the possibility of getting rich pushed fears to the background and the city filled with migrants as well as immigrants.

Some blamed poor sanitary conditions for the terrible diseases tormenting New Yorkers while others pointed an accusing finger at the sickly among new immigrants. Both fears pointed at issues that were partially responsible for pestilence. But cleaning up the town, first attempted by Peter Stuyvesant in 1647, and quarantining contagious immigrants, which was never quite mastered until after the Second World War, were only part of the story.

The role of microbes (pathogens) in illness was not understood until the early 18th century. When it came to disease, early New Yorkers did not know what they were fighting against. Even when the cause of disease was more fully comprehended, antidotes to bacterial and viral infections were seldom obtainable until recently. Antibiotics, which fight bacterial infections, were not available to the public until 1946. Antiviral drugs, a late-20th century discovery, are still being developed.

When large-scale epidemics struck, potter's fields were opened to receive the corpses of those without money to buy a cemetery lot. Such grim burial places for the poor, often in common trenches, were established in numerous places in the city. The two largest were located southwest of Foley Square (Negroes Burial Ground) and in Washington Square (Greenwich Village Burial Ground).

The most notorious and feared killers over the last four centuries were smallpox, yellow fever, cholera, typhus, typhoid, diphtheria, measles, tuberculosis, influenza, pneumonia, and polio. AIDS, West Nile Virus, and SARS are relatively recent epidemics. Asthma, while not a communicable epidemic, has recently reached epidemic proportions in New York City.

Smallpox was a serious affliction during colonial times and through much of the 19th century. The disease, which had killed most of the Lenape Indians, also killed about one-quarter of the colonial settlers. Many of those not killed by smallpox, a variola virus, suffered disfiguring pockmarks all over their bodies, and damage to the eyes and ears. Smallpox is contracted by protracted face-to-face contact and announces itself with a high fever, rash, malaise, and achiness. In the 19th century it killed as many as thirty percent of those stricken.

Smallpox cases, as with most contagious diseases, could appear at any time, but they visited death in great numbers on colonial New Yorkers in 1679, 1690, 1731, and 1752. The 1731 epidemic was fatal for almost eight hundred people, approximately eight percent of the population of ten thousand.

English physician Edward Jenner noted that milkmaids rarely contracted smallpox. He discovered that vaccination with cowpox virus would give recipients immunity to smallpox. The vaccinations began on a very limited scale in New York in 1801. Despite mandatory vaccinations in the 1890s, the disease continued to kill residents until shortly after the Second Word War.

In 1856, New York City opened the Smallpox Hospital on Blackwell's Island (now Roosevelt Island) to segregate victims and attempt treatment. Vaccination does not work after the patient contracts the disease, so the Smallpox Hospital functioned primarily to isolate the victims while the disease ran its course. The institution was packed with patients during the late 19th century when smallpox reached epidemic proportions in the city. It was closed in 1889 after charges of corruption and ineffectiveness were leveled against its managers by the Health Department. A new smallpox facility was opened on North Brother Island, also in the East River. The hospital on Roosevelt Island is now an eerie gray ruin. Its crumbling walls and Gothic-style crenellated top is a haunting reminder of the scourge of epidemics in the past.

A 1947 smallpox episode was stanched early when five million people were vaccinated by thousands of volunteers during a two-week period. Only twelve New Yorkers contracted the disease, and two died from it. Declared eradicated from the entire planet in 1980 by the World Health Organization, authorities in the United States and Russia have kept samples of the smallpox virus for research in Atlanta and Moscow.

Blackwell's Island was used to segregate victims of other contagious diseases, as well. The skinny island, which measures 1.75 miles long and just two hundred sixty yards wide, is located in the middle of the East River between Manhattan and Queens. For much of the 19th and 20th centuries, it was used as a secluded place to house incurables and others who the society wished to keep at arm's length.

Yellow fever, a viral infection spread by mosquitoes, thrived in the squalor of New York's rookeries and tenements. In the early years, when there was no effective sanitation, dead animals, mostly horses, were left to rot along the docks, in alleys, and in backyards. Outhouses were emptied along the riverbanks by *necessary tubmen*. Garbage was thrown in the Collect Pond, or left to rot in backyards, or in makeshift dumps. By 1860 there were at least thirty thousand horses in the city, each leaving the streets with prodigious amounts of excrement. Flies swarmed over carcasses, sewage, garbage, and horse manure. Yellow fever kills its victims through its complications: severe hepatitis and hemorrhaging. Creation of the Metropolitan Board of Health and the non-governmental New York Sanitary Association raised awareness, educated residents, and took steps to clean the city. Public health measures, garbage collection, proper sewage disposal, insect repellents, and the development of a vaccine greatly reduced the risk of yellow fever.

Epidemics of yellow fever were recorded in 1702, 1731, and 1742. It spread through the city annually in the 1790s. The 1798 epidemic, the most severe, killed two thousand eighty-six people, almost one out of twenty inhabitants. The last major outbreak was in 1822 and by 1825 yellow fever epidemics subsided.

Cholera is an epidemic intestinal infection that exists where sanitation is poor. Contaminated feces finds its way into the water supply. Mild diarrhea is, at first, the main symptom, though steady loss of fluids leads to death. Treatment depends on antibiotics (tetracycline or doxycycline) and a regimen of re-hydration. Cholera epidemics struck New York City in 1832, 1849, and 1892. The 1832 epidemic, the most intense, left 3,513 dead. From 1850 until 1870, cholera killed approximately sixteen hundred New Yorkers each year.

Typhus is an epidemic not communicable directly between individuals. It is an arthropod-borne disease, which causes high fevers, severe headaches, muscular aches, and a rash. In severe cases vascular and neurological complications cause death. Body lice, fleas, mites, and ticks carry variants of typhus. Body lice, not head lice or pubic lice, carry the most common type of typhus. Typhus outbreaks often occur during disasters and mass dislocations when a breakdown in hygiene, especially during wars and natural disasters, occurs. Presently, typhus is prevented by aggressive action against body lice, fleas, mites, and ticks with insecticidal dusts. Once contracted, typhus is treated with tetracyline class antibiotics. In the 1840s and 1850s typhus killed more than five hundred New Yorkers annually.

Typhoid fever is an acute infectious bacterial disease passed by fecal discharges in areas with poor sanitation and sewage disposal. The bacteria congregate in the small intestine and can cause, after initial discomfort marked by high fever, headache, general pain, and coughing spells, the perforation and hemorrhaging of the intestines, a consequence that is often fatal. Prevention depends on good sanitation and avoidance of exposure. Vaccination against typhoid fever has been largely successful. Typhoid became a serious threat between the Civil War period and 1900 when it killed between three hundred and five hundred people each year.

People who do not exhibit symptoms can carry typhoid. The celebrated case of *Typhoid Mary*, a New York immigrant from Ireland, demonstrates the point. In 1906, a sanitary engineer (health inspector) discovered that seven out of the eight families Mary Mallon worked for as a cook had contracted typhoid. She resisted testing and was arrested by five policemen who had to chase her through a series of backyards to take her to a hospital on Roosevelt Island. She was quarantined against her will from 1906 until 1910. Mary was freed on condition she would cease working as a cook. She promptly changed her name to Mary Brown and got a job as a hospital cook. In 1915, she was again incarcerated at Roosevelt Island after twenty-five cases of typhus were discovered at the hospital where she worked. Typhoid Mary died in 1938 after twenty-eight years of enforced quarantine.

Diphtheria is an acute contagious bacterial infection of the upper respiratory system chiefly affecting children. Complications often involve the heart and include serious inflammation and enlargement. Muscle paralysis may also result from diphtheria. The disease can be prevented with immunization with an antitoxin. Between 1870 and 1900 diphtheria killed an average of two thousand people each year, most of them children.

Measles (*rubeola*) is a highly contagious childhood disease infecting the respiratory tract. Symptoms include runny nose, hacking cough, high fever, generalized aching, and a red rash. Complications include cornea infections and possible blindness, middle ear infections, severe diarrhea, and brain damage. Prevention is conferred by a live-virus vaccine, which was introduced in 1967. Presently an MMR (mumps-measles-rubella) vaccine is administered to infants and young children. Mumps is a viral infection of the salivary glands, and rubella (German measles) is a viral infection of the neck glands. Rubella in a pregnant woman can lead to congenital defects in the unborn child. Measles killed from three hundred to one thousand people each year from 1850 until 1930.

Tuberculosis is an ancient disease never completely eradicated. It is also known as TB, and was formerly called *consumption* or the *workers disease*. It is a pulmonary bacterial infection, which still infects one-third of the world's population in the early 21st century. New Yorkers living and working is poorly ventilated, crowded conditions were especially susceptible to tuberculosis, which, between 1840 and 1955 killed from two thousand to nine thousand people each year. In New York City it is still rampant among prisoners, drug users, and the homeless, though the death rate from tuberculosis was down to about two hundred per year in the 1990s.

Influenza is an exceptionally contagious viral infection. All age groups are susceptible though the illness is particularly dangerous to young children and older adults. Though it is an illness frequently recurring in history, *influenza* (Italian for intangible visitation) received its present name during a 1743 epidemic. Previously it was called the *grippe.*

In 1918, the worldwide outbreak of influenza, sometimes called Spanish flu or Swine flu, was referred to as a *pandemic.* Globally, it killed about twenty million people, five hundred thousand in the United States, and ten thousand in New York City. Soldiers returning from the First World War, and trans-Atlantic travelers, were ordered to wear gauze masks by the Health Department. People in houses with cases of influenza were quarantined. Another outbreak in 1957 killed several hundred New Yorkers.

Seasonal inoculations now offer protection from the strains of influenza which each year are estimated by the Centers for Disease Control and Prevention to be the most widespread. Early detection is important because complications from influenza include bronchitis, bacterial pneumonia, and occasionally encephalitis and myocarditis (inflammation of the heart muscle).

Pneumonia is an inflammation of the lungs, which can result from more than thirty causes. Bacteria, viruses, yeast, fungi, chemical agents, and allergic reactions to foreign particles can all cause pneumonia's symptoms: shortness of breath, chest pains, and *pleurisy* (inflammation of the membranes enveloping the lungs). Blood tests and X-rays allow diagnosis, and antibiotics are used to counteract the disease. In the 19th century between two thousand and nine thousand New Yorkers died each year from pneumonia, and in the 20th century the figures ranged from two thousand four hundred to thirteen thousand.

Poliomyelitis, commonly called *polio,* or sometimes *infantile paralysis,* is a viral infection, which usually attacks children. Passed by infected feces, it attacks the central nervous system and can cause permanent paralysis of the arms and legs, or even the lungs. It was one of the most feared communicable diseases. Once contracted, no treatment is effective in restoring use to affected areas of the body. Before vaccines virtually eliminated the poliomyelitis, large full-body mechanical respirators (iron lungs) kept alive those whose lungs were paralyzed, though their quality of life was dismal. For others, wheelchairs and crutches provided some semblance of individual mobility. The Salk and Sabin vaccines were introduced in the early 1950s and school children and adults alike lined up to receive inoculation. Since then, cases of polio have been very rare.

Franklin Delano Roosevelt contracted polio at his summer home on Campobello Island, New Brunswick, Canada, in 1921. Initially paralyzed in all four limbs, he later regained full use of his arms, but needed a wheelchair or crutches to move about. Nonetheless, Roosevelt served as governor of New York State from 1929 to 1933, and president of the United States from 1933 to 1945.

While some of the old scourges are still active, three recent epidemics have also inflicted discomfort, death, and debilitation. Electronic and print media coverage gets the word out quickly to New Yorkers. Modern medicine in the 21st century has answers to many of the contagious diseases, which once terrified city residents. Nonetheless, while the numbers of those succumbing to pestilence is down, and life expectancy up (age 50 for men in 1900, age 74.5 for men in 2000), there are still contagious diseases which assault people in New York City.

AIDS, an acronym for *Acquired Immune Deficiency Syndrome,* was first isolated in 1983 at the Curie Institute in Paris. It is caused by a virus known as HIV-1, which leads to progressive degeneration of several organ systems. Unprotected homosexual and heterosexual sex, shared needles by drug users, and blood transfusions with AIDS-contaminated blood can transmit the virus. Treatment with powerful antiviral drugs can slow, but not cure, the disease. In the 1990s, about five thousand AIDS sufferers died each year.

West Nile Virus, a *flavivirus* from North Africa and the Middle East, was first identified in New York City in 1999. The disease is closely related to St. Louis encephalitis found in the United States. It causes flu-like symptoms, which last a few days and rarely cause long-term health problems. Closely related viruses include West Nile encephalitis and West Nile meningitis, which inflame the membrane around the brain and the spinal chord, often causing death. West Nile Virus can infect humans, birds, mosquitoes, and horses. Mosquitoes are the most common carriers of West Nile

Virus in New York City. There is no vaccine available, but using DEET mosquito repellent in the summer, and spraying areas of the city, which have stagnant water (empty lots, parks, cemeteries) with pesticides can control the disease.

SARS is an acronym for *Severe Acute Respiratory Syndrome*. It first appeared in New York City in 2003 from its point of origin in south China (Guangzhou and Hong Kong). The respiratory disease, a mutant strain of the virus that causes the common cold, is in the *coronavirus* family, and is spread by person-to-person contact. Its worldwide dissemination was sped by air travel.

Asthma, while not a communicable disease, has been an increasingly menacing problem in New York City. The condition causes inflamed airways, coughing, wheezing, throat irritation, and chest tightness that make it difficult to breathe. The causes of asthma are numerous and include genetic predisposition, allergies, and high levels of ozone. According to the Centers for Disease Control and Prevention, the percentage of Americans suffering from asthma has doubled between 1980 and 2000. New York City has the highest rate in the United States and may be as high as twenty percent among children under age 13.

Environmental factors often bring on asthma attacks and may even cause the disease. They include pollen, dust, flaking plaster, cat and dog dander, cockroach feces, dust mites, cigarette smoke, and air pollution from cars, trucks, busses, and factories. In 2003, a survey undertaken jointly by several hospitals and children's advocacy groups, examined all children age 13 and under in a 24-square-block area of central Harlem and found that more than twenty-five percent suffered from asthma.

The notion that infected immigrants disseminated diseases was a traditional suspicion of some New Yorkers. The answer was to give new arrivals medical examinations and refuse entry to the diseased. For immigrants at Castle Clinton or Ellis Island, a finding of a serious communicable disease could mean being sent back to the country of origin. If the examining doctors thought there was a chance of recovery, the individual was kept in isolation at Blackwell's Island, or, after 1892, in a set of special buildings on the south part of Ellis Island.

Another disheartening possibility for immigrants was being

incarcerated on Swinburne or Hoffman Islands, two lonely islets, which were places of quarantine and death. Staten Islanders had objected to quarantine stations placed in their borough at Tompkinsville, Stapleton, and Prince's Bay, for those suffering from typhus, typhoid, yellow fever, and smallpox. Riots ensued in 1857 and residents burned the hospitals. The two islands in the outer bay, just beyond the Verrazzano Narrows, were used as a substitute. Swinburne Island formerly held a small crematorium for those who died. The bodies of the dead were burned to prevent the spread of pestilence.

There is no longer a need for a quarantine station for immigrants. New York City's immigration station is now located at John F. Kennedy International Airport and all immigrants are examined at the United States embassy facility in the capital city of their country of origin before flying to New York.

Historically, finding cures or limiting the impact of contagious epidemics was attempted by instituting street cleaning and public garbage collection, establishing sources of fresh drinking water, founding a Health Department to investigate illnesses, publicizing the need for cleanliness, and treating the poor who could not afford private doctors. Visiting nurse services, school health clinics, and laws prohibiting spitting and public urination helped prevent the spread of disease. Recent preventative and curative methods rely heavily on preventative vaccines, and diagnosing the illness and treating it with powerful drugs.

Notations:

Roosevelt Island

First called *Minnehanonck* by the Lenape Indians and *Varcken* (Hog) Island by the Dutch, it managed to ultimately gain three more names. Ownership passed to the English Crown after the 1664 change in colonial sovereignty. In 1685 Captain John Manning received it as a grant from King Charles II. Manning's son-in-law, Robert Blackwell, inherited the island and farmed it. New York City bought it in 1828 for $32,000 and incrementally established various institutions on it: a prison, almshouse, workhouse, charity hospital, smallpox hospital, and lunatic asylum. In 1921 it was renamed Welfare Island to reflect its melancholy functions. The New York State super-agency known as the Urban Development Corporation, gained control of the island in 1969, and, as the U.D.C. planned on constructing middle income housing on the island, a more uplifting and positive name was sought. In 1973, the name was changed to Roosevelt Island in honor of President Franklin Delano Roosevelt.

There are still two long-care facilities on Roosevelt Island. At the north end is the Bird S. Coler Memorial Hospital, built in 1952, to provide shelter for the seriously ill who are not expected to recover. (Nearby is the Octagon Tower, which resembles the setting for a Gothic novel, now all that remains of the Municipal Lunatic Asylum which was constructed in 1839.) On the south end of Roosevelt Island is the Goldwater Memorial Hospital, which still functions as an institution for the chronically ill. The Goldwater facility was constructed in 1939 in a sprawling manner to provide patients with maximum sunshine.

Hoffman and Swinburne Islands

Hoffman and Swinburne Islands were built on Orchard Shoals in the lower bay, about one mile from South Beach, between 1870 and 1873. Landfill from the leveling of Manhattan was used. Hoffman is ten acres and Swinburne covers just 2.5 acres. Hoffman is named for former mayor and governor John T. Hoffman, and Swinburne for John Swinburne, the medical doctor who supervised the development of both islands. With more than one million immigrants arriving in the United States annually around the turn of the last century, the islands were filled with detainees. In 1901, almost eight thousand people were held on Hoffman Island. During the First World War immigration slowed, and harsh new laws passed by Congress in 1921 formally restricted it to very low levels. Swinburne Island was closed in 1928, and Hoffman ceased holding banished immigrants in 1938. The Coast Guard used it for training until 1947. Plans to use the two islands for city parks were never carried out because of the expense in establishing ferry service from South Beach. The city turned over Hoffman and Swinburne Islands to the federal government in 1972. They are now components of Gateway National Park though they are closed to the public. Thousands of birds, especially egrets and herons, nest on the islands. Fishermen now report seeing harbor seals sunning themselves on the cement and rock retaining walls.

CHAPTER 47
Benjamin H. Day & the Penny Press

New Yorkers have always been avid readers and the news of the day has been a familiar talking point for generations of people interested in current events. In the 17th and 18th centuries, newspapers were expensive, priced comparably to modern glossy magazines. Because of the high price they were often shared among neighbors and friends. In the early decades of the republic there were several *six-cent journals* published in New York City. For the price of a six-cent journal a New Yorker could purchase two or three loaves of bread, or eat an inexpensive lunch at a tavern. Among the six-cent journals were the *New York Journal of Commerce, Mercantile Advertiser and New York Advocate, Morning Courier and New York Enquirer*, and the *Evening Post*.

Benjamin H. Day, a printer at the *Journal of Commerce*, introduced the *New York Sun*, the first successful *penny newspaper*, in 1833. Day had been born in West Springfield, Massachusetts in 1810 and had learned the rudiments of the printing trade from age 14 as a general apprentice at the *Springfield Republican*. At age 20, Day came to New York hoping to start his own business. Three years later he launched a new enterprise in one small room on William Street where, with just one assistant, he served as publisher, editor, reporter, pressman, and distributor.

Day was innovative in three ways. He marketed his paper aggressively by enlisting newsboys to hawk it on the sidewalks. He followed the principle that he could make a good profit by selling large quantities of papers at an inexpensive price. And he covered human-interest narratives, local political news, and sensational police stories of crime, domestic violence, scandal, and sex. It worked. By 1836 the *Sun* had a daily circulation of thirty thousand copies at a time when the city's population had reached about a quarter of a million. *The Sun* had become the largest selling newspaper in the United States. In 1835 the seven morning and four evening six-cent journals ranged in circulation from twelve hundred to forty-five hundred. Three years later Benjamin H. Day sold *The Sun* to his brother-in-law, Moses Yale Beach, for $40,000.

In the first issue of the *New York Sun*, Day placed a classified ad calling for newsboys, though the precise term was coined sometime later. *To the Unemployed --- a number of steady men can find employment by vending this paper. A liberal discount is allowed to those who buy to sell again.* Ten-year-old Barney Flaherty was the first to answer the advertisement and became the city's first newsboy. (It was not unusual for children to be on the street at that age instead of in school.) Newsboys called attention to their wares, particularly special editions, by shouting, *Extra! Extra! Read All About It!* Far from being romantic, a newsboy's life was usually the result of severe poverty or an abusive home life.

The Sun began as a modest experiment. Day's statement of purpose was published the first day on the front page. *This object of this paper is to lay before the public, at a price within the means of every one, all the news of the day, and at the same time afford an advantageous medium for advertising.* Each issue was only four pages and the size, 11 1/4 x 8 inches, had about the dimensions of a sheet of computer paper today. But Day's stories were lively and it was accessible since newsboys sold it in the streets.

Some of the early stories that *The Sun* covered with great intensity and depth were the Fire of 1835, the fall of the Alamo in 1836, and the publication of Maria Monk's *Awful Disclosures* in 1836. Monk had claimed all manner of salacious activities took place in the Hôtel Dieu Convent in Montreal. Anti Catholic stories appealed to many readers at a time when some Americans felt the country was being inundated by Roman Catholic immigrants from southern Germany and Ireland. Later, Maria Monk's story was unmasked as pure fiction.

The most famous editorial in American journalism was published by the *Sun* in 1897 in response to a doubting letter from an eight-year-old girl. *Yes, Virginia, there is a Santa Claus...* began editor Francis P. Church. In 1950 the *Sun* was absorbed into the *New York World-Telegram.*

The Sun Building, formerly A.T. Stewart's Department Store, at 280 Broadway, between Chambers Street and Reade Street, became home to the newspaper in 1911. A.T. Stewart's Department

Store opened in the opulent seven-story *marble palace* in 1846. It was New York City's first marble-faced commercial building. Lavish and elegant on the inside it offered reasonable prices and encouraged browsing, the prototype of future department stores. Two large, four-sided, Roman numeral clocks were added by the newspaper and adorn the building's corners. They are engraved in Old English lettering: *the Sun, it shines for all.* In 2002 a neo-conservative newspaper took the name of *The New York Sun* and began publishing a few blocks away from the site of the historic *Sun* headquarters. The *Sun* closed in 2008.

Until the first decades of the 20th century, the area southeast of City Hall, especially the southern three blocks of the Bowery, now called Park Row, was the center of New York's newspaper and printing business. The statue of Benjamin Franklin, printer and publisher, stands in testament to his trade at Park Row and Nassau Street.

Most of New York City's newspapers are gone, victims of intense competition with each other and with the electric media: radio, television, and Internet. United States newspaper circulation was approximately the same in 2005 as it was in 1945, though the population has doubled. At the beginning and end of the same sixty-year period, New York City's population stood at eight million, but daily newspaper readership diminished a little less than fifty percent. A dwindling number of people still prefer the tactile touch of a newspaper while relaxing in an easy chair, sitting at the breakfast table, or riding the subway.

Up until the Age of Television there was a superabundance of daily newspapers in the city. At the end of the Second World War the following daily English language papers were available: *New York (Evening) Post* (since 1801), *Brooklyn Daily News* (1886-1947), *Brooklyn Citizen* (1886-1947), *Brooklyn (Daily) Eagle* (1841-1955), *Daily Mirror* (1924-1957), *Daily News* (since 1919), *Daily North Side* [Bronx} *News* (1901-1958), *Daily Worker* (1927-1958), [Bronx} *Home News* (1906-1948), *Long Island (Daily)* [Jamaica] *Press* (1926-1977), *Long Island* [Flushing] *Star-Journal* (1938-1948), *Morning Telegraph* (1897-1972), *New York Herald Tribune* (1924-1966), *New York Journal-American* (1937-1966), *New York World-Telegram* (1931-1950), *Staten Island Advance* (since 1886), and the *Wall Street Journal* (since 1889).

Of this large selection, plus two new entries, *New York Newsday* (since 1985) and *The New York Sun* (since 2002), only the *Daily News, New York Post, Staten Island Advance, Wall Street Journal,* and *The New York Times* exist.

One of the city's prominent and progressive early newspapers was *The New York Daily Tribune,* founded in 1841 as a penny newspaper by Horace Greeley who endorsed collective bargaining by labor unions, the cooperative movement, and the ten-hour workday. He supported the Homestead Act that gave land to settlers and issued his famous appeal to young males: ***Go west, young man***. During the American Civil War, Greeley hired Karl Marx, then living in London, to write several articles for *The New York Daily Tribune*. Marx wrote about English public opinion toward the two sides, the effect of the cotton trade on English textile mills, and the French intervention in Mexico. Greeley distanced himself from the Radical Republicans during the Reconstruction of the South, and ran against Ulysses S. Grant in the 1872 presidential election on a Democratic-Liberal Republican fusion ticket. He lost the popular vote 3,597,132 to 2,834,125 and the electoral vote 286 to 66. Controversial, though popular among many New Yorkers, he has two statues in the city: one just east of City Hall near the old Park Row headquarters of his abolitionist Whig, and later Republican, newspaper, and the other at Greeley Square, the intersection of 6th Avenue and Broadway between West 32nd and 33rd Streets.

Trolley, bus, and subway travel fostered reading during long commutes and newstands were everywhere. *The Cricket in Times Square,* George Selden's popular children's book published in 1960, tells the story of Chester, a cricket, Harry, a cat, and Tucker, a mouse, who all live near the Times Square newstand operated on the station's shuttle level by the family of young Mario Bellini. The setting is the chaos of a busy subway station and many of the references are to a rich variety of newspapers no longer in existence.

The *Evening Post,* now the *New York Post,* released just six hundred copies of its first issue in 1801. One of the *Post's* founders was Alexander Hamilton, and the paper reflected a federalist perspective. Most newspapers, regardless of whether they admit it, reflect a political point of view in their editorials and catchy headlines, and to a lesser extent in their news columns. Time can change politics, none more than the *New York Post* which has gone though several alignments, from Federalist to Whig to Republican to Democratic to Republican.

There were several newspapers that called themselves *The New York Times.* The first came out in 1813, and others in 1822, 1826, 1834, 1838, and 1846. *The New York Times* of today began in 1851. Henry J. Raymond, who had been Horace Greeley's associate editor at *The New York Daily Tribune,* founded *The New York Times.* While *The New York Times* was part of the penny press movement and became loosely aligned with Republican Party principles, Raymond opposed Greeley's interest in radical social reform and strident abolitionism, and gave *The New York Times* a very moderate voice. An early example was how the two newspapers viewed the Fugitive Slave Act of 1850. The *Tribune* called for its repeal while the *Times* urged caution since it was the law of the land.

The Gray Lady, as the *Times* is sometimes called for its formal appearance and writing style, had a way of equivocating on important issues. Raymond had explained that policy in his first editorial. *We shall be conservative in all cases where we think conservatism essential to the public good; -- and we shall be radical in everything which may seem to us to require radical treatment and radical reform. We do not believe that everything in society is either exactly right or exactly wrong; -- what is good we desire to preserve and improve; -- what is evil, to exterminate, or reform.* It was a policy followed by most editors over the years until the last quarter of the 20th century when *The New York Times* moved in its glacial way from a centrist Republican to a liberal Democratic newspaper. (Times Square, second home of the *The New York Times,* was known until 1904 as Longacre Square.)

In terms of readership, *The New York Daily News,* a popular tabloid that calls itself *New York's First Picture Newspaper,* is the city's paramount paper. *The Wall Street Journal,* established in 1889 by Charles H. Dow and Edward D. Jones, founders of the Dow Jones Company, focuses on business news. *Metro New York* and *AM New York,* two super-tabloids, are distributed free at subway stations and on street corners. Their news coverage is minimal; they make money by carrying advertisements.

More than two hundred local tabloids are found in the city's neighborhoods. They cover local items of interest, announce shop and restaurant openings, give gushingly favorable restaurant reviews, and provide classified sections. Some, like *The Village Voice,* serve Greenwich Village though the readership of *The Village Voice* is wide since it covers many cultural and political issues that go well beyond the neighborhood. *The Amsterdam News* in Harlem also has a large readership outside its neighborhood. The *Staten Island Advance* exists for the entire borough.

Religious newspapers reflect each major religious group in the city. *The Tablet,* the official voice of the Roman Catholic Diocese of Brooklyn and Queens, and *Catholic New York,* official paper of the Archdiocese of New York (Manhattan, Staten Island, the Bronx, and several upstate counties) provide worldwide, diocesan, and parish news. They are distributed in Catholic churches each Sunday.

The Jewish newspaper with the largest circulation in the city is the English language *Jewish Press.* It covers mostly Orthodox and Hasidic news and its editorials and columns reflect the very observant point of view. At the turn of the last century there were several Jewish newspapers written in Yiddish, but most were secular. Chief among them was the *Jewish Daily Forward,* published in the Lower East Side at Straus Square on East Broadway. The last Yiddish language newspaper, *Algemeiner Journal,* serves an Orthodox and Hasidic readership.

There are a plethora of ethnic newspapers in New York City. *The Irish Weekly,* founded in 1871, is the oldest. Other newspapers that serve the Irish diaspora include the *Irish Echo,* and the *Irish Voice,* weekly papers that are available at newsstands and shops and give a sense of the neighborhood and other places of Irish concentration: Bainbridge, Woodside, Bay Ridge, Yonkers. The pages are filled with articles and advertisement of special interest to Irish immigrants and expatriates. The same is true with Hispanic, Chinese, Jamaican, Haitian, Indian, and other ethnic newspapers. Some of the ethnic newspapers are published daily such as the Spanish language *El Diario La Prensa.*

Labor unions, led by the Newspaper Guild, the Communications Workers of America, and the International Typographical

Union organized newspaper employees early in New York City. The unions represented reporters, pressmen, typesetters, clerical workers, and delivery drivers. In the last quarter of the 20th century computerization of the printing process and competition from television and the Internet reduced the significance of newspapers for reporting the news and their capacity to raise money through advertising. Employment in the industry dropped and unions felt they had less clout with newspapers that were on the ropes.

Several recurrent political issues have divided public opinion about the press. The First Amendment to the United States Constitution is brief yet far-reaching. *Congress shall make no law respecting an establishment of religion, or prohibiting the free exercise thereof; or abridging the freedom of speech, or of the press; or the right of the people peaceably to assemble, and to petition the Government for a redress of grievances.* The free speech and free press clause in the First Amendment, forbids the government from *abridging the freedom of speech, or of the press.* Yet there are times when the governments objects to full reporting in the press.

Confidentiality of sources is another contentious issue. The right to keep sources and notes secret is claimed by reporters. They assert a protected confidential relationship similar to what is generally held to be the case between priests and confessants or psychiatrists and patients. Government prosecutors sometimes subpoena a journalist's notes from an interview with a suspect or a *person of interest* to the prosecutor. Reporters have been jailed over the issue of confidentiality of sources.

Sometimes newspapers do the government's work for them. All of the city's newspapers have shown the propensity for self-censorship and jingoism during the first phase of wars. This was especially true with the Gulf of Tonkin Incident in 1964, which was the precipitant for the escalation of the Vietnam War, and the Weapons of Mass Destruction charge beginning in 2001 that was the pretense for the invasion of Iraq in 2003. The Gulf of Tonkin Incident never occurred, and there were no WMDs, yet the newspapers ran scores of front-page stories fed to them by the government, accepting the erroneous charges by Lyndon B. Johnson and George W. Bush, respectively, and providing those leaders with political cover. Uncritical parroting of government pronouncements is sometimes later regretted though the pattern seems never to end.

Notations:

The Plight of Newsboys

The plight of newsboys and other street children became a *cause célebrè* by the end of the 19th century. The former Newsboys' and Bootblacks' Lodging House, now an apartment building at 127 Avenue B at East 8th Street, was an attempt to provide them with housing. It was one of many private charity-operated shelters for children. The Newsboys' and Bootblacks' Lodging House was operated by the Protestant-dominated Children's Aid Society founded in 1887 by Charles Loring Brace. He eventually determined that an *Emigration Plan* would be a better way of handling the surfeit of orphans or runaways in New York City and other large metropolitan areas. *Orphan Trains* sponsored by Brace and other groups such as the Catholic-run Foundling Hospital sent a quarter million children to upstate New York and points far to the west to be taken-in and sometimes adopted.

Jewish Daily Forward and the Forward Building

Under the large electric Yiddish sign, journalists throughout the eleven-floor structure at 175 East Broadway produced a daily paper that was the heartbeat of the Jewish settlement. It began publication in 1897, and under the editorship of the legendary Abraham Cahan from 1901 to 1951, the *Forvertz* (*Forward*) was a democratic socialist newspaper with many non-political features, such as book and theater reviews, serializations of new writers, and the popular column, *A Bintel Brief* (*A Bundle of Letters*), where Cahan exhorted Jews with reason and humor to Americanize and leave behind many Eastern European customs, prejudices, and superstitions. Readership peaked in the 1920s when two hundred fifty thousand copies of the paper were sold daily. The Americanization of Jewish immigrants succeeded too well for the newspaper. In 1974 the building was sold and the Yiddish paper was edited and printed in a string of other locations. By 1990 the *Forward* was being printed in English as a weekly from offices in New Jersey. A small Yiddish edition is also published. After a few years housing garment factories, the *Forward* Building was converted into a Chinese-sponsored luxury condominium, though the Yiddish sign will stay because it is landmarked.

Yes, Virginia, there is a Santa Claus... Editorial in The Sun by Francis P. Church, 1897

On September 21, 1897, three months before Christmas, *Sun* editor Francis P. Church answered a letter from a young lady on the Upper West Side in an editorial. The inquiry and response appeared together.

DEAR EDITOR:

I am eight years old.
Some of my little friends say there is no Santa Claus.
Papa says "If you see it in the Sun it's so."
Please tell me the truth, is there a Santa Claus?

VIRGINIA O'HANLON
115 West Ninety-fifth Street

Virginia, your little friends are wrong. They have been affected by the skepticism of a skeptical age. They do not believe except they see. They think that nothing can be which is not comprehensible by their little minds. All minds, Virginia, whether they be men's or children's, are little. In this great universe of ours man is a mere insect, an ant, in his intellect, as compared with the boundless world about him, as measured by the intelligence capable of grasping the whole of truth and knowledge.

Yes, Virginia, there is a Santa Claus. He exists as certainly as love and generosity and devotion exist, and you know that they abound and give to our life its highest beauty and joy. Alas! How dreary the world would be if there were no Santa Claus! It would be as dreary as if there were no Virginias. There would be no childlike faith then, no poetry, no romance, to make tolerable this existence. We should have no enjoyment, except in sense and sight. The eternal light with which childhood fills the world would be extinguished.

Not believe in Santa Claus! You might as well not believe in fair-

ies! You might get your papa to hire men to watch all the chimneys on Christmas eve to catch Santa Claus, but even if they did not see Santa Claus coming down, what would that prove? Nobody sees Santa Claus, but that is no sign that there is no Santa Claus. The most real things in the world are those that neither children nor men can see. Did you ever see fairies dancing on the lawn? Of course not, but that's no proof that they are not there. Nobody can conceive or imagine all the wonders there are unseen and unseeable in the world.

You tear apart the baby's rattle and see what makes the noise inside, but there is a veil covering the unseen world, which not the strongest man, nor even the united strength of all the strongest men that ever lived could tear apart. Only faith, fancy, poetry, love, romance, can push aside that curtain and view and picture the superal beauty and glory beyond. Is it all real? Ah, Virginia, in all this world there is nothing else real and abiding.

No Santa Claus! Thank God! he lives, and he lives forever. A thousand years from now, Virginia, nay, ten times ten thousand years from now, he will continue to make glad the heart of childhood.

CHAPTER 48
Department Stores & Shopping

New York City is a shopping paradise. Over the last three centuries it has had all the important ingredients for commercial success: a vibrant apparel manufacturing sector, an active harbor for importing foreign goods, numerous financial institutions and private investors, a strong entrepreneurial tradition, an appreciation for style, and many people with money. Since the 1920s New York has had advertising companies and modeling agencies, and since the 1970s millions of people with credit cards. One of the leading reasons New York City attracts tourists is its stores.

Both wholesale and retail commerce loom large in the city's economy. Real wholesale shopping is behind the scenes and generally restricted to shopkeepers and large companies that buy in bulk at discounted rates. What most people see and participate in is retail activity. Shopping can be high-end or bargain basement, a reality unchanged over the centuries. In the 19th century retail contrast was between gleaming department stores on one hand, and pushcart vendors and itinerant peddlers on the other. (Pushcart vendors who *made it* were able to rent storefronts and expand their inventories and profit.) Today's chic boutiques can be contrasted with contemporary outdoor vendors who sell from card tables or spread their goods below them on the sidewalk.

Until after the American Civil War the price of ready-to-wear clothing was very high and few people showed interest. The women of the house sewed each family's clothes. Prices for ready-to-wear garments came down with mass production methods introduced in the early 19th century as part of the Industrial Revolution. The introduction of uniform sizes also helped. *Sizing* was first used by companies, which had contracts with the Union Army for shirts, trousers, coats, and boots. Brooks Brothers may have initiated the new procedure that took into account different body shapes. Sizing made buying clothing much more convenient for customers.

A.T. Stewart (1803-1876), an immigrant from Ulster (Northern Ireland), came up with the idea for a *department store*. His plan was to sell clothing and accessories for men, women, and children under one roof. He founded A.T. Stewart's Department Store on lower Broadway in 1823. Twenty-three years later he opened a seven-story *Marble Palace* at 280 Broadway, between Chambers and Reade Streets. It was New York City's first marble-faced commercial building. Stewart's concept was to make shoppers feel welcomed and pampered. Lavish and elegant on the inside, the store had doormen, greeters, restaurants, live music, potted plants, and public rest rooms. It offered reasonable prices and encouraged browsing, the prototype of a century of department stores. John Wanamaker, owner of a Philadelphia-based department store empire, bought A.T. Stewart's Department Store in 1896.

The Wanamaker Department Store was once the largest department store chain in the United States. The six-story *Cast Iron Palace* was on Broadway between 9th and 10th Streets. In 1907, Wanamaker opened a 15-story annex across 9th Street connected to the original building by a remarkable three-tiered bridge. The annex also had an entrance in the Astor Place IRT subway station. Wanamaker's New York store was initially profitable but finally closed its doors in 1955 long after the department store district had gravitated uptown to 5th Avenue north of 34th Street. The *Cast Iron Palace* burned in 1956. Various offices now occupy the upper floors of the annex. Its ground floor commercial space houses K Mart, Ann Taylor, and Chase Bank.

R.H. Macy's, began doing business in 1858 on 14th Street and 6th Avenue and was the first department store to move uptown to chase after the business of wealthier New Yorkers. It opened the *world's largest department store* on 34th Street ultimately filling the entire square block between 6th and 7th Avenues.

The rich kept moving uptown and the stores followed them. *Ladies Mile* is the name historians now give to the area of lower midtown between 14th and 23rd Streets where many department stores selling ready-to-wear clothing clustered in the last half of the 19th century. Strikingly majestic cast-iron and Neo-Classical buildings and large illuminated display windows publicized the stores that opened along 6th Avenue and Broadway. Elevated railroad tracks brought in more customers but destroyed the architectural beauty of the shopping esplanade, and at night the area attracted prostitutes and men who sought them.

The original stores all moved from *Ladies Mile* but many of the buildings are still there, and after a stint as warehouses and offices they have been renovated and once again contain stores. The buildings that housed elite department stores on 6th Avenue are now occupied by large chain stores, including Dave's New York, Old Navy, Barnes & Noble, Men's Warehouse, Burlington Coat Factory, and Staples. The two most imposing face each other between 18th and 19th Streets. Number 625 is now home to Today's Man and Number 620 holds Bed, Bath, & Beyond, Filene's Basement, and T.J. Maxx. Along Broadway the buildings now holding ABC Carpet, Villeroy & Boch, Restoration Hardware, and The Bombay Company were once *Ladies Mile* establishments.

Late in the 19th century the most refined (and expensive) department stores drifted further uptown along 5th Avenue. Benjamin Altman opened his new B. Altman's department store in a particularly ornate building on 34th Street and 5th Avenue in 1914 where it remained until it ceased operations in 1989. (The building now houses the City University of New York Graduate School.) In 1826 by Samuel Lord and George Washington Taylor founded Lord & Taylor as a small dry goods shop on Catherine Street in the Five Points district. Their fourth location was opened in 1914 on 5th Avenue at 38th Street. Andrew Saks founded Saks in 1902 at Herald Square. His son Horace sold out to Bernard Gimbel in 1923, and the next year Saks opened a lavish store on 5th Avenue at 50th Street across from St. Patrick's Cathedral. The new store was called Saks's Fifth Avenue. Bloomingdale's, which had two earlier locations, opened on Lexington Avenue at 59th Street in 1931. Gimbel's stayed near Macy's at Herald Square. Bonwit Teller, owned by Paul J. Bonwit and Edmund D. Teller, opened on 5th Avenue and 56th Street in 1930, and closed in 1990. Bergdorf Goodman, formed as a small tailoring and furrier for women in 1894, moved to 5th Avenue and 57th Street in 1928 and now occupies the entire block between 57th and 58th with a men's annex across the street.

Later, after Union Square lost its *panache*, low-end department stores, S. Klein, Hearn's, Ohrbach's, and Mays, grouped around it. Elsewhere, especially in the outer boroughs, other cut-rate department stores, such as E.J. Korvette and Century 21, opened. Eventually, working-class department store chains from other cities moved into New York: Sears, J.C. Penney, Target, Home Depot, K-Mart, and Wal-Mart.

For customers, shopping at either high-end or low-end stores can bestow status. Bargain hunters and people who parrot phrases like *I never pay retail prices*, achieve status through real or perceived bargains. Another kind of status is achieved by expensive purchases in luxury stores, especially when inconspicuous labels are manipulated so they are noticed.

Unlike most American cities, New York has very few malls though the borough of Manhattan is filled with large and small retail stores located in hundreds of clusters in crowded areas. Exceptions exist and some of the best known are Kings Plaza Shopping Center in Brooklyn, the Staten Island Mall on Richmond Avenue, Queens Center in Elmhurst, and Coliseum Mall in Jamaica, Queens. The only places in Manhattan that might be considered malls are the South Street Seaport, Chelsea Market, and the Chelsea Piers Sports and Entertainment Complex. Since most art galleries left SoHo for Chelsea in the 1980s their commercial spaces have been occupied by retail shops, many of them part of large national and international chains. SoHo also resembles a mall.

The wholesale and retail trade employs large numbers of New Yorkers. In 1950, New York City had 35,000 wholesale companies employing 318,000 workers, and 105,000 stores with 438,000 employees. Many of the department stores employed more than five hundred clerks and warehouseman though small-scale stores made up the bulk of employees.

Labor activities centered around the Retail, Wholesale and Department Store Union (RWDSU) that formed in 1935. It had great success in the 1930s and 40s and won such benefits as the 40-hour week, overtime pay, sick days, and paid vacations. The union created a subculture by sponsoring sports teams, book discussion clubs, theater groups, educational classes, dances, picnics, and parties. The union refused to cooperate with a Cold War demand by the federal government to extract pledges from the union's leadership that they were not communists. As a result the Congress of Industrial Organizations (CIO) placed the RWSDU under receivership between 1948 and 1954. The RWSDU regained its independence and was a pioneer in the supporting the Civil Rights Movement's drive to integrate the retail workplace.

On one level it was relatively easy to organize retail clerks into unions for collective bargaining because they had many grievances in common and worked in close proximity. But the wholesale and retail workforce reflected more or less white-collar occupations, and some employees felt they did not need union protection as much as factory workers.

The threat of a strike or an informational picket line was particularly intimidating to owners and management. They were especially adverse to union activity in front of their stores because they feared negative publicity. Sometimes the far of bad publicity caused them to make concessions and settle quickly. On the other hand, clerks are much easier to replace than skilled machine operators and other technical workers.

The decline of manufacturing, the rise of the service economy, and the tremendous decrease in services offered to customers by stores have led to an erosion in the number of wholesale and retail workers and a lowering of their ability to win concessions from employers. In 1990, wholesale jobs dipped to 132,000 from its all-time high in 1950. Retail positions declined less dramatically from a high of 457,000 in 1970 to 429,000 in 1990. Much of the service economy since the 1990s has been in retail stores, as well as restaurants and other places of entertainment. A large percentage of the retail segment of the service economy has been in low-paying positions, producing what critics deride as McJobs.

Notation:

E. J. Korvette's Name

From 1948 until 1981 E.J. Korvette's was a noted discount department store with two outlets in Manhattan, Herald Square and 5th Avenue, and the remainder in the other boroughs. The widespread rumor was that the name stood for *Eight Jewish Korean Veterans*. The facts turn out differently, starting with chronology.

E.J. Korvette's opened its doors for business two years before the Korean War began. The name was taken from the first names of its owner, Eugene Ferkauf and his colleague Joseph Zwillenberg, and from a Canadian anti-submarine ship, the Corvette, in the Second World War.

CHAPTER 49
Street Grids in Manhattan & Queens

What we now call neighborhoods in New York City were once small villages or housing developments. In each case they had their own street systems. As the developed areas grew together the street systems came together at odd angles. In Brooklyn, Queens, Staten Island, and the Bronx, a close look at a map will show the different systems, which have fused together.

New York City, at the southern tip of Manhattan, acted in 1811 to prevent eventual street chaos on the entire island by creating a uniform grid plan, also known as the Commissioners' Plan or the Randel Plan. The purpose was to make straight streets and avenues, which would help vehicular traffic flow smoothly. The commission was appointed in 1807 and given the responsibility to devise a plan that would be approved by the state legislature. The streets and avenues were to be wide enough to foster a healthy circulation of air and to lessen the possibility of fires leaping across streets to engulf an entire section of the city.

The grid plan was to begin all across the east-west width of Manhattan starting at Houston Street and continue north to 193rd Street in Washington Heights. Twelve numbered avenues would run north and south. That created a grid of more than 2,100 rectangular blocks. Much of the northern part of the Lower East Side (1st Street to 14th Street) was still farmland and would also be mapped out. Greenwich Village and Inwood were already partially developed so they were not included.

The plan aimed at being rigidly rational and avoided embel lishments like parks, circles, ovals, squares, and alleys. The commissioners felt anything except streets and avenues was a waste of space. The original plan was altered over the years and Madison Square, Union Square, Tompkins Square, Stuyvesant Square, and Gramercy Park were added. Broadway was allowed to run diagonally all the way to Inwood. Fourth Avenue shed its number and received a name: Park Avenue. Two new avenues were squeezed into the scheme. Lexington Avenue was placed between 3rd Avenue and Park Avenue, and Madison Avenue was placed between Park Avenue and 5th Avenue.

Lots for potential buildings received house numbers. The systematic numbering of houses and the posting of street signs was initiated in 1793 in the developed sections of the city. House numbers in the new plan ran from south to north for the avenues. House numbers for streets began in the center, 5th Avenue. On the east side of 5th Avenue the numbers went progressively higher until they stopped at the East River. On the west side of 5th Avenue they went progressively higher until they reached the Hudson River.

A weakness in the commission's house numbering system is apparent in the avenues. The street house numbers are predictable starting from the center (5th Avenue) with east and west numbers getting progressively higher as streets approach the rivers on either side of the island.

But the house numbers of the avenues begin wherever the avenue starts. So, 1st and 2nd Avenues are numbered similarly since both avenues begin at Houston Street. But 3rd Avenue begins at 4th Street, Park Avenue begins at 14th Street, 5th Avenue at Washington Square, 6th Avenue at Canal Street, etc. Broadway, of course, begins at Bowling Green at the southern end of Manhattan. The result is that the house numbers on avenues differ greatly. At 59th Street, for example, a 1st Avenue building is 1065, a Park Avenue building is 476, 7th Avenue is 922, and Broadway is 1792. The solutions are either a good memory or a complicated formula, which is different for each avenue. To find 240 1st Avenue, drop the last digit, divide what's left --- 24 --- in half and *add* three. Presto! You get 15th Street. To find 2241 Broadway, drop the last number, divide 224 in half and *subtract* 31. Easy! You get 81st Street. The problem is to remember the formulas.

The grid plan was made irrespective of the natural topography of Manhattan, which included rocky outcrops, hills, ridges, valleys, streams, and ponds. The hills were shaved off and the low areas were filled in. Manhattan now appears flat, but a look in

Central Park, Morningside Park, and Mount Morris-Marcus Garvey Park will show a glimpse of Manhattan's original geography. It was covered with rock outcroppings. Some prominent New Yorkers including Clement Clark Moore roundly criticized the severity of the new street plan.

New Yorkers often have trouble with the grid system in Queens. It was set up to bring some unity to a system, which, like all the outer boroughs, reflected their origins as small villages, which eventually grew together.

In Queens the avenues start at 2nd Avenue in Whitestone, the northernmost part of the borough and run to 155th Avenue in Howard Beach just before crossing Jamaica Bay and Broad Channel into Rockaway, a peninsula that has its own grid system, i.e. Beach 2nd Street at the eastern edge of Far Rockaway west to Beach 222nd Street in Breezy Point. (There is no 1st Avenue in Whitestone or Beach 1st Street in Rockaway.) In the main part of Queens, the streets start at 1st Street along the East River near the Triborough Bridge and work their way up to 271st Street in Glen Oaks at the Nassau County border.

Then there are Roads, Drives, Places, Terraces, Lanes, and even a Court or two. Drive, Road, Terrace, and Court go with Avenues. Place and Lane go with Streets. Be careful! If someone says, "I'll meet you at 60th and 60th," chances are that person doesn't want to see you. In Middle Village, there are the following corners: 60th Avenue and 60th Street, 60th Avenue and 60th Place, 60th Avenue and 60th Lane, 60th Road and 60th Street, 60th Road and 60th Lane, 60th Drive and 60th Street, 60th Drive and 60th Place, 60th Drive and 60th Lane, 60th Court and 60th Street, and finally 60th Court and 60th Place. That can drive people crazy.

A newcomer to Queens driving along Queens Boulevard in Rego Park and Forest Hills must concentrate on the traffic and not get too distracted about seeing street signs on consecutive blocks reading: 102nd Street, 67th Drive, 67th Road, 67th Avenue, 66th Road, 99th Street, 66th Avenue, 98th Street, and so on. This is very confusing until you realize Queens Boulevard in that area is heading toward Manhattan in a northwest direction, so it makes sense that it crosses both north-south streets and east-west avenues.

Another surprise occurs when driving along Ditmars Boulevard in Astoria. Heading east into Steinway you pass 41st, 42nd, 43rd, 44th, 45th, 46th, 47th, 48th, 49th --- all streets. Perfect, just as it should be. Next is Hazen Street. Okay, not every street in Queens is numbered. But after Hazen Street, two short blocks beyond 49th Street, you cross 70th Street, then 71st Street and so on. What happened to 50th through 69th? If you check a map, you'll figure it out when you see how neighborhood street grids collide.

Before Queens adopted this theoretically rational system using numbers, the streets and avenues had non-numerical names. The Metropolitan Transit Authority still uses the original names for some of the subway stops. The #7 train has stops at 33rd Street - Rawson, 40th Street - Lowery, 46th Street - Bliss, 52nd Street - Lincoln, and 69th Street - Fisk. The N train has stops at 39th Avenue - Beebe, 36th Avenue - Washington, 30th Avenue - Grand. There are no longer streets named Rawson, Lowery, Bliss, etc.

An interesting non-numbered ordering of avenues occurs in Flushing, Queens, which also has its share of numbered avenues. Driving south on Kissena Boulevard, you pass many named avenues: Ash, Beech, Cherry, Elder, Geranium, Holly, Juniper, Kalmia, Laburnum, Mulberry, Negundo, Oak, Poplar, Quince, and Rose. This is a real alphabetic tribute to nature.

CHAPTER 50
John Jacob Astor

John Jacob Astor was the wealthiest New Yorker in the first half of the 19th century. He possessed a fortune based on North American furs, the China trade, and real estate. The story is sometimes presented as a rags-to-riches tale, though the facts indicate otherwise. Astor, like many immigrants was not among the poorest of the poor, for the truly impoverished were seldom able to afford the trans-Atlantic voyage or start-up money in the United States. Astor was from an artisan family, what we now would call the lower middle class. His father was a butcher, who probably owned farmland, and possessed enough money to educate his four sons.

John Jacob Astor was born in 1763 in the German village of Waldorf, located in the Duchy of Baden, eight miles from the Rhine River city of Heidelberg near the edge of the Black Forest. Three of the four Astor brothers left Waldorf at an early age. His older brother, George, joined an uncle in London and became a manufacturer of musical instruments. His brother, Henry, had fought for the English with a Hessian contingent at the Battle of Brooklyn. After the Revolution he stayed in New York City and opened a butcher shop. In 1779, at age 16, John Jacob left home to join his older brother in London. Of the four brothers, only John Melchior, remained in the Waldorf area as a farmer.

In London, John Jacob Astor learned much about the production and sale of flutes, violins, and pianofortes. Shortly after the Treaty of Paris ended the American Revolution in 1783, he immigrated to the United States. He landed in Baltimore in 1784 and stayed with a local shopkeeper. Tradition holds that he arrived with seven flutes. While perhaps true, he also had connections in the music business and became an agent for his brother, George, in London. After three weeks he traveled to New York City and stayed with his brother Henry.

Soon after arriving, he began buying furs in New York, traveled to London to sell them, and buy more instruments to sell in

New York. His merchandising pattern was set by the time he was age 23. Upon his return in 1786 he married Sarah Todd, shared her $300 dowry, and opened a musical instrument store in a building owned by his mother-in-law. He also opened a small fur shop in Lower Manhattan where he arranged to buy furs from white and Indian trappers and sell the pelts. Within two years he also had fur business centers in Albany and Montreal, places closer to the Great Lakes region, at the time the main source of furs for New York City. Somewhere along the way he discarded the musical instrument business.

John Jacob Astor took a gamble on settling in New York City. At the time of his arrival in 1784, Philadelphia, Boston, Baltimore, and Charleston were larger cities. The population of New York City ranged wildly during the years surrounding the Revolutionary War. In 1776 there were twenty-two thousand people living in the city. After the Battle of Brooklyn and the Revolutionary War Fire, which followed, both in 1776, the population fell to five thousand, but swelled again to thirty-one thousand between 1777 and 1783, when the English used New York City as their command headquarters and many Loyalists fled there for protection. When the English troops evacuated in 1783, thousands of civilian Loyalists also left and the population plummeted to eleven thousand. By 1790 the city had grown to thirty-three thousand residents.

During Astor's first six years in New York, the population tripled, which gave many new opportunities for an eager and dynamic entrepreneur. By the time Astor died in 1848, the population reached a half million and New York had become the largest city in the country and an unsurpassed engine of economic growth.

By 1793, Astor had made a fortune from furs and soon became the city's first millionaire. But the fur pelts were no longer from upstate New York; they came from the Great Lakes region, Rocky Mountains, Pacific Northwest, and Canada. The eastern sources of furs were being depleted. Nonetheless, the Erie Canal, which opened in 1825, made it easier for New York City fur dealers to obtain furs from western sources and stay in business.

Astor set up offices and trading posts in many locations in the northern part of the United States, the Northwest Territory, and the Louisiana Territory to buy, process, and trade furs. Mackinac

Island, in the Straits of Mackinac between Lakes Michigan and Huron, was an example of a profitable outpost. It was a complex of several one, two, and three-story buildings from which the American Fur Company engaged in the procurement of furs, mostly from the Indians. United States military officials sometimes protested that Astor was trading alcohol for furs. The commander of the U.S. Army outpost in Detroit, Colonel Snelling, complained in a report to the Secretary of War James Barbour, that in 1825 Astor's American Fur Company had brought thirty-three hundred gallons of whiskey and twenty-five hundred gallons of wine to Mackinac Island to trade with the Indians. The military concern was that drunkenness created disorder. *I will venture to add,* wrote Snelling, *that an inquiry into the manner in which the Indian trade is conducted, especially by the American Fur Company, is a matter of no small importance to the tranquillity of the border.*

The China trade soon captured Astor's imagination. His usual plan was to fill a ship with American products, sail it to China, reap a profit from the sale of American goods, and spend part of the profit buying items to bring back to the United States to sell. Beginning in 1796, Astor exported furs and hides (beaver, mink, fox, rabbit, raccoon, muskrat, buffalo, deer, otter, sea otter, seal) and *ginseng*. The gnarled roots of the ginseng plant were used in China as medicine and tea. (Ginseng grows well in the cool, damp climate of Tennessee and Kentucky.)

To his discredit, he also regularly bought opium off the coast of China, probably from English privateers or Chinese pirates, and sold it at a profit. This was before the English defeated the Chinese in the Opium War (1839-1842) and Arrow War (1856-1858), and forced China to legalize the opium trade in the Treaty of Tientsin (1858). Astor knew selling opium in China was illegal, if not immoral, and instructed his agent Nicholas Ogden on the need for secrecy and vigilance. *I should think opium must towards the last of the season get up, in a few hands. I believe no one knows of our having any on board the 'Seneca', except Captain Clark, and it is put up in casks as if furs.*

Astor imported black tea, green tea, silk, carpets, ivory, jade, porcelain, and *cloisonné* (finely decorated enamelware). Chinese products, often called *chinoiserie* (Chinese objects), were all the rage in the United States and Europe in the early 19th century. Astor's ships used the ports of Guangzhou (Canton) and Whampoa (near present-day Shanghai) in China. American ports proved more a problem since at the time there were none on the Pacific Coast, which was claimed by Russia, England, and Spain. American ships had to round Cape Horn in order to reach United States ports on the East Coast.

The Corps of Discovery (1804-1806), an expedition led by Meriwether Lewis and William Clark, had been sent by President Thomas Jefferson to investigate and chronicle the enormous tract of land the United States had bought from Emperor Napoleon of France in 1803. The $15 million Louisiana Purchase (at 3 cents per acre) increased the size of the country by one-third. John Jacob Astor was an active proponent of expansionism as it aided his business ventures.

Understandable curiosity led Lewis and Clark to exceed their orders and travel all the way to the mouth of the Columbia River through what is now Idaho, Washington, and Oregon, land claimed by both England and Russia. In 1805 they built Fort Clatsop (named for the Clatsop Indians) as secure quarters to spend the 1805-06 winter.

Seven years later Fort Astoria was constructed near the abandoned remnants of Fort Clatsop to shelter a trading party Astor had sent around Cape Horn. Throughout 1811, Astor's agents, who worked for the newly established Pacific Fur Company, traded with the Indians to obtain a large inventory of furs for the China trade. They also explored the Columbia River with an eye toward establishing more trading posts. Fort Astoria was small, just two log buildings surrounded by a stockade and guard towers.

The War of 1812, which lasted through 1814, doomed Astor's project on the Columbia River. In September 1813 a party of seventy-five trappers in the employ of the North West Fur Company, which operated out of English-owned Canada, and was once partly owned by Astor, laid siege to Astoria, and Astor's men surrendered both the fort and a great quantity of furs.

The American Fur Company and the Pacific Fur Company, Astor's creations, never achieved a monopoly on furs, but by 1811 he had the largest share of the United States fur business. It was the basis for his enormous wealth and, while he may be criticized for urging self-serving political policies on the nation, his dedicated expansionism and exploitation of resources played a role the development of an ever-larger United States. In 1834 John Jacob Astor got out of the fur business.

He did not rest on his financial laurels. In 1810 he began buying land in Manhattan assuming a land boom would occur. In fact, Astor's entire life in New York City was lived during a period when real estate prices grew at an enormous rate. Recognizing the obvious, that Manhattan real estate values soar because the space on the island cannot expand horizontally, he reputedly told a friend: *You should buy Manhattan. They aren't making any more of it.* Another frequently quoted line was: *Could I begin life again, knowing what I now know, and had money to invest, I would buy every foot of land on the island of Manhattan.*

He speculated increasingly on land, often buying newly laid-out lots close to the edge of city, waiting until the land appreciated, and selling the lots as development neared, or, more often, constructing rental buildings on them. According to his rent rolls, Astor had an income of $194,000 in 1848 from four hundred fifty tenants.

Astor also built stores, theaters, and hotels. He got into the hotel business in 1828 when he bought the City Hotel, at Broadway just north of Trinity Church, for $101,000. Astor did not refurbish the City Hotel because he planned to build a new structure nearby which would be the most opulent in the city. In 1832 construction began on a magnificent granite building on Broadway, between Vesey and Barclay Streets on the west, and Park Row on the east. Park Row was where almost all New York City newspapers were located, and the blocks behind it constituted the city's theater district. The new hotel, initially called the Park Hotel when it opened in 1836, was located across Broadway from City Hall and across Vesey Street from St. Paul's Chapel. The palatial six-story Greek Revival building, which was ultimately renamed the Astor House, cost $400,000 to build. (The hotel was demolished in 1913.) There are Astor hotels in many American cities. They took the name of Astor's hotel on Broadway in an attempt to transfer elegance to their establishments.

Astor, like Peter Cooper, J.P. Morgan, John D. Rockefeller and other 19th century millionaires, needed to establish intellectual credentials to gain genuine social acceptance. One way to do that was to endow cultural centers. The Astor Library, a superb example of *Rundbogenstil* architecture, a German form of Romanesque Revival, was built as much a tribute to himself as a gift to the community. The library, which opened to the public in 1854, was located on Lafayette Street between East 4th Street and Astor Place. (Presently the building houses the Public Theater.) Across Lafayette Street from the library was Colonnade Row, a set of nine elegant granite townhouses with Corinthian columns, where the Astors, Vanderbilts and other financial notables lived in mid-century when the area was fashionable. (Four of the townhouses survive.)

Astor was sensitive about criticism concerning his Astoria adventure on the Pacific Coast, as well as charges that he had been a war bond profiteer during the War of 1812, and less than honest in his fur business and real estate ventures. In 1832 he hired popular author Washington Irving to write a favorable, one-sided account of his life. Astor and Irving spent much time together at Hell Gate, Astor's two-story Greek Revival country mansion on the East River (near East 96th Street today), working on the book. The product, printed in 1836, was entitled *Astoria, or Anecdotes of an Enterprise Beyond the Rocky Mountains.*

One of the minor stories that harmed Astor's reputation involved the respected naturalist and artist John James Audubon, painter of *Birds in America,* a published folio, which the painter created between 1820 and 1826. Astor ordered a copy, accepted delivery, and then refused to either pay for the folio or surrender it. Audubon, according to the widely circulated story, made five trips to Astor's home to try to collect the money.

John Jacob Astor died in 1848 at age 84. Among the pallbearers was his official apologist Washington Irving. Because of his great wealth there was significant interest in the disposal of his estate. *The New York Herald* published details of his will on its front page a week after his death. Astor's estate was valued at $8 million. He left only $500,000 to charities and public causes, and $400,000 of that went to the Astor Library, which his family controlled. He left token amounts to the German Society of New York, the German

Reformed Church, the New York Lying-In Asylum, the Society for the Relief of Half-Orphans and Destitute Children, and the Institution for the Blind. The rest went to his family. New Yorkers considered him in death as well as in life to be miserly.

Notations:

Some Places Named Astoria

Astoria, Oregon, is on the Columbia River, just a few miles from the Pacific Ocean. Astor did not start the town but the fort he commissioned is nearby. The region around the present town of Astoria was home to two stockade-protected trading posts, which were primitive forts. In 1805, the Lewis and Clark Expedition, or Corps of Discovery, built Fort Clatsop. It was named for the Clatsop Indians and was a safe place to spend the winter of 1805-1806. It accommodated all thirty-three members of the group as they rested from their cross-country journey and waited for spring when they could return to St. Louis. Fort Astoria was constructed nearby in 1811 for the trading party sent by Astor around Cape Horn. His hope was to use it as a Pacific Coast base for the growing China trade.

Astor, Wisconsin was a town organized in 1835 by American Fur Company investors along the east bank of the Fox River a half-mile from Green Bay. John Jacob Astor owned three-quarters of the shares in the company town. His hope was that it would become a center of the immense German immigration then occurring. But Green Bay was too far north to attract farmers, and while many Germans and Scandinavians went to Wisconsin, most chose to live further south where the soil was richer and the climate less harsh. The settlement never grew beyond a few buildings and is now part of central Green Bay. All that remains of Astor is the name of a pleasant residential neighborhood of late 19th century Victorian houses known as the Astor Historic District.

Astoria, Queens had nothing directly to do with John Jacob Astor, though it was named for him. William Hallett received title for the wooded northwest corner of Queens in 1654 from New

Netherlands Governor Peter Stuyvesant. For decades the riverbank and beech forest had only one settlement, Hallett's Cove, on the East River across from the north point of Roosevelt Island between what is now Broadway and Main Avenue.

The Hallett's Cove area of Astoria was established as an important ferry link between Queens and Manhattan in 1815 with its first scheduled steam-powered ferry. At the time, Queens and the other Long Island counties were prolific garden farming centers and supplied Manhattan with much of its produce. Wealth did come to Hallett's Cove and mansions were built on 27th Avenue and along 12th and 14th Streets. Over the years Hallett's Cove became Hallets Cove losing a "t" and its apostrophe. Beyond the village and a few scattered farms it remained largely undeveloped until 1839.

That year, Stephen A. Halsey, an entrepreneur who made his fortune as an independent operator in the fur trade, persuaded the New York State Legislature to detach Hallett's Cove from the Town of Long Island City and incorporate it separately as a town named for the richest New Yorker, fur trader John Jacob Astor, hoping it would attract investments by the mogul. Halsey believed that Astoria's location was a promising inducement because Astor's country residence, Hell Gate, was located just across the East River. Astoria, Queens never attracted Astor's interest, but the name stuck.

The Waldorf-Astoria Hotel

There have been two Waldorf-Astoria hotels in New York City. They serve to underscore John Jacob Astor's interest in hotels though each Waldorf-Astoria was built long after his death. The first Waldorf-Astoria Hotel, really two hotels, was built by feuding Astor cousins. They were great grandsons of John Jacob Astor, and they built on adjacent land inherited from their parents. The eleven-story Waldorf Hotel built by William Waldorf Astor in 1893 and the sixteen-story Astoria Hotel built by John Jacob Astor IV in 1897 were designed by the same architect and constructed in the German Renaissance style. They functioned as a unit and together featured thirteen hundred guest rooms and forty party rooms. The location of the sumptuous Waldorf-Astoria, the most celebrated and opulent hotel in New York City at the turn-of-the-century was 5th Avenue between 33rd and 34th Streets. In 1929 it was torn down to make way for the Empire State Building.

The Astor family opened a new Waldorf-Astoria Hotel in 1931 taking the entire block between Park and Lexington Avenues and between 49th and 50th Streets. The new structure had forty-two stories, fourteen hundred guest rooms, and twenty-five party rooms including the renowned Empire Room. The lavish hotel was built during the Interwar Years in the darkest period of the Great Depression. The Astor family chose to build in the art deco style, which was at its height at the time. The Chrysler Building (1930) and the Empire State Building (1931) are also art deco structures. In 1949 the Hilton Hotel chain bought the Waldorf-Astoria but retained the original name. The famous *Waldorf salad,* first created for the hotel, and still served in its dining rooms, is composed of thinly sliced apples, grapes halved and seeded, diced celery, and crushed walnuts. A light mayonnaise-based dressing is used.

CHAPTER 51
Peter Cooper

Peter Cooper, noted engineer, inventor, and entrepreneur, was born in 1791 to a merchant family in downtown Manhattan. His father was a hatter who also sold groceries. The surname, Cooper, which is a mechanic's name meaning barrel-maker, was appropriate in the sense that Peter Cooper made his fortune from mechanical skills and inventions, as well as business.

Cooper always felt handicapped by his sparse education, which, due to poor health, his father's business troubles, and his own disinterest, amounted to just a few months. One of his reasons for later founding Cooper Union, a tuition-free college, was to assure talented students a fine education. *If I could have had such advantages as we can give the poorest boy now, how much more could I have done.*

As an adult, Cooper deplored games of chance, including the stock market, which he considered gambling. He was the kind of undeviating capitalist who only likes making money from inventions and manufacturing. He explained his point of view in an anecdote. *When quite a small boy I once made a little wagon. In giving one of my little brothers a ride in it one day, a friend of my father's came along and offered me six dollars for it, which I was glad to take, although I had spent a good deal of time and labor on it with the few tools I had. In some way, which I scarcely now remember, I succeeded in adding four dollars to the amount, and I used the ten dollars in buying lottery tickets. My uncle persuaded me to do this, as it was his business, and he was authorized by the state to sell lottery tickets. I had the 'good luck' to draw nothing but blanks, which I consider one of the best investments of my life, for I then learned that it is not my forte to make money at games of chance.* The painful childhood experience guided his career.

As a boy he was apprenticed to a carriage-maker and soon mastered the trade. When freed from his apprenticeship obligation he chose to take a job with a machinist in Hempstead, Long Island. The company produced devices for shearing cloth. Cooper was a serious worker who shunned smoking and drinking. He married his employer's daughter, Sarah Bedell, in 1813, and the next year bought a house in Hemstead. In 1818 he tried something different. Cooper moved back to Manhattan and opened a grocery store on the Bowery near Stuyvesant Street and East 9th Street, at the time a semi-rural location. (The city limits only reached to Houston Street in 1818.) Peter and Sarah Cooper's nuclear family provides a telling note about the high rate of infant mortality in the 19th century. Between 1815 and 1830 they had six children, but only the last two, Edward and Sarah Amelia, survived infancy.

The grocery store was unchallenging, so Cooper began tinkering with mechanical devices and putting his mind to inventing solutions to problems. The steam engine fascinated him and he began using his imagination and mechanical aptitude to work on ways to apply steam power to transportation.

Meanwhile, a manufacturing opportunity arose. In 1820 Cooper bought a small glue factory in east-central Manhattan near Sunfish Pond, at the edge of the hamlet of Kip's Bay. To be near it, he moved his small family to a house at East 28th Street and 4th Avenue (now Park Avenue South). During the 1840s, the Peter Cooper Glue Factory moved to Bushwick, Brooklyn. The odoriferous factory had outlived its welcome in Kip's Bay, and Sunfish Pond had been so polluted by Cooper's factory that in 1839 it had to be filled in. The reason the glue factory was a foul-smelling place was that waste material (bones, skulls, hoofs) from slaughterhouses and butcher shops was gathered after cows, sheep, goats, pigs, and deer had been butchered. The animal remains were boiled down with crushed limestone, zinc, coal, sulfuric acid, and water in large vats. The resulting pure glue stock, which no longer smelled, was packaged in containers for sale.

Peter Cooper also produced *gelatin* at his glue factory. There is very little difference between gelatin and glue. Gelatin is purer, which means the extracted substance from animal parts, usually hoofs, is scraped clean with all fat and blood removed. The resulting pure protein product is tasteless. It is used as a base for many desserts and candies, as a thickener in cooking, and as a food preservative. He packaged the first commercial gelatin available in the United States. Prior to that, housewives made their own gelatin by boiling down calves' feet.

In 1878 the glue factory was moved again as protests about the smell mounted from nearby residents of Bushwick and the City of Brooklyn. This time it was relocated to an 11-acre site on Smith Island in Newtown Creek. The island no longer exists, but was near Maspeth Avenue and Gardner Avenue where English Kills flows into the Newtown Creek. The streams were later reconfigured and part of the waterway, which forms a portion of the Brooklyn-Queens border, was filled in. The former site of Peter Cooper's glue factory now belongs to Keyspan National Grid, the successor company to Brooklyn Union Gas.

In 1828 Cooper opened the Canton Iron Works in Baltimore. He also started wire-rope factories and rolling mills for steel plating. Cooper produced many iron and steel products including the first functional steam engine for a railroad. The makeshift engine was small and seemed insignificant, so Cooper called it *Tom Thumb*, after P.T. Barnum's popular midget.

Cooper had caught railroad technology right at its start and his jerrybuilt engine helped launch a whole new industry. Cooper's engine-operated railroad was challenged to a race in 1830 by Baltimore, Stockton & Stokes, a company that operated stagecoaches. The company wanted the steam engine to race one of their horses. The race was neck and neck until almost the end. Near the finish line a band on the engine broke and the railroad car came to a halt. The horse won. The stagecoach company loudly proclaimed that steam engines would never be a serious threat to their stagecoaches. They were wrong. Soon railroad tracks with trains pulled by steam engines reticulated the country. The eastern and western railroad systems were connected in 1869 at Promontory, in the Utah Territory. The Union Pacific Railway, building westward from Omaha, and Central Pacific Railway, building eastward from Sacramento met at Promontory.

Cooper's ideas never stopped. In 1842, water from the Croton Reservoir in Westchester County was brought across the Harlem River over High Bridge to Manhattan. Cooper's steam engines powered pumps which were used to move the water into the holding reservoir in the future Central Park and the distributing reservoir at 42nd Street and 5th Avenue, the site today of both the New

York Public Library's Main Branch and Bryant Park.

Always interested in education and technology, Peter Cooper organized and built a college. He founded The Cooper Union for the Advancement of Science and Art to promote study in the fields he most appreciated. Cooper Union is divided into three schools: engineering, architecture, and art. The large 5-story fireproof brownstone building at Astor Place (St. Mark's Place between 3rd and 4th Avenues) was constructed between 1853 and 1859.

Cooper designed it for the future using the most modern technology. Steel beams were used in its construction, and a cylindrical shaft was built into the structure to hold an elevator, which Cooper anticipated would be necessary in the future for tall buildings to be practical. An elevator was installed only after Elisha Graves Otis developed the *safety elevator* with catch-devices to insure against falls. For more than a century a square elevator operated inside the cylindrical shaft until 1972 when John Hejduk designed a tubular stainless steel carriage to fit the way Peter Cooper had intended. (On the eighth floor the simple mechanical workings that drive the large clock visible on the south side of the building are on view.)

The college was built by Peter Cooper, but not endowed by him. Tuition would be free if the costs could be covered by public donations. The public did not respond generously despite some large gifts by wealthy New Yorkers, among them J.P. Morgan and Andrew Carnegie. Cooper's grown children finally came forward in 1903 with sufficient money to create a sizable trust. Along with continuing public donations, the trust was large enough so the college only began charging tuition in 2012.

Abraham Lincoln spoke in the Great Hall of Cooper Union on February 27, 1860. The Illinois lawyer had come to New York City to test the waters in his quest to get the Republican nomination for president. At first, muffled laughter erupted throughout the hall at the sound of his Midwestern twang and the sight of his tall lanky body. But soon he won the audience with his eloquence and earnestness. The Cooper Union speech was the turning point in Lincoln's pursuit of the nomination. He became the Republican candidate and defeated two Democrats, Stephen A. Douglas and John C. Breckinridge, and Union Party candidate, John Bell. Inside

Cooper Union the low ceiling and obstructive pillars give the windowless Great Hall an inelegant appearance, despite the Lincoln connection.

In Cooper Square, just south of Cooper Union, a statue by sculptor Augustus Saint-Gaudens of the engineer and manufacturer sits regally on a chair on top of a pedestal flanked by two columns and shielded from the sky by a canopy of granite. Architect Stanford White designed the base. It was installed in 1897.

Peter Cooper died in 1883 and was buried in Brooklyn's Green-Wood Cemetery. He lived during a century of tremendous industrial progress and he contributed to it significantly. His life spanned meteoric growth for New York City. When Cooper was born only about twenty-five thousand people lived in the city but the population had reached almost two million at the time of his death. Peter Cooper died the year the Brooklyn Bridge was completed, a symbol of 19th century industrial and engineering strength for the city and the world.

CHAPTER 52
Santa Claus & Christmas Get Makeovers in New York and Become Americanized

The Santa Claus that we know is a modern character that has evolved over the last two centuries. He gained many of his widely recognized attributes in New York City. His image evolved from a popular 4th century Christian bishop who was proclaimed as a saint after his death. He also had something to do with gifts and children. That is the historical part; the rest is much newer and centered in Manhattan.

So what do we know about the historical Saint Nicholas? He was the son of a wealthy early Christian family and lived in the Roman province of Lycia, Asia Minor. Later he became bishop of the seaside town of Myra (now Demre, Turkey). Nicholas of Myra was known for doing good deeds, especially for children. One story tells that he learned that a poor man nearby had three daughters but no dowry money. That meant that the daughters would be unable to get married and might end up as servants or slaves. Nicholas took some of his personal money, divided it into three bags, and tossed them through the family's open window, thus saving the girls. He was also credited with raising three young merchants from the dead after they had been murdered at an inn.

Another story that was repeated widely about Nicholas was that he had appeared to the Roman Emperor Constantine in a dream and told him to release three men falsely accused and condemned to death. Nicholas had boldly threatened the emperor in the dream. Constantine followed the advice that the dream character had given him and wrote a letter to Nicholas pleading that he never be threatened again. Such stories about his zeal and fearlessness spread the fame of Nicholas. A public assembly of the clergy and people elected him bishop of Myra.

We know that in 325 Nicholas attended the first ecumenical

(worldwide) council of the whole Christian Church, held in Nicaea, not too far from Myra. He was one of 318 church fathers, mostly bishops, who attended the assembly (or synod), to solve various religious problems. The delegates decided on the first part of the Christian Creed, and defined the divinity of Jesus. We know that Nicholas believed strongly in the Trinity. In fact, when Arius professed his belief that Jesus was not the same as God, Nicholas slapped him in the face. (Church leaders imprisoned Nicholas briefly for his behavior.) In another outburst he destroyed a local temple of Artemis, the Greek goddess of hunting and the moon.

Because he was an effective church leader, a devout believer, and constantly helped needy people he was popularly recognized as a saint. His feast day was set on December 6th, the anniversary of the day he died in 346. Nicholas was hailed as the patron of travelers on land and the protector of sailors at sea. He gained great popularity in Eastern and Western Europe. Often he was called Saint Nicholas Wonder-Worker. He became the patron saint of Greece, Sicily, and (along with St. Andrew) Russia. A bizarre note is that his fame grew so great that following eastern Turkey's conquest by Muslim Turks, the body of Saint Nicholas was kidnapped by Christians from its grave in Myra in 1087 and taken to Bari, Italy.

Over the centuries Christians in some countries began giving small gifts to their children in the name of Saint Nicholas either on December 6th or on December 25th. That tradition passed to the United States through Dutch Protestants in New Amsterdam. Saint Nicholas lost his religious connection and was presented as a kind of cheerful magician who simultaneously gave presents to all children in December. Even the date shifted from December 6th to Christmas.

In Dutch, the short name for Nicholas is Klaas, so Sinter Klaas, or Sanckte Klaas was the common name used for Nicholas of Myra when parents gave gifts in his name. Following the 1664 take-over, English colonists in New York readily adopted the Dutch gift-giver.

Christmas, however, was celebrated very differently in colonial New York. Some people went to church on Christmas Eve or Christmas Day, but the holiday was far less important than Easter.

Rowdy celebrations at Christmas erupted all over the city. Groups of drunken men, usually poor people, would stagger from house to house in upscale neighborhoods singing crude songs and demanding liquor. The merrymaking usually included rock throwing and fist fights. As the city grew and the mobs became more dangerous, efforts were made in the press to enlarge and transform the celebration of Christmas.

The point was to move the celebration indoors and cut down on the rowdiness. Christmas began to be presented as a holiday for family dinners and gift giving. Presents were given to children but also exchanged among adults. Children's gifts soon evolved far beyond the few nuts and pieces of fruit that were at first deposited for them in stockings or under the Christmas tree. German influence had added Christmas trees to the celebration in the 1830s, and the first retail Christmas tree lot in the United States was set up in New York City in 1851. Decorations, elaborate dinners, and gifts expanded Christmas into a major holiday. It was no longer deemed appropriate to celebrate Christmas in the streets.

Clement Clark Moore's poem, *A Visit from St. Nicholas*, was originally composed for his own children as he rode home to his farm in Chelsea from the Wall Street area one evening in 1822. The next year it was published in the *Troy Sentinel*, an upstate newspaper. Soon it was printed widely and regularly throughout the city and the country and was known popularly as *The Night Before Christmas*. The poem ushered in a new concept of St. Nicholas. He kept his formal name but *he was dressed all in fur*, carried *a bundle of toys*, clenched *the stump of a pipe*, and *he had a broad face and a little round belly that shook when he laughed like a bowlful of jelly.*

Thomas Nast, the renowned 19th century American cartoonist, began drawing a Santa for *Harper's Weekly*, a popular New York literary magazine, in 1862. He drew him as a white bearded, chubby, merry symbol of joy riding in the sky on a sleigh pulled by reindeer from his home in the North Pole. The image stuck and spread throughout the United States. The image of Santa Claus has even become internationalized.

Presents under the tree, dinners, parties, music concerts, ballets, holiday-released movies, and television specials are part of the contemporary Christmas celebration. *The Nutcracker*, *A Christ-*

mas Carol, It's A Wonderful Life, and *Miracle on 34th Street* have become important parts of the holiday. That is how Santa Claus got a makeover in New York City and how the whole celebration of Christmas changed.

CHAPTER 53
Weeksville, Brooklyn

Weeksville was a community of free blacks located in central Brooklyn's agricultural lands where former slaves gravitated to farm and carry on mechanical trades. The community developed in 1838 after James Weeks, a New York *stevedore* (dockworker) born in Virginia, purchased land for a farm from the estate of the Lefferts family who owned vast acreage in central Brooklyn. In 1827, slavery was abolished in New York State, though emancipation was not fully completed until 1841. Sensing better days ahead, many free blacks aspired to buy land and establish their own communities. Some may have also been encouraged by the desire to comply with the $250 property requirement imposed on black men as a prerequisite for voting. Slavery had been a major institution in colonial Brooklyn. Dutch farmers, in particular, used African slaves to tend their vegetable, grain, livestock, and dairy farms.

The Weeksville community developed churches, a cemetery, a school, an orphanage, and old age home. While no trace of the cemetery has been found, other institutions thrive. The Bethel Tabernacle African Methodist Episcopal Church, organized in 1847, and the Berean Missionary Baptist Church, started in 1851, still function as congregations, though the original buildings were demolished. Colored School #2 was formed in 1847. The Brooklyn Howard Colored Orphan Asylum was founded in 1866 and named for Freedman's Bureau leader General Oliver O. Howard. The Zion Home for the Colored Aged was established in 1869 to provide for the impoverished elderly. None of the community buildings survive.

By 1890 Brooklyn's black population had reached 10,000. The immense European migration from Germany, Ireland, Russia, and Italy greatly outpaced black settlement. By the 1920s farmland had disappeared, and row houses and apartment buildings lined the streets. Roman Catholic churches and Jewish synagogues became far more numerous than either black or white Protestant churches.

Weeksville ceased to exist as a separate community. It was left off maps and gradually forgotten by most New Yorkers.

In the 1940s and 1950s the area changed again. Caribbean and American blacks moved into north central Brooklyn. By 2000 Brooklyn's black population reached 500,000, two-thirds in Bedford-Stuyvesant. Not much of Weeksville endured all the building projects and ethnic changes.

Only four modest houses from Weeksville remain. They are along the last remnant of Hunterfly Road, a rural north-south artery built to connect 17th century Dutch settlements in Bushwick and Canarsie. Hunterfly Road itself was displaced by later street grids except for two short sections: the one block stretch that remained as an unmarked alley with the four houses, and Hunterfly Place, a one-block street four blocks northwest. Hunterfly Place, like the rest of this portion of Bedford-Stuyvesant, lacks any original buildings from Weeksville.

The four remaining Weeksville houses are listed as 1698-1708 Bergen Street. The confusing addresses on the east-west Bergen Street are used because Hunterfly Road is no longer an official city street. The four houses are located on the former Hunterfly Road, which runs north to south in the middle of the block, parallel to the streets on either side, Rochester and Buffalo Avenues. Unofficial Hunterfly Road (with no vehicles allowed) is entered from Bergen Street.

Four unadorned wood cottages built for workmen between approximately 1840 and 1870 line the narrow lane. Hunterfly Road's name may be an Anglicization of the Dutch term *Aander Vly* (*Swampy Place*). The four houses are the only buildings left from this sprawling 19th century community of free blacks. The one and two-story clapboard houses were restored in the 1990s and now constitute a preserved local historic monument.

Weeksville Houses are a work-in-progress, and historical researchers and community fund-raisers are busy supporting the endeavor. Professors and graduate students from Pratt Institute and the City University of New York worked on the early research. Support galvanized in 1968, and the *Society for the Preservation of Weeksville and Bedford-Stuyvesant History* was formed in 1971.

The preservation society has gathered a trove of household

artifacts, lanterns, and furniture to use in setting up displays of late 19th and early 20th century African-American life in Brooklyn. The plan is for each house to be outfitted for a different period: one for the 1840s, two for 1900, and one for the 1930s. The buildings and their common yard have undergone dramatic reconfiguration. (The site may be visited by appointment only with the Society for the Preservation of Weeksville and Bedford-Stuyvesant History.)

CHAPTER 54
Robert Fulton

Robert Fulton's early years moved with great speed. He was born in 1765 on a farm in eastern Pennsylvania near Lancaster. His parents were Scots-Irish immigrants, Protestants from Northern Ireland with antecedents in Scotland. At 15, Robert Fulton moved to Philadelphia where he was apprenticed to a silversmith. Within a few years he left the apprenticeship and established himself in a shop as a miniaturist, engraver, hairpiece weaver, gunsmith, and oil painter. In 1786 Fulton contracted a lung disease, probably tuberculosis, and spent time at a spa in Bath, Virginia. When his health improved he returned to Philadelphia.

At Bath he met James Rumsey, a carpenter and engineer, who interested him in canals, especially a proposal to build a canal with locks alongside the Potomac River to bypass rapids. George Washington enthusiastically supported the canal project. Fulton's interest would later return to canals.

In 1786 Fulton moved to London, England to study painting with the portrait painter and landscape artist Benjamin West. The relationship with West was a long one, even after Fulton decided to pursue engineering. Though Fulton was energetic and persistent in studying art, and worked on establishing a full range of styles in oils and watercolors, his penchant for mechanics came to the fore. He invented a successful marble cutting and polishing machine, and then turned his attention to designing small-gauge locks for use in rural England.

After almost a decade in England, Fulton decided in 1797 to return to the United States where canal building had become widespread. On the way home he visited Paris. He had been bold enough to visit Paris in 1790, at the height of the French Revolution, so his 1797 trip could focus on his real purpose, the reputation the French had for supporting experimental science.

The experiment that Fulton had in mind was the submarine, a fantasy in the minds of many for hundreds of years, but one that

Fulton was determined to make functional. His political and economic pitch to the French government was that it could be used to destroy the advantage the English navy enjoyed.

Back in the United States, Fulton rented a workshop to design and test models of his prototype, the *Nautilus*. He set up the Nautilus Company, and researched previous designs and attempts, including the 1776 *American Turtle* constructed by David Bushnell in New Haven, Connecticut.

His initial plan envisioned an elliptical submarine 21 feet long and 6 feet 5 inches high at the center. Water would be pumped by a hand crank into an iron ballast tank to descend, and pumped out to ascend. Below surface the submarine would advance by a hand-cranked, four-bladed propeller. On the surface it could progress by propeller or use a sail connected to a mast that could be raised or lowered at will.

In 1798 he presented his plans to a French commission. They were favorably impressed and called it a *bateau-poisson* (boat-fish). It took until summer of 1800, however, before Fulton was able to mount a demonstration using a full-size *Nautilus* in the Seine River. Further demonstrations were held at the ports of Rouen and Le Havre. Napoleon was First Consul (in reality, dictator) of France and the country was at war with many of its continental neighbors. After the public demonstration, some charges were made that Fulton's submarines were immoral because they would change warfare drastically. He rejected the accusations out of hand predicting that ultimately many countries would use submarines.

Between September and October in 1800 the *Nautilus* sailed into the English Channel several times, once for five days, trying to sink English ships. It failed because the rough seas made it impossible to maneuver close enough to an English vessel to plant a torpedo into its hull. Fulton realized he needed to develop larger, sturdier submarines. The other problem, of course, was that the torpedoes needed to be self-propelled, but that technology was almost a century into the future. Robert Fulton had advanced submarine technology as far as it could go for the moment.

While Fulton worked on his submarine plans, he earned money from other inventions. He planned a system of small-gauge canals in France and was awarded a 15-year patent. He also designed a machine (*cordelier*) to mechanically twist four strands of thick yarn that could produce three miles of strong, naval-quality rope per day. Fulton also experimented with steam engines.

In 1801, Robert R. Livingston was appointed United States ambassador to France. He was a wealthy New Yorker who owned a large estate, called *Clermont,* along the Hudson River near the Catskill Mountains. The ambassador professed great interest in mechanics and envisioned a steamboat connecting New York City with Albany. Livingston and Fulton became close friends and the steamboat idea took root in Fulton's mind, especially after Livingston promised to underwrite the project. James Watt had made the steam engine practical. What needed to be done was develop a light ferry able to be powered by vertical wheels.

Despite his work aimed at harming the English navy, Fulton sailed to England in 1804 to supervise the construction of a steam engine to transport to the United States. Seeming to profess loyalty to no foreign entity, Fulton stayed in London until 1806, spending a great deal of his time trying to sell his submarine ideas to the English to use against the French. In fact, while England and France were mutual enemies, England was also acting belligerently to the United States. (In 1812 the hostilities erupted into warfare.)

Fulton arrived in New York City in December 1806, and left almost immediately for the Federal City, as Washington, D.C. was called. While interested in Livingston's idea of a Hudson River steamboat, Fulton also had his eye on the Ohio and Mississippi Rivers. In fact, he stayed in the national capital until January so he could attend President Thomas Jefferson's gala banquet honoring Meriwether Lewis who had just returned from exploring the Louisiana Territory with William Clark.

In Manhattan, Fulton and Livingston went to Corlear's Hook (at the far east end of where Grand Street is located today) and contracted with Charles Browne, a well-known shipwright, to build a hull 146 feet long and only 12 feet wide for their steamboat. On August 9, 1807 the flat-bottomed steamboat was launched in the East River for a test run which proved completely successful.

On August 17th Fulton launched the maiden voyage of his steamboat from the Christopher Street dock on the Hudson River in Greenwich Village to Albany, with a stop at Livingston's estate, *Clermont*. The ship averaged four and a half miles per hour going upstream. Eventually he added pleasing amenities to his steamboat: an awning, deck chairs, sleeping accommodations, commode, and bar. The project was a much-heralded success.

Fulton's mind, however, was elsewhere. He wrote a smug letter to Livingston the day following the trial run in the East River: *Whatever may be the fate of steamboats for the Hudson, my thing is completely proved for the Mississippi.* He then asked Livingston for more money.

The steamboat was registered as the *North River Steam Boat*. (The North River was still the official name for the Hudson River.) During Fulton's life he always referred to the *North River Steam Boat* as simply *Steamboat*, though ultimately people called it the *Clermont*, in honor of the country estate of Robert Livingston, which was one of the regular stops on the steamboat's route between New York City and Albany.

Though he continued to work on plans for steamboats on the Mississippi River and its tributaries, Fulton did not ignore New York City. He designed and sometimes managed steamboats on several important routes along area waterways. Soon the *Firefly*, *Paragon*, and *Car of Neptune* joined the *Clermont* on the Hudson River. The *Fulton* ran on the East River and Long Island Sound between the Coenties Slip near Wall Street and Westport, Connecticut. He designed a catamaran 78 feet long called the *Jersey* with the paddle wheel between the two hulls. The *Jersey* ran between Hoboken and Vesey Street in Manhattan. In 1808 Fulton secured from the legislature in Albany a monopoly on all steamboat routes in New York State.

Fulton's steamboats encouraged development in communities separated by water from Manhattan. Brooklyn Heights was New York City's first suburb. It began when land speculator Hezekiah B. Pierrepont began surveying and subdividing farmland along the dirt road from Fulton Street to his house on the heights above the East River in 1816. The first regularly scheduled steam-powered ferry between Fulton Street in the developed portion of the Town of Brooklyn (centered at the foot of Fulton Street north of Brooklyn Heights) and Fulton Street in Manhattan began in 1814 with the *Nassau*, a new vessel designed and owned by Robert Fulton. Commerce increased and led Pierrepont, who became a significant investor in Fulton's ferry company, to begin advertising his lots in 1823.

Daniel D. Tompkins, land speculator and vice president of the United States under James Monroe (1817-1825), developed Tompkinsville as a New York City suburb in 1815. Tompkins sought to take advantage of New York's growth as a commercial center by establishing his suburb on cheap land at the south side of the inner bay. He quickly grasped that it would be dependent on steam power that could provide ferry service to Manhattan. Consequently, he organized the first regularly scheduled steamboat service between Staten Island and Manhattan using the *Nautilus* (a steamboat, not the submarine), designed by Robert Fulton, in 1817.

Outside the New York area, Fulton established steamboat companies on the Potomac River using the *Washington*, and on the James River in Virginia with the *Richmond*. He did establish routes on the western rivers. Fulton owned the *Harriet* that plied the Ohio River, and the *New Orleans* and *Vesuvius* on the Mississippi River.

During the War of 1812 Fulton designed armed steamboats for the United States Navy to use against the English. He developed the *Steam Frigate* and the *Fulton I* but the war was over before Fulton's steamboats could have any effect on naval battles.

Robert Fulton died in 1815 at age 49 and was buried in the underground vault owned by his wife's family in Manhattan's Trinity Church graveyard just a few blocks from their mansion on State Street near Bowling Green. While often self-serving, Fulton was also an idealist about the power of new forces unleashed by the Industrial Revolution. Premature with his submarines, he was right on target with his promotion and design of canals, and his development of steamboats.

CHAPTER 55
Erie Canal

In 1825 New York was the third largest city in the United States. It ranked behind Philadelphia and Boston. Baltimore threatened to overtake them all by becoming the eastern beneficiary of the federally financed National Road, which would eventually run westward across Ohio and Indiana from Cumberland, Maryland to Vandalia, Illinois. Cumberland was in western Maryland and was connected by roads to Baltimore. Cumberland was also on the Potomac River, which gave it water access to Baltimore.

Roads in the United States were few in number, narrow, and in terrible condition, usually pocked by potholes. Rain and snow often made them impassable. County and town governments were in charge and they approached the task of road building and maintenance with little enthusiasm and few resources.

The cost of shipping overland was very high so commerce was impeded for those far from rivers and lakes. Even the National Road would do little to help, though its anticipated success frightened communities not on its route. Shipping goods on water was the least expensive way to move heavy, bulky items.

How could New York City participate directly in trade with the Great Lakes region of the United States? Nature provided two key parts of the answer: the Hudson River and the Great Lakes. The answer was to build a canal across the center of New York State to connect the Hudson River with the Great Lakes. That would give New York's port direct shipping access to Cleveland, Detroit, Milwaukee, Chicago, Duluth, and their agriculturally rich hinterlands.

De Witt Clinton wanted New York City to get the largest share of the Midwest trade. A former United States senator and unsuccessful presidential candidate against James Madison in 1812, the well-connected Clinton had been mayor on and off from 1803 until 1814. In 1810 he headed a commission of politicians and businessmen looking into the feasibility of a canal. Clinton and a group of engineers crossed the state to make a preliminary report and popularize the concept.

Out of office from 1815 to 1818, Clinton spent his time promoting the idea of the canal. He was elected governor in 1818 and with the exception of one two-year term, he served until his death in 1828. He was an eloquent spokesman for the project both playing on people's fears of divisive sectionalism and their dreams of prosperity. This long passage shows Clinton's commitment, vision, and appeal. There is something for everybody in the way he envisioned and promoted the canal.

As a bond of union between the Atlantic and Western states, it may prevent the dismemberment of the American Empire. As an organ of communication between the Hudson, the Mississippi, the St. Lawrence, the Great Lakes of the north and west and their tributary rivers, it will create the greatest inland trade ever witnessed. The most fertile and extensive regions of America will avail themselves of its facilities for a market. All their surplus productions, whether of the soil, the forest, the mines, or the water, their fabrics of art and their supplies of foreign commodities, will concentrate in the city of New York, for transportation abroad or consumption at home. Agriculture, manufactures, commerce, trade, navigation, and the arts will receive a correspondent encouragement. The city will, in the course of time, become the granary of the world, the emporium of commerce, the seat of manufactures, the focus of great moneyed operations, and the concentrating point of vast, disposable, and accumulating capitals, which will stimulate, enliven, extend and reward the exertions of human labor and ingenuity, in all their processes and exhibitions. And before the revolution of a century, the whole island of Manhattan, covered with inhabitants and replenished with a dense population, will constitute one vast city.

Those who scoffed at the idea pointed out the difficulty of constructing a long canal through terrain that was often swampy or rocky. The cost would be high and the population of all New York State was fewer than one million. Detractors labeled it *Clinton's Ditch* and *Clinton's Folly*. Thomas Jefferson said to New York Assemblyman Joshua Forman, a supporter of the idea who unsuccessfully sought backing by the federal government: *Why, sir, you talk of making a canal of 350 miles through the wilderness --- it is little short of madness to talk of it at this day!*

The expensive project was beyond individual or corporate financing and needed state sponsorship. De Witt Clinton again toured the state in 1817 answering questions and portraying his dream of economic development and prosperity for the city and the state. That year the state legislature approved public financing for the canal and the ceremonial first spade of dirt was turned at the town of Rome on July 4, 1817.

The race was on with Baltimore. By 1818 the National Road had made some progress and it stretched from Cumberland, Maryland to Wheeling in western Virginia. However it took until 1850 to reach Vandalia, Illinois.

Though the engineering and planning for the Erie Canal was technologically sophisticated, the actual work was low tech. Workers used axes to chop down trees and picks and shovels to dig a ditch 4 feet deep, 40 feet wide, and 362 miles long. Parts of the canal followed the Mohawk River and the Tonawanda River, but most of the canal had to be excavated.

Local farmers and townsfolk along the way were hired to clear the forest and dig the trench. They soon fell behind the rapid timetable set for the project. Irish laborers and free blacks were then hired to do most of the work.

Some innovative machinery was used. One invention pulled down smaller trees by using a cable. Another yanked out stumps of big trees. Some of the work was exceedingly difficult owing to natural obstacles. At Little Falls and Lockport the workers had to cut through solid rock to build the canal bed. Montezuma Swamp at the north head of Cayuga Lake was a vexing problem because mud kept slipping back into the excavated ditch. Wood frames and pumps were used to complete the difficult stretch. Mosquitoes were nightmarish in the swamps. Workmen struggled to continue through incessant attacks. Some of the mosquitoes carried malaria and many workers died. Cold weather relieved the mosquito and malaria problem but snowy, cold upstate winters also proved difficult.

Every time a river crossed the canal's path the canal had to be raised on wooden or granite troughs (aqueducts) to go over the river. Raising or lowering the water level in the canal meant building 83 locks altogether. Canal locks are a kind of ladder of water to raise and lower boats. Crossing a road meant constructing a bridge so the road could pass over the canal.

The canal was finished in eight years and opened on October 26, 1825. To draw attention to the completed project, Governor Clinton organized a grand opening. He embarked on a canal boat procession from Buffalo to New York City. His decorated barge was called the *Seneca Chief* and displayed a painting of the governor wearing a Roman toga. Several more canal barges followed *The Seneca Chief.* One called *Noah's Ark* contained a zoo of caged wild and domestic animals from around the state. Bands played and canons were fired in towns all along the way as Clinton led an aquatic procession over a ten-day period. He had ceremoniously filled two barrels of water from Lake Erie and at the end of the trip poured them into New York City's Outer Harbor. (His symbolic act is memorialized in a mural, entitled *The Marriage of the Waters,* in the library of De Witt Clinton High School on West Mosholu Parkway in the Bedford Park section of the Bronx.)

When the barge and flotilla of accompanying ships landed at the Battery, they proceeded in a parade of 7,000 marchers and several bands up Broadway to City Hall. An estimated 100,000 people, out of a total population of about 150,000, watched the procession. De Witt Clinton knew how to organize civic theater and the onlookers sensed they were watching a momentous celebration that would usher in great changes.

Results from the Erie Canal were immediate. The cost of shipping a ton of wheat from Buffalo to New York City dropped from $100 to $5. Wheat, corn, apples, potatoes, cheese, corn whiskey, furs, hay, live hogs, pickled pork, lumber, and coal were the mainstay of canal traffic.

Canal barges were small and had no power of their own. They were pulled by teams of mules or horses walking on a pathway adjacent to the canal. Young boys called *hoggees* led the draft animals on the towpaths. Most of the barges hauled products, but some were passenger barges.

In ten years the canal was deepened and widened to accommodate increased traffic. The original canal closed in 1917 and much of it was filled in though a few segments have been preserved. Some of the towpaths are now used for bicycle and walking trails. A new canal, which is still used, called the New York State Barge Canal, was completed in 1925 and runs parallel to the original canal. It is presently used for shipping and pleasure boating. Reproductions of old canal boats can be rented for day trips or overnight journeys along the new canal.

After 1825, New York City commerce grew quickly and the city became a magnet for rural migrants and foreign immigrants. The city's population grew from 123,706 in 1820 to 312,710 in 1840. By 1860 the city was home to 814,000 people. Real estate prices soared and personal wealth increased. New York City became the main point of entry for imported goods from Europe and South America and place from which American made goods were exported. The Erie Canal helped New York City become the manufacturing center of the United States, the country's banking and finance center, and its largest city. Brooklyn's waterfront also profited greatly. Previously New York had no dockside facilities for grain storage. At Gowanus Bay, Brooklyn a grain elevator with a capacity for 2,000,000 bushels was constructed to handle wheat and corn from the canal.

Secondary canals were built to connect the Erie Canal with other parts of New York State: the Oswego Canal to Lake Ontario, the Champlain Canal to Lake Champlain, and short canals to three of the Finger Lakes (Lake Seneca, Lake Cayuga, and Lake Owasco). That extended the reach of the canal and spread its benefits. Towns along the canal also grew: Albany, Schenectady, Amsterdam, Herkimer, Utica, Rome, Oneida, Syracuse, Palmyra, Lockport, Tonawanda, and Buffalo.

The revolution in transportation was not solely limited to the Erie Canal. It also included railroads and steamships. However, New York City got a head start on urban growth and development engendered by the industrial revolution because of the canal.

Railroads followed closely behind canals. In 1826, the year after the Erie Canal opened, the state legislature authorized the incorporation of the first railroad company, the Mohawk and Hudson line, to build between Albany and Schenectedy. It opened in 1831 with just 16 miles of track. That modest start set off a torrent of railroad construction. By 1850 there were already thirty railroads in New York State with 1,649 miles of track.

In the 21st century trucks and airplanes transport most products in the United States. (Ships and trains have been largely eclipsed.) The infrastructure contains thousands of miles of highways and hundreds of airports. Though geographic location is no longer as important as it was two centuries ago, New York City still benefits from the resolute actions of De Witt Clinton in the early 19th century. The city seized preeminent economic power when it was up for grabs. Today, with eight million people living in the five boroughs and six million in the suburbs, New York City has become the commercial hub of Clinton's dreams.

Lyrics from *Erie Canal*
I've got a mule and her name is Sal,
Fifteen miles on the Erie Canal.
She's a good old worker and a good old pal,
Fifteen miles on the Erie Canal.
We've hauled some barges in our day,
Filled with lumber, coal, and hay,
And we know every inch of the way
From Albany to Buffalo.

CHORUS
Low bridge! Everybody down.
Low bridge! We're a-coming to a town.
You'll always know your neighbor,
You'll always know your pal
If you've ever navigated on the Erie Canal

We'd better get on our way, old pal,
Fifteen miles on the Erie Canal.
You can bet your life I'd never part with Sal,
Fifteen miles on the Erie Canal.
Get us there, Sal, here comes a lock;
We'll make Rome 'fore six o'clock.
One more trip and back we'll go,
Right back home to Buffalo.

(Repeat CHORUS)

CHAPTER 56
Irish Famine

There is much more to the story of the Irish Famine, Irish Potato Famine, or the Great Hunger, than meets the eye. The broad facts are that from 1845 to 1849 a potato blight destroyed the most important food crop available to the Irish people, killing many and prompting approximately one million to emigrate. In 1840 the population of Ireland was 8,175,000 and in 1850 it was down to 6,552,000. Death certificates rarely existed and burials were usually unrecorded, so it is impossible to ascertain how many perished and how many fled the country.

The enormous migration out of Ireland changed American and New York demographics. Between 1840 and 1860 about two million Irish immigrated to the United States. Many came during the years of the potato famine. New York City and Boston were the main points of entry for Irish immigrants to the United States, and while some continued their migration westward, many remained in the New York and Boston metropolitan areas.

Ireland was England's first colony. It had first been invaded in 1169 by French speaking Normans from England, and for the next 600 years the Irish people were subjected to arbitrary acts by a hostile foreign power. Periodic confiscation of land and its redistribution to settlers from England and Scotland was an economic disaster for the Irish, who lapsed into poverty and misery. In 1841, half the families in rural Ireland lived in windowless mud cabins with a single room and virtually no furniture. They had been reduced to sleeping on the floor, wearing rags, working as periodic day laborers on English-owned farms and estates, and subsisting on potatoes, the food that would provide the highest yield for them on their tiny patches of land. Few Irish Catholics had farms more than one acre in size, and only one-quarter possessed full-time jobs.

The ethnic hostility between conqueror and vanquished had, after the Protestant Reformation in the 16th century, added a religious dimension. The English under Henry VIII established the Anglican Church (Church of England), independent of the pope and hostile to Rome. Ireland remained Catholic and its people were seen by the English as ready to serve the interests of England's Catholic rivals, France and Spain.

In 1690, followers of the Stuarts and its deposed Catholic monarch, James II, raised his standard in Ireland to oppose the Protestant king, William III of Orange. In 1689, William had been invited by the English Parliament to rule the country as joint-sovereign (co-ruler) with his wife Mary, the Protestant daughter of King James II. (William had been Dutch *stadtholder* of the province of Zeeland, and the Captain-General and Admiral-General of the United Provinces. These were titles created for House of Orange royalty within the *republic,* which was eventually named the Netherlands.) English supporters of William and Mary defeated the Stuart army supporting James II at the Battle of the Boyne, near Drogheda, on July 1, 1690. What the English Protestants called the *Glorious Revolution* was an ignominious defeat for the Irish.

The Penal Laws of 1695 aimed at outlawing the Roman Catholic Church. Until 1829, Catholics were barred from the army and navy, all commercial activities, and denied the protection of English laws. Catholics could not vote, serve on juries, or become Members of Parliament. They could not purchase land, and at the death of a Catholic farmer, his land had to be divided evenly among his male heirs, unless the eldest became a Protestant, in which case he would inherit everything. Catholics could not attend school, organize their own schools, or go abroad for an education. Catholic churches, seminaries, convents, and schools were closed or converted into Protestant institutions. Catholic priests were forbidden from saying Mass and were not allowed to enter cemeteries. The practice of the Catholic faith was forced underground.

The 1801 Act of Union between England and Ireland dissolved the Irish Parliament in Dublin (from which Roman Catholics were barred), folded Irish laws into the English legal system, and integrated both economies. In every case, the Act of Union favored the English and further alienated and suppressed the Irish.

In the 18th and early 19th centuries, many English landlords ordered their tenants, even those who paid their full rent, evicted so they could turn the croplands into grazing farms for cows and sheep. For the English entrepreneurial farmer in Ireland, exporting beef and mutton to the growing middle class in England was more profitable than collecting ground rent from Irish tenant farmers. John Mitchel, advocate for Irish independence, wrote: *During all the famine years, Ireland was actually producing sufficient food, wool and flax, to feed and clothe not nine, but eighteen millions of people.* The process of selling Ireland's products abroad aggravated the precarious economic state of Ireland's rural masses.

Seventy-five percent of Ireland's population was Catholic. Most Protestants in Ireland lived in Ulster, the six counties in the northeast. Overwhelmingly they were Presbyterian Scots. There had been a steady flow of Irish immigrants to the Thirteen Colonies before the potato famine. Most were Scots-Irish Presbyterians who integrated easily into American colonial society. During the late 18th and early 19th centuries, the population of Ireland rose sharply, the pressure on the land increased, and Catholics began to join Protestants in leaving Ireland for the New World.

The potato blight was a new menace added to all the other problems plaguing the people of Ireland. Its peasants were familiar with the unreliability of weather and had, over the years, suffered many poor crops. Usually the culprit was weather that poured too much rain on the island.

In 1844, a previously unknown disease had attacked crops along the northern Atlantic coast of the United States. While it hurt many farmers in potato raising areas of Maine and Massachusetts, most American farmers had large farms and raised a variety of crops and livestock, so the failure of one product would not destroy their entire yield. When it spread to Ireland, its effects were disastrous.

The 1845 potato crop in Ireland appeared to be good until harvesting started in mid-October. When farmers dug into the sandy soil to pull out the tubers they found they were covered with mold and had turned black. Putrid, rotten potatoes were unearthed throughout Ireland. *Phytophthora infestans*, the technical name for the potato blight, was a fungus, which destroyed the potatoes and spread rapidly as its tiny airborne spores drifted throughout Ireland.

Nothing was cheaper than the potato. It was the last bastion of the Irish against hunger and starvation. Lacking sustenance for working, and with absolutely nothing to sell, thousands of peasants lost their plots and huts because the English landlords demanded the timely payment of rent despite the unfolding famine. Dispossessed people, with no place to live, dug holes in the ground along the roads and lived in shallow pits. Some went to the seashore and lived in shacks made of stones and driftwood.

Following in the wake of the Great Hunger came *typhus*, an arthropod-borne disease, which causes high fever, severe headache, muscular ache, and rash. It was popularly called *famine fever*, and in severe cases it lead to death. Body lice, fleas, mites, and ticks carry typhus. Typhus usually accompanies disasters and mass dislocations when a breakdown in hygiene occurs. Another plague upon the Irish was *scurvy*, an illness produced by a diet lacking in Vitamin C. Those ailing from scurvy suffered painfully sore gums and joints. In severe cases teeth fall out, the afflicted lost the use of their limbs, and blood vessels under the skin burst.

The English made a modest effort to help the Irish, though it was half-hearted at best. The government imported corn from the United States and yams from the Caribbean to distribute to the hungry. They organized public works projects employing, at its height in December 1846, 450,000 destitute people, and set up some soup kitchens. Much of their emergency work was done with an undertow of contempt. Some of the English thought that divine justice was killing off the Irish. Sir Charles Edward Trevelyan, permanent head of the treasury in London, lamented that the Irish did not understand the will of God. *It is hard upon the poor people that they should be deprived of knowing that they are suffering from an affliction of God's providence.* The English authorities pronounced the famine over in 1849, though suffering continued and the Irish emigration continued.

Most Irish were too poor to afford passage to emigrate from Ireland. Those who could afford to leave went to several countries. The United States was a popular destination because it seemed to promise the most economic possibilities and religious freedom. Irish people also emigrated to England and the various English settler-states: Canada, Australia, New Zealand, South Africa. Some went to Argentina, Chile, Brazil, and elsewhere. Because of its close proximity and inexpensive steamship fares, more Irish went to England than to any other destination. Fortunate emigrants secured passage on safe ships, but many took chances, for cheaper fares, and bought tickets on dangerous old ships, some which were never built for oceanic travel. Uninspected and overcrowded vessels often carried few provisions and water, and quickly earned the name *coffin ships*, a reference to their likeliness to go down in bad weather, or arrive at their destination with sick and emaciated passengers.

Some American non-governmental agencies aided the Irish in their homeland and upon arrival as new immigrants. Roman Catholic relief organizations and Irish fraternal groups (Ancient Order of Hibernians, Irish Emigrant Society, and Friendly Sons of St. Patrick) led the way, though other societies such as the Friends Meeting House (Quakers), Congregation Shearith Israel (Jewish), and Tammany Hall (Democratic Party political club) also helped

The Great Hunger exacerbated the bitterness between Ireland and England. In 1824 the first disturbances around the anniversary of the victory of the forces of William III over James II broke out in New York City. Protestants attacked Catholics in the first of many *Orange Riots*. Orange Day Parades began in the 1870s when Irish Protestants marched to trumpet the victory of the Protestants at the Battle of the Boyne in 1690. They led to riots as Irish Catholics attacked the Irish Protestant (*Oranngemen*) celebrants and the Protestants fought back.

November 25, known as *Evacuation Day*, marked the 1783 withdrawal of English troops from New York City. The local holiday, celebrated by turbulent parades and forcefully patriotic and anti-English speeches, attracted many Irish participants. It continued until 1917 when the United States allied with the English in the First World War and such sentiments became an embarrassment.

In New York City, Irish-Americans and Natives (generally meaning English-Americans) often fought in pitched street battles. The Irish lived in alarming poverty and became an underclass trapped in a cycle of overcrowding, ignorance, unemployment, alcoholism, violence, prostitution, child abandonment, gang warfare, and street crime. Their appalling poverty and disproportionate numbers involved in lawlessness, fed a backlash of anti-foreignism and anti-Catholicism in the city. The *Know Nothings* became the nickname of the American Party, organized on a nation-wide scale, as well as in New York City, to oppose immigrants, especially Catholics.

Ireland finally received independence from the United Kingdom in 1921, except for the six counties in the north, which, as Northern Ireland, remained part of the United Kingdom. Bad feelings between the U.K. and Ireland lingered. During the Second World War, when England and Germany fought, the Irish opted for neutrality.

Notation:

Irish Hunger Memorial

The Irish Hunger Memorial, also called the Irish Stone Cottage Memorial, located in the north part of Battery Park City near Stuyvesant High School, recalls the potato famine in a simple yet powerfully moving monument. An actual stone cottage, transported from County Mayo, is presented in the midst of a very small yard with potato furrows and stone walls. The two-room roofless cottage has neither furniture nor written descriptions. Resembling an artist's palette, the lot is tilted upward to the west. The memorial, which is dedicated to people throughout the world who have suffered hunger, shows a scene of mid-19th century Irish rural poverty, the underlying reason so many died and others emigrated. The Irish Hunger Memorial is located at the corner of North End Avenue and Vesey Street opposite Nelson A. Rockefeller Park, Manhattan.

CHAPTER 57
Seneca Falls Reverberates in New York City: Women's Suffrage

Women were left out of the Declaration of Independence and the United States Constitution. Like enslaved and *free* blacks, Indians, and white men without property, women were excluded from the political process in the American Republic. Women had very few political, economic, or religious rights and could only exercise influence within the family at home.

There were women who managed to agitate for gender equality in colonial days and in the earliest years of the United States. Some had been influenced by European voices such as Mary Wollstonecraft, English philosopher and feminist who wrote *A Vindication of the Rights of Woman* (1792), in which she argued that women are not inferior but have been kept out of civic leadership by being denied education and the right to participate in public affairs.

Dutch New Amsterdam, much more focused on commerce than religion, was by default, marginally tolerant of women leaders. It attracted strong women from elsewhere. Anne Hutchinson, a Biblical scholar and unauthorized Puritan study group leader in Boston, was banished from Massachusetts in 1643 for usurping male roles. She established a tiny settlement at Pelham Bay, now part of the Bronx, but soon afterward she and her family were killed in a Lenape Indian raid. In the same year that Anne Hutchinson and her family were murdered, Lady Deborah Moody, another exile from Puritan Massachusetts, established the small English settlement of Gravesend in Dutch colonial Brooklyn. She was an Anabaptist, one of the few Christian denominations that allowed women some participation in religious life. In 1657 a group of Quaker families settled in Gravesend and used Moody's house as their meeting place.

There were some prominent figures in the late 18th century arguing for women's rights including Abigail Adams, wife of John

Adams, the second president. She is best known for her March 1776 private letter to John Adams and the Continental Congress, requesting that they *...remember the ladies, and be more generous and favorable to them than your ancestors. Do not put such unlimited power into the hands of the Husbands. Remember all Men would be tyrants if they could. If particular care and attention is not paid to the Ladies we are determined to foment a Rebellion, and will not hold ourselves bound by any Laws in which we have no voice, or Representation.* John Adams, lacking in sympathy, responded *...as to your extraordinary code of laws, I cannot but laugh...Depend upon it, we know better Than to repeal our masculine systems...*

The organized movement to repeal those *masculine systems* began in earnest at the Seneca Falls Convention in 1848. The meeting pulled together people who had been active in various reform movements. New York State had at least 104 local societies dedicated to antislavery agitation. Many abolitionists also supported rights for women and other progressive reforms. Three hundred women and men participated in the convention that met on July 19-20, 1848 in the Wesleyan Methodist chapel in Seneca Falls. They sought to launch a larger, unified national movement to alter conditions for women both through legislation and attitude changes. Elizabeth Cady Stanton was the main force organizing the meeting. She supported the right to vote for women, though her scope was far larger than suffrage. Stanton wanted women to be free to enter professions and trades in order to obtain self-confidence and economic independence.

Traditional patriarchal ideas of male supremacy and female inferiority, often reinforced by religious beliefs and culture, needed to be changed. Feminists and their male supporters battled the *cult of domesticity*, the idea that women were emotional and delicate and needed protection from men, who were perceived as strong and capable. That men supported the notion of the *gentle sex* is not surprising, but many women also accepted the idea.

In the popular *Godey's Lady's Magazine*, Sarah Josepha Hale wrote in 1830: *Women may, if they exert their talents and the opportunities nature has furnished, obtain an influence in society that will be paramount with authority. They may enjoy the luxuries of wealth, without enduring the labors to acquire it; and the honors of office, without feeling its cares, and the glory of victory, without suffering the dangers of battle.* Hale, author of the poem *Mary Had A Little Lamb*, was an influential journalist who edited *Godey's Lady's Magazine* from 1837 until 1877. She had many successes, including her agitation to make Thanksgiving a national holiday, which Abraham Lincoln promulgated in 1863. Her conservative voice was difficult for the women's movement to overcome. It was more complicated because Sarah Josepha Hale supported economic independence for women, and backed Elizabeth Blackwell's struggle to become a physician, but opposed women gaining political rights.

The document produced at the Seneca Falls Convention was a masterpiece of political promotion and marketing. The *Declaration of Sentiments* was a reconfiguration of the second clause of the second sentence in Jefferson's Preamble to the Declaration of Independence. *All men <u>and women</u> are created equal, that they are endowed by their Creator with certain inalienable rights, that among these are life, liberty, and the pursuit of happiness.* Inserting *and women* into the document gave enormous change to its meaning.

Of the three hundred people that participated in the Seneca Falls Convention, 68 women and 32 men, including Frederick Douglass, signed the declaration. The Quaker orator and women's rights activist Lucretia Mott had said to Elizabeth Cady Stanton: *The convention will not be so large as it otherwise might be, owing to the busy time with the farmers, but it will be a beginning.* She was referring to the mid-July dates of the two-day conference. As no woman volunteered to chair the meeting, James Mott, husband of Lucretia Mott, presided.

Susan Brownell Anthony also attended the Seneca Falls Convention. She was a tireless advocate for women's suffrage who also raised the issues of religious, economic, and cultural equality. Together with Elizabeth Cady Stanton, Susan B. Anthony founded the National Women's Suffrage Association in 1869.

Susan B. Anthony and Elizabeth Cady Stanton moved to New York City in 1862. As a result, more of the focus of the national women's movement was on New York City. Taking advantage of a loophole in the law, Stanton ran for Congress in Manhattan in 1862. The law barred women from voting but was silent on running for office. She received only a handful of votes. The debate over the 15th Amendment to the U.S. Constitution, ratified in 1870, provoked strong comments from Anthony and Stanton who contended it excluded half of the black population as well as all the white women. The 15th Amendment states: *The right of citizens of the United States to vote shall not be denied or abridged by the United States or by any State on account of race, color, or previous condition of servitude.*

Elizabeth Cady Stanton is interred in Woodlawn Cemetery in the Bronx. The dark gray granite stone lists her husband, Henry Brewster Stanton, as *philanthropist, journalist, lawyer, senator,* but there is no inscription in the empty space below her name. The space is not big enough to chronicle her activities on behalf of women in the fields of voting rights, educational opportunities, equal pay for equal work, birth control, divorce laws, and child custody rights. She also opposed slavery and supported labor unions and prohibition of alcohol. Neither Elizabeth Cady Stanton, who died in 1902, nor Susan B. Anthony, who died in 1906, lived to see the passage of the 19th Amendment that gave women the right to vote.

There were many other women who were prominent in the 19th century women's movement. Amelia Bloomer edited a newsletter and designed a new less restrictive garment for women that came to be called the *bloomer*. She explained her idea: *The costume of women should be suited to her wants and necessities. It should conduce at once to her health, comfort, and usefulness; and, while it should not fail also to conduce to her personal adornment, it should make that end of secondary importance.*

Victoria Woodhull, champion of women's rights and labor reforms had claimed that the 14th Amendment, ratified in 1868, used language that was inclusive and that women ought to use radical direct action to gain access to the ballot box. The 14th Amendment states: *All persons born or naturalized in the United States, and subject to the jurisdiction thereof, are citizens of the United States and of the State wherein they reside. No State shall make or enforce any law, which shall abridge the privileges or immunities of citizens of the United States; nor shall any State deprive any person of life, liberty, or property, without due process of law; nor deny to any person within its jurisdiction the equal protection of the laws.* Woodhull was nominated for president of the United States in 1872 though she received no electoral votes. Woodhull scandalized traditionalists with her support of *free love*, a doctrine that held marriage to be a form of social bondage for women. She embraced the anarchist or libertarian philosophy that neither the state nor the church should have any authority over personal relationships.

Carrie Chapman Catt, two generations younger than Anthony, Stanton, and Woodhull came to New York City in 1909 from the Midwest. She had been born in Ripon, Wisconsin in 1859 and raised in Charles City, Iowa. Catt was an organizer of the New York City Woman Suffrage Party and active in the final stages of the crusade to obtain voting rights. She was an organizer of the National American Woman Suffrage Association and the League of Women Voters. While rejecting the Nativist label, Catt publicly drew the distinction between more prosperous and educated whites with Western European backgrounds and newer immigrants from Southern and Eastern Europe who she claimed had beliefs that were *universally anti-woman suffragist*. One of the reasons she supported birth control was to keep down the growing population of recent immigrants. Catt was not alone having those sentiments. According to *Report of the Debates*, by Bishop and Attree, John A. Kennedy from New York City spoke at the Seneca Falls Convention and included in his remarks his position *that females of a mature age, of our own race* should be enfranchised *before a people who were foreigners in our midst.*

Women took aim at the established legal doctrine of *feme covert*, meaning that economic and the civil rights of married women were controlled by their husbands. Women had no separate legal identity beyond that of their husbands. They could not own property, keep bank accounts, buy life insurance, or control their own salaries or inheritance. In a divorce a wife could not have custody of her offspring because only a husband could be legal guardian of children.

Both feminists and conservative women opposed *feme covert*. Conservatives wanted to protect themselves against irresponsible spouses who gambled, drank excessively, or made poor investments. Feminists agreed but saw it as part of a whole process to gain equality. Without protection, an irresponsible husband could squander a wife's inheritance. The initial successes of the 19th century women's movement came in property rights. Beginning in 1840 the State Legislature began modifying the *feme covert* doctrine by allowing women to buy life insurance and put their inheritance under trusteeship. In 1850 women were permitted to keep separate bank accounts, and in 1860 women were allowed to keep their salaries and have joint guardianship of the children during marriage.

Reform issues were often bundled together in the women's movement. In 1861, just as the Civil War was commencing, New York City physician Elizabeth Blackwell, the first American woman to earn a medical degree (1849), spoke to a meeting of 3,000 women at Cooper Union where several key reform issues were discussed: abolition of slavery, women's suffrage, temperance, and universal education.

Numerous restrictive colonial laws and practices had been rolled over into the state statutes after the American Revolution. For example, the English Test Act of 1673 kept Catholics and Jews from voting or holding appointed positions. New York State retained property qualifications that excluded most white men from voting. The idea, couched in disarming republican sentiment, was that voters and elected officials needed to own enough property to be politically independent. In the first two decades after independence only about 25 percent of white males in New York City were entitled to vote or hold office. By 1825 the Test Oath for Catholics had been abolished and the property requirement was adjusted to include renters who paid high rents. Governor DeWitt Clinton was an advocate of many of these reforms. It proved very difficult, however, for white men to extend enfranchisement to women.

Margaret Sanger, one of the founders of Planned Parenthood, advocated contraception to regulate family size. They called contraception *birth control* and proselytized among both wealthy and poor New Yorkers. The Comstock Act, passed by Congress in 1873, defined contraception as *obscene*, and made it illegal to disseminate either information or devices through the mail. In 1914 she began publishing a feminist and socialist magazine, *Woman Rebel*, considered incendiary by her many opponents. In the opening issue, she wrote: *Woman is enslaved by the world machine, by sex conventions, by motherhood and its present necessary child-rearing, by wage-slavery, by middle-class morality, by customs, laws and superstitions.* Sanger opened her first Planned Parenthood clinic in Brownsville, Brooklyn in 1916 where the group advocated *child spacing* to the neighborhood's poor Italian and Jewish residents. She was repeatedly arrested and indicted for her speech and activities. Ultimately Sanger's ideas caught on with the vast majority of New Yorkers.

Some of the political positions seen as progressive by earlier feminists are not considered progressive in the 21^{stt} century. Eugenics, aimed at blacks and immigrants, was originally an American idea that carried a racist and anti-immigrant bias. It was finally discredited after German fascists used it as public policy in the 1930s and 1940s. While Margaret Sanger supported eugenics, few progressives would do so today. Almost all feminists once supported the temperance movement. As a law that prohibited all alcoholic beverages it was a failure and today is seen as overly intrusive nanny-state interference with personal lifestyle choices.

Less effective than most feminists was the colorful Emma Goldman. A plaque marks the tenement building in the East Village where the Russian-born anarchist and feminist, lived in a sixth floor apartment from 1903 until 1913. Goldman championed free speech, birth control, and free love. She was arrested by federal prosecutors for opposing American entry in the First World War and deported to the Soviet Union in 1919. Though Goldman was a Leftist, and the Soviet Union had given women the right to vote in 1918, she opposed the heavy-handedness of the regime. Unhappy with Bolshevik leadership she left the Soviet Union and spent the rest of her life espousing radical politics and feminism in various countries in Western Europe. She died in 1940 in Canada.

Voting rights for women came piecemeal in the United States and the first nine states to accept women's suffrage were in the West. Wyoming entered the Union in 1870 and granted suffrage rights in local and state elections to women in the body of its constitution. Other Western states followed: Colorado (1893); Utah and Idaho (1896); Washington (1910); California (1911); and Oregon, Kansas, and Arizona (1912). From 1910 large suffrage marches were held in many American towns and huge processions were organized in New York City and Washington, D .C. Victory for women's suffrage in New York State finally came in 1917. Only one signer of the *Declaration of Sentiments* survived to celebrate victory in New York State. Rhoda Palmer had attended the Seneca Falls convention in 1848 at age 32. In November 1919 she cast her first ballot at age 102. She died the next year.

Passing an amendment to the United States Constitution is usually a lengthy and difficult process. Two-thirds of the House and Senate must approve a proposal and send it to the state legislatures for a vote. Then, three-fourths of the states must ratify the proposed Amendment. In May 1919, the House of Representatives passed the amendment by a vote of 304 to 89, and in June the Senate followed by a vote of 56 to 25. Finally, on August 26, 1920, Tennessee became the 36th state (out of 48) to ratify it and the 19th Amendment became part of the Constitution. In November 1920 white women in all states were able to cast ballots in federal elections.

CHAPTER 58
Industries

Almost every neighborhood within the five boroughs once had industry. There was no zoning until the 20th century so in the late 19th century, at the height of the Industrial Revolution, property owners could construct factories, mills, tanneries, breweries, and foundries wherever they wished.

The Industrial Revolution involved the application of new scientific and technological principles and inventions to production. While factories had existed for at least two millennia, the factories of the Industrial Revolution were much larger and infinitely more efficient. Mass production was made possible by the steam engine. The fuel for producing steam was wood, coal, and later, oil. Whatever substance was used for fuel to heat the boilers badly polluted the surrounding area. The dates of the Industrial Revolution are imprecise because in New York City it occurred over a long period of time, though it would be accurate to view the entire 19th century as a period of constant industrialization.

The industries of the Dutch colonial period were marked by simple exploitation of the land and waterways. It involved preparing fur, tanning leather, and milling lumber. Tall, straight tree trunks were exported for ship masts. Food processing, mostly waterfront facilities for salting and drying fish (especially cod), packaging grain in barrels, and brewing beer, were found throughout the early city.

Eighteenth century industries in the English period included food processing, wool and cotton mills, and iron foundries. Sugar refining grew during the English period as a consequence of the heavy trade with the Caribbean. In the 18th century the area around the Collect Pond (Foley Square and Chinatown), the Manhattan side of the East River below Turtle Bay (United Nations), and eastern Harlem developed into a series of poor hamlets clustered around dirty industries such as slaughterhouses, tanneries, and breweries. By 1800 New York City's port became the busiest in the new nation and a host of small factories emerged to process imports and to prepare and package American goods for export.

As the pressure of population raised property values, Manhattan's industrial plants were replaced by housing. Corlear's Hook, east of the confluence of Grand Street and East Broadway, had been home to a thriving shipbuilding industry and subsidiary industries such as rope, sail, and barrel making. When Irish and German immigrants poured into the city, Corlear's Hook landlords converted their properties into cheap housing for workers.

The Gashouse District, a notoriously smelly area between 14th and 28th Streets, and between the East River and Park Avenue South, was home to three large and numerous small gas tanks and kerosene refineries, which emitted foul odors. In between the petroleum factories were tenements housing poor workers. In the 1940s most of the area was razed and Metropolitan Life Insurance Company, with political and financial help from Robert Moses and his Washington connections, completed two large middle-income housing complexes, Stuyvesant Town and Peter Cooper Village.

The garment industry began in the 1830s as men began to desire ready-to-wear clothing rather than depend on their wives and daughters to sew their clothes or commission them at a tailor shop. Much of the garment trade in the 19th century was *outwork,* when women picked up bundles of cloth from manufacturers and took it home to sew. The process involved little overhead and kept prices (as well as wages) very low. The garment industry received a boost after the Civil War with the advent of *sizing,* a practice, which further popularized the ready-to-wear trade. The garment industry increased in importance until the late 20th century when competition from China, Malaysia, Mexico and other countries with low labor costs put New York companies out of business or caused them to close down here and take their production abroad. In 1967 there were 243,300 garment workers employed in 10,026 shops. Twenty years later there were only 78,400 workers in 3,119 shops.

Staten Island had food processing plants, breweries, lumber mills, and industries based on high quality clay. In colonial times, Kreischerville (now called Charleston), the southern section of Arthur Kill Road, was a center of oyster gathering in the river.

Clay pits, brick works, and terra-cotta plants took over in the 19th century and into the 20th. Balthazar Kreischer owned the largest brick manufacturing plant.

There are only three identifiable remnants of the brick and terra-cotta industry left in Charleston. Clay Pit Ponds State Park Preserve on Nielsen Avenue off Sharrotts Road, now a haven for hikers and birders, was once the source of clay for Staten Island's former brick industry. The park's five ponds, which appear natural, were once clay pits, which filled up with rainwater transforming them into *clay pit ponds*. Killmeyer's Old Bavarian Inn & Beer Garden, corner of Arthur Kill Road at Sharrotts Road, managed to survive the 20th century. The present restaurant has been in business only since 1995, but the building had housed a series of inns, beer gardens, and bars catering to German workers since 1855. Outside, the sidewalk is made from bricks embossed with the Kreischer name. Located on a hill above the forgotten back end of Staten Island is the home built by Balthazar Kreischer's son Charles, which proudly possesses the highest ground in the area. The large white Victorian residence with cupola and gingerbread lattice-work was built in 1885 for the brick baron who had founded the Kreischer Brick and Terra-cotta Works in 1854. His employees worked in the nearby clay pits and brick kilns and lived in the company town, which kept his name until 1927. Today the area has a lot of weed-filled empty lots, tumbled-down houses, and two dry-docks

The Bronx was best known commercially for forest products and garden farming. The Lorillard Snuff Mill, now a cafeteria and conference center at the Bronx Botanical Garden, once housed Pierre Lorillard's tobacco curing, drying, cutting, and packing operation, which he began in 1760. For a time, P. Lorillard and Company produced more snuff in this building than was produced anywhere else in the United States. The Lorillard family diversified their holdings and became prominent in banking, shipping, and tanneries. In 1870 the company sold the building, and in 1891 moved out of New York City.

City Island, near Orchard Beach, briefly flirted with the possibility of becoming a major shipbuilding center. It received its present name from developer Benjamin Palmer in 1761. He had hoped the village would grow into a city and thought of it as an actual rival to New York City at the southern tip of Manhattan Island. (New York City had only about 8,000 people in 1761.)

Before shipbuilding, island residents had earned income from oystering, clamming, and fishing in nearby waters. A salt works was established in 1830 to make salt by evaporating sea-water. Shipbuilding companies lined the long coast and a profitable yacht construction niche was soon developed. However, the last shipyard closed in 1982, though sail makers, dry docks, and motor assembly and repair shops still thrive.

Astoria was the first section of Queens to industrialize. German brewers set up beer manufacturing facilities and German carpenters opened furniture factories and piano companies. The area's stands of tall beech trees and reasonable rents attracted the German woodworkers. In 1870 piano manufacturer William Steinway began putting together a tract of 400 acres of land in the northeast corner of Astoria. He named the central road Steinway Street and built company housing for his workers. The piano factory was located along the shore of the East River in a part of Astoria that came to be called Steinway. As a real estate developer, Steinway was also partner in a working-class beach resort at nearby North Beach, on land now occupied by LaGuardia Airport.

Long Island City, in Queens industrialized later than most areas, but it has retained its industrial base. As transportation routes were established and housing for workers was built, industries moved in with increasing rapidity. Oil refineries, chemical plants, paint manufacturers, sawmills and lumber yards, furniture factories, ceramic and terra-cotta works, iron foundries, metal factories, glassware companies, textile mills, shoe factories, marble and granite cutting works, and food processing plants established themselves in the area. By 1938 there were more than 1,400 industrial corporations operating in Long Island City.

Just as Long Island City reached the height of industrialization from the 1920s to the 1940s, heavy industry began to move out due to high labor costs. After the Second World War the flight of heavy industry continued, and clogged highways, which slowed distribution of finished products became another reason to relocate. The area remained industrial but shifted to light industry and

warehousing. Two of its food processing plants, Silvercup Bakeries and Adams Chewing Gum, were known throughout the metropolitan area. Other food processing companies produced sugar, candy, and pasta products.

The period of heavy industry was a long one and still has life in some sectors such as tool and die factories, hydraulic cranes, industrial pumps, and chemical works. Many small factories in Long Island City engage in finishing basic items produced elsewhere. There are companies, which cut aluminum siding and awnings, frame glass windows, and produce, store, and install automobile parts and supplies. L.I.C. is known as a place to find automobile components, install new mufflers, repaint vehicles, rebuild engines, and repair cars damaged in collisions. Other industries include photographic equipment, ceramic tiles, furniture, paint, wholesale florists, construction contractors, taxicab yards, carpet cleaning, marble and granite, printing and binding, and moving and storage.

Following the Second World War modern transportation routes for cars and trucks reconfigured the face of the area by driving paths of iron and cement through Long Island City, cutting it into slices, and overshooting it for more distant Queens. The riverfront was no longer important after river traffic ceded its role to bridges and tunnels, and the riverfront became a deserted backwater. Most of the remaining housing was demolished to make room for warehouses, taxi garages, and more light industry plants. By the 1970s there were very few blocks of houses and most were isolated and tucked between manufacturing plants. Gentrification began in the 1990s as factories were converted into housing and new high-rise apartment buildings were constructed along the East River.

Red Hook, Brooklyn was established as a Dutch fishing and farming village in 1636. For a century and a half there was very little growth in the area. By 1818 steamboats had entered the region's commercial activity and there was a rush for waterfront property to use as wharf space, storage facility, and for manufacturing. The opening of the Erie Canal in 1825 increased trade exponentially and Red Hook and the Gowanus Basin experienced rapid development. James Stranahan, a major port developer, reconfigured the shoreline and built enough piers by 1850 to handle 150 ships at a time. Grain and coal from the Midwest, hops from upstate New York (for beer), crushed limestone from New England (for concrete), tea from Asia, sugar from the Caribbean, cocoa from Africa, coffee from Brazil and Colombia, as well as lumber, clear sand (for glass), naval stores (sails, rope, pitch, tar), and clay (for bricks and terra-cotta) was unloaded at the Red Hook docks and either repackaged for distribution or manufactured into a synthesized product in the area. Red Hook became one of Brooklyn's important manufacturing centers.

Fishing declined and shipping and shipbuilding increased through the 19th century. Storage elevators handled thousands of tons of sugar, wheat, hops, corn, and barley. During the first half of the 20th century shipping, shipbuilding, storage, and manufacturing composed the employment base of Red Hook. The neighborhood was a busy community of workers and shopkeepers. As the century progressed, industries began to leave in search of cheaper labor and more space. Containerization of ship cargoes was the final nail in Red Hook's coffin. The novel, *Last Exit to Brooklyn*, by Hubert Selby, Jr., and the 1989 film by the same name, depict Red Hook and its rough longshoremen in 1952, long after the area's prime. Matty Rich's bleak 1991 film, *Straight Out of Brooklyn*, also presents a debased neighborhood. Novels and films portrayed the brawling, raw side of Red Hook's social disorganization.

Williamsburg, Brooklyn was a pioneer in industrial enterprises. In 1848 Charles Pfizer, a German immigrant, began manufacturing chemicals in a plant on Bartlett Street. Havemeyer and Elder, a sugar refinery eventually bought by Domino, was established near the corner of South 4th Street and 1st Avenue. Pottery manufacturers produced drainpipes, cooking ware, plumbing supplies, and flowerpots. Porcelain and glassware manufacturers, iron foundries, spice mills, printing companies, ink manufacturers, woodworking shops, distilleries, breweries, an oil refinery, and America's largest glue factory (owned by Peter Cooper) huddled near the increasingly environmentally degraded river. The shoreline, which had consisted of sandy bluffs over the East River, was rapidly developed, and the early bucolic look was completely transformed by factories, mills, and warehouses. A handsome business district with several large, impressive banks built as temples of commerce developed at the intersection of Broadway and Roebling Street.

Greenpoint, Brooklyn was the most heavily industrialized neighborhood in the city. After the opening of the Erie Canal in 1825, East River commerce increased exponentially. Greenpoint's heyday of shipping and shipbuilding was the mid-19th century. It became a significant industrial center in the two decades before the Civil War. During the war it was the birthplace of the Union's celebrated ironclad vessel, the *Monitor*, which was launched on January 30, 1862. The *cheese box on a raft* gained naval distinction by engaging the South's re-outfitted ironclad, the *Virginia*, formerly the North's *Merrimack*, in an epic battle on March 9, 1862 in the watery expanse of Hampton Roads, between Hampton and Norfolk, Virginia. They fought to a draw; neither could defeat the other, but together they signaled the end of wooden warships. (Late in December 1862 the *Monitor* sank in a storm of Cape Hatteras, North Carolina. In 2002 divers lifted the remains of the vessel.) The Sneeden and Rowland Shipyard, where the *Monitor* was built from components produced by the Hecla Iron Works, also produced huge cast-iron pipes to carry drinking water from Westchester County reservoirs to Manhattan.

Greenpoint was the home of the *five black arts*: printing, pottery, gas, glass and porcelain, and iron. The name *five black arts* came from the black smoke and soot that poured out of their factory chimneys. Each of the industries needed extremely hot furnaces and coal yards dotted the landscape.

Charles Pratt founded the Astral Oil Works for high-quality kerosene refining in 1867. It was one of scores of refineries set up near the waterfront of Williamsburg, Greenpoint, and Long Island City. Crude oil was shipped to Greenpoint, refined, and then sent out to communities throughout the east coast. In 1875, Charles Pratt's Astral Oil Works merged with John D. Rockefeller's Standard Oil Company.

Greenpoint became a beehive of production. Beside the *five black arts*, it was once the home of the Schaefer Brewery, Kirsch Beverages, and Eberhard-Faber Pencil Company, corporations still extant, but doing business elsewhere. Distilleries, chemical plants, glue factories, and paint manufacturers also thrived in Greenpoint. The heavy industries began leaving in the 1920s seeking cheaper labor and more room to expand. In the years after the Second World War Greenpoint further de-industrialized as the light industries also left, frequently because of high labor costs and transportation bottlenecks. By the 1960s, shipping had been eclipsed by trucking and what little ship traffic remained in Brooklyn gravitated to newer docks in Red Hook and Sunset Park. By 1980 Greenpoint had become a residential community without a substantial industrial base.

Industry's gain was a great loss for Newtown Creek, the body of water separating the northern part of Brooklyn from Queens. The waterway, which was used in colonial times to transport agricultural products on small barges from riverside farms to Manhattan, became the repository for sludge and acids from the new industries in Greenpoint, Williamsburg, and Long Island City. Constantly dredged and widened, the channel now resembles a fetid canal rather than a creek. Fortunately, by 1980 the Sanitation Department stopped discharging raw sewage into the waterway. Today, Greenpoint sits on top of a massive sludge repository from years of poor stewardship by the companies which had routinely rid themselves of waste by pouring industrial effluent into the ground or discharging it into nearby waterways.

Brooklyn had a considerable food processing industry, which included Barricini's Chocolates, Bonomo's Taffy, Drake's Cakes, Eskimo Pies, Black Jack Gum, and Topps Bubble Gum. Local beverages from Brooklyn included Yoo-hoo Chocolate Drink, Manhattan Special Espresso Coffee Soda (produced on *Manhattan* Avenue in Greenpoint), and Dr. Brown's Sodas. Of the many sugar refineries were once located in Brooklyn, none remain. Sweet 'n Low sugar substitute and Ex-Lax (*the Chocolated Laxative*), not exactly food products, also originated in Brooklyn.

The era of heavy industry in New York City ended in the years after the First World War. Today, even light industry hangs on perilously. The city and its workforce have entered a post-industrial phase. Service industries, especially financial services, and the tourist and hospitality industry (hotels and restaurants), are the dominant engines of the economy.

CHAPTER 59
Row Houses: Brick, Brownstone, & Limestone

Since the 1960s there has been a striking revival of interest and appreciation for New York City's row houses. In response to the demolition of the beautiful and venerable Pennsylvania Station in 1965, an act of cultural barbarism carried out by its owner, the cash-starved Pennsylvania Railroad, the Landmarks Preservation Commission was established as a city agency. It immediately marked Brooklyn Heights, a neighborhood of row houses, as an *historic district* and prohibited knocking down or altering the outside of any of the district's existing buildings.

The practice of building a group of houses *in a row* originated in 18th century English Colonial New York. To save space, row houses were built next to each other and filled an entire block. That process escalated after the Commissioners' Plan in 1811 surveyed Manhattan and established a street grid. Builders were able to know exactly where to construct lines of new residences anywhere in Manhattan. By the 1840s row houses were being built in settlements in Brooklyn and Queens.

Row houses have many different styles and can be made of brick, brownstone, or limestone, or in rare cases, wood. Middaugh Street in Brooklyn Heights and Sylvan Terrace in Washington Heights are lined with wood-frame buildings dating from the 1820s and 1882 respectively. The wood houses on Middaugh Street are located between Willow and Hicks Streets, and were built at a time when wood was plentiful and simple residences were much more common than elaborate brick or stone structures. Relatively few exterior alterations have been made to this concentration of Jacksonian-period wood houses over the past 180 years. Eventually combustible exterior building materials were banned throughout New York City.

Brick row houses were the first to be built and there are many early examples left, especially in Greenwich Village and along Grand Street on the Lower East Side. Brick sizes were usually uniform except for the occasional use of narrow-gauge Roman bricks, which have a thin appearance. Patterns of brick-laying varied though most bricklayers used the *English bond* system where *stretcher* and *header* bricks alternated every row, or the *common bond* system where most bricks were laid as *stretchers* and only every five rows would a line of *headers* be added. (The *stretcher* side of the brick is the long side and the *header* side is the end side.) Brick colors ranged from dark red (the most popular) to pink, beige, and brown. Clay pits, brick works, and *terra-cotta* plants in western Staten Island along the Arthur Kill and the Kill Van Kull supplied many of the millions of bricks used in New York City's row houses. Brick row houses are sturdy but the concrete between the bricks wears down and needs periodic *re-pointing.*

Brownstones were built with soft, porous sandstone quarried in Connecticut and New Jersey. Hematite iron ore in the sandstone caused its brown coloration. The building material had been used in the 18th century but mostly for stoops and decorative lintels. Its texture was valued because it allowed easy cutting and carving. Rows of brownstones began appearing in Manhattan and Brooklyn Heights in the 1840s, and despite complaints by some people about the visual monotony of their single color they became popular. The structural drawback showed up decades later when the surfaces became so weathered that chips and flakes fell to the ground. Rather than replace the brownstone blocks, generally four to six inches thick, owners covered the façades with a layer of concrete, dyed brown. Some brownstones have endured this process repeatedly and their surfaces are as much colored cement as they are brownstone.

Blocks of limestone, also four to six inches thick, were used for limestone row houses, which comprised the most sturdy, and weathering-resistant residential building material. Many limestone and brownstone houses have rounded fronts, to gain more sunlight, expand the view from inside, and provide some architectural diversity.

The main, or *parlor floors,* of row houses were often built five to six feet above the sidewalk level to allow for working basements underneath. In an age before electricity, the cellar could be partially lighted by front and back windows. A heavy, imposing, high stoop was necessary to reach the parlor floor, and there was usually a *service entrance* directly to the basement built under the front steps. Holding the house together was a skeleton of squared wood beams and a covering of rough bricks. Today, the main wood beams in the cellar need steel braces to insure they continue to hold up the whole edifice above.

A house's individual expression is muted with row houses and must be primarily exhibited by decorations. Decorative elements often make the houses constructed later more interesting and architecturally valuable than the austere older row houses. Some, however, are termed *no-style* houses because they lack sufficient architectural merit to evoke any style. Groups of plain no-style houses, especially on Manhattan's Upper East Side, are often excluded from historic districts and deprived of landmark protection.

Middle and upper middle class row houses predominated in Greenwich Village, Chelsea, Grammercy Park, Upper East Side, Upper West Side, Harlem, Brooklyn Heights, Fort Greene, Bedford-Stuyvesant, Clinton Hill, and Park Slope. They had four or five floors and often exhibited stylish embellishments. Ornamentation in the more substantial row houses could include a half-rounded window or triangular pediment and tympanum above the door, a portico, side columns or pilasters, decorative terra-cotta or marble lintels, molding, finials, tracery, trefoils and quatrefoils, stained-glass windows, corner quoin-work, a decorative cornice, or a cast-iron railing. In the early 19th century it was seen as embarrassingly showy to decorate a row house, but as the century closed the houses with adornments and frills became increasingly accepted. In Brooklyn the most austere row houses are the early examples in Brooklyn Heights while Park Slope and especially Fort Greene, which were developed decades later, contain homes with the most ostentatious embellishment.

Much smaller row houses (two and three floors) built for workers predominated in Park Slope South, Windsor Terrace, Greenpoint, Boerum Hill, Long Island City, and Steinway. Many were unadorned or decorated only by a small amount of tracery.

The north side of 9th Street between Prospect Park West and 7th Avenue in Park Slope contains humble three and four-story abodes built for artisans and workers. Several of the houses have rounded fronts and a few have a bit of simple tracery over windows and on cornices. The building materials on those two blocks alternate between limestone, brownstone, and brick. On the north side of 49th Avenue between 5th Street and Vernon Avenue in Long Island City, Queens, is a long row of two-story proletarian row houses, simple, functional, and kept up carefully.

New York City has some outstanding examples of very old row houses that managed to survive fires and the constant frenzy of building new structures to replace the old. Many early 19th century row houses were built in the Federal style or Greek Revival style. The Edward Mooney House (now occupied by Summit Mortgage Bankers), 18 Bowery, stands at the corner of Pell Street in Chinatown. While not the oldest house in Manhattan, it is the oldest row house. It was completed in 1789, the year the United States Constitution went into effect and combines elements of the new Federal style as well as the older Georgian style popular in Great Britain. It was once part of a row of impressively grand houses built on the east end of Werpoes Hill, the high ground favored by the wealthy.

Another example of a row house stands three blocks south of Bowling Green across from the Staten Island Ferry Terminal. The rectory of the Shrine Church of St. Elizabeth Ann Bayley Seton, 7 State Street, named for Mother Seton, the first American-born Roman Catholic saint, is the only existing row house in the Wall Street area. The rectory, originally the James Watson House, was finished in 1806 and is the last of the townhouses, which formerly surrounded Bowling Green and extended south to the harbor. The house is Federal style with some Georgian style decorations.

Colonnade Row, on Lafayette Street between Astor Place and East 4th Street, was Manhattan's most elegant block of row houses. The four worn-down remnants of nine once stately four-story Greek Revival town houses stand out because their collective front is a line of magnificent Corinthian columns. Colonnade Row, where all the facing and columns are marble, was built in 1831 on LaGrange Terrace (named for the country estate of the

Marquis de Lafayette), and intended to provide elegant homes for wealthy people moving north from lower Manhattan. At different times Astors and Vanderbilts lived in Colonnade Row. Only four of the attached houses remain. The southern five were demolished in 1902 for a truck garage, a reminder of how fast New York City's neighborhoods can rise and fall.

The Merchant's House Museum at 29 East 4th Street between the Bowery and Lafayette Street near Astor Place is an 1832 Federal style building with a front entrance decorated by a semi-circle window above, and *ionic pilasters* (flat outlines of scroll columns) flanking the door. The Greek Revival style was more concerned than the Federal style about the symmetrical proportions of a building. A Greek Revival house often included a columned *portico* (broad porch) holding up a triangular *pediment*, reminiscent of an Ancient Greek temple. Pilasters, not actual columns, were added to the corners or next to the door. The Sailors' Snug Harbor buildings in Staten Island exemplify Greek Revival architecture.

Greenwich Village has many valuable blocks of row houses. The two blocks on Washington Square North, between MacDougal Street and University Place, hold many of the treasures of early 19th century Federal style and Greek Revival architecture. Most of the row houses were built in the 1830s and have suffered very little modification. The southwest corner of Greenwich Village, especially Bedford, Morton, Commerce, Barrow, and Grove Streets, are rich in well-preserved brownstone and brick row houses.

West 138th Street and West 139th Street, two blocks of Harlem called Strivers' Row, reach from Frederick Douglass Boulevard (8th Avenue) to Adam Clayton Powell, Jr. Boulevard (7th Avenue). They were constructed as the King Model Houses between 1891 and 1893. Basically Georgian architecturally, the grouping reflects different stylistic interpretations but fits together harmoniously.

In Steinway, or the eastern part of Astoria, a *company town* owned by the Steinway Piano Company was built in 1879 by its president William Steinway on 41st Street between 20th and 21st Avenues. The handsome two-story red brick attached houses represented Steinway's attempt to provide a comfortable lifestyle for his employees, as well as to control them. The small row houses decorated only by embellished eaves were served by a company trolley, company library, and company church.

Carriage houses can still be found in New York City, though without horses or carriages. The ground floors were built for horses and the carriages they pulled. The upper floor held hay and grain, and sometimes rooms for groomsmen and stable boys. Many alleys and less attractive city streets once held boarding and storage facilities for horses and carriages. At the time of the Civil War about five percent of New York families owned a non-commercial carriage, though the concentration was much higher in upper middle class neighborhoods. Many carriage houses have been demolished and replaced by private automobile parking garages and others have been converted into residences.

North of Greenwich Village's Washington Square a block of carriage houses lines Washington Mews between 5th Avenue and University Place. The mews is paved with rectangular blocks made of trap stone and its north side contains several 19th century two-story wisteria-covered carriage houses remodeled for humans in 1916. (The stucco cottages on the south side were built in 1939.) Similarly, MacDougal Alley, a nearby *cul-de-sac* of carriage houses runs parallel with Washington Square North and West 8th Street with a single opening on MacDougal Street. In Brooklyn Heights there are carriage houses north of Pierrepont Street on College Place, off Love Lane, between Henry and Hicks Streets. Just south of Remsen Street are two other Brooklyn Heights carriage house locations: Grace Court Alley, off Hicks Street, and Hunts Lane, off Henry Street.

The fundamental attraction of row houses is spatial. Limited to lots measuring 100 feet by 25 feet (or even 20 feet), space was always at a premium, and, unless a family could afford a double lot, there was no choice but to build a house from one end of the lot to the other. A small space for a coal chute and a stairway or *stoop* was left in the front, and approximately 20 feet was set aside in the back for outhouses, water cisterns, and area for hanging the clothes to dry in the summer.

There are several drawbacks to brownstones. In her autobiography, Eleanor Roosevelt recalled growing up in a brownstone on East 37th Street in the 1890s. *Our old-fashioned, brownstone house was much like all the other houses in the side streets, fairly large and comfortable, with high ceilings, a dark basement, and inadequate servants' quarters with working conditions which no one with any social conscience would tolerate today. The laundry had one little window opening on the back yard and, of course, we had no electrical light. We were modern in that we had gas!* The monotony of very similar houses was a drawback to building in rows. Often an entire city block styled with cookie-cutter precision had the look of a 19th century version of Levittown.

The interior design of most row houses was predictable. It was virtually impossible to design a floor plan other than the standard arrangement. About two feet into the ground was the cellar with kitchen and laundry facilities (Now real estate agents euphemistically call a cellar the *garden floor*.) Dark, damp, and cramped, it was where much of the unseen support work for the family was accomplished, especially food preparation and laundry.

The parlor floor, with large windows and high ceilings, was always the most elaborate because that was where guests were entertained. It contained a parlor in the front, a small music room in the center, and a dining room in the rear. Generally all three rooms had fireplaces and mirrors. Sometimes there was a small butler's pantry next to the dining room where chinaware, utensils, and table linens were kept and where prepared food came up from the kitchen in a dumb waiter. The middle room on each floor was windowless and dark.

The second floor had three bedrooms with the parents usually taking the quieter room at the rear. The other two rooms were for children. Just like in *Mary Poppins*, children under twelve usually stayed together in one room, a nursery, with their servant or nurse. The third floor rooms were used as more bedrooms for children, or, in the case of small families, as a playroom, library, or sewing room. The top floor had the smallest rooms, usually four to six, and was where the house staff lived. Servants always worked on a *live-in* basis in the 19th century.

Row houses lacked attached facilities for a horse and carriage so most horses were boarded in private facilities. A notable exception is Strivers' Row in West Harlem where a private alley reached by a narrow opening in the center of the block, leads to a string of individual carriage houses. Backyards were tiny and did not hold gardens. It was, at best, a disagreeable workplace. Row houses were sometimes later extended back to the rear lot line once plumbing and electrical technology erased the need for privies, cisterns, and outdoor clotheslines. (A few owners even built upward, adding extra floors on the roof of their row houses.)

To live in an upper middle class row house in the 19th century required several servants. The houses were not subdivided as most are today, and only one family lived in each house. The servants, usually unmarried immigrants, many from Ireland, tended to fall into two broad categories: young people who eventually got married and then left their employment, and long-time servants who stayed with their employing families for their entire lives. The servants were on call as needed around the clock and they generally worked six and a half days each week. They labored for room and board and a token salary.

There were no nursery schools, kindergartens, or daycare facilities, so each family needed a nurse to look after the children. Fireplaces needed constant tending through the colder half of the year and required the service of a separate servant. Sometimes the fireplace tender doubled as the groom and took responsibility for the horse and carriage. Laundry, cleaning, and cooking were unimaginatively labor-intensive. At least one servant was required as a laundress, two maids for cleaning, and one or two cooks for preparing meals. The supervisor of the entire staff was often the butler, who also answered the door and presided over the maids as served the family at each meal.

Row houses declined with the growing popularity of large apartment buildings, which could have all rooms on the same floor and present more creative floor plans. Apartment buildings towered above row houses and could fit scores of substantial apartments on a relatively small collection of lots. The new subway system, which opened its initial line in 1904, and the growing popularity of the automobile after the First World War, meant people of abundant economic means were able to travel far greater distances and afford much larger free standing homes. As increasing numbers of the upper middle class sold their row houses and moved to Bay Ridge, Flatbush, Forest Hills, Riverdale, and the suburbs, the old row houses were transformed into multi-family dwellings and rooming houses.

After the Second World War, newer row houses were built for the lower middle and working class population. They were constructed with poorer quality building materials and an unpleasantly conspicuous lack of architectural vision. Columns of 1960s row houses can be found in each borough. Their construction gives a bad name to architecture in many newer parts of the city. The west side of Steinway Street, between Ditmars Boulevard and 23rd Avenue, in Astoria is an example of a long, dreary stretch of three-story red brick attached houses with a garage occupying the front half of every ground floor. Each front *yard* is almost completely filled by a concrete driveway and the second floor sports a narrow balcony with crudely crafted wrought-iron grillwork. Apparently the misguided inspiration was a poor imitation of the French Quarter in New Orleans.

Some new developments build a line of connected row houses each with a separate style. The southern and western ends of Staten Island offer numerous examples of developers aping classic European architecture. The burlesque of designs grouped together generally includes diverse styles: Spanish, Tudor, Gothic, and American Colonial Revival.

Some people tired of apartment buildings and the enormous modern high rises proposed by Le Corbusier and often built by large developers. Row houses captured the *cachet* of small-scale urban habitation and are now considered by many New Yorkers to be highly desirable. Time changes perspectives, and the row house design, developed to save space by building high and completely across each lot, has, after decades of infatuation with apartment houses and the suburbs, come to represent, despite its drawbacks, a popular structure in which to pursue an elegant and romantic way of life.

CHAPTER 60
Tenements & Apartments

Scattered farmhouses of wood and fieldstone predominated in the area northeast of the city during the Dutch and English periods. Using stones quarried from nearby outcroppings was common, and a few buildings made with this basic construction material still exist. Surviving examples are St. Mary's Roman Catholic Church on Grand Street, First Chinese Presbyterian Church (formerly Northeast Dutch Reformed Church) on Market Street, and the Bialystocker Synagogue (formerly the Willett Street Methodist Church) on Willett Street.

In the early 19th century the city grew toward the northeast, along the East River, as newcomers, migrants from Upstate New York and New England, and immigrants from Europe, needed more housing. Germans composed the initial European influx. A steady stream of people from Ireland soon surpassed large-scale immigration from Germany. The newest New Yorkers had very little money and the accommodations available to them reflected their poverty.

Landlords in the area now occupied by Chinatown and the tract under the Brooklyn Bridge quickly converted their dwellings into *rookeries,* a name applied to subdivided houses, warehouses, or factories with jerrybuilt additions. Many buildings were built to be rookeries, and whole families were packed into small, cramped rooms with little or no ventilation.

The term *tenements* applied to structures built in a standard form to cash in on the rush of immigrants. In the early 19th century the typical pattern was to construct two tenement buildings (front and rear) on a standard city lot 25 x 100 feet. These were Spartan four-story buildings with four apartments on each floor. A small courtyard divided the two buildings and was the site of one or more outhouses and rainwater cisterns. Tenement life, dark and poorly ventilated, was a breeding ground for cholera, tuberculosis, typhoid, and smallpox. Reformers managed to get a number of changes ordered by state law and city ordinance shortly after the Civil War.

Legislation was first enacted in 1867, and subsequent laws were passed in 1879, 1901, and 1929. Each added a few amenities to squalid tenement life: space between front and rear buildings (just 11 feet), minimum room size (70 square feet), indoor toilets, air shafts, fire escapes, running water, electricity, and heat.

In the last two decades of the 19th century, terra-cotta and marble ornamentation produced by immigrant Italian craftsmen was used by builders to enhance buildings and assure higher rents. All but a few tenements had terra-cotta panels inserted on the *cornice* (the crown of a building) and above the entryway and windows. Some of those decorations are now treasures since there are few contemporary craftsmen capable of such work.

An example of a highly decorated tenement is the twin entrance building at 14-16 Orchard Street, near Canal Street. It is prominently trimmed with two rows of eight large molded terra-cotta *Stars of David* and surrounded by intricate flowery finials and tracery. The building exhibits elaborate oversized hooded cornices in a style, which became residential tenement *heraldry* in old New York City neighborhoods. In this case the terra-cotta molds showed religious pride that was a way for the landlord to attract Jewish tenants.

None of the earliest rookeries exists in Chinatown, though an 1824 tenement still stands at 65 Mott Street. Most tenements were built after the 1879 legislation. Manhattan had no public parks or playgrounds before Central Park opened in 1859. The Five Points (Chinatown) district desperately needed open space and recreation areas. Children were forced to play in the courtyards and narrow streets. Jacob Riis, a Danish immigrant who became a prominent photojournalist, published his award-winning *How the Other Half Lives* in 1890. He became friends with Police Commissioner Theodore Roosevelt and was able to obtain support for his pet project, tearing down two square blocks of particularly bleak slums on Mulberry Street and constructing Mulberry Bend Park. The park, now called Columbus Park, provided breathing space for the neighborhood as well as a site for recreation and relaxation.

New York City continued its expansion northward until the

vast section known as the Lower East Side was covered with tenements. Jacob Riis gained credibility among White Anglo-Saxon Protestant reformers by taking photographs of tenement squalor and successfully advocating slum clearance. While Riis' pictures seem to express sympathy, the accompanying descriptions in his book harshly chastised immigrants, blaming them for their misfortunes and suggesting that their religious, ethnic, and racial backgrounds were to blame. Riis lumped the disparate new inhabitants of the Lower East Side together as he lambasted them for their poor housing. *Hardly less aggressive than the Italian, the Russian and Polish Jew, having overrun the district between Rivington and Division Streets, easy of the Bowery, to the point of suffocation, is filling the tenements of the Old Seventh Ward to the river front, and disputing with the Italian every foot of available space in the back alleys of Mulberry Street. The two races, differing hopelessly in much, have this in common: they carry their slums with them wherever they go, if allowed to do it... Between the dull gray of the Jew, his favorite color, and the Italian red, would be seen squeezed in on the map a sharp streak of yellow, marking the narrow boundaries of Chinatown.*

Russian-born Abraham Cahan, editor of the *Jewish Daily Forward* from 1901 to 1951, portrayed the Lower East Side much differently than Danish-born Jacob Riis. Cahan had his protagonist in his vaguely autobiographical 1917 novel, *The Rise of David Levinsky,* reflect on the Lower East Side: *The great thing was that these people were better dressed than the inhabitants of my town. The poorest-looking man wore a hat (instead of a cap), a stiff collar and a necktie, and the poorest woman wore a hat or a bonnet.*

Apartments served as places to eat and sleep, but many were transformed into day-time factories as housewives and older children made contracts with factory owners to take home items (usually garments) for processing and finishing. This system of *outwork* engendered unseen child labor among the very young since every set of hands was useful in making needed money from the piecework process.

By 1890, most Germans in the Lower East Side below Houston Street had been replaced by Eastern European Jews and Italians. In 1910 the population of the Lower East Side reached 373,000. At the end of the 19th century the area had an unparalleled population density. A report issued by the Tenement House Committee in 1894 measured the population density at 986.4 people per acre, exceeding the 759.6 found in the most congested part of Bombay, India. The streets, too, were crowded, mostly with pushcarts. For immigrants unable to pay rent on a store, a pushcart was a way to try and break into retailing.

Upscale apartment buildings were first introduced in 1869 and called *French Flats* to make a connection between them and the perceived glories of Second Empire France under Napoleon III. The first *French Flats* were five-story apartments built on 18th Street between 3rd Avenue and Irving Place in Gramercy Park, Manhattan. Luxury apartment buildings were a new way to live and included elevators, doormen, basement laundries, and garbage chutes.

The Dakota Apartments, which opened in 1884, symbolized the highest level of elegance in apartment living. Built across from Central Park on Central Park West and West 72nd Street it was named to emphasize that it was so far uptown it may as well have been in the Dakota Territory. Resembling a French country *chateau*, the Dakota had many hotel-style comforts including a *concierge*. The eclectic architecture included Gothic, Romanesque, and Dutch Renaissance styles. The Dakota was built around a large interior courtyard for carriages and contained 85 suites all served by elevators. The largest suite had twenty rooms. Upscale apartments were built surrounding Central Park, overlooking Riverside Park, and along Park Avenue from 59th Street to 86th Street. (The Dakota's most famous resident was John Lennon who was assassinated in 1980 at the main entrance.)

Elevators had an immense impact on buildings in New York City. Without them it was impractical to build too high. Once Elisha Otis developed the *safety elevator* in 1852 the green light was on for skyscrapers. The public was assured that the elevator carriages would not slip and fall down the shaft. Once elevators began to be used in all new buildings the city grew vertically. As the population rose to eight million, not only Manhattan, but each of the four outer boroughs had some high-rise apartment buildings.

In the prosperous 1920s six-story elevated apartment buildings for the middle class caught on in Manhattan. Row houses and tenements were knocked down to make space for middle-income apartments. Most had no special amenities except an elevator, lobby, garbage chute, and laundry room. They were preferable to tenement walk-ups and were also constructed throughout the Bronx, Brooklyn, and Queens.

Apartment buildings on the grand avenues like Eastern Parkway and Ocean Parkway in Brooklyn, Northern Boulevard in Queens, and the Grand Concourse in the Bronx, drew people out of Manhattan with the promise of large, spacious apartments on tree-lined boulevards. Architectural designs included Art Deco, Egyptian Revival, and Tutor Revival styles. Lobbies were considered luxurious. They were large, marble-paneled spaces with tile floors that sometimes included overstuffed chairs. Tenements had no lobbies and no elevators, just narrow entryways and stairwells the width of the front door.

As space got tighter in all sections of late 20th century New York City, apartments in newly constructed and remodeled buildings got smaller. Prices became high, even in rent stabilized units. Many people who once preferred to live in Manhattan have been priced out and have sought somewhat less expensive housing in the other boroughs.

CHAPTER 61
Abolitionists & Other Reformers

Reform movements were a recurring theme in 19th century American political and social history. Abolitionism, women's rights, and temperance were the most wide-spread, but there were others including housing, medical access, clean government, election law, food purity, environmental, and industrial working conditions. The labor movement was also a reform movement. Its aims were to reduce working hours, establish safety conditions in the workplace, and increase pay. Reform is often a contentious term. The word *reform* means *to change*, but what a reform is to some, can be a terrible mistake to others.

While a variety of New Yorkers joined one or more of the reform movements, a clear profile emerged. Reformers tended to be upper middle class white Protestants. Many were not native to New York City, but had migrated from small towns and rural districts in New England and Upstate New York. They came to the city to help themselves, usually in business enterprises, but they also came to help uplift the benighted. Reformers often operated from deep-seated religious convictions about the *Manifest Destiny* of the United States and the perfectibility of mankind through the taming influence of religion. And, from a distance, they wanted to help the poor and disadvantaged. Their opponents interpreted the reformers' sense of *noblesse oblige* as self-righteous, sententious, and smug. Some of the people they wanted to help viewed them as meddling, self-appointed do-gooders.

There are many examples of this clash of values and lifestyles by those who wanted to make changes, both wealthy and poor alike. Reformers detested Tammany Hall, the largely working class political machine that helped the poor by getting them jobs and spreading about money diverted from the government. Reformers wanted to replace the political club with civil service exams as a vehicle for distributing employment. Tammany viewed the clean government reformers as naive and missing the point.

Machine politicians felt the best way to help the poor was to get them jobs quickly, and all they expected in return was loyalty at the ballot box and a modest donation to the club.

The issue of alcohol was especially divisive. Temperance movement advocates ascribed a whole list of social ills to alcoholism, and wanted to abolish liquor, wine, and beer for everyone. Working class men wanted to be able to drink beer at home or in a tavern after work. To them the temperance promoters were wild-eyed fanatics bent on destroying an important part of working class culture. In this case, the constrained Protestant outlook, often permeated by self-denial, was completely at odds with the Irish, Italian, German, and Polish Catholic lifestyles. While true in large part, this characterization is a generalization. There were some Protestants who came from cultures where responsible social drinking was acceptable, especially among the Germans and Swedes. And some Roman Catholics, especially the Catholic Total Abstinence Union, led by Fr. Theobald Matthew, opposed any use of alcohol.

A survey of some of the prominent New York City abolitionists will explain their passion for reform. Henry Ward Beecher was a nationally known abolitionist and reformer. He was pastor of Plymouth Church of the Pilgrims, the most influential house of worship in Brooklyn in the mid-19th century. A spellbinding orator who was well connected with opinion leaders throughout the country, Beecher was from a large New England family of reformers. His father, Lyman Beecher, was a distinguished Protestant theologian in Massachusetts, and his sister, Harriet Beecher Stowe, was author of *Uncle Tom's Cabin*, the popular novel exposing the horrors of slavery.

Plymouth Church and the Brooklyn Heights neighborhood had a close association with Abraham Lincoln, which began when he attended a Sunday service while seeking the presidency in the 1860 campaign. He addressed groups on two occasions at Plymouth Church during the course of the Civil War. There is a stained glass window featuring Abraham Lincoln in the back of the church and a bas-relief in the grassy courtyard featuring the 16th president. It is unique for a Christian church in the United States to have images of a political leader.

Beecher and his fellow abolitionists turned Plymouth Church into a center of agitation against slavery. He raised money to send rifles to the abolitionists in Kansas and marked them *Beecher Bibles*. He held fund raising slave auctions at Plymouth Church to fund abolitionist projects.

Politically, Beecher is hard to categorize. He was a liberal on many social and cultural issues, even supporting Darwin's ideas on evolution, but a conservative and stridently anti-labor agitator and apologist for big business on economic issues. In 1877, *The New York Times* carried a report on his Sunday, July 22 sermon castigating and mocking the labor strife rampant throughout the country that year. *It was true that $1 a day was not enough to support a man and five children, if a man would insist on smoking and drinking beer. Was not a dollar a day enough to buy bread? Water costs nothing [Laughter.] Man cannot live by bread, it is true, but the man who cannot live on bread and water is not fit to live. [Laughter.] When a man is educated away from the power of self-denial, he is falsely educated. A family may live on good bread and water in the morning, water and bread at midday, and good water and bread at night. [Continued laughter.]*

Beecher was also tinged with anti-Catholicism, a prejudice that ran through his family. His father, Lyman Beecher, had written *A Plea for the West* in 1835, a book raising the alarm that the pope was coordinating an effort to conquer and control the Mississippi Valley and the western half of North America. Henry Ward Beecher's brother, Edward, wrote a rancorous anti-Catholic book in 1855 entitled *The Papal Conspiracy Exposed*.

Beecher, who served as minister of Plymouth Church of the Pilgrims from 1847 to 1887, was discredited in the eyes of many by a widely publicized sex scandal. He was alleged to have had an affair with a prominent parishioner's wife, and though acquitted by the court, the 1874 trial unleashed a torrent of negative publicity. Beecher kept his job until he died but was diminished by six months of trial testimony.

Horace Greeley, newspaper editor and prominent reformer, was founder of the *New York Tribune*, and an activist in several reform movements. He was from a poor Massachusetts farm family that migrated to Vermont and Pennsylvania in an unsuccessful quest for a farm that could financially support them. Moving to

New York City as a young man in 1831, Greeley landed a job in a commercial printing shop.

Concerned over the plight of the poor, Greeley became a leader of *Fourierism,* a plan put forward by French writer Charles Fourier. Greeley described the philosophy in an 1843 letter to Noah Webster. *Fourier's leading inculcation is that the evils, which mainly afflict mankind are social in their nature, and to be removed only by a re-organization of society upon principles analogous to those of a joint stock company. Each community is to consist of 500 to 2,000 persons, living in a spacious edifice, cultivating a noble domain, prosecuting industry in common, but sharing the proceeds according to their capital, skill, and labor. By this means vast economies are attainable, and a guarantee of plenty, comfort and expenditures to all may be secured.*

In the 1850s Greeley repeatedly issued his famous call: ***Go west, young man, go west!*** That advice was his favorite solution to urban poverty and overcrowding. He had seen the new lands for himself. Greeley took a trip to the west in 1859 and stopped in Salt Lake City, Utah to interview Mormon leader Brigham Young. He sent a dispatch to the *New York Tribune* reporting on polygamy, at that time practiced by the Mormons (Church of Jesus Christ of Latter-day Saints). *No woman indicated by word or look her approval of polygamy. That women acquiesce in it as an ordinance of God I believe, but I am confident that there is not in all Utah a woman who does not wish that God had not ordained it.* And then in a prophetic comment, Greeley continued: *On the whole I conclude that as polygamy is a graft on the original stock of Mormonism it will be outlived by the root --- that there will be a new Revelation ere many years whereby the Saints will be admonished not to marry more than one wife.* Indeed, in 1890, Wilford Woodruff, president of the Mormon Church, under severe pressure by the United States government, received a divine revelation instructing the Mormons to give up polygamy.

Regarding the Great Plains Indians, abolitionist and reformer, Horace Greeley, said in 1859: *These people must die out --- there is no help for them. God has given this earth to those who would subdue and cultivate it, and it is vain to struggle against his righteous decree.* This was the same Biblical argument that the first wave of European settlers used to justify genocide. It is their flawed interpretation of Genesis I:26: *And God said, Let us make man in our image, after our likeness: and let them have dominion over the fish of the sea, and over the fowl of the air, and over the cattle, and over all the earth, and over every creeping thing that creepeth upon the Earth.* With great inconsistency, Greeley supported wiping out the Indians but giving African-Americans equal rights.

Carl Schurz, born in 1829 near the German city of Cologne, was an example of an immigrant who became influential in the reform movement. He was a German-American writer, statesman, brigadier general in the Union Army during the Civil War, cabinet member, and prominent leader of the Republican Party

Schurz had been a participant in the nationalist and republican uprisings in the German states in 1848 and had been an associate of Karl Marx and Frederick Engels. He fled the German states and lived in the United Kingdom, France, and Switzerland before immigrating to New York in 1852. After Schurz moved to the United States he lost contact with his former compatriots, and, while still politically progressive, he became involved in reform politics, a stance, which earned him their scorn. In an 1864 letter to Joseph Weydemeyer, German-American communist, newspaper editor, and, like Schurz, a Union Army brigadier general, Engels wrote scathingly about Schurz: *And Schurz, the valiant Schurz, who p..... under a hail of bullets, what enemies is he annihilating now?*

Once in the United States, Schurz embraced the English language and general process of Americanization. In an 1897 speech, he said: *Nobody will dispute that the German-American in America must learn English. He owes it to his new country and he owes it to himself. But it is more than folly to say that he ought, therefore, to give up the German language. I have always been in favor of sensible Americanization, but this need not mean a complete abandonment of all that is German. It means that we should adopt the best traits of American character and join them to the best traits of German character. By so doing we shall make the most valuable contribution to the American nation, to American civilization.*

Schurz quickly became involved in American politics. He met Abraham Lincoln in Illinois in 1858 and sat on the platform with the future president during several speeches, including one of the Lincoln-Douglas debates. Schurz was valuable to the Republicans because he was active in German-American fraternal groups and could help draw votes. After his election in 1860, Lincoln appointed Schurz ambassador to Spain. He returned to join the war effort and was raised to brigadier general. After the Civil War, Schurz served one term in the United States Senate (from Missouri, not New York), and was later appointed Secretary of the Interior by President Rutherford B. Hayes. Schurz had been an active abolitionist and peripherally involved in other reform movements. He made his mark as an advocate of clean government and a foe of political machines. As Secretary of the Interior he used his influence to popularize the idea of civil service reforms. Tammany Hall and the other political machines in the United States opposed using test scores to gain employment because it cut them out of the process of gaining government jobs. He battled Tammany Hall continually as head of the New York Civil Service Reform League

Schurz died in 1906. He was honored in New York City when the park between East 84th and 90th Streets between East End Avenue and the East River, where the mayor's official residence, Gracie Mansion, is located, was named Carl Schurz Park. A monument in Schurz's honor was erected on Morningside Heights overlooking Morningside Park with the inscription: *CARL SCHURZ, MDCCCIXXX - MCMVI, A DEFENDER OF LIBERTY AND A FRIEND OF HUMAN RIGHTS.*

Dr. Sylvester Graham, born in West Suffield, Connecticut in 1794, believed in the necessity of total commitment and resolute action to reform American society through individual self-improvement. To that end, Graham believed in controlling and suppressing personal passions.

He was a proto-Victorian who believed ill health (especially cholera), indolence, and general weakness came from sexual excess caused by poor diet. He was convinced that a vegetarian diet could reign in sexual impulses, which he equated with good mental and physical health. To that end he advocated total abstinence from alcohol, meat, tea, coffee, and salt. He recommended eating primarily unsifted wheat and rye flour, fruit, and vegetables. Graham thought that alcohol, meat, caffeine, salt, and condiments weakened the internal organs while at the same time inflamed sexual desire. He argued *that flesh meat is decidedly more stimulating and heating than proper vegetable food, and increases...the animal instincts and propensities.*

Graham lived in Newark, New Jersey and lectured throughout the metropolitan New York area on the Bible, personal hygiene, chastity, temperance, cold showers, hard mattresses, and loose clothing. Some of his authority concerning health came from his title, but he was not a medical doctor. He was licensed as an itinerant Presbyterian preacher at the age of thirty-two in Massachusetts without benefit of a college degree or training in a theological seminary. He had no scientific or medical education at all. Graham simply appropriated the title *doctor*. He became famous for urging Americans to eat crackers made from unsifted, whole-wheat flour, which became known as *graham crackers*. Graham, who was obsessed by sex, was often the butt of jokes. He died in 1851.

Some of the most important reformers were women. Ida Tarbell was born in a log cabin in Hatch Hollow, Pennsylvania in 1857. Her father, a small oil entrepreneur, could not compete successfully against John D. Rockefeller's Standard Oil Company and was squeezed out of the business. The lesson Tarbell learned from this experience was not to love the rich. At one point she wrote of the ideas in her youth: *There was born in me a hatred of privilege --- privilege of any sort. It was all pretty hazy to be sure, but it still was well, at fifteen, to have one definite plan based on things seen and heard, ready for a future platform of social and economic justice if I should ever awake to my need of one.*

After college, Ida Tarbell traveled in Europe before settling in New York City where she moved to Greenwich Village and lived a bohemian life while she wrote for *McClure's Magazine*. As a journalist she was never content with merely reporting the facts. Ida Tarbell dug below the surface to try to find a larger story, often a tale of conspiracy and intrigue. She had become a turn-of-the-century *muckraker*, a journalist who seeks to bring to light previously undisclosed facts and stories. She wrote articles about the Triangle Fire and the difficulties of surviving in New York's Lower East Side.

In 1901, after writing nineteen articles on John D. Rockefeller's oil monopoly, she wrote *A History of the Standard Oil Company* exposing and documenting the heavy-handed manner, which

Rockefeller used to amass his economic empire. (Earlier in her career she had written biographies on Napoleon Bonaparte and Abraham Lincoln.)

Tarbell was an investigative journalist following the reform tradition of the Progressive movement in American politics. Progressives celebrated the independence of the individual farmer and the entrepreneurial skill of the small businessmen. They disliked monopolies and their ideas fueled the trust-busting efforts of Presidents Theodore Roosevelt and William Howard Taft.

In later years she took a number of conservative positions on social issues. Tarbell questioned the merits of the feminist movement in *The Business of Being a Woman* where she extolled the value of the homemaker. In a letter to Florence Kelley, founder of the National Consumers League, she expressed why she was uncomfortable with feminism. *We seem to me in our effort to enlarge our lives and to serve society better to look too much to the way men try to do these things. That's what I mean by my ugly and unsatisfactory phrase Making a Man of Herself. I have done it myself and I have watched hundreds of other women do it. Somewhere in there something is wrong, my dear Mrs. Kelley.* Ida Tarbell infuriated the labor movement by endorsing the *Taylorism* of industrial planner of Frederick W. Taylor, known to his critics as the father of the assembly line speed-up.

Lillian Wald was born in Westport, Connecticut and grew up in Rochester, New York. In 1889 she moved to New York City to attend the New York Hospital School of Nursing. Her grandparents were German Jews who emigrated following the abortive nationalist uprisings in the German states during 1848. Lillian Wald became well known for her activities on the Lower East Side where, in 1893, she established the celebrated secular social service organization called the Henry Street Settlement House. The organization is still operating out of two very old row houses at 265 Henry Street (built in 1827) and 267 Henry Street (built in 1834). The Henry Street Settlement House also has a large modern facility at 466 Grand Street between Willett and Pitt Streets.

The *settlement house* was a place for neighborhood people, usually poor immigrants, to come to for help with medical problems, naturalization documents, legal problems, and housing issues. The settlement house provided free milk for infants, childcare,

English classes, reading material, health instructions, recreational activities, and theater productions. It was established by Lillian Wald with help from Mary Brewster, another nurse, and financed in part by wealthy German Jewish philanthropists Betty Loeb and Jacob Schiff, who were interested in aiding their less fortunate Eastern European co-religionists. (Another leading settlement house is Hull House, located in Chicago and founded by Jane Addams, who became close friends with Lillian Wald.) Not everyone applauded settlement house work. Emma Goldman represented a radical position that dismissed reformist measures and favored a socialist reconfiguring of society. She scoffed at settlement house work as *teaching the poor to eat with a fork.*

Wald was attacked from the right as well as the left. She was accused by the Daughters of the American Revolution of being a communist in 1928. She defended herself from the ultra-conservative group's charges. *I have never taken the label Communist seriously. I am not a Communist. I do not know what their definition of a Communist is. I do believe in the brotherhood of man. I do think that one's life is too little to give for bringing about better relationships between human beings, and I feel there is no human being on this earth of ours, irrespective of race, creed or nationality, who should not be included among those to be served and helped. It is a simple philosophy, after all, and not unprecedented. The activities, which have absorbed me should speak for themselves.*

In her ministration delivering medical care to the poor, Wald coined the term *public health nurse*. She founded the Visiting Nurses Association of New York City, which aimed to deliver nursing care and health education to people where they lived and worked. As public health nurses the Visiting Nurses Association taught mothers the importance of regularly bathing their children, giving them adequate milk, fresh air and exercise, and taking whatever steps were possible to protect them from scarlet fever, diphtheria, smallpox, polio, tuberculosis,

Wald was a intrepid advocate for progressive social legislation including the drive to abolish child labor, and to obtain reforms in health care, education, industry, and housing. She was a peace advocate and an activist in the American Union against Militarism.

In many ways Lillian Wald was part of the process of Americanizing immigrants, yet she found unique value to be emulated in the young Russian women she worked with through the Henry Street Settlement House and the Visiting Nurses Association. *They have a vision of a better society, where opportunity for real life will be made possible. and they have an intellectual hunger as well as a pronounced love of beauty. Life to them is incomplete that offers them nothing but soul-stultifying labor, without sufficient recompense to give them what they hunger for, and they are willing to struggle to obtain what they seek, not for themselves as individuals but for their weaker sisters who cannot struggle unaided by them. Their vitality is sapped, and many of them are old before their time, but they have gained something of the glory and beauty of life, and their spirit of sacrifice knows no limit when once they have seen the vision. The combination of this ardor with the more executive power of organization that the Americans possess would be a most effective combination. American complacency needs divine discontent, and those of us who are in the Settlement believe that we are getting a very definite contribution from these young immigrants.*

Margaret Higgins Sanger was born into a family of eleven children in Corning, New York in 1879. Her parents, of Irish Roman Catholic descent, were *freethinkers* (non-religious). After attending nursing school in White Plains she moved to New York City where she practiced her profession at Manhattan Eye and Ear Hospital and later became a visiting nurse in the Lower East Side specializing in obstetrical care. After working among poor immigrants with large families she began to advocate birth control to help women prevent unwanted pregnancies.

But if birth control involved contraceptive devices, limiting the size of families was illegal in New York State, and most other states. Sending articles, books, pamphlets or contraceptives through the United States mail violated the federal Comstock Law. Margaret Sanger vigorously challenged the laws against contraceptives and went on to become the leading American advocate for birth control.

She began her crusade in 1914 by making speeches and writing articles. Conservative politicians, Roman Catholic priests, fundamentalist Protestant ministers, and Orthodox Jewish rabbis denounced Sanger. To bolster the authority of their arguments some of her opponents quoted God's command in Genesis 1:28: *Be fruitful and multiply.* In turn, she quoted Ecclesiasticus (Sirach) in the Apocrypha 16:1: *Desire not a multitude of unprofitable children.*

Margaret Sanger was definitely at the radical left end of the reform movement's spectrum, just as Comstock and Graham would be considered at the radical right end. Margaret Sanger and her husband William joined the Socialist Party in 1913. She described her segment of the reform movement in *My Fight for Birth Control*: *In those years before the war, a new religion was spreading over the country. It had no definite name and its adherents would have been the first vociferously to deny that they were religious. This new faith was made up of the scoffers, rebels, revolutionists, anarchists, socialists of all shades from the pink tea intellectual to the dark purple lawbreaker. The term* <u>*radical*</u> *was used to cover them all. But while all were freethinkers, agnostics or atheists, they were as fanatical in their faith of the coming revolution as ever any primitive Christian was for the immediate establishment of the Kingdom of God.*

In 1916 Sanger opened the first birth control clinic in the United States in Brownsville, Brooklyn. Five thousand handbills written in English, Yiddish, and Italian were distributed on opening day. In part, they announced: *MOTHERS! Can you afford to have a large family? Do you want any more children? If not, why do you have them?* While her clinic was popular with many of the neighborhood's Jewish and Italian women, parish priests regularly denounced her. A Jewish writer charged that by opening in a predominantly Jewish neighborhood, Sanger was trying to do away with Jews. Because she also believed in the right of a woman to decide whether or not to have an abortion, doctors at the clinic gave abortion information. The actual procedure was prohibited by state law.

She wrote several books including *Married Happiness, Motherhood in Bondage, The Practice of Conception,* and *My Fight for Birth Control.* Her articles, especially *What Every Mother Should Know* and *What Every Girl Should Know* were widely reproduced as pamphlets. Over the years Sanger was jailed eight times. She welcomed the publicity that trials and imprisonment gave to her cause and accepted it as being part of the tradition of civil disobedience.

At first her efforts were aimed mostly at the poor. She viewed it from a socialist perspective as part of the liberation of the working class. During the early 1920s she changed her strategy, and while still advocating family planning among the poor, she began to appeal to middle and upper class women as well. She presented birth control to them as an issue of privacy and personal freedom. When asked about the shift in strategy, she replied: *To make club women, the women of wealth and intelligence, use their power and money and influence to obtain freedom and knowledge for the women of the poor.*

Sanger formed the American Birth Control League in 1921 to disseminate information to the public about contraception. Over the next two decades a number of birth control advocacy groups, including the American Birth Control League, merged to ultimately form Planned Parenthood of America in 1942.

Margaret Sanger traveled on speaking tours throughout the United States, the Soviet Union, Europe, and Asia. In India to address the All-India Women's Conference in 1935, she met with Mohandas Gandhi to discuss population policy. They agreed only that in many cases it was wise to limit the size of families. He viewed sexual relations as mere lust and advocated total sexual abstinence between married couples after the first few children were born. She gave sixty-four lectures and traveled ten thousand miles in India. Unlike the *mahatma*, many of her listeners were impressed with her message.

The sexual revolution of the 1920s provided increased support for her mission and the birth control pill, which was released to the general public in 1960, also changed attitudes. Increasingly people considered the efforts of Margaret Sanger and Planned Parenthood to be informative, useful, and liberating. In 1963 the sponsors council of Planned Parenthood included two former American presidents, Harry Truman and Dwight Eisenhower. Truman gave a ringing endorsement to her work. *I have come to believe that the population explosion is the world's most critical problem. In some areas it is smothering economic growth; it can threaten world peace. Millions of parents in our country --- hundreds of millions abroad --- are still denied the clear human right of choosing the number of children they will have. Governments must act and private citizens must cooperate urgently through voluntary means to secure this right for all peoples. Failure would limit the expectations of future generations to abject poverty and suffering and bring down upon us history's condemnation.* Margaret Sanger died in 1966.

Eleanor Roosevelt, wife of President Franklin Delano Roosevelt, was also a prominent reformer. She had been an activist First Lady while her husband was president from 1933 to 1945. Eleanor Roosevelt was called the *president's eyes and ears* for reporting to him how poor and working class Americans were faring while he was battling the Great Depression and the Axis Powers in the Second World War. While officially domiciled at the White House and the Hyde Park estate she shared with her husband, she spent much time in her New York City home. Eleanor Roosevelt was well known for advocating civil rights, providing public housing, expanding welfare benefits, and creating jobs for the unemployed.

The reform tradition lasted in New York until the 1970s. With the triumph of many of its social and economic goals, the end of political machines in New York, and the educational and organizational role of political parties increasingly usurped by paid political operatives and television advertisements, reform politics entered a period of abeyance.

CHAPTER 62
P.T. Barnum

P.T. Barnum's connection with New York City was limited to his numerous business ventures. He was born in Bethel, Connecticut, later kept his main residence at a mansion 20 miles away in nearby Bridgeport, and retired there. He served as a State Assemblyman in Connecticut and mayor of Bridgeport. He died in Connecticut and was buried there. But his most important work, which is his contribution to the American entertainment business, took place in Manhattan on Broadway.

Phineas Taylor Barnum was born in 1810. The Congregational Church dominated Bethel. It was a bastion of Calvinist Protestantism, which opposed amusement or frivolity. Barnum's father, a farmer with several side occupations (tailor, grocer, bartender, stable owner), died when his son was 16 years old. P.T. Barnum left home, moved to New York, and worked in a Brooklyn grocery store at Sands and Pearl Streets near the East River. He worked for Oliver Taylor, an unrelated acquaintance from Danbury, Connecticut. *In the fall of 1826, he offered me a situation as clerk in his Brooklyn store, which I accepted, and before long was entrusted with the purchasing of all goods for his store. I bought for cash entirely, going into the lower part of New York City in search of the cheapest market for groceries, often attending auctions of teas, sugars, molasses, etc., watching the sales, noting prices and buyers, and frequently combining with other grocers to bid off large lots, which we subsequently divided, giving each of us the quantity wanted at a lower rate than if the goods had passed into other hands, compelling us to pay another profit.* Barnum proved to himself he could be a sharp businessman. The next two years he operated a *porter-house* in Manhattan, a small carting agency that transported groceries locally.

He moved back to Bethel in 1828 and the following year married Charity Hallett from nearby Fairfield. For three years Barnum engaged in a flurry of occupations. He started a candy and nut store, which later added pocketknives, combs, rings, and toys to its inventory. He bought and re-sold lottery tickets, he began a houseware store, and worked as an auctioneer. In 1831 he founded a newspaper, *The Herald of Freedom,* and operated it until 1835. His publishing career included a turbulent incident where he was sued for libel by Seth Seelye, a church deacon, for accusing him of swindling an orphan by charging *usury* in managing the boy's trust fund. Barnum was found guilty in court and sentenced to pay a $100 fine and serve 60 days in prison. (Usury is the Biblical term for interest.)

Dissatisfied with the many false starts in his career, Barnum moved to Manhattan in 1835, rented a building, which his wife operated as a boarding house, and purchased half-interest in a grocery store. A trip to Philadelphia changed everything and sent him in a completely new direction.

In Philadelphia he saw an announcement in a newspaper advertising a 161-year-old black woman alleged to have been George Washington's nurse. After checking her birth certificate and borrowing half the $1,000 purchase price, he bought Joice Heth. *She was quite garrulous about her protégé, 'dear little George,' at whose birth she declared she was present, having been at the time a slave of Elizabeth Atwood, a half-sister of Augustine Washington, the father of George Washington.* Barnum rented a room in Philadelphia and exhibited her to paying customers. His handbills called her *The Greatest Natural and National Curiosity in the World.* P.T. Barnum had become a showman and a slaveholder. (Slavery was legal in New York State until 1827.)

Joice Heth died a few months later but not until Barnum had taken her to Albany, Providence, Boston, Bridgeport, and New York City to exhibit. Distributing leaflets, selling tickets, and making exaggerated claims in front of a curious and gullible audience would soon open up a new career for Barnum. (When she died, the autopsy surgeon, Dr. David I. Rogers, suggested that *she was probably not over eighty.*)

In his autobiography, P.T. Barnum wrote about his commercial epiphany: *At the outset of my career I saw that everything depended on getting the people to think, and talk, and become curious and excited over and about the 'rare spectacle'. Accordingly, posters, transparencies, advertisements, newspaper paragraphs --- all calculated to extort attention*

--- *were employed, regardless of expense.* On another occasion Barnum wrote: *I thoroughly understood the art of advertising...*

After Heth's death in 1835, Barnum engaged the services of Signor Antonio, a juggler, who balanced swirling plates on the ends of sticks balanced on his hands, feet, and nose. For five years Barnum sponsored variety acts, musicals, comedies, and black-face minstrel shows. (In between productions he sold Bibles door to door.) Sometimes the shows were taken on the road and other times they were kept in the city, usually in bars and playhouses on the Bowery.

Minstrel shows were popularized in the North partly through the efforts of P.T. Barnum. The white singers and dancers would paint their faces black, dress in excessively colorful costumes, put on skits, and sing denigrating and racist songs to the accompaniment of a banjo. *Old Zip Coon,* and *Jimmy Crack Corn* were favorites. The point was to show blacks as fun-loving, lazy, ignorant slaves to the delight of the prejudiced lower class white audiences.

Barnum alternatively traveled and stayed in New York adding curiosities to his show until 1841 when he bought Scudder's American Museum, a failing exhibition hall for oddities. After the purchase, Barnum dropped the name Scudder's. The imposing building was in Lower Manhattan on the corner of Broadway and Ann Street. At the time, New York City's theater district was centered on Ann Street. The American Museum was across from St. Paul's Chapel, around the corner from Park Row, where most newspaper offices were located, and one hundred yards from City Hall. Matthew Brady had his famous *daguerreotype* shop (an early form of photography) a half-block away. Brady took many pictures of Barnum's exhibits and helped popularize the Great Showman. The most elegant hotel in the city, the Astor House, had been built across the street on the same intersection in 1835. The American Museum's location was excellent.

What Scudder's had lacked was extravagant promises, constantly changing exhibits, aggressive promotion, and vision. P.T. Barnum made the difference. He was the perfect visionary huckster who knew what the common people wanted to see and gave it to them with great pizzazz. Astonishing the public became Barnum's lifelong calling. *The American Museum was the ladder by which I rose to fortune.*

Barnum understood lowbrow mass culture and scoured the earth in search of human and animal oddities to display. He claimed high culture for himself, which may have been part of his dapper charm: *I myself relished a higher grade of amusement, and I was a frequent attendant at the opera, first-class concerts, lectures, and the like; but I worked for the million, and I knew the only way to make a million from my patrons was to give them abundant and wholesome attractions for a small sum of money.* The American Museum was always the anchor of his business empire, but he also sponsored traveling sideshows and exhibitions, and founded the Barnum Circus, one of the predecessors of today's Ringling Brothers Barnum & Bailey Circus. In all his dealings he was adept at separating the curious and gullible from their money.

In the days before movies and television, when photography was just beginning, and the world seemed to be shrinking because of the telegraph, steamships, and railroads, people were learning about the earth's great varieties of plants and animals, and the vast differences in human cultures. They wanted more. At the same time New York City's population was surging because of industrialization, new commerce facilitated by the Erie Canal, and European immigration. It went from 312,000 people in 1840 to 814,000 in 1860. Many newcomers were from isolated farms and villages in upstate New York, New England, or Europe and were easily astonished.

The amenities offered by the American Museum were intended to make customers feel important. The handsome five-story building was kept clean and decorated with flags and posters. It had a lecture hall and a rooftop restaurant. Lectures were given on scientific, technological, and naturalist topics, all big attention-getters in the 19th century. Most of the building was devoted to small stages and cases exhibiting oddities. Admission price was usually 25 cents, not cheap, but within range of the working class. It was about the price of a lunch.

By today's standards, many of P.T. Barnum's exhibits would violate every sense of decency and ethics. But not all of his exhibits were in poor taste. Ventriloquists, jugglers, snake charmers, pantomime, a dog who could operate a modern knitting machine, trained chickens and fleas, a collection of medieval armor, enactments of scenes from the Bible, taxidermy (stuffed animals), and animated dioramas showing the Creation, Circus Maximus, Christian Martyrs (from a novel by Harriet Beecher Stowe), Fall of Rome, and the Burning of Moscow were harmless entertainment. Even the *Fejee Mermaid*, an embalmed fish with an ape's head supposedly from Fiji was too ludicrous to take seriously. But many human specimens were cruel.

Human curiosities sold tickets and Barnum sought out every abnormality of nature and every type of disability to put on a stage or in a case. He always exhibited an obese child such as the *Carolina Fat Boy* or the *Great Wisconsin Boy* or the *Highland Mammoth Boys*, three brothers supposedly from Scotland. Vantile Mack, a 257-pound seven-year-old was a great hit. He used many overweight adults in his shows. Barnum also featured *Living Skeletons* like 54-pound adult, Alexander Montarg, and 46-pound, 5-foot-5-inch tall Isaac Sprague.

In 1842, Barnum secured the services of four-year-old Charles Stratton, a midget, from his embarrassed father, a Connecticut carpenter for $12 per month including room and board for the boy and his mother. At 2-feet-1-inch and weighing 15-pounds, Charles was renamed *Tom Thumb* and eventually called *General Tom Thumb*. He was an enormous draw and regularly performed for audiences by singing or reading lines from plays. He was often dressed as Napoleon including on European tours where he met Queen Victoria of England, King Louis-Philippe of France, King Leopold of Belgium, King Victor Emmanuel of Italy, and Pope Pius IX. In his Napoleon costume he met the Duke of Wellington who had actually defeated Emperor Napoleon at the Battle of Waterloo in 1815.

Along with *Commodore Nutt*, another midget, *Tom Thumb* was taken to meet President Abraham Lincoln and his entire Cabinet in the White House in 1862. P.T. Barnum related some of the banter between Lincoln and Commodore Nutt in the room where the Cabinet was seated: *Mr. Lincoln then bent down his long, lank body, and taking Nutt by the hand, he said: 'Commodore, permit me to give you a parting word of advice. When you are in command of your fleet, if you find yourself in danger of being taken prisoner, I advise you to wade ashore.' The Commodore found the laugh was against him, but placing himself at the side of the President, and gradually raising his eyes up the whole length of Mr. Lincoln's long legs, he replied: 'I guess, Mr. President, you could do better than I could.'*

Chang and Eng, the *Siamese Twins*, were hired from their home in Bangkok, Thailand and exhibited in Europe before Barnum hired them. Connected by a thick five-inch ligament in their lower chests, they shared the same liver and blood circulation. They were one of the American Museum's most popular attractions.

To add to the sense of freakishness, Barnum arranged marriages for the *Siamese Twins* to Sarah and Adelaide Yates. Chang and Adelaide had ten children, and Eng and Sarah had twelve. *General Tom Thumb* was married to the *Queen of Beauty*, 32-inch-tall Lavinia Warren Bump. P.T. Barnum publicized each wedding with vigor. After the 1863 wedding of Stratton and Bump at Grace Church in Greenwich Village, a reception for 2,000 guests was held at the Metropolitan Hotel.

Madame Josephine Cloffulia of Switzerland had 5-inch whiskers and was exhibited as the *Bearded Lady*. Annie Jones, a small child with facial hair, was shown as the *Bearded Girl*. He featured an *Albino Lady* for display. *Living Aztec Children from the Lost City of Iximaya*, Maximo and Bartola, were probably retarded dwarfs from Central America. The seven-foot-tall *Giantess of Nova Scotia*, Anna Swan, and seven-foot-eight-inch-high *Belgian Giant*, Monsieur Bihin, were among the displayed giants. *Jo-Jo the Dog-Faced Boy* was a 16-year-old Russian, Feodor Jeftichew, with hair growing all over his face. Anna Eliza Leak, who was born without arms, was displayed doing tasks with her feet and toes. Charles Tripp, an armless Canadian, excelled in neat penmanship and paper cutting using his toes. Hoomio and Iola, mentally limited *microcephalic* (small headed) children from Ohio, were passed off as *Wild Australian Children* who formed the missing link between humans and monkeys.

Native Americans captivated the fantasies of Easterners and Barnum responded by exhibiting individual Indians as well as groups. Exhibiting several Indians who purported to be chiefs, Barnum would tell the audience of their bloodthirsty character. *This little Indian, ladies and gentlemen, is Yellow Bear, chief of the Kio-*

was. He has killed, no doubt, scores of white persons, and he is probably the meanest, black-hearted rascal that lives in the Far West. Barnum told the audience that he could speak freely because the Indian did not know English.

Rare beasts infatuated audiences so Barnum exhibited tropical fish, various apes, giraffes, and elephants. He brought over a rhinoceros (which he called a unicorn) and even a small whale. In 1843 he bought a herd of young buffalo and staged a roundup, a *Grand Buffalo Hunt,* on a racecourse in Hoboken, New Jersey. Barnum chartered ferries to take the crowds across the Hudson River. In this way he cashed in on the *mystique of the West* to curious New Yorkers. The most famous animal exhibit and circus performer was Jumbo the Elephant, twelve feet tall at his shoulders and weighing 13,000 pounds.

In a spasm of good taste, P.T. Barnum sponsored a series of performances by Jenny Lind, the *Swedish Nightingale,* at Castle Garden at the Battery in 1850. *I then began to prepare the public mind, through the newspapers, for the reception of the great songstress.* The task was not difficult since the young Swedish singer already had a tremendous reputation in Europe. Frédéric Chopin, Hector Berlioz, and Richard Wagner had praised Jenny Lind. As *impresario,* P.T. Barnum gave her access to American music lovers. He rented Castle Garden, the covered circular brownstone fort, formerly Castle Clinton or Fort Clinton, and renovated it for Jenny Lind's performances. She sang and received accolades at each performance. Barnum knew how to sell accessories: *We had Jenny Lind gloves, Jenny Lind bonnets, Jenny Lind riding-hats, Jenny Lind shawls, mantillas, robes, chairs, sofas, pianos, --- in fact, everything was Jenny Lind.* Afterwards he took her on a national tour to Philadelphia, Boston, Baltimore, Washington, D.C., St. Louis, Cincinnati, New Orleans, Memphis, and even a performance in Havana, Cuba. P.T. Barnum sold one thousand tickets the first night for $10,141. In 35 concerts over a nine-month period at Castle Garden, ticket sales reached $282,216. Together, the entire concert series was enormously profitable: Jenny Lind grossed $176,675 and Barnum grossed $535,486.

P.T. Barnum's later years were increasingly occupied by his circus, lectures against the evils of alcohol and prostitution, and politics. He was a Republican and became involved in politics, not from New York City, but from his voting residence in Connecticut. In 1865 he was elected to the Connecticut General Assembly. In 1875 he was elected mayor of Bridgeport. He crusaded against saloons and prostitution and supported lower utility rates, a better water supply system, and public baths. In 1888, at age 78, he tried unsuccessfully to win the Republican nomination for the Presidency. Instead, it went to Benjamin Harrison who defeated the incumbent Grover Cleveland, but was, in turn, defeated by Cleveland in 1892.

P.T. Barnum died in 1891. He was a great showman and the first American to use advertising to sell entertainment on a massive scale. Some of what he did was shameful, though he has to be seen in terms of the sensibilities of his time, which were very different than today.

CHAPTER 63
Antonio Meucci & Giuseppe Garibaldi

Revolutionaries George Washington and Giuseppe Garibaldi are featured prominently in Washington Square Park. A white marble memorial arch with two statues, one as general and the other as president, honors Washington. A triumphal likeness of Giuseppe Garibaldi pulling his sword from its scabbard stands high on a pedestal just east of the center of the square in Greenwich Village.

Giuseppe Garibaldi was a colorful figure, born in Nice, who became intensely involved in revolutionary movements in Italy, Switzerland, France, Argentina, Uruguay, and Brazil. He was a passionate and eloquent internationalist and fought with republican forces wherever they clashed with monarchs or dictators. Most of all, Garibaldi was committed to the unification of Italy. Before 1861 Italy was not a country but a peninsula with several independent kingdoms. Austria, Spain, and France controlled some regions. The pope was the ruler of Rome and the Papal States in central Italy. Garibaldi and other Italian patriots organized military insurrections to unify Italy. Some nationalists like Garibaldi wanted to establish a republic, while others wanted a monarchy.

Garibaldi's connection with New York City is that he lived on and off in Staten Island from 1850 to 1854. He spent part of his exile with his friend Antonio Meucci, who rented a simple Gothic-style frame cottage in Rosebank. They passed time talking politics, hunting, and fishing. To make ends meet they produced candles on the property. Garibaldi returned to Europe to pursue his political goals.

In 1860 Garibaldi and a force of 1,070 republican revolutionaries were given passage on two old British paddle steamers to Marsala, Sicily. (The British hoped an independent Italy would ally with them.) Garibaldi quickly added thousands to his army and led them through Sicily, across the Straits of Messina, and up the boot of the Italian peninsula. His forces fought against regional royalty, nobility, and the temporal holdings of the Roman Catholic Church in Sicily, Calabria, Basilicata, and Campania, the southern sector of Italy, during the successful struggle for unity.

Approaching Rome, they converged with forces led by fellow republican Giuseppe Mazzini, and monarchist prime minister of Piedmont, Count Camillo di Cavour. The result was a political compromise and the establishment in 1861 of a unified Kingdom of Italy with its capital in Turin. The King of Piedmont, Victor Emanuel II, became King of Italy. (Turin was Italy's capital from 1861 until 1865 when the government moved to Florence, and finally to Rome in 1871.)

In 1870, despite the bitter protests of Pope Pius IX, Rome was annexed to Italy, which was then effectively united and the capital was moved to Rome. The pope retreated to the 101-acre Vatican City, a neighborhood in Rome and site of St. Peter's Basilica, which was recognized by most countries as a separate religious monarchy.

Garibaldi, well known throughout the world, had many admirers in New York. Italians in the United States lionized Garibaldi as they did Christopher Columbus. The local Italian community, many who lived in the southwest section of Greenwich Village, raised money to place his statue in Washington Square Park.

After the deaths of Garibaldi in 1882 and Meucci in 1889, their partisans transformed the house in Rosebank into an unofficial political and ethnic shrine. The Garibaldi Society of Staten Island bought it in 1906. They built a large white structure, very much like an ancient Roman temple, over and around the cottage. Ownership of the shrine passed to the National Order Sons of Italy in 1919. The bizarre wood and stucco protective edifice was finally dismantled in 1956 but the modest four-room house, remained a museum dedicated to both Garibaldi and Meucci. Some of the flamboyant revolutionary's personal effects are on display including one of his signature red shirts, a sword, and some books.

The Garibaldi-Meucci House Museum, at the corner of Tompkins and Chestnut Avenues in Rosebank, is especially interested in telling the story of the less known Meucci. He was a Florentine who had lived in Cuba before immigrating to the United States in

1850. In Havana he had been the chief mechanic at one of the city's opera houses for 15 years. After relocating to Staten Island he had several business ventures including electroplating sword hilts for the Spanish army, making candle molds, and manufacturing paper. He invented the paraffin wax candle.

Meucci also invented the telephone, which he called *teletrofono,* obtained a patent from the United States government in 1871, but was unable to improve or market it. Though skilled in science and technology he never learned to speak English and had a difficult time navigating American culture. He claimed he had been swindled by lawyers and investors, and especially by Alexander Graham Bell.

Meucci was also plagued by bad luck. In 1864 he had survived a powerful explosion on a steam-operated Staten Island Ferry and was hospitalized in Manhattan for several weeks. Destitute, his wife sold his original *teletrofono* prototype and all his working models for $6 to a scrap dealer. Long after Garibaldi had returned to Italy, poverty and illness prevented Meucci from renewing his patent in 1873. Bell took out a patent on a strikingly similar mechanism in 1876.

A short film at the Garibaldi-Meucci House Museum relates the story and points to the greed and duplicity of Bell. In the side yard is an oven for heating candle wax and the front yard features a large bronze bust of Meucci. Interred at the base of the monument are his ashes.

Before the idea of multiculturalism gained widespread popularity, immigrant groups often felt a need to spotlight the accomplishments of their star achievers in politics, music, literature, science, technology, sports, law, education, and entertainment. Various ethnic groups erected many of the statues in New York City to make a positive statement about their homelands and their fellow countrymen. The Garibaldi-Meucci House Museum itself, like the Ellis Island National Monument, is part of the history of immigrant groups seeking acceptance and integration.

CHAPTER 64
John Hughes, Roman Catholic Archbishop

Born in 1797 to a family of poor tenant farmers in Ireland, John Joseph Hughes immigrated to the United States at age 20, driven by grinding poverty and the unrelenting discrimination against Irish Catholics by the English Protestant overlords. He landed in Baltimore, briefly worked on a plantation as a slave overseer, later relocating to Pennsylvania where he earned a livelihood as a day laborer and gardener. He enrolled at Mount St. Mary's Seminary in rural Maryland in 1819. At the time the seminary was just a collection of rough log cabins. Hughes earned his room, board, and tuition as gardener for the school and overseer for the seminary's slaves. He was ordained a priest in 1826. Later, John DuBois, the French priest who was president of Mount St. Mary's Seminary, was installed as Bishop of New York. Eventually John Hughes went to New York to assist him.

From the start, Hughes found Protestants irritating. They insisted the United States was a Protestant country. Most Protestants and some Catholics did not think the hierarchical nature (graded ranks and positions) of the Roman Catholic religion could fit into the democratic political framework of the United States. He also saw as his mission the task of helping poor immigrants who were struggling in their new country.

Hughes took over the day-to-day leadership operations of the Catholic Church in 1838 when Bishop DuBois, had a stroke. John Hughes was appointed bishop of the New York Diocese in 1842, archbishop in 1851, and served tirelessly until his death in 1864. (A *diocese* is a unit of church government. It was used as an administrative designation in Ancient Rome. Presently, the New York Archdiocese of the Roman Catholic Church is composed of Manhattan, Staten Island, the Bronx, and seven upstate counties. The Brooklyn Diocese was separated from the New York Diocese in 1853 and is made up of Brooklyn and Queens.)

Shortly after he was enthroned bishop, the Irish Potato Famine (or Great Hunger) became one of the defining tragedies of the age. It complicated Hughes' tenure but gave him the possibility for greatness, to which he rose admirably.

Two million Irish fled to the United States in the next fifteen years, many to New York City. They lived in frightful poverty and became the city's underclass. The poorer Irish seemed stuck in a condition of overcrowding, ignorance, unemployment, alcoholism, violence, prostitution, child abandonment, gang warfare, and street crime. In the two decades before the Civil War more than half the people arrested in New York City were Irish. They filled the prisons; the police vans that picked them up were called *paddy wagons*. A street fight was known as a *donnybrook* (after the Irish town Donnybrook), and iron bars in ground floor residential windows were called *Irish bars*. The appalling condition of the impoverished Irish fed a backlash of anti-foreignism and anti-Catholicism.

Anti-foreignism (or *nativism*) existed before the arrival of the Irish and had been aimed at other groups, especially Germans and French Canadians. Fierce anti-Irish sentiments combined with anti-Catholic bigotry physically threatened the minority Catholic community in New York City. Bishop Hughes was energized by the responsibilities of his office and vigorously defended the Roman Catholic Church. His combative nature and the way he signed his name earned him the nickname *Dagger John*. He signed his name with a cross in front of it, which is usual for bishops, but John Hughes made the cross look like a sharp dagger. He wanted everyone to know that he meant business.

He defended the Irish, but he also preached strongly, or *evangelized*, to Irish immigrants about personal responsibility, discipline, hard work, and religious faith. Bishop Hughes preached against a whole list of sins. He also promoted the work of the Society of St. Vincent de Paul whose members, clergy and laity, collected food and clothing for the poor, visited prison inmates, organized youth groups, and set up reading and writing workshops. He nurtured the activities of the New York Foundling Hospital, a Roman Catholic institution operated by the Sisters of Charity of

Saint Vincent de Paul. The Foundling Hospital cared for *foundlings* and tried to place them in adoptive homes.

Bishop Hughes supported the temperance activities (abstinence from alcohol) of Fr. Felix Varela, a Cuban immigrant working in an Irish parish (Transfiguration Church on Mott Street), and Fr. Theobald Matthew, Irish immigrant and leader of the national anti-alcohol group, the Catholic Total Abstinence Union of America, based in Philadelphia.

Anti-Catholic feelings erupted periodically. In 1806 a disrespectful mob of Protestants had harassed Catholics worshipping at St. Peter's Church (Barclay Street) on Christmas Eve. As they fled, Protestants pelted the congregants with snowballs. In 1831 anti-Catholics burned St. Mary's Church on Grand Street in the Lower East Side.

Pope's Day attacks on Catholics were commonplace. Pope's Day (November 5th) was the Americanized version of England's Guy Fawkes's Day, a popular holiday to celebrate the failure of the Catholic attempt to blow up Parliament in 1605. New Yorkers traditionally celebrated it with public fireworks, torch light parades, and anti-Catholic effigy processions, featuring, of course, the pope, whose effigy was thrown into a roaring bonfire. In the 1790s nativists added straw effigies of St. Patrick in order to insult the Irish.

Though the United States economy needed immigrants to solve the chronic shortage of labor, the mood across the country was frequently anti-immigrant. The Alien and Sedition Acts, sponsored by President John Adams against radical French Revolutionary ideas and people, had the effect of stirring up anti-immigrant feelings. Increased immigration from Catholic areas in Europe (Ireland and southern Germany) stoked the fires of hate.

During anti-Catholic riots in 1844, Bishop Hughes recruited three thousand armed men to guard Catholic churches. He had no faith that the city government would protect Catholic property and warned the authorities: *If a single Catholic Church is burned in New York, the city will become a second Moscow.* (The Moscow reference drew attention to the fate of the Russian capital during the Napoleonic invasion.) At a meeting with Mayor Robert Morris, Hughes was asked: *Are you afraid that some of your churches will be burned? No sir,* Hughes responded, *but I am afraid that some of yours will be burned. We can protect our own. I come to warn you for your own good.* No more churches were burned.

Secret societies of nativists against a perceived *alien menace* proliferated in Manhattan and Brooklyn, areas where increasing numbers of Catholics were settling. Members of the Supreme Order of the Star-Spangled Banner, it appeared, were told to answer *I know nothing* when questioned about their nativist group. The *Know Nothings* became the nickname of the American Party, organized on a nation-wide scale to oppose immigrants and Catholics. Know Nothings went on an Anti-Catholic rampage in Brooklyn in the summer of 1854. Irish Catholics fought back and the mayor of Brooklyn had to call for the National Guard to quell the disturbance. The *Know Nothings* scored several victories in the fall elections. Together with Prohibitionists and Whigs, *Know Nothings* controlled the City Council. By 1855 the majority of New Yorkers were foreign-born, many of them Catholics, which gave the nativists a sense of urgency and led them to increasingly venomous attacks on immigrants.

Nativists were prejudiced against anyone who was not a white Protestant. Some nativists expressed the political fear that Catholics would undermine democratic institutions in the American republic by answering to the pope in Rome. That point of view had many followers. The pope, Pius IX, gave Protestants much ammunition. He was pope from 1846 until 1878, roughly the same time John Hughes was bishop in New York.

Pope Pius IX inspired many anti-Catholic political cartoons including some from the sharp pen of the famous New Yorker artist Thomas Nast. The pope had opposed the unification of Italy, especially since the newly unified Italian kingdom included the Papal States and the city of Rome, areas where he ruled as monarch. When Italy's new King Victor Emmanuel I held a *plebiscite* (election) in 1870 on the incorporation of Rome into Italy as the new capital, it won 153,681 to 1,507 in Rome. Pius retreated to the 108-acre Vatican neighborhood and church center as a self-styled prisoner. (Since 1861 the capital of Italy had been first in Turin then in Florence.) The pope lashed out at the Italian state, calling on Italians to boycott the new Italian government. But in 1864, Pius had also opposed democracy and the free press, and claimed control of all science, culture, and education for the Roman Catholic Church. When he composed the *Syllabus of Errors* in his encyclical, *Quanta Cura*, he attacked *progress, liberalism, and modern science.*

Pope Pius IX rejected the idea of freedom of religion for other faiths. And he proclaimed complete independence of the Roman Church from any government controls. Pius signed an 1851 Concordat (treaty) with Isabella II of Spain and a similar agreement in 1855 with Austria's Franz Josef opposing religious rights for anyone except Catholics. His opposition to democracy, republicanism, and freedom of religion provoked adverse reaction in many countries.

Pius convened the Vatican Council in 1870 where he proclaimed the dogma (basic church teaching) of *papal infallibility* as well as the universal episcopacy (supremacy in church government) of the Bishop of Rome, giving him *ordinary* (routine, or basic) jurisdiction over every diocese in the world. In the United States, the pope's opposition to public schools and the social work of Protestant benevolent associations intensified nativist sentiments and anti-immigrant hostility.

Most Roman Catholics, while loyal to their church, ignored the pope's attacks on democratic government and public schools. Priests in the United States downplayed Rome's stand against republicanism. At any rate, the 1929 Concordat of Rome ended the Catholic Church policy against the republican form of government.

Other religious and ethnic groups that had come under attack in the United States also formed various fraternal and mutual aid societies to protect themselves against bigotry and discrimination. The *B'nai Brith* (Sons of the Covenant), a Jewish group, was formed in 1843 at Sinsheimer's Saloon on Essex Street in the Lower East Side, in part to counter nativism. (An affiliate, the Anti-Defamation League, was formed in 1913 to concentrate on combating negative stereotypes of Jews.) The Ancient Order of Hibernians, an Irish group, founded at St. James' Church in what is now Chinatown, was formed in 1836 to protect church buildings, priests, and nuns, and to guard against anti-Catholic disruptions during Mass. The Sons of Italy, formed on Grand Street in Little Italy in

1905, aimed at protecting Italian interests. Blacks organized the National Association for the Advancement of Colored People after a series of meetings beginning in New York in 1909. The purpose was to fight racial injustice by legislative, judicial, and educational methods.

Many other issues came to the fore during the time of Archbishop Hughes. He embarked on a vigorous fund-raising campaign in New York City to reduce serious parish indebtedness. He ended *trusteeism* in Catholic churches in New York City. That was when parish members assumed control of church property, made policy, and appointed the priests. Hughes opposed the Public School Society because it taught anti-Catholic history and literature, and scriptural readings from the King James translation of the Bible, a Protestant translation. He said he would settle for tax money for parochial (church sponsored) schools. When his request was refused he set about organizing a vast Roman Catholic school system.

The secession of the Confederate States in 1861 presented more difficult choices for Archbishop Hughes. Despite his stint as a slave overseer, he disapproved of slavery. Yet he opposed both slavery *and* abolitionism. There were political pressures on him from both sides. The Catholic Church had opposed slavery since Pope Gregory XVI condemned it in 1838. But Hughes wrote an insulting comment in the *Metropolitan Record,* a newspaper that covered church politics. He described the supposed terrors of African society and took the position that slavery had liberated blacks from their native continent. He wrote: *We of course believe that no genuine Christian, no decent man --- would be engaged in this kind of business; still, we cannot discover the crime, even of the slaver, in snatching them from the butcheries of their native land.*

Archbishop Hughes also described slavery as a sickness, but went on to waffle some more in another statement. *There are in the southern states four millions of slaves. Abolish slavery all at once and what is to become of them? What is to become of their masters? What is to become of those articles which are the produce of their toil and which Europe so much needs? The abolition party in North America makes but little account of this.*

Hughes disliked the abolitionists intensely. He said they were *not authentic.* Mostly Protestant, many abolitionists were stridently anti-Catholic and had openly questioned the patriotism of Roman Catholics. He also had sympathy for Irish day laborers because they feared competition from newly freed blacks. In fact, in 1863 a shipping company brought in free blacks as strikebreakers to destroy a strike by predominantly Irish dockworkers. When President Abraham Lincoln began enforcing Civil War conscription (the draft), a provision was included that a draftee could buy a replacement by paying the federal government $300. Impoverished Irish workers were outraged and a riot exploded in New York City. The enraged crowd lynched eleven black men and burned the Colored Orphan Asylum during the Draft Riots. Lincoln sent five Union Army regiments from Gettysburg and 105 rioters were shot dead. Numerous buildings were burned during the street fighting.

When asked by city officials to calm the rioters, Hughes balked. During nativist attacks on their churches Catholics had to defend themselves with no help from the police. Now the civil authorities were asking him to calm the situation, a task that they had been unwilling to perform in the past. Nonetheless, he complied.

Through the turmoil of the period, he managed to sponsor an enormous building campaign. He raised money to construct new churches, schools, and cemeteries. By the end of John Hughes's life the archdiocese had 61 churches, 43 schools, and three cemeteries: Holy Cross in East Flatbush, Brooklyn, and Calvary and Mount Olivet in Maspeth, Queens.

Finally, Archbishop Hughes began the construction of the new St. Patrick's Cathedral, a grand Gothic structure on the east side of 5th Avenue between East 50th and 51st Streets. It was completed in 1879, fifteen years after his death. It is an important stop for the participants of the annual St. Patrick's Day Parade each year on March 17th. (The walled former St. Patrick's Cathedral on Mulberry Street just south of Houston Street became Old St. Patrick's Cathedral and was demoted to a parish church.)

When John Hughes died in 1864, the City Council, reflecting enormous changes in New York during two decades, ordered all municipal offices closed and the flags flown at half-mast. Over 100,000 people gathered outside St. Patrick's Cathedral for his funeral. He is buried in the cathedral's vault.

Within two generations the Irish newcomers had entered the American mainstream. Already in 1890, one-third of the city's teachers were Irish, and the descendants of those who fled impoverished Ireland had achieved important positions in the priesthood, business, the professions, civil service (especially police and firefighters), and politics. Nativism also abated with Rome modifying its political positions and non-Catholic Americans becoming more open to a multi-cultural society. In 1961, John Fitzgerald Kennedy, a Roman Catholic from an Irish family in Massachusetts, became president of the United States.

CHAPTER 65
Raising New York Fighting Units for the Civil War

There were three primary ways that combat groups were organized in the North during the Civil War (1861-1865). Many men were organized into battle units by the federal government itself. Soldiers were either recruited or drafted into the Army or Navy. States and individuals could also raise brigades, regiments, battalions, or companies and then charter the units and place them under the leadership of the War Department.

The idea of a decentralized recruiting system came from colonial times and is referenced in the Second Amendment to the U.S. Constitution as *a well regulated militia.* Each state raised units through recruitment. States also set the rules and procedures for individuals or groups that raised fighting units. While the process had a populist ring to it, the money-saving aspect was paramount. The negative factor was that only the rich could afford to raise units because the sponsors were responsible for paying salaries, feeding, clothing, arming, and transporting their soldiers. Recruitment standards were lax and uneven and medical exams were cursory.

Some of the groups that raised units and chose the colonels or captains to lead them were ethnic organizations. Germans organized militia units based on a shared background from a region in Germany, occupation, or sponsored by a *verein* (society, political club, or even a saloon). There were militia units representing mechanics, bakers, and tailors. German examples were the New Yorker Sozialistischen Turnverein, the DeKalb Regiment, and the Steuben Guard that formed regiments to fight for the Union. There was also a Polish Legion and the Pulaski Cadets; the Garibaldi Guard was composed mostly of Italians; the kilt-wearing 79th Regiment was Scots; the 55th Regiment was French. The 69th Regiment was almost entirely Irish as were seven other regiments. The

Fighting 69th and the other Irish regiments were commanded as a brigade by Brigadier General Thomas F. Meagher, Irish nationalist who the British had once exiled to Tasmania. Bowery thugs from the Dead Rabbits gang were rumored to dominate New York's 6th Regiment. The Committee for Colored Volunteers sponsored the 20th United States Colored Regiment.

Tammany Hall, the powerful Democratic club with a prepon derance of Irish members, initially opposed to the Civil War, but eventually sent the 42nd Regiment to fight for the Union. Mayor Fernando Wood, a Democrat opposed to Tammany Hall, organized the 40th Regiment, called the Mozart Regiment, named for the music hall at Broadway and Bond Street where Wood's supporters met. (Wood had originally opposed the war and called for New York City's secession from the United States.) The Union League Club of New York was established in 1863 as a political and social group by Republican abolitionists during the Civil War. It funded the Committee for Colored Volunteers that sponsored the 20th United States Colored Regiment.

Even some religious groups were involved in organizing units to fight against slavery. Many Quakers, who normally oppose war, dropped their opposition to the Civil War and helped raise fighting units because they felt strongly that slavery must be ended. When the Civil War began the militant abolitionist minister Henry Ward Beecher led his Brooklyn congregation, Plymouth Church of the Pilgrims, in raising money to equip and support a volunteer regiment. Earlier Beecher had sent crates of rifles labeled *Beecher's Bibles* to anti-slavery forces in Kansas during the vicious Border War, also called Bloody Kansas or Bleeding Kansas, between 1854 and 1858.

Three decades later, during the Spanish-American War (1898), Theodore Roosevelt formed the Rough Riders, a cavalry regiment that took its name from a popular circus-like attraction: Buffalo Bill's Wild West Show and Congress of Rough Riders of the World. Raising and commissioning battle units by individuals and groups did not last very far into the 20th century. The practice was discontinued before the First World War as part of the professionalizing and modernizing of the U.S. military, a key aspect of the ascent of the regular army.

Among the motives compelling wealthy individuals to spend large sums of money, as much as $20,000, on raising fighting units are strong political beliefs and the quest of fame. Regimental sponsors who actually commanded their recruits may have sought fame by being perceived as romantic swashbucklers.

Media attention often lionized commanding sponsors: a colonel of a brigade, regiment, or battalion, or a captain of a company. Theodore Roosevelt was able to use the fame he received from his charge up San Juan Hill to catapult himself into state and national politics. Photos in the popular press and prints of the *Charge of the Rough Riders at San Juan Hill* by painter Frederic Remington turned the battle in which the Americans suffered three times the casualties of the Spanish into a great victory.

The motives of common soldiers were more timeless. Through their letters and journals they tell of being moved by solidarity with their friends, a kind of peer pressure, or by popular ideals of manhood and masculinity. No one wanted to be labeled a coward. Some hoped to better their poor economic prospects or find adventure. Hatred and vengeance may have motivated a few. Deeply felt political convictions, especially abolitionist feelings, caused many to volunteer. Political patriotism often included the desire shared with Abraham Lincoln, to maintain the unity of the country. Christian fatalism probably bolstered recruitment. On one hand the war could be viewed as carrying out the will of God, and on the other that the personal outcome was preordained.

Some Irish-American soldiers fought with the memory of English oppression in their homeland on their minds. But many others were opposed to freeing slaves, a reality that became increasingly clear as the war progressed. Blacks in New York City competed at the bottom of the wage structure where many Irish were trapped. According to Civil War historian James M. McPherson: *Despite the fighting reputation of the Irish Brigade, the Irish were the most under-represented group in proportion to population, followed by German Catholics. Other immigrant groups enlisted in rough proportion to their share of the population.*

Following the Civil War, military units, many of them organized and supported by anti-labor and conservative political groups and individuals, were used to suppress strikes and demonstrations. As the labor movement gained popularity and strength, state governments moved to protect corporations and used police, state troopers, state militias, and national guard units to attack workers and break their strikes. A prolonged series of strikes and boycotts around the country began in 1877 when railroad workers protested a wage cut. A July demonstration in Tompkins Square provoked strident denunciations from conservative politicians and a skull-cracking attack by the police.

An enormous armory for the for the 7th Regiment of the New York State National Guard was built between Lexington and Fourth Avenues at East 66th Street on the city's Upper East Side. The purpose of armories was to place fortress headquarters of military units in population centers. The 7th Regiment's central hall was used for drills and troop maneuvers, but during a labor strike, political march, or riot it could be converted to a prison. The walls were several feet thick with crenellated towers and slits for rifles. The 7th Regiment Armory was built with $589,000 in private donations, mostly from big corporations, though most armories in the city and throughout the country were constructed with government funds authorized in 1877 by the War Department.

Twenty-nine of these curious medieval-looking fortresses were built in New York City, ten are still used by New York State National Guard units. Others have been sold, converted to other uses, or utilized by the city as homeless shelters or storage facilities. Today the site of the Squadron A Armory on Madison Avenue between East 94th and 95th Street is occupied by Hunter College High School though the Madison Avenue armory façade was preserved. The cavernous 23rd Regiment Armory on Atlantic and Bedford Avenues in Brooklyn, for many years a homeless shelter, is being converted into a commercial venue. Their original purpose of armories was more psychological than military.

Militia units had often been used for policing in New York City's early history. A partial list of incidents when the government used troops would include the Flour Riots of 1826, Abolition Riot of 1834, Stonecutter's Riot of 1835, Stevedore Riots of 1837, Astor Place Riot of 1849, and Draft Riots of 1863. In the particularly bitter Brooklyn Trolley Strike of 1895, at least 7,000 state militiamen from Brooklyn and Manhattan attacked the strikers.

When New York University's first building was constructed on the east side of Washington Square Park, on the present site of the Silver Building, the university contracted with Elisha Bloomer's marble works, a company that used unpaid prison labor at Sing Sing to fabricate the building blocks. Marble workers picketed the building site and attacked Bloomer's company headquarters on Broadway and East 4th Street smashing its windows. The governor used the 27th Regiment to suppress the marble workers union and the strike was ended.

Armories were placed throughout the city to intimidate those who threatened the capitalist system, the established government, or the pre-eminence of corporate power. The aggressive use of soldiers to battle strikers and the construction of armories were widely denounced by liberal voices and was another reason why private support for raising military units was discontinued.

CHAPTER 66
Draft Riots

The American Civil War began when Abraham Lincoln rejected the secession of eleven Southern states in 1861. Though the United States Constitution is silent on the issue, President Lincoln's position was that once a state was accepted into the Union it could not withdraw. Whatever the legal merits of that case, it was obvious that if states were allowed to secede, the United States might shrink drastically, decline in importance, and lose power and influence abroad. The cause of the Civil War was slavery. Southerners used the issue of *states rights* to justify their secession though the primary reason they wanted *states rights* was so that they could continue to have the *right* to own slaves.

Almost all states had originally allowed slavery, though only the South and the border states (Missouri, Kentucky, Maryland, and Delaware) were still slave states in 1861. Embarrassingly, Washington, D. C. also had slavery. The slave system was a bulwark for the Southern aristocracy whose prosperity rested on keeping four million African-American in bondage and stealing their labor-power. The business community in the North had determined that wage-labor was a more efficient system as long as pay was kept low, no benefits were offered, and workers could be laid off or fired when they were not needed, or when they became injured, or failed to keep pace with others.

Slavery began in New Amsterdam in 1626, the second year of the colony's existence, when the Dutch West India Company imported slaves to labor on its farms, buildings, and fortifications. Later, individual Dutch residents bought slaves to work on their farms and in their homes. After the English takeover in 1664 slavery became a big and profitable business and public slave auctions were held at several locations. New York became the largest slave importing and auctioning center in the English colonies. New York City (southern Manhattan) was about one-fifth black, and Brooklyn's black population was about one-quarter. At the time of the

American Revolution fifteen percent of New York City's population was enslaved.

Because of the influence of the Abolitionists, and the steady stream of European immigrants willing to work for low wages, New York began to move away from slavery. In 1817 the legislature in Albany committed itself to freeing slaves throughout New York State. The Act of 1817 stipulated that every slave born before July 4, 1799 would be freed on July 4, 1827. The law allowed one exception as a favor to Southerner cotton merchants doing business in New York City. It permitted residents of slave states to bring their slaves to New York State for up to nine months. That arrangement was to end in 1841. When the Civil War started virtually every adult New Yorker had witnessed slavery and some had formerly owned slaves.

Free black communities, called *Little Africas*, existed in the southwest section of Greenwich Village and in what ultimately became SoHo, Hell's Kitchen, and Columbus Circle. Weeksville (now Bedford-Stuyvesant), Flushing, and Stapleton also had free black communities. New York was not a welcoming destination for blacks. Few jobs were open to blacks and a radical discrimination in housing forced them into several scattered ghettoes. The enormous European immigration marginalized the number of blacks in the city, so that in 1860 the black population was only 12,500 out of a total New York City (Manhattan) population of 814,000.

Many New Yorkers did not favor war with the South and there were several reasons for their attitude. New York merchants and bankers were involved in the financing, shipping, and manufacturing ends of the cotton trade. The South, which had very little industry, imported many finished products from New York City, which in the 19th century was the manufacturing center of the United States. Several New York hotels, restaurants, and theaters catered to Southern businessmen.

On the other end of the economic spectrum were poor whites, mostly immigrants from Ireland and southern Germany. They made dire predictions about lowered wages if freed blacks flooded the labor market. Already at the bottom of the economic ladder they feared being pushed even lower.

Mayor Fernando Wood called for New York City to secede in

1861. Wood wanted the city to be a *free city-state* and not belong to any country. He wanted New York City to be neutral in the Civil War and retain business relations with both the Union and the Confederacy. But, cities to not have independent standing in the U. S. Constitution, and all local laws (ordinances) are liable to review and possible rejection by state legislatures. Certainly the pro-Union legislature of New York State would have never accepted the secession of its largest city. And if Lincoln fought to bring the eleven Confederate states back into the Union, he would certainly have done the same if New York City used armed force to gain independence. Mayor Wood's idea went nowhere.

Horatio Seymour, like Wood, an anti-war Democrat, or *Peace Democrat*, was elected governor of New York State in 1862. Republicans referred to Peace Democrats by the pejorative *Copperheads*. He made inflammatory speeches against Lincoln, the war effort, and the draft. Just a week before the riots started he spoke at the Academy of Music comparing Lincoln to King Charles I of England, who was beheaded, and warned that the people would rise up against what he called *Lincoln's tyranny*.

In the 1860 presidential election Abraham Lincoln had received 32,641 votes in New York City and his three opponents (Stephen A. Douglas, John C. Breckinridge, and John Bell) together received 59,728. New Yorkers, and many other Americans, believed that if Lincoln won the election, the South would secede. In 1864 Lincoln was defeated in New York City by former general George B. McClellan. The vote was 73,709 to 36,737 and Lincoln carried only one ward in the entire city. McClellan supported continuing the Civil War until the Southern states were forced back into the Union but opposed emancipating the slaves.

Though the city's voters twice rejected Lincoln, he won on the national level. In 1860 he captured a plurality, not a majority, garnering 1,866,452 votes compared to a combined total of 2,813,741 for his three opponents. In the electoral college he won 180 to 123. In 1864, with the traditionally Democratic Southern states not voting, Lincoln received 2,213,655 to McClellan's 1,805,237, and won the electoral contest 212 to 21. This is all to say that history has been kind to Lincoln and for good reason, but the voters in New York City rejected him, and he was not very popular in the rest of the country either.

Not only did the Civil War divide the United States, it divided New York City. Nonetheless, when Fort Sumter, a federal military outpost in the harbor of Charleston, South Carolina was bombarded on April 12, 1861, many New Yorkers rallied round the flag and supported Lincoln. Even Tammany Hall, which had opposed the war, issued a proclamation of support and raised a regiment to send to the Union Army. A pro-war rally of 100,000 people was held at Union Square and even Fernando Wood pledged loyalty to the North.

Economically the war both helped and hurt New York City. While trade with the South ended with the Union's naval blockade, military orders for the Union Army were a huge stimulus. All the supplies a soldier needed could be made in New York and many companies earned a great deal of money producing uniforms, boots, rifles, knives, mess pans, kettles, coffee, *hardtack*, dried beef and pork. The city's kerosene refineries, iron foundries, shipyards, and manufacturers of naval stores (pitch, tar, rope, sails) did a brisk business on war contracts. Regardless of their political feelings some New Yorkers volunteered because their army pay was more than they could make in low-paying jobs in the city.

Though both sides initially believed that the war would be brief, it dragged on as soldiers were killed and wounded in astounding numbers. (Ultimately more than 620,000 Americans died.) The initial string of Union defeats dulled enthusiasm for the war, as did the daily listing of the dead.

Lincoln had originally called for 75,000 three-month volunteers. Later, the North invited three-month and three-year volunteers and paid cash bonuses to the recruits. Some private groups and wealthy individuals paid additional bonuses to encourage enlistment. Modern methods of warfare killed and wounded soldiers faster than recruiters could induce volunteers and both sides turned to conscription, or the draft. The Confederacy introduced the draft in April 1862. In March 1863, realizing there was no longer an adequate supply of volunteers for the U.S. Army, Congress passed of the National Conscription Act. New York State Governor Horatio Seymour challenged the legality of the draft, but lost.

An aspect of conscription that infuriated working-class and

poor New Yorkers was a provision that allowed a draftee to buy his way out by paying $300. (John D. Rockefeller avoided service in the U.S. Army in that manner.) New York City was divided into special districts where draft offices were set up.

On Saturday, July 11, 1863 public drawings began and 1,200 names were pulled out of revolving wire-mesh lottery wheels. The following day the names of the inductees were printed in the city's newspapers. Anger and resentment built among the pool of young men liable to be conscripted. Two days later, when the drawings were set to resume, groups of irate men opposed to the draft gathered on street corners on the Lower East Side to denounce the Conscription Act, the Civil War, and blacks. Most in the crowds were Irish but the speeches and excitement attracted participants from several other ethnic groups.

Irish wrath had intensified the month before when Lincoln sent federal troops to protect hundreds of black strikebreakers during a strike by 3,000 mostly Irish Longshoreman. The bitter racial hostilities were complicated. Twenty years earlier free blacks drove out Irish immigrants from low-paying jobs by.

The crowds began to march north toward the draft office at 46th Street and 3rd Avenue. They carried posters reading *No Draft, Down With The Rich Men, A Rich Man's War But A Poor Man's Fight,* and *No $300 Arrangements With Us,* which alluded to the $300 exemption clause. The throng surged forward and in the street-brawl that ensued the draft office was burned and the lottery wheel smashed. The mob raced to other draft offices to repeat their vandalism.

The violence was widespread in Manhattan and included arson, window smashing, cutting telegraph lines, chopping down telegraph poles, attacks on draft officers and policemen, clashes with the police and militia, and murderous assaults on blacks. The city erupted in a spasm of violence with mobs operating in scores of locations. It ranged from the area northwest of the Battery up to 86th Street, though much of it took place in Five Points (Chinatown), *Kleindeutschland* (Lower East Side), Greenwich Village, Grammercy Park, and in the 30s and 40s in midtown. Rioters also attacked Brooks Brothers clothing store (which made uniforms for the U.S. Army), the Temperance Union headquarters (a Republican stronghold), and Horace Greeley's *New York Tribune*. *The New York Times* defended its building by placing gunmen on the roof.

At first the violence was directed against the draft stations and the federal troops who staffed them. The eruption had a clearly discernible class element. Rich people were attacked because they could easily evade the draft. But also because the poor were enraged that their dream of a good life had been deferred or ruined by the harsh economic conditions they faced as they tried to eke out a living. The rioters could recognize the rich by their clothes and carriages, and easily spot their well-appointed row houses.

The Draft Riots were also race riots. Those who opposed conscription did not want to be drafted to fight and perhaps die in the struggle to defeat the South to free the slaves. They feared the freed slaves would migrate north and take their jobs. Eleven black men were lynched and seven shot by mobs. As their corpses hung from telegraph poles they were set on fire. The Colored Orphan Asylum at 5th Avenue and 43rd Street was burned. Miraculously all 200 children escaped, led out a back door and hurried to a barge on the East River to safety on Blackwells Island.

Mayor George Opdyke, a Republican who supported Lincoln, tried to call a special session of the City Council, but lacked a quorum. The police rushed to some of the scenes of destruction but were unable to handle the rioting. Opdyke, faced with anarchy in the streets, wired President Lincoln and requested New York regiments be sent to the city to quell the disturbance. On the third day of rioting, Wednesday, July 15th, a heavy morning rain turned the city steamy. The City Council met and tried to appease the rioters. They issued a proclamation denouncing the draft and appropriated $2,500,000 to pay the $300 replacement fees of New Yorkers who wanted to escape the Civil War. Despite their actions sporadic rioting continued and spread to the Brooklyn docks and Stapleton, Staten Island.

Five regiments with 10,000 men rushed back from the Battle of Gettysburg and entered the city later on Wednesday. Fearing the arrival of regular soldiers, the mob built street barricades along 9th Avenue in Hell's Kitchen, and north of Tompkins Square. They were designed to block the soldiers and provide safety for the crowd. The barricades were built of upended wagons and carriages, barrels, and boxes. Items were tied together to make dismantling difficult. Stones and bricks were dug up from the streets to use as weapons.

Wednesday evening there were several violent clashes between small roving crowds and the soldiers, especially the 7th Regiment. Rioters were shot dead as troops marched up and down streets looking for remnants of the mob. Many of the bodies were never identified.

Thursday, the newspapers and the mayor were urging people to return to work. Signs were posted throughout the city announcing that the next day Archbishop John Hughes would deliver a speech from the balcony of his residence. Four thousand Catholics gathered to hear the archbishop. During the upheaval Hughes had been asked by city officials to pacify the rioters. He hesitated until Friday when the riot had effectively ended. Hughes' position was that during nativist attacks on Roman Catholic churches the police and civil authorities looked the other way. Ultimately, he acquiesced and asked his listeners to return to their daily lives.

In his youth Hughes had been a slave overseer in Maryland and Pennsylvania though he accepted the Catholic Church's opposition to slavery following an 1838 encyclical by Pope Gregory XVI. Nonetheless, Hughes thought blacks, despite slavery, were better off in the United States than in Africa, and he was apprehensive about the economic impact of four million freed slaves. The archbishop's position reflected his intense dislike for Reformers and Republicans, mostly Protestants, who stridently opposed the Catholic Church and Irish immigration.

The Draft Riots stirred the ire of those who fervently supported the war. Herman Melville said of New York: *The town is taken by its rats.* Walt Whitman wrote: *It had been the devil's work all through.* Most of the blame was placed on the Irish. George Templeton Strong, a founder of the Union League Club and Trinity Church vestryman, wrote in his diary: *I would like to see war made on Irish scum as in 1688.* (Strong's 1688 reference was to the English army of William and Mary defeating the Stuart army supporting James II at the Battle of the Boyne, near Drogheda in 1690. A brutal repression against Irish Catholics followed the Protestant victory.

Strong was mistaken about the date.)

The number of people killed in the Draft Riots remains unclear. Police Superintendent John A. Kennedy calculated 1,155, Governor Seymour put the number at 1,000, and others estimated 2,000. Most contemporary historians place the number far lower: 17 blacks, 16 soldiers, and between 85 and 120 rioters. Conscription resumed at new draft offices on August 19th.

The Draft Riots of 1863 composed a very ugly chapter in New York City's history. The meteoric growth of the city, its deep division between rich and poor, and the clashing aspirations and interests of its diverse groups blew up under the stress of the Civil War. Not all the battles of the war were fought in the South.

CHAPTER 67
Edgar Allan Poe

Edgar Allan Poe, the American writer most often cited as the favorite author in high school English classes, has a connection with New York City. He spent a few months of his short life living at 85 West 3rd Street in Greenwich Village. In 1845 Poe began *The Cask of Amontillado* in a four-story rooming house one block from Washington Square. The next year he left Manhattan for a part of Westchester County, which is now in the Bronx.

The Edgar Allan Poe Cottage, preserved by the Bronx County Historical Society is in Poe Park at the intersection of the Grand Concourse and Kingsbridge Road. It was there that he finished *The Cask of Amontillado* and the poems *Annabel Lee* and *Ulalume*. The tiny cottage was leased to Poe for $100 a year from 1846 until his death at age 40 in 1849. He moved there because he thought the country air would strengthen his wife Virginia, who was ailing from tuberculosis. At the time the area was in the southern part of rural Westchester County. Relocation did not cure Virginia and she died the next year.

Poe had been orphaned at age two. He was born in 1809 and by 1811 his father had disappeared and his mother had died. A middle class family in Richmond, headed by John Allan, raised him. Between 1815 and 1820 he lived in England with the Allans, where he attended school. At 17 he enrolled in the University of Virginia but gambled and lost $2,000, at the time more than the yearly income of an attorney. John Allan refused to pay Poe's debts, the two disagreed bitterly, though Allan helped him gain entry to West Point in 1830. Within a year he was expelled for unexplained absences. Between 1831 and 1849 he resided at numerous addresses in Philadelphia, Baltimore, Richmond, and New York.

He became very close to his father's sister, Maria Poe Clemm, and her daughter Virginia. With the blessing of his aunt, Poe married Virginia in 1835 when she was 13 years old. Poe made a meager living as an editor and writer. In his stories we find his feisty personality, restlessness, and romantic sense of adventure. He excelled at probing the concealed workings of the human mind, a notion that had gained much attention in the mid-19th century. He was a master of presenting strange, hypnotic experiences. The anticipation of fear and horror in his characters has a mesmerizing effect on his readers. Excitement, suspense, and horror are his tools in *The Black Cat, The Cask of Amontillado, The Telltale Heart, The Pit and the Pendulum,* and *The Fall of the House of Usher*. Poe had a daring sense of creativity and could evoke dark moods with the rhythms and sounds of carefully chosen words.

His sense of darkness and personal loss comes through in *Ulalume*:

The skies they were ashen and sober;
The leaves they were crisped and sere---
The leaves they were withering and sere;
It was night in the lonesome October
Of my most immemorial year;
It was hard by the dim lake of Auber,
In the misty mid-region of Weir ---
It was down by the dank tarn of Auber,
In the ghoul-haunted woodland of Weir.

More wistful is his *Annabel Lee,* also written after Virginia's death:

It was many and many a year ago,
In a kingdom by the sea,
That a maid there lived whom you may know
By the name of Annabel Lee;
And this maiden she lived with no other thought
Than to love and be loved by me.

The Raven, a poem with haunting repetition, first gained Poe national attention:

Once upon a midnight dreary, while I pondered, weak and weary,
Over many a quaint and curious volume of forgotten lore ---
While I nodded, nearly napping, suddenly there came a tapping,
As of someone gently rapping, rapping at my chamber door.

"'Tis some visitor," I muttered, "tapping at my chamber door---
Only this and nothing more."

Poe also popularized the first detective stories. His character, Dupin, became the model for Sherlock Holmes stories by Conan Doyle. The rational methods, scientific approach, and careful line of questioning of the brainy sleuth in *The Murders in the Rue Morgue* and *The Purloined Letter*, Monsieur C. Auguste Dupin, are still used in popular *whodunits* whether short stories, novels, or films. Sure of his methodology, Dupin asserts himself in *The Murders in the Rue Morgue*: *My own examination was somewhat more particular, and was so for the reason I have just given, because here it was, I knew, that all apparent impossibilities must prove to be quite possible in reality.* Poe's characters are reflected in Sherlock Holmes, Miss Marple, Joe Friday, Inspector Clouseau, and Columbo.

After leaving Manhattan, he moved to the cottage in the Bronx hoping the fresh air would heal Virginia's tuberculosis. While living there, the family was so poor that Poe's mother-in-law (and aunt), who was residing with them, picked dandelion stems in the orchard and foraged in nearby meadows for food.

Crushed by Virginia's death in 1847 Poe became increasingly depressed and dependent on alcohol. In 1849 he left the Bronx and spent two months in Richmond preparing to relocate in the state capital. Returning north to Philadelphia to collect a debt, he stopped off at Baltimore, drank heavily, ended up in a hospital and expired from what the doctors called *congestion of the brain*. Edgar Allan Poe was 40 years old.

Notation:

Edgar Allan Poe Cottage

Located in Poe Park at the intersection of the Grand Concourse and Kingsbridge Road, the ground floor of the Poe Cottage contains a comfortable living room and a minuscule bedroom where his wife Virginia died. Two more bedrooms, a little more than six feet high, are up a narrow flight of stairs. The house is furnished with period pieces though only three items belonging to the author. The one-and-a-half story wood frame building was constructed in 1812 as a bunkhouse for farm laborers on the Valentine garden farming estate. It was saved from destruction by the Shakespeare Society in 1890, and is now owned by the Bronx County Historical Society. The house was moved from the other side of Kingsbridge Road in 1913.

CHAPTER 68
Walt Whitman, Romantic Poet

Born on a farm in upstate New York in 1819, Walt Whitman moved with his family to Brooklyn at age four where his father found work as a carpenter. Whitman grew up in New York City during the time of its most rapid expansion. He was on his own early in life after leaving school at eleven to be an office boy in a law firm. The next year he worked in a printing office and became a journeyman printer at sixteen.

Whitman is identified with many places in Brooklyn and Manhattan. He lived in several buildings in Fort Greene and Brooklyn Heights, and later on Centre Street in Manhattan. For his poetry he used a printer on Henry Street in Brooklyn Heights near the intersection of Cranberry Street. (The modern apartment building there is now called Whitman Tower.) He loved the city's nightlife, energy, and fast pace. He regularly took long walks exploring the city and outlying towns that would ultimately be joined together in 1898. He frequented the famous Bohemian hangout, Pfaff's, an underground saloon on the corner of Broadway and Bleecker Street. Throughout his life he continued to write commentaries defining what the city was becoming, and poetry glorifying its dynamic nature.

Whitman was a Romantic poet. He differs from many others in the Romantic tradition because he includes the city as part of his Romantic vision. He appreciated the natural beauty of the rivers and hills, but he also cherished the large, imposing buildings and the crowds of people.

Romanticism was primarily an artistic and intellectual movement. It was a feisty response to political, economic, and social events of the period from about 1750 until at least 1870. The movement burst forth in our country as well as in Europe, especially in England, France and the German states.

By the beginning of the nineteenth century many Europeans and Americans were tiring of the artistic element of the Enlightenment, which stressed rationality, order, control, symmetry, and restraint in the arts. Neo-Classicism, which artistically went hand in hand with the Enlightenment, used ancient Greek and Roman images as its models and stressed esthetic rules and consistent standards. The cultural pendulum of taste always swings back and forth, and as the popularity of Enlightenment and Classical themes waned, the ebullient themes of the Romantic Reaction gained dominance.

In rapidly modernizing areas of Europe and the United States the Romantic Reaction also targeted industrialization and urbanization, which were seen as ugly and unnatural. They felt the dehumanization caused by factory conditions and city life could be countered by following natural artistic emotions. Walt Whitman departed from this aspect of Romanticism. He appreciated cities and industrial achievements.

Romantics loved powerful emotions and intense feelings. They let their assertive egos show in art, literature, music and architecture. They were unabashedly spiritual and loved nature, often portraying the enchanting or frightening aspects of the wilds as well as longing for the unusual and exotic.

Composers like Beethoven, Berlioz, Liszt, Chopin, Schubert, Tchaikovsky and Paganini added enthusiasm and range in music, greatly enlarging orchestras by adding wind instruments and percussion as well as using more strings. Concert halls were built. Music was composed for enjoyment as an end in itself and not just as a background for religious services and elegant dinner parties. The period of Romantic operas like those of Giuseppe Verdi and Richard Wagner had begun.

In art, subjects were likely to be common people doing ordinary tasks or struggling with tempest-tossed seas or ensconced in remote or phantasmagorical locations. Either nature or political upheaval could be the setting. French Artist Eugène Delacroix painted the Greek War of Independence against the Ottoman Turks in *Massacre at Chios*, and the French Revolution in *Liberty Leading the People.*

The Romantic painting style known as the Hudson River School focused on nature. The setting was often the Hudson River or the Catskill and Adirondack Mountains. The powerful, realistic paintings glorified the wildness of New York State's landscape. Paintings usually included tempestuous skies, beams of light breaking through clouds, rugged terrain, and hunters (man, raptors, and wild felines). Its theme was the ambiguous relationship between man and nature: tantalizing but dangerous. The intensity of nature evoked a spiritual presence of God. Thomas Cole, Frederic Church, Asher Durand, John F. Kensett, and Thomas Doughty are the main representatives of this tradition. The Brooklyn Museum of Art has a spectacular collection of their paintings.

In literature, Romantics abandoned formal poetry for direct, ordinary speech and often endowed simple subjects with lofty importance. Examples from Europe and America are *The Sorrows of the Young Werther* by Johann Wolfgang von Goethe, *The Captain's Daughter* by Alexander Pushkin, the *Leather-Stocking Tales* by James Fennimore Cooper, and Edgar Allan Poe's detective stories and spooky poem, *The Raven*. In *Daffodils*, William Wordsworth shunned the noble rose for wildflower simplicity. In a similar way Henry Wadsworth Longfellow wrote a poem entitled *Seaweed*.

The Romantics had moved as far away from Enlightenment and Neo-Classical restrained order as they could. All of life and all of life's emotions, including tragedy, were fit subjects for their attention. Whitman was New York City's chief Romantic poet in the mid 19th century. Many of Whitman's articles and poems were devoted to New York City. His rosy attitude can be found in individual poems collected in his work *Leaves of Grass*, published in 1855. They include *Broadway Pageant, Manahatta I*, and *Crossing Brooklyn Ferry*.

In *Crossing Brooklyn Ferry*, which was first published as *Sun-Down Poem*, Walt Whitman told of his ferry commute from the Fulton Street pier in Brooklyn to the Fulton Street pier of Manhattan. He traveled with other Brooklyn commuters on their way to jobs in downtown Manhattan. He compared his crossing with what others would do in the future.

Others will enter the gates of the ferry and cross from shore to shore,
Others will watch the run of the flood-tide,
Others will see the shipping of Manhattan north and west, and the heights of Brooklyn to the south and east,
Others will see the islands large and small;

Fifty years hence, others will see them as they cross, the sun half an hour high,

A hundred years hence, or ever so many hundred years hence, others will see them,

Will enjoy the sunset, the pouring-in of the flood-tide, the falling-back to the sea of the ebb-tide.

Just fourteen years after Whitman's poem construction began on the Brooklyn Bridge. It was finished in 1883 and the East River commute became quicker and less reflective than Whitman's. In 1904 the I.R.T. subway (4 and 5 trains now) tunneled under the East River and Romantic visual images were sacrificed to speed.

Whitman had abounding esteem for America and especially loved New York City. His long hikes gave him admiration for the area's landforms, and he freely mingled with people in its neighborhoods. He personalized the city in *Crossing Brooklyn Ferry.*

I too lived, Brooklyn of ample hills was mine,

I too walk'd the streets of Manhattan island, and bathed in the waters around it...

At one point Whitman burst forth with Romantic enthusiasm for New York:

Stand up, tall masts of Manahatta! stand up, beautiful hills of Brooklyn!

He was a prolific writer and contributed articles, stories, and poetry to the *Long Island Democrat, New World, Democratic Review,* and *Long Island Star*. Later in his career he served as editor of the *Long Islander, Aurora,* and the *Brooklyn Daily Eagle*. He was active in politics especially the Free Soil Party, which opposed allowing slavery in the western territories. During the Civil War he moved to Washington, D.C. and worked as a hospital attendant. For several years following the war Whitman worked as a clerk in the Attorney General's office. After suffering a stroke in 1873 and moved to Camden, New Jersey to stay with his brother. He recovered from partial paralysis but with the exception of trips to Philadelphia, Boston, and New York, he stayed rooted in Camden where he died in 1892.

CHAPTER 69
Parks by Olmstead and Vaux

New Amsterdam and early New York were without parks. The town was so small that it was only a short walk, about a dozen blocks at the most, to the countryside. There was a town common, but it was not really a park for humans. It was a pasture for grazing cows, sheep, and goats. The idea of a park for public recreation is a new one.

As New York grew and reached 600,000 by 1850, a quick trip to the country had become too far to travel, and the notion of green space within the city became increasingly appealing. There were some private open spaces like Bowling Green and several beer gardens, but nothing public and free. Spare time outdoors for children and adults was spent on stoops or in the streets. Children sometimes went to swim in the East River during the summer.

In the early 19th century the popular Romantic idea of bringing countryside experiences to cities took root. Cemeteries led the way, especially Brooklyn's Green-Wood Cemetery, which was patterned after the Père-Lachaise Cemetery in Paris.

What *was* the Romantic model? Romanticists detested the Industrial Revolution and the excesses of urban life: smoke belching from dark factories and mills, foul water, noise, overcrowded tenements, narrow streets, crime, and poverty. To them, the city contained mostly evil, and good came from the countryside. In their view, a *greenspace* would provide a nearby escape for New Yorkers. Romanticists liked their nature unrestrained and untamed. Their idea of a greenspace was not formal, pristine, and manicured, but enchanting, emotional, and asymmetrical.

Green-Wood Cemetery, completed in 1840 on 478 acres of land that had retained its original hills and lakes, was planned to reconstruct (and even *invent*) rugged nature. Hills and bluffs were kept. Narrow winding roads and footpaths were built, and trees, shrubs, and flowers were planted to look like the random placement of nature. Romantics held nothing back. When they placed carved tombstones in Green-Wood they opted for designs that captured intense feelings like beauty, love, friendship, fear, loneliness, and mourning.

The success of Green-Wood inspired organizers of a Romantic style park for Manhattan. New York City bought most of the 843 acres of land in the heart of north central Manhattan from individual owners in 1856. A Board of Park Commissioners was established by New York State to operate the project. Frederick Law Olmstead and Calvert Vaux won a planning contest with their design called *Greensward* in 1858. Olmstead had an appealing, far-sighted vision: *The time will come when New York will be built up, when all the grading and filling will be done, and when the picturesquely-varied, rocky formations of the Island will have been converted into foundations for rows of monotonous straight streets, and piles of erect, angular buildings. There will be no suggestion left of its present varied surface, with the single exception of the Park.*

Few people lived in the rectangle chosen for the park in 1853. It was still far to the north of the heavily populated parts of Manhattan. But squatters and residents of Seneca Village, populated mostly by poor free blacks and Irish immigrants, did live there. Detractors claimed the area held only a garbage dump, tannery, animal bone-boiling company (for gelatin products), and grazing land for pigs and goats. The 264 residents of Seneca Village were evicted, often violently, by application of the law of *eminent domain,* which allows the government to take private land, with compensation, for a *higher purpose*. Their three churches and two schools were destroyed, and their three cemeteries covered up. Seneca Village was located near Central Park West at about West 85th Street.

Central Park partially opened in 1859 though it was not fully finished for 20 more years. When completed, the magnificent park did resemble the idealized countryside. The dramatic landscape had rocky ridges, valleys, woods, and open spaces. Some areas were constructed to be wild: The Ramble, The Cliff, the area around Belvedere Castle, and the Bird Sanctuary. Several lakes were created: Harlem Meer, The Pool, Belvedere Lake, The Lake (for rowboats), Conservatory Water (for model boats), and The Pond. The largest meadows were: North Meadow, the Great Lawn (once the site of a very early reservoir), and the Sheep Meadow.

Central Park is at the center of Manhattan but it has no central area itself. The park is inviting but once inside, it is easy to get lost. How can you remember where you are and orient yourself? The architects were striving to create a forest, or wilderness experience, and using curvilinear roads and paths while resisting a central hub helped make their idea work. Olmstead and Vaux wanted people to experience getting lost in the great outdoors. In a sense, they were creating a Hudson River School painting that New Yorkers could physically experience by stepping into a picture of upstate wilderness.

To build the park 20,000 laborers were hired to move ten million cartloads of dirt, reconfigure rocky outcroppings, build roadways, paths, and meadows, construct a reservoir, and plant 270,000 trees and shrubs. The park project was popular with most New Yorkers. It appealed to Reformers who had been scandalized by the poverty further downtown. They thought a glimpse of the countryside would uplift the lower classes. (The irony is that most of the poor had come from rural parts of Ireland, Germany, and elsewhere.) Tammany Hall, the Democratic Party political organization, was ecstatic that the park would employ thousands of workers. Tammany Hall distributed those jobs to its favorites. Land speculators, both Reformers and Tammany Hall people, bought up land near the park waiting for land values to rise. In fact, the really wealthy New Yorkers focused on large lots along 5th Avenue and Central Park West, the streets on the park's two long sides, to construct mansions. With this project it seemed everyone would win.

The lower classes, however, were initially locked out from fully enjoying Central Park. Olmstead and Vaux were elitists who shared prejudices about immigrants and did not want their creation *ruined* by working class and poor people. Olmstead distrusted their habits and discipline. He explained his belief: *It was to be expected as the city should in effect be brought nearer, year by year, to the park, and it thus came to be more easily, familiarly and numerously visited, that the means used for instructing and reminding visitors of their duty would be found less effective.*

There were numerous restrictions. To begin, there was no

walking on the grass. No picnic lunches or beverages. No spontaneous sports were allowed. *Boys* could play baseball only if they had a note from their principal. Olmstead had seen rough children around town and he did not want them endangering *his* park. He explained to a newspaper reporter from the *New York Sun. The rich as a general thing know how to behave themselves but unfortunately the poor boys, at least those whom I have seen on the playgrounds, manifest a strong propensity to deviltry and cannot control themselves, being invariably very boisterous and rowdy in their activities.*

If you wanted to drive your horse-carriage through the park's winding roadways, it had to be a pleasure vehicle, one without any business lettering. It couldn't say *Moishe's Seltzer Delivery* or *Giuseppe's Fish Market*, for example. Only five percent of New Yorkers owned carriages, which were purely for pleasure. Complaints poured in against the restrictions. *The New York Times* published an editorial declaring: *The rules about not walking upon the grass are now enforced so rigidly that sending children to the Park is rather a punishment for them than a treat.*

Only four restaurants were allowed in the park: the Casino, Mount Saint Vincent, and Mineral Springs Pavilion were all costly. A less pricey snack bar called the Dairy specialized in milk, ice cream, pastries, and coffee. It was forbidden to bring in food from home or a store, or buy from a surreptitious vendor, though each of these transgressions sometimes occurred.

In 1870 a new City Charter gave Central Park over to local control. The mayor appointed new park commissioners who began the democratization process. Changes included walking on the grass and climbing the rock outcroppings, bicycling, rollerskating, lawn tennis, goat rides, pony rides, a carousel, and a zoo. In 1880, after strenuous protests by some Protestant clergymen (usually *Sabbatarians*), free Sunday afternoon concerts were initiated. Political rallies remained barred from the park until the 1960s. Labor unions and political groups continued to use Tompkins Square Park, Union Square, and City Hall Park for their activities.

Frederick Law Olmstead was greatly displeased by the new openness that was fundamentally altering his perception of Central Park. His idea that it be a kind of outdoor nature museum, mostly just for looking, had been turned into a democratic place for people to actively enjoy their leisure. He wrote to a friend in 1874 showing his bitterness: *I tell you that I think the park is going to the devil and have grave doubt whether the undertakings to provide a* <u>*rural*</u> *recreation ground upon such a site in the midst of a city like this was not a mistake, was not doomed to failure because of the general ignorance of the conditions of success and the impossibility of getting proper care taken of it.*

Parks also functioned as common ground meeting places for new Americans. Immigrants from diverse backgrounds and insular ghettoes could see each other strolling, picnicking, playing games, or relaxing in public spaces. They could break out of their ethnic enclaves and slowly learn to coexist and mix. It demystified strangers and has been credited with being an important part of the assimilation process.

In 1934 Governor Herbert H. Lehman gave control of the city's park system to urban planner and master builder Robert Moses. Further opening the park to the people, he reconfigured some of its original Romantic image. He built twenty playgrounds, athletic fields, a swimming pool, a theater, and two skating rinks. Eventually he added the Conservancy Garden, a beautiful maze of symmetrical walkways through flowerbeds. It was decidedly un-Romantic plan. But, wedding parties, which often take photographs there have been forever grateful.

Mayor John Lindsay further opened the park in the 1960s by allowing rock concerts, hippie *be-ins,* parades, political demonstrations, sporting events, and speeches to take place there. Later, Pope John Paul II and the Dalai Lama came to speak in Central Park.

In the 1970s severe budget cuts led to a reduced staff and Central Park rapidly decayed. The grass wore down in favor of large patches of exposed soil. The 1970s was called the park's *dust bowl* period. Its deterioration into shabbiness raised the ire of people in nearby fashionable buildings. In 1980, neighbors and businessmen organized the Central Park Conservancy that raised contributions for repairs and upkeep, and in 1998 took over maintenance and control of the park. By 2000, Central Park was in excellent condition.

Olmstead and Vaux went on to create many more greenspaces

in New York City as well as in Chicago, Boston, and Washington, D.C. (They were the landscape architects for the National Zoo in the capital.) They designed Tompkins Square Park, Riverside Park, and Morningside Park in Manhattan, and Fort Greene Park and Prospect Park in Brooklyn. All followed the same Romantic vision of bringing the country to the city.

The story of Brooklyn's Prospect Park is similar to Central Park. Citizens wanted greenspace for the rapidly growing independent City of Brooklyn. A 526-acre area was designed by Olmstead and Vaux, which they made even more woodsy than Central Park. A *berm* (banked-earth mounds) around the diamond-shaped park and lower height of residential buildings around the periphery made it seem very detached from urban life. The park opened in 1868 to a vast, enthusiastic throng of visitors.

Special features of Prospect Park included the boomerang-shaped, mile-long, 75-acre Long Meadow, Nethermead (lower meadow), Lookout Hill (highest point in the park at 170 feet), two ponds (The Pools), the Ambergill (a brook), the Lullwater, Prospect Lake, the secluded and steep-sided Ravine, and the Vale of Cashmere (a hollow). Along Flatbush Avenue near Empire Boulevard stands the rebuilt Lefferts Homestead, a Dutch house that was burned by the Redcoats in 1776 during the Battle of Long Island (which happened in Brooklyn). The house, just inside the park, has a typical Dutch-style overhanging roof and split front door. The house, now a museum, was once part of a 240-acre farm established in 1660.

The 15-acre Friends Cemetery located inside the west central part of the park, established by Brooklyn Quakers in 1846, was left intact and remains active. (Consider the difference between how the black cemetery in Central Park and the white cemetery in Prospect Park were treated.)

Robert Moses, the tremendously powerful park and highway commissioner, made changes in Prospect Park as well. He added several playgrounds, a skating rink, and a zoo. In a move that now causes constant controversy, he also widened and straightened purposefully winding roads for the convenience of automobiles.

Each borough has a park that is a special treasure: La Tourette Park in Staten Island, Flushing Meadows Park in Queens, and Van

Cortlandt Park in the Bronx. Brooklyn's Prospect Park and Central Park in Manhattan belong in this fine tradition thanks to Frederick Law Olmstead and Calvert Vaux.

CHAPTER 70
Cathedral of Saint John the Divine (Episcopal)

New York City has the largest cathedral in the world: the Cathedral of Saint John the Divine, at 112th Street and Amsterdam Avenue in Morningside Heights, Manhattan. It is surpassed in size by only two other large Christian churches, Our Lady of Yamoussoukro in the Ivory Coast, and the Basilica of Saint Peter in the Vatican, neither of which is a cathedral. (While the Pope is the Bishop of Rome, the cathedral of the Diocese of Rome is Saint John Lateran, not Saint Peter's.)

How big is Saint John the Divine? It is 200 yards long and has a floor area of 121,000 square feet. The Statue of Liberty could fit in the center of the cathedral. It is twice the size of Saint Patrick's Cathedral on 5th Avenue, the seat of the city's Roman Catholic archbishop. The rose window at the west end of Saint John the Divine (shaped like a rose) is 40 feet in diameter and the figure of Jesus in the center is six feet high. The organ has 8,035 pipes. Behind the high altar are eight imposing granite columns, 55 feet in height, quarried as monoliths on Bear Island off the coast of Maine. Each weighs 130 tons. In order to polish and transport the columns, they were cut in half for the barge and steam-tractor journey to the cathedral in 1903. They broke every manhole cover they passed over.

Cathedral comes from the Greek word *kathedra*, meaning chair or throne of the bishop. In the early Christian community each city or town had a bishop, and his headquarters was a church with a special throne reserved for him. One bishop for each city was enshrined in church law by the First Ecumenical Council which met in Nicaea in 325 A.D. Roman Catholic, Eastern Orthodox, Episcopal, Methodist, European Lutheran and some other branches of Christianity follow the tradition. The Cathedral of Saint John the Divine is the *ecclesiastical* (church government) center for the Diocese of New York of the Episcopal Church.

Traditionally, cathedrals were not just the office of the diocesan bishop they were places of beauty and special meaning. Important ceremonies were held in cathedrals, especially ordaining new priests. In Europe, kings and queens were crowned in cathedrals. Religious pilgrims and tourists visited cathedrals to see relics of saints or pray in front of famous statues or paintings. The square in front of the cathedral, or cathedral yard, was a common place to hold religious and government ceremonies.

All these things are still true about cathedrals. Saint John the Divine has added some modern elements to a cathedral's purpose. There are special memorial side altars to AIDS victims, Holocaust victims, those who suffer today under political dictatorships, and a monument to the environment. The cathedral operates a 50-bed homeless shelter, a soup kitchen, a recycling center, a crisis intervention center, and senior citizen programs. It rents inexpensive loft space to 17 artists, and has a job training program and stone carving company. The church is very active in neighborhood affairs.

Stoneyard Institute is a job-training program for neighborhood young people who work for Cathedral Stoneyard learning stonecutting, sandblasting, and masonry construction. Stoneyard wins contracts to work on many building projects in New York City. They have done renovation on the Woolworth Building, Rockefeller Center, and Grand Central Terminal. The money they earn pays their salaries and pays for making more stone blocks and decorations, like gargoyles and statues, for the cathedral. The stoneyard is just north of the cathedral and is filled with large blocks of granite and limestone. Unlike medieval stoneyards, this one uses very modern equipment: diamond-tipped blades on computer operated saws, high-tech polishing machines, pneumatic drills, sandblasters, and vacuum air cleaners to remove dust.

Festivals and pageants are important events at the cathedral. The yearly celebration in October marking the Feast of Saint Francis, patron saint of animals, attracts widespread media attention and an audience of 5,000 people. They are accompanied by at least 1,000 pets --- dogs, cats, birds, guinea pigs, snakes, even fish in bowls. Blessings are given to the animals during a joyful service full of singing and dancing.

The eccentric pomp, for which Saint John the Divine has become famous, is achieved on the Feast of Saint Francis by a combination of ornately robed priests in a medieval procession to the altar, followed by animal handlers in church garb leading an elephant, camel, donkey, snake, owl, turtle, spider, and finally a bowl of green algae resting on a purple satin pillow. The celebration is really about the miracle of diverse life and while people sing songs, barking and other animal noises fill the cathedral.

During the 100th birthday party for the cathedral in 1992 the procession was led by high-wire acrobat Phillippe Petit balancing a globe in the air at the end of a very tall pole. Angels on stilts, circus clowns, Scottish bagpipers, and West African drummers followed.

The *ecumenical* movement (sharing common values and beliefs) is frequently seen at the cathedral. Leaders of other Christian denominations, and non-Christian religions, are invited to give speeches. The Dalai Lama, leader of Tibetan Buddhists, often speaks at Saint John the Divine.

The initial eclectic design for the cathedral included a pointed octagonal dome and rounded columns, which reflect the Byzantine style but with some Romanesque and Gothic features. In 1913 the plans were re-drawn to feature more pinnacles, pointed arches, and flying buttresses in the Gothic style. At the time Gothic architecture was making a comeback after being unpopular for at least two centuries. It had been considered representative of Medieval Europe, which was disparagingly called the Dark Ages. After 1913 the Gothic style predominated but all three styles can be found in the cathedral.

The way the interior is decorated reflects traditional European cathedrals, but also has some very distinct American elements. The low dividing walls between the two ends of the choir section and the high altar, called *historical parapets,* include statues of Christians of historical importance: Saint Paul, Saint Augustine, and Saint Gregory the Great. But they also include Christopher Columbus, George Washington, and Abraham Lincoln! (At the very end is an empty niche with an uncarved block waiting for the right person to come along.)

The sanctuary includes two cloisonné Shinto vases given by Emperor Hirohito of Japan and two Jewish menorahs presented by Arthur Ochs, former publisher of *The New York Times*. American multiculturalism is also evident along the ambulatory, the walk way behind the high altar, where there are seven chapels, each dedicated to a representative saint of the most prominent Christian immigrant groups at the beginning of the 20th century: Scandinavian, German, Irish, French, Italian, Spanish, and Levantine (eastern Mediterranean area including Greece, Syria, and Lebanon).

Along the nave (the main part of the cathedral) are fourteen side altars and bays, each dedicated to an occupation. The stained glass windows are high, and strong focused eyes or binoculars are needed to tell what is being portrayed. In the Sports Bay, we find Samson killing the lion and Jacob wrestling with an angel, as well as modern boxing, soccer, baseball, football, polo, fishing, tobogganing, bowling, bicycling, and golf. The Arts Bay shows Byzantine Emperor Justinian planning his cathedral, Hagia Sophia, in Constantinople, as well as Shakespeare, and Homer. It also features contemporary metalworkers, stonecutters, embroiderers, and painters. The American History Bay portrays Henry Hudson, George Washington, Thomas Jefferson, Benjamin Franklin, Betsy Ross, Francis Scott Key, Abraham Lincoln, and the 1912 sinking of the *Titanic*!

Considering that the English replaced the Dutch as masters of New York in 1664, it took a very long time to build an Episcopal cathedral. One reason is that all Episcopal churches in America were organized as part of the Anglican Diocese of London. After the American Revolution ended in 1783 the Episcopal Church separated organizationally from the Anglican Church and secured a bishop in 1787, but political ill-will prevented construction of a cathedral.

In 1828, Episcopal Bishop John Henry Hobart met privately with New York City Mayor Philip Hone to float the idea of an Episcopal cathedral. Fear of popular outrage in the city against people of British ethnicity, and opposition of the State Legislature to construction of a prominent symbol of the American branch of Great Britain's Anglican Church stalled the project until 1872.

Protestant hostility, especially upstate, and fear of offending Roman Catholic sensibilities in the city (especially among new Irish immigrants), put the idea on hold. The Episcopalian denomination was not popular in the United States in the years immediately following the American Revolution and the War of 1812, when the Episcopal Church was seen as a Tory, or pro-British institution.

The New York Diocese eventually received permission from the State Legislature to begin building the cathedral. In those days a state charter was necessary to build a church. It was built on Morningside Heights next to Saint Luke's Hospital and down the block from Columbia University (formerly King's College), at the time both Episcopal institutions. Construction began in 1892, helped by a $500,000 donation by banker J.P. Morgan. In 1913 enough progress had been made that the cathedral began holding regular services in its crypt chapel.

The Episcopalians chose to name the cathedral for Saint John the Divine, also called Saint John of Patmos. He was the author of the final book in the Christian New Testament known as *The Revelation of Saint John the Divine, The Revelation to John,* or *The Revelation of Jesus Christ.* He was called *the Divine,* which does not mean he was divine, but rather that he could *divine* (predict or foresee) the future. The book of prophesy is filled with mystical symbolism. It contains many visions including a great battle between Archangel Michael's legion of angels and an evil dragon, punishment of the wicked, the Battle of Armageddon, the defeat of Satan, and an account of the Last Judgment.

The cathedral is not finished. Many European cathedrals took centuries to complete, and some were never finished. Mayor Edward Koch, speaking at the cathedral in 1979, joked: *I am told that some of the great cathedrals took over five hundred years to build. But I would like to remind you that we are only in our first one hundred.* Saint John the Divine may never achieve the fullness of the original plan with north and south transepts and a large central squared spire, but the nave is done and the two front towers are slowly rising above the roof level.

Whether the Cathedral of Saint John the Divine is ever completely finished may not be so important. It is a monument in stone to an important religious and cultural tradition and a repository of many Christian and American symbols. The role of the cathedral in neighborhood people's lives and New York City's arts is also significant.

CHAPTER 71
Elizabeth Blackwell & Hospitals in New York City

Elizabeth Blackwell was a prototypical 19th century social reformer who exerted great effort to help women, children, and the poor, and to change minds about the abilities and qualifications of women to engage in occupations formerly held exclusively by men. Her primary field of endeavor was medicine, but she was active in many causes.

She was born in 1821 in Bristol, England to middle class parents. Her father, Samuel Blackwell, a sugar merchant, was an active reformer and supported the establishment of public schools (there were none at the time), removal of the property qualification for voting, abolition of slavery, temperance, and equal rights for women.

In 1832 the Blackwell family emigrated from England to the United States, initially staying at the elegant City Hotel on Broadway, then settling in New York City before relocating to nearby Paulus Hook (Jersey City). She attended a private school, took family vacations, and traveled often on short trips around the area, especially in Staten Island and the New Jersey Shore. From across the Hudson River, Blackwell witnessed the Great Fire of 1835, which ravaged southeast Manhattan.

In 1838 the Blackwell family moved to Cincinnati, Ohio and bought a house near the Ohio River. Elizabeth continued her schooling and studied mathematics, English composition, and French, German, Latin, and Greek. She read broadly and attended lectures, hearing, for example, the educator Horace Mann and the theologian Lyman Beecher (father of Henry Ward Beecher and Harriet Beecher Stowe).

Blackwell had been encouraged by her parents to study whatever interested her, and ultimately that freedom led her to plan a career in medicine. *At the time I had not the slightest idea of how to become a physician, or of the course of study necessary for this purpose. As the idea seemed to gain force, however, I wrote to and consulted with several physicians, known to my family, in various parts of the country, as to the possibility of a lady becoming a doctor. The answers I received were curiously unanimous. They all replied to the effect that the idea was a good one, but that it was impossible to accomplish it; that there was no way of obtaining such an education for a woman; that the education required was long and expensive; that there were innumerable obstacles in the way of such a course; and that, in short, the idea, though a valuable one, was impossible of execution.* In the mid 19th century a student could go directly to medical school, and so she applied to 29 medical colleges. No one, including Elizabeth Blackwell, was surprised when 28 rejected her application. What was astonishing was that she received an acceptance, the first time in American history that a woman had been invited to study medicine.

Geneva College, which later became a component of Syracuse University, offered her admittance to the medical class of 1847. Many years later Blackwell learned that the medical faculty had voted unanimously to reject her application, but that the student body voted unanimously to admit her. The faculty, when notified of the student vote, acquiesced. The student body passed a welcoming resolution, which read, in part: *...and in extending our unanimous invitation we pledge ourselves that no conduct of ours shall cause her to regret her attendance at this institution.*

Her experiences at medical school were positive. The faculty and students respected Blackwell without hazing or rudeness. *The behavior of the medical class during the two years that I was with them was admirable. It was that of true Christian gentlemen. I learned later that some of them had been inclined to think my application for admission a hoax, perpetrated at their expense by a rival college. But when the 'bona-fide' student actually appeared they gave her a manly welcome, and fulfilled to the letter the promise in their invitation.*

After graduation in 1849 she became the first woman to earn a medical degree in the United States. Dr. Elizabeth Blackwell traveled to London, Paris, and Germany to study informally with some of the physicians she had read and heard about while at Geneva College. In Paris, she volunteered for a while at La Maternité, a convent hospital for women, located on the Boulevard de Port

Royal, which specialized in obstetrics.

She returned to New York City in 1851 eager to practice medicine at a hospital or dispensary but was prevented by the hostility of male physicians. She rented a floor of a row house on University Place, furnished it, and hung a modest shingle advertising her services as a women's doctor. *I took very good rooms in University Place, but patients came very slowly to consult me. I had no medical companionship, the profession stood aloof, and society was distrustful of the innovation. Insolent letters occasionally came by post, and my pecuniary position was a source of constant anxiety.* Sometimes she had fewer than three patients each week. Eventually Blackwell began attracting a number of Quaker women and their children.

In 1852 she began offering a study course of six lectures, not just on medicine, but on a whole array of social reform topics. The health issues she was most interested in expounding were the need for wholesome food, physical exercise, fresh air, proper sanitation, and adequate housing. Blackwell urged women to understand their bodies and presented physiological lectures on the circulatory, muscular, skeletal, and reproductive systems.

From her first stay in New York, and again when she returned as a doctor, Elizabeth Blackwell socialized with the most well known reformers of the day: William Lloyd Garrison, Henry Ward Beecher, and Harriet Beecher Stowe (abolitionists), Lucy Stone (women's rights advocate), Horace Greeley (journalist), Peter Cooper (industrialist and inventor), and Charles Loring Brace (social worker). They encouraged her in providing medical care for women and children, and she, in turn, helped them advocate for some of their causes.

After being rebuffed again when she applied for a position as staff doctor at a dispensary in 1853, she raised enough money to open her own dispensary on East 7th Street near Tompkins Square in the Lower East Side. The small suite was located in an area of recent German immigrants called *Kleindeutschland* (Little Germany), and many there were too poor to afford traditional medical care. Her dispensary operated as an outreach clinic seeking patients and charging them little or nothing. For those women with more money at their disposal, Elizabeth Blackwell provided an opportunity to have a physician of their own gender. Choosing to be close to her work, she bought a house on East 15th Street.

Ultimately, her modest dispensary became the New York Infirmary for Women and Children, changing its location to East 3rd Street and then Bleecker Street. The name was changed again to the Women's Hospital of New York in 1855, and in 1860 she secured enough funding to move to larger quarters at 2nd Avenue and St. Mark's Place, and at length to the east side of Stuyvesant Square between East 15 and 16th Streets.

Blackwell hired female nurses and midwives to assist her in the busy clinic. Her sister, Emily Blackwell, who had graduated as a physician from the Medical College of Cleveland, Ohio, joined her at the Women's Hospital. In 1868 a medical college was added to the Women's Hospital to more rapidly train staff to meet the enormous demand for women's medicine. Blackwell's ideas and innovations were fought all along the way by the male medical profession, but, as she raised her own funds and trained her own staff, they were unable to stop her. It helped, of course, that she had cultivated some well-respected and powerful friends.

In her later years, Elizabeth Blackwell continued to manage the Women's Hospital and speak out publicly on a variety of social and political issues. She traveled often to Europe to visit family and friends, including Florence Nightingale, and to share ideas on medicine. While in England she became increasingly impressed with the ideas of Christian Socialism popularized by Charles Kingsley, an Episcopal priest. Always concerned about poverty and uneven distribution of wealth, Blackwell supported the moral reforms and cooperative ventures (housing, farming, workshops) advocated by Christian Socialists. She died at age 89 while visiting Hastings, England in May 1910. Her sister Emily died four months later.

Women's Hospital became the New York Lying-In Hospital, then the Stuyvesant Square branch of Beekman Hospital. Presently, the building is the Bernstein Pavilion, a component of Beth Israel Hospital. The only reference to Blackwell is a small plaque in the foyer, which reads: *Dedicated to Elizabeth Blackwell, M.D., 1821-1910, whose pioneering efforts overcame the prejudices of her day and opened the doors of equality to allow women to study and practice medicine in the United States.* Elizabeth Blackwell would be gratified to know that by the end of the 20th century almost half of the physicians graduating from U.S. medical schools were women.

From its colonial beginnings, New York City had medical doctors, pharmacies, and facilities for treatment, recuperation, and quarantine. Wealthy people through the 19th century preferred to be treated at home. A doctor came to the home to examine a patient and the prescription was filled at a pharmacy or a charity-supported dispensary. In dispensaries examinations by doctors could be done for poor people who lacked suitable quarters, or money, for a private doctor. Pharmacies were very different before the dawn of modern medicine. Much of their stock was patent medicines. (What was patented about patent medicines was the brand name, shape of the bottle, and color of the substance, not its content, which was almost always water, alcohol, sugar, flavoring, and sometimes codeine.) Pharmacies, alternatively called drug stores, usually had a soda fountain where a young male employee, called a *soda jerk*, would mix soft drinks, malted milks, root beer floats, and egg creams while customers waited for the pharmacist to mix ingredients and put the powder in capsules. There were no x-rays, CAT-scans, or blood tests, so medical laboratories were not yet part of medicine. In the 20th century the dispensaries have been replaced by city, corporate, pharmacy, or charity walk-in clinics and the emergency rooms of hospitals.

The few hospitals that served New Yorkers in the 19th century were Protestant establishments. Roman Catholic and Jewish hospitals were founded for similar reasons. Since the city's hospitals were either Protestant-owned or private entities, which regularly and exclusively invited Protestant clergy to offer prayers, operate chapels, place religious material in the rooms, and visit patients. Support for patients from Roman Catholic and Jewish clergy was prohibited. There were credible accusations that Protestant missionaries attempted deathbed conversions from non-Protestant patients.

The first Roman Catholic hospital was St. Vincent's Hospital, operated by the Sisters of Charity, which opened in 1850 in Manhattan. Throughout the next century there were many others including Our Lady of Mercy Medical Center, opened in 1888 in the Bronx, and the New York Foundling Hospital, operated by the Sisters of Charity of Saint Vincent de Paul, which cared for *foundlings* and tried to place them in adoptive homes. Mother Frances Xavier Cabrini, superior of the Missionary Sisters of the Sacred Heart, opened Columbus Hospital (now Cabrini Medical Center) in 1892 catering to Italian immigrants who were often refused treatment by New York's medical doctors. (The Roman Catholic Church later canonized Mother Cabrini and her remains lie behind glass under the altar at the Shrine Chapel of Cabrini High School in Washington Heights near Fort Tryon Park.)

The first Jewish Hospital was The Jews' Hospital in Manhattan, later renamed Mount Sinai Hospital, which opened in 1855. Others include Beth Israel Hospital in Manhattan, which was organized in 1891, Montefiore Hospital in the Bronx, and Maimonides Hospital in Brooklyn. Maimonides Hospital, named for Moses ben Maimonides (1135-1204), medical doctor and the European Jewish scholar who lived in Moorish Spain, has a history of mergers shared by many hospitals in New York City. The Maimonides' antecedents began with the New Utrecht Dispensary in 1911, which became the Israel Hospital of Brooklyn in 1919. It merged with Zion Hospital in 1920 and formed the United Israel Zion Hospital. In 1947 it merged with Beth Moses Hospital to form Maimonides Hospital.

There were also some ethnic hospitals such as the German Hospital, formed in 1868, which later became Lenox Hill Hospital, French Hospital, and Swedish Hospital. Black patients had the Colored Home, founded in 1841, which ultimately became Lincoln Hospital.

Protestant-affiliated hospitals included: St. Luke's (Episcopal), Presbyterian Hospital, now Columbia-Presbyterian Hospital, founded in Manhattan in 1872, Methodist Hospital, Norwegian Deaconess Hospital (Lutheran), and St. John's Hospital (Lutheran) which merged with Brooklyn Jewish Hospital in 1983 to form Interfaith Hospital. In general, religious affiliation has been played down or abandoned by most traditionally religious hospitals in the 20th century.

Private non-religious hospitals in the city include New York Hospital, New York University Hospital, Flushing Hospital, and Long Island College Hospital. Some private hospitals are affiliated with universities and others are organized as not-for-profit corporations.

Among the City of New York's municipal hospitals are Bellevue Hospital in Manhattan, which traces its lineage to the Almshouse Infirmary in 1736 (essentially a prison for the poor with chronic illnesses), Kings County Hospital in Brooklyn, which dates from 1831, Harlem Hospital, founded in 1877 as Reception Hospital, Metropolitan Hospital in Manhattan, and Bronx Municipal Hospital, which opened in 1954, The Veterans Administration of the United States Government operates VA Hospitals in Brooklyn, Manhattan, and the Bronx.

Since 1965, both city and private (religious and non-religious) hospitals have received indirect aide from the state in the form of reimbursements from Medicare and Medicaid programs. State regulators monitor all hospitals in New York State, and the New York Health and Hospitals Corporation, a city department, governs municipal hospitals.

Medicine has changed greatly since Elizabeth Blackwell's day. Advances in all aspects of medical technology have increased greatly over the past two centuries. When Elizabeth Blackwell died in 1910, the actuarial age (life expectancy) for an American male was 51. In 1935 when the Social Security System was established and retirement benefits were set to begin at age 65, a man's life expectancy was 64. By 2000 it had climbed to 74. Inequities still exist and the debate over heath care continues to capture the attention of the public. There are many unresolved issues over who should pay, or share, the cost of advanced medical treatment, which includes routine check-ups, testing, hospitalization, rehabilitation, and pharmaceuticals.

CHAPTER 72
Sunday School Movement

The Sunday School Movement was started by Protestants in the United States who were concerned that Enlightenment ideas, rural isolation, and rapid urbanization had all contributed to a lack of religious sentiments in the young. They were also concerned that poverty in solitary rural areas and crowded city slums kept young people without money for tuition from receiving a basic education. The Sunday School Movement addressed both issues in the days before the establishment of public schools.

The Sunday School campaign began in England in the first two decades of the 19th century and quickly caught on in the United States. In some communities the concept was broadened to include classes for adults. Local groups organized to *evangelize* (convert to Christianity) the unchurched and illiterate. Quakers organized a First-Day Society was organized in Philadelphia in 1790. Several independent Sunday Schools were opened in New York City before the War of 1812. The first Sunday School was started by two women at the home of Mrs. Leech on Mott Street in 1803. Later, the founders of the Mott Street School, Isabella Graham and her daughter Joanna Graham Bethune, opened two more Sunday Schools for poor children in Greenwich Village, and one for indigent adults. The four schools welcomed black students.

Divie Bethune (Joanna's husband) and Eleazer Lord established the New York Sunday-School Union Society in 1816. Richard Varick was elected president. Varick had been secretary to George Washington during the Revolution, and mayor of New York City from 1789 to 1801. By the following year they had established twenty-eight schools and enrolled 3,000 students. In 1829 the Kings County Sabbath School Society was formed to coordinate Sunday School activities in Brooklyn.

The American Sunday-School Union was organized in 1824 to coordinate efforts and share instructional materials and strategies. Morris Ketchum Jessup, banker and president of the Young

Men's Christian Association, served as president of the American Sunday-School Union from 1896 to 1908. He spoke laudably of its universal (catholic) appeal and its proselytizing (evangelical) nature. *The American Sunday-School Union took hold of my heart when I was a boy. I remember very well --- one of the earliest recollections of my life --- when my father told me about this Sunday-School Union, and he became so interested in its work that he contributed toward the expenses of a missionary in Virginia. I like this work also because it is so catholic. It is a type of what we want as Christian unity. I like it because it is so thoroughly evangelical. I like it because it has stood the test of these seventy-two years and has never been found wanting....I like the Sunday-School Union because it has a fixedness of purpose, and because it has principle behind its work.*

The movement was part of a high point of Protestant influence though it was not started by any of the denominations, and some, especially the Episcopalian, Dutch Reformed, Lutheran, Congregationalist, and Presbyterian church leadership were skeptical. Methodists and Baptists were, from the start, more sympathetic. In the early years of the movement it was not officially connected with the churches, so the classes were held in parlors and kitchens of private homes and taught by unpaid volunteers.

Despite the separation of church and state clause in the First Amendment of the U.S. Constitution, there was a strong patriotic aspect to the Sunday School Movement. Many Protestants saw patriotism and religion as linked concepts. Francis Scott Key was a manager of the American Sunday School Union and wrote a rhapsodic description of the group's work. *By means of it, the ignorant have been taught; drunkards have been reformed; infidels have been converted; and the thoughtless have been alarmed. By its influence, light has been brought out of darkness and order out of confusion; domestic peace has been established; the altar of domestic worship has been reared; the Sabbath has been consecrated; congregations have been gathered; churches of the living God have been planted, and in solitary places where no voice was, notes of joy and gladness, thanksgiving and the voice of melody are now heard.* Key had composed a poem during the British bombardment of Baltimore's Fort McHenry during the War of 1812. When put to the music of an old English song, the poem became *The Star-Spangled Banner,* later adopted as the national anthem of the United States. Francis Scott Key was an icon of American patriotism and Protestant education.

Sunday Schools marked a significant change in the way the impoverished young were instructed in religion. Previously only the sons of the upper and upper middle class attended church-affiliated private school where religion, as well as secular subjects, was taught. Collegiate, Trinity, and Fordham Preparatory were private schools connected with religious traditions. Collegiate opened in 1687 as a Dutch Reformed school, Trinity in 1709 as an Episcopal school, and Fordham Preparatory in 1841 as a Roman Catholic school.

Those who lacked tuition remained unschooled and had to pick up reading and writing skills from their parents or other adults. This was not impossible, and some who had little or no formal education grasped literacy quickly and became impressively erudite. Benjamin Franklin, Frederick Douglass, and Abraham Lincoln are striking examples. Bible stories and religious doctrines were passed down in the home or gleaned from Sunday sermons.

Before the organization of mandatory and free public education the classes set up by the Sunday School Movement were an important vehicle to teach literacy, Bible stories, and religious doctrines. After public schools were instituted in the United States, religion from a Protestant perspective became part of the curriculum.

Literacy had been an important bedrock principle of Protestantism where each individual was expected to be able to read the Bible and was encouraged to do so. Martin Luther had celebrated the autodidactic expertise of laymen as part of *the priesthood of all believers*. Reading was taught in the Sunday Schools so that the children could proceed with their studies. Many who signed up were illiterate working class youths who had never been to school.

Children love stories, and Bible stories were probably the most enjoyable to learn and the easiest to teach. Many are colorful and filled with action. Religious doctrines had to be accepted on faith and were generally taught by rote memorization followed by analysis. The Lord's Prayer, Nicene Creed, Ten Commandments, Beatitudes, Books of the Bible, and denominational *catechism* (summary of basic beliefs in question-and-answer form) were learned this way.

A few church leaders remained skeptical of Sunday Schools and considered them too populist. They doubted the qualifications of the teachers and the substance of the curriculum. Henry C. Potter, the Episcopal Bishop of New York, issued a warning in *Principles of Religious Education*, written in 1901: *This is not so much of a Service as to appear to make the Sunday-school a substitute for the Church. At the same time, it is enough to give the children that familiarity with the book [Book of Common Prayer], which will prepare them to take an intelligent and devout part in the Church service.* Potter explained his suspicions of teacher expertise. *A striking difficulty with the majority of Sunday-school teachers is the fact that their knowledge is in a chaotic state. Having studied one lesson at a time, with little reference to what preceded or followed, they may have become acquainted with many details, but these are not organized, and their knowledge lacks unity.* There were others who thought it was a desecration to teach the poor and ignorant to read. Some felt that basic doctrinal concepts should be learned either in the home or from the minister during a church service.

During the middle of the 19th century, states began to establish public school systems. The schools had a religious dimension but some critics contended they needed to be more religious. Horace Mann, father of the public school system in Massachusetts, felt compelled to defend the public schools from the charge that they were not teaching religion. In 1839, he wrote in his diary: *The fundamental principles of Christianity may and should be inculcated.... After this, each denomination must be left to its own resources, for inculcating its own faith and creed.* Mann believed that the public schools should teach *general* Protestant values, prayers, and doctrines, and use the King James translation of the Bible. Beyond that, the individual Protestant denominations had the responsibility of teaching their specific doctrines.

McGuffey Readers, popular reading primers in use throughout the country, were filled with Bible stories, poems, and essays on Christianity from a general Protestant perspective. Between 1836 and 1890 over one hundred million *McGuffey Readers* were sold in the United States. The 19th century was the high point of American Protestantism. The Sunday School Movement, the widespread campaign to build churches and colleges, and the spiritual impact of the Second Great Awakening, a new wave of revivalism that swept the nation at the turn-of-the-century, created an enormous impact on American culture.

On the last Sunday of May 1887, more than 100,000 children participated in the Sunday School Anniversary Parade in the Long Meadow of Brooklyn's Prospect Park. The *Brooklyn Daily Eagle* reported on the event: *The parade in Prospect Park began promptly at 3 p.m., and others were scheduled to begin at later hours, so that the drumbeats scarcely died away in one part of the borough before they began in another section. Altogether 27 divisions were scheduled to march in the afternoon.* The Brooklyn Sunday School Union organized the annual march.

The importance of the Sunday School Movement waned as compulsory and free public education was established in every state, and as the Protestant denominations began to prefer operating their own sectarian Sunday School classes to teach their specific catechisms and prepare students for confirmation. The generalist strategy ceased to be useful

Notation:

Brooklyn-Queens Day

The Sunday School Movement was behind the New York State Legislature's 1905 declaration reserving the first Thursday in June as a yearly public school holiday in Brooklyn to honor *the founding of the Sunday School Movement in Brooklyn* in 1816 and to allow Protestant children to march in Sunday School parades. The group had been staging processions on Sundays since 1860. In 1959 the legislature added Queens, so *Brooklyn Day* became *Brooklyn-Queens Day*. It was also sometimes referred to as *Anniversary Day* or *Kidsday*. The organization behind the movement is the Brooklyn Sunday School Union which still exists. Most Christian churches (Protestant, Roman Catholic, and Eastern Orthodox) maintain Sunday Schools but the Sunday School Movement itself is a pale shadow of its former self. In 1887, more than 100,000 children marched in the annual parade in Prospect Park, while in 2003 only 300 marched.

CHAPTER 73
Orphanages & Orphan Trains

Poor children in the city faced many problems in the 19th century. The worst was loss of parents either through death or abandonment. If no relative was available to take care of an orphan, it meant homelessness. The problem was made worse because there were no government agencies to help destitute families or individuals survive. The industrialization of New York City and the immense immigration boosted the population from 33,000 in 1790 to 814,000 in 1860, and up to two and a half million in 1890. The flood of people into the city made housing scarce and kept wages low.

Seriously impoverished families sometimes sent their children off to fend for themselves. Other times a child would escape the long hours and boredom of a factory job by running away. Official estimates for homeless children ranged from 15,000 to 40,000 in the middle of the 19th century.

There were many pejorative names for a homeless child: *ragamuffin, waif, urchin, vagabond, stray, guttersnipe,* and the racist terms, *Gypsy* and *Street Arab*. The variety of negative names suggests the rock-bottom status of the homeless and the cold hearts of some citizens. Jacob Riis, a photo-journalist who sought to reform the problems of the city, but also a harsh critic of the poor, wrote this about homeless children: *The Street Arab has all the faults and all the virtues of the lawless life he leads. Vagabond that he is, acknowledging no authority and owing no allegiance to anybody or anything, with his grimy fist raised against society whenever it tries to coerce him, he is as bright and sharp as the weasel, which, among all the predatory beasts, he most resembles.*

Street children lived by their wits and survived on the edge of society. They earned money shining shoes, selling newspapers, peddling flowers, neckties, matches, and cigars. Some children worked as street musicians singing or playing an instrument for donations. They used their small earnings to buy food. Some stole from crates and bushels outside grocery stores. Gangs often recruited young boys to act as decoys and lookouts. Though the gangs had colorful names like the Plug Uglies, Dead Rabbits, Roach Guards, Short Boys, Bowery Boys, and Shirt Tails, they committed serious crimes.

Sleeping quarters for street children were empty spaces between buildings or under stairs, hidden spots in alleys, or in the bushes in parks. In the winter they slept on steam gratings or broke into basements or storage rooms for shelter. When caught, they had their ears boxed and were kicked out.

Orphans endured a terrible life and the solutions offered by adults did little to help. In the early colonial period, Dutch charities and churches raised funds to build the first *almshouse* in New Amsterdam in 1653. An almshouse was a place where the homeless poor, both young and old, were sent to work, sleep, and eat. Disruptive paupers were put in cells. The almshouse was really a government sanctioned private prison since clothing, food, and work hours were all regulated and no one was allowed to leave. Disobeying rules meant an isolation cell, bread-and-water diet, and chains. In 1736 the New York City Poorhouse opened. It was a public facility with rules that were much the same as the private almshouse.

The New York Orphan Asylum, built in 1807, ushered in a slightly less prison-like environment for homeless children. At first, Protestant charity organizations or churches operated all orphanages. Many of the children were from Catholic and Jewish backgrounds, but Protestant ministers preached to the children on Sundays and before each meal. Catholics and Jews eventually formed their own orphanages and children's relief agencies such as the Catholic Orphan Asylum and the Jewish Board of Guardians. Blacks organized the Colored Orphan Asylum. *Little Orphan Annie*, both a play and a movie, portrays the negative side of a mythical orphanage run by mean-spirited Miss Hannigan, in New York City. (Annie, of course, had the good fortune to be adopted by Daddy Warbucks, a millionaire.)

The New York Orphan Asylum came up with a new idea to get children out of institutions and into homes. It was called the *cottage system*. Young children, divided by gender, lived together in cottages in groups of about 20 until they were 12 years old when they were indentured to families to work until they reached age 18.

The most daring idea came from Charles Loring Brace, who was born in a small town in Connecticut and moved to New York City in 1848. He was shocked at the misery of street children and decided to do something about it. To him, the problem was an embarrassment to our industrial system and to democracy. Brace came up with a completely new idea, which he thought would solve the problem. He wrote: *As Christian men we cannot look upon this great multitude of unhappy, deserted, and degraded boys and girls without feeling our responsibility to God for them.*

At first, Brace started the Children's Aid Society, an orphanage, to provide a safe place for vagrant children to sleep and eat. Fearing the task was too large for a handful of private orphanages to solve, he proposed gathering homeless orphans and shipping them off to families in upstate New York or in the West. He called it the *Emigration Plan*. Between 1854 and 1929, a quarter of a million children, many from New York City, were sent to live with rural families. About half the children were sent by the Children's Aid Society, the rest by other groups. The New York Foundling Hospital, where unwanted babies were dropped off, organized Baby Trains to the West.

An advocate of a strong family, hard work, thrift, and religion, Brace came to oppose institutionalizing orphans because the ideas he most cherished were difficult or impossible to pass along in the bleak setting of an orphanage. He regularly made four points to defend his Emigration Plan: *Individual influences and home life as better than institutional life; Lessons of industry and self-help as better than alms; The implanting of moral and religious truths in union with the supply of bodily wants; Entire change of circumstances as the best cure for the defects of children of the lowest poor.*

When an Orphan Train arrived at its destination, local residents gathered in town halls, churches, or railway stations to take a look at the orphans. Posters had publicized the arrival of the Orphan Train and the organizers had appealed to farmers to do a good deed and at the same time gain an extra pair of hands. Farm families were often short of labor.

There were some real problems with Orphan trains. No one ever verified that the children were actually orphans. Many were *half-orphans* who had left an impoverished home for the streets. Some were runaways from abuse. No reliable contact was ever kept between the children and the groups that sent them to monitor their condition and happiness. The potential for abuse was never explored. The trauma of being separated from whatever family and friends existed, and from familiar urban surroundings, and taken in by strangers hundreds of miles away, was ignored. Some of the children may have learned useful trades and become successful, though many of the boys were used as unpaid farm laborers and the girls as maids.

There was a big cultural issue, too. Brace was a Protestant minister from the Baptist denomination. He was profoundly prejudiced against other religions. Almost all the receiving families were Protestant and many of the orphans were Catholic. New York City's population was about half Catholic by the Civil War. The Roman Catholic Church strenuously opposed Orphan Trains and Bishop John Hughes saw the program as a plot to kidnap Catholic children and turn them into Protestants.

On the other hand, the New York Foundling Hospital, a Roman Catholic institution operated by the Sisters of Charity of Saint Vincent de Paul, started its own emigration program for infants in 1870. Parish priests notified most of the rural or small town adopting families. The Catholic families presumably raised Protestant, Jewish, and Eastern Orthodox infants in the Catholic faith.

Some of the placed-out orphans from these programs stayed and melted in with the local population. About half eventually returned to their familiar hometowns, and siblings or parents rescued others.

Today there are far fewer orphans because parents usually choose to limit the size of their families to what they can afford. Genuine adoptions (not indentured jobs) are much more common, and foster care, which is supervised by the city government, monitors the children's living conditions in homes where they have been placed. While all problems have not been solved, there are far fewer homeless boys and girls living on the streets than in the past.

CHAPTER 74
Brooklyn Bridge

The Brooklyn Bridge, which spans the East River between Manhattan and Brooklyn, solved a serious transportation problem, boosted economic expansion on both sides of the river, and became the world-renowned emblem of Brooklyn. The need for a bridge was palpable. Though the East River was important for the region's commerce, it was also a barrier to trade and movement. There was tremendous growth in both cities, and commuters from Brooklyn and Manhattan overwhelmed the ferries. Severe winters made river traffic difficult and winter storms or ice floes sometimes halted ferry service for several days in a row. The particularly cold and icy winter of 1866 proved to be the catalyst.

To build a bridge across the East River would be a Herculean task, but 19th century civil engineers and architects had made great advances in bridge building, especially with suspension bridges. In 1857 John Roebling submitted to the public a detailed design for a bridge connecting Manhattan and Brooklyn.

The New York Bridge Company, with 39 investors, was organized in 1867 to raise private funds and seek money from the City of Brooklyn and the City of New York. The investors were businessmen and politicians from Brooklyn. To get his support, the company gave $65,000 to Boss Tweed to pass along to City Councilmen, and granted him, for his own profit, stock in the company worth $40,000. John Augustus Roebling was hired by the New York Bridge Company as its chief engineer.

Roebling, a gifted engineer and master builder, had emigrated from the German state of Thuringia. He was an experienced bridge-builder as well as a visionary and brilliant polymath. He was an engineer, mathematician, astronomer, and musician. Roebling had already built three *suspension* bridges: the *Suspension Bridge* at Niagara Falls, the *Delaware & Hudson Aqueduct Bridge* at Lackawaxen in Pennsylvania, and the *Ohio River Bridge* in Cincinnati.

The roadway of a suspension bridge hangs from thousands of miles of cables, tightly twisted steel wires that are firmly tethered in the center to large *pylons*, granite towers of immense size and weight built in the water. The towers, in turn, are anchored on the land to bulky 60,000-ton *anchorages* at each shore. On top of the anchorages run the approach roads to the bridge. Roebling, who owned a wire-cable works in Trenton, New Jersey, had ample experience making wire rope. In the late 19th century, steel, and in this case wire rope fabricated from steel, was the chief measure of a nation's industrial strength.

The granite towers were built slightly offshore, which necessitated constructing two rectangular boxes called *caissons*, each measuring 172 feet by 102 feet. The caissons were placed in the East River and men inside dug out rock and sand at the bottom while the box lowered. A sealed top was put on the box before it sank below the surface to keep it watertight while the laborers dug. Kerosene lamps were used for lighting. The dark, smoky environment was uncomfortable and dangerous. The digging ceased when the caissons rested on solid rock at the bottom of the river, 44 feet below high tide on the Brooklyn side and 78 feet below high tide on the Manhattan side. Cement was poured through supply shafts, and when it hardened the granite base of the tower was built over it.

Work on the Brooklyn Bridge commenced in 1870, five years after the Union victory in the Civil War. It took thirteen years to complete. When finished, the bridge cost $16 million dollars, a very high price. Regrettably, some of the money ended up in the hands of the *Tweed Ring*, the political opportunists who hovered around Mayor William Marcy Tweed.

As it turned out, the Brooklyn Bridge became a family affair. Conceived by John Augustus Roebling, supervised by Washington Roebling, and finished with Emma Warren Roebling explaining her husband's directions. The bridge took its toll of tragedy on the family who planned it.

John Roebling died in 1869, just before work on the bridge began. A ferry crushed his foot in a dockside accident and he died a few weeks later either from gangrene, lockjaw, or tetanus. Washington Roebling, his 32-year old son, also an engineer, took over.

In 1872 he contracted the *caisson disease* (*the bends*, or *nitrogen narcosis*) when he ascended too rapidly from an underwater construction chamber. He had been fighting a fire started by a kerosene lamp inside one of the sunken bridge caissons. Washington Roebling was incapacitated and became an invalid for most of his life. For the duration of construction, bedridden at his house located on nearby Columbia Heights, he watched the progress through a telescope. Emily Warren Roebling, his wife, was not an engineer, but assumed a large role by assisting him and relaying his instructions to the foremen.

For the employees, the project was hazardous. It involved precarious heights, risky underwater work, and dangerous heavy equipment. Twenty-six of the 600 workers were killed constructing the engineering and structural sensation. Some fell off the towers and drowned, others were crushed, and several died from the *bends*.

When it opened, gas burners and calcium bulbs illuminated the Brooklyn Bridge. Its roadway had separate lanes for pedestrians, horse-drawn trolleys, railroad trains, and individual carriages or wagons. The trolleys were removed in 1944 and all lanes except the elevated pedestrian walkway were reserved for automobiles.

The Brooklyn Bridge opened on May 24, 1883, and was recognized as an engineering marvel, a modern Gothic superstructure of great beauty. James Stranahan, a company trustee, who was also Brooklyn parks commissioner responsible for supervising the construction of Prospect Park, presided over the gala celebrations that inaugurated the bridge.

President Chester Arthur with several members of his cabinet, New York State Governor Grover Cleveland, and New York City Mayor Franklin Edson led the parade from the Manhattan side. When the party reached the center it was joined by Brooklyn Mayor Seth Low, as they all proceeded to the Brooklyn side. Fourteen tons of fireworks lit up the sky for an hour that evening as tens of thousands of people celebrated the grand achievement. Washington Roebling, who suffered from illness, as well as increasingly strained relations with the New York Bridge Company, did not attend the festivities.

Stretching 1,595 feet, the Brooklyn Bridge was at the time

the longest suspension bridge in the world. The soaring height of its 25-story towers surpassed the steeple of Trinity Church as the highest structure in the metropolitan area. In fact, at the time the bridge was the highest man-made configuration in the United States. It became a symbol of New York City and the chief icon of Brooklyn, where it assumed mythical proportions. Its web of cables creates a beautiful pattern with interesting shadows. The present beige and brown tones are true to the original color scheme. The Gothic arches are significant because they soften the architectural modernism of the structure by making a connection with Europe's medieval cathedrals. It has inspired many artists and countless photographers. The Whitney Museum of American Art owns and displays modernist Joseph Stella's well-known abstract painting entitled *Brooklyn Bridge*. The bridge has become a popular tourist attraction and the renovated bridge walkway is situated between and above vehicular traffic and offers unsurpassed views of the busy city.

There had been three primary interest groups opposed to constructing the Brooklyn Bridge. While the elevated structure would solve a fundamental and growing transportation problem, ferry operators knew it would eventually destroy their East River business. The ferry industry had grown large and several ferry companies operated routes across the river. In the 1870s there were as many as 1,200 crossings each day. Nativists were horrified that an easy and inexpensive way to cross the river would bring a swarm of new immigrants to Brooklyn. A group of Protestant clergy also opposed the bridge, warning that it would bring the perceived sins of Manhattan to pristine Brooklyn, an independent and reserved cluster of communities known as the *city of churches*, a center of moral righteousness (or *self-righteousness)*, and a stronghold of the Protestant-dominated political reform movement.

In each case, the fears of the opponents came true. The Brooklyn Bridge soon destroyed the ferry business leaving only one company with limited service. The last Fulton Ferry crossed the river in 1924. The bridge rapidly changed the unsullied semi-rural character of Brooklyn. Immigrants flocked across the bridge to settle throughout Kings County that grew to be the most populous of the five boroughs. Brooklyn's collection of towns fused into one city and, by a slim margin voted to merge with New York City in a referendum held in 1898.

The proponents who had promised economic benefits had also been right. The bridge brought greater prosperity to both New York City and the City of Brooklyn. By 1900, an estimated 50 million crossings were made each year. The Brooklyn Bridge allowed commuters and shoppers to go about their business quickly, and it facilitated shipping manufactured goods and agricultural products for the growing metropolis that soon became a unified city.

Notation:

DUMBO

The Brooklyn Bridge spurred Brooklyn's economic growth, but because it was built very high to allow sailing ships safe passage underneath, the bridge's roadway overshot the old Village of Brooklyn, which had been the commercial center of the City of Brooklyn, and marginalized the original settlement. The area around Old Fulton Street lost retail businesses and residences and soon became a manufacturing and warehouse district. By the 1980s most manufacturing had ceased and artists and other urban pioneers began moving into the area, eventually called *DUMBO*, an acronym for Down Under the Manhattan and Brooklyn Overpass.

CHAPTER 75
Anthony Comstock & the New York Society for the Suppression of Vice

Anthony Comstock fashioned himself a reformer, though millions of Americans considered him a meddling, sententious prude. His life's work was to restrict public access to the many evils he saw swarming around American life. To that end he formed the New York Society for the Suppression of Vice and led a national campaign to persuade Congress to pass a law, popularly dubbed the *Comstock Law*, outlawing *obscene, lewd, or lascivious material* from distribution by the Post Office.

As with many New York City reformers, Anthony Comstock was born in rural Connecticut near New Canaan. His ancestors had lived in the area for almost two centuries before his birth in 1844. He was never too revealing about his childhood except to repeat on several occasions that it was then that he learned about the vices of small boys and their impure thoughts. It apparently bothered him for the rest of his life.

Comstock enlisted in the Union Army during the Civil War, joining in 1863 and being honorably discharged in 1865. He clerked briefly in a store in New Haven and then migrated to New York City to seek fulfillment. He worked in a clothing store progressing from clerk to salesman. His real interest, however, was finding a way to enforce his ideas of morality on the public, and he began to actively campaign as an individual against society's sins in 1868.

As a lone operator, seeing material he considered obscene at a newsstand, for example, and reporting it to the neighborhood police precinct, got him nowhere until he formed an organization. In 1872, Comstock enlisted powerful financial backers from the realm of New York's reformers and formed the *New York Society for the Suppression of Vice*. Morris Ketchum Jessup, banker and president of the Young Men's Christian Association and the American Sunday-School Union, Peter Cooper, inventor and manufacturer,

Abram S. Hewitt, industrialist and mayor, Anson Phelps Stokes, banker and philanthropist, and eventually J.P. Morgan, railroad magnate and powerful banker. (Morgan was only interested in reforming personal immorality, not social or economic problems.)

In 1872, Comstock began receiving attention in the press. A *New York Tribune* reporter and a police captain accompanied Comstock to two stationary stores where he purchased books he declared obscene. Six employees of the stores were arrested on Comstock's complaint and the adults were convicted of selling pornography and sent to prison for terms ranging from three months to one year. Between 1872 and his death in 1915, Comstock sent 3,600 men, women, and children to prison for violating various laws against vice.

The term *vice* is nebulous, and, in general, it means something like lechery, indecency, depravity, pornography, abomination, lasciviousness, sinfulness, debauchery, dissolution, iniquity, and immorality. Most of these words have a sexual subtext and, without ever being too specific to be embarrassing, Congress tried to define vice in the Comstock Law in 1873. President Ulysses Grant signed the bill and it became law as the *Act for the Suppression of Trade in, and Circulation of, obscene Literature and Articles of immoral Use.*

Section 148 of the Comstock Act specified: *That no obscene, lewd, or lascivious book, pamphlet, picture, paper, print, or other publication of an indecent character, or any article or thing designed or intended for the prevention of conception or procuring of abortion, nor any article or thing intended or adapted for any indecent or immoral use or nature, nor any written or printed card, circular, book, pamphlet, advertisement or notice of any kind giving information, directly or indirectly, where, or how, or by whom, or by what means either of the things before mentioned may be obtained or made, nor any letter upon the envelope of which, or postal-card upon which indecent or scurrilous epithets may be written or printed, shall be carried in the mail, and any person who shall knowingly deposit, or cause to be deposited, for mailing or delivery, any of the hereinbefore-mentioned articles or things, or any notice, or paper containing any advertisement relating to the aforesaid article or things, and any person who, in pursuance of any plan or scheme for disposing of any of the hereinbefore-mentioned articles or things, shall take, or cause to be taken, from the mail any such letter or package, shall be deemed guilty of a misdemeanor, and, on conviction thereof, shall, for every offense, be fined not less than one hundred dollars nor more than five thousand dollars, or imprisoned at hard labor not less than one year nor more than ten years, or both, in the discretion of the judge.*

The lengthy one-sentence long paragraph imposed steep fines and harsh prison sentences without really defining the crime. In fact, the paragraph used the vague word ***thing*** six times. The inclusion of *any article or thing designed or intended for the prevention of conception or procuring of abortion* meant that birth control and abortion had become federal crimes.

Comstock received an appointment from the Post Office Department as a special agent in charge of enforcing the new law. He refused to accept a salary for his new post because his wealthy backers in the New York Society for the Suppression of Vice provided him a yearly salary of $3,000. In 1873, $3,000 was about what a New York City lawyer earned, a more generous remuneration than what he could have received from the federal government.

In 1883, Comstock published *Traps for the Young,* to specify how vice could enter the hearts and minds of the nation's youth. The book is a survey of all the abominations Comstock found in New York City. Among his obsessions was rooting out what he called *evil reading* material. In his preface, Comstock writes: *This book is designed to awaken thought upon the subject of Evil Reading, and to expose to the minds of parents, teachers, guardians, and pastors, some of the mighty forces for evil that are to-day exerting a controlling influence over the young. There is a shameful recklessness in many homes as to what the children read.* He made many general statements such as *evil thoughts, like bees, go in swarms, and lewd thoughts soon overcome native innocence,* but one substantive point he made was that bright and ebullient children are more at risk to the perils of *evil reading* than others. *Children of strong affections, lively imaginations, and animated characters are more easily dazzled and drawn away by the opinions and expressions of those with whom they come in contact, than those possessing more sluggish natures.*

According to Comstock, the way *evil reading* harmed children was by affecting their imaginations. *Cheap works of fiction* and love stories especially agitated Comstock. *They defraud the future man or woman by capturing and enslaving the young imagination. The wild fancies and exaggerations of the unreal in the story supplant aspirations for that which ennobles and exalts. In brief, these stories, that make day-dreamers of our children and castle-builders of the student, are harmful just in proportion as these results are produced. In the home, at school, and even in the sanctuary during the solemn hours of worship on the Sabbath day, the day-dreamer wanders away in thought from all that is real and of highest importance, captivated by pictures and scenes that never can be realized.* Comstock provided specific examples of some titles to which he objected and offered a list including stories about *a man murdered by being blown up by explosives...a beautiful girl, by lying and deceit, seeks to captivate one whom she loves...six assaults upon an officer while resisting arrests...a burglary...an illegitimate child...two attempts to coerce a girl to marry against her wishes...an attempt to murder a child...a massacre by Indians...,* and *one woman who dies in New York and comes to life in Italy.*

Newspapers were dangerous to children because they contained *sickening details of loathsome crimes.* He portrayed how a seemingly innocent father with a daily newspaper could adversely affect children. *The father looks over his paper in the morning to ascertain the state of the market, to inform himself as to the news of the day. His attention is attracted by the heavy headlines designed to call especial attention to some disgusting detail of crime. A glance discloses its true character. He turns away in disgust, and thoughtlessly throws down in the library or parlor, within reach of his children, this hateful, debauching article, and goes off to business little thinking that what he thus turns from his child will read with avidity.*

Comstock devoted other chapters to warning against *rum traps* where a *smiling, coaxing, bowing, and scraping* bartender can initiate the young into a life of alcoholism. He railed against two particularly flagrant forms of gambling, shooting pool and playing the lottery, calling that category of gambling *one of Satan's most fascinating snares.* A particularly odd target was the neighborhood candy store. He accused it of tempting children to waste their money on candy and other treats.

Traps for the Young also attacked high culture, the novels, plays, paintings, and art books that *gild some of the most obscene representations and foulest matters* in the cloak of classical culture. In short, his attacks all had to do with nudity and sex. Curiously,

Comstock only mentioned one example, the 14th century Renaissance masterpiece, the *Decameron*, written by Giovanni Boccaccio. The book is a compilation of one hundred tales of wit, love, fortune, deception, religion, and sex told by ten Florentines who fled the city for the countryside during the Bubonic Plague in 1348. To entertain each other, each of the ten told ten ribald and outrageous stories during their voluntary exile.

Comstock was lampooned by opponents throughout his long reign as guardian of the nation's morals. They used the term *Comstockery* to mean narrow-minded and backward. National magazines ran cartoons poking fun at him. Despite attacks on his philosophy and methods, Comstock remained pugilistic until the end. At one point he took on dramatist George Bernhard Shaw, calling him ***an Irish smut peddler***. One of his last cases involved the prosecution of William Sanger, husband of Margaret Sanger, the leading birth control advocate, for distributing her pamphlet, *Family Limitation*. Comstock died of pneumonia in 1915, shortly after representing the United States at the Ninth International Purity Congress.

Traps for the Young, and Comstock's crusade against vice under the guise of reform, represented a serious cultural divide between two large amorphous groups in America. At that time it often pitted rural and small town conservative white Protestants against urban liberal immigrants, often Roman Catholics and Jews. The Scopes vs. Tennessee case, a 1925 legal battle over evolution, was also a benchmark in the American culture wars. Modified culture wars continue in the 21st century.

CHAPTER 76
How Marble Hill Joined the Mainland Geographically

The geographic face of Manhattan has had many changes since the Europeans settled in communities throughout the five boroughs. The Indians had lived in close harmony with nature. Because of their technological limitations, they would have had a difficult time changing the landscape had they wished to do so. The Europeans began altering the landforms immediately on arrival. They laid out a street grid south of the wall, smoothed the surface of the land by knocking down hills and filling in gullies and ponds, building docks, and a canal at Broad Street.

A later large-scale example that stands out is the engineering change that gave the Spuyten Duyvil Creek a new pathway. The broad creek took its colorful name from a Dutch saying, *spuit den duyvil* (in spite of the devil), which early settlers gave to the twisting waterway with dangerous tides. Or, alternatively the name can mean *devil's spout* for the treacherous eddies found in the tidal waters. It is a strait connecting the Hudson River with another strait, the Harlem River. (Henry Hudson once sheltered the *Half Moon* in the Spuyten Duyvil Creek during a storm in 1609.)

To early New Yorkers the only thing positive about the Spuyten Duyvil Creek was that it was compressed enough to be the first place where a link could be built between Manhattan and elsewhere. Kingsbridge Avenue, an Indian path and later a colonial trail, went on an east-west axis from Manhattan to the Bronx at a narrow point (about West 225th Street) in the course of the Spuyten Duyvil Creek. The first bridge constructed from Manhattan to anywhere was built there in 1693 and called King's Bridge to honor William III of England.

Where the bridge was built (Marble Hill neighborhood) is no longer water since the construction of the Harlem River Ship Canal, completed in 1895, cut off the northern loop of the Spuyten

Duyvil Creek and left Marble Hill connected to the Bronx by a dry riverbed which was soon filled in and raised to the level of the surrounding land for construction of houses.

Civil engineers dynamited through rock to straighten out the creek's passageway for construction of the Harlem River Ship Canal. Blasting left the northern tip of Manhattan, called Marble Hill because of an old stone quarry, as an island. Within twenty years the old creek at the northern part of Marble Hill was filled in and the neighborhood, still a political part of Manhattan, became geographically attached to the Bronx. The name Spuyten Duyvil was used for the western portion of the natural creek that remained. If you live in Marble Hill, you live in Manhattan, though you have to cross the Spuyten Duyvil Creek - Harlem River Ship Canal to get to the rest of the borough.

There were many other significant physical changes in New York City. Landfill smoothed out the surface of much of Manhattan. Garbage, as well as soil and rocks from outcroppings, was tossed into the Collect Pond. Measuring approximately 40 acres, and 60 feet deep, it was a valuable asset, the largest source of fresh water in the city. After being degraded for decades by dumping, and serving as the repository for the run-off from surrounding tanneries, breweries, and slaughterhouses, it was filled in between 1803 and 1813. Its outline can still be noticed where the land in and around Foley Square (Worth and Centre Streets) forms a slight depression.

Streams were filled in all over the city. The rationale was that they were inconvenient for construction of housing and other buildings, and necessitated bridges. The Collect Pond Stream ran northwest of the Collect Pond to flow into the Hudson River. A trench lined with logs was built over it, but it soon collapsed. The street built on top was called Canal Street. Minetta Creek, beginning just north of Washington Square Park, meandered through the square, then down what is now called MacDougal Street, Minetta Lane, and Minetta Street to the Hudson, before it was filled in.

In Queens, most of Flushing Creek was used as a town dump and covered up. The Newtown Creek, part of the borderline between Queens and Brooklyn, was once a waterway with numerous feeder streams before it was forced into a corset of wood and stone, and found its feeder streams covered up. Brooklyn's Bushwick Creek, Wallabout Creek, and Gowanus Creek had their tributaries filled in and were turned into putrid inlets and canals. Only the Bronx River, Hutchinson River, and Westchester Creek, all in the Bronx, are intact. Serious efforts have been made, especially with the Bronx River, to clean them up and respect these rivers as valuable natural resources.

Turtle Bay (where the United Nations is located), Stuyvesant Town - Peter Cooper Village, and Battery Park City were all built with landfill, the latter from the foundation excavation of the World Trade Center. The eastern three blocks of Lower Manhattan were filled with excavated rock. The East River's shore was originally at Pearl Street; Water Street, Front Street, and South Street are intrusions into the river.

Most of Ellis Island was built of landfill. Governors Island doubled in size from 90 acres to 172 acres after landfill from the Interboro Rapid Transit excavations (1901-1904) was dumped off the southern end of the island. Rock and sand from the Brooklyn-Battery Tunnel (1940-1950) was also deposited at the southern rim of the island.

The Manhattan street grid was mapped out in 1811. To make it fully operative meant rearranging nature. Rocky outcrops, hills, and ridges, had to be shaved off and valleys, streams, swamps, and ponds needed to be filled in. Though much of Manhattan now appears flat, a visit to Inwood Hills Park, Fort Tryon Park, Central Park, Morningside Park, and Mount Morris-Marcus Garvey Park will show a glimpse of Manhattan's original geography. It was covered with rocky outcroppings made of *Manhattan schist*, a combination of quartz and mica. A closer look at Murray Hill and Foley Square will show that the city is not completely flat.

For maritime commerce, it was necessary to deepen passages in several waterways such as the Kill Van Kull and Arthur Kill (separating Staten Island and New Jersey), Buttermilk Channel (separating Governors Island from Red Hook, Brooklyn), the Gowanus Bay and Erie Basin (off the south shore of Red Hook and the west shore of Sunset Park). Dredging by the Army Corps of Engineers goes on continually at these sites.

Blowing up rocks in the East River was the dramatic solution to a navigation problem, which had plagued ship captains from the colonial period. A narrow and treacherous section of the East River called Hell Gate needed to be altered. Rushing tides and rocky outcroppings conspired to cause many shipwrecks. In 1876 the Army Corps of Engineers blasted away the rocks to clear the waterway. Hell Gate can be seen from East 96th Street in Manhattan, the north tip of Roosevelt Island, the south end of Ward's Island, or Pot Cove in Astoria, Queens, just west of Astoria Park.

CHAPTER 77
Statue of Liberty

New York City is filled with well-known symbols proclaiming its identity. Among the most celebrated, Central Park (1859), the Brooklyn Bridge (1883), the Statue of Liberty (1886), and the Empire State Building (1931), the *lady in the harbor* takes first place. Often thought to embody the closeness of French-American relations, a better way of putting it historically would be as a testament to the debt each republic owes to each other over the years. To most Americans, however, it represents all the good things we believe about our country, especially our hopes and aspirations. It has special resonance for descendants of immigrants who passed through the New York Harbor on their way to Castle Clinton or Ellis Island.

The symbolism of *Miss Liberty* to the French was as *Marianne,* their metaphor for liberty. French artist Eugène Delacroix depicted her gloriously in an 1831 painting entitled *Liberty Leading the People.* The symbol of *Marianne* is unknown to most Americans but since 1886, the personification of liberty as a woman is perfectly understood. Over the years the *colossus* has come to represent both the spirit of freedom and a policy of welcoming immigrants.

The idea for the Statue of Liberty was first tested at a dinner party in Paris in 1865. Édouard-René de Laboulaye, a French politician and historian, who popularized the idea at the social gathering, greatly admired the United States. He had written a *History of the United States* and a book about a Frenchman living in New York City. After presenting his vision to enthusiastic friends, he began to promote his idea with vigor. As an historian, de Laboulaye was well aware that during our Revolutionary War the 28-ship French Caribbean fleet led by Admiral Comte de Grasse had made victory possible for the Continental Army at Yorktown in 1781. The Americans were led by George Washington and his French assistants the Marquis de Lafayette and the Comte de Rochambeau. The surrender of General Charles Cornwallis finally caused the British, the world's superpower of the 18th century, to give up their fight to hold onto the Thirteen Colonies in North America and sign the Peace of Paris in 1783.

The irony was that the French benefactor of the American republicans was the absolute monarch, Louis XVI. He helped the republican colonists as he practiced the political principle: *my enemy's enemy is my friend.* Militant French republicans during the French Revolution sent Louis XVI and his wife to the *guillotine.* As a testament to the timely intervention of the French monarch, no matter what his motivation, large oil paintings of King Louis XVI and Queen Marie Antoinette still hang in the two chief committee rooms of the United States Senate Chamber in Congress Hall, Philadelphia, the American capital city from 1790 to 1800.

De Laboulaye began raising funds in 1865. Emperor Louis Napoleon Bonaparte, the nephew of Napoleon Bonaparte was then emperor. Because de Laboulaye was adamantly republican, he chose to raise funds from the people, not the imperial government of France.

It was Frédéric-Auguste Bartholdi who designed the monument. He had been present at the banquet and was a celebrated French sculptor and a friend of de Laboulaye. It is significant that Bartholdi designed the statue to portray the promise of a new and better life, not imperial power. This was not to be a militaristic, triumphant statue extolling empire and portraying flags, eagles, and warriors.

In 1871 Bartholdi traveled throughout the United States looking for an appropriate site for the grand sculpture. San Francisco, Salt Lake City, Chicago, and Niagara Falls were first considered, and then rejected. He chose Bedloe's Island, renamed Liberty Island in 1956, because of its striking location on the west side on the New York Harbor. Bartholdi met with United States President Ulysses Grant, received his endorsement, and the federal government, which owned the island, gave its approval.

Both Barthodi and De Laboulaye were ceaseless promoters. In 1875 the Franco-American Union was formed to raise funds. De Laboulaye increasingly gained standing in France and was elected a member of the Chamber of Deputies in the Third Republic. He envisioned the statue as a way of cementing republican virtues across the Atlantic. He loved to extol the heroic deeds of Lafayette and other Frenchmen who helped win the American Revolution. *There you have the basis of the American feeling for the French --- an indestructible basis. The feeling honors the Americans as well as us, and if a monument should rise in the United States as a memorial to their independence, I should think it only natural if it were built by united effort --- a common work of both our nations.* Approximately $250,000 in donations was collected from common people in France to commence building the statue in Paris.

The structural engineer who designed the statue's skeleton of iron beams and bars was Gustave Eiffel. Work began on the project by 50 workmen at the foundry of Gaget, Gauthier & Company in the northern part of Paris. They built four models of wood slats covered with plaster, the final model was full size. While under construction at least 300,000 Parisians came to view the colossus. Bartholdi took the torch-bearing right arm to the United States for display as a fundraising attraction at the Philadelphia Centennial Exposition in 1876.

Eiffel solved the technical questions. He was an engineering genius, who designed France's great symbol, the Eiffel Tower for the Paris International Exhibition in 1889. The main concern was to make it sturdy enough to withstand powerful winds. Issues of financing in the United States proved more difficult. Bartholdi's plan called for the statue to stand on a pedestal. As the statue neared completion is Paris, insufficient money had been raised in the United States. The $125,000 collected by the Union League Club and the American Committee of the Statue of Liberty was not enough to build the pedestal.

A Hungarian Jewish immigrant and journalist, Joseph Pulitzer, rescued the plan. Earlier, when he lived in St. Louis, Missouri, he bought and merged the *St. Louis Post* and the *St. Louis Dispatch* to form the *St. Louis Post-Dispatch* a widely respected newspaper. Pulitzer came to New York City and bought the *New York World,* promptly turning it into a crusading reformist newspaper. He used the *World* to promote donations for the pedestal. Pulitzer scolded the rich for their lack of interest and turned to the common people. *Let us not wait for the millionaires to give this money. Let us hear from the people.* He listed each person who donated money, even a few pennies, in the *New York World*. Contributions flowed in from school children, workers, and middle class people. More than 121,000 contributors to the *World* raised more than $101,000, three-quarters of it in sums less than $1. The New York State Legislature added another $50,000, and the pedestal was soon constructed.

The statue had been fully built in the foundry yard in Paris. It was disassembled and its parts packed aboard crates and shipped by rail to the Seine River port of Rouen. The French ship *Isère* carried the segments across a particularly stormy Atlantic. Workers unloaded the crates at Bedloe Island and began riveting the iron beams and copper plates together. The Statue of Liberty was dedicated on October 28, 1886. The ceremony, presided over by President Grover Cleveland, included numerous speeches, readings, songs, fireworks, and a 21-gun salute.

The Statue of Liberty is impressive for its beauty, symbolism, and sheer size. The dimensions of the sculpture are filled with superlatives. The 225-ton statue measures 151 feet from head to toe, and 301 feet from the base of the pedestal to the tip of its torch. Its waist measures 35 feet, its mouth is 3 feet wide, and its index finger is 8 feet long. The pedestal and statue were illuminated by light bulbs and electrical current supplied by the new Edison Light Company.

Emma Lazarus, a young Jewish immigrant from Russia, sent in a modest donation to the *World* and included a *sonnet*. Pulitzer published her poem, *The New Colossus*, and it helped give the Statue of Liberty a special meaning to immigrants. The reference to a colossus referred to the Colossus of Rhodes, a torch-holding statue of the sun god Helios, which stood on a pedestal overlooking the harbor of Rhodes in ancient Greece. An earthquake brought it down in 224 B.C. In 1903, the last five lines of Emma Lazarus's poem were engraved in a bronze tablet laid in the pedestal:

Give me your tired, your poor,
Your huddled masses yearning to breathe free,
The wretched refuse of your teeming shore.
Send these, the homeless, tempest-tost to me.
I lift my lamp beside the golden door!

Notations:

Louisiana Purchase

In 1803, the French Emperor Napoleon Bonaparte sold the Louisiana Purchase to the United States for reasons similar to why Louis XVI helped the Americans defeat the British at the Battle of Yorktown. Fearing France could not hold Louisiana, Napoleon wanted to keep it out of the hands of the British, who were perceived by the French as enemies of the United States. (Americans and British soon fought each other in the War of 1812.) Napoleon also needed the $15 million President Thomas Jefferson paid for the enormous Louisiana Territory to help fund his wars against Great Britain, Austria, and Russia.

The New Colossus by Emma Lazarus (November 2, 1883)

The ent*ire text is on view at John F. Kennedy International Airport in Queens. Immigrants come to New York City on airplanes, not ships, and Ellis Island is no longer a port of entry.*

Not like the brazen giant of Greek fame,
With conquering limbs astride from land to land;
Here at our sea-washed, sunset gates shall stand
A mighty woman with a torch, whose flame
Is the imprisoned lightning, and her name
Mother of Exiles. From her beacon-hand
Glows world-wide welcome; her mild eyes command
The air-bridged harbor that twin cities frame.
Keep, ancient lands, your storied pomp! cries she
With silent lips. Give me your tired, your poor,
Your huddled masses yearning to breathe free,
The wretched refuse of your teeming shore.
Send these, the homeless, tempest-tost to me.
I lift my lamp beside the golden door!

CHAPTER 78
Prisons

Incarceration is punishment inflicted by the government on someone convicted of breaking a law. As a form of punishment it is comparatively new. Public trials and private imprisonment for people committing felonies is now common. Previously, trials were private and punishments were public. Whipping, branding, or execution, were the prevailing punishments. In each case, either the public trial or the public chastisement was a teaching tool to discourage felonies. The penalty for a misdemeanor, then and now, was usually a fine. It was during the 19th century that the idea of correcting behavior through removal from civil society became popular. High recidivism rates now make it a very questionable notion.

Civil law refers to cases involving two individuals or companies, or between an individual and a company. Civil cases are usually about money or contract obligations. The outcome is rarely imprisonment. A criminal case is when the state, in the form of the police, apprehends a suspect, and the district attorney prosecutes a defendant who has injured another individual personally, or harmed the property of an individual or company. The state acts on behalf of the whole community in bringing a criminal to justice.

Jails are places of confinement where suspects accused of committing a crime await trial. In New York City a jail is now called a *house of detention* or a *correctional facility*. They are located within the five boroughs. Only if the judge orders the accused released on his own recognizance may the person go free until the trial occurs. If the judge sets bail, and the suspect can post it, he may also remain at liberty until the trial begins.

Prisons are places of incarceration. Those convicted in a court are sent to prison by the judge. They may be maximum, medium, or minimum-security facilities. Separate prisons exist for men and women. All prisons in New York are now operated by the state and all seventy are located upstate, mostly far from the city.

In the colonial period and in the early 19th century, the government operated jails and prisons for those accused or convicted of crimes. A judge could remand the poor, indebted, homeless, orphaned, or ill (physically or mentally) to a private facility where they were held against their will for a set period of time or forever. Workhouses, poorhouses, orphanages, industrial schools, retirement homes, hospitals, and asylums were often prisons. Such institutions were operated by private charities and funded by wealthy citizens to get *undesirables* off the streets. Sailor's Snug Harbor on Staten Island, a home for old sailors was an example. It operated on grounds facing the Kill Van Kull in West Brighton from 1831 to 1975. The worn out sailors, many of them rough, destitute characters with an excessive fondness for alcohol, were prisoners at their retirement facility where they were kept behind a guarded iron fence.

Roosevelt Island, the third name for the long, narrow sliver of land in the center of the East River, housed several facilities that prevented free movement. The English Crown owned the island after the 1664 change in colonial sovereignty. Charles II gave the island to Captain John Manning in 1685. Manning's son-in-law Robert Blackwell inherited the island and farmed it. The New York City government bought it in 1828 for $32,000 and established various institutions on it: prison, almshouse, workhouse, charity hospital, smallpox hospital, and lunatic asylum. Inmates in those institutions had no rights and could not leave unless an administrator or judge released them. The name Blackwell's Island was changed to Welfare Island in 1921 to better reflect its melancholy functions. The City Council renamed it Roosevelt Island in 1971.

The first jails in the Dutch colony of New Amsterdam were located in Fort William and in the *Stadt Huys,* at Pearl Street and Coenties Slip. The *Stadt Huys* (State House) is often called the first City Hall. In British colonial days there was a jail in the basement of the second New York City Hall, built in 1699, at the corner of Wall and Nassau Streets. In 1758 a separate jail was constructed in the *common* or the *fields,* the present site of City Hall Park. A *bridewell* was built in the same area in 1775 to replace an earlier *bridewell* established further south in 1734. The term *bridewell* comes from London's Bridewell Prison, built by Edward VI in 1552 near

St. Bridget's Well, also called Brideswell. A bridewell was a workhouse or poorhouse for vagrants, debtors, drunken rowdies, and prostitutes where they were incarcerated and forced to work. The forced labor could be farm work, piecework for area factories, or the dreaded treadmill where inmates were forced to spend hours each day walking on a large step-wheel that ground grain.

During the Revolutionary War, 1776 to 1783, the British controlled the city and established several prisons for captured Americans who supported Washington and the revolutionaries. Livingston's Sugar House, just east of today's City Hall Park, was transformed into a notorious prison where Americans suffered and died from starvation and disease at the hands of the British.

Eleven old and disabled British frigates were anchored in Wallabout Bay where captured American soldiers were held in miserable conditions. Approximately 11,500 American patriots died on the prison ships. They succumbed to malnutrition and a variety of contagious diseases: smallpox, dysentery, typhus, and yellow fever. Their bodies were unceremoniously tossed into the bay. Many washed up on the shore and were buried by area farmers in graves near the water. After the Revolution the remains that could be found were re-interred in a vault on a hill that is now Brooklyn's Fort Greene Park. To memorialize their sacrifice the Prison Ship Martyrs Monument was constructed on the summit in 1906.

During the early years of the republic New York State constructed several prisons in the city. A state prison was built in a rural spot near the Hudson River near Greenwich Village in 1796. Another was built at Bellevue near the East River.

A reform school, called the House of Refuge, was built in 1825 on a four-acre plot at Madison Square. The Society for the Reformation of Juvenile Delinquents, a Protestant religious group, operated the facility. Judges remanded young people to the House of Refuge who had been brought in by the municipal police on various charges. In 1850 the institution was moved to Ward's Island.

The Halls of Justice, better known as the *Tombs*, New York County's main jail, was erected in 1838. The present Tombs was built in 1902 and enlarged and remodeled in 1983. It is located at 100 Center Street between Hogan Place and Walker Street. It is the third House of Detention built on the same site.

Rikers Island, the main House of Detention for New York City, is the country's largest prison complex holding approximately 25,000 prisoners. The caged island city is in the East River, where it makes an eastward turn toward Long Island Sound, lies between Queens and the Bronx. When detainees cross the long causeway from Steinway, near LaGuardia Airport, they vanish into the complex. A daunting sign welcomes prisoners: *City of New York --- Correction Department, Rikers Island --- The Boldest Correction Officers in the World.*

About 70 percent of the inmates are awaiting trial and could not post bail. The others are either serving prison terms of one year or less or are waiting for transfer to upstate prisons. The city spends about $70,000 annually to confine each inmate at Rikers. Almost 75 percent of Rikers inmates return at least once, some many times.

Notations:

Federal Hall

Little is known about the basement jail's holding cells but much is understood about the building and what took place in it. Built in 1699, the city's second City Hall was where the Continental Congress met in 1785. Pierre Charles L'Enfant remodeled the building in 1788. (L'Enfant later laid out the street grid of Washington, D.C.) The city government gave the building to the new government of the United States as its capitol after the adoption of the U. S. Constitution. The city offices moved out and the third and present City Hall was constructed. (The first City Hall, called *Stadt Huys* by the Dutch, was on the second floor of a tavern on Pearl Street facing Coenties Slip.)

Renamed Federal Hall, the second City Hall was where George Washington was inaugurated president from the second floor balcony in 1789. The capital of the United States moved to Philadelphia and the old building was demolished and a Greek Revival structure was constructed on the site in 1842. The new building became the United States Custom House and then the United States Subtreasury Building. A gargantuan statue of Washington was erected on its front steps in 1883. The building is now a museum.

John Peter Zenger Trial in Old City Hall

The celebrated 1735 libel trial of John Peter Zenger took place in the upstairs courtroom of the Old City Hall. The accused was held downstairs for ten months before the colonial government tried him and then lost to a jury that nullified the law and the judge's instructions.

Zenger's newspaper, the *New-York Weekly Journal,* had published many articles and poems that criticized Governor William Cosby. They accused him of bribery, graft, and rigging local elections and court cases. It was widely believed that the accusations were true. The critical articles were anonymous or signed with pen names. Unable to discern the identity of the writers, the governor had Zenger, who published and edited the *New-York Weekly Journal,* arrested and charged with libel.

New York's attorney general, the government's lawyer, claimed Zenger was guilty of *libel* because he knew the charges against Governor Cosby were lies, and the lies had harmed the governor's reputation. Libel is a false, malicious statement that harms the accused. Andrew Hamilton, Zenger's lawyer, had come to New York City from Philadelphia to argue the case. Hamilton argued that the charges printed in the newspaper were true. The attorney general countered that even if true, the governor had special rights protecting him from criticism. Two prominent judges, Chief Justice James DeLancey and Judge Frederick Philipse, jointly presided over the trial. The governor had appointed the judges. They agreed with the prosecution and instructed the jury to decide only if it was true that Zenger published the newspaper. If the jury found that Zenger had published the newspaper stories, then he would be guilty of libel. The jury went into deliberations and rejected the notion put forth by the attorney general and the instructions of the judge. They found John Peter Zenger *not guilty* of libel because the newspaper stories were true. They had nullified the practice of protecting the governor, an appointee of the King of England, from criticism.

The significance of the John Peter Zenger case was twofold. It enshrined the notion that free people have the right to free speech and free press. It also was a case of a jury nullifying a law it believed to be unfair despite the instructions of the judge.

Sailor's Snug Harbor

Sailor's Snug Harbor, a retirement home for sailors, opened its doors in 1831. The complex of Greek Revival temple buildings constructed between 1833 and 1892, provided for *aged, decrepit, and worn-out sailors* and was funded by Robert Richard Randall, a wealthy maritime merchant. The retirement facility moved to Sea Level, North Carolina in 1975, and in 1976 the buildings on Richmond Terrace became the site of the Snug Harbor Cultural Center. The facility opened with twenty-seven residents, numbered 1,000 in 1900, and had only 150 when it moved. The compound contains twenty-six large and small buildings, the front five in magnificent Greek Revival style, located on an 80-acre site just one-and-one-half miles from the Ferry Terminal includes galleries, museums, studios, concert spaces, and gardens.

The former retirement facility for sailors solved the societal problem of how to handle single men too old to work on ships. Many drank heavily, had no families, and soon became homeless. Sailor's Snug Harbor was essentially a prison to keep impoverished, potentially raucous old seamen off the streets and out of sight. In the early years the former sailors were compelled to wear uniforms, follow a strict daily schedule, and attend church services. No drinking was allowed and inmates needed written permission to leave the premises, which were surrounded by a high iron fence and guarded gates.

CHAPTER 79
Elisha Otis & Elevators

Real estate became increasingly more expensive as the city's population grew. In 1860, Manhattan had 814,000 residents and there was a pressing need to build the city vertically. Tall buildings required elevators and most people were reluctant to use them.

The power source for elevators in the early 19th century could be either horses or mules pulling a cable connected to an elevator carriage, or steam-operated hoists. Cables could be fashioned from rope, wire rope, or iron chains. People feared fatal accidents caused by snapped cables. Without safety devices, the public resisted taking elevators, so multi-storied buildings were not built.

Elisha Graves Otis changed that by inventing a *safety brake,* which prevented an elevator *carriage* from falling even if its cables broke. He developed a spring that would activate *pawls* on either side of the carriage forcing them to engage ratcheted racks at the sides of the elevator shaft and hold the elevator in place. A *pawl* is a pivoted device made to fit into a notch in a rack to prevent backward motion. The invention of the safety break was necessary for New York City to solve its space problem and become the skyscraper capital of the world.

In 1852, Otis produced his new elevator but could not sell it. He needed to show off his invention in a dramatic way, so he demonstrated the first *safety elevator* outfitted with a safety brake at the newly built Crystal Palace in 1854. He designed an elaborate set with an elevator open on all sides except for an iron and wood framework. Otis stood up inside the elevator carriage to add some drama to the demonstration. As crowds gathered, he took a knife and sliced the rope cable with great flourish. Instead of plunging down, the carriage slipped an inch until the pawls caught on the racks and halted the elevator. Each demonstration was greeted with applause. More importantly, Otis was building confidence in his product.

Otis, a Vermonter born in 1811, had a mechanical and business background. From 1838 until 1845 he manufactured wagons and horse-pulled carriages in Brattleboro. He relocated to Albany, New York, and, fascinated by *ergonomics*, developed several labor saving machines. He moved to Yonkers in 1852 to organize and install machinery for a bed manufacturer. It was in the vicinity of crowded New York City that Otis became interested in elevators. Otis founded a small elevator company in 1853 in the Westchester community of Yonkers and sold his first models for $300 each.

The first Otis safety elevator that was used on a daily basis was installed in 1857 by Otis in the Haughwout Store at 488 Broadway, corner of Broome Street. Some of the early buildings with elevators in Manhattan were the Equitable Life Assurance Building (1871), the Western Union Building (1875), and the Tribune Building (1875). After safety elevators, it made little sense not to build straight up. Otis remained active in the booming elevator business. He patented a steam-engine elevator in 1861.

Elevators changed the rent structure of apartments and offices. Before dependable elevators the lower floors rented for the highest prices while the higher floors fetched less money. Climbing steps was an impediment to business and a disincentive to live or operate a business on a high floor. After the invention of the safety elevator it was the higher floors that became expensive and the lower floors were discounted. Good views trumped the street level as long as there was a reliable, safe elevator.

After the death of Elisha Otis in 1862, his sons, Charles and Norton, re-configured the company and named it the Otis Brothers Elevator Company. By 1873 they had sold and installed more than two thousand Otis elevators throughout the United States. In 1878 they began producing a hydraulic elevator and in 1889 an electric elevator. In 1899 the Otis Company branched out and produced *moving stairs*, the first escalators. Impressive new skyscrapers including the Flatiron Building (1902), the Woolworth Building (1913), and the Empire State Building (1931) used Otis elevators. Over the years the Otis Brothers Elevator Company bought out fourteen other elevator firms and shortened its name to Otis Elevator Company. By the late 20th century rapid computer-controlled *Autotronic* elevators could climb a hundred-story building in 55 seconds. In the 21st century Otis remains the largest elevator company in New York City.

Otis went through many changes in the last quarter of the 20th century. United Technologies Corporation bought Otis Elevator Company in 1975 and its Yonkers plant was shut in 1982. All of its production is now abroad, mostly in China. The Otis Division of United Technologies Company became the largest manufacturer of elevators, escalators, moving walkways, and airport trains in the world, capturing 27 percent of the global market. There are 1.5 million Otis elevators in operation. While his company took on a life of its own, Elisha Graves Otis' invention had a dramatic impact on the skyline of New York City and the way New Yorkers live.

Notation

New York's Crystal Palace

The site of the safety elevator demonstration, the Crystal Palace, was a glass and cast-iron exhibition hall at 42nd Street and 6th Avenue. The domed structure was patterned after the Crystal Palace in London. It was primarily used for exhibitions of art, science, and technology. New York's Crystal Palace burned to the ground in just fifteen minutes in 1858. Bryant Park was built on its site.

CHAPTER 80
Flatiron Building & the Skyscraper Phenomenon

The Flatiron Building, standing twenty stories and completed in 1903, was the first modern skyscraper in New York City. Officially christened the Fuller Building, its popular name comes from the uniquely elongated triangular plot on which it rises at the intersection of 5th Avenue and Broadway at 23rd Street. People thought it resembled a giant old-style *flatiron*. The iconic beauty of its limestone façade stands out because of its graceful lines and striking shape. Placed at an intersection and across from Madison Square gives its sight-line protection from the north. Though many buildings now exceed its 300 feet height, the Flatiron Building remains a significant symbol of the skyscraper era.

The need for vertical buildings in the island city was both spatial and economic. The water that surrounds the city creates a natural barrier to horizontal expansion, and population pressure on the land within the boundaries causes land value to rise. The economical response has been to build upward. The need for large buildings was magnified toward the end of the 19th century with the growing popularity of corporate consolidation.

After Elisha Otis successfully demonstrated his safety elevator in the Crystal Palace at the New York World's Fair in 1854, the age of tall buildings was inevitable. Prior to reliably safe elevators, builders rarely went above five or six floors since neither commercial nor residential tenants wanted to climb too many stairs. There were numerous buildings built between 1870 and the turn of the last century that were called skyscrapers, but the *Age of Skyscrapers*, the time when architects and builders raced to outdo each other in height, began with the Flatiron Building. After the Flatiron Building, height records were exceeded every few years.

The ability to construct tall buildings also rests on some technological advances. Engineers need to be able to accurately test the soil and rock below and construct foundations strong enough to support enormous weight, and most of the mass needs to rest on an internal skeleton of steel beams. At first steel beams were held together by rivets; beams are now fused together by welded steel bolts. Much of a building's frame needed to be made of lightweight glass, a strong substance that will not stress the frame, and will allow sun and air to light and ventilate each floor. A rusticated limestone skin was built over much of the Flatiron Building's steel frame.

Through the first half of the 20th century New York's skyscrapers left a singular architectural mark and Manhattan was considered the *city of skyscrapers*. In the 21st century there are several cities in the world that have taller buildings and many American cities have a central core of skyscrapers, though not as many as New York. Numerous skyscrapers have also sprouted in Downtown Brooklyn and Jersey City, to the east and west of Manhattan.

A decade after completion of the Flatiron Building, Frank Winfield Woolworth built his cathedral of commerce at 233 Broadway across from City Hall as headquarters for his retail empire of five-and-ten cent-stores, or *dime stores*. The 60-floor building, rising 792 feet, used a steel frame covered with numerous windows and a surface of bricks and baked terra-cotta blocks to give it a Gothic look. On the other side of City Hall Park the two towers of the Brooklyn Bridge also used a Gothic design. In a sense, the late medieval Gothic design softened the mass and height of the two large downtown edifices.

The Woolworth Building, opened in 1913, is covered with extraordinarily intricate detail. The lobby is decorated with Gothic finials, elaborate tracery, and whimsical corbels (like gargoyles), including images of architect Cass Gilbert holding a model of the building and owner F.W. Woolworth paying for the project with nickels and dimes. (He always paid cash, including for the Woolworth Building.) It remained the tallest structure in the city and the world until 1929.

The Chanin and Chrysler Buildings, the first large Art-Deco skyscrapers were built across the street from each other at the intersection of Lexington Avenue and 42nd Street. Irwin S. Chanin, who made his fortune constructing houses, offices, and hotels, built his company's 54 story headquarters of brick, limestone, and terra-cotta capped by a ribbed rectangular-topped roof. Inauspiciously it opened in 1929, the year of the Great Depression.

Walter P. Chrysler built the city's most dramatic Art-Deco building for his automobile corporation's headquarters. Rising 77 stories the sleek and elegant marble and polished chrome building is crowned by a several-layered tiara and spire that reaches 1,046 feet in the air. Steel eagle gargoyles and radiator cap finials decorate the structure that was completed in August 1930 and became, for just eight months, the tallest building in the world.

The Empire State Building soon became the city's tallest structure. The 102-story building, when you count the 14-story dirigible mooring mast and the two-story basement, was constructed in 18 months and finished in May 1931. The massive Art-Deco edifice that stands 1,250 feet became one of the city's major symbols.

On a foggy July morning in 1945, a U.S. Air Force bomber making its way to Newark Airport hit the Empire State Building. The plane was traveling at about 250 miles per hour when it struck the Empire State Building between the 78th and 79th floors killing eleven office workers and three crewmen. There was no structural damage to the skyscraper though there was considerable damage to the offices affected.

The 1933 film *King Kong,* in which a giant ape climbs to the top of the mooring mast to escape capture, was the most famous representation in popular culture of the building. There were remakes of the original film in 1976 and 2005.

The World Trade Center was a massive complex of seven stainless steel and glass buildings on a sixteen-acre site and included the Twin Towers which each rose 110 stories and 1,350 feet in the air. The filigreed towers had 198 elevators and ten million square feet of office space. The first buildings were opened in 1970, the Twin Towers in 1976, and 7 WTC not until 1988. In 1993 an underground garage sustained serious damage when a car bomb exploded in an attempt to demolish the compound. The complex was destroyed in an attack by two jet airplanes on September 11, 2001.

After the Second World War, New York skyscraper architects almost uniformly used the Bauhaus style. Noted examples are the Met Life Building (originally Pan Am Building), the Secretariat Building in the United Nations complex, McGraw-Hill Building, the ziggurat glass city office building at 250 Broadway, New York Hilton and other office towers along 6th Avenue in Midtown Manhattan, the former World Trade Center, and the green glass Citicorp Building in Long Island City, Queens. Critics called them rectangular glass boxes. In the 1980s several Bauhaus boxes attempted to soften their look by incorporating multi-storied interior atriums. Examples include the atriums in Trump Tower, the Ford Foundation, and New York University's Bobst Library.

The Bauhaus style got its name from the design principle worked out at the architecture school south of Berlin led by Walter Gropius. Bauhaus architecture and design flourished in Germany in the 1920s until 1933 when the Nazis outlawed it. (Hitler permitted only traditional Germanic or Neo-Classical architecture.) As it became internationalized in the 1960s the Bauhaus style was often called the International style.

Gropius's principle of *form follows function* meant that the choice of building materials would follow the intended use of the structure. Since most were workplaces they were designed to be economical and supplied with much natural light. The prescribed design included clean, straight lines without embellishments, and the building materials were primarily concrete, glass, and steel. Variety would be achieved by coloring concrete, glass, or the brushed steel or aluminum on the superstructure. The trio of concrete, glass, and steel were also the least expensive building materials.

Concrete was first used by the ancient Romans to hold bricks together, but in the 20th century it became a basic building material itself. Concrete is formed when water is added to an aggregate of crushed stone and *Portland cement*. The Portland cement is a mixture of limestone and clay ground to a fine powder and baked in a kiln to evaporate moisture. Once water is added to the aggregate and cement the resultant concrete hardens into a solid mass.

By the 1980s a post-Bauhaus style began to take precedence over Bauhaus designs, though the new structures incorporated only minor design changes and the basic building materials remained the same. The point was to break the monotonous shape of the big glass box. Examples of post-Bauhaus style include the SONY Building (originally AT&T Building) sporting a Chippendale top, glass pyramids topping Zeckendorf Towers on Union Square, Citicorp Center with its steeply sloped asymmetrical roof, the vaulted glass and steel Winter Garden and the red domed Merrill Lynch World Headquarters within the World Financial Center complex, and the swooping concave-bottomed office building at Nine West 57th Street.

Throughout New York City's history there has been very little permanence with buildings. In Manhattan nothing at all is left from the 17th century and only a few 18th century residences remain. As population pressure increased old structures were torn down and larger buildings put up to house more shops, offices, and apartments. Skyscrapers, the fundamental template for 20th century buildings, are no longer just for major corporate headquarters. Almost every edifice that is built is now a skyscraper and low-rise portions of the city are increasingly interspersed with tall buildings. The city never tires of rebuilding itself and seems never to reach a saturation point in the volume or height of new structures.

CHAPTER 81
Samuel Gompers & the Labor Movement

Born in London in 1850, Samuel Gompers ultimately became the embodiment of the American trade union movement. At age 13, during the American Civil War, he emigrated with his Dutch Jewish family from the poor East End of London to the United States and settled in the Lower East Side of Manhattan. *On the first day we found a home in Houston and Attorney Streets. Those four rooms signified progress from the little London home. Our neighbors were chiefly American, English, and Holland Dutch.* His description of the neighborhood was decidedly unappealing: *Our house was just opposite a slaughterhouse. All day long we could see the animals being driven to the slaughter pens and hear the turmoil and the cries of the animals. The neighborhood was filled with the penetrating, sickening odor. The suffering of the animals and the nauseating odor made it physically impossible for me to eat meat for many months --- after we moved to another neighborhood.*

Initially apprenticed to a shoemaker, Gompers decided to return to his father's trade and roll cigars at home for a tobacco company. Each day father and son would walk to a tobacco company, pick up tobacco leaves to carry home to be cut, rolled, and pressed. The following day the finished cigars would be returned to the company and Solomon and Samuel Gompers would be paid for their labor. Doing piecework at home, in both the food industry and the garment industry, was common practice at the time. Years later, arguing that working conditions at home were unsanitary and cramped, Gompers, with the help of young Assemblyman Theodore Roosevelt, got the state legislature to outlaw tenement house cigar work.

Gompers had attended a Jewish primary school in London where he learned basic literacy in Yiddish, Hebrew, and English. In New York City he joined a debate club and attended classes at

Cooper Union. He worked in a small cigar-rolling factory in the Lower East Side and joined the Cigarmakers Union. When rolling cigars in the shop, fellow workers recognized his outstanding reading ability and took up a daily collection so Gompers would be free to read aloud to them while they worked. By 1881 he was active in union affairs and in 1885 elected president of his local union.

Samuel Gompers was sensitive to social injustice and economic inequality and became a convinced socialist. His colleagues included P.J. McGuire, founder of the Carpenters Union, and father of both Labor Day (1882) and May Day (1886), J.P. McDonnell, Irish republican and socialist, and fellow Cigarmakers Union activist Adolph Strasser. Gompers participated in the International Workingmen's Association that had been founded in London in 1864 by Karl Marx, the Economic and Sociological Club in Manhattan, and the Workingmen's Party of the United States. Gompers also allied with a group of progressive thinkers and liberal reformers in New York City including Felix Adler, the Jewish philosopher who founded the Society of Ethical Culture.

Gompers increasingly moved toward a gradualist, or *pure and simple* position, as opposed to revolutionary socialism, after he saw several examples of police repression against socialist and labor groups, notably at an 1874 rally in Tompkins Square. He realized that there were powerful class interests arrayed against the labor movement. Mayor William F. Havemeyer was effusive in his praise of the police for breaking up the Tompkins Square demonstration. A great deal of repression followed three years later during a period of tumultuous strikes nationwide. Conservative religious leaders in New York City preached against labor from their pulpits. An 1877 sermon delivered by the Reverend Henry Ward Beecher of Plymouth Church in Brooklyn Heights was quoted in *The New York Times*: *It was true that $1 a day was not enough to support a man and five children, if a man would insist on smoking and drinking beer. Was not a dollar a day enough to buy bread? Water costs nothing [Laughter.] Man cannot live by bread, it is true, but the man who cannot live on bread and water is not fit to live. [Laughter.] When a man is educated away from the power of self-denial, he is falsely educated. A family may live on good bread and water in the morning,* *water and bread at midday, and good water and bread at night. [Continued laughter.]* Gompers feared that the capitalist class would not hesitate at using sustained violence against workers who wanted fundamental changes in the society.

Gompers was criticized by former allies for pursuing narrow monetary goals, *economism* in the words of his opponents, and for being vice president of the National Civic Federation, a group dominated by business leaders and bankers that sought to do away with strikes and encourage stable labor relations through collective bargaining.

In 1925, the year after his death, radical socialist, feminist, and labor leader Emma Goldman wrote a scathing attack on the effect Gompers had on the American labor movement. *One has but to examine into the nature of the American Federation of Labor, over which Mr. Gompers lorded for so many years, to see the evil results of leadership. It cannot be denied that the late President raised the organization to some power and material improvement, but at the same time, he prevented the growth and development of the membership towards a higher aim or purpose. In all these years of its existence the A. F. of L. has not gone beyond its craft interests. Neither has it grasped the social abyss, which separates labor from its masters, an abyss which can never be bridged by the struggle for mere immediate material gains. That does not mean, however, that I am opposed to the fight labor is waging for a higher standard of living and saner conditions of work. But I do mean to stress that without an ultimate goal of complete industrial and social emancipation, labor will achieve only as much as is in keeping with the interests of the privileged class, hence remain dependent always upon that class. Samuel Gompers was no fool, he knew the causes underlying the social struggle, yet he set his face sternly against them. He was content to create an aristocracy of labor, a trade union trust, as it were, indifferent to the needs of the rest of the workers outside of the organization. Above all, Gompers would have none of a liberating social idea. The result is that after forty years of Gompers' leadership the A. F. of L. has really remained stationary, without feeling for, or understanding of the changing factors surrounding it.*

Gompers had defended himself against charges from the left for decades. In 1911 he said: *Our mission has been the protection of the wage-worker, now; to increase his wages; to cut hours off the long workday, which was killing him; to improve the safety and the sanitary conditions of the workshop; to free him from the tyrannies, petty or otherwise, which served to make his existence a slavery....But while our Federation has thus been conservative, it has ever had its face turned toward whatever reforms, in politics or economics, could be of direct and obvious benefit to the working classes. It has never given up its birthright for a mess of pottage.* Gompers represented one side in the polarized view of how to organize workers throughout the country.

The trade union movement had been the first type of labor union organized in the United States. For many workers, especially artisans and skilled mechanics, it made sense to organize around their vocation. In some ways it was a modern extension of the guild system but without the participation of the owners. Workers wanted to increase their wages, decrease their hours, gain some control over work rules, and protect their members against cheap labor.

Almost all early labor unions discriminated against non-white workers and did not represent them in matters of economics or politics. Some labor leaders stirred up racist sentiments by indirectly attacking immigrants, especially Chinese workers. While the real fear may have been competition from cheap labor, the tactic used against the Chinese was to connect them with opium and level accusations about using the drug to seduce young white women. Samuel Gompers, in a pamphlet entitled *Some Reasons for the Chinese Exclusion*, wrote: *What other crimes were committed in those dark fetid places when these little innocent victims of the Chinamen's wiles were under the influence of the drug, are almost too horrible to imagine.* Gompers and others played to racist sentiments of the time by stoking fears of the *yellow peril* and hurling charges of opium addiction, white slavery, and filthy living and eating habits at the Chinese. They supported the Chinese Exclusion Act of 1882 that barred almost all immigration from China and the rest of Asia.

In a 1921 letter to a professor at Haverford College, Samuel Gompers explained his position on immigration restriction as a reaction to high unemployment. *The American Federation of Labor made an earnest effort to have immigration restricted for at least two years. It also urged that an immigration law be enacted containing the provision that after that period of two years an order can be issued abso-*

lutely prohibiting immigration during times of unemployment...Every citizen of the United States should make protest against the influx of people from other countries. It is estimated that there are 5,000,000 unemployed in the country at the present time with the number increasing rapidly. The 1921 letter deleted the usual racist and anti-foreign sentiments.

Women, because they composed a large number of the first factory workers, especially in apparel manufacturing, organized labor unions and lead a number of early strikes. Women organized the United Tailoresses Society of New York and in 1831 held a five-week strike. In 1864 women organized the Working Women's Union that cut across industry lines.

The American labor movement has a long history in the United States. The first large union, the Knights of Labor, reached a membership of one million by 1886. Uriah Stephens founded the Knights of Labor in 1869 in Philadelphia. Stephens was a tailor and a radical Baptist minister. The group was an oath-bound secret society (Noble and Holy Order of Knights of Labor) that borrowed much pageantry and rituals from the Masonic Order. Despite its romantic infatuation with ceremonies and secrecy, it was not a craft union but an *industrial union*, meaning all workers in all industries were included. Terrence V. Powderly, who led the Knights of Labor from 1879 until 1893, continued the political utopianism of Uriah Stephens and worked to organize women and blacks. His all-inclusive, highly politicized labor movement steadily lost ground to the more parochial American Federation of Labor after 1886.

Uriah Stephens, Terrence V. Powderly, and Samuel Gompers were not alone in supporting organized labor. Many social reformers and some religious leaders supported labor. Jane Addams of Hull House in Chicago and Lillian Wald and Jacob Schiff of the Henry Street Settlement on the Lower East Side were pro-labor. In 1891, Pope Leo XIII, Roman Catholic pontiff from 1878 until 1903, issued the encyclical *Rerum Novarum* on the relations between capital and labor, and presented a forceful impulse to social movements along Christian lines. (Conservative Catholics argued that the pope leaned too much towards socialism and republicanism.)

As the labor movement gained popularity and strength, governments moved to protect corporations and used police, state troopers, state militias, and national guard units to attack workers and break their strikes. The series of strikes and boycotts around the country in 1877 began when railroad workers protested a wage cut. A July demonstration in Tompkins Square provoked strident denunciations from politicians and a skull-cracking attack by the police.

An enormous armory for the for the Seventh Regiment of the New York State National Guard was built between Lexington and Fourth Avenues at East 66th Street on the city's Upper East Side. The purpose of armories was to place fortress headquarters of military units in population centers. The Seventh Regiment's central hall was used for drills and troop maneuvers, but during a labor strike, political march, or riot could be converted to a prison. The walls were several feet thick with crenellated towers and slits for rifles. The Seventh Regiment Armory was built with $589,000 in private donations, mostly from big corporations, but most armories in the city and throughout the country were constructed with government funds authorized by the War Department in 1877. Armories were placed throughout the city to intimidate those who threatened the capitalist system, the established government, or the pre-eminence of corporate power.

In 1886 the American Federation of Labor, composed of craft unions, was formed and Gompers was elected president, a post he held continuously until his death in 1924, except for 1895 when John McBride of the United Mine Workers served as president. Gompers had soured on politics and within the next decade cut ties with former socialist allies and accepted the capitalist system. His belief was that by collective bargaining through their unions, workers could achieve a decent lifestyle. Gompers gave up on the idea that a revolutionary economic and social change was needed to effect a more equitable distribution of wealth and opportunity.

Politically the A.F.L. and many of its member unions moved to the right even before the turn of the last century. In 1896 Gompers, who distrusted farmers, refused to support the populist candidacy of William Jennings Bryan, and in 1898 supported William McKinley in the Spanish-American War.

Gompers, the Cigarmakers, and his colleagues in the American Federation of Labor had deep suspicions about political parties. Called *pure and simple* unionists, they preferred to depend on contracts reached between labor and capital rather than look to politicians to help through legislation. Gompers believed politicians were unreliable and fundamentally dishonest. Gompers and other pure and simple labor union activists knew they needed alliances but did not want to permanently harness themselves to a political party. Nor did they wish to start a Labor Party as British and other unionists abroad had done.

The trade union movement was exclusionary in terms of skills, family, and ethnic connections. Most of the organized union workers in a particular trade were drawn from the same ethnic group. Often they were *father and son* unions where membership depended on having a father, or an uncle, already in the craft union. Though modern laws and social pressure have integrated and opened up some trade unions in New York City, some unions still operate on a father and son basis. Many trade unions moved rapidly to the right politically in the late 1960s opposing the Civil Rights Act and supporting the War in Vietnam. Since the 1980s many regularly endorse Republican candidates for public office. The triumph of the A.F.L. unions was that at least for a while they did achieve a middle class economic base for their members.

CHAPTER 82
Tammany Hall & Boss Tweed

Tammany Hall was a colorful political organization, which dominated New York City politics several times in the 19th and 20th centuries. It evolved into an urban political machine that fused patronage and private welfare with politics. Tammany Hall, always interested in money, was seldom driven by ideology. One of its most powerful leaders, William M. Tweed, gave the group its symbol, the *Tammany Tiger,* and also its well-deserved reputation as a callous and corrupt den of thieves.

Tammany began as a fraternal club, the answer by middle class professionals and mechanics (artisans) to rich men's clubs from which they were excluded. Formed in 1786 as the *Society of St. Tammany or the Columbian Order*, it lionized a mythological Delaware Indian chief *Tamanend* and chose Indian-related names for its clubhouses and officers. Meeting halls were called *wigwams,* leaders were *sachems*, and members were *braves*. During meetings they put on war paint, dressed in Indian garb, carried tomahawks, passed around a peace pipe, and marched single-file, or *Indian-style*. Except for the terminology, they outgrew the Indian paraphernalia by the 1820s.

The reference to *Saint* in the club's name was an anti-Catholic taunt. At first, Tammany's members were nativists, but as they became more involved in politics they grew to realize that to be successful in New York they would need to be inclusive. In 1860 the first Roman Catholic, James Conner, was elected *grand sachem* of Tammany Hall. His sponsor was William M. Tweed. By the 1850s the fraternal organization had become thoroughly politicized and after the Civil War the society became a disciplined Democratic Party political machine.

Tammany built its strength in poor immigrant neighborhoods by swapping votes for services at a time when the government offered none. So, if a widow needed a bucket of coal, or a returned veteran needed a job, the organization would oblige. Tammany politicians are sometimes recollected as lovable rogues. In truth, they were neighborhood oligarchs with absolutely no appreciation for democracy. Tammany Hall was a collection of thieves, embezzlers, and swindlers. They provided bread and circuses for the masses, especially the poorest immigrants, but granted no long-term relief for the needy. When Tammany supported park construction and other public works it was always to supply more patronage jobs to dispense and more opportunities to fleece the taxpayers.

William M. Tweed rose to power in the neighborhood where he was born, on Cherry Street in the area under where the Brooklyn Bridge was later built. (Tweed's middle initial was sometimes written out as Magear, his mother's maiden name, and other times as Marcy.) Before entering politics he worked as a chair maker, saddle maker, clerk, bookkeeper, and partner in a brush shop. It was his extracurricular activity that started him off in politics. While still quite young he joined a volunteer fire company and then helped form the Americus Engine Company in 1848 at age 23. Volunteer fire companies were as much about socializing as they were about rescuing people and putting out fires. Tweed was sociable and was chosen foreman the next year. The Americus Engine Company was also called Fire Company No. 6, and nicknamed *Big Six*. They soon adopted the representation of a wild Bengal tiger as their symbol

Tweed ascended quickly in the political world. In 1851 he was elected alderman at a time when the Board of Aldermen was so corrupt it was commonly called the *Forty Thieves*. The next year he won election to the United States Congress. Bored with the legislative process, ignorant of national and international affairs, and feeling out of touch in Washington, D.C., he declined to run for re-election and returned to the city to run for alderman. He was defeated by a member of the American Party, a *Know Nothing*. The experience impelled him to redouble efforts to bring more immigrants into his political following.

In 1854 Tweed was elected to the New York County Board of Supervisors and to the New York City Board of Education. He was the undisputed leader of the 7th ward, a position he kept by making alliances with Irish Catholics. In 1863 he was chosen to lead the county-wide political club called Tammany Hall.

Never mayor, Tweed derived his power from his position at grand sachem of Tammany Hall and as president of the Board of Supervisors of New York County (Manhattan). Under an earlier city charter, the legislative and administrative duties of Manhattan were split between the county and the city. Among other things, the County Board of Supervisors operated the court system.

Tweed bought controlling interest in a printing company and a stationery company; he then awarded all contracts for paper and official municipal printing to his companies. As Commissioner of Public Works he planned where civic improvements would be located and then before releasing the information to the press he bought up real estate in the area that he knew would appreciate in value.

Tweed made an alliance with robber barons Jay Gould and Jim Fiske to take control of the Erie Railroad from Cornelius Vanderbilt. They rewarded him with company stock. In 1867 Tweed added to his list of government positions by getting elected to the New York State Senate. He sponsored a new municipal charter in 1870, which replaced the County Board of Supervisors with a smaller County Board of Audit to which he was elected president. The new board supervised all expenditures for both city and county.

In 1866 he was rich. Tweed began wearing elegant clothes and expensive jewelry, riding in an ornate carriage, and dining in fashionable restaurants, especially Delmonico's and the Astor House. He and his family left their unpretentious house in the 7th ward (now Chinatown) and moved to a stylish brownstone on 36th Street off 5th Avenue. The hard drinking 300-pound political kingpin had a peaceful home life. Tweed appeared to be happily married and proud of his eight children. Being a good family man, however, did not deter his critics.

The product of his most outrageous scandal is the legendary Tweed Court House, which is doomed to perpetual association with the unsavory Tweed. The stately Roman Revival structure, formally the Old New York County Courthouse, is located at 52 Chambers Street between Centre Street and Broadway. The opulent building, constructed between 1858 and 1878, became a monument to brazen graft and corruption which netted the Tweed

Ring at least $12 million dollars in thievery and kickbacks. The interior, for example, was rebuilt three times to generate more opportunity for theft of public funds. Twice when finished, Tweed ordered the plaster and marble ripped out and a new interior installed. Each time the contracts went out Tammany Hall collected a new set of payoffs.

The group around him was dubbed the *Tweed Ring* from a Thomas Nast political cartoon. Tweed was always self-serving. It took a $40,000 bribe to get him to approve the building of the Brooklyn Bridge. He strenuously opposed construction of a subway system because he owned considerable stock in several streetcar and surface railroad companies. Alfred Ely Beach, editor of *Scientific American* and a patrician of independent wealth, secretly built an underground pneumatic tube subway under Broadway just one hundred feet west of City Hall. The one-block subway between Warren and Murray Streets opened in 1870. Furious at the end-run, Tweed blocked Beach's proposal in the State Legislature for permission to build a subway line under the full length of Broadway. The problem for Tweed and Tammany Hall was that they could see no way of making money from Beach's venture and it would harm their interest in streetcar and railroad lines.

Tweed had no qualms about being a crook. *The fact is that New York politics were always dishonest --- long before my time. There never was a time when you couldn't buy the board of aldermen. A politician coming forward takes things as they are. This population is too hopelessly split up into races and factions to govern it under universal suffrage, except by the bribery of patronage or corruption.* George Washington Plunkitt, Tammany district leader and state senator, was able to conceptualize a difference between what he called honest and dishonest graft. *Just let me explain by examples. My party's in power in the city, and it's goin' to undertake a lot of public improvements. Well, I'm tipped off, say, that they're going to lay out a new park at a certain place. I see my opportunity and I take it. I go to that place and I buy up all the land I can in the neighborhood. Then the board of this or that makes its plan public, and there is a rush to get my land, which nobody cared particular for before. Ain't it perfectly honest to charge a good price and make a profit on my investment and foresight? Of course, it is. Well, that's honest graft.*

The end came for Boss Tweed as Republican, Democratic, and non-partisan reformers clamored for his removal from government. *The New York Times* issued a scathing (though condescending) editorial in 1870: *No Caliph, Khan or Caesar has risen to power or opulence more rapidly than Tweed I. Ten years ago this monarch was pursuing the humble occupation of chairmaker in an obscure street in the city. Now he rules the State as Napoleon ruled France, or as the Medici ruled Florence.* Other newspapers including the *Nation* and *Harper's Weekly* joined the chorus of attack. Perhaps most damaging was the way Tweed was continually lampooned by Thomas Nast, the German-born political cartoonist whose well-known drawings appeared in *Harper's Weekly* and other periodicals in mid-century.

Tweed was arrested in 1871 on charges of grand larceny. The leadership of Tammany Hall, watching out for their interests, quickly deposed him as grand sachem. In January 1871 he went on trial but the result was hung jury. In November he was re-tried and convicted on 204 counts of theft. Tweed was fined $12,000 and sentenced to 12 years in prison. He was released after one year when a friendly judge ruled the sentence excessive and reduced the fine to $250. The year Tweed spent in the Tombs was made uncharacteristically pleasant since the warden carpeted his extra-large cell, installed a sofa, rocking chair, and five other chairs to accommodate visitors.

Tweed was arrested the same year he left the Tombs on a civil charge and sent to the Ludlow Street Jail in the Lower East Side. The warden gave him his personal quarters, allowed him to bring in meals from the outside, and to entertain guests. Each afternoon he was driven by guards to visit his wife and dine with her. Tweed was allowed to escape during a visit to his family in 1875, but was recaptured in New Jersey.

Tweed was tried on new civil charges in 1876 and a $6 million judgment was leveled against him for fraud and theft. He escaped again, fled in turn to Staten Island, Florida, and Cuba, and ultimately to Spain, but was returned to prison in New York by Spanish authorities. Boss Tweed ended up dying of bronchial pneumonia in prison in 1878. Estimates of the total cost of his rule, from 1863 until 1872, range from $50 to $200 million. The public was duly outraged at Tweed's crimes and Mayor Smith Ely, Jr. refused to lower the flag to half-mast at City Hall on the day of his funeral. He is buried in Brooklyn's Green-Wood Cemetery. Tweed deserved what he got, but he also took the fall for the whole corrupt system that included bankers, contractors, politicians, judges, and bureaucrats.

Notation:

New Use for the Tweed Court House

The Tweed Courthouse was used for trials until 1926 when a much larger courthouse was built at nearby Foley Square. Between 1926 and 2002 the building was a storage facility for municipal records. Its undignified placement, squeezed between City Hall and Chambers Street, created aesthetic and structural difficulties. The courthouse's grand stairway crowded the narrow street. Highway Commissioner Robert Moses ordered the front stairway removed in 1942 in order to widen Chambers Street. The amputation left the front portico an ungainly stump for six decades. In 2001 Chambers Street was constricted from four lanes to three in the middle of the block to rebuild the lower portion of the stairway. It was part of an $85 million restoration. In 2002 Mayor Bloomberg moved several top officials of the Department of Education (formerly the Board of Education) from 110 Livingston Street in Brooklyn to the Tweed Courthouse to keep them under his watchful eye. It is now the official headquarters of the city's Department of Education.

CHAPTER 83
Water Tanks

New Yorkers cannot help noticing thousands of wooden water tanks perched high above buildings throughout the city's five boroughs. They seem as anachronistic as they are ever-present, giving the modern city a bit of a nineteenth-century look. The weathered but sturdy tanks, alone or in sets of two or more, top off six-story apartment buildings as well as the highest skyscrapers. On the taller buildings, tanks are often camouflaged by walled enclosures, or even put inside buildings. Some skyscrapers, including the former World Trade Center, have water tanks spaced evenly throughout the building.

Skyscrapers use tanks to regulate the pressure. As the water flows down from the highest levels the result is more and more pressure. Water pressure increases with depth. Deep-sea divers experience tremendous weight because of being under so much water. A water pipe also contains great pressure, which needs to be relieved. In the science of physics, there is a mathematical formula to express this: pressure = weight divided by area (the higher the pipe, the greater the weight and pressure). In New York City buildings, the speed of the water is caused by gravity as it flows down through the pipes. Tanks are placed every ten floors in a skyscraper to relieve the pressure so it never gets too strong.

The Rosenwach Tank Company of Williamsburg, Brooklyn is responsible for more than half of New York's tanks. Operated by the family's third generation, the company was formed when Harris Rosenwach, an immigrant tub-maker from Polish Russia, bought the company from the Dalton family in 1896 for $55. The Daltons had started it in downtown Manhattan in 1866, the year after the Civil War ended.

Other American cities outfit their multi-story buildings with high-pressure electrical water pump systems. New York is alone in choosing the older technology. The standard explanation is that pump systems are expensive to maintain and use a great deal of electricity. They also need a standby gas generator in case the electricity fails. Respect for tradition also plays a role.

There are several New York City ordinances that affect the industry. One directs that buildings more than 83 feet high (the level city aqueduct pressure will reach on its own) must have a *roof reservoir* for satisfactory pressure. Another local law states that tanks must be *cleaned and chlorinated once per year.*

The tanks exist to increase water pressure in buildings for home or industrial use, especially at peak periods. That insures that there will be enough water pressure to take showers, flush toilets, and wash the dishes. Periodically during both day and night, an electrical pump keeps each rooftop tank filled.

There are two other reasons mandated by city law. Tanks are needed for sprinkler systems and for hallway standpipe reserves. Those reserves are not used by the fire department, which depends on their own water pumping system from fire hydrants, but are needed to *wet down a means of egress* in case of fire and to *fight fire* before the arrival of the fire department.

Some commercial and industrial buildings have several tanks and use them separately for their water supply, standpipe reserve, sprinkler system, and various industrial uses. Apartment buildings with only one tank must divide it for three uses: normal water supply, standpipe reserve, and sprinkler system.

Steel tanks are sometimes used, but in New York City they have the negative reputation of being expensive to maintain and last only about twenty years. Surprisingly, wooden water tanks may last a lifetime or at least a generation. An example is the tank on the Aberdeen Hotel in Manhattan, first installed in 1919, replaced in 1954, and again in 1992.

Rosenwach and other tank companies use wood, though only Rosenwach manufactures the tanks locally. The favored wood is California redwood, but Western yellow cedar, Alaska cedar, or white juniper, are sometimes substituted. *Green* lumber cannot be used, so the carefully sawed wood staves are air-dried for four years. The cone-like plywood covers, designed to keep down the snow load and provide space for insulation, are placed on top. Heating most tanks is unnecessary because the thick wood insulates the water from cold winter temperatures. Some commercial tanks use heating coils because the weekend use is minimal or absent and on very cold days the still water could possibly freeze.

The average 10,000 to 15,000 gallon tank sits 25 feet above the roof. An old tank can be removed and a prefabricated replacement put together all in one day. Rapid installation is important to minimize water service disruption. Construction follows a simple technology. Staves are pre-cut with tapered sides, to be fitted together in the familiar circular shape. Wooden dowels (pegs) hold the staves together, and threaded steel bands bind them as they are tightened with handled lugs. The finished product is leak-proof and functional. Water tanks are a classic skyline symbol of New York City.

Notation:

Steam Coming Up from the Streets

It is a curious sight to see wafts of steam billowing up from manholes in Manhattan streets, especially in winter. It is neither dangerous nor an ominous sign from the Underworld! Why, then, does the steam surge up in both winter and summer? It is because Consolidated Edison, Manhattan's publicly regulated private electrical monopoly, provides heat to some Manhattan office buildings and residences in winter, and air conditioning in summer. In both seasons, excess steam is released through the Con Ed manholes. In winter the steam is used directly for heating, and in summer, steam-powered turbines run compressors to cool the air in offices and homes. Most buildings have their own energy systems for heating and air conditioning. For those that do not, the Con Ed system, which reticulates under Manhattan's streets, is the cause of those mysterious geysers.

CHAPTER 84
Jacob Riis & the Plight of Immigrants

Jacob Riis was a Danish immigrant who became a prominent photojournalist and published an award-winning book of photographs with lengthy descriptions, which turned a spotlight on the plight of immigrants. *How the Other Half Lives* came out in 1890, but Riis had been active as a reformer much earlier.

His own background gave him direct contact with immigrant poverty. Born in 1849 in Denmark, Riis came to New York City by himself as a 21-year-old in 1870. After four days of looking unsuccessfully for work, he had completely run out of money. He left Manhattan and spent the next several years as a day laborer, agricultural worker, and door-to-door salesman in New Jersey, Pennsylvania, and upstate New York. Returning to Manhattan, Riis found employment, learned photography, and got a newspaper job.

From 1877 to 1888 he was a reporter for the *New York Tribune* and afterwards for the *New York Sun*. His investigative specialties were crime stories and human interest articles, which always came with a photograph. Riis had a good eye for presenting heartfelt pictures, which helped the readers evaluate the story.

He forced middle class readers to confront the squalid conditions endured by many immigrants in New York City. Poverty and overcrowding were constant themes for Riis. The lighter side of immigrant life --- festivals, beer gardens, sporting events, church picnics --- were largely absent from the scenes he presented. Riis was considered an advocate for the poor and homeless, and his pictures of filth and deprivation were meant to elicit a response from government officials and the business community.

What Riis wanted was to close the police lodging houses (homeless shelters) in the basements of police stations where people slept on narrow wooden planks with no bedding. He advocated tenement regulation, and care for street children. He put great effort into a campaign for playgrounds and parks. (There were no public parks or playgrounds in Manhattan south of Central Park and none at all before Central Park opened in 1859.)

Riis made progress in each of these quests. His photographs helped him build a case for social reforms. He also gave lectures to church and civic groups with slide shows to bolster his case. Riis made friends with Theodore Roosevelt when the future president of the United States was president of the Police Board of New York City. Roosevelt, who was the city's top police official from 1895 to 1897, gave the order to close all police lodging houses.

Roosevelt's support for another pet project was crucial: tearing down two square blocks of particularly bleak slums on Mulberry Street and constructing Mulberry Bend Park (now Columbus Park). The park opened in 1897. It provided breathing space for the neighborhood as well as a site for recreation and relaxation.

Despite his good ideas, Riis can be criticized on two counts. First, plans were not made for displaced people. Closing police lodging houses made no provisions for the homeless. Tearing down two square blocks of tenements at Mulberry Bend meant the evicted tenants were thrown out of their apartments with no place to go.

Second, as much as Riis helped by putting the spotlight on the problems faced by some immigrants, he also was prone to blame the victims. In fact, many of his characterizations of immigrant groups in *How the Other Half Lives* are racist. There are numerous examples.

Early Chinatown, which Riis described, was huddled along Mott, Pell, and Doyers Streets. Commercial specialties included chop suey-chow mein restaurants, laundries, and gift shops. By 1900, New York Chinatown's population was about 5,000. Jacob Riis knew Chinatown well as it was 50 yards from his project at Mulberry Bend. He seemed to be looking for something to criticize. He portrayed the neighborhood as quiet compared to the Irish, Italian, and Jewish areas: *Chinatown as a spectacle is disappointing.* But the noted reformer meant no compliment. *One thing about them was conspicuous: their scrupulous neatness. It is the distinguishing mark of Chinatown, outwardly and physically. It is not alto-*

gether by chance the Chinaman has chosen the laundry as his distinctive field. He is by nature as clean as the cat, which he resembles in his traits of cruel cunning and savage fury when aroused.

Faulting immigrants in *How the Other Half Lives,* Riis represented the contradictions of reformers, who were mostly upper middle class people with family antecedents in northwestern Europe. Another reformer, Rev. Richard Salter Storrs, pastor of the Church of the Pilgrims in Brooklyn Heights, warned of being overtaken by the *political sewage of Europe.*

Many reformers decried the tenement neighborhoods and blamed the inhabitants. Despite Riis' moving photographs of poverty, the text of his book leaves no doubt that his reformist instincts came from racial, ethnic, and religious bigotry. He even criticized Buddhism, the religion of most Chinese immigrants. *Ages of senseless idolatry, a mere grub-worship, have left him without the essential qualities for appreciating the gentle teachings of a faith whose motive and unselfish spirit are beyond his grasp.*

Jacob Riis lumped together the immigrant inhabitants of the Lower East Side as he lambasted them for their poor housing. *Hardly less aggressive than the Italian, the Russian and Polish Jew, having overrun the district between Rivington and Division Streets, east of the Bowery, to the point of suffocation, is filling the tenements of the Old Seventh Ward to the river front, and disputing with the Italian every foot of available space in the back alleys of Mulberry Street. The two races, differing hopelessly in much, have this in common: they carry their slums with them wherever they go, if allowed to do it...Between the dull gray of the Jew, his favorite color, and the Italian red, would be seen squeezed in on the map a sharp streak of yellow, marking the narrow boundaries of Chinatown.*

Prejudiced sentiments such as those written by Riis are offensive and deeply disappointing, especially when they come from a reformer. But American sensibilities were vastly different during his life than they are today.

In 1904 Jacob Riis was stricken with heart disease. He retired to Barre, Massachusetts and died there in 1914. His 1890 book, *How the Other Half Lives,* is still in print. And hundreds of people, mostly children and the elderly, make good use of Columbus Park every day.

CHAPTER 85
1898 Consolidation of New York City

In the late 19th century the business community desired to enlarge New York City in order to unify economic development of the harbor and rivers, railroads, bridges, and roads. The merchants behind the proposal wanted to local governments in New York, Kings, Queens, and Richmond Counties rolled into a single municipality. In addition, they intended to detach several communities in southern Westchester County and merge them with the *Annexed District* of the mainland in New York County north of the Harlem River and Spuyten Duyvil Creek. Those areas would comprise a new county, the Bronx, which would also become a borough of New York City. Altogether the plan was for forty municipalities to be fused into one city covering five counties.

The city kept moving north in Manhattan at the same time it was adding suburbs across the rivers. It incorporated Greenwich Village, the village of Harlem, and smaller hamlets as houses and streets filled up the island. Steam railways connected New York City with Harlem in 1837 and over bridges to the Bronx and Westchester in 1844. Since the commercial, political, and cultural center of the metropolitan area was in downtown Manhattan, it was an appealing thought to many that the whole region be united.

Consolidation promoters led by Andrew Haswell Green, a former law partner of 1876 presidential candidate Samuel J. Tilden, drummed up support for a unified metropolis. Green had also been a member of the Board of Education, president of the New York State Central Park Commission, and a well-known historic preservationist. At the time of consolidation he was active in merging three private libraries (Astor, Lenox, and Tilden) to form the New York Public Library. Though the opposing sides that developed over the consolidation issue blurred party lines, there was a political component to the program of the Manhattan business elite. Mostly Republican, they wanted to dilute the power of Tammany Hall, the Democratic organization in Manhattan, which was not organized in the other four counties. On the other hand, many of the foes of consolidation, especially in Brooklyn were Republicans.

Support for consolidation, which required approval by the New York State Legislature for New York City to annex the other communities, was lead the Consolidation League and supported by the Chamber of Commerce. Most of Manhattan's newspapers, the *World, Sun, Tribune, Herald,* and *Times,* supported unification. Editorials pointed to the success of unifying the police, fire, and health departments of Brooklyn and New York, a pre-consolidation merger that occurred in 1857. They also warned that New York City could lose its competitive edge against newer cities, especially Chicago, if unification and capital improvements to the infrastructure were ignored. Opponents in Manhattan protested against their tax money going to develop outlying rural areas in the other counties, and upgrading commuter lines for the comfort of people who spent only their working hours in the heart of the city.

Brooklynites who supported consolidation cited several compelling reasons. The opening of the Brooklyn Bridge in 1883 had been a great boost to Brooklyn businesses. Construction of new residences and factories increased as people and goods could be more efficiently transported across the East River. Farmers in Brooklyn and Queens were able to speedily ship perishable dairy products and produce to Manhattan. It was pointed out that London and Paris, straddling the Thames and Seine Rivers respectively, were consolidated cities and had constructed many bridges so that their rivers were no longer impediments to commerce or travel. Residents in Brooklyn and Queens, especially in Williamsburg and Long Island City, clamored for more bridges that they expected a unified city would construct.

Because Brooklyn, Queens, Staten Island, and southern Westchester were spread out it was costly to construct roads, sewer lines, and water mains in their territories. Most of the municipalities had borrowed heavily to support growth. The growth was largely residential so the burden fell on homeowners and landlords who looked with envy across the waterways at New York City where taxes were lower because a larger share of the burden was paid by businesses. A greater tax base would also mean more money for schools, fire stations, and police stations. (The same uneveness in tax assessments was true in 2005 when Brooklyn paid 14 percent of the city's property tax while Manhattan, with half Brooklyn's population, paid 59 percent.)

Water was another big issue. Brooklyn, with 900,000 residents in 1895, was almost out of water. Wells had to be dug deep and water mains running to ponds, streams, and wells in Nassau and Suffolk Counties supplemented what the Brooklyn wells could provide. Drawing water from Nassau and Suffolk provoked opposition by residents who feared it would lower the water table in eastern Long Island and pass on to them the water crisis of Brooklyn. In 1896 the New York State Legislature barred Brooklyn from drawing any more water from Long Island. There was no water crisis in Manhattan. New York City had opened the Croton Aqueduct (1842) and New Croton Aqueduct (1890) to tap water in the Croton system of reservoirs in Westchester County and had plenty of drinking water. (In 1917 the aqueducts and reservoir system would be extended across the Hudson River and the bulk of the unified city's water would come from reservoirs in the Catskill Mountains and the Delaware River.) Staten Island's population was too small to have a water crisis.

Brooklyn also had commercial waterfront operations in Greenpoint, Williamsburg, Brooklyn Heights, and Red Hook. Queens had active docks in Long Island City, Astoria, and Flushing. Staten Island's north shore had an active maritime industry. Pier improvement and a unified waterfront authority were appealing concepts to maritime companies and longshoremen.

There were powerful forces in Brooklyn that supported unity. The Municipal Union Society of the City of Brooklyn, led by Stranahan, Litchfield, Low, and Gaynor was a powerful voice for development interests. James S. T. Stranahan had built the Atlantic Basin docks in Red Hook, played an important role in funding the construction of the Brooklyn Bridge, and was president of the commission that built Prospect Park. Electus B. Litchfield was a streetcar and land developer active in promoting Park Slope and

Borough Park. Seth Low was a former mayor of Brooklyn known for advocating capital improvements, trustee of Columbia University, and was to be elected mayor of newly consolidated New York City in 1901. William Gaynor was a lawyer and judge, a political reformer, who went on to win election as mayor in 1909.

Most of the opposition to city consolidation came from Brooklyn, the only municipality in the five counties other than New York City to be chartered as a city. It was centered around the *Brooklyn Eagle*, Protestant churches in Brooklyn Heights, and the Loyal League of Brooklyn. Many consolidation opponents were descendants of New Englanders and while they earned a living in New York City, wanted to keep a separate cultural and political identity. They were already concerned that the Brooklyn Bridge had made it easier for immigrants, meaning Catholics and Jews, to move to Brooklyn. They were sentimental about Old Brooklyn and feared increased immigration and the political intrigues of Tammany Hall.

Brooklyn opponents also used local control as an argument, that small government is best. But the Town of Brooklyn itself had once practiced consolidation within Kings County. After it was chartered by the state legislature as the City of Brooklyn (1834) it began to annex bordering towns. By 1894 the City of Brooklyn had subsumed all other political entities in Kings County.

From Plymouth Church and the Church of the Pilgrims came a steady stream of bigoted invective against consolidation. Little of it was aimed at structural or political issues; most was directed at the religion, culture, and politics of immigrant groups. The Reverend Dr. Storrs, minister of the Church of the Pilgrims on Henry and Remsen Streets, warned Brooklyn voters not to *vote away our religion and to reject the political sewage of Europe.* A letter to the *Brooklyn Eagle* asked that Brooklyn remain free *of Fifth Avenue millionaires, free of huddled masses, and free of Hell's Kitchen.* Opposition to consolidation from the old elite in Brooklyn Heights did carry some weight.

In 1894 a non-binding referendum was held and proponents of unification with Manhattan won most areas by large margins. In Manhattan 96,938 supported merger and 59,959 opposed it. In Queens sixty percent favored consolidation. In Staten Island, with

67,000 inhabitants, the vote was a lopsided 5,531 to 1,505 for consolidation. The results in southern Westchester were complicated. The Town of Mt. Vernon voted no by a large majority and the Town of Westchester voted no by one vote. Those towns remained in Westchester County. Eastchester, Pelham and other towns supported consolidation and soon became part of the Bronx County and the City of New York.

By an exceedingly small majority, Brooklyn was on its way to becoming one of the five boroughs of an expanded New York City. The vote was 64,744 to 64,467, a difference of just 277 votes. In 1896 the Consolidation Act passed the State Legislature and was signed into law by Governor Levi Morton to take effect on January 1, 1898. At midnight a crowd of 50,000 celebrants marched down Broadway to City Hall. The next morning die-hard opponents of Brooklyn staged a mock funeral for their city on the steps of the former Brooklyn City Hall.

The economic fruits of consolidation did not take long to materialize. The Interborough Rapid Transit subway line was extended under the bedrock below the East River four stations into Brooklyn in 1904. In the first two decades of the 20th century the Williamsburg (1903) and Manhattan (1909) Bridges were built over the East River and five more subway lines were tunneled below it. The Queensboro Bridge, connecting East 59th Street in Manhattan with Long Island City, was completed in 1909.

New York City's population jumped from 2 million to 3.4 million in 1898. Much of the four outer boroughs had been farmland dotted with villages. Why did the majority vote yes? Probably because they believed their tax rates would go down. Manhattan has an enormous tax base because it is filled with businesses. Consolidating the five counties together into one city would keep taxes down for homeowners while still promoting expansion of public services. And some voters may have been influenced by local chauvinism wanting to be part of the largest city in the United States.

Notation:

City Hall and the Borough Halls

The present Georgian style City Hall with some ornate French Renaissance details was constructed in 1812. After the city consolidation in 1898 it became the center of the unified government of the five boroughs. The sprawling elegant white two-story structure with a particularly tall cupola cuts a dashing figure amidst the neighboring skyscrapers. It houses the office of the mayor, the 51 member City Council Chamber, and a large hearing room that was formerly the chamber of the now defunct upper house of the New York City government, the Board of Estimate. (The Board of Estimate was declared unconstitutional by the United States Supreme Court in 1990 for violating the one person-one vote principle). City Hall has also been the scene of special festivities, award ceremonies, and somber occasions. In 1865 the body of President Abraham Lincoln reposed here for a week while on a roundabout funeral procession from Washington, D.C. to Springfield, Illinois. Unfortunately, intimidating fences, gates, and guard posts installed by Mayor Rudoph Giuliani have cut off public access to the building. Brooklyn City Hall became Brooklyn Borough Hall and new borough halls were built in Queens, Staten Island and the Bronx. The offices of the Manhattan borough president, lacking a borough hall, use one floor of the Municipal Building at Centre and Chambers Streets. Some of the Town Halls such as the Long Island City Town Hall were converted to courthouses. The Flushing Town Hall is now a museum.

CHAPTER 86
Architecture of the 19th Century

Georgian architecture in the English period (1664-1783) had been based on ideas of symmetry and proportion that were valued by new interest in Classical Antiquity following the Renaissance. By the end of the 18th century the appreciation of Greece and Rome intensified, particularly after the discovery of Herculaneum (1783) and Pompeii (1793). It also got a boost from the widely publicized Greek struggle for independence in the 1820s. In the United States, Neo-Classical ideas developed into two styles: Federal, which was based on Roman patterns, and Greek Revival, based on Greek models. Many examples still exist in New York City.

The Federal style was plain with elegant, reserved lines and a minimum of decoration. It was particularly appealing to Americans who had just set up a new republic without the frills of monarchy.

Round and oval spaces appeared in the Federal style. The dome, originally developed by the Romans, had delighted Thomas Jefferson and continued to intrigue Americans. Jefferson designed his own mansion, Monticello (a likeness is found on the back of the nickel), and the University of Virginia's main building, with domes. In New York City, houses were too small for domes, but they were included in three noted structures in Brooklyn (though two were not finished until the opening decade of the 20th century): Williamsburgh Savings Bank (1875) at Broadway and Driggs Avenue in Williamsburg; Brooklyn Museum (1905) at Eastern Parkway and Washington Avenue in Prospect Heights; Greenpoint Savings Bank (1908) at Manhattan Avenue and Calyer Street, in Greenpoint.

Indoors, round and oval spaces appeared as designs on ceilings and walls. A popular structural feature was the semi-circle window often appearing on the front of a house over the entry and above windows. *Pilasters* (flat version of a column used for decorative purposes) were often found flanking the front door or at the ends of the house. Columns were sometimes included in front of a building.

Federal Hall, built in 1701 as New York's City Hall, was completely remodeled in Federal style in 1789 by Pierre Charles L'Enfant. It served as the capitol building of the United States for one year (1789) before the federal government moved to Philadelphia, and ultimately to Washington, D.C. President George Washington took his first oath of office on the second floor balcony. Unfortunately, the historic Federal style building was demolished in 1812. The site, at Wall Street and Broad Street, is now occupied by the old Custom House, built in 1842, and renamed Federal Hall National Memorial. The Federal-style City Hall (1812) at Broadway and Park Row was mixed with some ornate French Renaissance style details. The sprawling building managed to combine republican simplicity with monumental majesty. The Merchant's House Museum at 29 East 4th Street between the Bowery and Lafayette Street near Astor Place is an 1832 Federal style building with a front entrance decorated by a semi-circle window above, and *ionic* (scroll) pilasters flanking the door.

The Greek Revival style, similar to the Federal style, was more concerned about the proportions of a building than the decorations. Large homes often included a columned *portico* (broad porch) holding up a triangular pediment, like an Ancient Greek temple. Smaller homes turned the gable toward the street so they achieved the triangular pediment effect. In modest buildings pilasters were added to the corners or next to the door in place of actual columns. Greek Revival buildings were invariably painted white. Inside, pilasters were found at entries into the parlor and dining room and flanking the fireplace. A common decoration was the Greek *meander* or key pattern (like the border on Greek diner coffee cups). The buildings in Staten Island's Sailors' Snug Harbor complex are superb examples of well-preserved Greek Revival architecture.

Row Houses existed in the Dutch and English colonial periods but achieved prominence by sheer number in the 19th century. Developers would buy an entire block and build a long row of houses each more or less the same, hence the name row houses. In the early 19th century most rows were either Federal style or

Greek Revival style. Individualism was asserted by decorations: pediments, pilasters, molding, wrought iron railings, and artistic finials like pineapples to symbolize hospitality. The Theodore Roosevelt Birthplace National Historic Site, at 28 East 28th Street between Broadway and Park Avenue South in Manhattan is a 1923 replica of the Roosevelt family's original 1848 row house.

Cast-iron architecture was developed in the 1850s. America produced iron in great quantities and New York City had many iron foundries, especially along the East River in Manhattan and Brooklyn, and in Mott Haven in the Bronx. In the foundries metal was heated and the liquid iron poured into desired molds. Cast-iron architecture combined a strong frame with a handsome look of slender columns. The columns were prefabricated at the foundries and sent to construction sites. It was much less expensive than labor-intensive building with bricks or stone (granite or marble). Today, there are many beautiful cast-iron specimens in SoHo and Tribeca, the two Manhattan neighborhoods whose names are acronyms: *South of Houston* and *Triangle Below Canal Street*. The most striking cast-iron edifice in the city is Grand Central Terminal (1869). It is located on 42nd Street and Park Avenue and was commissioned by railroad tycoon Cornelius Vanderbilt.

In 1904, a whole series of 133 ornamental cast-iron and glass kiosks for entrances to the new subway system, the I.R.T. (Interborough Rapid Transit, the numbered trains), were fabricated in Greenpoint, Brooklyn. By the 1960s they had all been demolished. Since 1985 two have been restored (recast from mold patterns) to their original locations: Astor Place Station in Manhattan and Court Street Station in Brooklyn.

Brownstones were row houses popularized by the Italian *palazzi* (palace) style in the 1860s. The material used was reddish-brown sandstone from New Jersey sawed in 4-inch thick blocks and placed over brick frames. Brownstones have high, imposing stoops with cast-iron railings, a raised cellar (only three or four steps down), floor-to-ceiling windows on the parlor floor, heavy cornices over the windows and front door, and a prominent patterned cornice over the top floor.

Grand brownstones of four or five floors were built for upper middle class New Yorkers. (The top floor had a series of small rooms for servants.) Modest two and three story brownstones served as homes for skilled craftsmen.

Darkness was a chief drawback for row houses and brownstones. Generally, just two rooms per floor (front and back) received light and air from windows. The houses were often built with cookie-cutter repetition and sometimes derided for their chocolate brownstone uniformity. Deterioration of the soft sandstone from weathering (cracks and flaking) can be repaired. The solution involves mixing brown-colored concrete and applying it on the remaining stone, like stucco. Brownstones are found in great numbers in Brooklyn's Fort Greene, Park Slope, Boerum Hill, Cobble Hill, Carroll Gardens, and Brooklyn Heights, and in Manhattan in the Upper West Side, Chelsea, Grammercy Park, and Greenwich Village.

Tenement houses developed in the mid-19th century for poor and working class people, mostly immigrants. The rent was low but there were no amenities. Rooms were arranged railroad style, each room in a row with access from the next room. There were no elevators, and there were no hallways within each apartment, and windows only in the front and rear. Kerosene lamps lit rooms without windows, and tenants shared backyard privies.

The Lower East Side Tenement Museum at 97 Orchard Street near Broome Street in Manhattan, is an 1863 five-story red brick tenement house which, from the time in opened until its abandonment in 1935, housed over 10,000 people from twenty-five countries. Four apartments have been meticulously restored and are historically connected with the families that lived there. The Gumpertz apartment is set up to look as it did when the family lived there in 1874. It includes kerosene lamps and coal stoves.

The Tenement House Law of 1879 set new rules for ventilation and hygiene. It standardized a required floor plan for new buildings called the *dumbbell* design, which left an air shaft between adjacent buildings giving some light and cross ventilation.

Upscale apartment buildings were introduced in 1869 and called *French Flats* to connect them with the perceived glories of Second Empire France under Napoleon III. The first *French Flats* were five-story apartments built on 18th Street between 3rd Avenue and Irving Place in Gramercy Park, Manhattan. Apartment buildings were a new way to live and included elevators, doormen, basement laundries, and garbage chutes.

The Dakota Apartments (1884) symbolized elegance in apartment living. Built on Central Park West and West 72nd Street, the building received its popular name to underscore its location so far uptown it may as well have been in the Dakota Territory. Resembling a French country *chateau*, the Dakota had many hotel-style comforts including a concierge. The eclectic architecture included Gothic, Romanesque, and Dutch Renaissance styles. The Dakota was built around a large interior courtyard for carriages and contained 85 suites (the largest had twenty rooms) all served by elevators. Following the Dakota, upscale apartments were built surrounding Central Park, overlooking Riverside Park, and along Park Avenue from 59th Street to 86th Street.

Terra-cotta decorations embellished many late 19th century buildings. Terra-cotta is a ceramic from clay. It may be whatever color is natural (brown, red, gray) or colored, glazed or unglazed. Much of the local terra-cotta was produced at Staten Island along the southern part of the Arthur Kill where clay pits, like Kreischer's, were located near the villages of Charleston and Port Socony. *Kilns* (ovens for ceramics) baked the molded designs. All but the meanest tenements had terra-cotta panels inserted on the *cornice* (the crown of a building), above the door, and around the windows. Once Italians began immigrating to New York the number of skilled stone carvers increased and builders could afford to hire them to carve marble or granite designs and tracery to adorn buildings.

Elevators had an immense impact on buildings in New York City. Without them it was impractical to build too high. Once Elisha Otis developed the safety elevator in 1853, the green light was on for skyscrapers. The first large buildings with elevators were in Manhattan.

Romanticism inspired architecture in the last half of the 19th century; it stressed irregularity and asymmetry in designs. There was a fascination with eclectic decorations, and tracery, sometimes called Victorian gingerbread. Gothic, Romanesque, Baroque, and Italianate styles from Europe were revived. Buildings resembled castles and chateaus; they were often decorated with spires, pinnacles, finials, gargoyles, quatrefoils, and no end of fancy tracery in stone or wood.

• 20th Century New York City

CHAPTER 87
Subways: Trains, Tunnels, Sandhogs, & Station Designs

Slow and chaotic travel in the rapidly growing metropolis had become a maddening problem by the middle of the 19th century. Commuting, shopping, or running errands took too long and had become decidedly unpleasant. There were no stop signs or traffic lights, which made both vehicular and pedestrian travel a chaotic free for all.

Getting around New York City was an especially unpleasant experience in the heat and humidity of the summer. Horse manure deposited on city streets caused an olfactory assault. Thousands of horses deposited tons of manure daily. A contemporary summer walk past the horse-drawn *hansom cabs* (two-wheeled carriages) along 59th Street at the south end of Central Park provides a dim sample of how the city once smelled. New York was in need of a streamlined transportation system.

Scores of competing horse-drawn omnibus coaches and fourteen separate track-bound horse-railroad systems (trolleys) remained captives of the street gridlock. Elevated train systems, popularly called the *el*, initially pulled by horses, but later powered by coal-burning steam engines, were faster, but spewed out smoke and produced a deafening noise.

In 1863 the world's first subway opened in London. The idea of underground travel was appealing though noxious smoke from the engines needed to be overcome. The key factor that inspired far-sighted engineers, technicians, and investors was the promise that subterranean trains could travel at swift speeds unimpaired by traffic. Even today, the subway is often the fastest way to travel in the city.

Alfred Ely Beach was New York City's first subway visionary to generate a plan, raise the money, mostly from his own investments, and actually build a model subway in 1868. Beach was the well-known editor of *Scientific American* and managing editor of the *New York Sun*. He wanted his subway to be tasteful and attractive as well as solve traffic congestion. In the station lounge there was a grand piano, a fountain with gleaming goldfish swimming in its basin, and a grandfather clock. The single wood paneled subway car had upholstered seats and held twenty-two people.

The demonstration tunnel was only 100 yards long, running under Broadway just west of City Hall and spanned Warren Street with Park Place. It was built covertly at night by tunneling from the basement of an adjacent clothing store. The secrecy was necessary because Beach had no city license to construct the system that was opposed by the streetcar companies and Boss William Marcy Tweed, one of the principal shareholders of a streetcar company. When the state legislature passed a bill approving construction of a larger system, Tweed persuaded Governor John Hoffman, a political ally, to veto it.

The single tubular car, which fit tightly in a round subterranean conduit, was propelled by pneumatic pressure provided by a large fan called a Roots Patent Force Blast Blower. The car was blown the 100 yards from one station to the other. The fan could be reversed to pull the car the other way. The model was successful but very limited and many people doubted that workable technology could be developed for longer trains plying a multi station system. Beach eventually ran out of money, his project died, and the one-block demonstration tunnel was sealed off. In 1912, workmen digging the tunnel for a precursor of the Brooklyn Manhattan Transit (BMT) came across Beach's tunnel and demonstration car. It was photographed and then destroyed. Today the R train runs under Broadway through that location.

In 1900, Interborough Rapid Transit (IRT), a subway construction and operating company led by August Belmont and John McDonald, leased the rights for tunnels, tracks, and stations, and constructed them for the city. The New York City system was operated by electricity, each car separately connected to the electrified *third rail*, but controlled as a single unit by the motorman in the front car. It pioneered the use of four-track service that facilitated express and local trains. Subway lines and stations greatly influenced real estate prices. Property values increased for housing and commercial space that was close, but not too close, to subway lines.

The 22-mile long IRT opened in 1904. Mayor George B. McClellan, Jr. (1904-1909) led the official delegation into the first car of the inaugural subway train. He took the controls and drove the train from City Hall station up to the 103rd Street station on the West Side. At the ceremony in City Hall prior to the first subway trip, McClellan declared: *Now I, as mayor, in the name of the people, declare the subway open.* McClellan was a strong supporter of the subway system as were all subsequent mayors. The subway quickly became a valued and indispensable aspect of daily life in the city.

The route followed by the first line that opened in 1904 is now part of three separate subway lines. It ran on the east side from City Hall to 42nd Street - Grand Central Station, turned west under 42nd Street to 7th Avenue and then north up to 145th Street. The next extensions, opening soon after, took the trunk line up to Van Cortlandt Park at 242nd Street in the Bronx, and another line veered eastward at 96th Street and then up Lenox Avenue before dividing again, one spur to 148th Street and 7th Avenue and the other crossing into the Bronx up to West Farms Square and East Tremont Avenue. More extensions followed. Using tunnels dug under the bedrock below the Harlem and East Rivers the IRT extended its system to the Bronx in 1905, Brooklyn in 1908, and Queens in 1915. In Brooklyn and Queens the IRT connected with the Long Island Railroad.

The purpose of the subway train system was to get people to work and to facilitate shopping. So the system was constructed to be Manhattan-centric with the downtown and midtown areas having the most lines and stations. Only the G train, running from Brooklyn to Queens, does not fit this paradigm.

The flurry of construction called for an army of *sandhogs*, men who tunneled underground and laid the tracks. Mostly Italian immigrants, sandhogs worked 12-hour days six days a week under frequently dangerous conditions. Most of the transit workers after the system was built were Irish. Presently, transit workers are predominantly African-Americans, many from the West Indies.

Their union, the Transport Workers Union (TWU) was organized in 1934 and fought for higher wages and improved working conditions. Fiery Irish-American Mike Quill led the union for many years. The strike he called on January 1, 1966, just one hour after John V. Lindsay took office as mayor, gained significant monetary and work rule concessions. The thirteen-day strike sent Quill and other union leaders to jail. The union president suffered a heart attack from which he succumbed by the end of the month. The strike inconvenienced many New Yorkers and the state legislature responded with a new law regulating union organizing, collective bargaining, and strikes by public employees the following year. The Taylor Law gave labor unions the right to bargain collectively and prescribed binding arbitration on the two sides, but mandated stiff penalties for striking: two days fine for each day on strike. Public servants never had the legal right to strike in New York State, but the Taylor Law made it easy to prevent work stoppages.

When TWU president Roger Toussaint called a subway and bus strike five days before Christmas in 2005 it lasted only two days. The contract negotiated by TWU leaders was narrowly rejected by a membership vote and, because the position of the MTA had hardened amidst public support, it took months to agree on a new contract. Meanwhile, to the cheers of Mayor Michael Bloomberg and much of the public, a judge sentenced Toussaint to ten days in jail, fined the union $2.5 million, took away their automatic paycheck deduction for union dues, and fined each union member two days pay for each day of the strike.

Railroads and trolleys had supported urban development. After the Civil War commuter railroad lines were built from Downtown Brooklyn to Coney Island. The Brighton, Culver, Sea Beach, and West End lines made it easier to spend a day or a week at the beach. A private transportation company, Brooklyn Rapid Transit, formed in 1896, and precursor to the Brooklyn Manhattan Transit (BMT), bought out the railroads and integrated them into its new mass transportation system. It was an amalgam of elevated lines, surface railroads, and electric trolleys. The Brooklyn Manhattan Transit became the successor to the BRT in 1923.

The IND, or Independent line, was the municipal subway system organized by the NYC Board of Transportation under the direction of Mayor John F. Hylan. Its first line, the 8th Avenue line (A and C trains) opened in 1932, and was followed by the Brooklyn-Queens Crosstown line (G train), 6th Avenue line (F train in Manhattan), and Queensboro line (E and F trains). Its stations are particularly large, often have ramps and medians, and are the least decorated.

In June 1940, Mayor Fiorello LaGuardia took control of the privately operated IRT and BMT systems and integrated them with the city-managed IND. The Transit Authority, later a component of the Metropolitan Transit Authority, New York City's subway and bus company, operated the newly unified system of 710 miles of track and 468 subway stations. The TA standardized as much of the three systems as possible. The IND and BMT use the same large-gauge tracks and bigger rolling stock compared to the IRT trains. So the numbered trains (IRT) and lettered trains (IND and BMT) cannot be integrated. IRT cars are approximately 51 feet long and 9 feet wide while BMT and IND cars measure 67 feet in length by 10 feet in width.

Today there are several mass transportation systems that are either associated with the Transit Authority (TA), the city's subway and bus system, or are linked to it as part of the network that New Yorkers depend on every day. The Metropolitan Transit Authority (MTA), created in 1968, includes the Staten Island Railway, Long Island Railroad, Metro North, Triborough Bridge and Tunnel Authority, as well as the TA. The Long Island Railroad has terminals in Pennsylvania Station and Brookyn's Atlantic Avenue Terminal while Metro North Railroad's three main trunk routes, Hudson Line, Harlem Line, and New Haven Line, terminate at Grand Central Station.

The Staten Island Railway reaches the eastern shore communities of Staten Island. This former section of the Baltimore & Ohio Railroad system, which had carried passengers since 1860, joined the Metropolitan Transit Authority in 1971. It runs the entire 14-mile length of Staten Island on its east side serving the public with twenty-two stations. Like the rest of the subway system it uses the same rolling stock, operates around the clock, and has the same fare policy, but only about 14,000 riders use it on a weekday, just a fraction of the crowds that pack the other lines. It is not exactly a subway since it does not go underground, but runs on surface level or in open trenches.

The Port Authority Trans-Hudson Corporation, part of the Port Authority of New York and New Jersey, has subway trains that link Hoboken, Jersey City, and Newark with Manhattan on two lines, one that terminates at the site of the World Trade Center and the other with stations at Christopher Street and four along 6th Avenue ending at 33rd Street. New Jersey Transit, a large system of trains and buses uses Pennsylvania Station as its New York City terminal.

Unlike later subway stations in Moscow, St. Petersburg, Beijing, or Washington, D.C., New York's stations, similar to the early stations in London and Paris, were built for pragmatic reasons alone. There was never the intent that the system would be an artistic and nationalistic showcase. In fact, there was a certain glorification of steel and concrete as the basic building blocks of an industrial society, so raw steel I-beams were unadorned. Yet there were exceptions to the stark practicality that characterized the IRT and later systems.

Great care was taken in the design and color of many of the entrance ways, especially the cast-iron and glass subway kiosks, original wooden ticket booths, lighting fixtures, vent covering grilles, directional signs, terra-cotta cornices, glazed wall tiles, and station name tablets. Plaques at some of the stations caught the historical significance of the place name or the area. Memorable and cherished examples are the beavers at Astor Place, the *Santa Maria* at Columbus Circle, the seal of Columbia University at 116th Street, the steam ferry that once crossed the Hudson to Jersey City at Cortlandt Street, the stone bridge over a canal and adjacent tavern at Canal Street, the Brooklyn Borough Hall at Court Street, and Robert Fulton's steamship *Clermont* at Fulton Street.

Squire J. Vickers, chief architect of the IRT and later of the integrated transit system, had an enormous impact on subway design. While retaining the dignified Victorian and Beaux-Arts look in older stations, Vickers moved the system into a Machine Age Aesthetic that straightened and flattened curves and favored simple yet colorful geometrics over flowering designs. His contributions are often called Art Deco or Civic Moderne and are most noticeable on the IND lines. In 1933 Squire Vickers, who held his post from 1906 until 1942, defended his vision. *The basic reason for the change probably lies in the fact that a new deal in architecture was overdue. The column pilaster, cornice, and string course of the classic style were not adapted to form the architectural clothing of the skyscraper nor of many other of our modern buildings. Now we see that the only solution to the problem was the discarding of the old forms and the creation of the new style.* His architectural vision articulated in 1933 was certainly consistent with two new popular skyscrapers, the Chrysler Building (1930) and the Empire State Building (1931).

The most beautiful station, the rounded City Hall terminal, has vaulted ceilings with multi-colored tiles. It is closed and inaccessible though the IRT Lexington Avenue #6 local train passes through it as it makes a loop at the south end of its run. Beaux-Arts, the rich, lavish, and heavily ornamented classical style, remained in favor as the 20th century dawned.

The worst days for the subway system were the 1960s and 1970s, a time when middle class flight to the suburbs decimated New York City's population and left it without adequate financial resources to fight crime or repair the crumbling infrastructure. The trains were dirty, over-crowded, occasionally dangerous, covered with graffiti, plagued by broken doors, and without air-conditioning.

However, there was romanticism in the old stations with the smells of hot dogs, hamburgers, and fried eggs wafting from independent food stalls and underground chains like Nedicks. Newsstands, and cheap shops, especially tie stores selling 50-cent neckties, were everywhere. Signage used endearing archaic terms like *To the City* and *From the City* in the Outer Boroughs, and *Canarsie Cross-Town Local* (L train), or *Lexington Line* (4,5,6 trains), or *Culver Line* (F train). Signs instructed riders with small children: *Little Enough to Ride for Free, Little Enough to Ride Your Knee.* George Selden's children's book, *The Cricket in Times Square* captures the feeling.

There are still problems with the subway system. New lines are needed in eastern Queens and Manhattan's illusive 2nd Avenue line, in the planning and fitful start-and-stop stages for six decades, is still unfinished. When acute problems arise, especially flooding after rains, track fires, or signal malfunctions, patrons at most stations are left in an information vacuum. In 2012 Hurricane Sandy's destructive flooding knocked out several subway tunnels under the rivers. The R train connection between Brooklyn and Manhattan was lost for two years. The TA has a poor track record in sharing accurate information. Ninety-two stations out of 468 have no reliable public address system, and announcements made at some of the other stations are often mangled. In the summer the trains are kept delightfully cool but the stations, especially large stations where trains idle while customers get off and on, are sweltering. Rats can be seen scurrying around the tracks and sometimes on the platforms. Food and paper goods carelessly dropped by transit customers exacerbates the rodent problem and causes track fires. Another problem is that cell phones will not operate when trains are underground.

The United States Census Bureau released data in 2006 showing that New Yorkers as more likely to use mass transit (subways, buses, trains, ferries) to go to work than people in any other American city. The average length of the commute was clocked at 39 minutes each way, though it took Staten Islanders 42 minutes to get to work. Two of every seven commuters in the entire metropolitan area, defined by the federal government as the five boroughs plus 18 surrounding counties in New York State, New Jersey, Connecticut, and Pennsylvania, used public transportation to get to their jobs.

Notations:

Mayor George B. McClellan

Mayor George B. McClellan, who took the controls of the first IRT train on opening day in 1904, was the son of controversial Major General George B. McClellan, Sr., organizer of the Army of the Potomoc, a meticulous planner but indecisive warrior and insubordinate military leader. After being fired by President Abraham Lincoln the general unsuccessfully ran against him as a Democrat in the 1864 election, unsuccessful nationally though popular enough here to carry New York City.

Unlimited MetroCards

For more than eight decades transit tokens placed in a slot at the turnstile were the way rides paid their fares. The little round tokens were phased out in the early 1990s and replaced by rectangular plastic farecards that required a quick swipe at the turnstiles. Computerization allowed for some helpful innovations and probably spurred commerce. Free transfers between subways and buses were instituted in 1997 and unlimited-ride cards were introduced in 1998. Ridership soared as people became much more willing to make extra stops to run errands on the way home from work, or to travel to another neighborhood during their lunch break.

CHAPTER 88
Ellis Island

Ellis Island has become a shrine honoring the trials, tribulations, and ultimate triumphs of millions of immigrants. Sixteen million immigrants passed through Ellis Island on their way to a new life in the United States.

The procedures for accepting immigrants changed radically over the centuries. During the colonial period each colony issued rules on accepting newcomers. After the establishment of the United States government in 1789, the states supervised immigration and several designed some regulations, though at most ports of entry there were few, if any, rules. Generally immigrants entered the U.S. at New York City, Boston, Philadelphia, Baltimore, or Charleston. As the ships docked the immigrants simply stepped onto the piers and entered American life.

In the middle of the 19th century New York State first began processing immigrants. Between 1855 and 1890 Castle Clinton at the Battery was the state's immigration center. Originally called Fort Clinton, the circular citadel overlooking the harbor had been built by the U.S. federal government in 1811 to defend the harbor. Twelve years later the fort was demilitarized and given to the city which outfitted it with a roof and renamed it Castle Garden. Between 1823 and 1855 Castle Garden was regularly leased by P. T. Barnum and others as an entertainment center. After 1855, under the name Castle Clinton, it became New York's intake center for immigrants. When the federal government took over immigration from the states, New York's center was moved to Ellis Island.

Ellis Island, named for Samuel Ellis, who purchased it in 1785, was bought by the State of New York in 1808. The state ceded it to the federal government to be used as part of a harbor defense system against foreign warships. Between 1892 and 1954 it was a federal immigration center. At first, makeshift wooden buildings were used for the inspection process. The large French Renaissance style Reception Hall was completed in 1900. The three-acre island was enlarged with landfill to twenty-seven acres, and thirty-four buildings were erected for examining, inspecting, interrogating, quarantining, and sometimes incarcerating would-be immigrants. The intimidating process was intended to screen out people suffering from contagious or debilitating diseases, as well as criminals, mental defectives, and polygamists.

Approximately 98 percent of the immigrants were accepted and most of them finished the process in less than eight hours. The remaining two percent were not all permanently rejected. Some of the ill were quarantined until they recovered or died. The others were sent back. The ships that brought unfit immigrants were obliged by American law to return them to their ports of embarkation. When a person under age twelve was returned, one adult could accompany the child. This de-humanizing immigration inspection process was ended by Congressional legislation in 1919 that mandated obligatory pre-embarkation physical exams. The bill was co-sponsored by Congressman Fiorello La Guardia, mayor of New York City from 1934 to 1945, who had once been an immigration translator at Ellis Island.

Not everyone had to go through the humiliating and frightening gauntlet of inspectors at Ellis Island. First and second-class passengers remained on their ships and doctors came aboard to give them private, individual exams. They were able to disembark directly in Manhattan. Only the *steerage* passengers were obliged to pass through Ellis Island. *Steerage* was the lowest class where impecunious passengers traveled in dark, crowded compartments below deck. The difficult immigration experience is much more romantic to the descendants of immigrants than it was to those forced to endure it.

In 1954 the Immigration and Naturalization Service moved its headquarters from Ellis Island to Manhattan, and Idlewild International Airport, renamed JFK International Airport in 1963, became the intake center. In 1965 President Lyndon B. Johnson declared Ellis Island a national monument to be operated by the National Park Service in conjunction with the Statue of Liberty on nearby Liberty Island. In 1982 President Ronald Reagan appointed a private commission to raise funds for restoring the island and transforming it into a museum of immigration.

Conceptually, the craze for information about immigrants who came at the turn of the last century and before was a reaction to the enormous historical emphasis previously put on the importance of Mayflower descendants and other very early arrivals. The children and grandchildren of Eastern and Southern Europeans struck back, popularizing and exalting the experience of their ancestors.

Lee Iacocca, former chairman of Chrysler Corporation, was appointed by Reagan to head the committee to raise money and promote the concept. The initial renovation of the site cost $162 million. The committee ultimately collected $450 million for both the Ellis Island project and refurbishing the Statue of Liberty. The choice of Iacocca was symbolic as well as pragmatic. His father had emigrated to the U.S. from Italy through Ellis Island as a 12-year old boy in 1902. At least 100 million Americans can trace ancestors who were inspected at Ellis Island. Raising funds and public awareness were both accomplished by Iacocca's committee.

The Ellis Island Immigration Museum is part of the National Park Service. Its mission is to preserve the historic site and allow visitors to see the complex where sixteen million immigrants passed through. The museum holds the American Family Immigration History Center that has extensive and attractive demographic displays on various aspects of the immigrant experience, a library, oral history project, search facilities for immigration records, and a gift shop.

Nineteenth century immigration to the United States was part of the Great European Emigration, the period between 1815, the end of the Napoleonic Wars, and 1914, the start of the First World War, when 60 million Europeans left their continent. During those years approximately 88 percent of the 34 million immigrants to the U.S. came from Europe, eight percent from Latin American countries, and four percent from other locations.

In the Dutch period when the population of New Amsterdam was below 2,000, visitors claimed seventeen separate languages could be heard on the streets. In 1850, nearly half of the city's 600,000 residents were born abroad. At that time two-thirds of all immigrants to the United States entered through the port of New York.

Europeans left their homes because of population pressure on agricultural and urban areas. From 1800 to 1900 Europe's population increased from 188 million to 432 million. Unemployment and underemployment were the chief causes of the mass departure. Other reasons included war, famine, and ethnic and religious discrimination. Those who emigrated were not the poorest because the lowest level of society could not afford ship fare. It was mostly small landholders unable to survive on minuscule farms, artisans marginalized by factories, shopkeepers, minor officials, and professionals.

Germans made up the largest 19th century group to arrive in the United States. They amounted to sixteen percent of the total. In the two decades before the Civil War, one-quarter of the entire population of Ireland left, many relocating to the U.S. The Irish comprised thirteen percent of all immigrants. Italians composed twelve percent, Great Britain (England, Scotland, Wales, Northern Ireland) eleven percent, and Russia, which included Finland, Estonia, Latvia, Lithuania, and most of Poland, ten percent.

European emigrants also went to other settler-states. The vast majority of the population in Argentina, Uruguay, Chile, Canada, Australia, and New Zealand is derived from the Great European Emigration. At the same time a smaller emigration occurred in Asia, mostly out of China, Japan, India, and the Philippines to Latin America, the Caribbean, Australia, East Africa, Hawaii, and California. In 1882 the Chinese Exclusion Act prevented Chinese and all other Asians from immigrating to the United States.

Not all immigrants to the U.S. stayed. Many Europeans ended up as *migrants* returning to their countries of origin after a period of years in the United States. About one-third of the immigrants returned home, though the likelihood of repatriation varied greatly by country. Seven out of eight from the Balkans returned, but only one of ten from Ireland, and one of twenty Jews returned. Some immigrants never intended to remain in the United States and had planned to earn enough money to go back to their home countries with greatly enhanced economic resources. Others missed ancestral ties, suffered religious or ethnic discrimination, or had trouble adapting to American culture and the English language.

Between 1914 and the 1970s there was little legal immigration. The National Origins Act of 1924 severely restricted immigration from Southern and Eastern Europe and reaffirmed the ban on all immigration from Asia. President John F. Kennedy liberalized immigration quotas in 1963 and by the late 1980s more than 1.25 million legal immigrants were entering the United States each year, a number higher than the previous peak of one million annually between 1900 and 1906. The difference in relative percentage makes the numbers less striking. In 1900 there were 60 million Americans and by 2014 there were 312 million Americans.

The top ten countries of *ancestry* for New Yorkers in 2000 were Italy, Ireland, Germany, West Indies (considered collectively), Russia-Ukraine, Poland, Great Britain, Greece, Hungary, and Austria. The census data is flawed because it does not count African-Americans where the country of origin would usually be unknown, or Puerto Ricans who are from a commonwealth of the United States. Jews are not listed separately but came mostly from Russia-Ukraine, Poland, Germany, and Austria.

With the exception of Puerto Rico the top twenty-six countries of *birth* gives a good view of the source of immigrants to New York City in 2000: Dominican Republic, former Soviet Union, China, Jamaica, Guyana, Poland Philippines, Trinidad & Tobago, Haiti, India, Ecuador, Ireland, Colombia, Bangladesh, Korea, Pakistan, Peru, Honduras, Great Britain, Israel, Italy, Cuba, Greece, Barbados, former Yugoslavia, El Salvador. Some of the countries at the top of the list one and two centuries ago (Ireland, Great Britain, Italy) are now at the bottom. Germany does not appear anywhere on the list. Nor does Mexico though anecdotal evidence indicates that there are many Mexicans living in New York City, especially in Corona, Sunset Park, East Harlem, and Washington Heights.

Why does the United States accept so many immigrants? The answer is partly romantic, and can be found in a profound appreciation for the immigrant experience, since all Americans except native people have immigrant ancestors. Mostly it is about cheap labor. Immigrants are generally young and hard working, and in the beginning many work for wages and under conditions unacceptable to Americans already here.

Notation:

Migrant, Emigrant, Immigrant

A *migrant* is a person who moves from one country to another, or from one state to another. We usually use the word to refer to *migrant workers* who follow the crops as they ripen beginning in southern Texas in July and working up through the Great Plains and the Middle West until October. An *emigrant* originally meant a person who permanently leaves or enters a country. In the 1920s the word *immigrant* was coined in American English. An *immigrant* is a person who enters a country and an *emigrant* is one who leaves a country, so, depending on point of view a person who changes countries is both an *emigrant* and an *immigrant.* That explains why the name of New York's Emigrant Savings Bank, a place for newcomers to deposit assets, makes sense. (People who leave the United States would not put their savings in a New York bank.) In 1850 Archbishop John Hughes had urged the Irish Emigrant Society to set up the bank as a service to poor Irish Catholic depositors. Despite the coining of *immigrant* the bank never altered its name.

CHAPTER 89
Coney Island

Brooklyn's beachfront communities of Coney Island, Brighton Beach, Manhattan Beach, Oriental Beach, and Sea Gate share a peninsula, formerly an offshore island, which became attached to the mainland of Long Island (Brooklyn) before the Dutch period. The peninsula was an island because Coney Island Creek and Sheepshead Bay were once connected. The D train to Coney Island (West End Line), passes through the immense Coney Island Subway Yard and over Coney Island Creek, which provides a good vantage point to view the waterway which once stretched the dozen blocks to connect with Sheepshead Bay making Coney Island a real island.

The Canarsie Indians, a tribal subgroup of the Lenape nation, set up summer villages near the ocean to collect the gifts of the sea: hand plucked oysters, clams, scallops, mussels, crabs, and lobsters. The Dutch called the peninsular sand spit at the southern end of Brooklyn *Konijn Eisland* (Rabbit Island) because of the large rabbit population.

By 1830 there were already inns and resorts in the sandy, seaswept area. Fraternal groups, chorale and gymnastics societies, political clubs, and church groups used the facilities for yearly gatherings. In 1884, the Elephant Colossus was built on Surf Avenue. It was an immense wooden frame covered with hammered tin and shaped like an Indian elephant. The extraordinary structure, which stood 150 feet high held a large party room, amusement stalls, and a museum. While a captivating landmark, the Elephant Colossus was a financial failure. It burned to the ground in 1896.

There were three horse race tracks in the vicinity (Brighton Beach, Sheepshead Bay, Gravesend) and they drew thousands of racing enthusiasts who often spent time in the area's hotels. Increasingly, Coney Island achieved a national reputation. Entertainment became a specialty of Coney Island and carousels, roller coasters, bars, brothels, gambling, and more innocent games of chance sprouted along the beachfront. Mixed bathing became popular on the beach. Eventually this all merged into the distinctly American phenomenon known as the *amusement park.*

Increased leisure time for the working class in the late 19th century and a growing population provided paying customers for Coney Island entrepreneurs. Technological advances brought electricity and more complex machinery to the service of the rides and amusements. Railroads and trolleys also facilitated development. After the Civil War, commuter railroad lines were built from Downtown Brooklyn to Coney Island. The Brighton, Culver, Sea Beach, and West End lines made it easier to spend a day or week at the beach. In the 1920s the private railroad and subway company, Brooklyn Manhattan Transit (B.M.T.), bought out the railroads and integrated them into its new mass transportation system.

By 1904 developers had erected three large amusement parks along Surf Avenue near the beach: Steeplechase, Luna Park, and Dreamland were three private and separate components of Coney Island with independent amusements sandwiched between them.

Steeplechase presented fifty amusements, many using mechanical force to entertain patrons, in a 12-acre area. The *Barrel of Love* was a dizzying centrifugal-force novelty and the Earthquake Floor simulated a natural upheaval. The signature *Steeplechase Race* featured mechanical horses carrying customers around a track.

Luna Park was a fairyland with a million incandescent bulbs outlining spires, minarets, and domes. Its *Trip to the Moon* show featured an imaginary ride on a simulated spacecraft for thirty passengers who looked down and viewed lighting effects and movie screens showing Coney Island and North America fade into the background as the craft sped along through an electrical storm to the moon. The ride was over when the spacecraft landed on the craggy surface of the moon where passengers disembarked, explored the *Palace of the Man on the Moon,* encountered moon creatures and finally exited the extraordinary ride.

Dreamland promoted civic improvement and its serene, spacious grounds mirrored the City Beautiful Movement. A popular show at Dreamland was *Fighting Flames,* where a fake tenement fire was put out and women and children saved by an imitation fire department. It also featured replicas and murals of famous

Western European tourist spots.

In 1910, small communities of year-round residents appeared, primarily Italians and Jews. A decade later both Coney Island and Brighton Beach developed sizable populations that stayed through the winter. The heyday of Coney Island was from 1900 until the Second World War. Afterwards, general prosperity and widespread automobile ownership beckoned Brooklynites to Queens, Long Island, Staten Island, and New Jersey for recreation.

From the record high attendance on July 4th, 1947, when an estimated 2.5 million people packed Coney Island, the number of visitors dwindled as the electric age matured and the electronic age dawned, automobiles made transportation easy, and modern theme parks sprouted around the country. The Coney Island style of entertainment became outdated and hoakey.

But, the pervasive tackiness and seediness remained part of the attraction for many people. And there was a sense of inverted snobbery about Coney Island that even attracted some upper middle class New Yorkers. Surf Avenue, the main drag, is filled with tumbledown buildings with street-level food and entertainment concessions and rooming houses on the top floors. The movie, *Went to Coney Island on a Mission from God* (2000), which portrays sad losers who inhabit the area and work at the concessions, gives an idea of the underside of the neighborhood.

The three large amusement parks did not survive very long, though much of their space was filled with newer small-scale rides and amusements. Dreamland burned in 1911, Luna Park was destroyed by fire in 1944, and Steeplechase Park closed quietly in 1964. City planner Robert Moses disliked the honky-tonk atmosphere of Coney Island and had several square blocks north of Surf Avenue razed. He commissioned developer Fred Trump to build twelve residential projects on the site. Today's Coney Island, while still fun, is just a ghost of its former self. Yet it has some compelling attractions. Chief among the enticements are the Atlantic Ocean, the broad sandy beach, and the Boardwalk.

The Boardwalk was built in 1923 by New York City and stretches four miles from Brighton Beach to Sea Gate. It is fifty feet wide, built just off the ground, and constructed of wooden planks placed in a zigzag pattern. Along its north side range a plethora of commercial establishments and toward the east a few basketball, paddleball, and handball courts. Full sensory entertainment is provided by the rides and shrieking laughter of their passengers, food smells, competing carnival music and hawkers pitches, and the beautiful Atlantic Ocean with a broad sand beach and a multitude of frolicking, tanning, and swimming New Yorkers. In the sky, small planes pull commercial advertisements through the air and large jetliners land and take off from Kennedy Airport.

Food and drink are available from a host of Boardwalk shops and kiosks where you can satiate your appetite on any number of traditional beach specialties. Gird your stomach for the assault of grease and salt from fried clams, onion rings, Italian sausages, pizza slices, hamburgers, French fries, hot dogs, and corn-on-the-cob whose peeled ears rotate endlessly on warming machines. Dessert could be ice cream or dyed cotton candy. The treeless beach and entertainment area is hot. To wash down the oily snacks and assuage summertime thirst, a wide variety of sodas, both national brands and Brooklyn favorites are available: Yoo-hoo Chocolate Drink, Manhattan Special Espresso Coffee Soda (produced on *Manhattan* Avenue in Greenpoint, Brooklyn), and Dr. Brown's Celray, Black Cherry, or Cream Soda, and international brands like Coca Cola.

The new $40 million Keyspan Park, built in 2001 for the Brooklyn Cyclones, one of the Class A farm teams of the New York Mets, is a small, comfortable stadium with a capacity of 8,000, intimate enough to see clearly from any location. With a keen eye on the past, the team's logo is a nostalgic Brooklyn Dodgers-like white **B** and an interlocked bright red **C**. The *Baby Bums* brought a semblance of the game back to Brooklyn 44 years after Walter O'Malley took the Dodgers to Los Angeles. The stadium, named for Keyspan, the local utility company and a chief corporate financial backer, is a concoction of metal, glass, and tile, part 1960s and part post-modern. An angular fiberglass canopy covers some of the bleacher seats. The animated crowd is all Brooklyn. When *Saturday Night Fever* is played on the loudspeaker, fans dance in the aisles. Brooklyn Cyclones is local ball. The outfield advertising boards tout the local patrons: *L & B Spumoni Gardens, Midwood Appliances, Sal's Transmissions, and Riviera* --- *Only One Wedding at* *a Time*. The team, of course, is named for the roller coaster. Coney Island was always risqué, even sleazy, and the Cyclones are meant to sanitize the neighborhood, the way Manhattan's 42nd Street was cleaned up. Coney Island always appealed to the newest immigrants and to nostalgics, and sanitization may not work.

The Parachute, next to the Boardwalk at West 17th Street, was abandoned when Steeplechase Park closed in 1964. Its Eiffel Tower-like frame hulk has always been a symbol of promise to Brooklynites that someday it would re-open and Coney Island would regain its old pizzazz. Across the Boardwalk from the Parachute is the Long Pier, connecting to the Boardwalk and extending 100 yards out into the Atlantic Ocean. It affords a spectacular view of the coastline, accommodates photo opportunities, and provides a free, convenient place for fishermen to try their luck.

The former Childs Restaurant Building, at the Boardwalk and West 21st Street, marks the western end of the Amusement Park area. It is an ornately decorated beige stucco building constructed in 1923 to house a Childs restaurant. The architectural style is Spanish Colonial Revival, though its esthetic elements reflect its beachfront setting. The fanciful terra-cotta reliefs and medallions colorfully invoke images of the sea: Neptune, mermaids, dolphins, seahorses, and ships. The baked clay is glazed with seven separate colors and is a spectacular example of the triumph of the local terra-cotta industry. The façade was declared a landmark in 2003. Childs, once the largest local restaurant chain, had been founded in 1889. It was a pioneer in self-service and showed a fetish for cleanliness and the color white. The Childs floors were white ceramic, walls were white tile, counters and tables were white marble, and the staff wore starched white uniforms. The fare was comfort food and the prices ranged from low to moderate. The founders were supporters of the Temperance Movement and did not serve any alcoholic beverages. Smoking was forbidden and lingering was discouraged. Childs, which numbered fifty-three outlets at its height in the 1920s, experienced hard times after the Second World War and was bought by the Riese organization in 1961 and ceased to exist as an independent restaurant chain. The abandoned building has been waiting for a new occupant for more than five decades.

West of the Childs Building is a cluster of high-rise apartment buildings owned by the New York Housing Authority. Beyond that is Sea Gate, a sleepy gated residential community of 7,500 with no access to the public. It was organized as a private community in 1892 under the auspices of the Sea Gate Association, which barred Roman Catholics, Jews, and non-whites. Today it is mostly Jewish and includes a community of Satmar Hasidim.

The New York Aquarium for Wildlife Conservation has entrances on the Boardwalk and on Surf Avenue between West 5th and West 9th Streets. Despite its name, this public facility straddles the line between animal habitat and sideshow. It is home to four hundred species of marine animals: fish, birds, and mammals. The most popular are the enormous whales, ponderous walruses, frightening sharks, electric eels, and the playful sea otters, dolphins, penguins, and seals. All feeding times are posted and watching animals gulp down fish provides great entertainment. In the *Aquatheater* sea lions do tricks at feeding time.

Many of the amusements at Coney Island are rides. Astroland Park owns the largest facility as well as several of the games of chance. Along Jones Walk, the main concourse of Astroland, is the Cyclone, Pirate Ship, Dante's Inferno, High Flyer, Astrotower, and Wonder Wheel. The venerable, slow moving Wonder Wheel (Ferris Wheel) offers a magnificent view of the oceanfront. It has a more frightening internal track where swinging carriages rock and slide as the whole ensemble turns. The Cyclone Roller Coaster, at the east end of Surf Avenue near the New York Aquarium, is a 1927 wooden landmark is one of the few old-style roller coaster survivors in the United States. Charles Lindbergh pronounced it: *scarier than flying solo across the Atlantic.* Howls of joy and screams of fear can be heard from blocks away. Delight through predictable terror has always been the draw.

The Freak Show, Fun House, Skee-ball Lanes, Shooting Galleries, and various games of chance line both sides of a lane called Bowery Street, which is often used as a backdrop for films. Bowery Street is the quintessential Coney Island walkway. This is the place to play, earn points, and perhaps win a doll or stuffed animal.

The point of the game at Eldorado Auto Skooter (Bumper Cars) is to drive the sleek little electric cars around the track crashing into everyone else without getting too badly bumped. The pulsating disco music, colored strobe lights, and yells of drivers racing toward excitement or whiplash is the attraction.

The B & B Carousel is one of the neighborhood's treasures. Brightly painted horses with riders, often sitting with a parent, gently ease up and down a pole as they rotate on the platform. Familiar *calliope* music accompanies the riders as they go around and around. B & B Carousel is in pretty good shape for an original fixture at the park. To add a little bit of fun for older children, a brass ring sticking out from a wooden armature taunts riders. If you can pluck it, you get a free ride.

Recently, there have been indications that Coney Island may survive the general American shift to high-tech amusement parks and retain an ambiance of century-old entertainment for New Yorkers. Keyspan Park and the Brooklyn Cyclones has been the single most important improvement in the area. The Parachute could prove to be an irresistible attraction.

Many new improvements were made and unveiled at the start of the 2014 season. The trick will be to retain enough of the old to keep its character yet update some of it to bring more people. Like comfort food, there is a timeless familiarity of Coney Island with its comfort-games and comfort-rides, the ocean, and the ageless Boardwalk. Whether in youth you visited it once or a hundred times, the cozy feeling always returns. Brooklyn is the most romantic borough, and Coney Island is a chief symbol of Brooklyn Romanticism.

New stores and artists moving into surrounding houses have been another boost for Coney Island's stagnant economy. Sculptors, painters, potters, and designers found Coney Island's cheap rents and large spaces enticing and added some new effervescence to the old scene. Irreverent artist groups sponsor live sideshow performances, *Sideshows by the Seashore*, with outrageously politically incorrect acts, and an outlandish annual *Mermaid Parade* along Surf Avenue with marchers and revelers in various states of nautical dress. (The Mermaid Parade is held the first Saturday after the Summer Solstice at 2:00 P.M.)

Two old-time Italian-American restaurants in Coney Island were remodeled in the 1990s. Both Gargiulo's, which dates from 1907, and Carolina, founded in 1928, are neighborhood icons. Nathan's Famous, is a local fast food stand that has not changed much since it opened in 1916. A hectic Independence Day hot dog eating contest is held in front on the curb of Surf Avenue and televised on all the local news programs. Garish green and yellow signs cover the entire building hawking hot dogs, French fries, fried clams, and corn-on-the-cob. Since the Brooklyn Cyclones and their fans joined the neighborhood, Nathan's greatly expanded its outdoor seating by knocking down the building to its west.

Brighton Beach is located just east of Coney Island and shares the same peninsula. It became a popular destination for New Yorkers soon after Coney Island achieved prominence as a recreational center. While Coney Island specialized in entertainment, Brighton Beach became home to resorts and family beach houses. The classy block-long Hotel Brighton opened in 1878, followed by a racetrack, music hall, and dance hall. In 1907 the Brighton Beach Baths opened, signaling a shift to Eastern European Jewish vacationers. The area was filled with summer cottages, most just three or four blocks from the ocean.

In the 1920s residents winterized and enlarged the small beach houses. In addition, six-story apartment buildings were constructed, and the summer community became a year-round, predominantly Jewish, neighborhood. After the Second World War the area went into a slow, steady decline. By 1970 many stores had closed, crime had soared, and the entire area had become a slum.

During the 1970s Brighton Beach was reinvigorated when thousands of Soviet Jews (*Refusniks*) came to New York City and settled in the area, attracted by its cheap rents, comparatively spacious old apartments, and proximity to the Atlantic Ocean. Shops that cater to Russian tastes and styles and advertise wares in Cyrillic-lettered signs announce their predominance.

Little Odessa, so named because a large proportion of the Russian Jews came from Odessa, a Black Sea city in southern Ukraine, remains a nickname for Brighton Beach, but increasingly new immigrants have come from the former Soviet Republics of Georgia, Kazakhstan, Tadzhikistan, and Uzbekistan.

An interesting way to experience the impact of Eastern European culture on Brighton Beach is to visit a *gastronom*, which means grocery store in Russian. There are several along Brighton

Beach Avenue. Each Brighton Beach gastronom is more like a deli than a grocery store, but the name from the old country stuck. Historically, Russian gastronoms had sparse shelves and post-1991 gastronoms were often foreign-owned and carried very expensive goods from Italy, the Netherlands, Germany, and Scandinavia. In Brighton Beach the prices are reasonable and the traditional foods are stacked everywhere, overflowing from the deli counters. Some Russian-style products, primarily the prepared foods, are made in the United States, but most goods are imported from Poland, Ukraine, Georgia, Romania, Bulgaria, with a few from Russia.

Meat counters are laden with prepared meats: breaded and fried duck legs, roasted pork knuckles, and lamb kebabs. Sausages hang down from above. Cheese counters offer various types of pastries are stuffed with cheeses, mostly forms of farmer cheese. They always stock *smetana,* delicious and fatty Russian sour cream. Among the beverages is bottled *kvass,* a Russian non-alcoholic near-beer made of slightly fermented stale black bread and raisons. The fish sections carry traditional Russian *farshirovanaya riba* (*gefilte fish* or stuffed fish), not the elongated, sad little patties swimming in gelatin found in American stores. True to its name, which means *refilled-fish,* the fish meat is removed, mixed with egg white, spices, and some sugar, then stuffed back into the skin of the carp or whitefish from which it came. Fish counters have mostly dried and smoked fish, but regularly carry caviar and sturgeon as well. The bakery sections sell strudel, cookies, cakes, sponge cake, buns, loaves of mandle bread, and fruit-filled tarts. Breads are generally *bielo* (white), but they also make *chorny* (black), and braided *challah.* Deli specialties are shish-kebab, blintzes, potato pancakes, fried fish, and stuffed cabbage. The chief grocery stores are on Brighton Beach Avenue: Odessa Gastronom, *Zolotoy Kluchnik* (Golden Key), and M & I International Food.

Brighton Beach is filled with interesting shops. There are Turkish sweet shops offering dried fruits, candy, juices, syrups, nuts and several varieties of sunflower seeds. Homemade pomegranate, peach, and apricot juice is served from large vats. Gift shops carry typical Russian souvenirs: *matryuska* dolls, enameled boxes, amber jewelry, and wooden spoons.

Mrs. Stahl's Knishes, formerly at Brighton Beach Avenue at

the corner of Coney Island Avenue, represented Russian Jewish immigrants at the turn of the last century. Knishes are fluffy potato filling with added salt and garlic encased by layers of soft, philo dough and baked, not deep-fried with thick batter. Originally, when the store opened in 1935, knishes were poor people's food (cheap and filling), and the Depression gave them a boost in popularity in New York City. Knishes are not a big hit in today's Russia, and this shop characterized the tastes of older immigrants who came from Belarus, western Ukraine, and Poland. Consequently many of the customers were not neighborhood people, but visitors who lived elsewhere. There were not enough customers to stay in business and Mrs. Stahl's Knishes closed in 2004. The storefront is now a Subway. Jonah Schimmel's on East Houston Street is the only knishery left in New York City.

Manhattan Beach and Oriental Beach are quiet residential communities at the east end of the Coney Island peninsula. Across Sheepshead Bay from Manhattan Beach is the Sheepshead Bay neighborhood. A footbridge between Dover and Exeter Streets offers a short cut across the bay. The docks along Emmons Avenue, Piers 1-10, are home to several party-boats for half-day or full-day fishing trips. Some of the lucky fishermen who catch more than they want, sell their fish, usually bluefish, striped bass, or porgies, from the docks.

CHAPTER 90
Drinking Water, Bathing, & Toilets

New York City was primitive in terms of drinking water, bathing, and toilet facilities until the beginning of the 20th century. Farmers had it easier than townspeople because they usually had a spring or pond on their property to supply drinking water, a reserve of firewood to heat water for baths, an outhouse placed at a discreet distance from the farmhouse, and empty space to dispose of garbage that their animals would not eat.

In the town, all of these daily functions presented difficulties. Drinking water was an absolute necessity. Wells were dug all over colonial New York, but if they were too deep or too close to the salty rivers or harbor, the water was undrinkable. The pump built over the spring feeding the Collect Pond (where Foley Square is now located) was a cherished source of fresh water and was dubbed the Tea Water Pump because housewives used it to brew tea. Other streams were also used, but the process entailed sending a family member, usually a child, to fetch water in buckets, or paying a water carrier to supply water from a huge cask mounted on a wagon. Everyone was thrifty with water use considering the difficulty of getting it.

Salt water from the rivers was unusable for laundry purposes. Water for washing clothes was gathered from the roof run-off down gutters and spouts into a backyard *cistern* (catch-basin for water). The cistern was usually round, lined with stones, and used clay or cement to seal the open spaces. It was often dug only a few feet away from the backyard outhouse. If there wasn't enough rainwater in the cistern, people took their laundry to a town well, or to ponds or streams.

Bathing was infrequent. Europeans at that time rarely washed themselves, except for hands and face, because bathing was thought to be a health hazard: a way to catch pneumonia. Many bathed only on a monthly or seasonal basis. Even when bathing was desired, it was a big production to heat enough water to fill a wooden tub (with no drain) and then dump it out or ladle it out afterwards. If bathing was on the schedule for the day, the whole family used the same water, one by one.

Toilet facilities were very different from today. The privy and the chamber pot took care of their excretory needs. A square-shaped dry-laid stone pit (without mortar) was dug in the backyard and an outhouse placed over it. Oyster and clamshells were commonly used as *bathroom tissue,* and have been found in large quantities during archaeological digs through the waste of outhouses. (Toilet paper was invented by Joseph C. Gayetty in 1857 and sold in bundles of separate sheets from his shop on Ann Street.) Chamber pots were often used at night or during rainstorms or snowstorms. When the pit below the outhouse filled with waste, it had to be shoveled out by *necessary tubmen,* usually slaves or free blacks, and dumped in the river. Local laws allowed *night soil* dumping only at night.

The backyard was a busy place. Clothes were washed there because of the proximity to the cistern, and were dried outdoors on lines stretched across the backyard. If the family had cows, goats, pigs, or chickens, that is where they were kept. It was not a place for gardening or relaxing. The backyard was an outdoor work area, barnyard, and toilet facility.

Garbage, the other waste, was something altogether different in New Amsterdam. There was not very much of it because paper and metal were very expensive, tin was not used for cans, and aluminum, plastic, Styrofoam, and polyurethane hadn't been invented. Their garbage --- animal bones, peels from potatoes and onions, coffee and tea grounds --- was thrown in the street to be gobbled up by dogs, pigs, and chickens. Ashes from burned wood and cinders from coal were also dumped in public places. In 1648 Governor Peter Stuyvesant, in a thundering rage over the filthy streets, put a stop to dumping garbage in public places and also forbade residents from letting their animals wander freely about town. So, people dumped their garbage and trash in fields just outside town or in the Collect Pond where they also got their drinking water, or in the rivers where they got their fish. In 1657 several town dumps were established, though river and pond dumping was still allowed.

Life did not improve much during the English colonial period. The city had 249 public wells operated by hand-pumps and numerous private wells by 1803, though the water was foul smelling and brackish (salty). People who could afford it, bought water in casks from springs further north in Manhattan.

The Collect Pond was the largest source of fresh water well into the English period. Forty acres and 60 feet deep, it was fed by several springs. The overflow went into its swampy surroundings and was drained through a meandering stream to the southeast emptying into the East River. It was a valuable asset, which both the Dutch and English colonists degraded by using it as a town dump, and building tanneries, breweries, and slaughterhouses along its banks. Eventually it became a foul menace and was filled in between 1803 and 1813 and its springs had their water diverted into storm sewers. (Today the site of the Collect Pond is known as Foley Square, Manhattan's judicial center, which remains a slight hollow. More geographically telling is a sign next to an apartment building on Park Row near Pearl Street reading: *Danger: Sinking Ground - Do Not Enter*.)

The English evacuation of New York City in 1783 ushered in a time of rapid population growth. Immigrants poured into the city, especially from Germany and Ireland. It became imperative to solve the problems of insufficient drinking water, a lack of laundry and bathing facilities, and disposal problems for sewage and garbage.

A brilliant scheme entailing a great deal of engineering mastery was developed to solve the water problem. It called for damming the Croton River in Westchester County and building the 40-mile Croton Aqueduct to Manhattan. Fresh water began flowing in 1842. The water filled a 31-acre receiving reservoir located in what is now Central Park, and was then pumped down to a two square block reservoir, built in Egyptian style, where the Main Branch of the New York Public Library and Bryant Park are presently located. A new Croton Aqueduct with twelve new reservoirs was built in 1890. The new aqueduct was actually an underground tunnel.

The system was expanded to the Catskill Mountains, one hundred miles north of Manhattan, on the other side of the Hudson River as the city's appetite for water grew. In 1917 water began flowing to the city from the Ashokan Reservoir, the first of many reservoirs to be built in the Catskills. The water tunnel, fourteen feet in diameter, was sunk 1,100 feet below the Hudson River on its way to the five boroughs. Some water is also diverted into the reservoir system from the Delaware River. Presently, Tunnel No. 1 (opened in 1917) and Tunnel No. 2 (opened in 1936) are fully operative. Tunnel No. 3 (begun in 1972) is partially operative while its construction continues. New York City's water is lightly treated with small amounts of *chlorine* (disinfectant), *fluoride* (tooth decay preventative), and *orthophosphate* (pipe-corrosion preventative).

Two problems threaten the system: occasional droughts cause the reservoirs to get dangerously low; continued residential construction around the watershed region increasingly pollutes the ground water, which seeps into the reservoirs. The only defense against droughts, which happen approximately twice each decade, is conservation. Laws exist requiring water-saving showerheads, sink faucets, and toilets. Someday, to induce conservation, individual houses and apartments may need to be metered so consumers will pay for the water they actually use.

During droughts the possibility of opening twenty-five closed wells in southeastern Queens, is a possibility. The unused wells once belonged to the Jamaica Water Supply Company. The problem is that they are polluted with bacteria and dry-cleaning chemicals and the water would need purification. If tapped, the Queens wells could yield 40 million gallons of water each day.

The New York City Water Supply System presently has nineteen reservoirs surrounded by 2,000 square miles of watershed land (where no people live), 346 miles of aqueducts and tunnels, and 5,814 miles of distribution water mains. Each day New Yorkers use 1.5 billion gallons of water from this system. About 1,000 aluminum boxes are places on city streets by the Department of Environmental Protection to take water samples for periodic testing.

Nicholas Denise established the first *Bathing House* open to the public in 1792. Bathing was available in either fresh cold, warm, or salt water at a cost of four shillings, a pricey fee. In 1849 the Association for the Condition of the Poor built the *People's Bathing and*

Washing Establishment on Mott Street (now Chinatown) as the first inexpensive public bathhouse. It cost from five to ten cents to take a bath and three cents per hour to do laundry. It closed in 1861 for lack of customers. The city government came to the rescue in 1870 when the Department of Public Works built a series of floating bathhouses on barges. By 1888 there were fifteen barges providing inexpensive baths: 2.5 million for men and 1.5 million for women each year.

As people understood more about germs, the city moved more rapidly to provide bathing facilities. In 1901 the first *free* public baths opened on Rivington Street on the Lower East Side. By 1914 there were seventeen free public bathhouses in Manhattan, seven in Brooklyn and one each in the Bronx and Queens. Most included swimming pools and gymnasiums, a bit like the Roman baths in the ancient world. By that time there were about 70 private bathhouses in New York City. They were social centers as well as places to get clean. The Russian & Turkish Baths, which opened in 1892, still does a lively business. It is located on East 10th Street in the East Village, and features both Russian steam rooms and Turkish hot air rooms.

Public places for baths and showers are now rare. Queens has the most since it has a large immigrant population from the former Soviet Union, where bathhouses are seen as a place for socializing. Most New Yorkers have bathing facilities in their homes and prefer to bathe privately. Public facilities now exist only for the very poor. Since 1990, Municipal Shelters offer free showers to homeless people.

Twentieth century technology and pressure for ecological reforms slowly brought New York City a long way. Sanitary sewage disposal remained a serious problem until very recently. In about 1800 the city began loading untreated sewage from designated collection places and dumping it into the East River and Harbor. Digging trenches and placing large cast-iron sewer pipes to take away effluent was started before the Civil War. In 1855 there were 70 miles of sewer pipes and the number grew to 1,400 miles in 1902. At that time the sewers all led to the rivers. There are presently 6,200 miles of sewer pipes in the five boroughs.

Repeated cholera epidemics, an often fatal disease spread by polluted water, and the filth of the city's waterways led the government to start the process of building fourteen sewage purification plants in 1930 when New York City was dumping 1.3 million gallons of raw sewage into New York Harbor every day. The first sewage treatment plant opened in 1937 in Coney Island, but the last two (Red Hook and Harlem) were not completed until 1987. They treat 1,6 million gallons of sewage each day. Dumping untreated raw sewage into the ocean finally stopped in 1992.

In the past, reeking garbage gave New York's streets an awful smell and appearance. Poor neighborhoods always fared worse. Charles Dickens, after visiting the Five Points part of Manhattan in 1842, remarked: *All that is loathsome, drooping, and decayed is here.* In 1881 the Department of Street Cleaning was organized to keep the streets clean and to collect garbage. It changed its name in 1929 to the Department of Sanitation. The Supreme Court outlawed ocean dumping in 1934, though it continued for six more decades. In 1948 a gigantic 3,000-acre dumping facility was established in Fresh Kills, Staten Island. Thousands of seagulls looking for a meal hovered routinely over the mountains of garbage. Mount Trashmore, or Mount Garbage, as it was sometimes called, closed in 2001, much to the relief of Staten Islanders.

Garbage disposal presents contemporary New York with expensive options for collection and disposal. Laws and common sense prohibit dumping any refuse in the ocean or burning it, which would emit toxic smoke in the air, so since the closing of Fresh Kills Landfill, it is hauled from curbsides by 12-ton capacity garbage trucks to sixteen smelly, slippery transfer stations, weighed, unloaded, compacted, and put in tractor trailers or railroad boxcars, and shipped to poorer rural areas in upstate New York, Connecticut, Pennsylvania, Virginia, and West Virginia, which accept it in gigantic dumps. A lot of New York tax money is used to ship the garbage and to pay the towns to accept it.

What about recycling? Some waste cannot be recycled, but cans and bottles can be returned and re-used. Laziness gets in the way of success. Some government agencies have also dragged their feet. What about excessive packaging? Stores and take-out restaurants routinely wrap up products with more layers of polyurethane, plastic, cardboard, and paper than is necessary. So far, some have cut back a bit, but not enough.

Our lives are immeasurably easier, cleaner, and healthier today in regard to drinking water, bathing, and toilet facilities. The irony of being surrounded by water, but not being able to use it because of the salt content, was not lost on early New Yorkers. It took over three centuries to provide everyone with fresh water for drinking, hot and cold water for bathing and laundry, and at least one toilet in each apartment or house.

CHAPTER 91
Kleindeutschland, the General Slocum, and Yorkville

Germans were among the earliest settlers in New Amsterdam. They lived interspersed with others in the disparate immigrant community south of the wall. When their numbers began to increase sizably in the early 18th century, a German neighborhood developed to the northeast in the vicinity of where the Brooklyn and Manhattan Bridges were later built. It also became home to some of the Hessian mercenaries who either defected or failed to leave when the British troops evacuated New York in 1783. Baron von Steuben, Washington's drillmaster at Valley Forge, was the hero of the German community and a symbol of their loyalty to the new republic.

In the 1830s large-scale German immigration brought thousands of people to the edge of the city where new construction was underway and old houses were being enlarged. The enormous German settlement called *Kleindeutschland* (Little Germany), ultimately stretched from East Broadway to East 23rd Street and from the Bowery to the East River. Between 1840 and 1860, almost thirty-two percent of all immigrants to New York were from the German states. Approximately 154,000 German-born New Yorkers lived in Little Germany by the Civil War when it was home to more Germans than either Berlin or Vienna. New York's German-born population exceeded by at least three times the respective German-born populations of Milwaukee, Cincinnati, St. Louis, and Chicago. However, the percentage of German-born in those cities was slightly higher than the sixteen percent in New York. Including second and third generation German-Americans, Kleindeutschland's Germans numbered about 250,000. In the early 20th century the area completely lost its German character and was called the *Lower East Side*. In the 1960s many people began referring to the portion north of Houston Street the *East Village*.

Much can be learned about the community by viewing its opinion leaders. Carl Schurz (1829-1906), arguably the most prominent and successful German, came to New York after the failed republican and nationalist Revolution of 1848-1850. Traveling from one German community to another, Schurz involved himself in Republican Party politics, and campaigned for Abraham Lincoln, who later appointed him ambassador to Spain. He fought in the Civil War as a brigadier general and following the war was appointed to the United States Senate from Missouri. During the presidency of Rutherford B. Hayes he served as Secretary of the Interior and used his influence to promote civil service reforms and battle New York's Tammany Hall and other political machines in the American cities. Returning to New York City he was elected president of the *New York Civil Service Reform League*. Schurz, even more than von Steuben, was a figure Germans respected as able to navigate American society while retaining his links to German culture. Political machines throughout the country opposed using test scores advocated by civil service reform groups because it cut them out of the process of providing government jobs. Schurz battled Tammany Hall continually as head of the New York Civil Service Reform League

Oswald Ottendorfer, publisher of the *New-Yorker Staats-Zeitung*, the leading German language daily, gained influence because his newspaper had the largest circulation of any German-language daily in the United States. Abraham Jacobi, a German Jewish physician, founded the field of pediatrics at the College of Physicians and Surgeons. He worked among the poor teaching hygiene and disease prevention. Both Ottendorfer and Jacobi had fought on the barricades as revolutionary *48ers* before emigrating.

The German community in New York, essentially secular, was readily characterized by its cultural, commercial and political activities. Few Germans were involved in the American social reform movement because of its driving religious nature and hostility toward drinking. The *biergarten* (beer garden), tavern, popular music concert, *verein* (association), *turnverein* (gymnastics club), *schutzenverein* (shooting club), group picnic, and outdoor festival were more reflective of the community than its connection to religious activity.

The *turners*, as the *turnverein* were called, were part of a Romantic Movement that developed in Germany before the 1848 revolutions and reflected a peculiarly German mixture of physical culture, nature, nationalism, and republican politics. The *Turnhalle of 1871*, named for the date of German Unification, stands at 66 68 East 4th Street between the Bowery and 2nd Avenue. The majestic building with *1871* emblazoned on its pedimental emblature rests on four city lots. It is a five-story, double-width building that reaches to East 3rd Street. Inside were meeting rooms, gymnasiums, bowling alleys, a theater, dance hall, shooting gallery, bar, and restaurant. Next door, at 64 East 4th Street is the building that once housed the *Labor Lyceum*, a hall used by German and Jewish labor organizations, where the *International Ladies' Garment Workers Union* was organized in 1900. The *Turnhalle of 1871* and the *Labor Lyceum* are now Off-Broadway theaters. Around the corner four blocks away at 291-293 Bowery is the partly abandoned two-story building that was a beehive of activity when it was the *Germania Assembly Rooms*.

Unterstutzung verein (sickness and death benefit society) were inexpensive insurance groups, which paid for funerals, sometimes owned sections of cemeteries, and organized social events. They were usually based, like *landsmannschaften* (Jewish mutual aid societies), on a shared occupation or a common hometown or region in Germany, and financed by monthly dues.

There were more than a dozen German Masonic Lodges in New York. Kleinedeutschland's Masons built a substantial neoclassical building at 220 East 15th Street at Rutherford Place, now used by Friends Seminary for some of its high school classes. The *Deutsche Gesellschaft* (German Society), once led by Baron von Steuben, figured prominently in sponsoring lectures and speaking out publicly for the community on key political and cultural issues. Other German societies included the *Harugari*, the largest German-American fraternal group in the United States, and the *Frei Gemeide*. Germans also organized militia units based on a region of Germany, occupation, or sponsored by a society or saloon. There were militia units representing mechanics, bakers, and tailors. Several fought in the Civil War.

In 1850, newspaper reporter George G. Foster published *New*

York by Gas-Light, and recounted the evening scene at *Mager's Concert Hall*, on Elizabeth Street close to Grand Street. Foster used the word *Dutch*, from the German word *Deutsch*, to refer to Germans.

It is an immense room on the second floor, elaborately and gaudily painted in fresco, with scenes from Dutch mythology (at least they are not from any other) in which naked goddesses, grim knights, terrific monsters and American eagles, are like Shelley's immortal combatants --- Feather and Scale inextricably blended. The floor, on ordinary occasions, is filled with rough tables and wooden benches, and partly across one end runs a balconied platform by way of orchestra. Every Sunday night takes place at this establishment a grand German and English concert, vocal and instrumental...These concerts are regularly attended by the respectable German men and women residing in the city, to the number of from twelve to seventeen hundred. In pleasant weather the number seldom falls below fifteen hundred...Sometimes in the dancing season this immense hall is put to worse purposes than those we have thus far enumerated --- being rented out to disreputable women for grand public balls and flare-ups, in the high faluting style.

Germans opened many businesses. There were numerous grocery stores, bakeries, butcher shops, *delicatessens* (from the words *delicacy* and *eat*), drinking establishments, music halls, and hotels in Kleindeutschland. The *Tenth Ward Hotel*, at Forsyth and Broome Streets, where Karl Marx relocated the *International Workingmen's Association* (or *First International*) from 1872 until 1876, was a leading German hotel.

Germans, like all New York's ethnic groups had niche occupations. They were dominant as tailors, shoemakers, furniture makers, and carpenters. Germans were also heavily represented as tobacco workers (mostly cigar rolling), printers, machinists, producers of musical instruments, and white-collar office employees.

Political sentiment in the neighborhood was overwhelmingly abolitionist and generally in favor of the Republicans. It also included a large socialist component and an active and radical commitment to the labor movement and social welfare organizations. American socialism began in Little Germany. Joseph Weydemeyer, a colleague of Karl Marx, organized the *Amerikanischen Arbeiterbund* (American Workers League) to promote trade unionism and socialist ideas. Social welfare groups included *landsmannschaften*, *unterstutzung verein*, libraries, clinics, lecture halls, and settlement houses.

Two adjacent buildings on 2nd Avenue between St. Mark's Place and East 9th Street were busy institutions in Kleindeutschland. The *Freie Bibliothek und Lesehalle* (Free Library and Reading Room), now the Ottendorfer Branch of the New York Public Library, and the *Deutsches Poliklinik* (German Polyclinic), now the Stuyvesant Polyclinic Hospital affiliated with Cabrini Medical Center were built of red brick with imaginative terra-cotta tracery

The German Free Library and Reading Room was magnificently housed in a red brick edifice with imaginative terra-cotta tracery featuring shells and globes to signify armchair travel. It memorialized Oswald Ottendorfer, publisher of the *New-Yorker Staats-Zeitung*. Today it is a branch of the New York Public Library. The *Deutsches Poliklinik* was once the downtown affiliate of the German Hospital, now Lenox Hill Hospital. Its façade incorporates head-finials of classical figures in medicine: Hippacrates, Celsius, Aesculap, and Galenus. The name of the clinic was changed in 1917, the year the United States entered the First World War, at the height of anti-German sentiment. Both buildings opened in 1884.

German-Americans had two important common bonds: the German language and a shared interest in Germany. There were many divisive factors as well. Religion (Catholic, Protestant, Jewish), region of origin, which was especially important before German Unification in 1871, politics, and class sometimes segregated and differentiated Little Germany's residents.

Tompkins Square Park played a central role in German life in Kleindeutschland. Physically, the park added significantly to the neighborhood's quality of life. It was a pleasant tree-covered place to gather and enjoy the fresh air. It provided breathing space for the community and gave it a focal point. Wealthy Germans built townhouses along its north side, some with elaborate cornices and emblatures, though the park's border on Avenue A was lined with saloons. Each year, a week long festival of public merrymaking, the *Volksfest*, was centered at Tompkins Square Park. A central meeting place, the park became the rallying point for the 19th century labor movement. In January 1874 it was the site of the first labor demonstration in New York City, which was organized by

Marx's *International Workingmen's Association*. The police attacked the workers and the *Tompkins Square Riot* ensued. (By the 1920s Union Square usurped the role of Tompkins Square as the labor movement's rallying place.)

The graceful *Temperance Fountain*, at the west center section of the park, close to the saloon row, was a provocation by New York reformers. The statue of *Hebe at the Well*, a zinc representation of the perpetually youthful daughter of Hera and Zeus, the cupbearer of the Greek gods who provided them with nectar as well as ambrosia, stands on a three-tiered canopy supported by four slender columns. Under the canopy is a water fountain, undoubtedly a service to the public, but also an advertisement for sobriety. To further drive home the point to thirsty passersby who may have missed the symbolism, the four entablatures carved in raised lettering call out: FAITH, HOPE, CHARITY, TEMPERANCE. The quote, with an anti-alcohol addition, came from St. Paul's letter to the Corinthians (I Corinthians 13:13) in the Christian Bible's New Testament: *And now abideth faith, hope, charity, these three; but the greatest of these is charity.* The temperance people had sneaked in a fourth virtue. The placement of Hebe in Tompkins Square Park in 1888 was a calculated gauntlet thrown down to German drinkers by Henry Cogswell, a San Francisco dentist and temperance advocate, who commissioned and donated the statue. Residents ignored the preachy challenge and the statue still stands, though in Buffalo an angry mob toppled a temperance statue.

The number of Germans in Kleindeutschland who were Jews grew from 7,000 in 1845 to 85,000 in 1885. Many were *Freethinkers* (non-religious) and Jews affiliated with the Reform Movement and active in the overall German community, while Orthodox Jews, a distinct minority, remained apart. Several eminent synagogues got their start in Kleindeutschland before moving uptown. *Central Synagogue*, established by a merger of two previous congregations dating from 1839 and 1846, and *Rodeph Shalom* (Persuers of Peace), organized in 1842, follow the Reform tradition, and *Anshe Chesed* (People of Mercy), founded in 1850, is a conservative synagogue. *Temple Emanu-El* (God Is With Us), a Reform synagogue, was organized in 1845. Felix Adler, son of Temple Emanu-El rabbi, Samuel Adler, established the *Ethical Culture Society*, primarily composed of German Jewish freethinkers.

German Jews organized The Jews' Hospital in Manhattan (later renamed Mount Sinai Hospital), which opened in 1855, and established Beth Israel Hospital in 1891. German Jews organized the *B'nai Brith, Free Sons of Israel, Educational Alliance,* and *Arbeter Ring* (Workmen's Circle). The founding site of B'nai Brith is marked by a small metal plaque set high in the brick wall of a modern apartment building yard and playground on the east side of Essex Street between Broome and Grand Streets. The *Jewish Anti-Nativist, Self-Protection, and Mutual Aid Society,* the secondary name of B'nai Brith, was established by secular Jews in 1843 who met in Sinsheimer's Saloon, 60 Essex Street, to organize a community response to anti-Semitism.

The preponderance of Germans had come from the Catholic states in Germany's south, especially, Baaden, Württemberg, Bavaria, and Hesse. Most Holy Redeemer Roman Catholic Church, the second parish to have German-speaking clergy, was a congregation established in 1852 by Redemptorist fathers from Germany. The present German Rococo structure, located at 173 East 3rd Street between Avenues A and B, was completed in 1875. For decades it was the tallest building in the neighborhood. Eighty-five of the Redemptorists are buried in the crypt of the interesting church. To the right of the altar stands an ornate tomb, a reliquary for the remains of St. Datian, a martyred Roman soldier so obscure as to be missing from most hagiographies. The pews in the nave are slightly elevated on four-inch raised wooden platforms to insulate the feet of the faithful from cold floors in winter, as is commonly done in many churches in Germany, Poland, and Scandinavia. St. Nicholas, the first Roman Catholic German parish, built a small church in 1833 on East 2nd Street between 1st Avenue and Avenue A. Only the rectory survives at 135 East 2nd Street. It is a five-story Gothic brick and limestone building built in 1867 and now converted into apartments.

Most of the other Germans who were affiliated with Christian religions were Lutherans, called the Evangelical Church in Germany. St. Mark's Evangelical Church was a leading Lutheran congregation, as was St. Matthew's Evangelical Church on Mott Street, noted for its religious and political conservatism. There were also other German Protestants.

One church and two cemeteries mark the German Reformed (Calvinist) presence. The Russian Orthodox Cathedral of the Holy Virgin Protection, at 59 East 2nd Street between 1st and 2nd Avenues, was originally Mt. Olivet Memorial Church, a German Reformed congregation. The cemeteries were established in 1831 as private non-sectarian cemeteries serving primarily as burial places for Protestants from Episcopalian, Dutch, and German Reformed denominations. At New York Marble Cemetery, 2nd Avenue between East 2nd and 3rd Streets, and New York City Marble Cemetery, 52-74 East 2nd Street midway between 1st and 2nd Avenues, underground family crypts hold the coffins of the deceased. Even German Methodism was represented in Little Germany. The building and name of the First German Methodist Episcopal Church, 48 St. Mark's Place between 1st and 2nd Avenues, still exists, but the converted row house is now home to Spanish-speaking and Korean-speaking Methodist congregations.

Freethinkers constituted a significant segment of Kleindeutschland's population. They followed Enlightenment ideas and established a few organizations and a newspaper to promote their concepts and provide a counter-balance to the influence of the churches. Freethinkers celebrated Thomas Paine's birthday, held Anti-Revival Meetings, and sponsored lectures explaining their point of view.

There were some non-Germans who also lived in Little Germany. People with English, Irish, Greek, Armenian, and Slavic backgrounds could also be found scattered in the neighborhood. Ensconced within Kleindeutschland was a small Italian enclave along East 11th, 12th and 13th Streets. A few signs of it can still be found: two remaining Italian spaghetti houses (from 1904 and 1908), two pastry shops (from 1894 and 1904), and a tiny grocery store (1909). Mary Help of Christians Roman Catholic Church (1917) was razed in 2013 for a new apartment building. A workers hiring hall at 231 East 14th Street closed decades ago but the sign, chiseled in granite above the second floor windows, remains: *Italian Labor Center.*

Germans established communities outside Kleindeutschland such as Yorkville, on Manhattan's Upper East Side, and in the surrounding counties of New York as well as in Hoboken, New Jersey. Germans could be found in Stapleton, Kreisherville, Astoria, Maspeth, Ridgewood, Middle Village, Williamsburg, and Greenpoint.

Yorkville had become predominantly German by 1850. Its western edge attracted middle class Germans who could afford townhouses. Working class Germans were attracted to the large tenements constructed in the eastern part of the neighborhood. By 1900 significant numbers of Czechs, Hungarians, and Eastern European Jews also lived in Yorkville. The neighborhood lost its German ethnic character by 1980 though there are still a handful of German shops and restaurants near East 86th Street.

By the 1860s, the Stapleton neighborhood on the north shore of Staten Island had attracted a significant German population who established several industries including furniture factories dependent on local hardwoods and breweries using spring water from the hills. Along the southern segment of the Arthur Kill in Staten Island, a German community of skilled workers labored in the nearby clay pits and brick kilns and lived in a company town, Kreischerville, which had existed since Balthazar Kreischer founded the Kreischer Brick and Terra-cotta Works in 1854. Finally, in 1927, when the German influence had ended, the town changed its name to Charleston.

German immigrants moved into the northern part of Astoria, Queens after the Civil War. They were drawn by cabinet and woodworking shops, stands of tall beech trees, and by attractive housing provided for them at reasonable rents by their trade group, the German United Cabinet Workers. Piano manufacturer William Steinway began putting together a tract of four hundred acres of land in the northeast corner of Astoria in 1870. He built company housing for his workers and named the central road Steinway Street. The piano factory was located along the shore of the East River in a part of Astoria that came to be called Steinway. William Steinway's father, Heinrich Steinweg, had emigrated in 1850 from what later became Germany, Americanized his name to Henry Steinway, and proceeded to become the largest producer of pianos in the United States. William Steinway, as a transit developer, sponsored the tunnel from Hunter's Point in Long Island City to Midtown Manhattan under the East River. The tunnel is now used for the subway system's #7 IRT Flushing line. As a housing developer, Steinway was partner in a working class beach resort at nearby North Beach, on land now occupied by La Guardia Airport.

Many Germans left crowded Kleindeutschland and moved across the East River to Williamsburg and Bushwick in Brooklyn, and Maspeth, Ridgewood, and Middle Village in Queens. After the failure of the 1848 Revolution in Germany, a broad band of German settlement took form stretching from Williamsburg through Bushwick and into Queens. Twelve German-owned breweries opened in Bushwick, and two, Rheingold and Schaefer, remained in business there until 1976. In 1850, two-thirds of the population of Williamsburg was German, and several German-style breweries, were established. Charles Pfizer, a German immigrant, began manufacturing chemicals in a plant on Bartlett Street in Williamsburg in 1848. Havemeyer and Elder, another company owned by German-Americans, established a sugar refinery near the corner of South 4th Street and 1st Avenue.

The opening of the Williamsburg Bridge in 1903 led to the rapid transformation of Williamsburg. Dubbed the *Jews' Highway* in the press, it carried thousands of Jewish immigrants from the Lower East Side to more spacious apartments in Williamsburg. It also carried German, Italian, and Slavic immigrants across the river. Peter Luger's Steak House, at 178 Broadway, between Bedford and Driggs Avenues, still one of New York City's premier steak houses, opened in 1876, has been a lasting example of the former German influence in Williamsburg.

Some Germans gravitated to Greenpoint, which, before the Polish influx at the turn of the last century, was a mixed neighborhood of Germans, Irish, Dutch, English, and Scandinavians. In the 20th century Washington Heights had a German presence, primarily middle class German Jews fleeing the Nazi regime.

Demographics changed rapidly as Germans prospered and sought to integrate in *American* communities in the city and elsewhere. After two or three generations, when most German-Americans lost their ability to speak German, it was easy to blend in with the *natives* whose background was usually British. New immigrants from Russia, Belarus, Ukraine, Poland, and Slovakia, both

Christians and Jews, pushed Kleindeuschland from the south. Shared German heritage and the generally satisfactory housing stock, especially north of Houston Street, kept portions of the German community intact until the 20th century.

The *coup de grâce* for Little Germany was the *General Slocum* ship disaster in 1904. The three-decked side-wheeler excursion boat, named for Civil War major general Henry Warner Slocum, left a dock at East 3rd Street in the morning of Wednesday, June 15 taking a group of women and children from St. Mark's German Evangelical Church on their annual Sunday School picnic. Their destination was Locust Grove on Long Island Sound. Near Randall's Island, off 125th Street, a fast-burning fire broke out in a cabin. The crew was unable to extinguish the blaze, and the captain, instead of beaching the *General Slocum* at one of the East River's shores, headed into the wind full-speed ahead toward North Brother Island where the burning ship ultimately beached. The increased speed had fanned the flames causing passengers to leap off the vessel or be burned alive. Police estimated that 1,031 of the 1,331 passengers died though not all bodies were recovered. St. Mark's Church minister, the Reverend George Hass, lost his entire family. Most victims were buried at the Trinity Lutheran Church Cemetery in Middle Village, Queens. Two years later the captain was sentenced to ten years in prison for criminal negligence. It was the greatest disaster in New York City until the attacks on the World Trade Center in 2001. Utterly disheartened, the remaining Germans migrated almost en masse to Yorkville and other communities. Ukrainian, Russian, and Polish Christians, and Eastern European Jews quickly replaced the Germans. A Jewish congregation bought St. Mark's German Evangelical Church on East 6th Street. It was established as the Community Synagogue in 1940.

A memorial to the General Slocum Ship Disaster was built in the north central section of Tompkins Square Park. It is a modest stele of light granite with a bas-relief of two children looking wistfully into emptiness, and a lion's head spigot and fountain. The monument memorializes the salient disaster for the area's German community.

Beyond the memorial, few traces of the German community exist anywhere on the Lower East Side. Exceptions are Most Holy

Redeemer Roman Catholic Church, Kiehl's (cosmetic store), the *Freie Bibliothek und Lesehalle* and the *Deutsches Poliklinik*, and buildings which were formerly the Turnhalle of 1871, Labor Lyceum, Germania Assembly Rooms, St. Mark's Evangelical Church, Mt. Olivet Memorial Church, and the rectory of St. Nicholas Church. Kiehl's, 109 3rd Avenue between East 13th and 14th Streets, opened in 1851 selling a high-end line of cosmetics, lotions, and shampoo.

German neighborhoods throughout New York City and the United States ceased to exist through both voluntary assimilation and the force of international events. The two World Wars, where Germany and the United States opposed each other, brought up anti-German feelings for those who had not Americanized, become fluent in English, changed their names, or integrated themselves in mixed neighborhoods. During the First World War most German language programs in American schools were terminated, ethnic organizations disbanded under pressure or because their membership dropped off precipitously, and surnames and pronunciation of names were changed. (Colonel Dwight D. Eisenhauer changed his surname to *Eisenhower*.) In 1919, the year following the First World War, German-Americans organized the *Steuben Society* to demonstrate their patriotism. After Adolf Hitler's rise to power in 1933, the Steuben Society took a strong stand against the Nazis. Some right-wing Germans in Yorkville, almost all foreign-born, affiliated with the pro-fascist *German American Bund* and were prosecuted by federal officials. On the farcical end, *sauerkraut* became liberty cabbage, *hamburgers* became liberty sandwiches, and *frankfurters* became hot dogs. Anti-German sentiments pushed Germans into giving up a separate ethnic identity.

<u>Notations</u>:

A Calvinist Presence in Little Germany

The German Reformed (Calvinist) presence in Kleindeutschland is marked in the East Village by one church building and two cemeteries. The German Reformed Church no longer exists as a separate religious body. The German denomination operated like its much larger Dutch counterpart. Peter Minuit, director-general of Dutch New Netherlands, chartered The *Dutch Reformed Protes-*

tant Consistory of four churches in 1628. The single consistory of ministers, deacons, and elders ruled four churches, and the ministers rotated pulpits. The shared governance ended in 1871 when the collegiate churches (Fort Washington, Middle, West End, and Marble) each organized independently within the new Reformed Church denomination as it ended its ethnic identity.

Russian Orthodox Cathedral of the Holy Virgin Protection (originally Mt. Olivet Memorial Church, German Reformed), 59 East 2nd Street between 1st and 2nd Avenues, across from the cemetery

Until 1970 this was a Russian Orthodox Cathedral. The congregation is now affiliated with the *autocephalous* (self governing) Orthodox Church in America. The priests and monks have recreated a bit of Old Russia by strictly observing traditional Orthodox canon law, hence there are no pews or instrumental music. Worshippers stand or kneel amidst scores of icons and the smell of liberal doses of incense. In 2001 a new *iconostasis* (icon screen) was installed to separate the chancel from the nave. A smaller Georgian Orthodox congregation also worships here at a side chapel dedicated to St. Innocent of Irkutsk.

New York Marble Cemetery, 2nd Avenue between East 2nd and 3rd Streets

This is a tantalizing hidden treasure, but difficult to get inside, or even to see into. Established in 1831 as a private non-sectarian cemetery, New York Marble Cemetery, served primarily as a burial place for Protestants from Episcopalian, and Dutch and German Reformed denominations. Now it is only open to the public once a year. Built as an innovative concept that never caught on elsewhere makes it a truly exceptional cemetery. It is situated in the core of a fully square, not rectangular, city block and has a high brick wall surrounding it. Imbedded in the wall are marble plaques denoting the interred that are buried in 156 individual crypts below the plain grassy lawn. A solid black metal gate on an alley leading from 2nd Avenue is the only access, but it is locked and offers no possibility to see inside. (Consult www.marblecemetery.org for dates and times of the periodic public openings.)

New York City Marble Cemetery, 52-74 East 2nd Street midway between 1st and 2nd Avenues

Established in 1831, just a few months later than its neighbor around the corner, New York City Marble Cemetery was built by the same corporation. It has its entire south side exposed through a cast iron fence to the public view. Underground family crypts hold coffins but tombstone are allowed and many are interspersed throughout the well-kept yard. One eye-catching name on a stone toward the front marks the interment site of New York patrician Preservéd Fish, who must have had enough respect for his parents, or fear of them, never to have changed his name. Another interesting case is James Monroe, fifth president of the United States, whose body rested here for twenty-seven years. Monroe expired while living with his daughter in a house, no longer standing, at the corner of Lafayette and Prince Streets. The former president died impoverished after selling his Virginia plantation, Ash Lawn, to pay his debts. He was interred in the New York City Marble Cemetery from his death on July 4, 1831 until 1858 when his body was re-interred in Richmond, Virginia.

CHAPTER 92
Abraham Cahan and The Forward

Abraham Cahan, editor and writer, led the most influential Yiddish-language newspaper in the United States from his appointment as editor in 1901 until his death in 1951. He had been born 1860 in Pabrade, Russian Lithuania, and attended teacher's college in the regional capital, Vilna. He fled Russia for New York in 1882 after members of his political group, *Narodnaya Volya* (People's Will), were found guilty of assassinating Tsar Alexander II the previous year.

Cahan helped launch the *Forward* (officially called *Jewish Daily Forward*) in 1897. The successful newspaper was housed in a new building at Straus Square in the Lower East Side beginning in 1911. Under the large electric Yiddish sign journalists in the eleven-story structure at 175 East Broadway produced a daily paper that was the heartbeat of the Jewish settlement. The *Forvertz* (Forward in Yiddish) was a democratic socialist paper with many non-political features: book and theater reviews, serializations of new writers, and popular columns. At the *Forward*, Cahan specialized in writing editorials urging Jewish people to support democratic socialism, the labor movement, and civic reforms in New York City.

A Bintel Brief (A Bundle of Letters), Cahan's question and answer column, gently exhorted Jews with reason and humor to Americanize and leave behind many Eastern European customs, prejudices, and superstitions. It also explained the importance of applying for citizenship, participating in democratic elections, organizing labor unions to gain higher wages, shorter working hours, and health benefits.

The printed readers' letters were for all to see and provided answers that were part common sense and part conscious attempt to help immigrants from disparate places adjust to American life while retaining some basic Jewish traditions. Using Yiddish, the mother tongue of Eastern European Jews, made the arguments more appealing. (Yiddish, meaning *Jewish,* is a mixture of Medieval German with some Hebrew words. Depending on the region where it is spoken, it also incorporates Polish, Russian, Hungarian, or Romanian words. It uses the Hebrew alphabet with some modifications in the sounds of letters.)

In the earlier years readers' letters tended to be about poverty, disease, housing, unemployment, gender relations, and labor union questions. Later they usually addressed family issues like complaints about in-laws, nagging parents, infidelity, disappointment with adult children, intermarriage, and retirement. The letters reflected the Americanization of the Jewish immigrants and the aging of Yiddish speakers. Selections from *A Bintel Brief* provide a good idea of some of the questions on the minds of immigrants.

In 1906 a letter from a jeweler who recently emigrated from Russia explained how he was a *greenhorn* (new immigrant) and had landed a job at $8.00 a week, barely enough to survive. *I come from Russia where I left a blind father and a stepmother. Before I left, my father asked me not to forget him. I promised that I would send him the first money I earned in America. Now I want you to advise me what to do. Shall I send my father a few dollars for Passover, or should I keep the little money for myself? In this place the work will end soon and I may be left without a job.* Cahan advised him to send some money to his father because even though there was no job security in the United States, he was better equipped to earn a living than his father.

Another letter the same year complained about regional prejudices within the Jewish community in New York City. It was written by a young woman from Galicia, the southern part of Poland, then part of the Austro-Hungarian Empire. *I am a girl from Galicia, and in the shop where I work I sit near a Russian Jew with whom I was always on good terms. Why should one worker resent another? But once, in a short debate, he stated that all Galicians were no good. ..According to him the Galitzianer are inhuman savages, and he had the right to speak of them so badly...Dear Editor, does he really have the right to say this?* Abraham Cahan patiently assured her that one group of people is as good as another.

A young man wrote in 1908 questioning an Old World superstition about dimples. *I am a young man of twenty-five, sixteen years in America, and I recently met a fine girl. She has a flaw, however, that keeps me from marrying her. The fault is that she has a dimple in her chin, and it is said that people who have this lose their first husband or wife. He explained that he had investigated the saying. I got so interested in this that whenever I see someone with this defect I ask about it immediately, and I find out that some of the men have lost their first wives, and some of the women's first husbands are dead...I've questioned many people. Some say it's true, others laugh at the idea. Perhaps you, too, will laugh at me for being such a fool and believing such nonsense, but I cannot rest until I hear your opinion about it.* He signed his letter: *Respectfully, The Unhappy Fool.* Cahan had no patience with that kind of superstition! He told the young man that he should consider the dimple a *beauty spot*. Cahan added: *It's truly shameful that a young man who was brought up in America should ask such questions.*

Cahan received a heartbreaking inquiry from another reader in 1908 who suffered from *the worker's disease,* this was the popular name for tuberculosis, also called consumption, an infectious scourge that spread easily in the crowded conditions of tenements and factories. *I am the father of a three-year-old girl, a clever, pretty child who attracts everyone's attention. All who know my child hug her and kiss her. But I may not. I know this all too well, yet I can't keep myself from kissing my little girl. Every time I hold the child in my arms and kiss her, my conscience bothers me...What can I do when I cannot control myself?* The editor responded to the man who signed his letter, *An Unhappy Father,* to be more responsible: *Control yourself and do not kiss your dear child.*

In 1910, during a period of ferment over women's rights, the editor received an anguished letter from a housewife who inquired: *I ask you to decide whether a married woman has the right to go to school two evenings a week. My husband thinks I have no right to do this.* She explained that her husband, who controlled the family's purse strings, suspected she had too much free time and would no longer allow her to send out the laundry out to be done. She ended by telling the editor about her husband's contradictory politics. *I want to say that my husband is an intelligent man and he wanted to marry a woman who was educated. The fact that he is intelligent makes me more annoyed with him. He is in favor of the emancipation of women, yet in real life he acts contrary to his beliefs.* Cahan was a strong proponent of education for everyone. He scolded the husband severely for wanting to enslave his wife's mind.

A 1911 letter told the story of poverty in a small fatherless household where the daughter had been killed in the terrible Triangle Fire and the son and mother were left to fend for themselves. The boy had come from Russia at age twelve. *I am a newsboy, fourteen years old, and I sell the Forvertz in the streets till late into the night. I come to you to ask your advice...My sister worked and supported us. She didn't allow me to work but sent me to school. I went to school for two years and didn't miss a day, but then came the terrible fire at the Triangle shop, where she worked, and I lost my dear sister. My mother and I suffer terribly from the misfortune. I had to help my mother and after school hours I go out and sell newspapers.* He explained that he wanted to go to high school and college. *But my mother doesn't want me to go to school because she thinks I should go to work. I tell her I will work days and study at night but she won't hear of it.* Cahan handled this sensitive letter very gently by comforting the bereaved mother but exhorting her not to stand in the way of her son's night school education.

In 1917, the year of the socialist revolution in Russia, a man who had fought against the *tsar* (or *czar*) and fled to the United States, wrote to Cahan asking him his advice about returning to his former country to help construct a new society. He explained that he had married an American girl and made a comfortable living as manager of a large wholesale firm. *The Russian freedom movement, in which I took part, has conquered Czarism. The idea for which I fought has become a reality, and my heart draws me there more than ever now. I began to talk about it to my wife, but her answer is that she hasn't the least desire to go to Russia...I can't leave my wife, whom I love very much, but it's hard to turn my back on my beloved homeland. I don't know how to act and I beg you to advise me what to do.* Cahan, who had also emigrated from the Russian Empire, warned the man that the Civil War was still going on there, and that in any event he had an obligation to his American wife who could not be expected to adjust to life in the Old World.

A 1933 letter showed how grown children were embarrassed when their parents spoke a foreign language in public. *We, the five brothers, always speak English to each other. Our parents know English too, but they speak only Yiddish, not just among themselves but to us too, and even to our American friends who come to visit us. We beg them not to speak Yiddish in the presence of our friends, since they can speak English, but they don't want to. It's a sort of stubbornness on their part, and a great deal of quarreling goes on between our parents and ourselves because of it...Imagine, even when we go with our father to buy something in a store on Fifth Avenue, New York, he insists on speaking Yiddish. We are not ashamed of our parents, God forbid, but they ought to know where it's proper and where it's not. If they talk Yiddish among themselves at home, or to us, it's bad enough, but among strangers and Christians? Is that nice?* The letter ended with a request made comical by the subject of the letter. *We beg you, friend Editor, to express your opinion on this question, and if possible send us your answer in English, because we can't read Yiddish.* Abraham Cahan, who was the editor of a Yiddish newspaper, reacted strongly! He told the brothers that there was nothing wrong with speaking Yiddish in public. He suggested that the parents might be embarrassed about speaking imperfect English in public. He softened his stand, somewhat, by declaring that ultimately everyone must learn the language of the new country.

Cahan also wrote *The Rise of David Levinsky* in 1917, a novel about an immigrant's struggle in New York City. The story was vaguely, or wishfully, autobiographical. Told through the eyes of David Levinsky, we learn that he emigrated from Russia just after the assassination of Tsar Alexander II, and the murder of his mother in an anti-Semitic incident. Young David arrived in New York City with four cents in his pocket yet went on to become a millionaire in the garment industry. Met by a labor broker at the immigration station outside Castle Clinton at the Battery (before Ellis Island), the man explained to him: *If a fellow isn't lazy or a fool, he has no reason to be sorry he came to America.* Through hard work and wise choices, David cashed in on success. He studied English, enrolled in a public evening school, read voraciously, attended City College, and put in long hours at work. Toward the end of the novel David Levinsky summed it up: *The able fellow succeeds and the misfits fail.* Abraham Cahan was a great booster for America.

Unbridled enthusiasm caused Cahan to be naïve about some issues. Regarding the achievement of success in the United States, he underestimated the severity of racial, religious, and ethnic discrimination and placed all emphasis on hard work. The day after the election in the German Reichstag in 1930, which catapulted Adolf Hitler to power, Cahan wrote an editorial in the *Forward* calling Hitler *no more than a windbag, stupid, filled with chutzpah, yet not one to be worried about.*

Americanization succeeded too well for Abraham Cahan's newspaper. By 1990 the *Forward* was being printed in English as a weekly newspaper from offices in New Jersey. The mission of the newspaper had changed. Americanization was no longer on the agenda. It became a journal of ideas and issues dealing with philosophical questions of Jewish life in Israel and America. After a few years housing small garment factories, the *Forward* Building was converted into a Chinese condominium, though the Yiddish sign stayed because it had been landmarked.

CHAPTER 93
Ritual Rules for Foods and Slaughtering: Kosher and Halal

Rules about food and the practice of ritual animal slaughtering accompanied Jewish and Muslim immigrants to America and introduced *kosher* and *halal* foods to the general public. Both Jewish and Muslim religions follow rules and regulations regarding food. Jews follow rules from the *Torah* (the Law, or Five Books of Moses) and later commentaries such as the *Talmud*. Most of the regulations in the Torah are found in the Biblical books of *Exodus* and *Leviticus*. Muslims obey the *Qur'an* (revelations from Allah) and the *Hadith* (accounts of the life of Muhammed). Together the Islamic rules are part of the *Shari'ah* (straight path, or law).

Many religions have food prohibitions and special methods of ritually slaughtering animals. Jews call acceptable foods *kosher* (clean or fit) and unclean foods *trefah,* literally *torn to pieces* (*treyf* in Yiddish). Muslims call clean foods *halal* and unclean foods *haram*. The reasons for the rules are speculative. Some supporters say they are for health reasons. Others think the purpose is for keeping the tribe or faithful together and preventing intermingling and intermarriage. Some believers say the rules should be obeyed without question because they accept that God decreed the dietary code.

Food rules are not present in Christianity. It is recorded in the *Gospels* of *Matthew, Mark,* and *Luke,* that Jesus, who was Jewish, told his followers it was no longer necessary to follow all the laws received by Moses. *Hear Me, everyone, and understand: There is nothing that enters a man from outside which can defile him; but the things which come out of him, those are the things that defile a man.* (Mark 7:14-15) His disciple, Peter, is quoted in the *Acts of the Apostles* as having had an elaborate vision of a great sheet descending from heaven holding all manner of clean and unclean animals. *Upon the which when I had fastened mine eyes, I considered, and saw four-footed beasts of the earth, and wild beasts, and creeping things, and fowls of the air.* (Acts 11:6) A heavenly voice told Peter that humans were allowed to eat whatever God had created. *But the voice answered me again from heaven, What God has cleansed you must not call common.* (Acts 11:9) Therefore, except for periodic fasts, Christians do not observe any religious rules about food. This became one of the early ways Christianity separated itself from Judaism.

There have been times in American history when differing religious views of food have fueled narrow-mindedness and bigotry. That was especially true before the widespread availability of kosher and halal foods and before the mass media often focused sympathetically on the customs and rituals of religions other than Christianity.

Kosher laws became well known in New York City when the large immigration from Eastern Europe began toward the end of the 19th century. *Matzoh,* yeast-free bread used at the Jewish holiday of Passover, was the first widespread ritual food introduced to America. Most matzoh bakeries were small shops on Manhattan's Lower East Side that flourished between 1880 and 1930 when the neighborhood was filled with new arrivals from Eastern Europe. Later, most of the small bakeries went out of business and large bakery companies produced most of the product. Some were on the Lower East Side, like Horowitz - Margareten on East 4th Street and Streit's on Rivington Street.

By 1930 there were several thousand food processors selling kosher foods. There were also several hundred kosher butchers, most of them poultry butchers. How would the buyer know if the product was actually kosher? Many observant Jews thought some kind of uniform regulation was needed. Rabbi Jacob Joseph (1840-1902) was called from his post in Vilna (then Russia, now Lithuania) in 1888 to serve the large Orthodox Russian Jewish community in New York City as their chief rabbi. He was a colorful figure and tireless organizer who operated a voluntary organization, the Association of the United Hebrew Congregations, attempting to tax kosher producers and send out inspectors to certify that the products were being prepared according to his interpretation of kosher laws. Many resisted the taxes and Rabbi Jacob Joseph's strict standards and the effort to unify kosher standards failed.

Hasidic Jews felt prevailing kosher standards were too low

and came up with their own certification: *glatt kosher,* which means *extremely kosher*. Since there are 200 Hasidic groups in New York, leading Hasidic rabbis often certified products using differing standards.

The Kosher Meat Riots of 1902, 1910, 1929, and 1937 were sparked by consumer claims of price gouging and lax food processing standards. State laws regulating products deemed kosher were passed fragmentarily beginning in 1882. Eventually the state government stepped in forcefully and the New York Department of Agriculture and Markets was established to enforce the law so that food represented as kosher really was kosher. In 2000, a federal judge in Brooklyn ruled the laws were unconstitutional because they violated the First Amendment separation of church and state by involving the government in religious practices. Judge Nina Gershon ruled: *The entanglements involved here between religion and the state are not only excessive in themselves, but they have the unconstitutional effect of endorsing and advancing religion.* In 2003, the United States Supreme Court left intact Judge Gershon's ruling. Kosher boards still exist but they are private and no longer under state authority. Since all boards are presently Hasidic, all kosher food products and eating establishments are also *glatt kosher.*

By the 1950s half the Jewish population was living in many scattered communities in the United States and large companies began accepting kosher oversight by rabbis to certify some of their products as kosher. Oversight meant that a rabbi would periodically visit the food processing plant to certify that the foods were being prepared in accordance with kosher rules. The mark indicating kosher found on many foods is a circle (standing for the letter O) surrounding the letter U, verifying approval by the Union of Orthodox Hebrew Congregations. (The symbol is called the O-U.) A letter K also signifies kosher. Crown Heights Kosher, symbolized by a small HK inside a larger C and topped with a crown is the emblem of the Lubavitch rabbinical authority overseeing kosher food.

Some food companies have produced traditionally Jewish foods exclusively, such as Manischewitz, Rokeach, Mother's, Wolff's, Gold's, and Goodman's. Others are mainstream corporations that choose to have some of their product lines certified as kosher to be acceptable to Jewish customers who wish to keep kosher kitchens. Common examples certified by O-U are Nestlé, Quaker Oats Company, McCormick & Company, General Mills, Mueller's, Ronzoni, Heinz, Wish-Bone, and Bumble Bee. Companies that use K are Post Cereals, Red Cheek, Kellogg's, Wesson, Sun-Maid, Red Pack, Hunt's, Del Monte, and Orville Redenbacher's. Not all the products of these large corporations are kosher. Heinz can have their ketchup certified as kosher, but not their pork gravy because kosher laws prohibit pork products.

Competitive pressure to open seven days per week has caused some popular Jewish delicatessens to give up on remaining kosher. They are *kosher-style*, but not kosher. Katz's and the Second Avenue Deli in Manhattan belong to this category. They are not kosher because they open on Saturday, the Jewish Sabbath, and because on Saturdays they are unsupervised by an orthodox rabbi, though the cuisine is kosher-style and the food was certified as kosher by the producers.

What are some of the specific rules that must be followed to be kosher? Certain foods are prohibited in the Bible. Chapter 11 of Leviticus presents a list of prohibited animals. It begins by classifying mammals in a way that excludes pigs, camels, and horses, but includes cows, sheep, and goats. *And the Lord spake unto Moses and to Aaron, saying unto them, Speak unto the Children of Israel, saying, These are the beasts which ye shall eat among the beasts that are on the earth. Whatsoever parteth the hoof, and is cloven-footed, and cheweth the cud, among the beasts, that shall ye eat.* (Exodus 11:1-3) The next verses specifically prohibit eating camels, rabbits, and swine. Many prohibited animals are listed in chapter 11: eagle, osprey, vulture, raven, owl, cuckoo, hawk, cormorant, swan, pelican, stork, heron, bat, beetle, weasel, mouse, tortoise, ferret, chameleon, lizard, snail, and mole. Exodus 11:42 prohibits snakes, caterpillars, and centipedes. *Whatsoever goeth upon the belly, and whatsoever goeth upon all four, or whatsoever hath more feet among all creeping things that creep upon the earth, them ye shall not eat; for they are an abomination.*

Certain sea creatures are prohibited. *These shall ye eat of all that are in the waters: whatsoever hath fins and scales in the waters, in the seas, and in the rivers, them shall ye eat. And all that have not fins and scales in the seas, and in the rivers, of all that move in the waters, and of any living thing which is in the waters, they shall be an abomination unto you.* (Leviticus 11:9-10) The prohibition includes eels, catfish, crayfish, squid, octopus, lobsters, shrimp, mussels, oysters, and clams.

In the slaughtering process (*shekhitah*), the Jewish *shokhet* (slaughterer) slits the throat of the animal with a horizontal cut across the windpipe and gullet, and carefully drains out the blood. The *chalaph* (knife) must be sharp and free of notches, dents, or cracks. If the knife is not sharp, it will cause *drassa*, pressing of the knife against the skin of the neck, that renders the process unkosher.

No blood may be ingested because it is prohibited in several passages in Leviticus and Deuteronomy. *Morever ye shall eat no manner of blood, whether it be of fowl or of beast, in any of your dwellings. Whatsoever soul it be that eateth any manner of blood, even that soul shall be cut off from his people.* (Leviticus 7:26-27) *Only be sure that thou eat not the blood: for the blood is the life; and thou mayest not eat the life with the flesh. Thou shalt not eat it; thou shalt pour it upon the earth as water.* (Deuteronomy 12:23-24) After the jugular vein of an animal is severed most of the blood runs out. Much of the rest is extracted by soaking the meat for one-half hour in warm water (but not more than 120 degrees) and sprinkling it with medium grain salt (kosher salt).

There are other prohibitions. Fat, which is not intermingled with flesh (*kheleb*) and forms a separate layer is forbidden, though fat that is intermingled with flesh (*shuman*) is allowed. The hindquarters of an animal (behind the 12th rib) are prohibited. Any adhesions between the lungs and the thoracic walls or discoloration of the lungs, liver, and spleen disqualify the animal as kosher food.

In the cuisine of Eastern Europe available in many New York City neighborhoods, some of the common foods eaten by Christians and Jews look similar but are very different. Pork sausage is popular with Christians while Jews make sausage from ground beef. *Kishka*, a non-meat sausage, is called *Jewish sausage* among Eastern Europeans because instead of using flour and onions held together with pork fat or pork blood, the Jewish variety mixes matzoh meal and onions held together with chicken fat. (The fat in this case is obtained from boiling chicken meat and skimming off the top layer of fat that forms on the water as the broth is cooled.)

The separation of meat and milk products and the division between meat and dairy restaurants, which is part of *kashrut* (dietary laws), comes from interpretations of three almost identical Biblical injunctions (Exodus 23:19, Exodus 34:26, and Deuteronomy 14:21). *Thou shalt not seethe a kid in his mother's milk.* Various kashrut rules regulate the amount of time that must pass between the two food categories. Some require that two hours pass between eating dairy products and meat, and six hours between consuming meat and dairy products. Others require a general three-hour break between the two groups. Foods that are neither meat nor dairy can be eaten with either category and are called *parve*. Separate dishes, utensils, and pots and pans are needed to comply with the rules.

Kosher regulations can be applied to any cuisine, so New York City has Chinese, Indian, and Italian kosher restaurants. Chinese and Italian kosher food may not use pork. Indian curries such as *kurma,* which combine meat and cream, are prohibited. Kosher dairy pizzerias serve nothing made with meat. Kosher cheese contains no *rennet,* the inner lining of the fourth stomach of a calf or lamb, which is an animal product. (Rennet as a dried extract is used to curdle milk in cheese making.) Kosher pizzas may have familiar vegetable toppings such as onion, pepper, mushroom, broccoli, and spinach along with rennet-free cheese.

Any edible product can be sold as kosher. Wine can be sold as kosher, though grapes are parve, or neutral (neither milk nor meat), and obviously do not need slaughtering. Imported wines from France and Italy as well as from Israel can be certified kosher. That has long been the case with local wines such as Mogen David, Kedem, and Schapiro's Wines. The kosher certification establishes that the vineyard does not have a Christian religious shrine, has not been blessed by a Christian priest, and that the barrels and vats were not previously used for non-kosher products.

Because kosher means fit or clean, even inedible products can be kosher. Dishes and utensils, pots and pans, refrigerators and ovens are kosher if they have been free from non-kosher foods. Items that have touched non-kosher foods can be purified. A polluted utensil or a plate can be *kashered* (purified) by being submerged in boiling water and left unused for 24 hours. A defiled oven can be purified with fire from a blowtorch. Newly purchased dishes can be taken to a ritual bath (*mikvah*) and washed.

Kosher laws also apply to clothing. The reason is a Biblical prohibition on blends. *Thou shalt not wear a garment of diverse sorts, as of woolen and linen together.* (Deuteronomy 22:11) Kosher clothing must be certified as free of mixed cloth. Rules in Leviticus 19:19 exhibits a general Biblical bias against mingling. *Ye shall keep my statutes. Thou shalt not let thy cattle gender with a diverse kind: thou shalt not sow thy field with mingled seed: neither shall a garment mingled of linen and woolen come upon thee.* Kosher laws are complex but an important part of the religion for observant Jews.

Halal dietary laws became commonplace in New York City only in recent decades as the Muslim population in the city has grown. Muslims have come from Arab countries, as well as Turkey, Iran, Pakistan, Bangla Desh, India, Indonesia, Central Asia, many parts of Africa, and Guyana in South America.

Islamic dietary laws are less complicated than kosher laws. They fit into three categories: *halal* is what is permitted, *haram* is whatever is expressly prohibited, and *makruh* is any action or food which is not expressly forbidden but is questionable and probably should be avoided. Cigarettes and late prayers are examples of makruh.

While most foods are permitted in Islam, some are forbidden. Muslims may not eat pork or blood, or drink alcohol. Meat from the carcass of an unslaughtered dead animal (carrion) is forbidden. Also prohibited are any foods that have been dedicated to idols. Gelatin, lard, and rennet are also banned because they are considered waste products of an animal. Gelatin is from a substance scraped from the hoof of an animal, lard is from excess animal fat, and rennet is from the wall of the fourth stomach of a young cow or sheep.

In slaughtering animals, Muslim butchers say a brief dedication prayer, *Bismillah*, or *Allah-u-Akbar* (In the name of God, or God is Great) and slit the throat with a sharp knife and carefully drain out the blood. As with kosher slaughtering, it takes the animal a minute of writhing to die. The process is considered a humane and painless death required by both Islam and Judaism. Care is taken not to rupture internal organs, especially the stomach, bladder, spleen, and intestines.

A whole body of etiquette (table manners) developed in Islam with regard to eating. Much of it came from the habits of 7th century Prophet Muhammed. Food must be halal, hands must be washed, and eating must be with the right hand. Three fingers should be used to take food from the common bowls into the mouth. *Eating with one finger is [indicative] of hatred, with two fingers arrogance, with three fingers Sunna [the sayings and actions of the Prophet], with four and five, greed.* (Muslim, Ashriba, 2032) Prayers are to be offered to God before and after eating, and when drinking water or milk.

Muhammed placed his food upon a *sufra* (tablecloth generally made of leather) on the ground or floor to eat, and while today using a table is permissible, to emulate the prophet is considered a distinguished and noble act. Eating in a group (family or friends) is preferred to eating alone. Muhammed said, *The best food is that over which there are many hands.* (Bayhaqi, Shu'ab al-Iman, VII, 9622) It is prohibited to eat or drink while reclining. Both meat and bread should be torn with the fingers, not cut with a knife.

Accommodations and substitutions can be made for popular ethnic foods in multicultural New York City. Halal pizza may mix meat and cheese, but the cheese may not contain rennet. Italian and Chinese food prepared in accordance with halal laws may not use wine sauces or pork. Precisely how many people who follow all the kosher and halal rules remains unclear. But both foods are widely available in all five boroughs, and restaurants serving kosher and halal meals can be found in many neighborhoods.

Notation:

Live Chicken & Meat Market, 31-37 20th Avenue next to the large Con Edison plant

This large Muslim abattoir is a *halal* slaughterhouse for an array of poultry (chickens, guinea hens, ducks, turkeys, quail, pigeons), rabbits, goats, sheep, and cows. Only whole animals may be purchased at the slaughterhouse. The most active time to visit is during the three days leading up to *Eid ul-Adha*, the Festival of the

Sacrifice, when Muslims believe both father and son were willing to obediently follow the commandment of God (*Allah*) that Abraham (*Ibrahim*) sacrifice Ishmael (*Isma'il*). God's angel intervened at the last moment and a sheep was substituted. About 300 sheep are slaughtered in each of the three days preceding the festival.

CHAPTER 94
Garment Industry and Fashion (Cultural)

New York was unexceptional in the colonial fashion world. Philadelphia, Boston, and Charleston, South Carolina, each with a greater population than New York City, tended to set the colonial pace. Of course, trends from Paris and London trumped any colonial ideas of fashion.

New York City excelled in fur production and the ready access to upstate sources drew furriers into the trade. Beaver, mink, otter, and muskrat dominated the fur traffic in hats, collars, and coats. By 1808, John Jacob Astor eclipsed most independent fur businesses both in New York State and the West. When the I.R.T. subway station at Astor Place in Manhattan was built, Astor was honored with several terra-cotta polychrome *bas reliefs* (colored partially raised sculptures made of tile) of a beaver gnawing on a tree stump.

Two phenomena elevated New York City to eventual leadership in American fashion: the explosive population growth after the 1825 completion of the Erie Canal, and the development and acceptance of ready-to-wear clothing. New York's population exploded from 242,000 in 1830 to 3,437,000 in 1900, providing garment workers and a large pool of customers. Business opportunities drew tailors, jewelers, shoemakers, furriers, and milliners (women's hat makers) to the city.

The Industrial Revolution applied machine precision and mass-production techniques to the time-consuming task of making clothing. Women still learned as girls to sew at home but increasingly they chose to buy *off the rack* in shops, especially in fashionable department stores.

Lower Broadway dominated high-end retailing. A.T. Stewart's Department Store, known as the *marble palace*, opened his seven-story building on Broadway and Chambers Street in 1846.

It was New York City's first marble-faced commercial building. Lavish and elegant on the inside it offered reasonable prices and encouraged browsing, the prototype of a century of department stores.

The fashionable shopping district gravitated northward to Astor Place, to Ladies' Mile (Broadway between 14th and 23rd Streets), and ultimately to 5th Avenue between 34th and 59th Streets. It was in the 19th and early 20th centuries that Lord & Taylor (1826), A.T. Stewart's (1846), Macy's (1858), Abraham & Straus (1865), Bloomingdale's (1872), Wanamaker's (1896), Sak's 5th Avenue (1902), Bonwit Teller (1905), and Gimbel's (1909) established themselves.

Ready-to-wear clothes first gained widespread notice from large military orders when thousands of items needed to be quickly produced and *sized* for specific physiques, especially during the Civil War. Most people preferred ready-to-wear clothing rather than homemade apparel by the 20th century. The garment industry became a big business, at its height employing 300,000 workers throughout the five boroughs. Popular nationally distributed fashion magazines produced here furthered New York City's hold on fashion. *Vogue, Mirabella, Harper's Bazaar,* and *Women's Wear Daily,* the trade journal of the industry, are published in the city. By the end of the 20th century New York ranked with Paris and Milan as an international fashion capital.

Thorstein Veblen, writing in *The Theory of the Leisure Class* (1899), observed that the value of clothes was related to price. *We find things beautiful, as well as serviceable, somewhat in proportion as they are costly.* Choosing a wardrobe had become very important in *fin de siècle* America.

Getting dressed *appropriately* in the big city was especially important during the wave of immigration from Europe and the country-to-city migration in the two decades before the First World War (1914-1918). Appropriate dress meant a conservative style that showed Americanization and urbanization. No one wanted to be taken for a foreign *greenhorn* or a rural bumpkin! A newcomer wanted to look just like a New Yorker. The wrong clothes provoked disdain and were thought to delay acceptance.

Nonetheless, a great change in clothing took place in the 1920s when Americans began wearing casual clothes. Women took the lead. Older generations were horrified that their children threw caution to the wind and opted for radical new styles. The process accelerated again in the 1960s and 1970s, and now the casual look dominates most sales.

Immigrants and migrants alike quickly felt at home in New York City and other American metropolitan areas. While carefully choosing clothes to look pretty or handsome, many in the postwar generation also sought a palpable sense of freedom and individualism through new fashions.

The chief style icon of the 1920's was the flapper. From head to toe it was a new look, which horrified the older generation as it set free the young women espousing it. Everything about the flappers contradicted established common sense norms of American style and sense of propriety.

The accent on a thin body contradicted ideas of good health and strength. But thinness was the desired frame for loose clothes. Bobbed hair was a new fad. Previously, unmarried women wore their hair long, and piled it in a bun after marriage. Flappers wore hats but scorned the flamboyance of large hats and bonnets festooned with ribbons, feathers, and rhinestones worn by their mothers for the close fitting, head-hugging *chapeau*.

A large portion of the arms and legs were exposed, often without nylons, and especially without the demure opaque stockings favored by the older generation. The new style turned its back on corsets, layered skirts, gloves, and long sleeves. Abbreviated skirts or dresses were the hallmark of the flapper. They flared elegantly while dancing the madcap *Charleston* and brazenly revealed body form. A flapper's shoes might be either comfortable moccasins or greatly exaggerated high heels. Whether for comfort (moccasins) or style (high heels), the shoe choice contradicted generations of wisdom about sensible shoes that kept the foot trussed up. But trussing was out of style with the young women called flappers. To complete the picture add the sleek mink coat to the knees only, a delicate wristwatch, and a minimal piece of jewelry, perhaps a single strand of pearls.

Novels, style magazines, advertisements, and movies magnified the image. It represented a girl who rode in cars, smoked cigarettes, drank whiskey with the men, and played golf and tennis. (Think of the characters in *The Great Gatsby* by F. Scott Fitzgerald.) The new style was a badge of freedom, and to some it was freedom itself. The flapper was the manifestation of the New American, concerned with personal freedom, self-expression, and action. (Sometimes it also signified a working girl with earned money.)

Young men favored a corresponding style called *jazz dressing*. The guiding principles were the same: loose fitting, informal clothes adhering to none of the past strictures on the propriety of dress. Colors were often loud and clashing with checks and broad stripes predominating. Black clothing and thin pinstriped suits were shunned. Men enjoyed freeing themselves from the tyranny of starch and the uncompromising adage: *a dark shirt for work and a white shirt for Sunday*. Collars, cuffs, cufflinks, and long sleeves were on the way out. Color and wild style crept into socks, shoes, handkerchiefs, suspenders, and especially ties. Young men began to shed the hat, especially the bowler, derby, or fedora. Straw hats for summer were okay, or a workman's cap, which was renamed a golf cap. If a fedora was worn, it could be brown or gray, but no longer black.

The notion that fashion leadership could exist outside Europe was known only by necessity in the buckskin frontier during colonial America and the early Federal period. Enormous changes occurred in New York City during the century following 1825. Industrial Revolution production techniques had a great impact on the garment industry. Styles also evolved. The 1920s was the first significant change in clothing styles in three generations. In many respects those new principles remain in force.

CHAPTER 95
Garment Industry and the Triangle Fire (Economics)

The greatest industrial tragedy in New York City's history occurred in a ten-story building one block east of Washington Square Park, at the corner of Washington Place and Greene Street. The structure, a former garment factory, is the site of the March 25, 1911 Triangle Shirtwaist Factory Fire where a conflagration that lasted only fifteen minutes killed 146 people, mostly young Jewish and Italian women, including sixty-four teenagers. The catastrophe motivated reformers to urge legislation regulating factory conditions and fire hazards.

A bronze plaque marks the fire's site at 19 Washington Place. The structure was originally the Joseph J. Asch Building, acquired in 1929 by New York University, subsequently renamed the Brown Building, and now used for chemistry laboratories. Each year on the anniversary of the fire representatives of the former International Ladies Garment Workers Union hold a memorial at the corner and leave flower bouquets and 146 long-stem roses lined up along the sidewalk. The New York City Landmarks Preservation Commission declared the site an historic landmark in 2003.

The 1911 fire began just before closing time on a table strewn with fabric and paper patterns. It raged quickly through the 8th, 9th, and 10th floors of the building where the Triangle Shirtwaist Factory was located. Though the city had at least 1,500 skyscrapers at the time, the fire department had no ladders that reached beyond the sixth floor. The firemen did their best but were hindered by inadequate equipment. The Fire Department of New York was still using horse-drawn fire trucks.

The *sweatshop,* owned by Max Blanck and Isaac Harris, had resisted unionization and cut corners to make as much profit as possible. The garment industry operated on a slim margin of profit and Blanck and Harris did what they could to *sweat* as much out of their workers as possible. They locked exit doors so the employees could not take unauthorized breaks or smoke in the stairways. Halls and stairways were clogged with boxes of shirt-waists (blouses) and bolts of cloth. Flammable scraps of material and paper were saved in scrap bins under the cutting tables, there were no sprinklers, no fire hoses, and the company had never had a fire drill. The proprietors had a poor track record with regard to fires. There had been four previous fires at the Triangle factory and three at another garment factory owned by Blanck and Harris.

The Triangle Shirtwaist Factory had been under pressure by its employees who worked 84-hour weeks for between $7 and $10 without overtime pay, sick days, vacations, or pensions. Many garment workers had joined either the International Ladies Garment Workers Union or the Amalgamated Clothing Workers Union but Blanck and Harris had successfully resisted unionization efforts. The Triangle Shirtwaist Factory Company fired union sympathizers and hired thugs to break up picket lines. Sympathetic Tammany-controlled police and judges always sided with the factory owners.

When the fire began some employees were able to use the stairway and elevator to leave the burning building. The elevator soon stopped working and flames blocked the stairway. The metal fire escape collapsed under the weight of too many panicking workers crowding onto it. A few escaped over a ladder placed horizontally by quick-thinking college students from the former Main Building of NYU. Ten thousand onlookers including many family members and friends crowded around Greene Street and Washington Place to witness the destruction of lives.

One hundred forty-six never escaped and the Triangle Shirtwaist inferno became the most disastrous factory fire in the city's history. The majority crowded around the windows and then, pressured by the flames behind them, jumped to their deaths. A reporter for *the New York Times* wrote: *A 13-year-old girl hung for three minutes by her fingertips to the sill of a 10th-floor window. A tongue of flame licked at her fingers, and she dropped to her death.* Many jumped into the fire department's nets, but they were not strong enough to hold the weight. *At a ninth-floor window a man and a woman appeared. The man embraced the woman and kissed her. Then he hurled her to the street and jumped. Both were killed. Five girls smashed a pane of glass, dropped in a struggling tangle, and were crushed into a shapeless mass.*

An estimated 350,000 people turned out on a cold rainy April 5th for the funeral procession. Speakers at several memorial services and mass meetings included Rose Schneiderman, union organizer; Abraham Cahan, editor of the *Jewish Daily Forward;* Meyer London, labor lawyer; Morris Hillquit, Socialist orator; Monsignor William J. White, director of Catholic Charities in Brooklyn; Rabbi Stephen S. Wise; Jacob Schiff, philanthropist; and Anna Shaw, suffragist and medical doctor. Most of the victims were buried in Mount Zion Cemetery in Maspeth, Queens, and Evergreen Cemetery in East New York, Brooklyn.

Max Blanck and Isaac Harris stood trial for manslaughter in December 1911. The Tammany-appointed judge instructed the jury that manslaughter convictions could only be returned if the owners had knowingly been negligent in the operation of the Triangle Shirtwaist Factory. The jury found the defendants not guilty. Because they were over-insured, Blanck and Harris collected $80,000 more in insurance claims than the cost of replacing their factory. They paid $75 to the families of twenty-three of the victims who had sued. The families of the other 123 dead employees received nothing after scornfully turning down an offer of one week's pay per victim.

Social reformer Frances Perkins, who later became Labor Secretary in the cabinet of President Franklin D. Roosevelt, Assemblyman Alfred E. Smith, and State Senator Robert F. Wagner, Sr. and others were appointed to the New York State Factory Investigating Commission. Samuel Gompers, president of the American Federation of Labor and Mary Dreir, president of the Women's Trade Union League represented organized labor on the commission. They held extensive hearings and visited several sweatshop factories. Their recommendations sparked fifty-five new laws including a 54-hour workweek, and numerous fire laws.

Since the beginning of the Industrial Revolution in the early 19th century there were people calling out for shorter hours, higher wages, safety devices on machines, and steps to minimize the possibility of fire. While most voices that were raised belonged to workers, many of the calls for reform came from clergy in the United States and abroad. Pope Leo XIII criticized employer greed at some companies. He wrote: *A small number of very rich men have been able to lay upon the teeming masses of the laboring poor a yoke little better than slavery itself.* Factory workers and their advocates sometimes referred to industrial labor as *wage-slavery.*

More than any other single factor, the moral authority for government regulation in Franklin D. Roosevelt's New Deal (1933-1945) can be dated to the Triangle Fire. It prompted legislation in New York and many other states to enact a wide variety of fire safety laws.

The publicity from the Triangle Fire also helped efforts to unionize more garment workers and increased the prestige and effectiveness of the International Ladies Garment Workers Union. Though organized in 1900, the ILGWU had achieved mixed success in unionizing the city's garment workers. Even after the 1911 fire the garment owners often intimidated their workers to block them from establishing an effective collective bargaining apparatus. With Frances Perkins installed as a pro-union Secretary of Labor, and the establishment of the National Labor Relations Board in 1935, the administration of Franklin D. Roosevelt made it easier to organize unions since most anti-labor practices by employers were outlawed.

Some sweatshops still exist in New York City and many other American communities. Their crowded conditions and sub-minimum wages are clearly illegal. Some of the garment shops ignore safety and fire laws. A shroud of secrecy surrounds the offending companies who manage to remain in business by hiring immigrants, especially those without legal documentation and with little or no knowledge of English or American labor and safety laws. The owners justify contemporary sweatshops by claiming they are the only way American companies can compete with similar shops in Mexico, China, Malaysia, Pakistan, and India. Critics respond that such a policy amounts to *a race to the bottom.* A new union of garment workers is fighting against modern sweatshops. In 1995 the International Ladies Garment Workers Union and the Amalgamated Clothing and Textile Workers Union merged to form UNITE, an acronym for Union of Needletrades, Industrial and Textile Employees, which is leading the struggle to organize sweatshop employees into unions and enforcing laws already on the books, many since the days following the Triangle Fire.

CHAPTER 96
Chinatown

There are three fully developed Chinatowns in New York City and several smaller Chinese communities. Brooklyn has the newest Chinatown, since the 1980s, and can be found along 8th Avenue between 40th Street and 65th Street including the surrounding area. It is located at the point where Sunset Park, Bay Ridge, and Borough Park meet. The middle section of Flushing, Queens has been an established Chinese community since the 1970s. The Chinese area surrounds Roosevelt Avenue, Main Street, and Kissena Boulevard. (To the north the neighborhood is Korean, and to the south it is Indian.)

When New Yorkers think of Chinatown, however, the first image that usually comes to mind is Manhattan's Chinatown, tucked in between Little Italy, the Lower East Side, and Foley Square. The area now known as Manhattan Chinatown has a long history. Before the arrival of the Europeans, a band of Lenape (Munsee) Indians known as Werpoes had a small village on top of a hill where Mott Street now bends and intersects with Pell Street. For some time after the Indians disappeared, presumably from Old World diseases like smallpox, the area was called Werpoes Hill. In the Dutch colony that area included the undulating hills that had given shelter to the Werpoes people and a stretch of sloping fields with a large freshwater pond called the Collect Pond at its western end.

In the 18th century the elevated area of Werpoes Hill, with its good views and breezes, was a desirable location for housing, and a number of fine homes were built by the wealthy. The only one still standing is the Edward Mooney House, built in 1789, now occupied by Summit Mortgage Bankers, at 18 Bowery, corner of Pell Street. As more people constructed houses and multi-dwelling buildings, the area became overcrowded and slid into disrepair developing a reputation for crime. Centuries before zoning laws, mixed residential and industrial areas lowered the area's desirability for housing. Breweries, tanneries, and slaughterhouses proliferated on the hillside where they could dump their waste into the pond below. (Three of the main streets were named after butchers: Mott, Pell, and Bayard.)

European population doubled within a century after 1750 and many chose relocation in America. The late 18th century saw the start of an immense German migration from the Rhineland Palatinate to the United States, and many who came to New York City settled in this area on the northeast edge of the city. Before the Civil War 1.7 million Irish emigrated to the U.S. Those choosing New York City often found housing in the swampy low area just south of Chinatown's present location. In time, as English and Germans exited and after Ireland's potato famine, the area became overwhelming Irish.

Absentee landlords quickly converted their dwellings into *rookeries,* a name applied to subdivided houses, warehouses, or factories with jerrybuilt additions. Some buildings were built as rookeries, and whole families were packed into small, cramped rooms with little or no ventilation. *Tenement* is a term applied to structures built in a routine form to cash in on the rush of immigrants. In the early 19th century the typical pattern was to construct two tenements (front and rear) on a standard city lot 25 x 100 feet. None of the earliest rookeries exists in Chinatown, though an 1824 tenement still stands at 65 Mott Street. Most tenements were built after the 1879 legislation.

Manhattan had no public parks or playgrounds before Central Park opened in 1859. The Five Points - Chinatown area desperately needed open space and recreation areas. Children played in the narrow streets. Jacob Riis, a Danish immigrant who became a prominent photojournalist, published his award-winning *How the Other Half Lives* in 1890 was able to obtain support for his pet project, tearing down two square blocks of particularly bleak slums on Mulberry Street and constructing Mulberry Bend Park (now Columbus Park) as a site for recreation and relaxation.

By the Jacksonian period gangs like the Short Boys, Dead Rabbits, Roach Guards, Plug Uglies, and Bowery Boys periodically rampaged through Five Points. Some exaggeration by the *Police Gazette* was natural since gang activity ranked high on the list of topics about which respectable New Yorkers enjoyed reading. Even Charles Dickens, an authority on London slums, called the area *loathsome* after a visit prior to the Civil War. The 2002 film, *Gangs of New York*, explored the violence of the Five Points area. Though it is true that the area had become overcrowded, disease-laden, and raucous by the 1830s, the Five Points was a popular whipping boy for the press and probably got more bad publicity than it deserved.

Al Smith grew up in Five Points and spent most of his life on South, Madison, and Oliver Streets, all part of today's Chinatown, though during Smith's childhood Chinatown was miniscule. Smith represented the progressive wing of Tammany Hall and agitated for rent regulation, workers' compensation, public housing, and more effective building and fire codes. He represented Five Points in the State Assembly from 1904 to 1915 and later served as sheriff of New York County, president of the Board of Aldermen, and governor. In 1928 he became the first Roman Catholic nominated by either party for president but was defeated by Herbert Hoover and Republican charges that Smith stood for *Rome, Rum, and Rebellion*. After his defeat he dedicated himself to private and Catholic charitable projects.

The Bowery, the main artery through Five Points-Chinatown, passed through several stages, from a rural road to an avenue of upper middle-class homes, to a street of rookeries, bars, transient hotels, and honky-tonk entertainment. When the Chinese first established a presence in southern Manhattan, the Bowery was at the eastern edge of Chinatown; now it runs through the enclave as the major north-south axis. As Chinese immigrants moved into the area, the Bowery began to lose the character it had assumed as a housing preserve for men of the underclass. At the end of the Second World War the Bowery had 100 flophouses providing sleeping cubicles for 10,000 men. Thirty down-and-out Bowery bars dotted the street. These were the gin mills so often featured in lurid dime novels and religious tracts. None is left, though a few flophouses remain.

The transcontinental railroad completion in 1869 made it much easier for Chinese immigrants seeking the *Gold Mountain* (America) to move to the East Coast of the United States. Prior to the railroad most Chinese-Americans lived on the West Coast or in the Rocky Mountain states. Early Chinatown was huddled along Mott, Pell, and Doyers Streets. Commercial specialties included *chop suey-chow mein* restaurants, laundries, and gift shops.

By 1900 New York Chinatown's population was about 5,000. Jacob Riis knew Chinatown well, as it was just 50 yards from his pet project constructing a park at Mulberry Bend. He portrayed the neighborhood as quiet compared to the Irish, Italian, and Jewish areas: *Chinatown as a spectacle is disappointing.* But the noted reformer meant it as a backhanded compliment. *One thing about them was conspicuous: their scrupulous neatness. It is the distinguishing mark of Chinatown, outwardly and physically. It is not altogether by chance the Chinaman has chosen the laundry as his distinctive field. He is by nature as clean as the cat, which he resembles in his traits of cruel cunning and savage fury when aroused.*

Faulting immigrants in *How The Other Half Lives,* Riis represented the contradictions of reformers, mostly upper middle-class people with antecedents in northwestern Europe, who decried the tenement neighborhoods but blamed the inhabitants. Despite Riis' moving photographs of poverty, the text of his book leaves no doubt that his reformist instincts emanated from racial, ethnic, and religious bigotry. *Ages of senseless idolatry, a mere grub-worship, have left him without the essential qualities for appreciating the gentle teachings of a faith whose motive and unselfish spirit are beyond his grasp.* The 1892 *King's Handbook of New York City* was also unkind: *The district is a veritable <u>Chinatown</u>, with all the filth, immorality and picturesque foreignness, which the name implies.* For decades Chinatown struggled to overcome this kind of negative publicity.

Until the First World War, sixty percent of all Chinese in New York came from one county in Guangdong province: Toishan, near Canton. Most of the others came from other counties in the same province. Reacting to the fear of cheap labor, revulsion to the cultural habits attributed to Chinese people, and racism, the Chinese Exclusion Act of 1882 kept Chinese immigration low. Furious prejudice was directed against the supposedly deviant habits of the Chinese: opium, gambling, prostitution, even baby eating.

Franklin Delano Roosevelt signed the bill ending the Chinese Exclusion Act in 1943, and the immigration of Chinese could begin again. However the yearly limit placed on the Chinese amounted to just 105 immigrants per year. Change came when John F. Kennedy liberalized the immigration law. Today, about half of Chinatown's residents refer to them selves as *ABC*: American Born Chinese.

Chinatown's population is about 100,000 today, making it the largest Chinese community in the United States. Initially it was just a tiny enclave on the border of two other immigrant neighborhoods: Irish and Italian. Now it dominates the section and has moved into surrounding areas, especially Little Italy and the Lower East Side. By the end of the 20th century other Chinese neighborhoods had established themselves in areas where property prices were much lower.

Chinatown has been a haven from the hostile outside world as well as a place for some immigrants to postpone assimilation. For most it has been a stepping-stone to middle class life in other less cramped parts of New York City. The Tong Wars, 1896 to 1925, between two powerful commercial organizations (*tongs*), gave the community a negative reputation. They were violent and invariably reported in lurid detail in the press. The *Hip Sing* controlled the Pell Street - Doyers Street area and the *Ong Leong* dominated Mott Street. These business associations were involved in legitimate as well as illegitimate activities. Control of gambling and drug traffic led to the violence and negative publicity.

Despite problems, an attempt at a unified public face was orchestrated by the *Chinese Consolidated Benevolent Association* from its formation in 1883 until the 1970s. It is a non-governmental organization community council and an umbrella association of many fraternal, occupational, business, and family groups. Chinatown split into two factions as immigration increased. On the surface the dispute seems to be about political orientation either to the People's Republic of China (nominally Communist regime in Beijing mainland) or the Republic of China (Nationalist regime in Taipei on the island province of Taiwan). But the dispute also is about how Chinese Americans see themselves in the United States: passive or activist. Chinatown's two statues, only a hundred yards from each other, speak volumes about this schism. Confucius, at the Bowery and Division Street, represents quietude and self-cultivation; Lin Ze Xu, at the Bowery and East Broadway, represents forcefulness and public action.

There are two National Day celebrations: October 10th (Ten-Ten) along Mott Street for the Taiwan regime, the Republic of China, and October 1st along East Broadway for the mainland regime, the People's Republic of China. The four Chinese language dailies and several weeklies are highly politicized and aligned with one or the other group.

Lion dances and dragon dances proliferate at Chinese New Year (late January or February) on Chinatown's primary streets. The elaborate lion or dragon-head, usually made of brightly colored *papier maché*, is trailed by a long body of cloth carried by several energetic dancers. Each ensemble is accompanied by a contingent of drummers, and a man ritualistically teasing the animal with a lettuce on a string. Eventually the lion, amidst bursts of exploding firecracker strings, gets to eat the lettuce that symbolizes a pearl. The streets are clogged with dancers and onlookers. Shopkeepers give donations to dancing teams willing to stop and perform in front of their stores that bring good luck to the sponsors. Various martial arts schools or clubs sponsor most of the troupes. Interestingly, the ensembles are composed of New Yorkers from every background, not just Asians.

CHAPTER 97
Breweries & the Temperance Movement

Dutch colonists began brewing beverages almost as soon as New Amsterdam was established. Specifically, the Dutch brewed beer, ale, and porter varieties, which were produced and consumed at warm temperatures. The Red Lion Brewery, owned by the Verveelen brothers, was an early example of the business. Surrounding towns also began breweries. Nieuw Haarlem had a brewery within a few years of its 1658 founding.

When German immigrants began arriving in the 18th century they introduced techniques that required cold temperatures and the result was known as lager. Breweries also thrived in surrounding areas. The largest brewery in the United States in 1877 was the Hell Gate Brewery. Manhattan had 78 breweries in 1879 and

Brooklyn had 43. Over the course of the twentieth century midwestern cities like Milwaukee, St. Louis, and Cincinnati became the beer industry centers. By the 1960s there were only four left in New York City. Piels closed its Manhattan plant in 1963, Schlitz left the Hell Gate Brewery in Queens (which it had bought) in 1973, and Schaefer and Rheingold departed from Brooklyn in 1976.

Brewing has made a small come back in New York City. Several micro-breweries opened in the 1980s. The Brooklyn Brewery, popular regionally, was established in Williamsburg, Brooklyn in a set of factory buildings and warehouses in 1988. By 2014 there were four established breweries in New York City, as well as some start-ups: Heartland Brewery and Chelsea Brewery in Manhattan, and the Park Slope Brewery and Brooklyn Brewery in Brooklyn.

The distilling business in New York City was never as large as beer making. It depended on imported West Indian sugar cane, which was distilled into rum. There were several distilleries located throughout the city. Likewise, while wineries have always existed in New York City, wine making was never a large business.

Alcohol consumption provoked well-organized opposition by the late 19th century. The opponents were known as prohibitionists because they wanted to prohibit alcohol, that is, make it illegal. They intended to save people from their bad habits. In 1808 the first of many local temperance societies was organized in Saratoga, New York. In 1833 the first National Temperance Convention met in Philadelphia and called for outlawing the manufacture, sale, or consumption of hard liquor. Meeting again in 1836 they broadened their target to include wine and beer.

Intoxicating beverages were a broad target for prohibitionists. Rum, beer, hard cider, wine, whiskey, and corn whiskey (bourbon) had long been an integral part of the social life of many Americans. In 1869 the crusade turned political and the National Prohibition Party was established in Chicago. The most effective groups were the Women's Christian Temperance Union, founded in 1874 and militantly politicized during the nineteen-year leadership of Frances E. Willard, and the Anti-Saloon League, organized in 1893.

Temperance enthusiasts opposed alcohol on three fundamental grounds. They felt drinking sapped the religious spirit and stood in the way of the human perfectionism they advocated. They held that new scientific and medical research found that alcohol destroyed good health by debilitating both mind and body. But the contention that seemed to appeal most persuasively to activists, especially the women, was the social and economic argument.

Promoters of prohibition thought alcohol abuse was a key force behind poverty, family abuse, accidents, lethargy, and unemployment. To them, drunkenness was the enemy of both domestic happiness and material prosperity.

At first, temperance groups used moral persuasion to achieve their goal. They developed many tactics including educational activities centering on literature, lectures, debates, and letter writing campaigns. They led rallies and marches. Coffee urns were placed in factories to dissuade workers from drinking alcohol on the job. They opened inexpensive liquor-free public cafeterias to help men resist the temptation of the customary free lunch or dinner in a bar. Church sermons often focused on temperance.

Moral suasion was never abandoned, but was supplemented

by increasingly militant activities. Crusades were organized in targeted towns or neighborhoods to browbeat dispensers of alcohol pharmacists, grocers, innkeepers, physicians, and restaurateurs --- to sign a public pledge not to sell any form of liquor. Protracted demonstrations and boycotts were used against holdouts with activists blocking doors, making speeches, praying, and singing inspirational songs, notably, *Onward Christian Soldiers*. Naturally there were excesses, and Carry Nation, a colorful crank from Kansas, stormed into saloons around the country smashing liquor bottles and furniture with a hatchet. (Her weekly newsletter was named *The Smasher's Mail.*) Eventually, it was political action used by temperance groups that finally achieved victory for them.

Public drinking fountains and statues were one small, but interesting part of the prohibition campaign. In the 19th century great weight was attached to political and military statues. Cultural associations, ethnic organizations, and religious groups competed with each other for public space to erect memorials, which would glorify their deeds or publicize their goals.

The last two decades of the 19th century saw speeches, mass meetings, marches, celebrations, and picnics accompanying the dedication of about sixty monuments aimed at stirring the souls of temperance advocates in their quest to free America from what they felt was the demonic effect of alcohol. Temperance agitation produced some intriguing monuments, which served as granite, marble, sandstone, and metal pieces of propaganda as well as water fountains.

Many of the sixty statues erected by various temperance groups honor water themes and advocate water or other unfermented beverages as acceptable and healthy substitutes for intoxicating drinks. Water and fruit juice became icons for the forces of temperance.

As evangelical Protestantism increasingly turned away from sacramental theology (Lord's Supper and Holy Communion) toward personal conversion and private morality, a strong attraction developed for plain living and self-denial. A striking example was a popular tract of the National Temperance Society, *Self-Denial: A Duty and a Pleasure*. In celebrating the Lord's Supper (Communion), evangelical Protestant churches such as Methodists, Baptists, Congregationalists, Presbyterians, and Lutherans had no trouble substituting grape juice for wine. Mormons used water

After a century-long dispute, little was resolved. Prohibition was instituted nationally in 1919 by amending the United States Constitution, and then abolished in 1933. Alcohol abuse continued and the effects surely caused harm to the families of problem drinkers. Responsibility with any obsession has proved difficult or impossible to legislate. The goal of moderation remains, for many, elusive. The enormous energy expended by thousands of well-intending temperance enthusiasts failed to solve the problem and unknowingly fostered the growth of organized crime. The fountains and statues, however, now old enough to have lost their intended impact, remain compelling testaments to bygone political excitement and an issue of great importance. And in their odd way, they add personality to our public spaces. *Hebe at the Well* is the best looking statue in Tompkins Square Park.

CHAPTER 98
From Horses to Automobiles

In one century the horse population in the United States dropped from sixty million to one million and in New York City the decline was more drastic. Though the term *horsepower* is still used to measure the units of power output for internal-combustion engines in automobiles, trucks, and buses, power produced by actual horses has ended. Except for the eighty horses of the NYPD Mounted Unit, established in 1871, there are only a handful of horses in contemporary New York City. Some pull hansom cabs in Central Park and a few people own horses for recreational riding in some city parks. Only about five hundred horses now live in the city.

In the 1940s and 1950s a few dairies still delivered milk products by horse-drawn cart. Until the 1970s an occasional fruit and vegetable vender, seltzer deliveryman, or knife-sharpener might be spotted using a horse and wagon, but automobiles marginalized horses very rapidly.

The Dutch and English colonists brought strong draft horses to plow fields, pull heavy loads, and operate mills. Later they added sleek trotters for riding or to pull coaches. The first of many local racetracks opened in 1665. Horses became ubiquitous in the 19th century and were used to deliver goods and transport people around the city. They were also used by firefighters to pull pump and ladder trucks.

Buying and keeping a horse was expensive, so few New Yorkers owned them. Upper middle class and wealthy residents owned or rented space in nearby carriage-houses to board their horses. A few blocks in the city had alleys lined with privately owned horse stables. Behind Strivers' Row in Harlem, West 138th and 139th Streets from Frederick Douglass Boulevard to Adam Clayton Powell, Jr. Boulevard, are private alleys reached by a narrow opening in the center of each block. Signs at the entrance still announce: *Walk Your Horse.*

Private use of horses included mounted riding, though most

horse owners used one of a variety of carriages. Hansom cabs were two-wheeled covered carriages for two passengers, pulled by one horse; the driver's seat was above and behind the cab. Broughams were light, two passenger four-wheeled horse-drawn carriages with an enclosed body and two doors. Barouches were four-wheeled, shallow vehicles with two double seats inside, arranged so that the people on the front seat faced those on the back. They had a collapsible half-hood over the back seat and an outside box seat high in front for the driver. Victorias were low four-wheel pleasure carriages for two with a raised seat in front for the driver. Chaises were two-wheeled carriage for one or two people usually drawn by one horse. Promenading in their carriages on Sunday afternoons along the main avenues and parkways and in Central Park was a popular social activity of well-heeled New Yorkers.

Larger horse-drawn vehicles were used for 19th century mass transportation. Horse-drawn taxicabs, elongated stagecoaches, even double-decker stagecoaches, plied the streets and avenues of the city before the Civil War. In 1836 the first horse-drawn streetcar running on tracks went into service in Manhattan and by the Civil War several lines ran north to Harlem. Horse-pulled carriages running along tracks could travel at speeds of about five miles per hour. The last horse-pulled railroad, which ran on the West Side, ceased operations in 1918.

In Brooklyn several surface-level railroads ran from Downtown Brooklyn to Coney Island, Brighton Beach, and Bay Ridge, but much of the borough was reticulated with horse-drawn trolleys. Trolleys connected newly emerging developments in Fort Greene, Clinton Hill, Bedford-Stuyvesant, Flatbush, and Borough Park with ferry terminals along the East River.

By 1870 public mass transit on the city's street consisted of fleets of horse-drawn stagecoaches and trolleys, or streetcars. They competed for space with horse-drawn commercial vehicles and pedestrians. Traffic jams clogged almost every corner since there were no stop signs or street signals until the end of the 19th century.

As trolleys became ubiquitous in Manhattan and Brooklyn, crossing the street on foot became dangerous. The initial name of the Dodgers baseball team was the *Brooklyn Trolley-Dodgers.*

Trolley workers often labored for 17-hour shifts without breaks. The exploitation was dangerous to their health and to the safety of their customers. A large strike in 1886 was directed against the Grand Street Line on the Lower East Side of Manhattan. Police violence and judicial intimidation broke the strike. More than 5,000 trolley workers went on strike against the large Brooklyn Rapid Transit Company in 1895 and were violently suppressed by 7,000 New York State militiamen.

One disadvantage of horse transportation was the inevitable excreta. Tons of manure was picked up each night and dumped into the rivers, but much was ground into dust on dry days or mixed with mud during rains. Edwin G. Burrows and Mike Wallace discussed the issue in *Gotham*: *Much of the muck followed from the still-unavoidable reliance on horses---forty thousand of them, who each working day generated some four hundred tons of manure, twenty thousand gallons of urine, and almost two hundred carcasses---exacerbated by municipal incompetence and corruption in garbage removal.*

Few New Yorkers could afford horses or the carfare for horse-pulled vehicles. Most working class people walked to their jobs or to the markets. As the city expanded so did the demand for faster, less expensive public transportation.

Experiments with internal combustion engines began in Europe and the United States in the 1870s. Production line manufacturing of affordable automobiles was pioneered first by Oldsmobile factory in 1902, and greatly expanded by Ford in 1914. Individual automobiles, even automotive taxicabs, made only a dent in the transportation needs of the city. It was the development of buses with gasoline or Diesel burning internal-combustion engines that began to create the modern mass transit system. At the turn of the last century New York City had several small factories that produced electric-powered automobiles. The internal combustion engine operated by gasoline proved more powerful and efficient. It gained the upper hand by the First World War and the city's electric-powered vehicles gave way to Detroit, which produced autos powered by internal combustion engines.

Subways, operated by electrical current, made their appearance in 1904. The internal combustion engine and electrical power changed daily life more than any other inventions between 1875 and 1925. In terms of mass transit the internal combustion engine powered buses and electrical power propelled subways.

Heavy traffic remains a problem in the city since solutions have never been able to keep up with population growth. During morning and afternoon rush hours only subways can transport people quickly. Sometimes walking is faster than taking a bus.

One novel attempt to weave in and out of traffic and gain speed is the pedicab, a two-seated carriage similar to a Chinese *rickshaw* pulled by a bicycle-riding driver. Pedicabs came on the scene in Manhattan in about 2000 and soon there were five hundred operating with city licenses.

The use of Select Service buses operating in dedicated express lanes with special tickets bought at self-service sales stands located at bus stops, and ingress and egress from all doors of three-door articulated buses, was an idea borrowed from Bogota, Colombia. Beginning service in 2012, the Select buses, which stop approximately every fifteen blocks, have carried people about thirty percent faster than regular buses. They have eliminated the bottleneck at the front entrance door when all passengers must dip their farecard or deposit their coins.

The use of bicycles for commuting and recreation has increased markedly since the 1990s. Increased bike lanes and the advent of Citibikes in 2013 gave a boost to the popularity of bicycling. Walking to and from work has increased in attractiveness as a healthy and free way to commute. A look at walkers along the Hudson River on the West Side Promenade or over the Brooklyn and Manhattan Bridges reveals thousands of hoofing commuters.

Motor scooters, two-wheeled motor vehicles with 4-stroke gas engines are popular in most urban centers in Europe, Africa, Asia, and Latin America, but have been slow to gain popularity in the United States. They may be the next wave in the story of commuting.

CHAPTER 99
Women in the Workplace

Traditional roles for women in the 19th century revolved around the home. Women were expected to wed, and married domestic life included all the unpaid work associated with the term *homemaker*. Those domestic duties included childcare, food preparation and cooking, gardening, cleaning, laundry, sewing, marketing, and often educating the children if there were no affordable schools available. Sometimes it included manual labor such as chopping wood, shoveling coal, or carrying buckets of water.

Some occupations outside the home were open to single women. Unmarried women could be grade school teachers, nurses, shop clerks, seamstresses, or maids. Industrial work, especially in cloth mills or garment factories, was open to women though wages were always significantly lower than those paid to men doing the same jobs. Employers preferred unmarried women though married women were sometimes hired. Occupations closed to women were those that demanded heavy labor, skilled craft positions (machinist, carpenter, bricklayer), business careers, and the higher professions. Those were the jobs that paid the most money.

The labor shortage caused by the First World War brought women and blacks into some occupations that had been previously held almost exclusively by men. After the war, which lasted only one year for the United States, most of the newly hired people were unceremoniously dismissed. But some new positions did begin to open up for women after First World War. They included several categories previously dominated by men: secretarial and other clerical positions in business, high school teachers, librarians, bookkeepers, and restaurant servers.

After the Second World War conditions changed more profoundly due to attitude changes by men and women, greater access for women to high school education, and union contracts providing equal pay for equal work. The 19th Amendment to the Constitution in 1920, the personal freedom engendered by the Roaring

Twenties, and various government campaigns, one starring *Rosie the Riveter*, contributed to an increase of confidence by women workers. During the Second World War, when eleven million men and one million women served in the Armed Forces, women were urged to work outside the home for patriotic reasons. After the four-year war it was impossible to slam the door shut on women.

New York City had more high-level positions outside the home available for women in the 1950s and 1960s than most other locations in the United States. Those fields included journalism, publishing, advertising, and retailing, each a major industry in the city.

In 1963 Betty Friedan published *The Feminine Mystique*, a serious critique of the role women played in modern industrial America. She focused on the full-time homemaker and declared it *stifling*. She portrayed the suburban housewife in particular as isolated, fearful, trapped, bored, and prone to anti-depressant drugs to keep going. The bestseller and Friedan's many appearances on television launched what came to be called Second Wave Feminism. In 1966 Betty Friedan and twenty-seven others co-founded the National Organization for Women.

By the late 1960s and through the 1970s feminism was the preeminent social movement in the United States. New York journalist Gloria Steinem, who had once worked as a Playboy Bunny, was its most prominent leader. Steinem co-founded the National Women's Political Caucus in 1971, co-founded the feminist-themed magazine *Ms.* in 1972, and co-founded the Coalition of Labor Union Women in 1974. Some of their key issues were reproductive rights, economic equality, sexual harassment, and violence against women.

A victory celebrated by feminists was *Roe v. Wade*, the 1973 decision of the Supreme Court that ruled a woman, in consultation with her physician, could decide to terminate a pregnancy. That decision galvanized conservatives who stepped up their attack on the Equal Rights Amendment. The Amendment, first proposed in 1923 read: *Equality of rights under the law shall not be denied or abridged by the United States or by any state on account of sex.* Between 1972 and 1982 supporters of the ERA lobbied, marched, rallied, leafleted, petitioned, picketed, and committed acts of civil disobedience, but not enough states ratified the Amendment by the Congressionally determined time limit.

The 1970s was a time of great achievement for advocates of women's rights. Many states passed equal pay for equal work laws, and more women than men began to graduate from high schools and colleges each year. There were openings in corporate positions, law, medicine, and college instruction. There are areas with few women represented, especially in New York City's uniformed services: police, fire, and sanitation. But a 21st century phenomenon in the city has been the shift in professional young people's earning power in favor of women.

New York City women began to successfully seek elective office in the 1970s. The *glass ceiling* was pushed upward and in some cases shattered by a number of dynamic women. Bella Abzug, labor and civil rights lawyer, elected congresswoman from the west side of Manhattan in 1970 and served until 1970, actively promoted feminist and environmental issues in Washington. Shirley Chisholm, an educator won a seat in Congress from her Bedford-Stuyvesant neighborhood in Brooklyn in 1969, the first African American woman to do so. She served until 1983 and was active in women's rights issues, education, healthcare, civil rights, and labor. In 1972 she sought the Democratic nomination for president and received 152 first ballot votes. Geraldine Ferarro, lawyer, businesswoman, and journalist, was elected congresswoman from Forest Hills and surrounding neighborhoods in Queens in 1978 and served until 1984. That year she was chosen by Walter Mondale as the Democratic Party's vice presidential candidate.

More recently Hillary Rodham Clinton and Christine Quinn have been in New York's political spotlight. Clinton, former First Lady of Arkansas and the United States, moved to Westchester County in 2000. That year she was elected senator from New York State, and reelected in 2006. As a lawyer, political activist, and senator she was especially active in healthcare issues. Hillary Rodham Clinton was the runner-up candidate in the 2008 Democratic Party presidential nomination. Christine Quinn, active in city politics since college, ran successfully for the New York City Council in 1999 to represent Chelsea, Greenwich Village, and Hell's Kitchen. In 2006 Quinn was elected City Council Speaker. As the first openly lesbian member of the City Council she was particularly involved in promoting legislation to guarantee parity in benefits between married spouses and registered domestic partners.

Women remain under-represented in the halls of political power, but that has been changing. New York City is a leader in providing equal access to many jobs in the private and public spheres. The aim of women's groups is to completely shatter the glass ceiling.

CHAPTER 100
City Wildlife: Pigeons, Seagulls, Rodents, Insects, & Fish

It would seem that New York City would not be the place to look for wildlife. The deer are gone. So are the beavers, pheasants, loons, oysters, lobsters, minks, foxes, and rabbits. Coney Island, which was named for the rabbit, called *konijn* in Dutch, because there once were so many, now has none.

A few wild animals have begun to come back, but only as vestige or rare oddity. Owls, red-tail hawks, eagles, parakeets, bats, rabbits, and muskrats are sometimes spotted in parks, cemeteries, and coastal ecosystems. Raptors nest on upper floor ledges of office towers or high-rise apartment buildings. They also build homes on bridge pylons, which are the towers that support cables or frames needed to hold up a bridge's roadway. These exceptions aside, today's New Yorkers see very few animals they classify as *wild* unless they go to the country or watch the Nature Channel.

That is not to say New York City is without animals. In fact, there are millions of wild animals in Gotham. They include birds, rodents, insects, fish, reptiles, and amphibians. Prominent members of the bird family are most noticeable.

Pigeons are not native to North America. They were originally brought from Europe during the 18th century and raised in rookeries, or cages, for food. (They are still available as poultry in Greek, Italian, and Arab meat markets.) New York's immense pigeon population descends from barnyard escapees. In the city they are scavengers subsisting on a diet largely of bread and seeds provided by bird lovers. From the 1920s to the 1960s it was common to see pigeon *lofts* on top of buildings. Hundreds of coop owners raised pigeons, exercised them in flocks that flew around in circles, and sometimes raced them. As a hobby, pigeon keeping has become rare.

A mystery surrounds baby pigeons. Why don't we ever see

them? Pigeons live on building ledges, bridge girders, and sometimes trees. Pigeons choose especially well-hidden spots to have their young. Baby pigeons grow up fast --- in about ten days --- which is why babies are rarely seen.

Pigeons bold enough to ride the subways amuse New Yorkers who have noticed it. When pigeons seeking crumbs fly into the Staten Island Ferry Terminals in St. George and the Battery, not much is made of it. But commuters who use the last stop on the above ground lines occasionally see train-riding pigeons. The explanation is simple. While the cars wait to reverse directions, their doors are left open. Pigeons amble through the doors to peck at bits of food. Some are trapped when the doors close, but usually saunter off at the next stop. Among non-humans, only pigeons seem bold, or foolish, enough to ride the subway. Train-riding pigeons can be seen at the following terminals: Pelham Bay Park and Woodlawn in the Bronx, Ditmars Boulevard and Far Rockaway in Queens, Stillwell Avenue and New Lots Avenue in Brooklyn, and Tottenville in Staten Island.

Pigeons are not popular with everyone. Their detractors find them filthy and call them *flying rats*. The main problem is their droppings, which make a mess out of sidewalks and corrode limestone, brick, and even some metals. Poisons are used to kill them, and models of owls are supposed to scare them. Raptors, mostly hawks and owls, spear them with their talons. But the city has very few raptors. Closely spaced spikes can be placed on window and door ledges so pigeons will be unable to perch and defecate there. An insidious tactic, which brings to mind Roald Dahl's story, *The Twits*, is a substance called *Tanglefoot*, bought at hardware and houseware stores. *Tanglefoot* resembles glue and is applied to roof or window ledges. It makes pigeons stick to it, not forever, but just long enough to force them to struggle free in a few seconds and then go elsewhere.

Seagulls are seen near all New York waterways, especially the shore, but they fly far inland when storms are brewing over the ocean. There may be over one million seagulls in the city, though they do not provoke as much controversy as pigeons. They squawk loudly, which annoys some people. They also rob unguarded lunches by the beach. Mostly they soar and look for small fish to pluck from just below the surface of the water.

Other common shorebirds are terns, black skimmers, oystercatchers, pelicans, egrets, herons, and red-winged blackbirds. Egrets and herons are wading birds. They step carefully with their long legs around the marshes and tidal basins until they find tiny fish or fiddler crabs to pull out of the water with their long bills.

Canada Geese have proliferated near park, cemetery, and golf course ponds. Their droppings make a mess on the grass as the amount of bird dung they leave behind is enormous. Canada geese, snow geese, some ducks, white-throated sparrows, and blackpoll warblers regularly migrate at high altitudes along Atlantic flyway routes near the coast, between summers in Canada and winters in Mexico or South America. (Monarch butterflies also use the Atlantic flyway to and from their winter quarters in Mexico.) Apparently, some Canada geese prefer to ignore migration and stay in New York all year.

Raptors are birds of prey with strong beaks and sharp talons. They either spear smaller birds with their talons or pick up small mammals or snakes with their powerful claws. Most are endangered species and some of them live in New York's tall buildings and bridge towers. Peregrine falcons, red-tailed hawks, barn owls, screech owls, and eagles never go hungry in the city. Their prey is usually pigeons, rats, mice, and meadow voles. (Some raptors are known to have died of poisoning after eating rodents that were themselves poisoned.)

Songbirds, like sparrows, warblers, swallows, robins, blue jays, and cardinals, add to the diversity of bird life. Their songs delight urban dwellers, and their movements and whereabouts intrigue *birders* (birdwatchers) who hike in the parks and wetlands looking for them through binoculars. Central Park, in the midst of Manhattan's skyscrapers, is the best place to see numerous bird species, especially during migrating times in the spring and fall. Early morning in spring and fall is prime time for birding, especially if there's a weather front advancing from the appropriate direction. Birds ride the front to conserve energy. Migrating birds typically fly at night, then stop and eat for a day or two.

Rodents are numbered in the millions in New York City. They breed profusely and are able to live anywhere. Many strike humans as loathsome creatures. They carry diseases and will bite if cornered. Rabies, a very serious though rare disease, can result from a rodent bite. Most city rats are Norway (or Brown) Rats, which came to the United States from Europe aboard ships in the late 18th century. Rats are responsible for occasional nightmares and several scary Hollywood movies. They are the object of fear and disgust.

Rats play a typically creepy role in a famous Christmas season ballet. In *The Nutcracker*, with music by Peter Ilyich Tchaikovsky and story by Ernest Theodor Amadeus Hoffmann, little Clara becomes tired during her parents' Christmas party and falls asleep in a chair. She has a vivid dream and fantastic things happen. The Christmas tree grows to the top of the high ceiling. A swarm of giant rats comes out of the baseboard and chases the Nutcracker all around the living room. The elaborately carved and painted Nutcracker had been a gift to Clara from Herr Drosselmeyer, the honored guest. Toy soldiers awake to help fight off the army of rats. Eventually, just the Rat King and the Nutcracker are left on the field of battle. Fearing the Nutcracker may lose, Clara flings her shoe at the Rat King and kills him to the great relief of the audience. Then the Nutcracker is transformed into a handsome prince.

Traditionally, government experts and exterminators have estimated that the rat population roughly equals the human population in the city. By that calculation there are eight million rats. Others believe the number of rats to be significantly higher. Rats thrive below the streets in subway tunnels, drains, and sewer pipes. Everyone has seen them from subway platforms as they scamper along the track bed looking for dropped *Cheetos* or discarded sandwiches. They prefer an underground habitat. Abandoned buildings are inviting to rats. They also live in occupied buildings, squeezing through cracks and holes, and scurrying between the walls from one part of the building to another. Rats are able to chew through plaster walls to make their own holes. Food is never a problem; they feed on the contents of garbage bags and littered food. Remember how Templeton, the bad-mannered, nasty rat in *Charlotte's Web,* the story by E.B. White, survived happily on garbage.

With all the rat poisons (arsenic, strychnine, anti-coagulants) and traps available to humans, the enormous numbers of rats seem immune to serious assault. Each year, adult females can bear five litters of six to twelve young. They have plentiful sources of food and can hide in buildings and beneath the surface of streets. Rats can gnaw through plaster, wood, concrete, bricks, and lead pipes. They can jump a yard high, climb up brick walls, and swim for hours at a time. Rats may be here to stay. (An evocative 1944 wartime short story by Joseph Mitchell, *The Rats on the Waterfront,* will send shivers along your spine. It is found in his collection, *Up in the Old Hotel.*)

Mice, gophers, and meadow voles are also rodents, but they lack the fearsome quality of rats. Mice live in buildings or outdoors. Gophers and voles live in parks, cemeteries, and residential backyards.

Gray and black squirrels, also rodents, were native to North America and lived in the region's forests before the arrival of European settlers. Their numbers have increased greatly due to the abundance of available food. Foraging for littered lunches is easy in New York. People also feed squirrels. Many of the bags of peanuts and mixed nuts on grocery store shelves end up fed to squirrels by their human admirers. Squirrels have few predators in the city and peacefully raise their young in leafy nests built high in trees. Unlike some people in rural Kentucky and West Virginia, New Yorkers are completely uninterested in *eating* squirrels. (See the *Game* chapter in the venerable *Joy of Cooking,* by Irma S. Rombauer and Marion Rombauer Becker, for squirrel stew and roast stuffed squirrel recipes. The authors even included a diagram showing how to skin a squirrel.)

Squirrels, more than any of the other New York wild animals, draw out both strong pro and con attitudes. *Squirrels at My Window: Life with a Remarkable Gang of Urban Squirrels,* is an endearing story of friendship between a human and some squirrels, by Grace Marmor Spruch. There is a pro-squirrel Web site called *Squirrel Rights League* (http://members.tripod.com/sr12/), and an anti-squirrel site called *Squirrel Defamation League* (www.deadsquirrel.com). A neutral site is set up as the *Squirrel Almanac* (http://spot.colorado.edu/~halloran/sqrl.html).

One marine mammal in our waterways is the harbor seal.

There may be a few hundred of them living along the city's coastline where they find fish to eat. Seals can be spotted swimming or occasionally sunning themselves on rock outcroppings or on docks in Brooklyn, Queens, and the Bronx.

No one loves insects, and the varieties we notice --- flies, mosquitoes, silverfish --- are greeted with screened windows, fly swatters, and cans of bug spray. Vermin infestations are more pronounced in the summer than in the winter, except for cockroaches.

Cockroaches are the insects, which bother New Yorkers most. They are present at all seasons. They like the homes of the poor as much as the mansions of the rich. Turn the lights on in the kitchen at night at watch them scatter from around the sink. Sometimes they are brave enough to go about their business in the daylight.

Estimates put the number of cockroaches in New York City in the billions. Exterminating them is impossible, and, before the development of *Combat*, even controlling them was difficult. They predate the dinosaurs and have been found in fossils 300 million years old. Cockroaches can adapt to any conditions though they prefer warm, humid environments. It is presumed they originated in regions of the world with tropical climates. Cockroaches, like so many urban animals, are scavengers. Their food supply consists largely of crumbs, though they also eat human hair, dandruff and other shed skin, and the carcasses of dead roaches. They like the kitchen and bathroom sink areas because of the moist surroundings and the myriad places to hide among cabinets and pipes.

German cockroaches, the thin, brown, lightening-fast variety, make up most city roaches. American cockroaches, also called waterbugs, are much larger (often two inches) and slow moving. (Similar outdoor roaches in Florida are called palmetto bugs.) Though people eradicate cockroaches because they are ugly and disconcerting, there is a common disease associated with them. Chronic asthma can be caused by *cockroach dust*, which is the proteins from their decomposing bodies, droppings, and shed skins. The allergic reaction to cockroach dust in infested surroundings can cause severe medical problems.

By 2005 it became obvious that scattered reports of bedbug infestations had become a plague and that the city, no longer armed with the synthetic pesticide DDT (dichlorodiphenyltrichloroethane), was under assault. They spread by hitching rides on people's clothing and can easily pass from person to person through contact in subways, buses, elevators, or seats in restaurants and movie theaters. The tiny nocturnal insects are about the size of apple seeds. They have flat reddish brown bodies and hide in beds and other furniture, carpets, books, and between floorboards. Initially their bites do not hurt, but later turn to large itchy sores. Bedbugs do not carry disease, but unnerve people because of their small size, nighttime activity, and difficulty of eradication. An outside exterminator usually needs to be called and the apartment treated by insecticides, steam cleaning, freezing, and washing.

Surprisingly, the city's waterways are filled with fish. Most are small, like killfish, menhaden, baby herring, and even seahorses, which serve as food for larger fish and for birds. Larger finfish provide food for New Yorkers and sport for amateur fishermen. Most fish in seafood markets, of course, come from commercial ships operating far out in the Atlantic Ocean.

Fish found in New York City's saltwater rivers and bays, and in the ocean, includes sea bass, striped bass, croakers, porgies, herring, skate, fluke, flounder, blackfish, and weakfish (sea trout). Bluefish, prized for their feisty nature, are found in the Atlantic Ocean, Long Island Sound, and all New York City waterways. Their young are called *snappers,* and grow up in the shelter offered by the harbor and the East River.

Some of the most popular places to fish in the city are in Brooklyn: Louis Valentino, Jr. Park and Pier in Red Hook, Public Pier at the foot of Shore Road in Bay Ridge, and Long Pier at the Boardwalk in Coney Island. In Queens, people can fish at Gantry State Park, which opened on the East River waterfront in 1998 at the Hunter's Point section of Long Island City, Hallets Bay in Astoria, and Broad Channel, an island in the middle of Jamaica Bay. In Staten Island, fishing can take place along the Arthur Kill, Raritan Bay, and Great Kills Park. Manhattan and the Bronx are more difficult, but there are Hudson and East River sites in each borough that are close enough to the water to cast fishing lines. Fishing is also done from secluded parts of Pelham Bay Park in the Bronx.

From Brooklyn's Sheepshead Bay, City Island in the Bronx, Broad Channel in Queens, and Staten Island's Great Kills Harbor, party boats for half-day or full-day fishing trips go far out into the Atlantic to pursue fish. Small motorboats can be rented at numerous locations to fish, or use a long-handled net or a mesh crab trap with fish or chicken for bait to seek blue crabs.

Since most of New York's ponds were filled in over the centuries, fresh water fish are limited to carp, sunfish, brown trout, and largemouth bass in the three Bronx rivers. The Hudson River has saltwater fish in its southern part, which is very briny, but is a spawning ground further north where the river's water is fresh. Some fish, called *anadromous*, are born in fresh streams and rivers, live in the salty ocean, and return each year to spawn (and die) at the place where they were hatched. Shad and Atlantic sturgeon are anadromous. So are American eels, but they choose to spawn in the more salty lower reaches of the Spuyten Duyvil Creek, the Harlem River, and the three rivers in the Bronx.

Lobsters, crabs, scallops, mussels, periwinkles, and clams are all native to New York's waters. Enormous oyster and clam beds in Raritan Bay and Long Island Sound were harvested until late in the 19th century when over fishing and pollution destroyed the industry. These bi-valves are increasingly present in local waterways, though not in the numbers a century and a half ago.

Can you eat fish taken from New York waters? Be careful. The advice from the New York City Department of Health for all women of childbearing age and all children under the age of fifteen is not to eat any fish caught in local waters.

New York has reptiles and amphibians in parks, cemeteries, and waterways. Garter snakes are the most common reptile. The more numerous amphibians include: red-spotted newts, bullfrogs, and Fowler's toads. Though they can be found in the city's big parks --- Central Park, Prospect Park, Van Cortlandt Park, Flushing Meadows Park, LaTourette Park --- remote sites close to the water are best for spotting amphibians. In Queens they can be found in Steinway Canal, Bowery Bay, Flushing Bay, Little Neck Bay, Breezy Point, Grassy Bay, and Broad Channel. They exist in Brooklyn's Floyd Bennett Field, Jamaica Bay, Mill Basin, Marine Park, Sheepshead Bay, Coney Island Creek, Gowanus Canal, Atlantic Basin, Wallabout Bay, Bushwick Inlet, and Newtown Creek. In the Bronx they live in Pelham Bay Park, Eastchester Bay, and along Westchester Creek, the Hutchinson River, and the Bronx River. Locations in Staten Island include Arthur Kill, Fresh Kills Creek, Old Place Creek, Silver Lake Reservoir, Grasmere Lake, and Clove Lake. There are several varieties of turtles: diamondback terrapins, painted turtles, box turtles, and snapping turtles. Some of the snapping turtles manage to survive in the most polluted waterways, the Gowanus Canal and Newtown Creek.

Alligator stories have delighted New Yorkers since Florida became a tourist destination and New Yorkers became familiar with them. Enormous alligators are rumored to live in the sewers beneath city streets. Alas, the closest thing to the rumors of killer-amphibians was documented in 2001. An 18-inch *cayman* (similar to an alligator) was captured in the Harlem Meer, which is a lake in the northeast corner of Central Park.

CHAPTER 101
Radical Unionism

As early 19th century New York City and much of the United States became industrialized, sharp conflicts between labor and capital developed. The answer for many working people was collective bargaining through unions. There had been craft unions in the 18th century but in the years after the completion of the Erie Canal (1825), when industrialization and immigration took quantum leaps, the quest for higher wages and better working conditions intensified. Often workers also wanted a restructuring of society to level the economic playing field.

Early examples of radical labor in New York City were the Working Men's Party (1829-1831) and the General Trades' Union (1833-1836). Of more lasting significance were ideas and strategies popularized by the Knights of Labor (1869-1949) and the International Workingmen's Association (1864 -1876), primarily a European group that raised and promoted political and socialist philosophy.

The Knights of Labor, a national union led by Irish immigrant Terence V. Powderly from 1879 to 1893, grew to 700,000 members at its high point in 1886. Considered too conservative and ineffective by many workers the Knights quickly lost adherents to the American Federation of Labor, the Socialist Trade and Labor Alliance, and the International Workingmen's Association. Membership in the Knights of Labor declined to 15,000 by 1900 and, though largely inactive in the 20th century, was not officially disbanded until 1949.

The International Workingmen's Association, founded in London and centered in Europe, split after a dispute on philosophy and strategy by partisans of the socialist Karl Marx and the followers of anarchist Mikhail Bakunin at The Hague Congress in 1872. The same year the IWA relocated to the Lower East Side in New York City. It disbanded in 1876 at its Philadelphia congress. The Second International, titular successor to the IWA was organized in 1889 and still exists. Member parties today include the Socialist Party USA, British Labour Party, French Socialist Party, and the Social Democratic Party of Germany.

The observance of labor solidarity on May 1st, with local rallies in Tompkins Square and later in Union Square, began in 1889. The demonstration became a yearly event and spread throughout the world as International Workers' Day, Labor Day, or May Day. The date was chosen to commemorate the execution of four Haymarket martyrs after a series of demonstrations in Chicago against the McCormick Harvesting Machine Company, May 1-4, 1886. As police tried to disperse the assembly a bomb exploded in the crowd, and the police opened fire. Seven police officers and four other people were dead, and more than one hundred persons were wounded, when the shooting subsided. In 1958, during the Cold War, the United States Congress designated May 1st as Loyalty Day to counter the socialist and communist association with May Day.

The Knights of Labor first sponsored Labor Day, celebrated in the United States on the first Monday in September, with parades and rallies. It began in 1883 in New York City, six years before the appearance of May Day. Fearing that May Day celebrations were divisive and kept alive the memory of the Haymarket Riot, the United States Congress proclaimed Labor Day as a legal holiday to celebrate all labor in 1894.

After almost a century of popular support with broad participation, labor parades and rallies became marginalized. By the 1980s participation in the Labor Day parade in NYC dwindled to 50,000 marchers and only a few hundred radicals gathered at Union Square on May Day. Labor Day, along with Memorial Day, a legal holiday celebrated on the last Monday in May, had become one of the two bookends of summer. The two three-day weekends became the unofficial beginning and ending dates of the summer season. Celebration has become individualized and moved from parades and rallies to parks, beaches, and the backyard barbecue grill. In 1996 Labor Day in New York City was even dislodged from its traditional date and the remnant parade along 5th Avenue moved to the Sunday after Labor Day due to competition on the same date from the two-million-strong West Indian American Day

Carnival and Parade along Brooklyn's Eastern Parkway. In 2007 the Labor Day Parade was canceled altogether, but resumed the following year.

The 1886 mayoral campaign of social reformer Henry George was a watershed for leftist unions and radical groups. His campaign was a broad front of socialist, progressive, and liberal groups demanding significant economic and social changes in the Gilded Age, a time that had left workers behind. George based much of his campaign on the demand for a single tax on land that would be steep enough to restructure society. Many of his ideas were found in *Progress and Poverty*, which he wrote in 1879. It sold three million copies and he became an important voice in American politics. He lost the mayoral election to Tammany Hall Democrat Abram S. Hewitt, son-in-law of Peter Cooper. The official tally was Abram Hewitt (Democrat) 90,552; Henry George (Labor Union) 68,110; Theodore Roosevelt (Republican) 60,435; others 895.

The defeat of Henry George taught Samuel Gompers and his followers to stay away from politics and concentrate on *pure and simple* unionism, keeping the focus on wage and work rule concessions from employers. But radical unionists saw politics as inseparable from unionism and emphatically rejected both the worldview and strategies used by Gompers that they disparaged as *economism*. The American Federation of Labor (AFL), formed in 1886, was the major vehicle for reform-minded unionism that worked within the capitalist system. Those who desired a fundamental, or radical change in the socio-economic system had to look elsewhere.

There were many domestic radical labor and political groups for workers to choose from. At the same time an enormous wave of immigration from Southern and Eastern Europe had started bringing new points of view from Europe that further radicalized American workers. One of the unions most closely identified with leftist ideas was the International Ladies' Garment Workers' Union, which, though it affiliated with the American Federation of Labor, remained a radical union. Their program included demands for a 50-hour workweek, overtime pay, and ten legal holidays.

Members of the International Workers of the World (IWW)

were proponents of *one big union*, a labor organization that would include all workers regardless of industry or craft. Nicknamed the *Wobblies*, the I.W.W. was an *anarcho-syndicalist* group, which meant it wanted to abolish all political systems and organize every aspect of society around voluntary cooperatives. The government would exist only as a *cooperative commonwealth*, a federation of local co-operatives. They favored *direct action* against companies and the government, and did not shy away from using individual violence against what they called the institutional violence of the corporations, government, or police.

IWW militants were active throughout the United States including in NYC. Elizabeth Gurley Flynn, a full time organizer for the IWW, was prominent in fighting for women's rights, civil liberties, and labor. She was active in many New York City struggles especially a drive to organize restaurant workers.

Carlo Tresca was an important voice in many campaigns throughout the country including the drive to free Arturo Giovannitti and Joseph Ettor during the *Bread and Roses* textile strike in Lawrence, Massachusetts, and the unsuccessful campaign to free anarchists Nicola Sacco and Bartolomeo Vanzetti. Tresca was an outspoken opponent of Italian fascist dictator Benito Mussolini and his American cheerleader, Generoso Pope,Sr. editor of *Il Progresso Italo-Americano*. In 1943 Tresca was assassinated just west of Union Square. It was widely believed to be the work of a Mafia crime family. Giovannitti was active in several strikes and Ettor was a leader of the barber strike and the restaurant waiters strike.

Irish-born labor leader, fiery orator, and political activist, Mary Harris Jones affectionately called Mother Jones, led a campaign against child labor and was an organizer for the coal mine workers in Pennsylvania and textile unions in New York City. (The Mother Jones Apartment Building at 3102-16 Brighton 1st Place just south of Brighton Beach Avenue is a testament to the socialist political sentiments of many Eastern European Jews at the turn of the last century.)

Emma Goldman, who emigrated from the Russian Lithuania, was a major anarchist theoretician and active in numerous movements in New York City. She was imprisoned three times for her beliefs. The first was for publicly urging workers to expropriate food. *Ask for work. If they do not give you work, ask for bread. If they do not give you work or bread, take bread.* She was also imprisoned for distributing literature advocating birth control and for opposing American entry into the First World War. Her former apartment at 208 East 13th Street just east of 3rd Avenue in the East Village has a plaque explaining that she lived in a sixth floor apartment there from 1903 until 1913. Goldman was expelled to Russia in 1919. Unhappy with the Bolshevik regime she spent the rest of her life espousing radical politics and feminism in various countries in Western Europe. She died in 1940 in Canada.

Alexander Berkman, Russian-born anarchist, close associate and partner of Emma Goldman, was infuriated by the violent role of three hundred Pinkerton agents during the strike at the Homestead Works of the Carnegie Steel Company. In 1892 he armed himself with a revolver and a sharpened steel file and shot Henry Frick three times and stabbed him twice. Frick, coal magnate and business associate of Andrew Carnegie, survived the attack and Berkman spent the next fourteen years in a Pennsylvania prison. After Berkman's release, he moved to Greenwich Village and resumed an active political life.

Along with thousands of others, Goldman and Berkman were ordered deported from the United States during the Palmer Raids in 1919. At an anarchist-sponsored farewell banquet for them in Chicago, Berkman, always irreverent, referred to the recent death of Frick, saying that Frick had been *deported by God. I'm glad he left the country before me.*

At noon on September 16, 1920 a bomb blasted the corner of Broad and Wall Streets, a prime capitalist target that had on its four corners the New York Stock Exchange, Bankers Trust Company, House of Morgan, and the Subtreasury Building. Thirty-five people were killed by the explosion and 130 injured. The crime was never solved though it was widely speculated in the press that the perpetrators were anarchists.

The 1930s saw a precipitous decline in the influence of independent radicals and anarchists. Most leftists were attracted to large political and labor organizations aimed at bolstering the impact of unions and easing the plight of the poor. The Congress of Industrial Organizations (CIO) was formed in 1936, during the midst of the Great Depression. Its organization was similar to the AFL, an umbrella group to which separate unions could affiliate for added strength in lobbying or in strike activities. Its affiliates were *industrial unions,* labor organizations that represented everyone working for a company, such as the International Ladies' Garment Workers' Union (ILGWU) and the International Brotherhood of Electrical Workers (IBEW).

By the end of the Second World War most individual unions were allied with the Democratic Party and backed their candidates in elections. The Communist Party heavily influenced some of the CIO unions until Cold War laws and the hostility of the House Un-American Activities Committee (HUAC) drove the communists out. The AFL and CIO remained separate entities until 1955 when the two groups merged to form the AFL-CIO.

The chief rallying point for left-wing labor and radical political groups in the 19th century was Tompkins Square. In January 1874 it was the site of the first labor demonstration in New York City that was organized by the International Workingmen's Association (or First International). The police attacked the workers and the *Tompkins Square Riot* ensued. By the 1920s Union Square usurped the role of Tompkins Square as the labor movement's rallying place. In the 1960s Tompkins Square again became a center of radical activities: rallies against the War in Vietnam, marijuana smoke-ins, and concerts by *The Fugs, Country Joe and the Fish,* and *The Grateful Dead.* From 1988 until 1991 Tompkins Square was the scene of violent confrontations between police and squatters who had constructed shacks in the park. The struggle pitted the remnants of the Hippie subculture and some of their neighborhood allies against the first wave of gentrification.

The Socialist Party influenced the International Ladies' Garment Workers' Union (ILGWU) and the Amalgamated Clothing Workers of America (ACWA). These unions, led by David Dubinsky and Sidney Hillman respectively, were particularly active in the cooperative housing movement and sponsored high-rise coops in the Lower East Side. (In the 21st century many of them have been privatized.)

Communists strongly influenced several of the industrial unions in the CIO, especially the United Electrical Workers, National Maritime Union, Transport Workers Union United Retail and Wholesale Employees, Fur Workers Union, and the American Newspaper Guild. They were also influential opinion-leaders in a few of the AFL unions, namely the American Federation of Teachers, Hotel and Restaurants Workers Union, and the Painters Union.

The Labor Movement today has lost much of its influence in the city. In part it suffered from its own successes in the 1940s through the 1960s when labor contracts, especially for skilled workers or those in very profitable industries gave members middle class lifestyles. There are many other reasons why organized labor's membership has fallen and its power has been diminished. Suburbanization, both in Long Island, Westchester, New Jersey as well as in the outer sections of Queens and Staten Island, reduced the cultural affinity of workers who formerly lived close together near their jobs. Automobile ownership after the Second World War exacerbated the flight from the city and lessened neighborhood bonds.

Runaway shops, outsourcing, automation, and immigration have hurt organized labor. At first the runaway shops in the textile, shoe, and printing industry relocated to the anti-union states in the American South. More recently whole industries have left NYC and relocated in Asian or Latin American countries. Even service industry jobs are often relocated abroad. The largest and most sustained immigration in American history has provided a vast supply of non-union workers willing to accept low wages and substandard working conditions. In the construction industry, only new buildings and public works built with government funds use union labor. Almost all demolition and new private construction is non-union, much of it immigrant.

Sustained hostility to unions from Ronald Reagan and George Bush, Sr. resulted in laws, regulatory agency decisions, and executive orders that harmed organized labor. Most notable was the dramatic signal that Reagan sent to the business community when he broke the Professional Air Traffic Controllers Organization (PATCO) strike in 1981. Declaring the strike by 13,000 controllers a *peril to national safety*, Reagan ordered them back to work under the federal Taft-Hartley Act. Only 1,500 complied so the president fired the 11,500 air traffic controllers remaining on strike and permanently banned them from employment in the federal government. The destruction of a powerful union, the arrest and shackling of its leaders, failed to elicit sympathy strikes or mass demonstrations. The era of powerful labor unions seemed to be over.

The North American Free Trade Agreement (NAFTA) shepherded into law in 1993 by Bill Clinton, a conservative Democrat, contributed to the job loss by bolstering inexpensive imports from Mexico. It also flooded Mexico with cheap American corn, heavily subsidized by the U.S. Congress, that sent millions of marginalized Mexican corn farmers across the border to compete with Americans and drive down wages. The U.S. labor movement, with little or no influence in the Carter, Reagan, Bush I, Clinton, Bush II, and Obama administrations, was unable to stop the race to the bottom in wages and benefits.

Though the labor movement in New York City has been wounded by globalization and right-wing politics, it still has a higher percentage of union members than most cities. About thirty percent of New York City's employees are unionized compared to only eleven percent nation-wide. Manufacturing jobs have fallen precipitously in the city though there are growth areas for organized labor. The main area of expansion for the labor movement in NYC has been in the government service sector. Uniformed city employees such as police, firefighters, sanitation employees, and prison guards are all unionized, as are teachers, professors, social workers, court employees, and public hospital workers.

The Taylor Law, enacted in 1967, gave public service labor unions the right to bargain collectively and prescribed binding arbitration on the two sides, but mandated stiff penalties for striking (two days fine for each day on strike). Civil servants never had the legal right to strike in New York State, but the Taylor Law made it easy to prevent work stoppages. Though the Taylor Law has weakened the effectiveness of public sector unions it has not stopped their growth.

In the first decade of the 21st century there has been a mild uptick in the labor movement in New York City with more aggressive organizing among non-union workers in universities, restaurants, demolition and construction sites, retail shops, and in the home healthcare industry. One of the new slogans is *The Labor Movement: The Folks Who Brought You the Weekend.* It rightfully takes credit for workers receiving two days off each weekend and reminds people that without organized labor they and non-union workers alike would not have many of the benefits presently enjoyed.

Notations:

Inscription in front of the Hillman Houses established by the Amalgamated Clothing Workers Union and the International Ladies' Garment Workers Union in the Lower East Side at the intersection of Grand, Henry, and Jackson Streets

There has been much gentrification in the Corlear's Hook section of the Lower East Side as cooperatives organized by labor union, socialist, and liberal activists have been privatized. Particularly thought-provoking in light of the privatization of the coops, is the inscription quoting Sidney Hillman, dedicated *to perpetuate the ideals for which he lived and died,* carved in granite and set in the brick and iron gate of the Hillman Houses. Hillman (1887-1946) was a Russian-born labor leader, socialist, and proponent of *industrial democracy* who, in 1914, became the first president of the Amalgamated Clothing Workers of America. *We want a better America, an America that will give its citizens, first of all, a higher standard of living so that no child will ever cry for food in the midst of plenty. We want to have an America where the inventions of science will be at the disposal of every American family, not merely for the few who can afford them; an America that will have no sense of insecurity and which will make it possible for all groups, regardless of race, creed or color to live in friendship, to be real neighbors; an America that will carry its great mission of helping other countries to help them selves.*

Dorothy Day & the Catholic Workers Movement

The ideology of the Catholic Workers Movement is a particularly unconventional form of radical labor philosophy. It exists without sanction from the Roman Catholic Church, and unlike Catholic workers movements in Europe, it has no connection with any labor unions. Never large, but doggedly determined, it has played a noticeable role in various anti-war movements, the struggle for Civil Rights, the fight to give amnesty to undocumented immigrants, and has supported the poor in their quest for jobs and housing. The group was in the forefront of a coalition of leftist and civil libertarian groups that opposed the nuclear arms race and the hysteria around civil defense. In the 1960s and 70s the Reverends Philip and Daniel Berrigan and Sister Elizabeth McAlister carried on Catholic social activism against racism and specializing in dramatic protests including burning draft records and intruding onto military bases. Catholic Workers are a utopian anarchist lay organization of pious Catholics unaffiliated with the Roman Catholic Church.

The French mystical utopian Peter Maurin, and Dorothy Day articulated the guiding philosophy of the Catholic Workers. Maurin, a former teacher in the Christian Brothers religious order, came to New York City after living for several years as a worker in Canada. He embraced poverty as God's gift and spent his life helping the poor. Dorothy Day was a Greenwich Village communist who converted to Roman Catholicism because at the time it was the religion of most industrial workers. She searched and found many points of confluence between communist and Catholic ideas. *The Catholic Worker*, founded by Maurin and Day in 1933, promoted their ideals. The newspaper still sells for one penny, a symbol of the movement's devotion to the poor.

Maryhouse, at 55 East 3rd Street between 1st and 2nd Avenues in the East Village, is the center of the Catholic Worker movement in the United States. St. Joseph House, around the corner at 36 East 1st Street, is the headquarters of the bi-monthly journal, *The Catholic Worker*.

What about the poor in New York City? How hidden are the poor and the working poor? Most of the poor are children, so they do not present themselves on the streets as homeless people, though some of them are without homes. The 2010 census revealed New York County (Manhattan) to be the richest per capita in the United States. It also showed that the borough had the greatest income disparity of any urban county in the United States.

CHAPTER 102
Wall Street Crash & the Great Depression

The effects of the Wall Street stock market crash in 1929 are easier to gauge than its causes. In large part it was a radical correction in the grossly overvalued stock market. After years of inflated stock prices it was time for the economy to bounce the other way. The prosperity unleashed after the First World War set off a spirited buying spree of stocks, housing, mechanized farm equipment, automobiles, and home appliances. There were twenty-three million cars in use by 1929, and movie theater attendance reached fifty million per week. Culturally the Great Depression occurred at the end of the Roaring 20s, a time of exploding personal freedom, new inventions, greater mobility, and risky finances. There was a buoyant feeling of optimism, an irrational belief that the good times would never end. Humorist Will Rogers commented: *You can't lick this prosperity thing. Even the fellow who hasn't got any is all excited over the idea.* Prohibition (1920 -1933), an event that seemed to refute the *zeitgeist,* was not really a contradiction to the upbeat spirit in New York City since many local bars remained open and it was rarely difficult to find alcoholic beverages in restaurants or nightclubs.

People borrowed money with abandon even buying stocks on ten percent margin meaning customers gave brokers ten percent of the cost of the stock and borrowed the remainder. There were strong elements of greed and folly to the run-up of the stock market. When the panic began, brokers called in the ninety percent loans and customers had to liquidate assets, often selling their cars and homes, to pay. The crisis on Wall Street quickly became a collapse of international capitalism as stock markets around the world went into steep decline.

There were some other problems with the financial system.

Technological advances in farm equipment and fertilizers had created a glut of agricultural products and the dominant laissez-faire policy prevented the government from taking steps to reduce farm products. There was also a worldwide overproduction of basic industrial commodities. The chaotic banking system in the United States was largely unregulated and ineffectively monitored.

Once the stock market crashed a bill squeaked through Congress that exacerbated the crisis. The Hawley-Smoot tariff of 1930 intensified protection from goods manufactured in Europe. Soon other countries followed and the result was a precipitous drop in international foreign trade that hurt exports and further drove down production.

There had been sell-offs, panics, and recessions before. The Panic of 1907 and the Recession of 1893-1896 remained vividly in the memory of older Americans. The 1929 collapse was more severe and became an international economic crisis. It began on *Black Thursday*, October 24th and the sell-off continued unevenly until it hit its bottom in June 1932.

On Wall Street shares of American Telephone & Telegraph (AT&T) had been at 310 in 1929 and fell to 69 in 1932. During the same period General Motors went from 91 to 7, Radio Corporation of America (RCA) from 114 to 2, Sears, Roebuck from 181 to 9, and United States Steel from 261 to 21. The Dow-Jones Industrial Average fell from 381.17 in 1929 to 41.22 in 1932 and the Gross National Product, the estimated sum of all goods and services produced, plummeted from $104.4 billion to $56.0 billion. Prices for agricultural commodities also collapsed: a bushel of wheat from $1.03 to $0.38, corn from $0.80 to $0.31, and a pound of tobacco from $0.18 to $0.10.

The collapse in stock and commodity prices spread quickly to banking, real estate, and all types of goods and services. Bank runs were common, foreclosures threatened homeowners, consumer buying power declined precipitously, factories and offices laid off workers, and the whole economy slowed to a crawl.

Lines formed outside of banks daily as depositors, savings passbooks in hand, sought to withdraw funds they incorrectly assumed banks kept inside their safes. Faced with overwhelming requests to withdraw deposits, many banks were forced to close their doors. There is a memorable scene in Frank Capra's 1946 film *It's A Wonderful Life* where George Bailey, played by James Stewart, successfully weathers a chaotic run on the funds of the Bailey Building and Loan Association. George Bailey tried to explain to his anxious depositors that money placed in bank accounts is not kept in vaults but is rather leant out for house and auto loans or invested in bonds.

Housing prices plummeted and rents plunged. Beyond deep discounts in rent New York landlords gave a free month's rent to tenants who accepted apartments that had not been repainted. Some tenants moved every year to get the free month's rent. For unemployed or under employed all rents were too high. Those who lost their homes often doubled-up and moved in with relatives or friends. Some became homeless. Riding the rails was an adventurous option to some young New York men as they rode freight trains around the country looking for jobs. Shantytowns, often called *Hoovervilles* sprouted in Central Park, the area of New Lots, Broad Channel Island and the larger islets in Jamaica Bay, and along railroad tracks and under viaducts.

People learned to live without items and services that they had previously enjoyed. New York's rich web of small shops was shattered by the Depression as barbershops, bakeries, florists, diners, and candy shops closed for lack of business. Trips to the doctor and dentist were postponed. The spiral continued from 1929 until 1932 when it bottomed out but remained flat.

The number of unemployed swelled to twelve million, which was twenty-five percent of the normal labor force, though that was before federal government statistics on employment included Blacks, Hispanics, Asians, or white women.

A group of unemployed First World War veterans, many from New York City, demanded to be paid their promised bonuses in a lump sum now that they were in dire straits. The veterans hitchhiked, rode freight trains, commandeered trucks, or walked to Washington, D.C. in May 1932 where they organized themselves into the Bonus Expeditionary Force. About 10,000 bivouacked in the Anacostia Flats and another 10,000 occupied derelict buildings or campsites between the Capitol and the White House.

In 1924, Congress had enacted a law, over President Calvin

Coolidge's veto, to provide $3.5 billion in compensation to veterans. Under the plan, based on length of service, veterans who were entitled to a bonus of $50 or less were paid in cash, but those entitled to more than $50 were to receive certificates that would mature in 1945. The Bonus Expeditionary Force staged daily rallies and marches to convince Congress to raise the funds and pay out the bonus thirteen years early. In June the House approved the change but in July the Senate soundly defeated the measure. The District of Columbia Commissioners ordered the demonstrators to disperse and leave the capital. When they refused, Hoover ordered troops to disperse them.

Mounted soldiers with loaded rifles and unsheathed bayonets used tear gas and tanks to destroy the camps. General Douglas MacArthur, who thought the demonstrators were communists trying to overthrow the U.S. government, exceeded his authority by burning tents and makeshift huts, and unleashing several armed volleys against the veterans. Hundreds were injured and three were killed. Major George Patton and Major Dwight D. Eisenhower aided General MacArthur. Photographs of thousands of veterans being attacked by mounted soldiers angered many Americans and further marred Hoover's reputation.

President Herbert Hoover's pronouncements concerning the Depression were not helpful and stoked opposition to the Republican stewardship of the economy. In December 1930 he said: *The fundamental strength of the nation's economy is unimpaired.* Hoover's optimism in the economy was not prophetic. In November 1929 he claimed, *Business and industry have turned the corner,* and in May 1930 the president said: *We have now passed the worst.*

There were some heroes. Will Rogers, Cherokee Indian, cowboy, master of the lariat, and gentle humorist, managed to capture the sense of frustration and tragedy and make some light-hearted jokes. In a way that is now very difficult to imagine, First Lady Eleanor Roosevelt became the main symbol of rescue from the plight poor Americans faced. She was the eyes and ears of the White House and went on hundreds of inspection tours around the country to bring first-hand information back to her husband, who, because of his paralyzed legs, had limited mobility. The First Lady received letters from adults and children across the land telling her of their predicaments and often seeking her direct aid.

Franklin Delano Roosevelt, former state senator and governor of New York State, handily defeated Hoover in the 1932 election. Though the collapse was over by the time he took office on March 4, 1933, the Roosevelt administration's program, the New Deal, sought to provide relief to those still suffering from the Depression and to stimulate the economy to recapture growth. He sought in his inaugural address to assure people that there would be significant change. *First of all, let me assert my firm belief that the only thing we have to fear is fear itself --- nameless, unjustified terror, which paralyzes needed efforts to convert retreat into advance.*

What unfolded through the New Deal was a massive restructuring of government and a shift in the way people thought about it. Previously most Americans believed that self reliance was enough to insure survival, but the complexities of increased urbanization and an advanced industrial economy convinced most people that the government had a central role in guiding the country and protecting its citizens from economic dislocations. Roosevelt's activist cabinet and his advisors, the *brain trust* of his administration, embarked on an ambitious program to change the role of the federal government.

During the New Deal, Congress approved and the president signed into law many new programs that helped relieve the effects of the Depression in New York City included the Emergency Banking Act, Glass-Steagall Banking Act, Truth in Securities Act, Securities and Exchange Commission, Civilian Conservation Corps, and Home Owner's Loan Act. Others were to follow: Social Security System, Works Project Administration, National Labor Relations Board, and the Works Project Administration. Since many new government bureaus used abbreviations such as SEC, CCC, SSS, NLRB, and WPA they were sometimes called the *alphabet agencies.*

Because the financial services industry is centered in New York City, Roosevelt's measures that aimed at shoring up banks and financial markets were crucial to the city's economic survival. The Emergency Banking Act sent an army of accountants out to review the records of all banks operating within the Federal Reserve System. Within three days seventy-five percent were reopened and the others were either reorganized or forcibly merged with fiscally sound banks. In one of his weekly *fireside chats* on the radio, Roosevelt told listeners that the bank crisis had ended. *I can assure you that it is safer to keep your money in a reopened bank than under the mattress.*

The Glass-Steagall Banking Act stopped banks from speculating in the financial markets by forcing them out of the investment business. It set up the Federal Deposit Insurance Corporation (FDIC), which initially secured small deposits up to $2,500 each. The Truth in Securities Act obliged companies to register all new securities with the Federal Trade Commission and provide accurate financial information to the public. The Securities and Exchange Commission policed the stock and bond markets in order to prevent manipulation of the markets or the use of privileged information by brokers called *insider trading*.

The Civilian Conservation Corps gave work to 300,000 young men from urban areas in 1,300 camps mostly tent-cities in undeveloped areas where they planted trees, dug lakes, constructed dams, built fire towers, lodges and roads in national parks, and cleared the Appalachian Trail. Each CCC participant was paid $30 monthly of which $25 was sent as a check to his family. Approximately two and a half million young men participated in the program that gave them employment, accomplished work that may not otherwise have been done, and provided needed funds to their families. Thousands of young white men from New York City served in the Civilian Conservation Corps.

The Social Security System was an admission that many people in an advanced industrial urban society were unable to save enough money to provide for their support in old age. The SSS was an insurance plan that enrolled almost all American workers regardless of economic position. It was initially funded by a one percent tax on payrolls. The money that was taken directly from paychecks, half paid by the employee and half paid by the employer. It provided an old-age pension based on a sliding scale that took into account how long and how much the worker contributed. The SSS also paid benefits to the blind, handicapped, and orphaned. In an unfortunate example of pandering to racial bigotry, Roosevelt agreed to exclude farm laborers, domestic workers, and restaurant employees in order to gain the support of Dixiecrats in the Democratic Party. (In the South many of the farm laborers, domestic workers, and restaurant employees were blacks.) The Social Security System began to slowly relieve pressures on indigent senior citizens.

The National Labor Relations Board aimed at regularizing the frequently violent and disruptive process of union certification and collective bargaining. The NLRB, which was detested by corporate leaders, protected workers from unfair practices and retaliatory firings and discrimination. It protected the *right of employees to self-organization and freedom in the choice of representatives for collective bargaining.* New York City was already heavily unionized but the NLRB boosted the success rate in unionizing efforts. The Wagner-Connery Act that set up the NLRB, and the Social Security Act were co-sponsored by New York Senator Robert Wagner, Sr.

The guiding idea behind the Works Projects Administration was to put the unemployed to work on public ventures. Between 1935 and 1945 over eight million Americans had worked on WPA endeavors. About half of the money was appropriated for construction and conservation projects. The agency accomplished a wide variety of disparate tasks including flood control, reforestation, dam and levee construction, and rural electrification. It built highways, streets, bridges, airports, libraries, hospitals, and schools.

About fifteen percent of the money spent by the national program was allocated to projects in New York City, the result of close political cooperation between Roosevelt, Mayor Fiorello LaGuardia, and *master builder* Robert Moses. Some were construction projects and others were community service programs that used the skills of historians, writers, poets, painters, sculptors, photographers, musicians, actors, and doctors and dentists.

Slum clearance, police station, firehouse, school, bridge, beach, park, and parkway construction were accomplished in New York City. The Works Project Administration built LaGuardia Airport, Jacob Riis Beach, Orchard Beach, FDR Drive, the Belt Parkway in Brooklyn, much of the public housing in all five boroughs, and seventeen public swimming pools and 250 playgrounds.

The WPA's Federal Arts Projects planned and supervised programs to photograph each building in the city, start orchestras in schools, record ethnic music, establish poetry workshops and sponsor readings, research and catalogue historical and genealogical records, refurbish public monuments and statues, and open medical and dental clinics. Theater groups were organized and plays were performed at public venues. The Federal Writers Project produced *The WPA Guide to New York City*, an exhaustive catalogue of interesting sights.

Thousands of unemployed artists were enrolled in the Federal Arts Project to paint murals in New York City. A small sampling gives an idea of the scope. In the Bronx murals were painted in Split Rock Golf Course in Pelham Bay Park, the Central Post Office, De Witt Clinton High School, and Theodore Roosevelt High School. Examples in Brooklyn include public spaces in the Red Hook Houses and Williamsburg Houses, Abraham Lincoln High School, Erasmus Hall High School, George Westinghouse Vocational and Technical High School, Midwood High School, several buildings at the Prospect Park Zoo, and the Brooklyn Public Library's main branch at Grand Army Plaza. In Manhattan, WPA paintings can be found in New York County Court House at Foley Square, the rotunda of the National Museum of the American Indian (originally the United States Custom House) at Bowling Green, Bellevue Hospital's Doctors' Lounge, Harlem Hospital's Women's Pavilion, main branch of the New York Public Library, Seward Park High School, Grant's Tomb, U.S. Passport Office in the International Building at Rockefeller Center, and in the Central Park Zoo's Concession Building. Queens murals include the Marine Air Terminal at La Guardia Airport, Astoria branch of the Queensboro Public Library, Forest Hills Post Office, Jackson Heights Post Office, Queensbridge Houses, Flushing High School, and Queens College. Staten Island's Borough Hall and Curtis High School also have WPA murals.

The endeavors of the WPA were not without controversy though it gave needed employment to at least 700,000 New Yorkers. The House Un-American Activities Committee investigated the WPA in 1938. Some members of HUAC charged that communists dominated the WPA, especially its projects for writers, musicians, and artists, who used the opportunity to make anti-capitalist statements. The WPA remains the largest example of federal non-military employment in the United States. It helped millions of American secure paychecks and produced some valuable physical and cultural contributions.

The Depression spawned an increase of radical politics on the left and the right. The strength and prestige of socialist and communist parties grew dramatically, and so did the influence of the right. Nonetheless, Roosevelt's New Deal held the middle ground. Many historians see the New Deal as the program that saved American capitalism by forcing its reform and regulation.

America First Committees, initially organized by Yale University law students led by R. Douglas Stuart Jr., quickly spread across the country. The organizing petition stated: *We demand that Congress refrain from war, even if England is on the verge of defeat.* Among those at Yale who joined the committee were architect Frank Lloyd Wright, John F. Kennedy, and Gerald R. Ford, who became presidents of the United States in 1961 and 1974 respectively, and Potter Stewart, appointed to the U.S. Supreme Court in 1958. In 1940 former General Robert E. Wood, chairman of the board of Sears, Roebuck, chaired the group's board of directors. Other board members included Henry Ford, the auto maker who had sponsored publication of *The Protocols of the Elders of Zion*, an old anti-Semitic tract from tsarist Russia, American Olympic Association president Avery Brundage, Chicago meat packing company executives Jay Hormel and Philip Swift, former Colonel Robert J. McCormick, publisher of *The Chicago Tribune*, and John T. Flynn, chairman of the New York City chapter. Flynn, who claimed to oppose fascism, wrote *As We Go Marching*, an analysis of German and Italian fascist regimes tried to make them palatable to Americans by stressing fascism's similarity to Roosevelt's New Deal.

The America First Committee called a mass rally for May 23, 1941 in Madison Square Garden. Ten thousand people attended and listened to Charles A. Lindbergh address the crowd. Lindbergh was the star speaker able to draw large crowds for America First rallies. He admired German work habits, precision and order, skill at engineering, science and industry, pioneering use of air power, commitment to eugenics, and ideas of racial purity. On trips to Nazi Germany as aviation consultant he dined with Adolf Hitler, propagandist Joseph Goebbels, and air force head Hermann

Goering. On one occasion he accepted a Nazi air force medal from Goering. Lindbergh, driven by extreme anti-communism and racist beliefs, was on the far right of the America First Committee. He regularly spoke of the *pressing sea of Yellow, Black and Brown and the semi-Asiatic hordes of the Soviet Union* as threats to American and European civilization.

The German-American Bund emerged from several German-American heritage groups that feared a repeat of anti-German measures that had been used indiscriminately against Germans in this country during the First World War. Some also subscribed to the goals of the Nazi Party. In 1936, Fritz Kuhn led the organization, which focused on producing films and pamphlets, sponsoring lectures, and staging rallies to oppose American intervention in Europe and to defend the Hitler regime. The bund, centered primarily in German areas of New York such as Yorkville in Manhattan, Bushwick in Brooklyn, and Maspeth and Ridgewood in Queens, was especially active in opposing a Jewish boycott of German goods. On February 19, 1939, the bund held a rally in Madison Square Garden that attracted 20,000 people. Kuhn defended Hitler's policies, warned of a global conspiracy masterminded by communists and Jews, and lambasted Roosevelt's call for American aid to England. Kuhn repeatedly referred to the president as *Frank D. Rosenfeldt* and called the New Deal the *Jew Deal.* During the Second World War, Kuhn was arrested and imprisoned in an internment camp in Texas. In 1945 he was released and deported to Germany. *The House on 92nd Street,* a 1945 film showed the F.B.I.'s efforts to infiltrate the bund in Yorkville.

Thousands of New Yorkers regularly listened to the right-wing radio priest Fr. Charles Coughlin's diatribes against Roosevelt's New Deal, Jews, and left-wing politicians. The Roman Catholic Church, staunch opponent of communism, had sided with Francisco Franco's fascists in the Spanish Civil War. Despite the best efforts of the right, New York City remained a left-liberal metropolis and the vast majority of its people supported the administration's New Deal and Roosevelt's response to the Japanese attack on Pearl Harbor by declaring war against Germany and Italy as well as Japan.

An evaluation of Roosevelt's New Deal, and his twelve-year-plus presidency, is inextricably bound up with international events and the Second World War. While the administration's employment programs generated few long-term jobs they succeeded in relieving acute economic misery and gave people hope for a better future. Bank and labor regulations were needed and the Social Security System saved millions of Americans from destitution in their old age. The New Deal shifted a great deal of emphasis and activity to the federal government and altered the country's traditional laissez-faire philosophy. Congressional acts and executive orders that stressed privatization and deregulation occurred during the Reagan, Bush Sr., Clinton, and Bush Jr. administrations as Roosevelt's legacy was challenged.

CHAPTER 103
Radical Politics

Christian Socialist communitarian experiments based on the Social Gospel were found in most parts of the United States in the 19th century. Examples of collective utopian communities were Brook Farm, Oneida, New Harmony, and the Icarian Settlement. But it was non-religious organizations that promoted the economic and philosophical ideas of Karl Marx and Friederick Engels, known at the time as *scientific socialism*, that were the prevalent radical groups in New York City. The International Workingmen's Association (1864-1876) and the Second International (1889 to the present) formed the ideological groundwork of most radical political parties.

The history of radical politics in New York City is complicated. In broad terms it can be seen as the advent of a variety of competing and colluding socialist organizations from the 1880s through the 1920s, then the supremacy of the Communist Party during the Depression and the Second World War. Following the war, the Communist Party and most other openly leftist groups declined precipitously, though progressive politics remained alive in the movements for Civil Rights, for Nuclear Disarmament, and against the Vietnam War. The Labor Movement, which lost much of its militancy after the war, nonetheless entered its golden age that lasted for twenty years largely due to the partial restructuring of society during Franklin D. Roosevelt's New Deal. Since the 1970s, however, labor has been in steep decline.

Curaçao-born Daniel DeLeon led the Socialist Labor Party (1877 to the present), an early pioneer among leftist groups, between 1890 and 1914. It opposed both the reformism of other nascent socialist groups as well as the harsh social and economic policies of the Bolshevik Party in the Soviet Union. The SLP supported industry-wide labor unions and a political system with people represented in a congress by their occupations, not geographic districts.

The Socialist Party of America, formed in 1901, had many adherents in NYC among Eastern European Jews, both intellectuals and workers, especially in the needle trades. The Socialist Party, the *Forwartz* (Yiddish-language paper), and the International Ladies' Garment Workers' Union led the fight for industrial reforms and fire codes after the March 25, 1911 fire that killed 146 workers at the Triangle Shirtwaist Company near Washington Square. Democrats and liberal reformers, notably Assemblyman Alfred E. Smith and State Senator Robert F. Wagner, took up the cause as well.

Despite some early national successes under the leadership of Eugene V. Debs and the election of Victor Berger to Congress from Milwaukee, the Socialist Party suffered numerous defections from its left to the Communists in the 1920s and from its right to the Democrats in the 1930s. The Communist Party became the primary radical political organization in New York City during the Depression.

Following the October Revolution in 1917, a coup d'état by Vladimir Lenin's Bolshevik Party in Russia, socialists worldwide were split on the question of support. Those who distrusted Bolshevik militancy and supported reforms within the capitalist system or the establishment of mixed economies stayed with their respective socialist parties. The more radical socialists began breaking away and forming communist parties, the name that was adopted by the Bolshevik Party in 1919. The Communist Party USA, formed in 1919, was first centered in Chicago but moved its headquarters to New York City in 1927. The national, state, and city offices were in a building on East 13th Street, one block south of Union Square. The *Daily Worker*, the party newspaper, and the *Morgen Freiheit*, a Yiddish-language Communist Party paper, each occupied adjacent buildings on the east side of Union Square, the area that had become the center of left-wing groups by the 1920s. *New Masses*, the party's literary journal, and International Publishers, the party's publishing house, were located nearby. The Jefferson Book Store on East 16th Street, one door off Union Square, carried books from the Soviet Union and all publications printed by International Publishers. The name of the store came from the Popular Front days when party chairman Earl Browder pronounced that *Communism is 20th century Americanism.*

Taking directions from the Third International in the Soviet Union, the Moscow-controlled directorate of scores of communist parties around the world, the American party had both public and secret members. Secrecy protected individual communists from being fired by employers or harassed by mortgage lenders or the police. The party organized clubs, which the popular press referred to as *cells*, in the workplace and the neighborhood. Associated organizations, labeled *front groups* by the press and the FBI's J. Edgar Hoover, included labor unions, tenant organizations, civic clubs, legal aid organizations, civil rights groups, and immigrant aid societies. Communists were also heavily involved in theater organizations and literary clubs. Allied groups, including housing cooperatives, summer camps, health clinics, and publishing houses, each separately incorporated and only nominally connected with the party, were part of the communist network and subculture. The party participated in electoral politics and two of its public members were elected to the City Council, Peter Cacchione of Brooklyn and Benjamin Davis from Harlem. Congressman Vito Marcantonio from East Harlem, though not a party member, ran on the American Labor Party ticket, received the strong support of Communist Party activists. He served from 1935-1937 and from 1939-1951, losing only when an opponent was endorsed by the Democratic, Republican, and Liberal Parties.

Communists were devoted to their cause and many of their actions were aimed at helping the poor at a time when most New Yorkers were poor. They could attract news stories and turn out big crowds at demonstrations. The largest demonstration, just months after the Stock Market Crash, drew an estimated 100,000 people to Union Square on March 6, 1930 to protest unemployment, hunger, and evictions, and demand government-sponsored jobs, food, and housing. At the time about ninety percent of the wealth in the United States was owned by fourteen percent of the population and many Americans thought some income and power redistribution was needed.

There were probably never more than 80,000 members of the Communist Party nation-wide, though almost half lived in New York City. But the Depression, Civil War in Spain, Second World

War, and Civil Rights Movement gave them many objective opportunities to magnify their impact on public policy. The fanatical opposition by the FBI, House Un-American Activities Committee, New York Roman Catholic Archdiocese led by Francis Cardinal Spellman, industrialists, and various right-wing organizations, especially during the Cold War, often over-estimated their influence on American politics.

Internally, many members grew disillusioned after the executions of Julius and Ethel Rosenberg in 1951, the anti-Stalin speech made by Soviet premier Nikita Khrushchev in 1956, and the Hungarian Uprising against the Soviet occupation the same year. The anti-authoritarian New Left stole much of the thunder from the weakened party in the 1960s and 1970s. By the collapse of the Soviet Union in 1991 there was little left of the Communist Party, USA.

There were many independent New York City leftists, usually intellectuals, who belonged to no political party, or changed parties often. Many lived in Greenwich Village or the northern part of the Lower East Side now called the East Village.

John Reed, who bounced from one leftist point of view to another, can best be described as an independent radical war correspondent; he wrote *Insurgent Mexico* (1914) and *The War in Eastern Europe* (1916). Louise Bryant, a journalist and independent leftist, married Reed and traveled with him to Russia during the 1917 Revolution. While in Russia, Bryant wrote *Six Months in Russia* (1918) and Reed composed *Ten Days That Shook the World* (1919). Reed died in Russia of typhus in 1920 and his cremated remains were interred in the Kremlin wall behind Lenin's tomb in Moscow. Bryant took many unorthodox positions, some from socialism and others from anarchism. *Reds*, a 1981 film starring Diane Keaton as Bryant, Warren Beatty as Reed, was based on their lives together. Others in their Greenwich Village circle included Sherwood Anderson and Eugene O'Neill.

Max Eastman, editor of *The Masses*, an independent leftist literary journal, visited the Soviet Union for a full year in 1923 and upon his return gravitated to the side of Leon Trotsky and the Trotskyist group, the Socialist Workers Party. By the Second World War Eastman was so alienated by Stalinism that he turned his back on the left and took a position as editor of the *Reader's Digest*, a right-wing popular magazine.

For the entire 20th century radical political groups played a vociferous role in New York City politics that was disproportionate to their numbers. They were instrumental in guiding many labor organizations and promoting leftist agendas. Some of the groups such as the Communist Party, Socialist Party, Socialist Workers Party, and Socialist Labor Party still exist in the 21st century, though as mere vestiges of what they once were. Many of their ideas have entered the agendas of other political and civic organizations including the Working Families Party, Green Party and other environmental groups, Metropolitan Council on Housing, Center for Constitutional Rights, National Lawyers Guild, Legal Aid Society, Amnesty International, and Coalition for Human Rights.

CHAPTER 104
Tammany Hall and Al Smith

By the Civil War, Irish immigrants were active in all aspects of city politics. They tended to favor Tammany Hall and soon dominated it. The birthplace of New York City Irish politics was the neighborhood along the East River between Fulton and Canal Streets stretching west to City Hall and Centre Street. In contemporary New York it would include the area around the South Street Seaport, the blocks between the Brooklyn and Manhattan Bridges, Chinatown, and the southern portion of the Lower East Side. Irish politics became inextricably linked to Tammany Hall.

By 1914 there were 50,000 public employees in New York City and almost all owed their jobs to Tammany. Many of them lived in crowded Irish neighborhoods where *ward-healers* and *precinct captains* provided aid in return for votes. The pinnacle of Tammany influence and fame, when it almost achieved respectability, came in the years surrounding the governorship of Alfred E. Smith, 1918 to 1920 and 1922 to 1924, and during his candidacy for president of the United States in 1928.

Al Smith, closely associated with Tammany, grew up in Five Points and spent most of his life on South, Madison, and Oliver Streets. Born in 1873, he grew up playing near the construction yards of the Brooklyn Bridge, which was completed when he was ten. He attended St. James Roman Catholic School but left before finishing the 8th grade to help his immigrant parents make ends meet. Smith was a man of New York City's neighborhoods and he knew them well. He was much less familiar with the rest of the state, except Albany, and his narrow local experience was a shortcoming when he became a national candidate.

Smith represented the progressive wing of Tammany Hall and advocated in the State Legislature for rent regulation, workers' compensation, public housing, and more effective building and fire codes. Though never a *sachem* of the powerful political organization, he symbolized it and frequently served as Tammany's spokesman. Smith sympathized with workers and as a State Assemblyman served as vice chairman of the New York State Factory Investigating Commission following the Triangle Fire. He represented southern Manhattan in the State Assembly from 1904 to 1915. He was elected, in turn, sheriff of New York County, president of the Board of Aldermen, and governor. In 1924 Governor Smith appointed Robert Moses president of the State Parks Council and the Long Island State Park Commission. The governor viewed the Moses appointment as a progressive act that would bring New Yorkers parks, beaches, swimming pools, slum clearance, public housing, bridges, parkways, highways, and tunnels. Moses remained a powerful and popular figure in New York until his methods and vision began to be questioned in the 1960s.

In 1928 Smith became the first Roman Catholic nominated by either party for president. His running mate was Joe T. Robinson, a Protestant from Arkansas. In November the Republican team of Herbert Hoover and Charles Curtis defeated the Smith-Robinson ticket. Hoover received 22,391,000 popular votes to Smith's 15,016,000, and 444 electoral votes to 87. The Democrats won only six states in their formerly Solid South plus heavily Catholic Massachusetts and Rhode Island. (Norman Thomas, the Socialist candidate, received 267,000 votes.) Republicans charged that Smith stood for *Rome, Rum, and Rebellion* referring to his religion, opposition to Prohibition, and the support of the Southern wing of the Democratic Party, men whose ancestors had supported the Confederacy. Republicans had used the same slogan without success in the 1884 election between Grover Cleveland and James G. Blaine.

As the first Roman Catholic presidential candidate, *The Happy Warrior*, a nickname affectionately used by his supporters, endured bigotry and hostility in many states during the campaign, and though he lost the presidency, he gained a special place in the hearts of American Catholics. Eleanor Roosevelt recalled: *Governor Smith was a Roman Catholic, and the kind of propaganda that some of the religious groups, aided and abetted by the opposition, put forth in that campaign utterly disgusted me.* It was not until the election of John F. Kennedy in 1960 that a Catholic was able to win a presidential election in the United States.

A devout Catholic with conservative social habits, Smith dedicated himself mostly to private and Catholic charitable projects following his defeat. In 1929, however, he accepted the presidency of the Empire State Building Corporation, which built the world's tallest skyscraper. Contracts were signed in September 1929, and though the Stock Market Crashed that fall, the Empire State Building was completed on schedule in 1931.

Eleanor Roosevelt, who knew Al Smith well, commented on his proletarian elitism (inverted snobbery), as she felt it was sometimes directed at her husband. *There are two kinds of snobbishness. One is that of the man who has had a good many opportunities and looks down on those who lack them. The other kind is rarely understood, that of the self-made man who glories in his success in overcoming difficulties and admires greatly people who have achieved the things he considers of importance. Governor Smith had a great deal of respect for material success, but tended to look down upon a man like Franklin who was content not to make a great deal of money so long as he had enough to live comfortably.* Alfred E. Smith attempted unsuccessfully to get the Democratic Party to nominate him for a second try at the presidency in 1932. Instead the delegates chose another New York governor, Franklin Delano Roosevelt from Hyde Park. Embittered by his defeat and increasingly conservative, he twice supported Republican opponents against Franklin Delano Roosevelt. Smith died in 1944. The Governor Alfred E. Smith Houses, built on the site of his birth, were named for him.

Some anti-Tammany voices claimed that Smith simply put a veneer of respectability on the Democratic machine. Norman Thomas, who had run against Smith in 1928, wrote: *Of late years, particularly while Al Smith was running for president, an effort has been made to throw a cloak of gentility about the early activities of Tammany. An egregious paper-bound history of the society has been put out which omits or distorts everything that a history should tell. The truth is that Tammany always has been a center of corruption and it has never reformed. It has on occasion modified its methods in the face of public indignation but as soon as the public indignation has cooled down it has gone as far as the law would permit.* Thomas charged police, judicial, zoning, building, and electoral corruption in his 1932 book entitled: *What's The Matter With New York?* Thomas excoriated

Tammany for corrupting the judiciary through bribes and the sale of judgeships. *Tammany has profoundly shocked even hard-boiled New York by creating a court system that has gone beyond all the limits of ordinary political manipulation.*

William M. Tweed and Alfred E. Smith, the two most famous Tammany Hall politicians, were very different. Few Tammany men resembled Smith. Well-known leaders of the club, Mayor Fernando Wood (who predated Tweed), John Kelly, Richard Croker, Charles Francis Murphy, John F. Curry, and Carmine De Sapio, were more analogous to Tweed. They were contemptibly dishonest and brashly manipulated the city's finances to enrich themselves and their cronies.

There were hundreds of prominent New Yorkers from a variety of political perspectives who stood up to Tammany, but usually lacked the votes to make a lasting difference. Beginning in 1892, the Rev. Dr. Charles H. Parkhurst, pastor of the Madison Square Presbyterian Church, spoke resolutely from his pulpit against police corruption. Parkhurst, a leader of the Social Gospel Movement among Protestants, believed that the Tammany-controlled police department protected criminals who preyed on the public. He also called on the city government to improve the quality of public schools, enforce health laws, provide adequate public bathing facilities, improve garbage collection and street cleaning, and modernize mass transit.

As president of the Society for the Prevention of Crime, Parkhurst led a crusade against police misconduct which helped lead to the election in 1894 of William L. Strong, a reform mayor, and the subsequent appointment the following year of crime-busting Theodore Roosevelt as chairman of the Police Board. Parkhurst supported the consolidation of the five counties into New York City in 1898 as a means of diluting the Manhattan-based power of Tammany Hall.

Parkhurst and his followers, while genuinely committed to the economic and social reforms, which characterized the Social Gospel Movement, were also obsessed with their view of public morality, including support for Prohibition, a stand that alienated them from many New Yorkers. Parkhurst often railed against prostitution and its protectors in the police department controlled by Tammany. Referring to the 11th precinct he wrote: *I know the larger number of disorderly houses that are located there, and their street addresses, and the number of vile women that ply their trade in each, and the confidence that these women have that they will not be interfered with by the Captain or his subordinates or superiors, if they continue to maintain their own part of the contract with the powers that be.* In 1894 Parkhurst urged his congregation to go to the polls and vote for William L. Strong, the Republican candidate. *In other words, avoid it as you like, and wince under it as you please, the election in this city next Tuesday will practically be nothing more nor less than a public vote on the Ten Commandments.* Strong defeated Hugh J. Grant, the Tammany Democrat, 154,000 to 109,000.

Judge Samuel Seabury, more than anyone else, succeeded in uncovering some of Tammany's dirty little secrets. From 1930 through 1933 he led three separate investigations into corrupt Tammany practices. Seabury, a gifted attorney and former judge, was asked by the Appellate Division of the New York State Supreme Court to investigate dishonest operations in the city's judiciary. President Franklin D. Roosevelt requested that Seabury look into corruption in the Manhattan District Attorney's office, and the New York State Legislature prevailed on Seabury to serve as chief counsel for a joint committee investigating criminal behavior in the city's government. In each case Seabury discovered evidence of wrongdoing, especially in the court system where he found cases where judgeships were bought, judges were bribed, evidence was doctored, court records altered, and relevant testimony suppressed. One result of years of headline news was the resignation of popular but corrupt Tammany-backed Mayor James J. Walker in 1932.

Tammany Hall spiraled in a downward trajectory after the Alfred E. Smith presidential race and the withering attacks by Judge Seabury's investigations. In the 1930s and 40s Tammany was weakened and lost any luster it had gained from Smith. Once again its leaders excelled only in placing personal power and graft above any semblance of community service. Carmine De Sapio, the first Italian-American to head Tammany Hall, breathed new life in the organization when he assumed leadership in 1949.

De Sapio, a life-long resident of Greenwich Village, understood that times were changing and he responded by running Tammany more openly. He supported several liberal Democrats, including Robert F. Wagner for mayor and Averell Harriman for governor. Even Adlai Stevenson, a liberal Democrat, who was his party's candidate for president in 1952 and 1956, welcomed De Sapio's support. *If I were to seek the Democratic nomination in 1956,* said Stevenson in 1955, *I would welcome the support of Carmine De Sapio and Tammany Hall.*

De Sapio placed blacks and Hispanics in district leader posts and generally supported Civil Rights legislation. None of that mattered to the Reformers. A formidable coalition of Reform Democrats arrayed themselves against Tammany and De Sapio in the 1960s. Reform clubs were started in neighborhoods throughout the city including in De Sapio's own backyard, Greenwich Village. The contentious Village Independent Democrats spearheaded the anti-Tammany struggle in De Sapio's district. Reformers were energized by the Civil Rights Movements and by Adlai Stevenson's two presidential campaigns. Later they would draw strength from the mass movement against the Vietnam War. On the top level, De Sapio's opponents were national figures: Eleanor Roosevelt, former Governor Herbert Lehman, and, despite his 1955 statement, Adlai Stevenson.

De Sapio, whose dark-tinted eyeglasses made him appear sinister, was an eloquent speaker and brilliant political strategist. (He wore the dark glasses because he suffered from ocular rheumatism.)

The Village Independent Democrats endorsed James E. Lanigan to run against Carmine De Sapio for Democratic district leader in 1961. They neighborhood had changed faster than De Sapio had, and newcomers outnumbered his traditional supporters, especially in the shrinking Italian-American community. Lanigan defeated De Sapio 6,165 to 4,245. In 1963 De Sapio attempted a come back but was narrowly defeated by Edward I. Koch 4,656 to 4,615. (Koch was later elected congressman and mayor.) A 1965 re match between Koch and De Sapio resulted in a second victory for the Reform Democrats. The vote was Koch, 5,895 and De Sapio, 5,282. Carmine De Sapio was convicted of bribery in 1969 and, after appeals, entered Lewisburg Federal Penitentiary in Pennsylvania for a two-year term.

There were objective historical reasons for the decline of Tammany that had nothing to do with corruption. They were factors that led to the disappearance of political machines in other American cities as well. The rise of labor unions and the activism of government, especially after F.D.R.'s New Deal policies, garnered higher wages, benefits, and better working conditions for many people. Government welfare programs aided the poor. Immigration, an important source of Tammany's strength, was effectively choked off from 1914 to 1965. And the political message was more likely delivered by radio and television than by a ward captain knocking on each door in the district. In short, the *need* for Tammany Hall declined at the same time it was attacked for its brazen corruption.

Notations:

Tammany's Several Headquarters

In its early years Tammany's meetings were held in several rented buildings east of City Hall. In 1868, under the leadership of Boss Tweed, Tammany built a lavish *wigwam* east of Union Square. The three-story building was located on the north side of the street in the middle of the block of East 14th Street between Irving Place and 3rd Avenue. Inside were meeting rooms and a large hall grand enough to host the 1868 Democratic National Convention that nominated Horatio Seymour to challenge Ulysses S. Grant. The clubhouse façade was noted for its decorative eaves and high entablature holding a statue of Chief Tammany. When it was demolished the site became the headquarters for Consolidated Edison.

In 1928, at the height of Al Smith's career and Tammany's prestige, the organization built a new clubhouse, a Federal Style building on Union Square at the corner of Park Avenue South and East 17th Street. Fifteen years later the club was unable to pay the mortgage and Tammany leaders sold the three-story brick and limestone building to Local 91 of the International Ladies' Garment Workers Union. Presently it houses the New York Film Academy and the Union Square Theater. On the 17th Street side of the building carved stone medallions of Christopher Columbus and

Chief Tammany (no longer *St. Tammany*) flank sandblasted lettering reading: *The Society of Tammany Or Columbian Order.* Dates on either side of the inscription read *1786*, the founding, and *1928*, when the headquarters was built.

Grave of Alfred E. Smith in Calvary Cemetery, Queens

One hundred feet southeast of the Chapel of St. Callixtus and three rows into Section 45 finds a simple low granite marker reading: *Alfred E. Smith, Governor of New York, Born December 30, 1873, Died October 4, 1944.* This is the gravesite of New York State Governor and 1928 Democratic presidential nominee Alfred E. Smith.

The nearby Chapel of St. Callixtus is well known to drivers on the Brooklyn-Queens Expressway. From the highway it appears as a bright white shrine set on a knoll in the midst of a patch of greenery in an undulated field of white and gray tombstones. From ground level its central elongated beehive tower looms majestically upward. The chapel was patterned after the Church of Sacré Coeur in Montematre, Paris. Its elongated, white, tile-covered dome rests on colonnettes rising over a red tile roof and is crowned by a life-size statue of the Sacred Heart of Jesus. The architecture is modified Romanesque Revival, particularly recognizable in the rounded triple set back arched entrance topped with a scene of Jesus surrounded by saints. The archway is inscribed with words from the Bible: *I Am The Resurrection And The Life.* The chapel's interior resembles a crypt with its vaulted ceiling and preponderance of marble and granite.

CHAPTER 105
Harlem Renaissance

Harlem exploded with artistic talent in the 1920s. Half the black population left the South in the two decades on either side of the First World War. Many, especially from Virginia and the Carolinas, moved to New York City where they joined an already established American black community, including new immigrants from the Caribbean. The 1920s is known as the *Harlem Renaissance.*

What was Harlem's background? Dutch Governor Peter Stuyvesant established Nieuw Haarlem in 1658. Its center would have been about 1st Avenue and East 125th Street near the Manhattan foot of today's Willis Avenue Bridge. It remained a very small farming village until late in the 19th century. Nearby along the East River an industrial center grew: tanneries, brickworks, and breweries. Increasingly, German, Irish, and Italian immigrants moved to the area to take low paying jobs in factories.

But the exponential leap in population came toward the end of the 19th century as improved transportation made the area attractive to real estate developers. Railroads were key. In 1837 the first railroad was constructed on Manhattan's Upper East Side along Park Avenue and in 1879 railroads from Downtown Manhattan were built through Harlem on 2nd and 3rd Avenues. The IRT subway (#2 and 3 trains) was extended along Lenox Avenue (6th Avenue) in 1908. Trains ran regularly around the clock and commuting became feasible.

In the 1880s and 1890s developers built upscale apartments and stately brownstone houses along broad Parisian-style boulevards. They were looking for upper middle class buyers and renters who were willing to commute to their jobs in Lower Manhattan. Many came from the southern part of Manhattan and others from Europe. By the First World War approximately 200,000 people lived in the thriving community including about 80,000 German Jews and a smaller settlement of African-Americans.

But at the start of the First World War in 1914 immigration

from Europe slowed to a trickle. To prevent immigration from resuming after the war Congress passed the *Johnson Act*, also known as the *Emergency Quota Act of 1921*, and the *National Origins Act of 1924*. They brought down yearly immigration to the United States from over one million before the war to 150,000 per year. New housing in Harlem went unsold and apartments went vacant.

At the same time the Great Migration of blacks from the rural South to northern cities was taking place. Much of the black migration to New York City came from the Carolinas and Virginia. In the mid 1920s there were 80,000 blacks living in Harlem. By the 1930s the black population topped 200,000. Harlem became the largest concentration of African-Americans in any American city and was quickly catapulted to national prominence. It became the focal point of black politics and cultural achievement, and residence for many black politicians, writers, artists, and musicians.

Adventurous whites in search of new forms of entertainment or novelty visited Harlem regularly. The idea of *prestige from below* was powerful among some avant-garde whites. They filled many of Harlem's clubs from the 1920s through the 1950s. But other white residents continued to move out of Harlem as blacks moved in, a situation which transformed many institutions, especially places of entertainment, churches, and synagogues.

Three decades before Harlem hit its lowest point in the 1960s and 1970s, a time when crime and drugs ravaged the area and depopulation resulted, the Harlem Renaissance occurred and the neighborhood became the cultural and political capital of Black America. Even as concentrations of blacks developed after the Second World War in Brooklyn, Chicago, Detroit, St. Louis, Memphis, Los Angeles, Cleveland, Baltimore, Philadelphia, Boston, Atlanta, and Washington, D.C., Harlem remained for some time the symbolic capital of Black America. It earned its preeminence by cultural achievements and by being a large settlement located in New York City. Long after the Harlem Renaissance ran its course many influential black opinion leaders and cultural innovators still gravitated to Harlem. Exploitation and neglect in the 60s and 70s failed to destroy the spirit of the neighborhood, and it remains a strong cultural icon of the national African-America community. Today Harlem is again on the way up as a desired place to live though gentrification has dulled its edge and much of the black middle class that had patronized the arts has dispersed and been replaced by whites.

The Harlem Renaissance was a literary and artistic movement that centered in a single American neighborhood. Participants were a cultural vanguard of a people striving to define themselves as a community. Questions about the shared African background, the effect of slavery, relations with whites, and the role of the black church were central literary and artistic themes that were vigorously debated through the arts and in political circles.

Most rejected the Back to Africa Movement supported by Marcus Garvey's Universal Negro Improvement Association, but most could understand it. Many supported the goal of the National Association for the Advancement of Colored People (NAACP) to integrate with white society, though in the 1920s that looked unlikely. Most agreed with writers Claude McKay and Alain Locke that further development of an intellectual black consciousness was needed. In 1925 Locke discussed his ideas in *Harlem: Mecca of the New Negro* and *The New Negro: An Interpretation*. He often looked to Africa for aesthetic guidance.

Important voices in the Harlem Renaissance included noted poets Countee Cullen, Claude McKay, and Langston Hughes. Cultural creativity and politics were often combined in single polymath personalities. Countee Cullen, poet, novelist, and teacher, examined the struggles of blacks in their urban neighborhood subculture. The respected research facility, the Countee Cullen Branch of the New York Public Library at 104 West 136th Street near Malcolm X Boulevard (Lenox Avenue), honors him.

Claude McKay's book of poetry *Harlem Shadows* (1922) was one of the first books published during the Harlem Renaissance. He wrote three novels including *Home to Harlem* (1928), and later wrote two autobiographies. It was the sonnet, *If We Must Die* (1918), McKay's first published work, that first drew literary attention to his ideas.

If we must die, let it not be like hogs
Hunted and penned in an inglorious spot,
While round us bark the mad and hungry dogs,
Making their mock at our accursed lot.

If we must die, O let us nobly die,
So that our precious blood may not be shed
In vain; then even the monsters we defy
Shall be constrained to honor us though dead!
O kinsmen! we must meet the common foe!
Though far outnumbered let us show us brave,
And for their thousand blows deal one deathblow!
What though before us lies the open grave?
Like men well face the murderous, cowardly pack
Pressed to the wall, dying, but fighting back!

Poet, novelist, columnist, and playwright Langston Hughes raised political consciousness by focusing on the lives of everyday characters with problems and aspirations common to many African-Americans. His voice spanned the middle of the 20th century from the Harlem Renaissance to the Civil Rights Movement. In the 1930s Hughes traveled the country, especially the South, giving poetry readings in poor communities. He visited the Scottsboro Boys imprisoned in Alabama. He spent a year working in the Soviet Union and espoused many causes backed by the Communist Party including racial equality and equal pay for equal work. In a powerful and memorable poem written long after the Harlem Renaissance, *A Dream Deferred* (1951), Langston Hughes asked:

What happens to a dream deferred?
Does it dry up
like a raisin in the sun?
Or fester like a sore--
And then run?
Does it stink like rotten meat?
Or crust and sugar over--
like a syrupy sweet?

Maybe it just sags
like a heavy load.

Or does it explode?

In the 1920s the United States was a rigidly segregated country, by law in the South and by convention in the North. The arts, however, were difficult for a segregated society to suppress or ignore. Artistic innovation and excellence came through, and Harlem burst forth with creativity. As it did, its fame became a magnet pulling black artists from around the United States to the northern part of Manhattan.

Aaron Douglas and William H. Johnson led the way in the visual arts. Douglas illustrated books, painted canvases and murals, and illustrated books often using broad bands of color and geometric shapes. Through color, design, and subject matter, Douglas tried to promote African-American spiritual identity. William H. Johnson grew up in South Carolina, traveled and studied in Europe and North Africa, and settled in Harlem. Each place influenced his work. Always colorful, many of his paintings combine van Gogh brushstrokes with a primitive style. Johnson focused on scenes of people in Harlem or the American South going about everyday tasks.

Duke Ellington, Bessie Smith, Count Basie, Louis Armstrong, Ella Fitzgerald, Billie Holiday, Nat King Cole, Fletcher Henderson and many others made music in venues like the Cotton Club and the Apollo Theater. In the 1920s and 1930s the Cotton Club and Apollo Theater were segregated and black performers played and sang for white audiences. It was in the 1920s that jazz was popularized.

Jazz, the undisciplined, vibrant, colorful music of blacks dominated by the saxophone and trumpet, led the way and gave the era one of its most legendary names, *the Jazz Age*. Countercultural because it was black, its soulful notes and spontaneity screamed out to be heard. The story it told had no lyrics, but it set a personal, introspective mood. From the jazz center of New Orleans it migrated up through the Mississippi Delta to clubs in the South Side of Chicago and Harlem. It was exotic because it flouted traditional and classical rules for music; many of the performers could not even read music. It was an ebullient product of the underclass.

There was an explosion of new musical forms in the 1920s as black and white counter-cultural music came to the fore. The general rise of popular folk culture set the tone for the period. Country-Western, bluegrass, and the blues all gravitated north. They gained prominence throughout the United States on the radio. Country-Western music, with its sad lyrics about drifters, love gone awry, and other tragedies was folk music of poor whites. The fast, plucky banjo, guitar, and mandolin sounds of bluegrass reflected the poor white mountain culture of Appalachia.

The blues, like jazz, is a popular black form of expression. It came from the Mississippi Delta, the poorest part of the United States and describes economic oppression, hardscrabble sharecropping lives, racism, prison, and violent personal relationships. Langston Hughes tried to explain it: *I know very little to tell you about the blues. They always impressed me as very sad, sadder even than the spirituals because their sadness is not softened with tears but hardened with laughter, the absurd.*

Photographer James VanDerZee documented Harlem life for six decades. His 75,000 black-and-white prints chronicled cultural icons, political and religious leaders, and street scenes of everyday life showing people shopping, working, praying, and sitting on stoops. (Since the 1980s Alix Dejean has been amassing photographs with similar themes in contemporary Harlem.)

John Henry Hammond II arrived on the scene a few years after the Harlem Renaissance and recorded many musical luminaries of the next generation. He was instrumental in furthering the musical careers of Charlie Christian, Billie Holiday, Count Basie, Teddy Wilson, and Big Joe Turner by taking their music to recording companies and radio stations. It was difficult for black performers to get booked by radio stations and large public spaces. Some foundations, like the Harmon Foundation of William Elmer Harmon, were interested in popularizing and cataloging the Harlem Renaissance and subsequent neighborhood artists. They recorded artists, published books, and sponsored art exhibits.

Arthur Schomburg (Arturo Alfonso Schomburg), an immigrant from Puerto Rico, was a noted educator with a special interest in Afro Latin culture. He amassed an enormous collection of art, sculpture, unpublished manuscripts, articles, books, slave narratives and other documents of black history and culture. The NYPL's Schomburg Center for Research in Black Culture, the repository of his vast collection, is named for him.

Only one cultural institution from early Harlem remains, though it did not become a black venue until just after the end of the Harlem Renaissance. From 1914 until 1934, the Apollo Theater had featured burlesque and played to a whites-only audience. New owners opened its 1,500-seat auditorium with a program featuring black musicians, dancers, and comedians entertaining mixed audiences. Over the years, Billie Holiday, Bessie Smith, Louis Armstrong, Duke Ellington, Charlie Parker, and Dizzy Gillespie were featured on stage. The Wednesday night Amateur Hour still draws large crowds.

CHAPTER 106
Passenger Liners

The first ships that can be called *passenger liners* were the *packet ships* that began to sail across the Atlantic between New York City and European ports in 1838. Packet ships were passenger craft with scheduled times of arrival and departure. Prior to the publicly posted service of packet ships, travelers had to go directly to the piers to find a ship heading in their direction. Sleek four-masted *clipper ships* operated only from 1843 until 1860. Steamships replaced the clippers. Passenger vessels used many of the one hundred docks that jutted into the Hudson and East Rivers. At least one trans-Atlantic departure each day occurred between 1900 and 1950. New York City was the most active port in the world during the first half of the twentieth century.

Sailing vessels, originally built of wood, were upgraded to cast-iron, and then re-enforced steel. Their source of power evolved from wind to steam-power (produced by coal or oil), and finally to diesel-powered electric engines. From small ships they graduated to truly immense size. Large ocean liners served the busy trans-Atlantic routes between New York City and European ports: London, Le Havre (for Paris), Marseilles, Genoa, Naples, Hamburg, Bremen, Danzig (now Gdansk), and Rotterdam.

The New York dockside scene, especially along the Hudson River, was bustling with passenger line employees and travelers. A voyage often attracted a crowd of relatives and friends to either wish travelers *bon voyage* or to welcome them home. The piers of the United States Line, France Line, Italian Line, North German Lloyd line, and the Cunard Line were the focus of the most coveted vacations. Foreign dignitaries arriving at the piers were often welcomed by a phalanx of reporters, photographers, and people curious about current events.

During the Second World War, the Cunard Line's *Queen Elizabeth* and the *Queen Mary* carried two million Americans to war in Europe. In 1945 and 1946 each ship made several voyages bringing soldiers home to resume their civilian lives.

The Cunard Line symbolized the romantic era of luxury passenger liners crossing the Atlantic between New York and London, or Le Havre. Cunard was an English company, which chose New York as its North American terminal port in 1847. In 1921 the Cunard Line built a spectacular headquarters at 25 Broadway across from Bowling Green. A majestic vaulted ceiling elaborately decorated with maritime themes tops its large Booking Hall. (The Bowling Green Station of the United States Postal Service now occupies the space.) A lavish corporate headquarters gave prestige and elegance to ocean travel from the point of ticket selection. Modern technology has erased the function of the booking hall. The company's office has moved to a midtown office and most customers buy their tickets online or by telephone using their credit cards.

Some of the Cunard Line's ships are still remembered in novels and movies: *Britannia, Mauritania, Lusitania, Queen Mary, Queen Elizabeth,* and *Queen Elizabeth II.* The *QE2* still operates and makes several trans-Atlantic crossings in the summer and cruises the Caribbean in the winter. The Queen Mary II joined the QE2 in 2004. With few visits from passenger liners, local cruise ships and dinner party vessels offer a weak reminder of the days when the Cunard Line symbolized refined and relaxed travel.

Cunard ships were not always comfortable and luxurious. First Lady Eleanor Roosevelt wrote about her 1902 trip to London. *In the little Cunard ships of those days (I think we were on the Umbria), a rough crossing meant that the steamer chairs, if they were out at all, were lashed to the railing. There were racks on the table, and when you tried to walk you felt you were walking up a mountain or down one.*

The *QE2* still operates and makes several trans-Atlantic crossings in the summer, cruises the Caribbean in the winter, and makes an occasional round-the-world tour. The Queen Mary II joined the QE2 in 2004. Passenger ships abandoned Manhattan in 2006. The only docks now servicing trans-Atlantic passenger liners are at the Atlantic Basin Piers in Red Hook, Brooklyn. With few visits from trans-oceanic passenger liners, Caribbean-bound cruise ships, local cruise ships, and dinner party vessels offer an appreciated but very weak reminder of the days when the Cunard Line symbolized refined and relaxed travel.

Princess Cruises operates several ships that specialize in Caribbean and East Coast cruises and occasionally schedule transoceanic trips to North Sea or Mediterranean ports. One popular northern route passes the coasts of Iceland, Greenland, Labrador, Newfoundland, and New Brunswick.

In recent years there has been an increase in cruises cut short by viruses sweeping through the passengers and crew. The so-called *Norwalk virus*, a gastro-intestinal bug, which generally lasts from 24 to 48 hours, is not dangerous but it is decidedly uncomfortable. The U.S. Centers for Disease Control and Prevention have guidelines that include a thorough cleanup of any affected ship before it goes out on another journey.

Accommodations are differentiated by class with the largest ships offering the most opulent suites and staterooms, dining facilities, recreation, and entertainment. The Cunard Line's *Queen Mary II* is a *city at sea* and offers a wide variety of accommodations and activities. Each liner has a variety of rooms, though staterooms predominate. The largest suites on the *Queen Mary II* measure 2,249 square feet. The smallest staterooms are a snug 194-square feet.

Room class determines dining facilities. The meals, which include items from various cuisines, are sometimes prepared under the direction of celebrity chefs, though all cooking is done on a large, institutional scale.

Dining attire is ranked *formal, informal*, or *casual*, depending on the dining room. Formal is defined as *tuxedo (alternatively a dark suit) for men, evening gown or other formal attire for women.* Informal is *jacket and tie for men, cocktail dress, dressy pantsuit or similar for women.* Casual is delimited as *slacks and a sweater or shirt for men, skirt or slacks with a sweater or blouse for women.* Bathing attire, shorts, or jeans are unacceptable dress for dinner.

To help wile away the hours on a long trip there are numerous recreation and entertainment possibilities. Recreational facilities include indoor and outdoor pools, paddle tennis, fitness center, jogging track, gymnasium, golf putting green, and platforms for hitting golf balls into the ocean. Aerobics classes and tai-qi quan instruction is provided. Entertainment includes ballroom dancing with an orchestra, popular theater, and movies. Other amenities include a *Purser's Office* (banking center), spa, afternoon tea, cigar lounge, library, book store, gambling casino, nightclub, wine bar, several pubs, gift shops, clothing stores, and video arcade.

Luxury liners are expensive. Rooms on higher decks cost more money than lower deck accommodations. Still lower in price on the *Queen Mary II* are inside rooms without windows. The price for a 110-day world cruise double-occupancy grand suite on the *QE2* is $375,000, though less commodious suites range from $209,000 to $107,000. The price for a 6-day Southampton (England) to New York trip in a high-end room ranges from $27,500 for a grand duplex to $5,900 for a junior suite, and from $3,200 for a standard ocean view to $1,900 for a standard inside room.

What happened to the popularity of trans-Atlantic passenger travel? Speed and frugality trumped elegance in cross-oceanic travel as business people and middle class tourists replaced the rich as the most numerous travelers to Europe. A two-week vacation to Europe is not possible if ten days are spent on a ship. Airplanes cost a fraction of the price (between $800 and $1,400) and reach Europe within a few hours: five to Dublin, six to London, seven to Paris, eight to Rome, and nine to St. Petersburg. New York City's passenger liners now exist on a very limited scale.

CHAPTER 107
The Bronx Zoo, New York Botanical Gardens, and the Bronx River

The Bronx Zoo and the New York Botanical Gardens, adjacent public spaces, have preserved a long stretch of the Bronx River, the largest free-flowing river within the five boroughs. The two outdoor cultural sites are important in and of themselves, and they also give a sense of what the Bronx River looked like before massive urban development.

The Bronx Zoo-Wildlife Conservation Park, originally established as the New York Zoological Park by the state-chartered New York Zoological Society in 1895, opened four years later on a 262-acre wooded site along the Bronx River. William Hornaday was the first director and presided over the construction of the initial buildings from 1899 to 1908: the Aquatic Bird House, Reptile House, Primate House, Lion House, Large Bird House, and Elephant House. In 1916 it became the first American zoo to open an animal hospital. The Bronx Zoo quickly became a favorite New York City recreational destination for children and many adults. By 2001, the number of visitors reached 2.2 million each year.

Under the leadership of William Conway, appointed director in 1966, the Bronx Zoo emphasized constructing naturalistic settings for the animals instead of confining them to cages, and became a breeding center for endangered species. The zoo has approximately 6,000 animals representing 600 species, and more than 1,000 live births occur there each year.

The Bronx Zoo is an intriguing place to visit and the zoo's carefully drawn maps and well-marked walkways make it easy to get around to exhibits of interest. Among the chief attractions are the Mouse House, World of Reptiles, Butterfly Zone, Monkey House, Congo Gorilla Forest, Birds of Prey, Aquatic Bird House, World of Birds, World of Darkness, Giraffe Building, Baboon Reserve, African Plains, Himalayan Highlands, and Bison Range.

The land occupied by the New York Botanical Garden was once part of the extensive Lorillard Estate. The 661 acres of gently rolling land includes a 250-acre garden component, a 40-acre tract of forest, meadows, a section of the Bronx River, and several buildings.

In 1891 the New York State Legislature created the New York Botanical Garden but sought significant contributions from private sources. Funding came in donations large and small. Among the substantial gifts were grants from Cornelius Vanderbilt, Andrew Carnegie, and J.P. Morgan. A noted botanist at Columbia University, Nathaniel Lord Britton, became the first director and took steps to point the institution toward scientific research as well as creation of a public recreational facility. More than 1,000 worldwide research expeditions have been conducted by the Botanical Garden to gather and study plants. Its library holds a broad collection of books and scientific papers on botany, and the Herbareum preserves six million plant specimens.

The facility sponsors scientific conferences, sponsors research projects, and is visited by 500,000 people yearly who come mostly to enjoy the botanical pulchritude offered by constantly changing displays of plants and flowers. Special events include weekend and summer gardening programs for children, lectures, gardening demonstrations, and concerts.

The words *botanic* and *botanical* are used by the two largest public gardens in New York City: the Brooklyn *Botanic* Garden and the New York *Botanical* Garden. Despite the different configurations of the term *botany*, the words have the same meaning.

The native old-growth forest, which preserves oak, beech, hickory, maple, hemlock, and tulip trees, is the most historically important aspect of the New York Botanical Garden. The trails are well maintained and carefully marked with color-coding. The *Orange Trail* leads through the forest foliage to the Bronx River.

Another important site is the Lorillard Snuff Mill, now a public cafeteria and conference center. The mill has an interesting background beginning with an immigrant French Huguenot tobacconist. Pierre Lorillard, a Manhattan snuff-maker, founded his tobacco business in 1760, by curing, drying, cutting, and packing snuff in containers. Lorillard, a patriot, was killed during the American Revolution, and his sons moved the manufacturing component of the enterprise to the mill on the Bronx River where they used waterpower to mechanize the manufacturing process.

The present three-story granite structure was built in 1840 to replace an earlier wooden mill. For a time, P. Lorillard and Company produced more snuff in the building than was produced anywhere else in the United States. The Lorillard family diversified their holdings and became prominent in banking, shipping, and tanneries. In 1870 the company sold the building, and in 1891 moved out of New York City altogether.

Meandering through both the New York Botanical Garden and the Bronx Zoo, the Bronx River flows south on its way from the uplands in Valhalla, Westchester County, to the East River between Hunt's Point and Clason's Point. The river is twenty-three miles long and travels over Cameron's Line, an ancient geological fault on the North American tectonic plate. New York City has only three freshwater rivers, all in the Bronx, and the Bronx River is by far the largest. (The other two are the Hutchinson River and Westchester Creek.)

While locally significant, it is a modest, shallow river; its southern two miles average only ten feet in depth. The frequently repeated Revolutionary War story about the Bronx River makes light of British understanding of North American topography. Admiral Lord Richard Howe was ordered by the British War Office to sail his fleet up the Bronx River to attack whatever American ships he discovered.

The river has tremendously varying shorelines. As it passes through the Botanical Garden it exposes outcroppings of glacial rock deposited as the Wisconsin Ice Sheet receded 10,000 years ago. Very shallow in spots, it forms a few rapids, and a waterfall at about the midway point of its journey through the Botanical Garden. The river turns into a tidal estuary as its fresh water commingles with the salt water of the East River, which is really an ocean strait.

For three centuries the Bronx River was ecologically degraded as a dump for the industrial waste products of factories, mills, tanneries, slaughterhouses, and breweries. Companies, such as the

Bolton Bleachery, which processed and dyed cloth, and the Bronx Wool and Leather Company, once lined the river's banks. For much of the 20th century riverside communities discharged human waste into the river, and it has been overshadowed and polluted by noise and emissions from the Bronx River Parkway and Sheridan Expressway, which shadow it along much of its course. By the Second World War, the river had essentially died and become an open sewer.

Most of those problems have been corrected and the Bronx River is coming back to life as a cherished community resource. River *aficionados* have formed several organizations to protect it and lobby for government support in cleaning up its banks and removing snags and blockages. Industrial and human waste is no longer spoiling the water and considerable wildlife has returned. Once again there are painted turtles, frogs, brown trout, largemouth bass, pickerel, carp, and American eels living in the Bronx River. Ecological and civic-minded groups have promoted community stewardship, creation of riverside pedestrian walkways, and canoe and kayak recreation. The Bronx River Restoration Project, Bronx River Alliance, Parks Department Urban Rangers, and the New York Botanical Garden are involved in these activities and sponsor public programs.

CHAPTER 108
Fiorello La Guardia

Fiorello La Guardia was arguably the best-loved mayor in the city's history. He served three four-year terms between 1934 and 1945. New Yorkers remember him for his courage and determination in leading them through difficult times. His tenure as mayor took place during the same years Franklin D. Roosevelt was president, the years of the Great Depression and the Second World War. He was a colorful figure who seemed to be everywhere, constantly waded into crowds and mingling with people. La Guardia visited street festivals, strolled on the beach, went to baseball games, attended funerals of city employees, and raced to fires to encourage firefighters and comfort victims. He is fondly remembered for reading the syndicated comics over WNYC, at that time the city-owned radio station, during a newspaper strike in 1945. La Guardia was a man of the people, a reformer, and champion of the underdog.

La Guardia himself seemed to represent the ethnic mosaic of the city. His father was a southern Italian from Foggia, in the Naples-dominated Kingdom of Two Sicilies, now in the province of Puglia. He was a non-practicing Roman Catholic. La Guardia's mother was a non-religious Jew, born in Trieste (now Italy) when it was owned by Austria-Hungary. Her family had come from Split, Croatia. Fiorello (*Little Flower*) La Guardia was born at 177 Sullivan Street, an Italian area of Greenwich Village, on December 11, 1882. His father, a bandmaster in the U.S. Army, moved the family out of the city when Fiorello was three years old. They lived in the Dakota Territory, upstate New York, and the Arizona Territory. From his father, Fiorello learned to play the trumpet, cornet, and banjo. In order to *fit in*, his parents enrolled him in an Episcopal Sunday School and he became a life-long Episcopalian. In 1898, when La Guardia was sixteen years old, his family returned to Italy. In 1906 he came back to New York City, worked for the United States Immigration Service on Ellis Island, went to law school, and established a law practice specializing in cases involving immigration and labor. He spoke English, Italian, and Yiddish fluently, and enough German, Hungarian, and Croatian to make himself understood. He was elected to the United States House of Representatives in 1916 and served seven terms in Congress. La Guardia was the first Italian-American to serve in the House. In 1917, while still in Congress, he enlisted in the Army Air Service, during the year the U.S. was involved in the First World War.

Though an archetypal New Yorker, La Guardia grew up in Arizona. *All my boyhood memories are of those Arizona days. To me that is truly God's country --- I love everything about it.* The Arizona he loved was the Arizona Territory, a rough and under-populated frontier that did not become a state until 1912. For most of his life La Guardia's distinguishing symbol of attire was a Stetson hat, perhaps a constant reminder of Arizona.

Not everyone loved La Guardia. He had enemies within the Republican Party, and conservative Democrats, especially Manhattan's Tammany Hall Democrats, detested him. Eleanor Roosevelt, on generally courteous terms with the mayor, nonetheless considered him to be a grand-stander, and less than fully substantive. In her autobiography she related the story of when, while trouble-shooting for her husband during the Second World War, she became critical of La Guardia's performance coordinating civilian defense. *His work as mayor of New York City prevented him from giving full time to organizing civilian defense. The few group meetings we had left me with the impression of great hurry and a feeling that decisions were taken which had not been carefully thought out...The mayor was more interested in the dramatic aspects of civilian defense, such as whether or not cities had good fire-fighting equipment, than in such things as building morale.* Mrs. Roosevelt invited the mayor to her 11th Street apartment in Greenwich Village for *a simple lunch* to discuss the issue. She never revealed the result of their talk but did disclose a humorous anecdote. The First Lady had assured the cook that *the mayor was an easy person to please.* Indeed, the rotund La Guardia loved eating. Mrs. Roosevelt related that La Guardia, on leaving, remarked: *My wife never asks me where I have been nor whom I have seen, but she always asks me what I have had to eat. Today, I can truthfully say I did not have too much!*

As a politician, La Guardia was straight talking and incorruptible. His political ideology was a mixed bag rarely seen in New York City. La Guardia entered politics as a Republican because of his disdain for the boss-controlled Democratic Party. Many silk stocking Republicans did not welcome his participation in their party. He was a Progressive Republican supporting many of the ideas of Senators Robert La Follette, George Norris, and Hiram Johnson, and Congresswoman Jeanette Rankin. As a younger man he had often found himself siding with the reform programs of Presidents Theodore Roosevelt and William Howard Taft. But while the reform impetus for these Progressive Republicans originated from a middle class, small town Protestant experience, La Guardia was an urban activist always concerned with housing accommodations, economic issues, legal rights, and safety conditions for New York's largely immigrant workforce. Furthermore, La Guardia opposed Prohibition, a touchstone issue for many Republicans.

In many ways La Guardia resembled activists on the Left, especially the Socialist Party. In fact, he sometimes ran with the endorsement of the Socialist Party, and in 1924, when the Republicans refused to re-nominate him, he successfully ran for Congress as a Socialist, even though he was not a Socialist. Other times he was a *red-baiter* and attacked the political positions of the Socialist and Communist Parties, often yelling at them to *go to Russia* when they questioned his political positions.

La Guardia broke with most Progressives and Leftists to support American participation in the First World War. He felt strongly enough to enlist in the U.S. Army Air Service and became a combat flyer. After the war, and a venomous and bruising Congressional battle against Scott Nearing, pacifist and Socialist, La Guardia joined the hysteria known as the *Red Scare,* aimed at Socialists, Communists, and Anarchists, especially immigrants. On the national scene the *Red Scare* was led by the U.S. Attorney General A. Mitchell Palmer, a self-styled super-patriot and bigot. It led to a broad attack on civil liberties, and the National Origins Act of 1924, which severely restricted immigration from Southern and Eastern Europe, thought to be hotbeds of Left-wing politics. (Reflecting anti-Asian racism on the West Coast, the National Origins Act banned all immigration from Asia.) La Guardia opposed restricting immigration, though his participation in the *Red Scare* helped cause the anti-immigrant backlash.

One of his chief reforms as a congressman was the Norris-La Guardia Act of 1932, legislation he sponsored to help labor unions by effectively stopping courts from prohibiting strikes or boycotts. Prior to the Norris-La Guardia Act, judges often issued orders prohibiting strikes as *restraint of trade*.

In *The Making of An Insurgent*, La Guardia's brief autobiography dictated as he lay dying in 1947, he recalled with great empathy the plight of immigrants in general, and especially garment workers. He had been deeply moved by the tragic Triangle Shirtwaist Fire in 1911 in which 146 young Jewish and Italian women died.

To humanize the immigration process he co-sponsored Congressional legislation in 1919 which mandated obligatory pre-embarkation physical exams so the humiliation, disappointment, and economic calamity of being rejected at Ellis Island would never again occur. His first-hand experience working at Ellis Island gave him a profound appreciation for the plight of immigrants.

La Guardia was intensely critical of the conditions suffered by garment workers. He denounced recruiting agents in Europe, *padrones*, who, for a large fee, arranged jobs for newcomers, and the deplorable conditions in the sweatshops. In his autobiography he wrote: *Many fortunes were made in this business. And they were made out of exploitation of labor. Ninety-five percent of the needle trades workers on dresses, cloaks and suits were newly arrived immigrants. They had to take whatever wages and working conditions were offered to them. The were crowded into dark, unsanitary workshops, worked ten to twelve hours a day, a 72- to 80- hour week, at shamefully low wages. The work was seasonal. For some fifteen to twenty weeks a year these people were unemployed. They lived in overcrowded, disease-infested old-law tenements that had been condemned years before but were still in existence.*

Fiorello La Guardia was elected mayor of New York City in November 1933. He won as a *fusion* candidate, essentially an independent running on the ballot lines of the City Fusion Party and the Republican Party, but not the Tammany-dominated Democratic Party line. His victory was not overwhelming. La Guardia received 868,522 votes out of 2,205,402. He won a 39.3 percent plurality against Recovery Party candidate Joseph McKee (609,053), Democratic Party standard-bearer John O'Brien (586,672), and Socialist Party candidate Charles Solomon (59,846). He did achieve a majority of the votes in his subsequent elections. In 1937, La Guardia received 58.4 percent running on the City Fusion, Progressive, American Labor, and Republican lines against Jeremiah Mahoney on the Democratic, Trades Union, and Anti-Communist lines. In the election of 1941, La Guardia captured 51.7 percent on the City Fusion, United City, American Labor, and Republican lines against William O'Dwyer on the Democratic line.

As mayor during the bad times of the Great Depression he managed to expand social services, develop new public health programs, keep the schools and libraries open, build hospitals and health clinics, and support Robert Moses's construction programs for new parks, beaches, pools, bridges, highways, and housing. In part, La Guardia supported the Moses agenda because it created jobs for the unemployed. The mayor unified the three separate subway systems (IRT, BMT, IND) and merged them into one city-owned agency. Always a lover of opera, concerts, and dance, La Guardia opened the City Center for Music and Drama where ticket prices were considerably less expensive than private halls, and founded the special High School for Music and Art now called La Guardia High School for Music and Art and the Performing Arts.

La Guardia fought Tammany Hall, the regular organization of the Democratic Party in Manhattan, and struggled against the *rackets*, both labor and mob controlled, which operated throughout the city's fabric. He tried to clean up the New York Police Department and the city's numerous inspection and building permit agencies, which had wallowed in a culture of bribery.

La Guardia made a big show against *vice*. He ordered the confiscation of slot machines and pinball machines, placed them on a barge, personally smashed them with a sledgehammer, and pushed them overboard into the harbor. He ordered garbage men to confiscate pornography from newsstands and truck it to the dump. He instructed the police to raid burlesque shows, houses of prostitution, and gambling dens, and to interfere with numbers running and betting on horse races. La Guardia's investigators pursued crime lords, especially loan sharks.

La Guardia was an energetic proponent of commercial air travel. The New York Municipal Airport, built on a peninsula projecting into the East River north of Jackson Heights, Queens, was sponsored and actively supported by La Guardia. It opened in 1939 and was re-named La Guardia Airport in 1947.

New York City received an official mayoral residence when the mayor accepted the gift of Gracie Mansion, overlooking the East River at East 89th Street and East End Avenue, from the Gracie family. The house, built in 1799, was refurbished at city expense and La Guardia moved into it in 1942.

While never supporting a sweeping slum clearance program, which destroyed entire neighborhoods, La Guardia was angered and embarrassed that some New Yorkers lived in primitive walk-up tenements reminiscent of a Charles Dickens novel. Their buildings often had no ventilation, a community *water closet* in the hallway, and coal cooking stoves. In *The Making of An Insurgent,* La Guardia recounted. *I had the chance thirty years later when I became Mayor to condemn, vacate and demolish some 160 of these very shameful dwelling units. Tuberculosis was particularly prevalent among these underpaid, underfed, badly housed garment workers. Yet, many of them survived and raised splendid families. Some gave their lives that their children might have a better existence than they themselves had ever known.*

Another aspect of crowded urban life that La Guardia disliked was the pushcart. The streets once bustled with pushcarts until he banned all of them in 1938 and drove them into newly constructed city-owned indoor malls. He did it to humanize the difficult lives of pushcart vendors though his opponents pointed out that it was an action enormously pleasing to rent-paying shopkeepers. Most retail markets have closed including the Borough Park Retail Market and the First Avenue Retail Market, though the Arthur Avenue Retail Market, a cavernous Depression era *civic moderne* structure, thrives in Belmont. It was built in 1940 and has preserved some of the older street atmosphere though the stalls are much larger than pushcarts and fully modernized with electricity and running water.

With respect to master builder Robert Moses, La Guardia rode the commissioner's wave of popularity even when he sensed the autocratic developer was violating important democratic principles. La Guardia was never comfortable with Moses's attempts to destroy the old-fashioned New York of ethnic enclaves that La Guardia loved. Moses thrived in an era when the interests of working people were increasingly dismissed as irrelevant. La Guardia owed his elections to Congress and City Hall to the support of poor and working class New Yorkers. The two visions of New York City were incompatible but La Guardia never took on Moses. *Robert Moses has too much power,* La Guardia said at the end of his third term.

La Guardia is difficult to evaluate on race. While in Congress he had been heralded as *a friend of the Negro people* by the *Amsterdam News*. As mayor he had ordered an end to discrimination in some agencies and commissioned a study to investigate poverty in black neighborhoods. Though La Guardia was an aggressive champion of rights for the white worker, he was often quiet when it came to black rights. He either lacked compassion for people in Harlem or was afraid that a forthright stand for their economic and social well-being would hurt him with white voters. There were times when he flirted with populist racism by describing jazz as ***primitive tribal music.***

In 1935 a race riot erupted in Harlem. The cause was the dire economic situation in the black community where at least sixty percent were unemployed, compared to the white community where thirty percent were jobless. Discontent against Harlem shopkeepers simmered because white proprietors did not hire black employees. A *Don't Shop Where You Can't Work* campaign had been going on for months. The riot's precipitant came when a 16-year-old black Puerto Rican was accused of shoplifting a penknife from Kress's dime store on 125th Street. A policeman was summoned and he questioned the youth, but as an angry crowd gathered on the sidewalk the manager declined to press charges and the boy was released out the back door. Rumors swept through the crowd that the youth had been lynched and by night bottles and bricks were flying through the air shattering shop windows. The all-white New York Police Department restored order by morning.

The police killed three blacks and arrested 125; windows in 250 stores had been smashed. A new report was commissioned but only token changes were made. The incident marked a turning point in black consciousness. Previously, as in the Draft Riots in 1863, race riots saw whites pour into black areas to beat up or kill people. This time blacks turned on white shops doing business in their community.

When the United States entered the Second World War in 1941, La Guardia, through his Emergency Control Board, ordered 2,500 Japanese-Americans living in New York City rounded up and sent to holding facilities on Ellis Island. He retreated into jingoism and racism by referring to Japanese as *Japs* and called his critics *friends of the Japs.*

La Guardia was a cultural conservative and in 1939 when British mathematician and philosopher Bertrand Russell was appointed visiting professor for a year at City College of New York, La Guardia, led a campaign against the Board of Higher Education for approving his appointment. Russell had written *Why I Am Not A Christian* and had come out for *free love* and alternative forms of sexuality. The episode ended when Russell withdrew acceptance of his academic appointment at CCNY and took a teaching post in Pennsylvania.

By the end of his third term as mayor in 1945 La Guardia was enervated. President Harry Truman named him to the American delegation of the United Nations Relief and Rehabilitation Administration, which aided war-torn countries rebuild. He began to suffer from pancreatic cancer and died two years after leaving the mayor's office at age 64. La Guardia died a poor man residing in a small walk-up apartment and leaving his wife only a small number of war bonds. Fifty thousand devoted followers waited patiently in line to see his body as it lie in state at the Episcopal Cathedral of Saint John the Divine.

CHAPTER 109
Reconfiguring New York City: Robert Moses v. Jane Jacobs

The same issue is behind all twentieth century disputes over city planning. The debate is about what kind of city urban planners envision. This broad topic can be personalized in New York City by powerful master builder Robert Moses and Greenwich Village grass-roots community organizer Jane Jacobs. Robert Moses represented aggressive city planning for a modern car-dominated society. He thought the city needed to be rebuilt to accommodate cars. Jane Jacobs championed the traditional city of small-scale neighborhoods for walkers. She reminded her protagonist that before automobiles the streets had been playgrounds for many New Yorkers. In some ways the visions can be dichotomized as the needs of motorists versus the needs of pedestrians, though that would over-simplify complex issues.

The career of Robert Moses, who once held twelve appointed government jobs simultaneously, began in 1924 and ended in 1968. Jane Jacobs arrived on the scene much later at a time when some influential New Yorkers began to doubt the wisdom of Moses's vision. She was a Greenwich Village mother and housewife, journalist, neighborhood activist, and recreational bicyclist who wrote *The Death And Life Of Great American Cities* in 1961 to combat the ideas and programs of Robert Moses and other urban planners.

Historically, the streets and bridges of New York City were created for pedestrians and horses. The Commissioners' Plan was activated in 1811 to make a grid of straight streets and avenues in most of Manhattan to help traffic flow smoothly, but the commissioners had horse-drawn vehicles in mind. Building regulations were sporadic during the 19th century and there was no zoning in the city until 1916. Houses, tenements, apartments, stores, factories, and warehouses were constructed privately wherever their sponsors owned land. New York City had developed in a haphazard manner, which, despite drawbacks, gave its neighborhoods architectural and spatial charm. The traditional city, which was sometimes crowded and chaotic, was the one that Jane Jacobs held dear.

Jane Jacobs believed that Moses's undertakings obliterated important historic places and neighborhood values that made the city attractive and livable. In the first sentence of *The Death And Life Of Great American Cities* she stated her opposition to Moses: *This book is an attack on current city planning and rebuilding.* Jane Jacobs did not stand alone. The New York City vision of Robert Moses was opposed by others including Ralph Fasanella, the urban primitive painter, who championed a humane, small-scale, democratic society that enshrines common working people, their homes and stores. Ralph Solecki, a New York City archaeologist, viewed Robert Moses as the one person who, more than anyone, *...can be blamed for more single-handed destruction of archaeological sites in the New York City area.* Rapid excavations and highway construction at Native American sites, especially in Inwood and along the Harlem River, left no time for archaeologists to research the areas.

Robert Moses was born to an affluent family and had all of society's advantages, a fine education at the Dwight School and Yale University, summer trips to Europe, and a wealth of New York City culture. He was an idealistic reformer and felt a need (*noblesse oblige*) to help the lower classes whether or not they wanted it. With great arrogance, Moses believed he knew what was best for them, and, since his plans centered on parks, beaches, highways, and modern housing, the poor and lower middle classes, and for many years almost everyone else, supported him.

Philosophically and politically, Robert Moses was a *futurist* and a *statist*. He believed that America had entered the age of the private automobile that people would welcome. He disliked cramped old buildings with narrow streets and a hodge-podge of little shops. He aimed to make the city modern by using the legal and financial power of the state to condemn land and build new public facilities. He received his chance when Belle Moskowitz, a Democratic Party fund raiser, reformer, and activist, took him to meet Governor-elect Alfred E. Smith in 1918. Moses was an independent Republican who allied himself with the Democratic governor. In six years Moses climbed through the state bureaucracy and achieved his first position of power. His career as a master builder lasted 44 years. More than any person in the 20th century, Robert Moses changed the face of New York City by knocking down many neighborhoods and replacing them with his vision of a new and modern metropolitan area. His undertakings were enormous and even listing his main projects takes several paragraphs.

Robert Moses, appointed president of the State Parks Council and the Long Island State Park Commission in 1924 by Governor Smith, began by constructing parks and beaches. He built numerous state parks in Nassau and Suffolk counties: Jones Beach, Valley Stream, Hempstead Lake, Bethpage, Robert Moses, Heckscher, Sunken Meadow, Caumsett, Connetquo, Wildwood, Orient Beach, Hither Hills, and Montauk Point. In New York City he built more parks: Wolfe's Pond, Great Kills, South Beach, Clove Lakes, Silver Lake, La Tourette, Willowbrook, Dyker Beach, Owl's Head, Marine, McCarren, Jacob Riis, Rockaway, Jamaica Bay, Spring Creek, Brookville, Baisley Pond, Cunningham, Alley Pond, Kissena, Flushing Meadows, Clearview, Astoria, Corlears Hook, Chrystie-Forsyth (now Sarah Roosevelt Park), Riverside, Inwood Hill, Highbridge, Randall's Island, Ward's Island, St. Mary's, Crotona, Van Cortlandt, Soundview, Ferry Point, and Orchard Beach. He built many smaller parks, plus 290 tennis courts, 669 baseball diamonds, and 658 playgrounds, including twenty in Central Park.

To get people to the parks, Moses built parkways. While they were quite clearly highways, his *parkways* exceeded a reasonable interpretation of his authority, but because the parks and beaches were so popular very few people complained. Car owners wanted more roads, not just to get to parks, but to allow them to move further from the city's center in eastern Queens, southern Staten Island, Long Island, and Westchester. By the Second World War there were more than one million cars registered in New York City. He constructed numerous parkways: Henry Hudson, Mosholu, Bronx River, Hutchinson River, Cross County, Saw Mill River, Belt, Interborough (re-named Jackie Robinson), Grand Central, Cross Island, Northern State, Southern State, Meadowbrook State, Wantagh State, and Bethpage State.

Moses also built multi-lane expressways: Long Island, Brooklyn-Queens, Prospect, Gowanus, Staten Island, Willowbrook, Richmond, Harlem River Drive, Major Deegan, Bruckner Expressway, Cross Bronx, Throgs Neck, Clearview, Van Wyck, Whitestone, and turned Astoria Boulevard into an expressway. The Van Wyck Expressway led to Idlewild Airport (renamed for John F. Kennedy in 1963). Rather than extend a subway line to the airport terminals, Moses favored private cars and paved over 8,000 acres of marshland for immense parking lots.

To ease travel between the five boroughs Moses constructed several important bridges: Henry Hudson, Alexander Hamilton, Triborough, Whitestone, Throg's Neck, Cross Bay, Marine Parkway, and Verrazano. Blocked from erecting a Brooklyn-Battery Bridge, he succeeded in constructing the Brooklyn-Battery Tunnel.

As chairman of the Slum Clearance Committee and construction coordinator of the Bureau of Public Housing, he was responsible for building many of New York's public housing developments, a process which was jump-started in 1937 by federal funds available through Title I of the United States Housing Act. His private housing complexes included Manhattan's Stuyvesant Town and Peter Cooper Village (owned by Metropolitan Life Insurance Company), housing 25,000 New Yorkers, and Co-op City in the Bronx (organized under the Mitchell-Lama Act and built on the former site of *Freedomland*, an amusement part), which is home to 65,000 people.

Moses built Shea Stadium, Lincoln Center, the New York Aquarium, and the United Nations Headquarters. He established the Prospect Park Zoo, Queens Zoo, and Staten Island Zoo. In Central Park he added playgrounds, the Delacourt Theater, Wollman Skating Rink, Conservancy Garden, and Tavern-on-the-Green.

There was an undeniable need for parkland in the five boroughs and beyond. The city's population reached 5,620,000 in 1920 and there were very few parks for recreation beside Central Park and Prospect Park. Al Smith supported parks and beaches and lashed out at those who opposed them for following their narrow self-interest to protect the privacy of their golf clubs, polo fields, and private estates. Moses took the same populist approach that was wildly popular with the park-starved public. The news media was soon showering Moses with accolades over his ambitious plans to increase park acreage and access.

The public authorities that Robert Moses controlled were remote from the people and completely insulated from public oversight. He was able to unilaterally float bond issues to raise money, decide how bridge and tunnel tolls were to be used, apply for federal assistance, and condemn private land. Because of the wording of the legislation enacted to set up the commissions he controlled, much of which he wrote, he needed no approval for his programs from the State Legislature or City Council, nor was he responsible to them.

Wherever Moses wanted to build something, the residents had to be moved and their houses razed. He pronounced as *slums* the areas he wanted to control and called for *slum clearance*, a popular catchword of the 1940s through 1960s. Those who disagreed were labeled *little people*, short sighted, or, communists. Moses was a red-baiter before anyone had heard of Senator Joseph McCarthy and the Cold War. He called his opponents within government agencies *planning reds*.

More than a quarter million New Yorkers in and out of the city were evicted from their homes while Moses demolished them and built his highways. Title I projects did not require that dispossessed residents be relocated. Those who were offered new apartments were inevitably moved into large projects rigidly segregated by race and class. The most egregious gashes caused by his highways were to Astoria, Elmhurst, the central Bronx, Carroll Gardens, Williamsburg, and Sunset Park. Astoria, already divided by a mammoth elevated railroad trestle, saw Astoria Boulevard transformed into a sunken six-lane highway connected to the Triborough Bridge. In central Queens, the Long Island Expressway eviscerated Elmhurst. Central Bronx, especially Mount Eden, Mount Hope, Bathgate, East Tremont, Crotona Park, West Farms, and Unionport were pierced by the seven-mile-long sunken Cross Bronx Expressway, which divided neighbors, and introduced a noisy, foul-smelling barrier into the effected areas. Its six-lanes carry 180,000 cars and trucks each day.

In Brooklyn, Carroll Gardens was sliced in two parts along Hicks Street by a sunken segment of the Brooklyn-Queens Expressway, which cut off Columbia Street, the neighborhood business corridor, from most of the community. Columbia Street merchants went out of business, the west end of Carroll Gardens deteriorated, and the shopping district gravitated east to Court Street. The BQE also severed East Williamsburg from its western sections, Northside and Southside Williamsburg. It was the second time Williamsburg had been traumatized by civil engineering. In 1903 the Williamsburg Bridge had destroyed Downtown Williamsburg by plowing into it at Roebling Street. That, however, was not the fault of Robert Moses. In Sunset Park, he refused to build the noisy elevated Gowanus Expressway over 2nd Avenue and insisted building it over 3rd Avenue, the main commercial street. The result chopped the area in half and left it without a central shopping area.

There is no doubt that much of the housing in older sections of New York City was in deplorable condition. As chairman of New York's Slum Clearance Committee, Moses had the power to seek court orders for the demolition of whole sections of the city for highways, parks, or new housing. Moses was never interested in renovating old buildings. He doomed his target districts by labeling them *slums* or *bombed-out areas* and ordered whole sections of the city torn down by decree. Residents were given ninety days to leave or the sheriff would remove them. He was scornful of any opposition and rarely made compromises. He called his housing policy *urban renewal* but critics labeled it *urban removal.* They countered that residents and historic buildings were removed, not renewed. Superblocks of dreary high-rises set in unimaginative geometric patterns replaced brownstones, tenements, and old apartment buildings. The scale was gargantuan and critics referred to the large projects as filing cabinets for people.

Moses's intention was to replace all the buildings in Manhattan's Lower East Side and East Village with housing projects. He did not believe in half-measures. In his book, *Working for the People,* published in 1956, he wrote: *There can be no real neighborhood reconstruction, no superblocks, no reduction of ground coverage, no widening of boundary streets, no playgrounds, no new schools, without the unflinching surgery which cuts out the whole cancer and leaves no part of it to grow again, and spread and perpetrate old miseries.* City blocks by the scores were leveled. In place of the 19th century structures rose Corlears Hook Houses, Baruch Houses, Lillian Wald Houses, La Guardia Houses, Governor Smith Houses, and Jacob Riis Houses. Demonstrators through the Great Depression had clamored for the government to build modern housing. Robert Moses answered their call.

He did not always get his way. Some projects, such as an upper deck of traffic on the Long Island Expressway, the Long Island Sound Crossing (from Nassau County to Connecticut), a Cross Brooklyn Expressway extending the Prospect Expressway through the center of Brooklyn by replacing Ocean Parkway with a limited-access highway, and an immense Atlantic Village housing complex in Breezy Point, Queens were too low on his list and he never got to them.

Moses had once said in a press conference: *I'll make as few compromises as possible.* But in a few projects he accepted a compromise, the most noted was the BQE route through Brooklyn Heights. The 19th century brownstone neighborhood escaped being cut in half the way Carroll Gardens and Sunset Park were because the Brooklyn Heights Association quickly offered an alternative plan to route the expressway in two levels around the western perimeter of the neighborhood, covering it, and adding a public Esplanade (Promenade) on top. Moses accepted the plan.

Three elevated cross-town Manhattan expressways never happened. Moses had wanted an Upper Manhattan Expressway at 125th Street, a Mid-Manhattan Expressway at 30th or 36th Street, and a Lower Manhattan Expressway across Broome Street (now SoHo). The latter elicited the most opposition because of its intrusive size in small-scale neighborhoods of the Lower East Side, Little Italy, and the southwest corner of Greenwich Village. The plan for the Lower Manhattan Expressway was to connect the Manhattan and Williamsburg Bridges with the Holland Tunnel and the Henry Hudson Parkway that would be extended south to the Battery.

The Brooklyn-Battery Crossing, a pair of enormous suspension bridges, was never built. In her newspaper column, First Lady Eleanor Roosevelt, timidly criticized the plan for the Brooklyn Battery Crossing that would turn the Battery Park into a gangle of approach roads. *I haven't a question that this will be done in the name of progress, and something undoubtedly needs to be done. But isn't there room for some consideration of the preservation of the few beautiful spots that still remain to us on an overcrowded island?* The Secretary of War, Harry H. Woodring, refused to approve the project because he claimed that if the proposed bridge was bombed its rubble would impede East River access to the Brooklyn Navy Yard. Moses and the Roosevelts never trusted each other and the master builder blamed the president and his wife for blocking his project. He converted his proposal into a tunnel, which was built and caused very little opposition.

Moses condemned Fort Clinton, also called Castle Clinton, in 1941 and was prepared to tear it down. The circular fort had been built between 1808 and 1811 by the U.S. federal government for harbor defense and was initially known as the West Battery. It was named for Governor George Clinton in 1815. The fort was decommissioned eleven years later. From 1824 to 1855 it was called Castle Garden and the city leased it to promoters such as P.T. Barnum who staged popular events there. From 1855 to 1890 it was the Emigrant Landing Depot for New York State, the largest east coast immigration center. Castle Clinton was transformed in 1896 to serve as the New York City Aquarium. Moses's plan to raze the historic structure met with widespread opposition. He moved the aquarium to Coney Island and left the fort as a fenced-off hulk. It was rescued in 1980 by the National Parks Service and presently contains the ticket booth where visitors can buy tickets for ferries going to Ellis and Liberty Islands.

His plans to take down the arch in Washington Square Park and run six lanes of 5th Avenue through it, and to build a Lower Manhattan Expressway across Broome Street, were stopped by a broad coalition of Greenwich Village activists including Jane Jacobs, Reform Democrat Hortense Gabel, housing activist Frances Golden, and author Grace Paley. They sponsored letter-writing campaigns, leafleted, posted placards, held demonstrations, and pressured Mayor Robert Wagner, the City Council, and the Board of Estimate. By unanimous vote the Board of Estimate (at that time the upper chamber of city government) killed Moses's Washington Square Park and Lower Manhattan Expressway plans. But the neighborhood coalition was unable to halt his condemnation of the area south of Washington Square, which he demolished and turned over to New York University for construction of five massive high-rises for faculty and graduate student housing.

Moses reacted angrily to opposition over his Greenwich Village projects. The depth of his disdain for the traditional city is palpable. *I realize that in the process of rebuilding south of Washington Square there would be cries of anguish from those who are honestly convinced that the Sistine Madonna was painted in the basement of one of the old buildings there not presently occupied by a cabaret or speakeasy, the Michelangelo's David was fashioned in a garret in the same neighborhood, that Poe's Raven, Don Marquis' Archie the Cockroach, and Malory's Morte D'Arthur were penned in barber shops, spaghetti works and shoeshine parlors in the pulieus of Greenwich Village, and that any one who lays hands on these sacred landmarks will be executed if he has not already been struck by a bolt from heaven.* (The meaning of the Latin word *pulieus* is unclear. If Moses meant *polieus*, it means *little city*, if he meant *pulieus*, it may mean *place of whining*.)

Moses wore many government hats. He was president of the State Parks Council and the Long Island State Park Commission, chairman of the State Power Authority, Triborough Bridge and Tunnel Authority, and Slum Clearance Committee. He had several offices but the one he chose to use was the executive office of the Triborough Bridge and Tunnel Authority, hidden next to and below the tollbooth plaza on secluded Randall's Island.

In Moses's corner were millions of motorists who appreciated new highways and parks, and many former tenement dwellers who preferred his housing projects because they had amenities: elevators, garbage chutes, door buzzer systems, dependable heat and hot water, and full bathrooms *inside* the apartments. His most important ally was public opinion by everyday New Yorkers who believed that their slice of the *American Dream* involved cars and the mobility they would facilitate. The public shared his vision of an automobile-centered society where the outer reaches of the city and the suburbs were primary and the deteriorating city center was to be modernized even if that meant it would be destroyed.

Labor unions supported his projects because they created thousands of new skilled and unskilled jobs. The Roman Catholic Church's Archdiocese of New York was won over when he gave Fordham University a four-square-block parcel of the land he condemned for Lincoln Center to be used as a Manhattan campus that included their law school. Fordham honored their benefactor with a bronze bas-relief in the central plaza of their Lincoln Center Campus in 1970.

In the 1960s the aging Moses began to see his power slip as he was removed from each of his positions except one. He finally lost out to Governor Nelson Rockefeller's will and was removed from his last post at the Triborough Bridge and Tunnel Authority in 1968.

At first glance it seems ungrateful to criticize the master builder since almost everyone in the city is appreciative for at least some of Robert Moses's creations. Among the problems cited were his haughty style, disrespect for public input and feedback, and his insistence on projects of immense size. Aligned against Moses were historic preservationists, romantics, walkers, people dispossessed of their homes, and residents where neighborhoods were disrupted. Jane Jacobs gave voice to their complaints in 1961 with publication of *The Death And Life Of Great American Cities.*

His absolute control over his dozen public authorities and his dismissive style galled Moses's opponents. To his critics he once responded: *There are people who like things as they are; I can't hold out any hope for them; let them move to the Rockies.*

Jacobs was leading and reflecting a newly emerging viewpoint that suburban automobile culture lacked the rich community life and cultural opportunities offered by cities. The early 1960s witnessed the start of a new interest in the old neighborhoods, especially Greenwich Village, the Upper West Side, Brooklyn Heights, and Park Slope. Beginning with Brooklyn Heights in 1965, significant portions of these neighborhoods were protected from demolition or alteration by the Landmarks Preservation Commission. In the 1980s the movement of young middle class people into the city became a torrent and widened to include Chelsea, Washington Heights, Inwood, Harlem, St. George, Bay Ridge, Cobble Hill, Carroll Gardens, Prospect Heights, Fort Greene, Williamsburg, Long Island City, Astoria and other neighborhoods. Even the East Village, Little Italy, the Lower East Side, and Downtown Brooklyn were being gentrified.

Jacobs's ideas opposed Moses on many changes he made to the face of New York City. She was horrified by the monotonous severity of his gargantuan housing projects and challenged his core assumptions. Jacobs wrote: *Low-income projects become worse centers of delinquency, vandalism and general social hopelessness than the slums they were supposed to replace.* She believed large housing projects for the poor would become devastating enclaves of concentrated poverty.

Jacobs charged that the aesthetics of Moses's housing projects were ugly and sterile. Several times she singled out Stuyvesant Town. *Middle-income housing projects are truly marvels of dullness and regimentation, sealed against any buoyancy or vitality of city life... Commercial centers are lack-luster imitations of standardized suburban chain-store shopping.* She railed against *...this degree of monotony, sterility and vulgarity,* and concluded that: *This is the sacking of cities.* Moses had rejected all aesthetic criticisms of Stuyvesant Town. *I can testify that the smarter visitors, not poisoned by jaundice and envy, whom we have guided along the East River, from Bellevue to Corlears Hook, have frankly expressed amazement and real admiration at the almost unbroken series of modern multiple houses for people of small and moderate means, built by a combination of public and quasi-public enterprise.*

The new high-rise buildings, though welcomed by most of the residents, had none of the architectural charm of their predecessors. Housing projects were made of bricks, uniform is size and color, and concrete. They lacked all the distinguishing character marks of old New York buildings: stoops, iron railings, entablatures, cornices, gables, dormers, pilasters, quoins, flower boxes, and finials and tracery made of terra-cotta or marble. Not until 2001 was a small portion of the remaining Lower East Side neighborhood along East Broadway and Orchard Street landmarked as the *Lower East Side Historic District.*

Many of Moses's housing projects began deteriorating within three decades. An August 9, 2003 feature story about Co-op City in *The New York Times* was entitled: *Utopia's $500 Million Repair Bill: Co-op City, Once a Working-Class Dream, Is Crumbling.* The article reported: *From the beginning, construction work at Co-op City, every-*

body agrees, was shoddy. The heating pipes were poorly laid, the concrete badly poured. Some buildings were built without the reinforcing bars needed to make them safe.

The roadways Moses built were derided as scars on the earth, and bleak strips of concrete cutting through and destroying neighborhoods. Jacobs scoffed at the *spaghetti-dish of ramps* that accompanied each highway as ugly and wasteful. Moses viewed wider and wider highways as a solution to traffic congestion; Jacobs saw multi-lane roadways as inviting more congestion.

Jacobs viewed Moses as the primary American apostle of the *Radiant City* ideas of Swiss architect and city planner Le Corbusier (born Charles-Edoard Jeanneret-Gris). She quoted Le Corbusier extolling the virtues of an imaginary Radiant City: *Suppose we are entering the city by way of the Great Park...Our fast car takes the special elevated motor track between the majestic skyscrapers: as we approach nearer, there is seen the repetition against the sky of the twenty-four skyscrapers; to our left and right on the outskirts of each particular area are the municipal and administrative buildings; and enclosing the space are the museums and university buildings. The whole city is a Park.* Le Corbusier believed cities had been rendered obsolete by automobiles and proposed a sleek new international-style replacement consisting of ribbons of broad highways connecting massive housing complexes set in fenced-off green spaces. Neither Le Corbusier nor Moses had any interest in commercial space.

Futurist ideas were very popular in Europe before and after the Second World War and can be seen in parts of London, Berlin, Warsaw, and Moscow. Fascists, communists, and capitalists alike embraced the architecture of the Radiant City in the middle of the 20th century. Paris and Rome banned Radiant City transformations within their central districts, though the southern edge of Rome has the EUR (Universale di Roma), a modern model city, and the western edge of Paris has La Défense, a modern model business and residential city. Le Corbusier was the architect for the concrete, aluminum, and glass Secretariat and General Assembly buildings at the United Nations Headquarters, built between 1949 and 1953, on land cleared by Robert Moses at Turtle Bay, Manhattan.

Many Americans were enchanted by Le Corbusier's concepts. The most popular attraction at the 1939 World's Fair in Flushing

Meadows Park was the General Motors exhibit, *Futurama,* which featured a ride around scale model relief map of the United States. What people saw was a car manufacturer's dream: an entire country dominated by highways and suburbs with reconfigured cities where old neighborhoods were replaced by multi-lane boulevards and mammoth housing projects resting on superblocks.

In *Working for the People,* Moses was candid about his determination to destroy old areas of New York City. *How far has central dry rot in the oldest parts of town developed into a spreading cancer, which threatens your taxes and integrity? Can you afford to leave it and let people and industry move out into the suburbs, or will you cut it out and rebuild at the heart of your community?*

How did Moses's critics view the value of traditional cities? They located its value in its collection of small neighborhoods reticulated by many streets. Instead of Moses-style superblocks with only a few stores clustered at the outer edge of large apartment complexes, Jacobs and her partisans liked street life. *This ubiquitous principle is the need of cities for a most intricate and close-grained diversity of uses that give each other constant mutual support, both economically and socially.* Street life meant more than the means to travel to and from a destination by street or sidewalk. What traditionalists extolled was the public and diverse social life of the sidewalk, street corner, and stoop. They believed sidewalks were important places for social interaction and were safer than parks or the fenced-off grassy spaces around housing projects. Jane Jacobs charged that futurists had a fetish about open spaces or urban breathing spaces, and retorted: *More Open Space for what? For muggings?*

Jacobs, always the romantic, waxed poetic about old buildings: *Cities need old buildings so badly it is probably impossible for vigorous streets and districts to grow without them. By old buildings I mean not museum-piece old buildings, not old buildings in an excellent and expensive state of rehabilitation --- although these make fine ingredients --- but also a good lot of plain, ordinary, low-value old buildings, including some rundown old buildings.* That was a radical call for a society where most people cherished almost anything new. Why did Jacobs like old buildings? *Chain stores, chain restaurants and banks go into new construction. But neighborhood bars, foreign restaurants and pawnshops go into older buildings. Supermarkets and shoe stores often go into new buildings; good bookstores and antique dealers seldom do. Well-subsidized opera and art museums often go into new buildings. But the unformalized feeders of the arts --- studios, galleries, stores for musical instruments and art supplies, backrooms where the low earning power of a seat and a table can absorb uneconomic discussions --- these go into old buildings.*

When evaluating the deeds of Robert Moses the question of race needs to be raised. Moses was a racist. The black population in the city reached 460,000 in 1940, but Moses built for whites and did everything possible to keep blacks and Hispanics out of the park system he created. Few blacks owned private cars in the 1930s and 1940s. Church groups organized most outings attended by black people, and they took buses to recreation sites. Moses had the parkway overpasses built too low for buses to pass underneath. Parking fees for cars and buses were steep to discourage the poor, both black and white, from visiting the parks. Buses needed a park permit to enter Moses's parks and black organizations had difficulty obtaining the permits.

While Moses constructed more than 250 playgrounds all over the city in the 1930s, he built only one in Harlem, New York's largest black neighborhood. He built ten swimming pools in the 1930s but only one in Harlem, the Thomas Jefferson Pool. Believing that blacks disliked cold water, he ordered that the Jefferson Pool remain unheated while swimming pools in white areas (Astoria, Corona, and Greenpoint) were heated to seventy degrees.

Public housing in New York City was segregated. The privately sponsored housing Moses facilitated with public funds was off limits to non-whites. The most notable case was Metropolitan Life Insurance Company's Stuyvesant Town and Peter Cooper Village whose chairman of the board, Frederick H. Ecker, had publicly stated upon its opening in 1947 that they would accept only white tenants. (Also barred were single people and unmarried couples.) Though the courts upheld the discriminatory policy, public demonstrations and negative publicity persuaded Met Life to voluntarily end racial discrimination when Ecker retired in 1950.

To facilitate building the Henry Hudson Parkway, the New York Central Railroad tracks, now used by Amtrak, along the

Hudson River were covered from Pennsylvania Station to 125th Street, but were left uncovered as they ran along the west edge of Harlem. President Franklin D. Roosevelt, who had provided funding for many of Moses's programs, and Mayor Fiorello La Guardia complained about the discrimination. Moses ignored Roosevelt and often tangled with La Guardia referring to him behind his back as a *dago, wop,* and *organ grinder.*

Unfortunately, many white Americans shared Moses's racist ideas. It was part of the prevailing national sentiment that began to change only with the Civil Rights Movement. Surely the City Council, and all the mayors, governors, and presidents he worked for between 1924 and 1968 could have influenced him had they been determined to end his discriminatory policies.

The legacy of Robert Moses is mixed. Some of Jane Jacobs's criticisms were valuable and others may be seen as strained. She never criticized his beaches, parks, zoos, or bridges. In the end, New York City was too big for Moses. After 44 years in a whirlwind of activity, he could not change everything in New York to fit into his vision, least of all Manhattan. Meaningful evaluations of his numerous projects must come from each individual's conception of what the city means, and there are many possibilities among eight million New Yorkers.

Notations:

Robert Moses and Cars

Though he built hundreds of miles of highways and parkways, and a plethora of parking lots, Robert Moses never drove a car. He took two driving lessons in 1922, did not like it, and rode in the plush leather-covered back seat of a chauffeur-driven limousine for his entire working life. The Parks Commission and later the Triborough Bridge and Tunnel Authority provided the limousine at taxpayer expense.

Rules Posted By Robert Moses At Coney Island

Department Of Parks Regulations Governing Use Of Bathing

Area & Boardwalk:

No Peddling, Advertising, Littering, Dogs Or Fires.

No Bicycling, Roller Skating, Vehicles Other Than Baby Carriages & Wheel Chairs For Invalids.

No Newspapers Other Than For Reading.

No Sitting On Railing Or Steps.

No Bathing Rings, Rafts, Inflated Or Buoyant Devices, Masks, Goggles Or Fins.

No Persons On Beach From Midnight To Dawn.

No Acrobatics, Ball Playing, Throwing Of Missiles Or Sand.

No Dressing Or Undressing, Tents Or Shelters.

No Chairs Or Picnicking On Boardwalk.

No Articles Hung On Signs, Benches, Baskets, Railings, Fences, Ropes Or Umbrellas.

No Boats Launched Or Beached.

No Fishing, Flying Of Kites, Flags Or Pennants.

No Digging Of Holes, Creating Hazards Or Committing Nuisances.

No Bathing Near Jetties. (Bathing Within Life Lines Only.)

CHAPTER 110
Corona Dumps becomes Flushing Meadows Park

The transformation from a salt marsh to a dump to a park illustrates two tendencies in New York City. It demonstrates the recklessness of early settlers and their descendants over the next three hundred years in degrading the natural landscape, and the later rescue of endangered places through ecologically sensitive restoration and development.

A salt marsh surrounded Flushing River as it flowed north into Flushing Bay from the hills in the center of Queens. Early Dutch and English settlers gathered shellfish and marsh grass in the area. As Queens developed, factories were built along the river's shore and industrial waste was dumped into the shallow waterway. The marshlands were transformed into a dump for ashes from coal furnaces in

the middle of the 19th century. In *The Great Gatsby*, F. Scott Fitzgerald described the industrial ash dump operated by the Brooklyn Ash Company (halfway to West Egg from Manhattan in the novel) in unflattering terms: *This is a valley of ashes - a fantastic farm where ashes grow like wheat into ridges and hills and grotesque gardens, where ashes take the forms of houses and chimneys and rising smoke and finally, with a transcendent effort, of men who move dimly and already crumbling through the powdery air.*

In the 1930s *the valley of the ashes* was covered over, its poisoned river routed into a conduit, and turned into a 1,316 acre park treasured by locals who use it to play soccer, picnic, and stroll. Set astride three intersecting highways and below the flight patterns for nearby LaGuardia Airport it sounds like a horrid place for either relaxation or sports, but proves that anyplace can be completely re-configured by competent urban planners. Use of Flushing Meadows Park is exceeded only by Central Park.

Flushing Meadows - Corona Park boasts several structures

and landscaping features left from two World's Fairs (1939 and 1964), which have been turned into attractions. Flushing Meadows Lake, a small, elongated body of water, is situated at the south end of the park. Each summer the Hong Kong Dragon Boat Festival, usually celebrated on the second Saturday in August, is held on the lake. The colorful boat race commemorates a Chinese Confucian morality tale in which the idealistic reformer, Qu Yuan, a scholar-bureaucrat in third century B.C. China, expressed his disapproval of the emperor's policies by drowning himself. Brightly colored and elaborately decorated boats race in the lake in a symbolic attempt to rescue the reformer's body from fish and dragons. A parade, lion dance, acrobatic performances, a traditional Chinese instrument concert, and Chinese food fill out the day.

Like the Statue of Liberty, the Unisphere is best seen from a distance which is how most New Yorkers know it: out the car window from the Long Island Expressway, the Van Wyck Expressway, or the Grand Central Parkway. It is left from the 1964 World's Fair. The spherical structure is twelve stories tall and made from 380 tons of stainless steel.

Rarely visited, the *Panorama* in the Queens Museum of Art is one of the most impressive tourist spots in the city. The main attraction is the panoramic model of all five boroughs with each feature crafted separately: 895,000 buildings, plus streets, bridges, piers, and airports. They are all there. For a spatial overview of the Big Apple the enormous diorama (15,000 square feet), conceived by regional planning tsar Robert Moses and built for the 1964 World's Fair, is terrific. A raised platform goes around the entire model to afford an elevated view of the perfectly scaled architectural replica from all directions. Lighting shifts from dawn to midday to dusk to midnight to make the capsule-shaped room even more sensually authentic.

Lovingly tended, the Queens Zoo is treasure hidden by lush woods, which almost shields visitors from the sounds of autos on nearby Grand Central Parkway and the overhead flights to and from LaGuardia. The showpiece is the innovative aviary where guests amble up and around on a progressively raised walkway to catch glimpses from the ground to the top of the trees. The zoo also has alligators, sea lions, buffalo, elk, prairie dogs, and other members of the animal kingdom. Next to the entrance is a carousel. Across the pathway from the zoo is a children's petting zoo featuring common farm animals.

In the New York Hall of Science, a children's favorite, the set-up is interactive, with more than 150 exhibits exploring color, light, optics, the atom, and elements of biology. An outdoor annex of slightly weathered spacecraft is adjacent to the Hall of Science.

The United States National Tennis Center is located at the north end of the park and is home to the U.S. Open. Shea Stadium, formerly part of the park, was built in 1964 to house the New York Mets. A new stadium, called CitiField, was built next to it in 2009 and seats 41,922 spectators. Shea Stadium had also accommodated a football team, the New York Jets, from 1967 to 1983. The old hulking behemoth with its jarring international style and blue and orange painted facade, was razed for a parking lot.

Flushing Meadows - Corona Park was not an attempt to recreate the unsalvageable ecosystem destroyed by the carelessness of previous generations, but the park project halted the further degradation of the Flushing River basin and turned it into valuable recreation area.

Though most of the environmental rescue operations have taken place since the 1970s it would be unfair to ignore the efforts of earlier preservationists who valued the idea of keeping some connection with the area's natural past. Mid 19th century romantics realized the need to recreate a country atmosphere and were responsible for building large parklands that preserve some of hills and lakes of pristine New York before colonization. They did a lot of rearranging of the natural setting, but the spirit was preserved. Central Park, which opened in 1859, offers a look at Manhattan's rough schist outcroppings. Green-Wood Cemetery (1840) and Prospect Park (1868) in Brooklyn have preserved the hilly moraine that runs through Brooklyn like a spine and kept a few of the ponds that once dotted the landscape. Frederick Law Olmstead and Calvert Vaux were the landscape architects responsible for Central Park and Prospect Park.

Since the 1970s a number of corrupted sites have been reconfigured and turned into useful public spaces that approximate nature, host wildlife, and provide valuable views of waterways. It marked a positive turning point for the city's dwindling natural treasures.

Gateway National Recreation Area, a littoral (shore area) of unconnected parklands stretching from several places in and around Jamaica Bay (Queens and Brooklyn), eastern Staten Island, and Sandy Hook, New Jersey, encompasses 9,155 acres of salt marsh and uplands, and about 16,000 acres of open bay. Prior to 1972 when the National Park Service created Gateway, partly out of the Jamaica Bay Wildlife Refuge (dating from 1953), much of the area had been used for illegal dumping.

Visitors to Gateway may hike along trails to catch a glimpse of egrets, sandpipers, plovers, killdeers, oystercatchers, snipes, woodcocks, swallows, geese, and swans. There are also raptors: owls and hawks. Reptiles and amphibians can be spotted around the ponds. The surrounding bay's waters, marshlands, islands, and fresh and saltwater ponds, located on a major migration route, give rest and sustenance to over three hundred species of birds. The American Littoral Society and Friends of Gateway periodically sponsor wildlife boat cruises in the bay.

State and city park authorities deserve accolades for three tiny access points to the East River. In Long Island City, Gantry State Park (Queens Landing), at the foot of 49th Avenue on the East River, opened in 1998 and received its name from the two giant industrial *gantry* cranes that once transferred boxcars from railroad tracks to cross-river barges. The park is a small gap in development and a breathing space and welcome opening to the East River. The four piers that make up much of the park each have a separate architectural feature, such as wooden chaise-lounge recliners for sun bathing. All have comfortable benches for skyline watching. The panorama is breathtaking. On the right is the 59th Street Bridge, at the center foreground is U Thant Island, and in the background is the United Nations, Trump Apartment Building, Citicorp Center, Empire State Building, and Chrysler Building. On the left are the Waterside Apartment Houses and Stuyvesant Town.

Grand Ferry Park, at the western foot of Grand Street in Williamsburg, Brooklyn is a minuscule park marking the former site of the Williamsburg to Manhattan ferry (from Grand Street to

Grand Street) which ran from 1802 until 1918 when the new bridge rendered it unprofitable. This is one of the only places where you can actually approach the shoreline of the East River, stand on the rocks, and touch the water. The park has a bit of grass, some benches, and a reconstructed round 70-foot smokestack from the old Pfizer Pharmaceutical Company's factory as an industrial monument. The park also affords a view of the high and graceless Williamsburg Bridge, which was tremendously significant to Williamsburg when it opened in 1903. It offered an escape for Jewish and Italian immigrants from the crowded Lower East Side to the comparative openness of Williamsburg. It also gave more commercial possibilities to both areas though it destroyed Williamsburg's downtown district by intruding into its center. The bridge has a pedestrian walkway, which offers unique views of both shores of the East River.

Louis Valentino, Jr. Park and Pier, at the foot of Van Dyke Street and Coffey Street in Red Hook, Brooklyn is a new public park (1997) with two hundred feet of waterfront that actually has a beach, though swimming in the harbor (more precisely Buttermilk Channel) is for the very brave or foolish. The park-beach-pier mostly draws sunbathers and fishermen. The spot is without trees to maximize the view. Anglers manage to catch bluefish, sea bass, croakers, herring, and porgies. This almost hidden site affords a unique surface-level view of the Statue of Liberty and Governors Island.

The part of Marine Park south of Avenue U in Brooklyn had been a place where scofflaws illegally dumped garbage and old cars. The tidal marshland, which empties into the Dead Horse Inlet of Jamaica Bay and ultimately the Atlantic Ocean, was cleaned up and turned into the Salt Marsh Nature Center. It has one-mile long salt marsh nature trail and a new discovery center for class visits. Birds, shellfish, small mammals, reptiles, and amphibians can be seen from the trail and marsh platform.

Some infamous sites have been passing through a process of slow improvement. The Gowanus Canal, once a fresh stream that in colonial Brooklyn had been a prime spot for gathering oysters, was transformed into a canal in the 1840s and became a putrid waterway and legendary gangland dumping place for bodies. An old flushing tunnel, which had not been operational for fifty years, was restored in 1989. It simulates the movement of the tides. The Gowanus Canal is on its way to recovery.

The Bronx River, which became a sordid sewer of industrial waste and junked autos, refrigerators, and garbage, is in its final stages of cleanup. Preservationists organize periodic canoeing and kayaking trips.

Fresh Kills Landfill, the city's enormous garbage dump from 1948 until 2001, is a smelly blight on the west side of Staten Island. Its closure delighted Staten Islanders. City garbage is now gathered in several transfer stations and shipped by rail and truck to communities in upstate New York, Pennsylvania, and West Virginia that are willing to accept it for a fee. It will take years to stabilize the landfill and transform it into a park.

Parts of the East River shoreline were improved in the 1940s when the F.D.R. Drive was constructed on the river's west side. Roosevelt Island stabilized and improved its shores in the 1970s. After the World Trade Center was completed in 1973 part of the Hudson River shore was tastefully developed, especially at Battery Park City. Still waiting for help is most of the East River and Harlem River shorelines, Newtown Creek, and Arthur Kill.

As people become more sensitive to preserving some semblance of New York City's natural surroundings the rescue of endangered or ruined places through ecologically responsible restoration or development will proceed. The last three decades of the 20th century give reason for cautious optimism.

CHAPTER 111
Airports

Originally airports in and around New York City were called *airfields* because they were relatively level, mowed fields of grass. Roosevelt Field, now a shopping mall in Nassau County, achieved fame as the place from which aviator Charles A. Lindbergh flew the *Spirit of St. Louis* to Paris in 1927. Flushing Field, formerly situated on three hundred acres between Flushing and College Point, Queens, west of the Whitestone Expressway, and Floyd Bennett Field, located at the edge of Jamaica Bay in Brooklyn near Marine Park, along Flatbush Avenue were two small early airfields. Flushing Field was abandoned in 1983 and the abandoned site is reverting to wetlands. The 1,500-acre Floyd Bennett Field opened in 1931 as the city's first municipal airport, but it was too far from Manhattan and was soon eclipsed by La Guardia Airport. Floyd Bennett Field was sold to the United States Navy and used as a Naval Reserve and Coast Guard station until 1972 when its ownership passed to the National Parks Service. The NYPD uses a portion for its helicopter fleet, and volunteers maintain a collection of old airplanes in two of the hangars.

New York City's first real municipal airport got a late start. Its chief booster was Fiorello La Guardia, mayor from 1934 to 1945, who had a personal interest in flying. He had been a pilot and had commanded an air squadron in the First World War. La Guardia was insistent that a commercial airport be built in New York City. To publicize his case, he refused to disembark a plane at the Newark Airport on a flight from Chicago to New York City because it did not land where the ticket promised. It was a publicity stunt and tipped-off reporters and photographers covered the story, which was favorably related in newspapers and on radio programs. The airplane took off again and landed at Floyd Bennett Field in Brooklyn where the flamboyant mayor emerged to a hail of photographers' flashbulbs.

North Beach Airport was constructed north of Ditmars Boulevard on a peninsula jutting into the East River between Bowery Bay and Flushing Bay north of Jackson Heights. The site was once called Bowery Beach and was partly landfill. It had contained a working class picnic area, beer garden, and carnival known as the Gala Amusement Park since the 1880s. Bowery Bay Beach was renamed North Beach in the 1890s. Prohibition killed the business and in 1930 it was transformed into the Glenn H. Curtiss Airfield, a private airstrip. The city bought it in 1935 and renamed it North Beach Airport.

Mayor La Guardia introduced commercial amenities to the 650-acre airport at the North Beach site in order to increase revenue and also offer services to the flying public. Other airports around the country quickly duplicated his idea. La Guardia Airport now includes a bookshop, French, Japanese, Italian, and Jewish cafés, fast food outlets, bars, hair-and-nail salon, health spa, clothing stores, cyber café, and even a resident dentist.

Most of the present airport complex was built under the direction of La Guardia, who, with his wife, often visited the site on weekends to watch the construction process. It opened as New York Municipal Airport in 1939 with 250,000 people attending the dedication ceremony. It has two main runways extended over water, ten hangars, and five terminals. The observation deck above the curved central terminal afforded air enthusiasts the chance to watch airport activities from a rooftop promenade for a ten cent fee. The thrill of watching take-offs and landings was new for Americans.

The beautiful art deco-style Marine Air Terminal was built to serve Pan American Airline's seaplanes which landed in Bowery Bay. One of President Franklin D. Roosevelt's New Deal programs supplied the artwork in its circular lobby. The Works Projects Administration (W.P.A.) engaged James Brooks to paint a wraparound mural, known as *Flight*, with the theme of *progress in the history of aviation*. It was dedicated in 1942, painted over in 1956, and carefully restored in 1980.

Shortly after La Guardia's death in 1947, the airport was renamed the New York Municipal Airport - La Guardia Field. When the Port of New York Authority assumed control in 1947 they changed the name to La Guardia Airport. In 2014 La Guardia Airport served 27 million travelers yearly.

In 1948, international flights were shifted from La Guardia Airport to the much larger Idlewild International Airport that was built on the south shore of Queens next to Jamaica Bay. Idlewild Airport was bordered by five neighborhoods: Howard Beach, South Ozone Park, Springfield Gardens, Laurelton, and Rosedale.

Idlewild International Airport, constructed on 4,930 acres of marshland, originally had five runways, fifteen hangars, and a series of nine individual and general airline terminals placed around a circular service road. The most notable terminals were built several years after the airport opened in 1942: the Pan American Airways Building (1961), United Airlines Building (1961), Trans World Airlines International Building (1962), and British Airways Terminal (1970). Most were award-winning international-style designs. In 1963 Idlewild was renamed the John F. Kennedy International Airport. Kennedy, the third largest American airport (following Atlanta and Chicago) employs 37,000 people. In 2014 approximately 51 million passengers passed through its terminals. Since the closing of Ellis Island's operations by the Immigration and Naturalization Service in 1954, JFK is now the point of entry for immigrants arriving in New York City.

The third airport considered by New Yorkers to be a New York City airport is in Newark, New Jersey. Newark International Airport, renamed Newark Liberty International Airport in 2001, has three terminals. Many suburbanites use Stewart International Airport in Newburgh (Orange County), Long Island MacArthur Airport in Islip (Suffolk County), and Westchester County Airport in White Plains.

In 1900, science fiction writers and artists predicted that by the year 2000 Americans would have individual flying machines. While that never occurred, a few New Yorkers use helicopters. There are landing platforms for helicopters on East River piers at Wall Street and East 34th Street, and at West 30th Street on the Hudson River. The Met Life Building Heliport, formerly Pan Am Building Heliport, dramatically and perilously perched on the roof of the skyscraper at Park Avenue and 45th Street, is no longer in operation.

Reaching the three major metropolitan airports is difficult

without a car. Highway access to La Guardia, Kennedy, and Newark Airports is efficient and they offer patrons both long-term and short-term parking lots. Private transportation to the airports includes taxicabs and car services, while public transportation includes express buses, regular buses, or a combination of subway and bus travel. AirTrain service to JFK or Newark involves a transfer.

Direct train service to the airports, which exists in many American cities (Chicago, Boston, San Francisco, Washington, D.C.), was never constructed in New York City due to the opposition from car-oriented commissioner of highways Robert Moses, and the taxi industry. Newark has a light rail system that connects its three terminals and the city of Newark, but the line was never extended to Manhattan. The PATH line (Port Authority Trans Hudson), New Jersey Transit, and Amtrak connect travelers bound for Newark International Airport with the light rail line at Newark's main railroad stations, Journal Square Station and Pennsylvania Station. AirTrain, a light rail system built over the Van Wyck Expressway, connecting the Jamaica Station of the Long Island Railroad with Kennedy Airport opened in 2004.

Air travel has become increasingly important mode of transportation for New Yorkers to and for moving commercial cartage. There are 55,000 flights each day in the United States and many of them start or end in New York City.

CHAPTER 112
Baseball in New York City

In the past century baseball fans in New York have had multiple choices of teams they could follow. Until the end of the 1957 season they could choose from the Yankees, Dodgers, and Giants. Since 1962 it has been the Yankees and Mets. There are other spectator and participatory sports as well, though baseball, often called the *national pastime*, has been the *city's pastime* for many sports fans.

The first recorded sporting activities in Dutch New Amsterdam were bowling on the green, at Bowling Green located at the foot of Broadway, sailing events, and horse racing held in pastures and along country roads in Manhattan and at the ocean beaches in Brooklyn.

Today, many sporting events are held in large venues such as Yankee Stadium, CitiField, Madison Square Garden, Aqueduct Race Track, or the National Tennis Center in Flushing Meadows Park, Queens. Spectator sports are viewed from paid seats or watched on television. Beyond baseball, popular spectator sports include football, basketball, soccer, boxing, hockey, and horse racing. Sports that are just as often participatory include tennis, golf, swimming, sailing, cricket, rugby, fishing, jogging, and three old-timers: bowling, stickball, and handball. The New York City Marathon, begun in 1970, attracts hundreds of thousands of spectators to cheer on the 37,000 runners along its 26.2-mile route passing through all five boroughs.

There is a longstanding dispute over where the game of baseball began, or what constituted baseball. New Yorkers often claim that the game was first played in Brooklyn or Manhattan. Evidence is scanty and contradictory because spontaneous games were rarely recorded. In 1846 the elite New York Knickerbocker Club issued a set of rules for baseball, though some semblance of the game had already been played in empty lots for decades. It is doubtful that common people were ever aware of the Knickerbocker Club's rules.

By the 1850s baseball had overtaken many other sports in popularity, and during the 1860s several teams were organized in Brooklyn, Manhattan, southern Westchester (now the Bronx), and other northeastern American cities. During the many idle moments between battles in the Civil War, soldiers played baseball, or a game very near to it. After 1865 the game spread rapidly as soldiers took it back to their hometowns. In 1876 the National League of Professional Base-Ball Clubs was organized in Manhattan to formulate common rules and organize games.

Until the turn of the last century there were many teams and small stadiums in Brooklyn, Manhattan, Queens, and the Bronx. In the early years of the 20th century the number of teams was reduced as baseball was professionalized and turned into a business. Early white teams included the New York Mutuals, Brooklyn Atlantics, Brooklyn Wonders, and Brooklyn Tip Tops. The New York Black Yankees, Brooklyn Eagles, and Cuban Stars were in the Negro National League. The Lincoln Giants and the Brooklyn Royal Giants were in the Eastern Colored League. The Bacharach Giants and the Cuban Stars East were in the American Negro League.

The New York Yankees started as the New York Highlanders in 1903 from a team originally located in Baltimore. The Highlanders played in Hilltop Park at Broadway and 165th Street in Washington Heights until 1913 when they moved a few blocks southeast to the Polo Grounds where they were tenants of the New York Giants. The same year they were renamed the Yankees and in 1923 moved to Yankee Stadium in the Bronx.

What does the term *Yankee* mean? Historically there are three meanings. It originally referred to New Englanders, especially descendants of Puritans. During the Civil War it was broadened to apply to all northerners. During the First World War Yankee was used by foreigners to encompass all Americans. But in baseball it refers only to the baseball team that plays in pinstripes at Yankee Stadium in the Bronx.

Babe Ruth was the first larger-than-life figure on the team. He had come to the Yankees from the Boston Red Sox in 1920, at a time when the Yankees were still playing at the Polo Grounds. As the game's home run champion he excited the fans with his swing-for-the-seats style and filled the stadium with paying customers.

In 1920, the first year Ruth played for the Yankees, attendance hit 1,289,422. The year before attendance had been 619,164. When Yankee Stadium opened sportswriters called it *The House that Ruth Built.* When Babe Ruth died in 1948, an estimated 75,000 people walked past his casket at Saint Patrick's Cathedral to pay their respects.

Lou Gehrig, the stately first baseman from 1925 until 1939 was beloved and respected as a powerful ball player, a native Manhattanite (from Yorkville), who managed a consecutive game streak of 2,130. He died in 1941 at age 37 of amyotrophic lateral sclerosis (ALS), now commonly referred to as Lou Gehrig's Disease. On July 4, 1939 he memorably addressed the crowd at Yankee Stadium: *Fans, for the past two weeks you have been reading about the bad break I got. Yet today I consider myself the luckiest man on the face of the earth. I have been in ballparks for seventeen years and have never received anything but kindness and encouragement from you fans...*

Some other Yankee titans have included Joe DiMaggio, Mickey Mantle, Roger Maris, Reggie Jackson, and Don Mattingly. The Yankees have dominated the sport for much of the 20th century and are the most famous team in American baseball.

The Brooklyn Base Ball Club was the official name under which the Brooklyn Dodgers were first incorporated in 1883. A series of nicknames in the popular sports press included the Atlantics, Grays, Bridegrooms, Superbas, and Trolley-Dodgers. *Trolley-dodging* was a skill reputedly mastered by Brooklynites as they navigated the borough's street-car filled roads and intersections. The team, which finally used the shortened name Brooklyn Dodgers, began playing in the storied Ebbets Field in 1913. (Ebbets Field was built on the former Pig Grounds, Brooklyn's main area of slaughterhouses.)

There were many luminaries playing for the Dodgers, especially in the 1950s: Pee Wee Reese, Duke Snider, Gil Hodges, Roy Campanella, Sandy Koufax, and Carl Furillo. But it was Jackie Robinson who became the icon of the team. Branch Rickey, executive director of the Dodgers, recruited Jackie Robinson to play for the Montreal Royals, the Dodgers' International League affiliate, for the 1946 season. The next year Rickey added Robinson to the Dodgers' roster, and he became the first black player in the modern major leagues.

In 1947 the Brooklyn Dodgers became an integrated team though not without hundreds of racial incidents in ballfields around the country including some at Ebbets Field. Rickey had chosen Robinson to integrate baseball because of his physical talents and his emotional steadiness. Branch Rickey was an innovator throughout his career. He developed the framework of the modern minor league farm team system and signed Roberto Clemente to play for the same Dodgers' farm team where Robinson had started. Rickey had done his homework researching Robinson's background. As a soldier at Fort Hood in Texas during the Second World War, Robinson was nearly court-martialed for protesting the rule that blacks had to sit at the back of military buses even as they were preparing to fight the racist Nazi regime in Germany.

In 1957 the Dodgers left Brooklyn for Los Angeles. The move, which came at the height of suburbanization, population loss, and the general decline of Brooklyn, broke the borough's heart for decades. Walter O'Malley, the Dodgers' president made the decision. Angry Brooklynites charged that he deserted the borough as Crown Heights, location of Ebbets Field, was changing racially, and that he lusted for lucrative California television rights. It was often repeated that the three worst persons in the 20th century were Hitler, Stalin, and Walter O'Malley. There was, of course, more to the story.

Citing steadily lowering attendance numbers, the small size and crumbling infrastructure of Ebbets Field, O'Malley wanted to build a new stadium and his team was willing to pay for it. His choice was the intersection of Flatbush Avenue, Atlantic Avenue, and 4th Avenue. It was centrally located in Brooklyn, easy to reach by car, and the Long Island Railroad and eight subway lines serviced the junction. O'Malley asked Robert Moses, New York City's power broker and development tsar, to provide the land. Moses refused and offered the north end of Flushing Meadows Park in Queens for a new stadium. Unable to reach an accord, O'Malley took his team to Los Angeles. Ultimately, Moses got a stadium in Queens but Brooklyn lost the Dodgers. Today, developer Bruce Ratner's Atlantic Center, constructed on the land O'Malley wanted for a new Ebbets Field, has a stylized façade with several baseball pennants flying on top to suggest the old stadium. In 2012 Ratner opened the Barclay's Center across Atlantic Avenue from the Atlantic Center. It is an indoor arena where the Brooklyn Nets play basketball, and is a popular venue for a wide variety of musical events.

Several factors sustained the romanticism of the Dodgers: local talent, an outer borough needing validation, an appealingly funky stadium, effusive and loyal fans, and the Dodgers Sym-Phony. The rag-tag five-member band, as in *phony symphony*, played popular baseball favorites since 1939. Their opening number would be *Take Me Out to the Ball Game*, and other thematic tunes: *Somebody Else is Taking My Place* when a pitcher was removed, *Would You Like to Take a Walk* when a Dodger got a base on balls, and *Three Blind Mice* to chastise an umpire who made a bad call for the Dodgers. The Sym-Phony never disbanded when the team left Brooklyn though the original members have one by one been replaced. They show up at Cyclones games, old-timers stickball reunions, and other Brooklyn events.

The New York Giants began in 1883 as the New York Gothams. The team played at the Old Polo Grounds across the street from the northeast corner of Central Park at 110th Street between 5th and 6th Avenues. The team was renamed the Giants in 1885 and in 1890 moved to the New Polo Grounds at 155th Street along the Harlem River. They were known for their bitter rivalry with the Dodgers culminating in the battle for the National League pennant in 1951 when a team featuring Willie Mays, Sal Maglie, and Bobby Thomson defeated the Brooklyn team. Bobby Thomson hit the pennant winning homerun for the Giants off Dodger pitcher Ralph Branca that became known *as the shot heard round the world.* In 1957 the New York Giants left Manhattan for San Francisco and the rivalry between the Giants and the Dodgers continued in California.

The New York Mets were organized in 1962 under the guidance of William A. Shea, who had been charged by Mayor Robert F. Wagner with obtaining a new team for the city as a consolation for having lost the Dodgers and Giants. The team colors fused the Dodgers' blue and the Giants' orange and the logo was a stylized version of the city's skyline. The Mets began playing in their modern blue and orange stadium named for Shea in 1964. Robert

Moses had arranged for the land between Flushing and Corona that was served by the #7 IRT subway and three of Moses' new highways: Grand Central Parkway, Long Island Expressway, and Van Wyck Expressway. The location made it readily accessible to residents in eastern Queens and Long Island.

In the early 1960s the Mets were derided as the worst team in baseball history. Under manager Casey Stengel the Mets had a dismal record of 40 wins and 120 losses in 1962. But by 1969 they were hailed as the Miracle Mets with players like Tom Seaver, Jerry Koosman, and Nolan Ryan. The Mets fielded impressive star power again in the 1980s: Dwight Gooden, Darryl Strawberry, Keith Hernandez, Gary Carter, and Howard Johnson. They won the World Series in 1986.

There are two minor league stadiums in the city where the endearing small town atmosphere during games evokes baseball before its commercialization. Both stadiums opened in 2001. The Brooklyn Cyclones, class A farm team for the New York Mets, play in MCU Park next to the boardwalk at Coney Island. The stadium holds 7,500 Brooklynites. (MCU Park was formerly KeySpan Park, but since 2012 naming rights have gone to the Municipal Credit Union.) The Staten Island Yankees, class A farm team for the New York Yankees, use Richmond County Bank Ballpark with views of the harbor and Downtown Manhattan just steps from the Staten Island ferry terminal in St. George. The ballpark seats 7,171 fans. In these minor league stadiums advertising signs in the outfield are for local businesses and during the 7th Inning Stretch local cub scout troops and other neighborhood groups are recognized and presented to effusive audiences of borough baseball boosters.

No matter how clear games are when seen on television, especially with close-up shots and instant replays, the appeal of attending a ballgame is enormous. There is something extraordinary about seeing the players live and being part of a sea of enthusiastic, boisterous fans. Like going to Jones Beach, or strolling down 5th Avenue at Christmas, it is something every New Yorker has done. Part of the appeal is the overpriced food and beverages, either hawked in the aisles or available in food stands. Sitting in the sun watching a close game while munching crackerjacks or a hot dog is a special summertime activity.

Notation:

Take Me Out to the Ballgame

The chorus of the song *Take Me Out to the Ballgame* is routinely sung during the Seventh Inning Stretch. Jack Norworth wrote it while riding the IRT in 1908. Though he had never been to a major league game he had seen a poster announcing a game at the Polo Grounds and managed to capture the feeling of attending a stadium game. Albert Von Tilzer provided the melody.

Take me out to the ball game,
Take me out with the crowd
Buy me some peanuts and crackerjack,
I don't care if I never get back.
Let me root, root, root for the home team,
If they don't win it's a shame
For it's one, two, three strikes you're oot,
At the old ball game.

CHAPTER 113
The Cold War in New York City

The Cold War, which is often dated from the end of the Second World War in 1945, had its beginnings almost as soon as the war began. It was clear to the two primary Allied Powers, the United States and the Soviet Union, that their alliance against Nazi Germany was for strategic purposes only. The two powerful countries had opposing social systems and the capitalist Americans and communist Russians each threatened the other. Each believed the other was attempting world domination.

Some aspects of the Soviet-American struggle date from Russia's Bolshevik Revolution in October 1917. Russians who liked elements of the American economic and political systems were persecuted and sometimes charged as foreign agents. Americans who supported some of the goals of socialism were considered spies or dupes. The KGB and FBI busied themselves keeping their respective citizens in line.

Communists or those accused of preaching ideas that would damage the capitalist system in the United States were spied on, fired from their jobs, blacklisted, and sometimes accused of treason. During the Palmer Raids, 1918 to 1921, foreign-born citizens or relatives were deported for supporting communist or socialist goals. A. Mitchell Palmer, Woodrow Wilson's attorney general, led the raids. J. Edgar Hoover intensified that tradition of actively rooting out dissent once he founded the FBI in 1924.

There were numerous outbreaks of anti-communist fervor in New York City. In 1935 charges were leveled that many public school teachers in the city were communists and socialists. The accusations were based on teachers' outside activities as well as their choice of novels and history texts in the classroom. In 1941 the New York Federation of Teachers, the local branch of the national union, was expelled from the American Federation of Teachers.

For the general public the start of the Cold War was about the atomic bomb. It came on August 6, 1945, shortly after the bombing of Hiroshima and Nagasaki. *Little Boy*, the world's first weapon of mass destruction, killed 140,000 Japanese, mostly civilians. The *Enola Gay*, piloted by Paul Tibbets, dropped the bomb. It was a top- secret flight so clandestine that the crew did not know the nature of the bomb. (The plane was named for the pilot's mother.) *Fat Man* was dropped over Nagasaki three days later and killed 74,000 Japanese people. President Harry Truman called the atomic bomb the *greatest scientific gamble in history* and pronounced it a complete success. Japan soon surrendered and the Second World War was over.

Japan, Germany, and Italy, former enemies, quickly receded in the public memory. The wartime cooperation that was symbolized by handshakes and smiles when Russian and American troops met at the Elbe River in 1945 was forgotten. Peace, the demobilization of eleven million soldiers, and the new economic boom intoxicated Americans, and distracted them from politics. The Depression did not return and a period of unparalleled prosperity began. The new enemy became the old ally: the Soviet Union.

In March 1946 British Prime Minister Winston Churchill delivered an articulate and thoroughly political commencement speech at Westminster College in Fulton, Missouri. The Iron Curtain speech presented the Anglo-American point-of-view on the Cold War.

From Stettin in the Baltic to Trieste in the Adriatic an iron curtain has descended across the Continent. Behind that line lie all the capitals of the ancient states of Central and Eastern Europe. Warsaw, Berlin, Prague, Vienna, Budapest, Belgrade, Bucharest and Sofia, all these famous cities and the populations around them lie in what I must call the Soviet sphere, and all are subject in one form or another, not only to Soviet influence but to a very high and, in some cases, increasing measure of control from Moscow. Athens alone -- Greece with its immortal glories -- is free to decide its future at an election under British, American and French observation.

Russian success at testing an atomic bomb in August 1949 polarized Americans still further. No longer was there an American monopoly on nuclear weapons. The result in the United States was tightened security at research installations, more appropriations for the military, and stepped up repression against leftist groups. In New York City even master-builder Robert Moses used Cold War rhetoric to attack his opponents. Moses was a red-baiter before anyone had heard of Senator Joseph McCarthy. He often labeled those who disagreed with his urban renewal projects as communists.

The Korean War, which began in 1950 and lasted until 1953, intensified the struggle between the Soviet Union and the United States. The Russians backed the North Koreans and the United States supported the South Koreans and also sent American soldiers to participate in the war. When the Chinese entered on the side of North Korea, Truman threatened to use atomic bombs. General Douglas MacArthur was overly enthusiastic and began making speeches opposing Truman for moving too slowly. Truman subsequently fired MacArthur.

In 1953, following the Korean War, the Soviets successfully tested a hydrogen bomb, one year after the U.S. tested its H-bomb. The explosion caused by just one hydrogen bomb dropped on New York City could destroy every building in the five boroughs. Powerful new military weapons further intensifying the mutual threat each side could potentially use against the other. *Sputnik*, a Soviet space station, was launched in 1957 and sent shock waves across the United States. While each side claimed the purpose of their space program was purely scientific and had communications, map-making, and weather predicting as its purposes, many people suspected that the military had goals that trumped the civilian objectives. Newspaper and magazine articles speculated that once space stations were established, nuclear bombs and lasers could be sent down bringing destruction to enemies on earth. The result was an atmosphere of crisis and fear.

Repression followed each new political and military event. Witch-hunts brought hundreds of government workers before Loyalty Review Boards after they had been denounced or accused by their co-workers. In New York City, the C.U.N.Y. faculty and public school teachers were especially hard hit. Interminable investigations by the House Un-American Activities Committee (HUAC) kept espionage and Cold War conflicts on the front page. In that period of continual crisis the big issues included the Berlin blockade and airlift in 1948 and 1949, the execution of Julius and

Ethel Rosenberg for espionage in 1953, Senator Joseph McCarthy's incendiary charges especially during the Senate Army-McCarthy hearings in 1954, and an American U-2 spy plane piloted by Francis Gary Powers shot down by the Russians in 1960.

The enigma was that all the solutions offered by Russian and American politicians to nuclear arms race were deficient, or even absurd. Waging nuclear war against an enemy also armed with nuclear weapons would be mass suicide. Superpower arsenals contained at least 50,000 nuclear bombs in the 1980s. Unilateral disarmament by either antagonist would be too risky and was unacceptable to both sides. Russians and Americans responded to the dilemma with the arms race, increasing their respective nuclear stockpiles. They increased propaganda at home and abroad, and set up civil defense procedures.

From Harry Truman to Ronald Reagan there were presidential platitudes about the horrors of nuclear war. *Starting an atomic war is totally unthinkable for rational men,* said Truman in 1952. Reagan stated in 1982 that: *A nuclear war cannot be won and must never be fought.* It is impossible to know why the Cold War never transformed into nuclear Armageddon. Conventional wisdom has it that deterrence came with the policy of Mutual Assured Destruction. Despite the unintended effectiveness of the MAD policy, there were many armed struggles where Russians and Americans backed opposing sides and where several million died. The wars in Korea, Vietnam, and Afghanistan were the most deadly, but there were also wars in Angola, the Congo, Ethiopia, Somalia, Nicaragua, El Salvador, and many other countries that were both local conflicts and theaters of the hot segment of the Cold War. One thing the smaller wars had in common was that no nuclear weapons were used in any of the struggles.

The 21st century finds more than a dozen countries possessing nuclear weapons, but since the Soviet Union collapsed in 1991, the world has, at least for now, only one superpower. Acting alone the United States has pursued various carrot and stick strategies to prevent most new countries from developing nuclear arsenals. The result has not been an American monopoly of power, but a United States with such overwhelming nuclear and conventional capability that challenges to American hegemony have been discouraged.

While much of the Cold War had to do with political and military leaders, and daily reports in the press, a program that touched everyday lives of most Americans was civil defense. Every war has a civil defense component that mixes political, military, and first aid responses to real or potential attacks. The policies and programs of the Federal Civil Defense Administration, created by Congress and signed into law by Harry Truman in 1950, gained credence as fear spread. People were frightened that if the D.E.W. line (Distant Early Warning) in Canada and Alaska failed to warn the U.S. military in time to counter in-coming bombers or missiles, or if submarines attacked from the Atlantic and Pacific Oceans, there would need to be a vibrant response at home. This was a chilling thought in a country that had not had death and destruction on its territory since the Civil War.

There were two equal and contradictory goals that can be discerned in the civil defense program. One was to ratchet up apprehension and anxiety over the Soviet threat in order to gain support for increased military appropriations and armed adventures abroad. The other was to soothe and calm down the public to combat defeatism and foster the notion that survival from nuclear blasts, radiation, and contamination was possible. To that end government propaganda and disinformation that civil defense procedures could save lives and claims that the domestic program of nuclear testing was not dangerous flooded the country. In its first year of operation the Federal Civil Defense Administration published *Survival under Atomic Attack* maintaining a cheerful optimism: *You can survive. You can live through an atom bomb raid and you won't have to have a Geiger counter, protective clothing or special training to do it.*

In some ways the Soviet civil defense system was similar. Participation was compulsory and was based on what Joseph Stalin called ***the inevitability of war*** between the capitalist and communist powers. (In 1956 Nikita Khrushchev softened Stalin's appraisal: *We deny the fatal inevitability of war. But, of course, no one can say categorically that there will be no war.)* Much of the Soviet preparation was similar to plans that they had used against the Nazis, especially the reliance on public shelters, evacuation, and gas masks. The subway systems in major cities had been built particularly deep so the stations could serve as bomb shelters. If the credibility of Soviet civil defense was stronger than in the United States, it was because the Soviet Union had been invaded by Germany in 1941 resulting in 25 million Soviet deaths. While there was little debate or dissent concerning civil defense in the United States in the early 1950s, none was allowed in the Soviet Union.

Because each state had the responsibility to set up its own civil defense program, with the federal government providing matching funds, the actual implementation of procedures varied widely by state and locality. New York City was one of the most committed to the civil defense program in part because it was assumed that with Washington, D.C., New York City would be one of the two primary targets in a nuclear attack.

The U.S. Army and the Federal Civil Defense Administration promoted news stories, public service announcements, films (one narrated by Edward R. Murrow), newsreel shorts at the movies, traveling lecturers with portable exhibits, and panel discussants on television talk shows to get out their message. Right-wing politicians, with Joseph McCarthy and Richard Nixon in the lead, stoked fear and paranoia. The federal government aimed at firming the resolve of the American people in case of a Soviet attack or a pre-emptive American attack on the Soviet Union. A compliant press and electronic media carried stories that underscored the government's position.

There was, of course, suspicion and skepticism among many intellectuals and even among some elements of the general population. A certain gallows humor evolved by the late 1950s as people tired of the tense situation and increasingly doubted that survival after a nuclear conflagration was possible. Jokes, popular songs, and flippant comments made the rounds. Eventually movies began conveying doubts as well as the fervent desire for an end to the Cold War and its strident politics.

By the 1960s there were several films that questioned key ideas of civil defense or poked fun at the imminence of a Soviet-American war. In *The Day the Earth Stood Still* (1951), an alien visits earth to warn leaders that if their conflicts spread to space they will face dire consequences. In *On the Beach* (1959), life on earth ends after fallout from nuclear war. *Dr. Strangelove: or How I Learned to Stop Worrying and Love the Bomb* (1964), shows an insane general who plans a nuclear holocaust that a war room of politicians and generals desperately try to stop. *Fail Safe* (1964), presents a scenario that ends with atomic bombs destroying Moscow and New York City. In *Thunderball* (1965), James Bond foils the SPECTRE plot to hold the world for ransom after having stolen a bomber with two nuclear bombs on board. *The Russians are Coming, the Russians are Coming* (1966), has eight sailors from a grounded Russian submarine landing on Martha's Vineyard where locals fear an invasion. In *Planet of the Apes* (1968), chimpanzees rule the world and humans are mere animals two millennia after a nuclear war. Though not a movie, Bob Dylan's *Talking World War III Blues*, stands up as a poignant attack on the whole idea of civil defense in a nuclear age.

Civil defense had several goals. An important objective was to establish public fallout shelters and promote the building of private fallout shelters. Public fallout shelters were established in every city and town in the United States. In New York City the subway stations, and basements of commercial buildings, apartment houses, schools, churches, and synagogues were declared to be fallout shelters. None, of course, could actually protect its occupants from nuclear fallout. Yellow and black signs heralding FALLOUT SHELTER below the nuclear symbol were ubiquitous throughout the five boroughs. Faded and weather-beaten, some are still affixed to buildings.

Leaders of the federal government had spent millions of dollars building special fallout shelters for themselves in Raven Rock, Pennsylvania, High Point, Virginia, and under the Greenbrier resort in White Sulpher Springs, West Virginia. Presumably the government leaders would attempt to administer the country from their shelters during and after a nuclear conflagration. The existence and location of the three facilities were secret at the time.

Very few private fallout shelters were built anywhere. They were expensive and only homeowners could construct them. Nelson Rockefeller, elected governor of New York State from 1959 to 1973 and appointed vice president of the United States from 1973 to 1977, was a vociferous advocate for both public and private fallout shelters. He failed in 1960 to persuade the New York State

Legislature to enact a billion dollar project for construction of shelters in each school building and to compel every homeowner to build a fallout shelter. Acting on his own, Rockefeller had shelters built under his apartment house in Manhattan and under the governor's mansion in Albany.

The focus of the government's advocacy campaign for fallout shelters did not dwell on the strategic issues involved. There was virtually no discussion of nuclear blast, firestorms, evacuation chaos, adequate storage and maintenance of uncontaminated food and water, half-life of radiated areas, and ultimate decontamination. Instead, the public was kept busy with the construction details and the tactics of supplying a fallout shelter. Endless suggestions for clothing, food, water storage, and first aid supplies were provided. The public shelters were stocked with modest amounts of water, crackers, bandages, and tranquilizers. Over the years the supplies disappeared.

When the air raid sirens shrieked and wailed, which they did once a year in New York City, all citizens were required to go into a public or private fallout shelter. Failure to comply was punishable by a $100 fine. The police enlisted thousands of neighborhood monitors to help enforce the rules.

Schools were an important theater of the campaign for civil defense. Children were asked to wear hats because the brims might prevent face burns, and they were given dog tags for identification in case of a nuclear attack. Lectures, films, and air-raid drills took place with frequency in New York City schools. The highlight was the *duck and cover* routine. It had several variations but the most common was, as soon as the siren sounded, the children would hide under their desks or work tables and protect their heads with their clasped hands. To help them remember, the Federal Civil Defense Administration and the National Education Association commissioned a song and a live-action, part animated film, starring Bert the Turtle. The live-action parts of *Duck and Cover*, the 1951 short, were filmed in P.S. 152 in Woodside, Queens.

There was a turtle by the name of Bert,
And Bert the Turtle was very alert.
When danger threatened him he never got hurt;
He knew just what to do:

Duck and cover, duck and cover.
He knew just what to do.

In school air raid drills, classroom lights needed to be turned out, shades drawn, and Venetian blinds closed before the children ducked under their desks or filed out into the corridor to crouch down along the wall. When in the playground, children were instructed to assume a hedgehog position and put their sweaters and coats up over their heads.

There were never evacuation drills, but maps of suggested methods and routes out of the city were printed in the newspapers and broadcast by radio and television. The Federal Emergency Management Agency (FEMA) had drawn up plans to simultaneously evacuate approximately four hundred cities and two thousand towns in case of nuclear war. The media refrained from questioning how a city of eight million inhabitants, 40 percent without cars, could evacuate New York City. How much warning time was needed? How long would it take? Would pets and baggage including clothing, food, and medical supplies be permitted? Could order be maintained? Where would the evacuees go? These questions were not raised by the press but New Yorkers, all too familiar with traffic jams every day during rush hour and quite experienced in negotiating the weekend rush out of and into the city, found plans for civil defense evacuation completely impractical. It undercut the credence of civil defense.

The Skywatchers Program of the Ground Observation Corps had 800,000 volunteer spotters at 16,000 observation posts looking for hostile aircraft. It enlisted adults and high school students to spend voluntary hours standing on top of buildings with binoculars scanning the sky for enemy planes and, in the meantime, taking down the identifying markings of any airplanes they saw overhead.

In New York City, the end for civil defense came with a whimper. Increasingly the public perceived air-raid drills, civil defense plans, and the arms race as enormous failures. Civil defense offered no real protection against the horrors of nuclear war and the clumsy attempt at controlling public perception was ridiculed.

There were many groups that opposed the arms race and the policies of civil defense: American Friends Service Committee,

National Committee for a Sane Nuclear Policy (SANE), Fellowship of Reconciliation, Women Strike for Peace, Women's International League for Peace and Freedom, War Resisters League, and the Catholic Workers movement. A focal point for their opposition came with the annual Operation Alert sponsored by the Federal Civil Defense Administration.

Operation Alert's first mass air raid drill in 1955 drew opposition from the War Resisters League, American Friends Service Committee, and the Catholic Worker movement. A handful of opponents gathered in City Hall Park and refused to seek cover when the sirens sounded. Twenty-seven, including Dorothy Day of the Catholic Workers and Bayard Rustin of the War Resisters League and the civil rights movement, were arrested. Over the next five years opposition began to grow. Demonstrations were held near nuclear test sites and *die-ins* became a form of street theater to capture attention for the anti-nuclear movement. In 1960 the protest at City Hall against Operation Alert included prominent writers, college and high school students. Posters ridiculed the whole idea of civil defense as a workable response to nuclear war and called for a policy of mutual disarmament.

In 1961, demonstrations took place at several high schools and college campuses as well as the main action at City Hall that drew two thousand participants. Only a few dozen random arrests were made. Unwilling to engender growing opposition and faced with an increasingly skeptical and lackadaisical response by the public, the 1962 Operation Alert air raid drill was quietly canceled and never held again.

Tensions had grown greatly during the early years of the Cold War. The United States alone possessed at least 30,000 nuclear warheads in 1960 and had tested 124 above ground and four underground nuclear bombs from 1946 to 1963. Finally, Soviet-American détente, or the policy of peaceful coexistence, lessened the fear engendered by the Cold War. President Ronald Reagan, trying to resuscitate the paranoia, postured against the Soviet Union calling it an *evil empire,* and attempted to get Congress to pass the greatest civil defense program ever, *Star Wars,* a plan to construct space stations and missiles to create a protective bubble over all fifty states. The reaction in New York City was a peace march against nuclear war in June 1982. One million marched from the United Nations to Central Park. Star Wars never passed Congress and Reagan failed to resuscitate Cold War fears.

There were two federal programs in the Cold War that were pushed through Congress by the Eisenhower Administration that few people, liberal or conservative, opposed. The National Highway Act created 43,000 miles of Interstate Highway between 1956 and 1991. It makes it possible for vacationers to drive their cars from coast to coast and for industrial and agricultural products to quickly reach their destinations by truck. It spawned a whole system of gas stations, fast food restaurants, motels, tourist shops, and made suburban life beyond commuter rail lines possible. The National Highway Act conceptualized the present National System of Interstate and Defense Highways passing the House by a vote of 388 to 19 and approved by the Senate on a voice vote of overwhelming approval. It was supported by the Pentagon as a bulwark against attack by the Soviet Union because it would allow for movement of weapons, soldiers, and supplies. Naturally it received the vigorous support of Wall Street investors, construction companies, the Teamsters Union, automobile manufacturers, the gasoline industry, and entrepreneurs involved with recreation, vacation, and roadside businesses.

Eisenhower also appealed to Cold War fears of Soviet technical and mathematical superiority after Sputnik to get the National Defense Education Act passed in 1958. The NDEA subsidized universities, colleges, and high schools by providing funds to bolster education in science, mathematics, modern foreign languages, technical education, area studies, geography, and libraries. Subsequent federal legislation guaranteed low-cost college loans. Some people joked that Joseph Stalin unwittingly gave the American people modern highways and better schools.

CHAPTER 114
Suburbia

The Latin derivation of *suburbia* is less than flattering: *sub* (under, below, or secondary to the) *urb* (city). By 1980, more than half of all Americans lived in the suburbs. Today, in Greater New York, eight million people live in the city's five boroughs and about eight million live in the ten surrounding suburban counties. Some have cheery names like Pleasantville, Fair Lawn, Valhalla, Lake Success, and Garden City, or countryside names such as Valley Cottage, Pine Island, Shrub Oak, Floral Park, Greenlawn, and Flower Hill. What has been their attraction?

For New Yorkers who felt cramped in small apartments the suburbs seemed wonderful. Families could have individual free-standing houses, a car or two with a garage, yards for playing, gardening, and barbecuing. An icon of suburbia was the basketball hoop attached over the garage door. Station wagons were the initial choice for the *second* car.

To qualify as a suburb in the 19th century, the distance had to be short enough to allow you to commute to your job and back each day. So early towns like Harlem, Flushing, Gravesend were not suburbs because they were too far away to commute on horseback or in a carriage. The first real suburbs of New York City (which was just the southern tip of Manhattan) were Brooklyn Heights, and Tompkinsville, Staten Island.

Farmer and land speculator Hezekiah Pierrepont laid out a grid of streets on his farmland on a ridge on Brooklyn Heights overlooking the East River and offered lots for sale. He began advertising his lots (25 x 100 feet) in 1823. Daniel D. Tompkins, land speculator and Vice President under James Monroe, bought farmland on the north shore of Staten Island and sold lots. He named the area Tompkinsville and gave some of the streets he laid out the first names of his children.

Key to both suburban developments was regularly scheduled steam ferry service, which had just been developed by Robert Fulton. Once the transportation was in place, the lots could be sold to people willing to commute across the water to their offices in Manhattan. The steam ferry to Brooklyn began in 1814 and to Staten Island in 1817.

Naturally the city kept moving north in Manhattan at the same time it was adding suburbs. It incorporated Greenwich Village, the village of Harlem, and smaller hamlets as houses and streets filled up the island. Steam railways connected New York City with Harlem in 1837 and over bridges to the Bronx and Westchester in 1844.

The four outer boroughs had been farmland dotted with villages. As they grew, votes were held and most of the Bronx joined New York City. In 1898 an election was held to incorporate the remainder of the Bronx, and all of Brooklyn, Queens, and Staten Island into New York City. The vote for consolidation was yes everywhere except in two Westchester County towns that remained part of Westchester County. Why did the majority vote yes? Their tax rates would go down. Manhattan has an enormous tax base because it is filled with businesses. Consolidating the five counties together into one city would keep taxes down for homeowners.

Suburbanization outside of the five boroughs was dependant on transportation. It had to wait for the railroads. By the early 20th century there were railroad lines running to Nassau County in Long Island, Westchester County, Fairfield County in Connecticut, and to several places in New Jersey. Eventually Metro North, beginning at Grand Central Terminal, would develop the Harlem Line and the Hudson Line through Westchester, and the New Haven Line with four branches to Connecticut. The Long Island Railroad built eight lines from Pennsylvania Station, plus one from Brooklyn and one from Queens, to Long Island. The Ronkonkoma and Montauk branches stretched to the two eastern tips of Long Island, 110 miles from Manhattan.

PATH Lines (Port Authority Trans Hudson) connected Manhattan to Hoboken, New Jersey, where commuters could catch the Port Jervis and Pascack Valley Lines to northern New Jersey and Rockland County suburbs in Upstate New York. From Pennsylvania Station, Amtrak offered stops along the way to Philadelphia.

New Jersey Transit ran the Morristown, Boonton, Raritan Valley, Northeast Corridor, and New Jersey Coast Lines.

Buses roll out of the Port Authority around the clock. The list of bus companies is long: Olympia Trails, Greyhound, Bee-Line, Red and Tan, Short Line, Spring Valley Jitney, Transport of Rockland, Leprechaun Lines, Bonanza, Arrow Line, Adirondack Trailways, Long Island Bus, Suffolk Transit, and Peter Pan Trailways. Ferries cross the rivers and harbor taking commuters shorter distances.

One and a half million New Yorkers live in Manhattan today, but four and a half million work there. Many of those people stream in from the suburbs as well as the outer boroughs in the complex commuter system that has developed over two centuries.

The first wave of suburbanization was mostly for wealthy people who could afford the expense of a daily round-trip train ticket. Early suburbs attracted people who could afford to build spacious stone houses on large lots. Many had cooks, housekeepers, and gardeners. Examples of the older suburbs were Rye, Tarrytown, New Rochelle, Garden City, Woodmere, Lawrence, and Teaneck.

The second wave of suburbanization came after the Second World War. It was a mad dash. By then, many things had changed. The Great Depression was over and a period of great economic prosperity began in 1945 and lasted until 1973. Middle class and working class people could afford cars, telephones, and more luxurious housing. The G.I. Bill of Rights gave veterans of the Second World War free college tuition and subsidized loans for home mortgages. Twelve million Americans were eligible for G.I. benefits. And there was the Baby Boom. More space was needed as families grew after the low birth rates during the depression and the war. The Baby Boom would last from 1946 until 1965.

There were other forces at work to help develop suburbia. Automobile companies, oil companies, construction companies for highways and housing, commuter train and bus lines, and restaurants along the roads all actively encouraged suburban development. The governments of the United States and New York State responded by constructing an enormous highway system with new bridges and tunnels to speed commuting. Master builder Robert Moses, officially head of the Triborough Bridge and Tunnel Authority, supervised the program for New York State. Moses had close working relationships with governors (beginning with Al Smith) and presidents (starting with Franklin D. Roosevelt). Besides highways, he also planned regional parks and beaches, most for the convenience and enjoyment of suburban people. His triumph was the gorgeous Jones Beach on the south shore of Long Island. Moses made sure to build all the overpasses too low for buses to pass under; Jones Beach was planned for suburban people who traveled in cars, not New York City people if they could not afford cars.

Technology and business practices also fostered the meteoric growth of the suburbs. William Levitt bought farmland in Long Island, subdivided it, and built tract houses in neat rows along curved roads. He built thousands of houses, sometimes finishing two hundred in a week. He did it with mass production techniques developed for other industries by Eli Whitney and Henry Ford. The key was uniformity; all the houses had four and a half rooms and they were all painted green and white. One architectural plan was all Levitt needed. Construction teams were specialized for their tasks: excavating, cement mixing, framing, roofing, cabinetry, plumbing, electricity, plastering, and painting. To speed up delivery of supplies Levitt began producing nails, shingles, cement, and lumber. The suburb William Levitt built, Levittown, was a remarkable achievement. His methods were used as a prototype throughout the metropolitan region.

Even with refugees entering New York from war torn Europe, and considerable migration from the American South, and immigration from Puerto Rico, the rush to the suburbs made a huge impact on the city. Its population decreased from eight million to seven million by 1970. It lost many middle class white families who sought the American Dream in the suburbs, not in the city. The negative impact was felt as crime rose, jobs were lost, subway and bus service deteriorated, schools suffered, and the city was filled with litter and graffiti. The 1970s were the truly bleak period in the 20th century for New York City.

Of course, everything was not idyllic in the suburbs. Some grew tired of the segregation. Suburbs were segregated by *race* (minorities were kept out), *age* (mostly young married couples with children), and *income*. Because each development was priced similarly, each attracted people in a similar income tax bracket. If someone made more money, they usually *traded up* and moved to a more expensive suburb. Few older people were interested in leaving the city to relocate to the suburbs. Blacks and Hispanics were barred until the Civil Rights Act (1964) outlawed all forms of segregation including property *covenants* designed to keep out minorities.

More pressing problems included the dependence on cars. No suburban bus service meant that when the kids weren't in the recreation room complaining that they had nothing to do, they needed to be chauffeured around everywhere, usually by mom. Some women complained about the boredom of suburban life. Dads tired of the train ride or the drive on the increasingly clogged highways. People began to call the Long Island Expressway, another project of Robert Moses, the *Longest Parking Lot in the World*.

Meanwhile, just as New York City hit its lowest point, national immigration quotas were raised and the city began attracting immigrants from all over the world, especially Latin America and Asia. They gave the city new energy and an enlarged workforce. Many suburban Baby Boomers chose not to return to the suburbs after college. They liked the activity of the city. Some of the people from the Second World War generation who left the city for the suburbs in the 1940s and 50s decided not to retire in Florida or Arizona, but to sell the house and buy a condominium in Manhattan to be close to plays, concerts, and museums. By 2000 the population was back to 8 million.

As we progress into the 21st century New York City is cleaner, safer, more efficient, and more exciting than in a very long time. People all around the world share the perception. Over fifty million tourists visit the city each year where 75,000 hotel rooms are ready to accommodate them. Modern suburbia posed a challenge for New York City, but after some hard times the city rose to the challenge and bounced back.

CHAPTER 115
Verrazano Narrows Bridge

Because four of the five New York City boroughs are on islands travel between them and to New Jersey or to the mainland of New York State depends on bridges and tunnels. King's Bridge, built in 1693, was the first span connecting Manhattan to the Bronx at a narrow point (West 225th Street) over the winding course of the Spuyten Duyvil Creek. King's Bridge, and Kingsbridge Avenue, was an Indian path that later became a colonial trail, honored William III of England.

The Verrazano Narrows Bridge, more popularly called the Verrazano Bridge, is the last link in a series of 2,027 bridges in the city. That surprisingly large number includes seventy-six bridges over bodies of water and 1,951 over land. They range from the large structures that span the Hudson and East Rivers to the small bridges that cross the Bronx River and the Gowanus Canal. Most of the land bridges are built over railroad tracks, subway lines, highways, and over roadways inside parks. Some are pedestrian bridges.

The Verrazano Bridge was named for Giovanni da Verrazzano, an Italian in the service of France, who sailed into New York Harbor in 1524. He led an expedition that navigated along the coast between what is now North Carolina and Cape Breton, Canada. Verrazzano was the first European to record entering New York Harbor. He found the area *hospitable and attractive* but did not stay long. In fact, he thought the Inner Harbor was a lake and named it Santa Margarita to honor the sister of Francis I, King of France. *La Dauphine*, Verrazzano's ship, anchored in the narrow strait between Brooklyn and Staten Island. Eventually the Narrows became the Verrazzano Narrows. The Verrazano Narrows Bridge opened in 1964 and the spelling of the seafarer's name was changed. Robert Moses dropped one z in the name. Moses was chairman of the Triborough Bridge and Tunnel Authority, the government agency, which built and owns the suspension bridge.

Moses ordered the alteration so it would be easier to pronounce the explorer's Italian name. (But don't we do just fine with *pizza*?)

Staten Island has a tenuous geographic connection to New York City. Three bridges connect it with New Jersey but only one bridge and a ferry connect it to the rest of New York City. The Verrazzano Narrows is a wide strait with choppy waters. Its width measures 2,500 feet. On the west side of the island, New Jersey is just a stone's throw across the Kill Van Kull and the even narrower Arthur Kill. The Kill Van Kull is a tidal strait about one thousand feet wide and the Arthur Kill, as the southern part of the same strait is called, is a bit narrower.

In the northwest corner of the island the Bayonne Bridge, constructed in 1931, connects Staten Island to Bayonne, New Jersey. The nearby Goethals Bridge, built in 1928, connects Staten Island to Elizabeth. At the southwest part of the island the Outerbridge Crossing, also built in 1928, attaches it to Perth Amboy. It might seem that the Outerbridge Crossing got its name by being the most southern, or *outer* crossing from New York City, but the bridge's name honors Staten Island resident, Eugenius Outerbridge, the first chairman of the Port of New York Authority. It is called the Outerbridge Crossing rather than the Outerbridge Bridge to avoid what would be a silly redundancy.

While Staten Island was a political segment of New York City, its commerce was much more closely connected with New Jersey until the construction of the Verrazano Bridge. Moses' Triborough Bridge and Tunnel Authority changed both the demographics and economy of Staten Island by building the new link with Brooklyn. Land prices increased exponentially in 1956 when the plans for the bridge were announced.

Not everyone was pleased with the bridge. On the Brooklyn side its approach roads took out hundreds of houses and apartment buildings displacing eight thousand people. Robert Moses ran the bridge's main approach, the Gowanus Expressway, through the block between 6th and 7th Avenues, which meant most of the buildings between 65th and 101st Streets had to be demolished. Bay Ridge, which had traditionally indistinct borders, was now defined solely by the Gowanus Expressway and Shore Parkway, which encircled it. The northern end of the neighborhood was grafted on to Sunset Park and the eastern end fused with Dyker Heights. Fortunately the highways were routed around Fort Hamilton and the 25-acre campus surrounding Polytechnic Preparatory Country Day School. Fort Hamilton dates from 1825 and Poly Prep was built in 1924.

On Staten Island it was different. Gay Talese, author of *The Bridge*, wrote: *On the Staten Island side, opposition to the bridge was nothing like it was in Brooklyn, where more than twice as many people and buildings were effected by the bridge; in fact, in Staten Island there had long been powerful factions that dreamed of the day when a bridge might be built to link their borough more firmly with the rest of New York City*. That linkage, of course, turned out to be a double-edged sword.

The Verrazano Narrows Bridge was a masterpiece of modern engineering technology. When it was built in 1964 it was the longest and most expensive suspension bridge in the world. The structure's length is 6,690 feet held up by 145,000 miles of steel wire twisted into four cables each three feet in diameter. The steel cables are connected to two large towers each 623 feet high and anchored into concrete and steel caissons sunk deep into man-made islands. Approximately 160,000 tons of steel and 570,000 cubic yards of concrete were used in the project. The center clearance at high tide is 228 feet, high enough to allow the tallest ships in the world to pass underneath.

The Verrazano Bridge is double-decked with six lanes on each level. The design, by Swiss engineer Othmar H. Ammann, is majestic and graceful. While some people opposed building the bridge, few disliked its design. Its function is to connect Staten Island and Brooklyn but its artistic value is as a monumental gateway to the city from the Atlantic Ocean. In *Saturday Night Fever*, a 1978 movie set in Bay Ridge, John Travolta and friends got out of their cars and played daredevil games at the bridge's edge.

Gay Talese celebrated the workers who constructed the enormous span. Tradition dictates that New York bridge builders are called *ironworkers* even though contemporary bridges are no longer built of iron but of steel. Sometimes the ironworkers call themselves *boomers* because they participate in *building booms*. Gay Talese described them romantically: *In appearance, boomers usually are big men, or if not always big, always, strong, and their skin is ruddy from all the sun and wind. Some who heat rivets have charred complexions; some who drive rivets are hard of hearing; some who catch rivets in small metal cones have blisters and body burns marking each miss; some who do welding see flashes at night while they sleep. Those who connect steel have deep scars along their shins from climbing columns. Many boomers have mangled hands and fingers sliced off by slipped steel. Most have taken falls and broken a limb or two. All have seen death.* Among the bridge workers were American Indians, both Mohawks and Caughnawagas, who have a long and proud history as ironworkers on New York City's skyscrapers and bridges. At the time most of them lived in Boerum Hill, Brooklyn.

The Verrazano Narrows Bridge changed Staten Island from a loose community of small towns to a thickly settled suburban area. The remaining farmland was sold to developers who built tract housing and the forests not included in La Tourette and other parks were chopped down and they too became neighborhoods of densely populated suburban housing.

After 1964, the population of Staten Island soared. It seemed possible to many newcomers, mostly from Brooklyn, that they really could escape urban decay and poor schools, buy a single-family or two-family house, have a backyard, and an above-ground pool if they relocated to Staten Island. Architectural historian Norval White characterized the resulting building frenzy on the island as producing *banal monotony and vulgarity.* It also fused together the distinct villages and settlements within the borough. The various village centers can still be discerned by looking closely at sets of older buildings clustered together. That is now one of the Staten Island's charms, but there are no longer clear borders or open space between former villages.

The population of Staten Island increased from 221,000 in 1960 to 468,000 in 2010. Most of the newer buildings are three-story houses. It has become increasingly obvious that almost all the open land was gone and construction had nowhere to go but up. The result is that Staten Island is beginning to look like the other three outer boroughs as it loses its old character and low-density population. The expense of crossing the bridge has not been a deterrent to travel or commuting. The toll was 50 cents one-way when the Verrazano Bridge opened in 1964. By the end of the 20th century the toll reached $7.50, collected only from westbound traffic. By 2014 the cash toll was $15.00 ($10.66 with E-Z Pass). Staten Island residents get a discount.

CHAPTER 116
Houses of Worship: Religious Buildings from Colonial Days

When New Amsterdam was founded in 1625 the world knew very little religious tolerance. The Dutch were an exception. The Netherlands was about half Roman Catholic and half Protestant, and the most religiously tolerant country in Europe. The prosperous 17th century Dutch Republic was obsessed with business and not keen to be sidetracked by religious disputes. These two factors created some semblance of pluralism. The Reformed Church (Protestant) was the official religion of the country, but other groups enjoyed freedom of religion. In fact, pluralism was popular and thousands of immigrants had moved to the Netherlands to enjoy religious toleration. (The Pilgrims, before they immigrated to Plymouth in 1620, had lived in the Netherlands for exactly that reason.)

The policy for the Dutch colony of New Netherlands was less tolerant than in the mother country, though more liberal than most places in the world. The colony was driven by the quest for money, not religious perfection, though only the Dutch Reformed denomination of Protestantism was permitted build churches. Other Protestants could live in town and worship freely in their homes, but could not construct churches. Catholics, Jews, and non-believers were not allowed to settle in the New Amsterdam at all. The penalty for a Catholic priest saying Mass in New Amsterdam was death. Eventually religious restrictions softened. Small Quaker communities were allowed to live in Flushing, Queens and in Gravesend, Brooklyn. Puritans from New England were permitted to settle in Long Island. During the English period, after 1664, permission was granted incrementally to various religions to settle in New York and build religious buildings for worship.

The unexpected arrival and ultimate acceptance of a group of Jews was the first official crack in the religious monopoly Peter Stuyvesant wanted for the Reformed Church. When twenty-three

Sephardic Jews from Recifé, Brazil arrived in New Amsterdam in 1654, Stuyvesant imprisoned them and refused to allow them to settle in the colony. The Dutch West India Company, which had Jewish investors, eventually overturned his decision and the refugees were allowed to remain.

The Flushing Remonstrance was the second crack in the religious monopoly of the Reformed Church. English settlers in Flushing, Queens wrote a Remonstrance (petition) to Stuyvesant against his policies prohibiting worship by Quakers. John Bowne had been arrested, imprisoned and fined in 1662 for allowing Quakers to meet in his house. He took the issue to the directors of the Dutch West India Company in Amsterdam. They upheld his position and ordered Stuyvesant to allow all Protestant worship in the colony.

Still, until the establishment of the United States with its First Amendment guarantee that no religion would be established above the others, the colony did have an established church just as the other twelve colonies had official government-supported religions. During the Dutch period (1625-1664) the established church was the Reformed Church, a Protestant denomination, and the Anglican Church was the established religion of the English period (1664-1783). At the end of the American Revolution, the Anglican Church in the American colonies became organizationally independent as the Episcopal Church. An *established* religion is an *official* religion. It means that public money is used to support the upkeep of the church and church school buildings and to pay the salaries of the clergy. It also means that the established church's clergy deliver public prayers and influence laws.

During the English colonial period the role of Trinity parish, officially part of the Diocese of London, dominated religion in the city. Other Anlican churches were just *chapels* of Trinity which centralized administrative and religious control in the colony. Trinity was the established church. In 1705 Queen Anne gave the parish an enormous land grant: from Fulton Street to Christopher Street and from Broadway to the Hudson River. It was called the Queen's Farm (or King's Farm when there was a king on England's throne) and parcels were rented out to tenant farmers to raise money for Trinity.

In the 18th century other people moved to New York and Anglicans became the minority. Still the Anglican Church was the official religion of the colony, Dutch Reformed Church members remained, and other Protestant denominations grew with the arrival of new immigrants: Congregationalists from New England, Huguenots from France, Lutherans from Germany and Scandinavia, and Presbyterians from Scotland and Northern Ireland. German and Irish Catholics began arriving in the late 18th century and their numbers increased enormously in the early years of the American Republic. Sephardic Jews (originally from Spain and Portugal) came by way of Brazil and the Caribbean colonies. Later, Ashkenazic Jews from Germany settled in New York. The much larger Jewish immigration came later in the 19th century when Ashkenazic Jews from Eastern Europe arrived.

The United States Constitution guarantees freedom of religion in the opening clause of the First Amendment: *Congress shall make no law respecting an establishment of religion, or prohibiting the free exercise thereof; or abridging the freedom of speech, or of the press; or the right of the people peaceably to assemble, and to petition the Government for a redress of grievances.*

Nonetheless, relations between various religious groups, especially Protestants and Catholics, have had a stormy past. Multicultural acceptance has made it possible for more peaceful relations between religious groups in the years since the Second World War. Today, New York City is home to members of virtually every religion on earth.

All religions have central meeting, praying, and gathering places. Their houses of worship differ in style and use. The congregations that presently use them built many of them. Some converted commercial or residential buildings into religious centers. Others purchased religious buildings from religious congregations that moved elsewhere or ceased to exist. Some houses of worship were very elaborate and others were quite simple. Most Christian churches and Jewish synagogues in New York City were constructed during the 19th century. But there are some examples from before that time, and many from after it.

The architecture of religious buildings often aimed at connecting the house of worship with a specific historical tradition or country. That was true of non-religious architecture also. For example, because the Islamic Cultural Center's mosque on East 96th Street and 3rd Avenue in Manhattan traced its ancestry to the Middle East, the sponsors chose to build a domed structure with a slender minaret that evoked the style of Middle Eastern mosques.

The Hindu Temple Society of North America (dedicated to Ganesha) on Bowne Street near Holly Avenue in Flushing, Queens was patterned after a South Indian temple. The Nichiren Shoshu Buddhist Temple in East Flushing was built in the austere, restrained form popular in Japan. The Jacques Marchais Center of Tibetan Art, in New Dorp, Staten Island, was made to look like a Tibetan Buddhist monastery and now functions periodically as a Tibetan Buddhist temple. A Daoist congregation in Queens built the elaborate and colorful Hua Lian Tsu Hui Temple in College Point in 2012.

The founders of Saint Nicholas Russian Orthodox Cathedral on East 97th Street near 5th Avenue constructed a tall building with one large onion dome and four small onion domes, each topped with a three-barred cross because that was how Orthodox churches were usually built in Russia. The designers of Saint Vartan's Armenian Apostolic Cathedral on 2nd Avenue and East 34th Street in Manhattan respected a time-honored Armenian practice of constructing churches with a circular dome topped by a conical roof. Saint George's Byzantine Rite Ukrainian Catholic Church on East 7th Street in the East Village was patterned after a synthesis of *two* churches in Ukraine: Saint George Cathedral in Lviv and Saint Sophia Cathedral in Kiev.

The organizers of Grace Episcopal Church on Hicks Street and Grace Court in Brooklyn Heights chose Gothic architecture because so many English churches used that style. In the former village of Woodside, Queens the board-and-batten Saint Paul's Episcopal Church at 39th Avenue and 61st Street was built in the style of many English country chapels.

The congregation of the West End Collegiate Dutch Reformed Church at West End Avenue and West 77th Street in Manhattan chose to design a stepped-gable roof with red tiles and yellow-orange brick façade with terra-cotta designs. The result closely resembled many churches in the Netherlands.

The Jesuits who built Saint Francis Xavier Roman Catholic Church on West 16th Street near 6th Avenue used Baroque architecture, an exceptionally lavish and ornamental arrangement (lots of chubby angels) that gained popularity among Catholics during their battle with Protestants at the time of the Counter Reformation. The Jesuits helped lead the Catholic Church in that struggle and the lavishly ornamented Baroque architecture, sometimes jokingly called Anti-Protestant architecture, helped define them.

Our Lady of Pompeii Roman Catholic Church on the corner of Carmine and Bleecker Streets in Greenwich Village, once predominantly Italian, was constructed in the Neo-Classical style found in many southern Italian churches. The overwhelmingly Polish parish of Saint Stanislaus Kostka, corner of Humboldt Street and Driggs Avenue in Greenpoint, Brooklyn, chose to include two tall, thin steeples, a feature found often in churches throughout Poland.

Jews were faced with an architectural dilemma when they began building synagogues. Many congregations did not want their buildings to look like churches. They wanted to have a distinct exterior. Though some used Federal, Greek Revival, or even Gothic styles, many opted for Moorish architecture, a style perceived as non-Christian because it reflected Judaism's golden age in Medieval Muslim Spain. (The great Jewish philosopher Maimonides lived in 12th century Spain.) Central Synagogue at Lexington Avenue and East 55th Street in Manhattan is an example. Its twin octagonal dome-topped minarets, *bichromatic* (striped) horseshoe arches, and decorative Islamic-style tracery are Moorish. Congregation Emanu-El, the largest synagogue in the world, at 5th Avenue and East 65th Street, has a Romanesque exterior but a decidedly Moorish interior.

Because they immigrated to the United States more recently than European Christians and Jews, most Muslim, Buddhist, Sikh, and Daoist congregations, converted pre-existing structures into their Houses of Worship so the exteriors showed little of the religion's traditional character. Small attempts were made to give buildings some traditional identity. The Madina Masjid (mosque) on 1st Avenue and East 11th Street in the East Village converted a corner grocery store into a mosque. They added a *faux* (model) minaret to the side. Too small to be used, the minaret gave the sense of a traditional mosque to the building. The perception of being a Buddhist temple was aided by placing a large white statue of the Bodhisattva Guan-yin in front of the Sung Tak Temple on Pike Street near East Broadway in Chinatown. The Buddhist temple had previously been a Jewish synagogue.

Buildings shifted from congregation to congregation, from use to use. The Orthodox Cathedral of the Holy Virgin Protection in the East Village had once been Mount Olivet Memorial German Reformed Church. The Mahayana Buddhist Temple on Canal Street was an independent movie theater in Chinatown, and Saint Sebastian's Catholic Church in Woodside, Queens was a Loew's movie theater until 1955. The Bialystocker Synagogue in the Lower East Side was formerly the Willett Street Methodist Episcopal Church. The Roman Catholic Church of the Transfiguration in Chinatown, Irish at first, then Italian, and now Chinese, was originally the Zion English Lutheran Church when Protestants predominated and the area was called Werpoes Hill. The list could be very long; as the ethnic make-up of neighborhoods changed, so did the religious buildings.

Whether the house of worship's size was large or small, whether it was ornate or showed studied plainness, the *sacred space* inside exuded a special feeling of mystery and majesty. There were, of course, many ways to show such sentiments.

Authority and majesty were certainly exhibited by three prominent Christian cathedrals in Manhattan: St. John the Divine (Episcopal), St. Patrick's (Catholic), and Holy Trinity (Greek Orthodox). Plain and simple architecture was evident at other Manhattan churches: St. John's Lutheran Church, 15th Street Meeting House (Quaker), and First Chinese Presbyterian Church.

The interior of a house of worship has many aspects to examine. Movement is a consideration. In many religious structures there are no chairs or pews. Muslims need open space because they form prayer lines when they recite group prayers in the mosques. Some Eastern Orthodox Christians (especially Russian Orthodox and Orthodox Church in America congregations) leave the centers of their churches open so that people may kneel and perform major reverences (prostrations), and walk about lighting candles and kissing *icons* (holy pictures) during the services. Hindus, Sikhs, Buddhists, and Taoists also keep the center space open. Sometimes they walk, stand, kneel, or sit on the floor, but no chairs are used.

Before the Protestant Reformation in the 16th century, all Christians stood during services. But Protestant sermons, the focal point of their services, were so long, sometimes up to three hours that benches, chairs, or pews were installed. Roman Catholics followed suit. Most Eastern Orthodox in the United States also added pews. Using pews or pew boxes as a way to raise funds by renting or even selling them to families began in colonial days. It finally ended, though it lasted at some Protestant churches far into the 20th century. (Saint Bartholomew's Episcopal Church on Park Avenue ended the rental of pew boxes in 1980.)

In the oldest Jewish synagogues in the Middle East and Europe, men stood at prayers, though a bench usually surrounded the prayer room. That is still true in some Hasidic synagogues in New York, such as the Grand Synagogue of the Lubavitch Hasidim on Eastern Parkway and Kingston Avenue in Crown Heights, Brooklyn, though most Jewish synagogues and temples have pews.

The focus of the congregation also distinguishes religious groups from each other. In most Christian churches attention is drawn to the chancel (front) where the altar and pulpit (lectern, rostrum, or podium) are located. Quakers, who usually sit facing each other from two or four directions without altar or pulpit, are an exception.

The seating arrangement in the nave is usually in two segments with an aisle in the center and an outer aisle at the left and right. That traditional form facilitated processions and focused on the altar, set in the center of the front. Nineteenth century Protestants developed a format to downplay the focus on the altar and prevent a clear processional path to the altar by installing three blocks of pews with two center aisles and two end aisles. The center aisle disappeared in the 1868 Akron Plan of Church Architecture that was jokingly called the anti-Catholic Plan.

Most Jewish Houses of Worship have a *bimah* (raised platform) with an *ark* (upright chest containing the Torah scrolls), a reading table, and a pulpit at the front. But some follow an older tradition of placing the reading table in the center of the room on another raised platform. In that case the seating arrangement is usually rows of pews on two sides of the room facing the open center. The service consists of prayers, songs, a daily reading from the Torah, and a sermon.

If possible, a mosque should be built with at least one minaret (tower) from which the faithful can be called to prayer five times each day. For Muslims the focus inside a mosque is always the direction of Mecca, the holy city located in Saudi Arabia. A *mihrab* (prayer niche) in the wall alerts worshippers to the correct direction and they form prayer rows facing this way. There are no chairs or pews. Near the prayer niche is the *minbar* (pulpit ladder of thirteen steps) from which the *imam* (clergyman) delivers his sermon.

In both Orthodox Judaism and Islam, public prayer is the obligation only of men. Women have a duty to recite certain prayers but not in the synagogue or mosque. If they do attend a prayer service, they remain in separate quarters, either behind a partition in a mosque, or in a balcony or behind a *mechita* (cloth used to divide a room between men and women) in a synagogue.

Hindu temples sometimes have a clear and open front where statues of the deities are placed in a row, but in more elaborate temples there will be a central granite *garbhagriha* (womb chamber) with a deity inside, and other *garbhagrihas* in the corners of the room. Hence, there is no clear front; people sit or stand facing whatever direction the opening of the *garbhagriha* faces. An important altar is the open table-like Altar of the Nine Planets where statues of the *Navagrahas* (nine planets) are placed. Hindu worship is closely connected with the placement of the heavenly bodies. The nine planets are: Sun, Moon, Mars, Mercury, Jupiter, Venus, Saturn, and two (*Rahu* and *Ketu*) that represent the ascending and descending pattern of the Moon.

A *puja* (individual worship) may be done at a home altar or at a temple. At the temple Hindu worshippers enlist a temple priest (always from the Brahman caste) to lead them in a *samskara* ritual offering food and flower sacrifices to one of the gods for rites of the life cycle: birth, food, school, work, marriage, illness, death. Veneration of the deities involves prayers and washing them with water, milk, honey, *ghee* (clarified butter), and festooning them with flowers and spices. The Hindu Temple Society of North America on Bowne Street in Flushing, Queens is an example of traditional Hindu architecture inside and out.

Buddhist temples have a front altar generally with one, three, or several statues. *Sakyamuni* (Historical Buddha) is the usual choice if only one statue is featured. If other statues are included in the front, they will probably represent other buddhas (Medicinal Buddha, Pure Land Buddha, or Buddha of the Future, for example), or a *bodhisattva*, or *arhat*. In the Mahayana tradition of Buddhism found in China, Korea, and Japan, *bodhisattvas* represent Enlightened Ones who, rather than progress to Nirvana (and becoming *one with the universe*), linger as spirits in the Sentient Being Realm to help humans achieve perfection. *Arhats*, in the Hinayana (Theravada) tradition of Buddhism found in India, Burma, Thailand, and Sri Lanka, represent Enlightened Ones who linger to more passively serve as models for perfection-seeking humans. Each *arhat* represents an attribute such as compassion or benevolence. In New York City, some temples mix Mahayana and Hinayana traditions.

Sakyamuni (or Siddhartha Gautama, the Historical Buddha), Earth Store Bodhisattva (Protector of Children and Liberator from the Torments of Hell), Medicinal Buddha, Pure Land Buddha (*Amitahba* or *O-mi-to-fo*), *Guanyin* Bodhisattva, and the eighteen *arhats* are commonly found in New York's Buddhist temples. On each altar the *five gifts* are placed: flowers, fruit, oil, pure water, and fire (candles). Worshippers come in and pray while bowing on prayer cushions and lighting incense. The Sung Tak Buddhist Temple on Pike Street just east of East Broadway and the Mahayana Buddhist Temple on Canal Street just off the Bowery (both in Manhattan's Chinatown) offer interesting examples of Buddhist temple plans.

Daoist temples are dedicated to a specific god or celestial spirit. There are often side altars with other honored deities. Families sometimes pray to their ancestors at a temple, though ancestral spirits are more often venerated at home. Outside a Daoist temple may be an octagonal metal furnace for burning paper money and paper food for deceased ancestors who have gone to another realm. An intricate method of telling fortunes is on most altars.

Two crescent-shaped ivory-like objects are shaken in cupped hands and dropped on the altar. If they land with their horns facing each other, the god on that altar will be receptive to your petition for an explanation of the future. Then, a cylindrical bamboo container resembling a large pencil-holder with numbered sticks inside is gently shaken until one stick falls out on the floor. The number is read and a drawer of a nearby cabinet with the corresponding number is opened. A piece of paper with a prediction is taken out but as it is often enigmatic it may need the expertise of a priest to decipher. Sometimes Chinese Buddhists incorporate these two Daoist practices in their New York City temples.

A Sikh *gurdwara* (temple) has a raised platform in the front where the *Sri Guru Granth Sahib* (book of holy scriptures) is kept and read. There are no statues in the monotheistic Sikh religion. Prayers and *mantras* (sacred sounds) are recited toward the *Sri Guru Granth Sahib*. Sikhs believe that Guru Gobind Singh, the last of ten Sikh *gurus* beginning in the 15th century, conferred the role of *guru* (teacher and spiritual guide) on the text. Accordingly, the *Granth* is treated with the respect accorded to a living guru. A whisk (fan) of yak hair, signifying royal authority, is waved over the open text while the priest, or *granthi*, reads from the *Granth*. Yoga exercises are sometimes practiced during prayers. A *langar* (communal meal) is regularly scheduled after each service. The largest Sikh *gurdwara* in the city is the Sikh Cultural Center at 118th Street and 95th Avenue in Richmond Hill, Queens.

Lighting influences moods and usually houses of worship prefer natural light through windows. When artificial light is needed they turn to candles, oil lamps, chandeliers, or light bulbs. Windows can be clear, *opaque* (purposely cloudy), or stained glass. Christians and Jews make the most use of stained glass windows. Designs can be simple symbols of the religion or elaborate reproductions of Bible stories. Jews are disinclined to use human figures in their stained glass.

Specific features in houses of worship in New York City vary from place to place but generalizations can be made. Among Christians, churches are usually divided into three parts: the narthex (lobby or vestibule), nave, and chancel (sanctuary).

In Roman Catholic churches there is always a front altar and a pulpit off to each side. Since the Second Vatican Council (1962-1965) the altar must stand out from the back wall to allow the priest to face the people. Often there are two altars in the front: the Altar of Repose and the Altar of Sacrifice, the latter where the priest consecrates the wine and bread. There are usually side altars and somewhere in the nave is a baptismal font. Along the sides attached to the walls (between the windows and side altars) are *bas reliefs* (partially raised sculpture) of the Stations of the Cross, a series of thirteen focal points arranged in order around the church to stop and recite prayers reflecting Jesus' Way of the Cross. Somewhere on the side or back are two-part confessional booths where a priest can hear a parishioner's private confession of sins. Catholic churches are often profusely decorated with paintings, stained glass, statues, and icons. In front of a statue or icon will be a kneeling bench and a rack of devotional candles.

Eastern Orthodox churches divide the nave from the chancel with an *iconostasis* (icon screen) that has a set of double-doors in the center (Royal Doors) and single-panel Deacons Doors at each side. The iconostasis, which is made of rows of icons sometimes reaching the ceiling, separates the priests from the people for parts of the service, though during much of it the center doors remain open. The priests bring the Bible and chalice out into the nave at points during the service. There is a lot of movement and pageantry in an Orthodox service with people visiting icons along the walls and lighting candles, and with priests using *censers* (incense vessels) to bless both people and icons with incense. A *Golgotha* shrine is off to the left in many Orthodox churches. It is a place to pray and burn oil lamps in remembrance of the dead. (*Golgotha*, or Calvary, was the name of the hill where Jesus was crucified.)

Protestant churches are difficult to categorize because there are more than one hundred denominations in New York City. Some Protestant churches are as elaborate as Catholic churches. Episcopal churches are good examples: Trinity Church, Church of the Ascension, and St. Thomas in Manhattan. The First Presbyterian Church and Riverside Church (affiliated with both Baptist *and* United Church of Christ denominations) are also elaborate Manhattan churches. Others are uncomplicated and plain: John Street Methodist Church, Abyssinian Baptist Church, and St. Peter's Lutheran Church in Manhattan; Riverdale Presbyterian Church in the Bronx; Flatbush Reformed Dutch Church and Bay Ridge United Methodist Church in Brooklyn; Bowne Street Community Church and Cathedral of Allen African Methodist Episcopal Church in Queens; New Dorp Moravian Church and Free Magyar Reformed Church in Staten Island.

Most Protestant churches prefer simplicity and some are strikingly plain, like a school auditorium. In general, Protestants focus most on the pulpit, the place where passages from the Bible are read, prayers are led, and sermons delivered. Protestants do not believe in a literal sacrifice (transubstantiation), so the altar, while often in the center of the chancel, is the focus of meditation only. Many Protestant denominations have a small table as an altar, or no altar at all. Some Protestant denominations place the pulpit in the center of the chancel since the main part of the service is the sermon.

New York City is not peppered with the street corner religious shrines found in many countries. In some neighborhoods, such as Carroll Gardens in Brooklyn, private front yards may have statues of Saint Mary, Sacred Heart of Jesus, or Saint Francis, but it is confined to a handful of areas. Only on holidays, especially Christmas time, do public displays of Christmas trees (Rockefeller Center, City Hall), lighted front yard decorations, wreathes, crèche scenes, and Jewish Hanukah menorahs proliferate. A new custom, however, is the emergence of instant (and temporary) street shrines after a death or murder of either a neighborhood person or a famous celebrity. A spontaneous memorial develops: votive candles, flowers, and personal cards, notes, and flowers. Tragedies like the deaths of Amadou Diallo and John F. Kennedy, Jr., or the destruction of the World Trade Center, sparked spontaneous non-denominational shrines.

CHAPTER 117
Fast Food

There is nothing new about fast food; it existed in Roman times and in the Medieval World. New Amsterdam's first popular fast food was shellfish, especially oysters. No cooking was necessary with oysters, clams, or mussels, just some salt, pepper, and a couple of drops of vinegar. Bi-valves were sold at street corner stands and on pushcarts. The city's bays and rivers contained enormous quantities of oysters and a few of them grew to as a foot in diameter. The 17th century Dutch gathered oysters from the rich beds around Oyster Island, renamed Ellis Island in 1770. They remained popular through the 19th century, especially as a fast food lunch treat, and after-hours bar food in any one of New York City's numerous and seedy oyster cellars or in the more upscale oyster bars. The rich ate them with champagne or white wine; the workers quaffed them with beer. Oyster consumption declined by the late 19th century as oyster beds were over-fished by commercial fishermen.

The number of places to eat in New York City fluctuates but it is now approximately 40,000. Many of them are fast food restaurants in that they serve meals quickly. The point of fast food is to rapidly serve busy people. In economic terms there is also an economy of scale: if you produce a lot of inexpensive meals for many people, you can still make money.

In English colonial days six-penny eating houses, bars that served free food to accompany purchased drinks, were popular in New York City as well as in some of the scattered villages in the other four counties that eventually joined to form the unified city. Coffee Houses were popular in the English period. They sold coffee and tea, as well as alcohol and food. They were places to eat and drink, relax and talk. The name was chosen because coffee was a new and attractive product. Many important political and civic meetings took place in Wall Street area establishments like the Exchange Coffee House, Merchants' Coffee House, and the Tontine Coffee House. By the 1830s they declined in number since the diversity of New York became so broad that each ethnic and class group chose their favorite spots, the workers to various pubs and the elite to exclusive private clubs.

Coffee houses that served primarily coffee and snacks appeared again around 1900 and catered to radical and bohemian groups. They served espresso and cappuccino and most were in Greenwich Village. A few of them, such as Le Figaro Cafe, Caffé Reggio, and La Lanterna di Vittorio Caffé, still exist. The Great Depression popularized the Horn & Hardart chain of cafeterias in the city. Much of the time people went in to drink the coffee and read the newspaper. Various diners were often referred to as coffee shops.

In the 1990s Starbucks, a chain of coffee shops, invaded New York City, opening ninety just in Manhattan. They and other new-style coffee shops specialize in expensive steamed milk coffee drinks like caramel mocha frappuccino, caffe lattè, and Tazoberry blended juiced tea and cater to young middle class patrons. The newest wave includes the Taiwan-inspired Saint's Alp Tea Houses found in Manhattan and Queens. The name and foot-shaped logo refers to the footprint made in stone by a Daoist immortal in the alps of Taiwan. The popularity comes from a wide variety of beverages, not tea as we normally think of it, but frothy tea with pearl tapioca, flavored milk teas (like coconut, peanut, taro, sesame, and ginger), milk shakes made of mung beans, honey dew melon, or coconut, green barley with lemon juice, kumquat lime juice, plum tea, as well as plain green, black, and jasmine teas. Cakes, shortbread, toast, and some cold chicken dishes are served for snacks.

Each group brought its ethnic touches to New York and some items were turned into fast food. Certainly the hamburger and frankfurter from Germany are the best known. Pretzels and the use of mustard as a condiment were also German traditions, which arrived in New York City before the American Revolution.

Nathan Handwerker started Nathan's Coney Island and built its success on the frank. Later, he added fried oysters, fried fish, and fried potatoes. Nathan's also included potato knishes (Jewish) and pizza and calzone (Italian) to its menu. Vendors all over the city sell franks, knishes, Greek souvlaki (lamb meat in pita bread), as well as a Mideastern grilled meat dish, shish kebab. Some offer Chinese and Vietnamese fast food.

The *delicatessen* was a 19th century German import. The compound word means *delicacy* and *to eat* (*essen* in German). Later, Jewish and Italian delis popped up all over the five boroughs. In a deli the customer could go straight to the counter, order food, and eat inside or take it away. Out-in-the-open merchandising, placing meats, cheeses, and breads right in front of the customer in a glass counter or hanging from hooks and strings, made the food all the more tantalizing. Cold cuts and warm meats were sold in delicatessens: salami, bologna, sausage, frankfurters, roast beef, corned beef, brisket, and tongue.

A Jewish deli had to choose to sell either meat or dairy products to keep in line with kosher laws prohibiting mixing of the two in the same meal. Most chose meat, but some, like Ratner's on Manhattan's Lower East Side or the B & H Dairy Restaurant in the East Village, sold only dairy-based foods, or vegetables (which are considered *pareve*, or neutral). A dairy restaurant could offer *latkes* (potato pancakes), cheese or fruit *blintzes* (crêpes), *kasha varnishkas* (buckwheat with bowtie noodles), cheese or potato *pierogis* (dumplings), egg or fish dishes (which are grouped with dairy foods), and soups like mushroom and barley, split pea, or *borscht* (beet).

An Italian delicatessen (called a *salumeria*) was free to sell cheese and meat and to include pork (sausages, chops, roasts) with their products. They also sold olives and *antipasti* (which means *before the meal*). The cold or warm antipasti could be *calimari* (squid), roast peppers, mozzarella cheese, or vegetables and pepperoni sausage marinated in olive oil, vinegar, and herbs.

Beer Gardens were another import from Central Europe, especially Germany and the Austro-Hungarian Empire. By 1870, in the days before fans or air conditioning, there were scores of outdoor eating and drinking establishments set amidst trees to simulate the countryside. You could eat quickly or linger. Very few of the old ones are left though in the early 21st century a few new beer gardens opened. You can get the general idea of an old-style beer garden from Bohemian Hall and Park, a Czech beer garden in Astoria, Queens, or Killmeyer's Old Bavarian Inn & Beer Garden (German) in Port Socony, Staten Island. In a sense, the popular outdoor restaurant L. & B. Spumoni Gardens in Gravesend, Brooklyn is very similar. Instead of German or Czech food, pizza, calzones, and spaghetti are served, along with spumoni.

Diners, often called Greek diners, serve hamburgers, hot dogs, sandwiches, and plate lunches with startling speed. They are like restaurants but the food is already prepared or semi-prepared and the customer can get a meal very fast. Breakfasts are available all day long in diners.

Hispanic parts of the city are dotted with small restaurants offering the food of the Spanish Caribbean, especially from Puerto Rico and the Dominican Republic. The aromas of *adobo* and *sazón*, commonly used Spanish spice mixtures, and long-simmering meats waft out the doors of restaurants in the South Bronx, Spanish Harlem, Washington Heights, and Sunset Park serving roast chicken and pork, beef stew, goat meat, and cod fish salad. Orders come with rice and beans, cassava, or plantains (green or yellow). *Cuchifrito*, a Puerto Rican specialty, is a combo plate of pig ears, blood pudding, *mofongo* (green plantains), and rice. Jamaican foods are common throughout the city, especially in Brooklyn's Bedford-Stuyvesant and East Flatbush neighborhoods. Jamaican beef patties, oxtails, curried goat, and fish cakes are sold in numerous restaurants and food stands.

South American fast food specialties from Venezuela, Colombia, Ecuador, and Peru are often found in Queens, especially Corona, Sunnyside, Woodside, and Jackson Heights. They include *arepas* (corn cakes stuffed with ham, shredded chicken, tuna, turkey, cheddar cheese, avocado, or vegetables), *empanadas* (plump wheat pastries filled with ham and ricotta, spinach and cheese, or eggplant and green pepper), and containers of *ceviche* (tartly marinated fish and shrimp).

Mexican food outlets all over town sell tacos, tortillas, burritos, fajitas, chili relleños, *tortas* (sandwiches), and *huaroches* (stuffed *slippers* of dough). Mexicans are the fastest growing immigrant group in New York City. The food has caught on fast and is often served as school lunches.

After the Second World War fast food chains sprouted everywhere in the United States. The appeal of sanitized chains (local or national) was speed, no tipping, cleanliness, predictable uniformity of taste, standardization of menu and ambiance. National chains, except for pizza chains, stuck with simple American cuisine. McDonald's, Burger King, Wendy's, White Castle, Roy Rogers, KFC, Subway, and Blimpie finally penetrated the New York City market by 1975. Au Bon Pain, California Burrito Company, Daikichi Sushi, Teriyaki Boy, Dunkin' Donuts, Domino's Pizza, Pizza Hut, Pizzeria Uno, and Sizzler came a decade later. Each eventually developed a loyal following. Detractors would say that part of their appeal is the generous use of salt, sugar, and grease.

One way that national chains stay in business is by constant evolution of their menu selections. Though familiarity draws and keeps customers, periodic change also entices new customers. National fast food chains also rely heavily on expensive national-wide advertising campaigns. After the turn of the 21st century Chipotle, Five Guys, and Shake Shack have garnered a significant share of the fast food market.

Local chains have been really very similar to national chains though they catered to localized tastes and to New York City nostalgia. Nathan's expanded in the 1960s and then pulled back a decade later. There have been several others: Chock Full O'Nuts, Nedicks (many of their one hundred restaurants and hot dog stands were located in subway stations), Kennedy Fried Chicken, Crown Fried Chicken (Brooklyn and Queens), and Orange Julius (now owned by International Dairy Queen and no longer in the city). Orange Julius had a secret recipe for its signature drink that seemed to be a combination of orange juice, sugar, and sherbet whipped into froth by a machine.

The first large-scale local chain restaurant was Childs, which was founded in 1889 and lasted until 1961. It featured a self-service counter, long communal tables with bentwood chairs, bright lights, white tile walls, no alcohol, and a policy of no loitering. Other local chain restaurants were Jahn's (Brooklyn, Queens, and the Bronx), Bickford's (Brooklyn and Manhattan), and Patricia Murphy's Candlelight Restaurants (Manhattan). They were more upscale because they featured padded seating and attractively decorated dining areas.

Tad's Steak House (there are only two left, both in Midtown

Manhattan), asked customers to pick up a tray and bring it along a line, order a quick char-broiled steak or hamburger, a potato, and salad. By the time the line moved down to the cash register, the meat had been cooked on a flaming grill. The chain began in 1957 with a T-bone steak priced at $1.09. At its peak it had eight restaurants in New York City.

Today, local chains like Two Boots (Park Slope, Brooklyn and Manhattan's East and West Village), Gray's Papaya, Papaya King, Bagelry, and Bagel World seem to do very well. Two Boots refers to geography as well as cuisine because both Italy and Louisiana are shaped like boots. The food includes Italian and Cajun specialties.

Upscale, national family-style chains (Olive Garden, Red Lobster, Cracker Barrel, Outback) have a hard time competing with other New York restaurants because their food is more expensive but too bland to capture a large share of the market. Motorized delivery was slow to catch on in New York City because the walking distance to the nearest restaurant was seldom far for the customer and because the delivery driver might have serious trouble finding a parking place. Today, deliverymen *on foot* or on motorized bicycles can be seen everywhere in New York City.

Cafeterias could once be found in almost every neighborhood. Notable examples were Garfield's in Flatbush, Dubrow's in Crown Heights, Garden Cafeteria on the Lower East Side, and several called Hoffman's. A Philadelphia-based cafeteria chain, Horn & Hardart Automats, began operations in 1912 and featured a technocratic food-dispensing system where the diner would obtain the required coins from a change booth, walk to an entire wall filled with little brass-framed glass cubbies, put in the change, and open the door to take out a plate of baked macaroni, chow mein, meatloaf, or apple pie. Coffee was 5 cents and no one chased out a lingering diner or newspaper reader. (The movie to see to catch the Horn & Hardart experience in Midtown Manhattan is *That Touch of Mink.*)

A thriving present-day cafeteria on Kent Street in Greenpoint, Brooklyn is the Polish and Slavic Credit Union Cafeteria. It is open to the public and serves an array of reasonably priced Polish mainstays: stuffed cabbage, *golonka* (pig knuckle with a thick layer of crispy fat), Hungarian potato pancakes (stuffed with goulash meat), *pierogi* (dumplings), *bigos* (hunter's stew), and pork cutlets. The soup selection usually includes *barszcz* (strained Polish-style beet borscht), Lithuanian borscht (with hard-boiled egg), *zurek* (fermented slightly sour soup with bits of sausage, a hard boiled egg, and a potato dumpling), and warm cucumber soup.

Food trucks achieved great popularity by 2010 with many trucks, such as Schnitzel and Things, Rickshaw, Korilla Dumpling BBQ (Korean), and Wafels & Dinges (Belgian waffles), selling unique fare. Cell phone apps give the location of the trucks.

Ice cream is more a snack than a meal, but vendors sell various forms of ice cream throughout the city in summer months. The early Good Humor ice cream came in pushcarts, and adult-size tricycles. Later it came in trucks. Trucks offering various soft ice cream (frozen custard) with their child-attracting melody took a share of the market beginning in the 1950s. In Hispanic neighborhoods ice vendors chip fragments from large blocks of ice into paper cones and pour flavored tropical fruit syrup on top: the result is called *frio-frio* or *raspado* (in Dominican Spanish) or *piragua* in Puerto Rican Spanish). The word *piragua,* from the French *pirogue,* refers to a canoe made from a hollowed-out log. The scraping motion of the vendor resembles the motion of the canoe-maker.

Soft drinks have always been popular refreshments in New York. Initially, drinks were made at a soda fountain, often located in a pharmacy. The *soda jerk* behind the counter would mix seltzer with flavored syrups. Even Coca Cola had to be mixed. It led to creative combinations like the Cherry Coke, Vanilla Coke, Lime Ricky, and Cherry Lime Ricky. A New York specialty, which was very popular in the early 20th century, was the *egg cream.* The irony was that it contained no eggs and no cream, but was a concoction of seltzer, milk, and chocolate syrup.

National drinks (colas, citrus, root beer) have the lion's share of the market here, but local drinks manage to hang on to a niche market. Local drinks from Brooklyn, Yoo-hoo Chocolate Drink, Manhattan Special Espresso Coffee Soda (produced on *Manhattan* Avenue in Greenpoint, Brooklyn), and Dr. Brown's Cel-ray, Black Cherry, or Cream Soda, retain some popularity. One reason Brooklyn became home to numerous soft drink companies was that the Havemeyer Sugar Refinery in Williamsburg, Brooklyn was the largest refinery in the world at the turn of the last century when these brands were developed.

At this point in the early 21st century, could anything be more New York than the neighborhood Italian pizzeria or Chinese restaurant? Their fares have become so common that many Americans consider Italian and Chinese food to be American food. In fact, American food seems to be anything that Americans regularly eat. And few Americans are more adventurous about food than New Yorkers.

For those who have neither the time nor the money to eat in New York City's many elegant restaurants, some version of fast food has been a choice from the Dutch period to the present. No one can ever complain that New Yorkers don't have much of a choice when it comes to eating out.

CHAPTER 118
Parades & Street Festivals

Private culture, always tolerated and sometimes cheerfully accepted, periodically bursts out of its natural environment in the home and house of worship right onto the streets with brashness, pride, colors, and noise. Ethnic parades and religious processions take place in every neighborhood of the city's five boroughs. There are over six hundred regularly scheduled ethnic and religious parades each year in New York City.

Political parades were once very common in New York. Marching bands set the pace and politicians were featured riding on horses (later in cars) surrounded by a sea of American flags. Night parades were illuminated by thousands of torchlights and usually ended in a park where a fireworks display was presented. Scheduled annual parades celebrated national holidays. Other parades promoted political candidates during election campaigns.

Evacuation Day was a very important political parade for a century. It celebrated the British evacuation of New York City in 1783. The yearly Memorial Day Parade began in 1896 to remember soldiers in our wars. Along with Flag Day and Veteran's Day, Memorial Day is still celebrated with a parade but its drawing power has greatly declined. Since the Vietnam War period, patriotic parades have ceased to include military components. Independence Day is no longer celebrated with a parade (except for neighborhood parades in Staten Island and Bay Ridge, Brooklyn), but rather with spectacular fireworks sponsored by Macy's Department Store. Macy's also sponsors a Thanksgiving Day Parade, which is a commercial event aimed at getting people interested in Christmas shopping.

There are two particularly bizarre parades that developed in the late 20th century. The Halloween Parade began as a small procession of revelers in outlandish costumes in Greenwich Village in 1974, but has grown into a large event routed along 6th Avenue in Manhattan. The much smaller Mermaid Parade along Surf Avenue in Coney Island began in 1983. It is a mixture of antique cars and marchers in various states of undress mimicking King Neptune and numerous mermaids. It is held the first Saturday after the Summer Solstice.

Manhattan's Tompkin's Square was once the focal point of labor and socialist parades and rallies, and in 1874 was the site of the first labor demonstration in New York City. By the 1930s thousands of union and socialist activists would march in groups to Union Square for rallies, especially on May Day.

Over the years, military parades and political movement processions have lost out to ethnic parades. There are two notable exceptions, the Gay and Lesbian Parade, and the Salute to Israel Parade, which in both cases are partly political.

Ticker-tape parades began in the 1880s on Wall Street and lower Broadway. The long thin strips of paper with stock market quotes were thrown from windows and became confetti falling on whoever was being honored. Notable ticker-tape parades honored Charles Lindbergh (1927), General Douglas MacArthur (1951), Pope John Paul II (1979), Nelson Mandela (1990), and Gulf War soldiers (1991). The Mets and Yankees have also received ticker-tape parades. (Because ticker tape is no longer used, similar looking scraps from paper-shredders are strewn from windows.)

Some parades, like those celebrating Pulaski Day and Von Steuben Day, rally around the names of famous military assistants to General George Washington during the American Revolution, but are really ethnic parades. The participants in the Pulaski Day event have Polish ancestry and Krakus Polish Ham, Lot Polish Airlines, and the Polish Credit Union sponsor the parade. Descendants of Germans march in the Von Steuben parade alongside floats sponsored by the Cannstatter Volksfest Verein and the Schaller & Weber German Meat Company.

Religious processions in New York are often ethnic affairs because Roman Catholic, Eastern Orthodox, and Protestant congregations were frequently organized around ethnic communities. So the parades honoring Saint Januarius (San Gennaro), Saint Paulinus, and Saint Anthony are unmistakably Italian, the parade honoring Three Kings Day (Epiphany) is Puerto Rican, and the parade in honor of Our Lady of Guadalupe is Mexican.

Two Roman Catholic congregations with the same name, Our Lady of Mount Carmel, sponsor particularly interesting religious processions in early June. In each case the tradition comes from 19th century Italy. Our Lady of Mount Carmel in East Harlem, Manhattan, celebrates the feast of Saint Anthony while Our Lady of Mount Carmel in Williamsburg, Brooklyn, honors Saint Paulinus. Parishioners at each church build an 85 foot 4.5 ton *giglio,* a highly decorated cylindrical tower (*giglio* means lily, a symbol of the Resurrection of Jesus), which is carried by 120 men in a procession through the surrounding streets. The *giglio* is *danced* along its way while Italian folk music is played and onlookers enjoy refreshments. Each *giglio* frame has colorful painted papier-mâché scenes about the saint's life.

There are four extra-large parades among the six hundred, each very different from the others. The subdued and sparsely attended parade along Manhattan's 5th Avenue that honors Christopher Columbus on the occasion of his October 12th European discovery of the New World also reflects the pride of all Americans of Italian background.

By far, the parade that attracts the most varied support is the Saint Patrick's Day Parade on March 17th, an event first organized in 1762 by Irish soldiers in the British army, and from 1853 on sponsored by the Ancient Order of Hibernians, an Irish fraternal group. It draws 150,000 marchers and more than two hundred marching bands, many with prominent bagpipe contingents. Half a million onlookers crowd the parade route. People of every ethnic group, race, and religion join the Irish in celebrating their patron saint. It is a day when many New Yorkers dress partially in green. When it passes the Roman Catholic Cathedral of Saint Patrick, the archbishop comes out to bless the participants. No politician or New York opinion-leader can easily afford to miss the event, which is covered on local and national television. In fact, many New Yorkers take the afternoon off from work and go to bars or office parties. The city is alive with revelers throughout the night.

Puerto Ricans constitute a large portion of New York's residents, and maintain a kind of dual cultural allegiance with the island because of the ease of going between New York City and San Juan. The Puerto Rican Day Parade in June is a particularly lively, gleeful assemblage. It has fewer bands and floats than many of the other parades, but sports an enormous number of cars packed with celebrants waving Puerto Rican flags from the windows. The day usually ends with picnics and home barbecues that go late into the evening.

Two million New Yorkers attend the yearly West Indian Day Parade each year, with at least 500,000 of them actually marching and dancing down the six lanes of Eastern Parkway in Crown Heights, Brooklyn. The parade begins in the afternoon and continues for six hours into the evening. Along the route entrepreneurs set up makeshift kitchen facilities to serve spiced rice, jerked chicken, Jamaican beef patties, roti, fried plantains, curried goat, lengths of sugar cane, and ginger ice cream.

The West Indian Day Parade is a parade and a festival at the same time. New York City is the home of the greatest concentration of West Indians in the United States, and Brooklyn is their first stop as immigrants. Music is everywhere: especially souk, reggae, and calypso rhythms of steel drums. The lavish kaleidoscope of colors and ornate costumes and floats represent a Mardi Gras spirit, though the parade is held in early September.

The West Indian Day Parade is inclusive and West Indians from most communities participate: Bahamians, Haitians, Grenadians, Guyanians, Trinidadians, and Caribbean coastal people from Panama and Nicaragua. In other ways, the West Indian Day parade, also called Carnival and Jump Up, is insular, choosing Brooklyn, which has the greatest concentration of West Indians, rather than Manhattan's high profile 5th Avenue, as the center for the joyful event.

Some parades are very small. The Museum of Tibetan Art in Staten Island sponsors the yearly Tibetan Parade, which is a small procession. The Hong Kong Dragon Boat Race is a maritime parade on Flushing Meadows Lake representing a segment of the Chinese community in Queens. In Broad Channel, Queens, the Volunteer Fire Department sponsors a yearly parade honoring its members. The religious parade recognizing the elephant-headed god Ganesha's birthday in September circles the block where the Hindu Temple of North America is located in Flushing, Queens.

With six hundred parades scheduled each year, it is clear that ethnic pride must also be a business. The floats used in parades are customized to reflect the various communities they represent. But under the floats are the same vehicles, gazebos, huts, steps, porches, pillars, urns, shrubbery, and cardboard cutouts. A handful of companies provide most of the vehicles and props. The same bamboo hut, for example, could be used in Cuban, Puerto Rican, Filipino, or Trinidadian floats. Redecorating float props keeps several small New York entrepreneurs busy. It may be a reasonable metaphor to see these prominent representations of ethnic pride as part of the greater society, which appear very different from each other on the surface, but are fully American underneath. *E Pluribus Unum.*

CHAPTER 119
Tourism & the City's Museums

New York City became a magnet for tourism once the meteoric increase in population and the growth of commerce and industry commenced in 1825. The city attracted business visitors from every section of the country, especially cotton merchants from the South and industrialists from New England and the Middle Atlantic states. By 1840 New York City had surpassed Boston, Philadelphia, Baltimore, and Charleston in population and became the center of financial services, publishing and printing, manufacturing, and fashion. People also came to the city to sample both high-end and low-end culture. Some attended the opera, ballet, symphony, or theater while others preferred bear baiting, dog fights, minstrel shows, and burlesque. Everyone sampled the restaurants. In the age before catalogue ordering or mass advertising shoppers came from every region to purchase stylish clothes and accessories. The temptation of A.T. Stewart's lavish department store at Broadway and Chambers Street proved too much to resist for Mary Todd Lincoln. During the Civil War the First Lady often took train trips from Washington, D.C. for extravagant shopping sprees at Stewart's *Marble Palace*. Her shopping trips included the purchase of over four hundred pair of gloves.

The cosmopolitan aspect of the city has always attracted domestic and foreign visitors. Business trips are often combined with tourism. New York City ranks second in domestic tourists sandwiched between first place Washington, D.C. and Orlando. Foreign tourists overwhelmingly choose New York City as their primary destination.

In 2014, about fifty million visitors came to New York City though many of those visits were repeat calls by business people. Among them were forty million domestic and ten million foreign visitors. Altogether, it is estimated by New York City & Company, the city's official tourism marketing organization, that the visitors, both from other parts of the United States and foreign countries, spend $30 billion each year. Most of the money is spent on hotels, restaurants, and stores. Broadway theaters take in about $850 million each year, much of it from tourists. Many people are attracted by the rich variety of restaurants.

Sightseeing is a favorite pastime for tourists who throng iconic places including Central Park, Rockefeller Center, Saint Patrick's Cathedral, the Empire State Building, and Chinatown. The Circle Line's river tour around Manhattan, a cross-harbor trip on the Staten Island Ferry, a visit to the Statue of Liberty and Ellis Island, bus tours, and walking tours are also popular.

More adventurous tourists visit the Bronx Zoo, New York Botanical Garden or Brooklyn Botanic Garden, New York Aquarium, Coney Island, Yankee Stadium or Shea Stadium, Battery Park City, the Brooklyn Heights Promenade, American Museum of Natural History, New York Public Library Main Branch, jazz clubs and other music venues, art galleries, and art museums. A handful of truly adventurous tourists go to Astoria or Flushing in Queens, Tottenville in Staten Island, Belmont in the Bronx, Roosevelt Island or Harlem in Manhattan, or Brighton Beach or Prospect Park in Brooklyn. Some visit historic houses in Manhattan's Washington Heights and Inwood, and in the Bronx, Brooklyn, Queens, and Staten Island.

Museums are an important component of the New York Experience for tourists and New Yorkers alike. Some museums are internationally famous for their world-class collections of art. The Metropolitan Museum of Art, and the Cloisters, its Medieval annex, surely ranks at the top of the list followed by the Museum of Modern Art (MoMA), the Whitney Museum of American Art, the Guggenheim Museum, Cooper-Hewitt National Design Museum, Frick Collection, J.P. Morgan Library and Museum, and the Brooklyn Museum of Art. Tourists are found in great numbers at these venerable institutions.

There are numerous niche museums that are interesting though they appeal to narrower segment of the population. Most niche museums are in Manhattan. Fraunces Tavern Museum, located upstairs from the Fraunces Tavern, 54 Pearl Street, has a collection of Revolutionary War memorabilia. The tavern was built in 1719 and was the scene of Washington's Farewell Speech to his officers in 1783. The National Museum of the American Indian, at 1 Bowling Green, is a branch of the Smithsonian Institution. Located in the former United States Custom House, it displays a broad collection of artifacts chronicling the culture of Native Americans throughout the continent. The Museum of American Finance, at 48 Wall Street, also an affiliate of the Smithsonian Institution, and contains artifacts and explanations of the American capitalist system. The Skyscraper Museum at 39 Battery Place features blueprints, photos, and models of New York City's skyscrapers. The Federal Hall National Memorial at 26 Wall Street features dioramas and video exhibits concerning the John Peter Zinger trial in 1735 and George Washington's 1789 inauguration. Exhibits at the South Street Seaport Museum, at Fulton and South Streets, are various ships including a schooner, oyster boat, and ferryboat that are docked at Piers 15, 16, and 17.

The New York City Police Museum at 100 Old Slip at Water Street presents the history of the New York Police Department. The New York City Fire Museum at 278 Spring Street is filled with old fire fighting equipment used by the Fire Department of New York and its predecessors. The Museum of Sex at 233 – 5th Avenue at 27th Street explores the history and cultural evolution of human sex. The Ukrainian Museum at 222 East 6th Street offers a glance at some elements of Ukrainian popular culture. The Jewish Museum of New York, 1109 - 5th Avenue at 92nd Street, explores Jewish history, culture, and art. The Museum of Jewish Heritage at 18 - 1st Place near West Street and Battery Place focuses on the Jewish experience in the 20th century.

The National Park Service operates Ellis Island and the Statue of Liberty National Monument. They may be reached by ferry at Castle Clinton at Battery Park. The museum in the base of the statue on Liberty Island explains the statue's construction. Ellis Island is a shrine to immigration and a museum. Its American Family Immigration History Center is a repository for books, photographs, artifacts, and audios, videos and CDs of immigrants telling their personal stories.

There are three notable old edifices open to the public in Flushing, Queens. The John Bowne House, 37-01 Bowne Street at 37th Avenue, is a 1661 colonial farmhouse. Around the corner is the Kingsland Homestead, at 143-35 37th Avenue, was built about 1785. It is presently home to the Queens Historical Society. The Friends Meeting House, 137-16 Northern Boulevard at Linden Place, is the oldest religious structure in New York State. The Quaker house of worship was constructed in 1694. Its high-pitched roof gives it a brooding medieval look. The Queens County Farm Museum in Floral Park, at 73-50 Little Neck Parkway, is a 47-acre parcel of land that passed to government ownership in 1926. The farm dates from 1697 and had been a 101-acre farm in the past. The farmhouse on the property was built in 1772, and expanded in 1856. The museum includes the house, outbuildings (barns, wagon shed, chicken coop, potting shed, and greenhouses), orchard, and fields.

In Staten Island, Historic Richmond Town, at 441 Clarke Avenue, off Richmondtown Road is a restored and reconstructed country village of twenty-eight houses from the 17th to the 19th centuries. The oldest buildings are the 1670 Britton House and the 1695 schoolhouse. The Snug Harbor Cultural Center, at 1000 Richmond Terrace between Tysen Street and Kissel Avenue, was a large retirement home for sailors that opened its doors in 1831. The Greek Revival buildings were constructed between 1833 and 1892 to provided for *aged, decrepit, and worn-out sailors.* The 80-acre site just one-and-one-half miles from the Staten Island Ferry Terminal includes galleries, museums, studios, concert spaces, and gardens. Conference House, Satterlee Street between Philip Court and Hylan Boulevard uses 7455 Hylan Boulevard as its street address, perches on a hill overlooking Raritan Bay at the confluence of the Raritan River and Arthur Kill. The 1680 stone house at the edge of Tottenville experienced a few hours of fame on September 11, 1776. Just as the American Revolution was beginning, three noted patriots met with Admiral Lord Richard Howe to see if the two sides could resolve their issues and stop the fighting. Benjamin Franklin, John Adams, and Edward Rutledge represented the Americans and traveled from Philadelphia for the conference. Nothing came of the meeting.

The oldest house in New York State is in Brooklyn. The Pieter Claesen Wyckoff House, built in 1652, stands at Clarendon Road and Ralph Avenue in East Flatbush. The Lefferts House, stands just inside Prospect Park at the intersection of Flatbush and Ocean Avenues and Empire Boulevard. The present structure, built between 1777 and 1783, is a successor to an earlier Lefferts house that stood nearby and was burned by the Redcoats in 1776 during the Battle of Long Island, fought in nearby fields and woods.

The Brooklyn Museum of Art holds the 1675 Jan Martense Schenck House, moved indoors from New Amersfoort (Mill Basin) to its location in 1952. Heavy Dutch farmhouse furniture including a walnut and cherry *kas* (Dutch cupboard) is displayed. The two-room one-and-one-half story house is built around a central *jambless fireplace.*

The Bronx features three interesting old homes. The Van Cortlandt House Museum at Broadway and 246th Street just inside Van Cortlandt Park is a spacious two-and-one-half-story fieldstone home was built in 1748 by Frederick Van Cortlandt and constituted an 18th century colonial manor. The Valentine-Varian House, 3266 Bainbridge Avenue at 208th Street, is the spacious fieldstone house built in 1758 by farmer and blacksmith Isaac Valentine. In 1792 the 260-acre property and house was sold to Isaac Varian, a farmer and butcher. Today it is a museum and research library owned by the Bronx County Historical Society. The tiny Edgar Allan Poe Cottage in Poe Park at the Grand Concourse and Kingsbridge Road was leased to Edgar Allan Poe for $100 a year from 1846 until his death at age forty in 1849. Poe wrote *The Cask of Amontillado* and the poem *Annabel Lee* while living there. The humble wood house was built in 1812 as a bunkhouse for farm laborers on the Valentine estate.

Manhattan's Dyckman Farmhouse, the only extant 18th century farmhouse in the borough, is located at 4881 Broadway at 204th Street. The present house dates from about 1785. It was substantially rebuilt after being destroyed by British forces during the Revolution. The farmhouse rests on a hill overlooking Broadway, and is surrounded by a wooded yard and herb garden. The Morris-Jumel Mansion, 1765 Jumel Terrace at West 160th Street, was built about 1765. The sumptuous Federal-Georgian mansion is the oldest surviving house in Manhattan. The house has a colorful past. Built by British landowner, Colonel Roger Morris, as a country retreat, it was used by General George Washington for his headquarters after he retreated to the area following the American defeat in the 1776 Battle of Long Island. Wine merchant Stephen Jumel purchased the 115-acre estate in 1810. His beautiful wife Eliza, an American from a poor Rhode Island family, redecorated the house in the showy First Empire style of Napoleonic France. She was never accepted in New York high society and remained socially isolated at her estate. A year after her husband died in 1832, she married pariah Aaron Burr, though the marriage ended in six months. Burr had been United States vice president during Thomas Jefferson's presidency, and had killed Alexander Hamilton in a duel in 1804. The Irish Stone Cottage Memorial is a humble roofless structure surrounded by potato furrows and stonewalls in memory of the Great Starving in the 1840s. It was transported from County Mayo, Ireland to the north end of Battery Park City at the corner of North End Avenue and Vesey Street opposite Nelson A. Rockefeller Park, in 2002.

Tourism is important to New York City's economy and flatters its residents. Because there is so much to see within the boundaries of the five boroughs, tourism in the city could be a life's work.

CHAPTER 120
Clean Drinking Water

Clean water is often taken for granted. New Yorkers now use approximately 1.7 billion gallons of water each day. Some is used for drinking and cooking, and much is used for showers and baths, laundry, toilets, commercial and industrial purposes. All of it is *potable*, or fit for drinking. Because the reservoirs are generally full and because our water taps runs with strong pressure we usually assume that plentiful drinking water has always been available.

Settlers in the Dutch and early English periods also took abundant, pure water for granted. They could find clean, clear drinking water in the streams, ponds, and small lakes that dotted Manhattan and surrounding communities. Those who lived far enough from the rivers and harbor could dig wells to obtain fresh water, though wells sunk too close to the East and Hudson Rivers or Harbor yielded brackish salt water. The Collect Pond, located in the area from Foley Square to Canal, was the greatest source of clean water in the city's first decades. During the early federal period the city owned and operated at least 250 wells throughout the city.

By the mid-18th century springs and creeks were being covered up as housing development progressed northward. The runoff from tanneries, breweries, and foundries defiled ponds. Waste from farm animals and outhouses polluted Manhattan's ground water and made drinking from wells dangerous. Seepage from cemeteries was also blamed for unsanitary ground water. Diseases from bacteria in the water supply included cholera and typhoid. Wood and coal ash accumulated on roofs and fouled the cistern water collected in barrels under drain spouts.

Small companies and individual teamsters hauled water that they sold by the barrel from wells and springs at the north end of the island. Small ships brought a limited amount of water in casks down the Hudson River from upstate springs. In 1799, the Manhattan Water Company opened a private reservoir fed by a well on Chambers Street. A primitive system of hollowed-out log pipes brought water a few blocks south. There was no effective distribution system beyond customers filling up barrels of water at the reservoir or at the end of the wooden water main.

Fire fighting in a city where most houses were built of wood was another reason the city needed for a dependable water supply. There had been significant fires that destroyed scores of residences in 1776, 1796, 1804, 1811, and 1833. Without water mains, hoses had to be put in the rivers and water laboriously pumped to fight fires.

Foresight as well as necessity propelled the city forward. In 1835 the City Council passed an enabling ordinance concerning a water system. The council sent it as a referendum to the voters who approved the plan and issued bonds to finance the Croton River reservoir and aqueduct project for supplying New York City with water from Westchester County. The project was also a jobs program; many of the workers were newly arrived Irish immigrants. That same year the Great Fire of 1835 destroyed seventeen blocks of the city and engulfed about seven hundred buildings, which underscored the need for urgent action.

Counting the planning, financing, and construction stages the project took seven years, beginning in 1835, and cost $12 million. A thick earthen barrier dammed the Croton River. The barrier was fifty feet high and 270 feet long, which flooded four hundred acres and held 36 million gallons of water. A great municipal celebration with a festive parade featuring marching bands and volunteer fire brigades, a concert, and laudatory speeches was held on October 14, 1842 at the conclusion of the project.

From the Croton Reservoir the water followed gravity south to Manhattan. An underground aqueduct was constructed of stone and brick. Water in the aqueduct ran through two iron pipes as it crossed the Harlem River over High Bridge. In Manhattan it resumed its downhill trajectory in a stone and brick conduit along Amsterdam Avenue until it veered east at 88th Street to make its way to the Receiving Reservoir. There was also an aqueduct bridge over the low spot between 98th and 100th Streets. At the time that area was called the Bloomingdale neighborhood but since the last decade of the 20th century it has been called the Manhattan Valley. The other Manhattan Valley, from 122nd to 135th Streets, was too large to span, so pumps were added at either end to push the water up its south end. (Today a Manhattan Valley Viaduct carries the #1 IRT local trains over the ravine.)

The Croton Reservoir in Westchester and its accompanying aqueduct produced a river of fresh water brought forty miles to Manhattan. The water was collected first at the Receiving Reservoir in what is now Central Park and then by aqueduct again to the Egyptian-style Distributing Reservoir at 42nd Street and 5th Avenue. The Receiving Reservoir was later filled in and is now the site of Central Park's Great Lawn. The above ground Distributing Reservoir was also dismantled and the land is presently the site of the 42nd Street New York Public Library and Bryant Park.

Everyone understood that the water project would ease the growing crisis of clean water; some felt it would begin to provide more cleanliness for an increasingly odoriferous population, and a few temperance leaders dreamt that clean, pure water might replace whiskey and beer as recreational beverages.

Croton water was pumped from the Distributing Reservoir through a 150-mile system of pipes under the streets. But to get water into their houses, homeowners had to pay a hook-up fee and a monthly charge of about one dollar. The city charged a water tax based on the size of the house or building. Two years after completion of the system only about six thousand residences and commercial buildings were connected. Free public spigots were placed throughout the city for the poor, who still needed to carry water to their apartments and were obliged to use backyard outhouses. Rich and middle class New Yorkers quickly connected with the water system and installed water closets, and pipes running to their sinks and bathtubs.

As the city's population grew the water system was greatly expanded especially after the 1898 Consolidation of the Five Boroughs. One by one, areas in the Bronx, Staten Island, Brooklyn, and Queens gave up their individual or town wells and hooked up to the city's water system. Brooklyn had been especially desperate for a reliable source of drinking water and it was one of the factors that caused Brooklynites to favor consolidation.

Only southeastern Queens, served by the Jamaica Water Supply Company, which drew its water from twenty-five wells tapping the Lloyd Aquifer under central Long Island, remained outside the system. In 1996 the affected neighborhoods with 400,000 people joined the city's system though occasionally the wells are activated to augment the water supply in Hollis, St. Albans, Cambria Heights, Springfield Gardens, and Rosedale. A problem has been that chemical analyses have shown the well water polluted with bacteria and dry-cleaning chemicals.

Eleven more reservoirs in the Croton system were opened in 1890. From 1907 to 1917 New York City constructed an expansive water system in the Catskill Mountains on the other side of the Hudson River. Thousands of acres of land were purchased, creeks were dammed and several large reservoirs were built. Water from the Ashokan and Schoharie Reservoirs crosses under the Hudson River in the Catskill Aqueduct as it flows into the lower part of the Croton System and then to the city. The Rondout, Neversink, Papacton, and Cannonsville water flows through the Delaware Aqueduct under the Hudson River to the upper section of the Croton System. Water is also taken from the Delaware River and sometimes even from the Hudson River.

Water coming into our taps is fluoridated, chlorinated, and aerated, but not filtered. The city's generally high quality water is increasingly compromised by sewage run-off into the ground water and various air-borne pollutants. To counter this looming problem a large multi-billion dollar water filtration plant is being constructed underground in Van Cortlandt Park in the Bronx.

Rainfall in the northeast most years is plentiful and the water system created in the last century has served the community well. Conservation, if not immediately critical, is something that needs to be seriously considered. Most of the water used by New Yorkers is unmetered so there is little connection between consumption and cost. Owners or co-op boards in unmetered buildings pay monthly charge based on a formula that takes into account the number of feet a building fronts on the street, amount of stories, and number of sinks, tubs, showers, and toilets. For individual rental units within each unmetered building there is no financial incentive to conserve water. Since the 1980s new buildings or gut-rehabilitations have had to install water meters, but in a city with

800,000 buildings that process could take centuries.

Surprisingly, large water main breaks are not very common, and when they collapse they are replaced with vinyl mains. Small leaks occur with greater frequency but can be readily patched up. At some point the old cast-iron water mains, many from the 19th century, will collapse with greater frequency and the new water mains may not last as long as the cast-iron pipes.

It is universally believed that drinking plenty of water is healthy. In recent years bottled water has come under attack by the New York City Department of Health because it is expensive, has no fluoridation, and is not inspected by the federal government's Food and Drug Administration. Tap water costs less than one percent as much as bottled water. Fluoridation drastically decreases tooth decay, but since the bottled water phenomenon began in the late 1990s dentists have reported significant increases in the number of cavities for young people. The F.D.A. exempts water from inspections because it is neither food nor drug. Bottled water, often with alluring names, attractively packaged, heavily advertised, and originating from seemingly pristine springs in Maine, France, Italy, or even Polynesia may contain high levels of bacteria. At any rate, there is nothing to fear from New York City's tap water and it is a healthy and economical alternative to commercial drinks with or without sugar and flavoring.

Notations:

Remnants of the Brooklyn's Former Water System

Brooklyn is not situated over Long Island's Lloyd Aquifer so water had to be piped in from wells in southeastern Queens and southern Nassau County. Though the water delivery system is gone, the trail can be followed through remaining place names. Water was pumped through a brick aqueduct built along *Conduit Avenue* in 1854 by the Brooklyn Water Works. It went up a hill along *Force Tube Avenue* into *Ridgewood Reservoir* in Highland Park, now a lake along the south side of the Jackie Robinson Parkway. From there the conduit traveled west along the glacial moraine ridge to a distributing reservoir located just below the 200-foot crest of Mount Prospect Park and Playground located between the

Brooklyn Public Library's main branch and the Brooklyn Museum.

Water Sampling Stations

Aluminum painted cast-iron boxes, rectangular, and perched on thick vertical water pipes are found throughout the city between the street and the sidewalk. They stand 4′ 6″ high with raised letters: N.Y.C. Drinking Water Sampling Station on one side and N.Y.C. - D.E.P. on the other. Department of Environmental Protection agents periodically check the purity of water running through underground mains by drawing samples from each box and testing them in the laboratory.

CHAPTER 121
ELECTRICITY & THE ELECTRONIC REVOLUTION

Through the 19th century New Yorkers used gas manufactured from coal, fish oil, whale oil, kerosene, candles, and fireplaces to light their homes. Each had a drawback: flickering light, odor, or danger. Several competing light companies had contracts to operate streetlights on major thoroughfares in the city. By 1880 electricity entered the market. The Consolidated Gas Company of New York, which became the city's largest gas and electricity provider, was formed in 1884. In 1936 it changed its name to Consolidated Edison, commonly called Con Edison or Con Ed. In 2008 the company had approximately $14 billion in annual revenues and $30 billion in assets.

The development of electricity spectacularly changed daily life for all Americans between 1875 and 1925. People whose lives spanned those years saw their whole world changed by electricity. And in future years, household and street lighting, traffic lights, subways, elevators, escalators, water pumps, washers and dryers, refrigerators, freezers, vacuum cleaners, radios, televisions, movies, fans, and air conditioners would dramatically alter everyday life. Only the development of the internal combustion engine came close to equaling the profound changes brought by electricity.

The electrical system had a few breakdowns, especially after almost everyone acquired numerous electrical appliances and gadgets. The three extensive breakdowns were the 15- hour power loss starting on the night of November 9, 1965, the 25-hour failure the evening of July 13, 1977, and the 29-hour outage beginning in the late afternoon of August 14, 2003. Reactions to the blackouts differed from neighborhood to neighborhood, and from person to person. While everyone was inconvenienced, especially the elderly and handicapped, many people enjoyed the day off from work and the sudden return to a semblance of the simple life before electricity. Of course, it was no longer so simple to cook, keep yourself clean, or get around. Some looting accompanied each of the blackouts, but while it was severe in numerous areas in 1977, mild in 1965, it was rare in 2003. Hurricanes and storms periodically cause blackouts as well.

New Yorkers like other Americans had become almost completely dependant on electricity. A blackout meant elevators, escalators, and subways stopped, trapping thousands and stranding millions. Buses, which continued to operate (even with air conditioning), could never make up for the subways, which carry four million riders each day. Water distribution in high-rise buildings ceased as soon as rooftop water tanks were drained. Traffic lights stopped and gas stations were unable to pump gasoline. Gas stoves worked, but they needed to be lit with matches. Many hallways and stairwells in apartment buildings lack windows, so a flashlight was needed to walk up or down the pitch-dark passages.

Sporadic disruptions in the power grid that delivers electrical current occur each summer in a few neighborhoods. They are usually weather-related and can be caused by flooding, lightning strikes, or burned cables unable to handle heavy demand on extremely hot days. But the widespread disruptions called blackouts are rare.

By the 1970s, almost every piece of equipment powered by electricity was termed *electronic*. Electricity produced by power plants and carried through cables and wires provides the energy to power hundreds of machines and gadgets. Electricity to operate a wristwatch or a laptop computer, or start a car engine, can also be stored in batteries. Electrical engineering or electrical appliances are general terms. Electronic refers to devices that use transistors, vacuum tubes, computer chips, or other solid state technology to provide a variety of functionality to the user. All of these devices use electricity as their source of energy. Televisions and computers are usually referred to as electronic.

Computers, powered by electricity, have changed businesses and personal lifestyles. Communications have become instant and worldwide. On the local level it has allowed New York City's businesses, especially financial services and retailing, to operate with greater latitude and speed. To the individual investor or banking customer it has meant that on-line financial services are no further than your personal computer or hand held device. ATMs and instant computerized credit card charging systems allow maximum flexibility in purchases and banking.

The computer has simplified many aspects of everyday life. The EZ Pass system allows cars to pass through highway, bridge, and tunnel tollgates without stopping. Computer systems have made the work of the police easier as well. Cameras photograph and ticket by mail those who run red lights. Packages sent by retailers, FedEx, UPS, or the U.S. Postal Service are automatically tracked. Grocery orders placed by computer are promptly delivered, and bills can be paid on-line.

Airplane, hotel, and rental car reservations can be made online by business travelers or vacationers. Diners can choose a restaurant, peruse its menu, and make reservations with computers. Goods may be purchased, old friends found, and entertainment enjoyed on computers. The dread is usually in passing through a *dead zone* in the Catskills or Adirondacks that effectively cuts the connection between an individual and just about everyone else.

There are negative aspects to a computerized society as well. Some people lost their jobs as computers automated office and factory work. Sitting in front of a screen all day puts strain on eyes, hands, and backs. Enormous sums have been spent to rewire office buildings to handle modern computer systems; ceilings were lowered and floors raised as contractors sought space to install wires and equipment. Many hours are whiled away on computers sending endless e-mails, shopping, or surfing the net. Time that is saved by computers can easily be taken back by the same technology. Many people complain that computers have made it too easy for government, businesses, or other individuals to intrude in our private lives.

In the late 1990s New York City developed a thriving computer industry known as Silicon Alley, named for Silicon Valley, California, home of the first large-scale computer industry. The name was originally applied to new dot-com companies located at first in SoHo and TriBeCa. The term became generalized to include all of NYC as dot-com companies spread out to other neighborhoods. Google's second largest office complex is in Manhattan. Many computer companies serve the city's vibrant financial services, advertising, and mass media industries.

Our growing collective carbon-footprint is partly a result of our enormous appetite for electric power. On a simple level we notice how air-conditioned subway cars idling in stations give off enormous heat, and how the sky is so brightly lit at night that we cannot see the stars. Global warming and climate change results from humans worldwide using enormous electrical power in our quest for an easier life. Few people would turn their backs on the labor saving devices and conveniences brought about by electricity and electronics, but ways need to be found to drastically lessen the negative impact of energy use on the environment.

CHAPTER 122
Shopping in the Age of Advertising and Direct Marketing

Advertising is an immensely important part of everyday life in New York City and a key component of American industrial culture. What does advertising actually do and when did it become important? Advertising brings products to the attention of the public and attempts to persuade people to make purchases. *If you build a better mousetrap, the world will beat a path to your door,* is an old adage that modern advertising negates. Advertisers sell their services to companies by promising them that customers will be much more likely to buy products if they are intermittently reminded of the commodity's desirability.

The importance of advertising came a full century after basic industrialization. It was not until the early 20th century that advertising became a corporate pillar in the developed countries. By the 1920s few companies could hope to succeed without having an active advertising department or hiring an advertising agency to publicize and popularize their products. People do not necessarily *believe* ads, especially the inflated claims often made by their producers, but people are likely to believe the *image* of the advertisement. Branding a company and its products is key to advertising.

Fashion drives many purchases, and can be conceptualized as a conspiracy by apparel manufacturers to increase sales, or as constantly evolving creativity by designers. The *fashion industry,* meaning the designers, models, photographers, and fashion magazines, is a very large industry in New York. In the 1970s New York City emerged as one of the top fashion centers in the world alongside Paris and Milan. Look at a stylish store's carrying bag and it will list its branches invariably located in all the world's fashion centers: New York, Paris, Milan Geneva, Tokyo, Miami Beach, Beverley Hills. Fashion certainly boosts sales by creating needs but it also expresses beauty and style. Some people care about fashion trends and others are oblivious to them, or reject styles and crazes outright.

Newspapers, fliers, and outdoor signs were the first forms of advertising found in New York. After the Civil War, magazines often carried more pages of advertisements than stories. Radio in the 1920s, television in the 1950s, and the Internet in the 1980s became new venues for the dissemination of advertisements.

Buying became easier when consumers were able to make purchases regardless how little cash was in their pockets. The importance of checks was felt in the years immediately after the Second World War when, for the first time, most Americans opened checking accounts. Large New York City advertising agencies such as Doyle Dane Bernbach, Young and Rubicam, Ogilvy and Mather, and Foote, Cone and Belding, helped direct consumer dollars to specific purchases. In the 1970s the importance of credit cards for large on-the-spot or telephone purchases began to seriously compete with the significance of checks. Credit cards for Internet purchases became important in the 1990s. Direct marketing takes place when companies contact potential consumers *directly* by mail, telephone, or computer. So, while advertising has been around for at least three hundred years, only in the past century has it become crucial to the success of a company seeking to sell its goods.

There are excesses related to yearning for items too deeply: shoplifting and compulsive buying. Shoplifting has its own pathology and is seldom related to actual need. The ultimate price paid by a shoplifter can mean arrest, community service, a fine, or jail. Compulsive buying probably affects most people at least occasionally, but the insatiable drive to possess can become an obsession. *Compulsive Shopping Disorder* is what some psychologists call a *soft addiction*. Though not detrimental to physical health it can be ruinous to financial health. Problem shoppers need to seek counseling to curb their disorder. Each year about 1.7 million Americans file for bankruptcy protection from their creditors. Most have debts of less than $30,000, though surprisingly the majority of bankruptcies are not caused by shopping addictions, but because of divorce, illness, or job loss.

The popularity of luxurious goods and the self-indulgent

egos of shoppers have propelled many retailers to financial success. The demarcation line between luxuries and necessities gets erased easily when people pay too much attention to advertisements. Prior to the 1950s there were no televisions, and before the 1980s nail salons and boutique apparel lines were rare, and cell phones did not exist. Now everyone *needs* these products.

Some people depend on obsessive shopping to help them leverage youth and beauty into success and happiness. Naturally the advertisements offer no end of advice on which beauty products to buy. Advertisers are happy to take down the hapless consumer a notch or two. They exploit personal apprehension, inferiority, boredom, and low self-esteem by suggesting that people's hair is ugly, teeth yellow and crooked, body and breath smelly, skin pimply, and clothes unfashionable. Subway ads often carry these messages questioning the adequacy of each individual. The advertisers, of course, have the remedy: buy their products. This is the pursuit of beauty and psychological reassurance through consumption.

Even in the acquisition of food and drink, the amount of *designer water*, take-out food, and prepared food from deli counters, as compared to unprepared grocery store items, has grown enormously in the past three decades. Many of the purchases are made to provide a real or illusory *pick-me-up* for the customer.

Responding to a September 2003 article in *The New York Times* on the excesses of teenage consumerism, a letter-to-the-editor from a woman in the Bronx lamented: *I feel sorry for these poor kids, who are the victims and the prey of screeched media advertising and who, upon looking into a mirror, see not themselves but a glossy composite of a dozen products.* Obviously it is not only teenagers who are swayed by advertisements.

Why do people enjoy shopping? For many there is a need to *get out of the house* and shop for a while. Some anthropologists consider it a primeval hunting and gathering (or *nesting*) instinct that propels people in the quest for commodities. Many keep buying objects to make a statement, establish authority, or improve self-esteem. That has been understood for a long time. Social critic and economist Thorstein Veblen explained what he called *conspicuous consumption* in *The Theory of the Leisure Class* in 1899. He believed people aspired to be rich and emulated the wealthy by purchasing items similar to those bought by the upper class. Put more bluntly, people often buy to show off.

There is a mystique about the power of things and the act of acquiring them. The term *reification* means becoming something through possession of its symbols and for some this may be the reason to shop. People also *window shop* as a social activity and make purchases only if they see exactly the right items at good prices. Often window-shopping is a social outing done with friends or family members. These factors operate in NYC as well as the rest of the country. The scope in the city is larger and has a high-end far more costly than in most cities. Few people judge others too much on their spending habits because consumption has become a private matter generally immune from criticism.

Holidays, especially Christmas, reinforce shopping. Gift giving is both an obligation and a source of satisfaction. By giving gifts the giver feels good and invites reciprocity. The gift-giving aspect of Christmas has become so universal that it is widely practiced in China and Japan where few people are Christians. Stores have tried to commercialize other holidays as well and have had considerable success with Halloween, limited success with Easter, and complete failure with Thanksgiving. Mothers Day and Fathers Day were established by greeting card companies and business enterprises and remain fundamentally commercial. One-day or weekend sales on New Years Day, Presidents Day, Memorial Day, Independence Day, and Labor Day have almost overshadowed the original reasons for celebrating those holidays.

Bazaars, market fairs, and periodic trade fairs have existed for thousands of years. New Yorkers have the opportunity to shop every day of the year and 24 hours per day in a few stores. The act of going to a specific place on a certain day to purchase items, the method of shopping since medieval days, was resurrected in its popular form for food items in the 1980s with the establishment of the Union Square Green Market. Other greenmarkets have opened in Brooklyn, Queens, Staten Island, and the Bronx though they represent a very small portion of the city's retail produce sales.

Small clothing stores, especially those selling a narrow range of items, still exist. There are shoe stores, hat shops, and bridal stores, just as there are butchers, bakers, sweet shops, coffee and teas stores, fish shops, spice stores, and bodegas. Most clothing and food purchases, however, are made in larger rather than smaller stores. Supermarkets, for example, were only introduced in the 1930s but by the 1950s they had become the chief source of kitchen, bathroom, and laundry supplies.

Two of the largest tourist attractions in contemporary United States are the Mall of America located outside Minneapolis, Minnesota, and King of Prussia Mall in eastern Pennsylvania, but much of New York City itself is a shopping paradise without being an artificially constructed mall. Shopping is a complex phenomenon that includes both needs and aspirations. Many New Yorkers make their livings from the shopping habits of others, and everyone in the city is also, one way or another, a shopper.

CHAPTER 123
Rise and Fall and Rise of the Harbor

At first, the harbor was the *sine qua non* of life in the city. It was the reason the site for New Amsterdam was chosen and the essential ingredient for the city's success, or, in Latin, *without which it could not be*. Deep water near the shore, generally ice-free rivers in the winter, and broad spaces to maneuver made the harbor, East River, and Hudson River attractive places to off-load cargo from large ships to small barges out in the water or build docking facilities on the shore.

The Dutch constructed the first dock at Schreyer's Hook in 1648, twenty-three years after the settlement was founded. The second dock was built in 1659 at the foot of Moore Street. Sometime between those years a ditch, built to drain a small swamp, was widened and named *De Heere Gracht* (Gentlemen's Canal). The site of that canal, now Broad Street, ran from Pearl to Beaver Streets. It had a narrow extension from Beaver Street to Exchange Place. Permanent piers were constructed along the East River in the 17th century and along the Hudson River in the 18th century.

Warehouses built next to the wharves held cargo until it could be sold. The first commercial storehouses were along Pearl Street and the little canals that were dug to facilitate off-loading barges from ships anchored away from the shore. (Pearl Street got its name because its surface was covered with crushed oyster shells.) Some of the most common products traded in New Amsterdam were animal furs and skins, Virginia tobacco, whale oil, Caribbean sugar, grain, vegetables, timber, dried fish, and liquor (wine, port, gin, rum, corn whiskey), ceramic tiles, and ceramic smoking-pipes. New York City became an *entrepôt* center as well as a major importer and exporter of goods. An entrepôt is a place where products are stored, bundled, and redistributed to other ports.

While the idea of the waterfront has an idyllic and picturesque mystique, it was the gritty workhorse of the city where ships rushed in to unload cargoes, buy necessary supplies and naval stores, load up again and depart as fast as possible in order to turn a profit. The workday began early and ended late. Perhaps a quarter of the city's dockworkers were slaves. The smell of fish and the residue of the emptied casks of the *necessary tubmen* (outhouse cleaners) filled the air. The bustle of dockside areas included food sellers, grog shops, flophouses, and cheap places of entertainment.

The five counties that were consolidated into New York City in 1898 have a waterfront of 770 miles, half of it at one time devoted to docking facilities. At its height, nine hundred wharves lined the shore. From the first decade of Dutch colonization, settlers in New Netherlands formed small communities in Queens, Brooklyn, Staten Island, and New Jersey. The broad expanse of the Hudson and East Rivers were transversed by sail and oar since it would be more than two centuries before the first bridge was built. Commercial ferry service was inaugurated in 1642 between Manhattan and Brooklyn. It was a rowboat operated by Cornelius Dirchsen. In 1812 Robert Fulton established steam ferry service between Manhattan and Paulus Hook (Jersey City). Popular routes connected various points in Manhattan with Astoria, Long Island City, Greenpoint, Williamsburg, Brooklyn Heights, Bay Ridge, Tompkinsville, Jersey City, and Weehawken. Cornelius Vanderbilt launched his career and took the title *commodore* operating ferry lines between Manhattan and Staten Island. There were a dozen routes by the Civil War and 45 in 1900.

The end of ferry service was at hand following the construction of bridges and tunnels. Subways and automobiles were faster than ferries. The City of New York assumed control of the route between South Ferry and St. George in 1905. When the Verrazano Narrows Bridge opened in 1964 the ferry between Bay Ridge and Staten Island ceased operations. A ferry revival began with fits and starts in the 1970s. Presently New York Waterways, which started limited service in 1986, operates several routes connecting New Jersey, Queens, and Brooklyn with piers in Manhattan.

New York City's harbor handled more volume of goods than any other by 1815. The landmark year for the city's growth, however, was 1825, the year the Erie Canal was opened and the city and its harbor erupted with activity. New York became a trading, manufacturing, shipbuilding, and banking center all at the same time. The population grew from 124,000 in 1820 to 600,000 in 1850. Looking for jobs in a the rapidly expanding local economy people flowed into the city from surrounding rural states, especially upstate New York and New England, and from Europe.

As ships increased in size the main impediment to navigation became the increasingly insufficient natural depth of New York Harbor, which is twenty feet. The Hudson, Raritan, Hackensack, and Passaic Rivers drain into the harbor carrying millions of cubic yards of sediment each year. Methodical dredging began when the Federal Rivers and Harbors Act of 1888 gave the U.S. Army Corps of Engineers authority to maintain all navigable waters in the United States. The Army Corps of Engineers and its subcontractors using enormous backhoe dredges preserve a central channel depth of forty feet in the rivers and fifty feet in the Kill Van Kull channel, which connects Upper New York Bay with Newark Bay, and serves as the main path for ships advancing to the busy New Jersey port facilities.

Another impediment to safe waterway commerce was the notorious Hell Gate Channel in the East River between Ward's Island and Astoria, Queens. Named *Hellegat* (*Gate to Hell*) by the Dutch, it was the cause of many shipwrecks and a constant threat to shipping. In the narrow channel of the strait's swirling crosscurrents was a jagged rock extending from Hallett's Point that was blasted out by the Army Corps of Engineers using fifty-two thousand pounds of explosives.

Sailing vessels lined the piers in the 17th and 18th centuries until steam-powered vessels were practical. Eventually, steamships became so large they needed to turn off their engines soon after they passed the Verrazano Narrows so they would not crash into piers while attempting to dock. Tugboats, powerful small vessels with great versatility, have been used to tow or push larger ships and barges, and guide the freighters and ocean liners to their berths. Columns of barges that were shackled together by wire rope and loaded with dry cement, coal, lumber, and petroleum products slowly pushed through the waterways. In the 19th century barges loaded with iron ore, bricks, grain, sugar, coffee beans, and livestock, mostly hogs and cattle were common sights. Tugboats became crucial to the functioning of the harbor. Companies founded by two Irish-Americans, Michael Moran and James McAllister, have dominated the business through the twentieth century.

In 1946 there were numerous strikes by longshoremen and other waterfront workers who had weathered the Depression and the Second World War with only paltry wage increases and wanted more money. Tugboat operators and laborers went on strike and had a powerful effect on the economy. Not only did tugboats guide large ships through the harbor and rivers, but they also shepherded barges carrying most of the city's coal supply and almost all its fuel oil. After three days President Harry S. Truman declared a national emergency and seized control of the tugboats.

There has been a romantic as well as economic aspect to tugboats. *Little Toot,* from the 1939 Hardie Gramatky children's story and the 1948 Disney short, was the coming of age story of an anthropomorphic tugboat. After a tempestuous childhood, Little Toot grew up and accomplished all the tasks of grown-up tugboats.

New York City became the world's busiest port in 1901 and remained so until shortly after the Second World War. The rivers were a beehive of activity and were lined with docks and warehouses doing brisk business. During the Second World War, the enormous Bush Terminal Warehouses were built on the Brooklyn waterfront between 39th and 66th Streets in the north part of Bay Ridge, now called Sunset Park.

In the first half of the 20th century the main competitor for shipping by sea were the railroads. Cargo was increasingly carried by airplanes, a new form of transportation, and trucks, a method made feasible by the construction of the Interstate Highway System between 1956 and 1991. Shipping declined rapidly after the Second World War and activity along the harbor and rivers withered.

By 1960 the development of steel containers radically changed the waterfront. Trucks and trains brought in the containers and deposited them in yards near the docks. Gantry cranes placed the containers on the ships. Some of the larger vessels hold eight thousand containers. Far fewer longshoremen were needed and the items in the containers were generally safe from inclement weather and pilfering. Mechanization cut down on payrolls and also prevented theft. Shipping had always been prey to pirates, privateers working on government commissions, slave-runners, smugglers avoiding taxes, and thieves. The modern harbor was rife with corruption.

Container terminals thrive in Brooklyn (Red Hook, Bush Terminal, Erie Basin, and Atlantic Basin), Howland Hook in Staten Island, and in New Jersey, but most shipping has moved to other cities. Even during the last twenty years when the Fulton Fish Market was located on the East River, one hundred percent of its fish was flown in to Kennedy Airport or trucked into Manhattan from other port cities.

The Port Authority of New York and New Jersey, originally formed in 1921 as the Port of New York Authority, managed the affairs of the complex shipping industry and expanded its port facilities to New Jersey. The compact signed between New York and New Jersey and the Congressional act approving the Port Authority gave it responsibility to *promote and encourage the movement of domestic and foreign commerce by land and water.* Since then it has constructed the George Washington Bridge, all three bridges connecting Staten Island and New Jersey (Bayonne, Goethals, and Outerbridge Crossing), and the Lincoln and Holland Tunnels. It also operates the Port Authority Bus Terminal and LaGuardia, Kennedy, and Newark Airports. Since the 1930s there has been intermittent talk of building a long tunnel under the harbor to connect Brooklyn and New Jersey.

Though the Port of New York is no longer the busiest port in the world, it is the largest port of the East Coast of the United States and the third largest in the country. More than ninety percent of the freight volume is loaded and unloaded in New Jersey at container ports in Newark, Elizabeth, Bayonne, and Jersey City.

While New York City's harbor was always gritty, it had been active. Once business slumped, the dockside areas in Manhattan, Brooklyn, and Staten Island became ghost-like. Even among the active sites, especially Howland Hook Marine Terminal in Staten Island, there were few longshoremen needed to operate the huge

Gantry cranes that loaded and unloaded giant containers brought in by truck or rail. Few passenger liners were berthed in the Hudson River as travelers preferred to jet to their vacation or business destinations. What business remained gravitated the newer facilities in New Jersey or Brooklyn.

In some areas the waterfront remained desolate for four decades. In the 1980s the long process of waterfront rebirth began. Chicago, Boston, Washington, D.C., and San Antonio had taken the lead in seeing the de-industrialized river, lake, and ocean shorelines as an asset rather than a liability. Mixed-use development included recreational parkland, commercial, and residential facilities. New York City's booming real estate market and population growth made waterfront development increasingly attractive.

There were a few waterfront places in New York City where parks had been placed earlier, most of them during the long tenure of State Parks Commissioner Robert Moses. They included Riverside Park, East River Park (east of the F.D.R. Drive along the Lower East Side and the East Village), Inwood Hill Park, and High Bridge Park.

In the new wave the first to open was the South Street Seaport, a small commercial and entertainment district on the East River, opened in segments between 1983 and 1985. It included a shopping mall on Pier 17, a Seaport Museum on Pier 16, a market building, and two blocks of restored buildings. Piers 59 through 62 on the Hudson River were transformed into the Chelsea Piers Sports and Entertainment Complex. The space between Piers 84 and 86, at West 45th Street along the Hudson, houses the Intrepid Sea, Air, and Space Museum in the Second World War vintage aircraft carrier *Intrepid*. Battery Park City from the Battery up to Chambers Street on the lower Hudson became a thriving residential, commercial, and recreational area. By 2004 the entire West Side along the Hudson River up to West 72nd Street, where Riverside Park begins, had been transformed into a thin ribbon of parkland for walking, jogging, and biking. Some of the piers on the Hudson River are still used by harbor cruise ships.

There are a few vest-pocket parks along the east bank of the East River in Astoria, Hunters Point, Williamsburg, and Red Hook. The nine-acre Empire - Fulton Ferry State Park, was established in

1978 between the Brooklyn and Manhattan Bridges in DUMBO. The Empire - Fulton Ferry State Park now connects with the new 85-acre, 1.3 mile long Brooklyn Bridge Park, reaching south to Atlantic Avenue below and west of Brooklyn Heights.

The future for the city's waterside looks lustrous compared with its bleak period of disuse. But the character has changed in response to a modern world and an increasingly de-industrialized city. Shipping, the industry that kept the waterfront booming for three hundred years, has moved out of the five boroughs and been replaced by demand for recreational facilities and luxury housing with salt air and open, river and harbor views.

Notation:

Tugboat Challenge

Annually, the Sunday before Labor Day a Tugboat Challenge is held in the Hudson River off Pier 86 at West 46th Street starting at noon. About a dozen boats participate, one outfitted to look like Theodore Tugboat, from a PBS children's show. The muscular harbor workhorses, some with four thousand horsepower engines, evoke nostalgia for the former swirl of activity in New York City's harbor. Activities include a parade of tugboats, tugboat race from 79th Street Boat Basin south to the Intrepid Museum Ship, nose-to-nose tugboat pushing contest (similar to an upstate tractor-pull), and for the crew, spinach-eating and line-throwing contests. Prizes are awarded for Best Looking Tug, Vintage Tug, Best Dressed Crew, Best Tattoo, and Best Mascot. Past winners of the Best Mascot title have been: a dog, a rabbit, an iguana, a duck, a ferret, a lobster, and a fish in a bowl.

CHAPTER 124
Immigration Changes Neighborhoods

One constant in New York City's neighborhoods is change. Modification and alteration is usually driven by successive waves of immigration. Once an ethnic, religious, or racial group begins to move into an area, usually where housing is cheap, the old residents begin to move out. The process can take a decade or longer to complete, and then at some later point it generally begins again.

A neighborhood like the Lower East Side was, in succession, Dutch and English, Irish and German, Eastern European Jewish, and then a mixed area of Puerto Rican, Dominican, and Chinese, with a present drive toward mixed, amalgamated middle class gentrification. Crown Heights was, in turn, Irish, Jewish, and West Indian, with a small Hasidic section in its center. Harlem was White Anglo-Saxon Protestant, Jewish, and American black. Crown Heights and Harlem are rapidly gentrifying. The West Village was Dutch, black, Italian, an artistic mix, and now increasingly gentrified by people from the business community. Before Chinatown was Chinese, the area had been Dutch, English, German, and Italian.

Only a few neighborhoods have remained within one ethnic camp for a long period of time: Italians in West Bensonhurst, Rosemont, and Belmont, and Irish in Far Rockaway and Woodlawn. There are several neighborhood that host two or more groups: Greeks, Italians, Arabs, and Latin Americans in Astoria, Koreans and Chinese in Flushing, and the mix of Irish, Scandinavians, Italians, Arabs, and Chinese in Bay Ridge.

Why do people from one background settle together? The word is spread in the home country once some compatriots find adequate housing and employment in an area and spread the word. At any given point in New York City's history its residence patterns have been complex. A given ethnic group usually had several enclaves or neighborhoods across the city. Today there are four Chinatowns: one in downtown Manhattan, another in Flushing, and two in Brooklyn.

Which ethnic groups get the best locations? Those that came first, or had the most money, did better than others with regard to housing. When the housing stock declined, or new and more advantageous possibilities opened elsewhere, the established group gravitated out and a newer, poorer group took its place. Sometimes the group vacated the city. Irish, who composed almost half the city's population in 1860, now comprise only three percent. Most Germans and Italians have also left the city for the suburbs. In 1950, Jews comprised 18 percent of the population; 12 percent in 1970; 8 percent in 2014.

Generally, areas that were initially affluent are still prosperous, though with a new population. Advantageous locations included hills or area with views of the harbor and rivers, or proximity to desirable parks. Brooklyn Heights, Park Slope, Bay Ridge, Fort Greene, St. George, Todt Hill, Little Neck, the Upper East and West Sides of Manhattan, and Riverdale fit the category. Usually such areas are near the business centers, though Little Neck and Riverdale are exceptions. Where the Bowery runs through Chinatown's Werpoes Hill, wealthy Dutch and English built four-story townhouses as country retreats during the 18th century. The sea breezes kept them cool during the hot summers. Tenements and commercial structures eventually replaced all townhouses except one as Germans, Irish, and Chinese in turn settled there. The lone survivor is the Edward Mooney House at 18 Bowery.

Some neighborhoods were never wealthy. Poor Germans first lived in the tenements of the East Village followed by poor Ukrainians, Russians, and Poles, then poor Hispanics. Today there is mixed gentrification, especially in buildings newly constructed or having gone through gut-rehabilitations. East Harlem was home to poor Italians, then Puerto Ricans, then increasingly Mexicans. The housing stock and proximity to public transportation are both important determinants of desirability.

As groups leave an area only remnants are left. In Harlem there are several black Protestant churches that were once synagogues, and in the Jewish enclave of the Lower East Side some of the synagogues were once Baptist and Methodist churches. A handful of stores and one restaurant is all that remains of the large German community in Yorkville in the Upper East Side. Reading the list of names on the First World War Memorial on Van Brunt Street in Red Hook shows that almost every name was Irish, Italian, or Scandinavian. Eventually each group's presence in an area is forgotten. Today, few remember that Swedes, Norwegians, Danes, and Finns once populated Carroll Gardens and Bay Ridge, or that German Jews lived in Washington Heights.

Why have immigrants been so attracted to New York City, especially in the past, but still true to a lesser extent? It was the lower middle class, the skilled workers, and small farmers who made up the bulk of 19th century immigrants. There were some desperately poor, like many of the Irish during the Great Famine, but immigrants needed money enough to get to a point of debarkation in Europe and to buy a one-way ticket to America. Because they came in ships their destinations were limited by geography. Some chose Boston, Philadelphia, Baltimore, or New Orleans, but most bought tickets to New York City. It was a magnet for newcomers because it had a powerful economy and there were neighborhoods of fellow countrymen. It had *caché,* as well, attractive because it was large, modern, and new.

Between 1815 and 1914, sixty million people left Europe. Most fled poverty, but others fled wars and persecution. Settler-states like Argentina, Brazil, Australia, Canada, and the United States received them. More came to the U.S. than to any other country. Between 1800 and 1910 the U.S. population increased from six million to ninety-two million people. Many of the Europeans were migrants, meaning they returned home for one of a variety of reasons. About one-third left after a few years. Some could not make the linguistic, cultural, or socio-economic adjustments. Others missed their families or homelands. There were no phone calls and very few people could afford to travel back and forth. Likelihood of repatriation varied greatly: eighty percent of the people from the Balkans returned home, but only ten percent of the Irish and five percent of the Jews went back. The majority of immigrants stayed and built new lives.

During the 19th century about three million Asians emigrated, mostly from China, Japan, India, and the Philippines. Their destinations included Southeast Asia, East Africa, Central America, Brazil, Peru, Ecuador, and Mexico. Asians who came to United States entered through Hawaii or California. There was a Chinese presence in many Western states drawn by the mining and logging industries. Few Asians came to New York City until after the trans-continental railroad was linked at Promontory, Utah in 1869. Chinatown was only a four-block area bounded along Mott, Doyers, Pell, and the Bowery until after the First World War.

There was considerable opposition to some 19th century immigrants from earlier arrivals. Wealthy New Yorkers who belonged to the Colony Club and the Knickerbocker Club, and who were listed by the *Social Register*, sometimes resented newcomers especially if they came from Eastern or Southern Europe. The Colony Club, founded in 1907 by a group of society ladies that included Mrs. John Jacob Astor and Mrs. Payne Whitney, was an affinity group of *socially distinguished women*, which meant that they had a great deal of money and that their families had lived in the United States for at least two or three generations. The Knickerbocker Club took its name from the term denoting old New York Dutch and English families. The *Social Register*, founded in 1886, was a directory of names and addresses, plus other biographical information, of the powerful and wealthy who form the social elite, though not necessarily the political or business elite. (It exists today in truncated form as a national directory.)

Among the common people, political opposition to immigrants, especially Roman Catholics, Jews, and Eastern Orthodox, found expression in the American Party, or the *Know Nothings*. Organized anti-foreign groups withered by the Great Migration's busiest years, 1895 to 1914, though the sentiment did not wholly disappear. Due to familiarity, more general tolerance of immigrants, and large numbers of Catholics, the Ku Klux Klan never got a foothold in New York City.

Between the very restrictive Immigration Act of 1924, also known as the National Origins Act or the Johnson-Reed Act, and the Immigration and Naturalization Services Act of 1965, also known as the Hart-Celler Act, there was little immigration to the United States. Restrictive laws kept most newcomers out. After

President Lyndon B. Johnson signed the 1965 legislation the sources of immigration changed greatly. Just prior to the First World War eighty-six percent of our immigrants came from Europe, while only three percent came from Latin America and four percent from Asia. By 1900 only thirteen percent came from Europe while forty-three percent entered from Latin America and thirty-nine percent from Asia. Most of the recent Europeans come from poorer Eastern European countries and Russia.

The enormous influx of immigrants to New York City, especially since the 1980s, has dramatically increased the percentage of residents who are foreign-born. The 2000 U. S. Census showed that those born outside the United States amounted to thirty-six percent of the city's population. The numbers vary among the boroughs: forty-six percent in Queens, thirty-eight percent in Brooklyn, twenty-nine percent in the Bronx and Manhattan, and sixteen percent in Staten Island. In 2000, there were 1,511,419 people from Latin America, 686,599 from Asia, 557,492 from Europe, 92,435 from Africa, 18,066 from Canada, and 4,982 from Australia and Oceania living in the city.

The 2000 U.S. Census showed immigration continues at a strong pace. New York State was the destination of the second-largest number of foreign-born people between 1995 and 2000. During that five-year period, 584,000 people entered, though the same period saw 1.2 million immigrants entering California. About forty percent of the newcomers, numbering 205,000, left New York for other states. New York City's share of the immigrant population remains very high. The foreign-born population stood at 2.9 million, which is thirty-six percent of the city's eight million residents. In 2000, the foreign-born population of the entire United States was 31.1, a fifty-one percent increase from 1990. Immigrants are not evenly distributed among the states. Just five states are home to 21.3 million of the 31.1 million immigrants: California, New York, New Jersey, Florida, Texas, and Illinois.

By the late 20th century immigrant day laborers could be seen lining up at certain intersections to wait for employers to offer them jobs. Each day, it is estimated that up to eight thousand immigrants congregate at about fifty places in the city to wait for jobs. Vans pull up, the driver shouts out what he is willing to pay, and those interested step forward. The driver chooses a few and drives off to the site. The employment can range from work in factories, yards, and kitchens. The pay usually ranges from $8 to $10 an hour off the books. Most male day laborers are from Mexico and other countries in Latin America. Others are Asians or Eastern Europeans. Women from Poland, Haiti, and Mexico line up daily at Hooper and Lee Streets in Williamsburg, Brooklyn for $8 an hour jobs cleaning houses in the Hasidic community.

Many of the *shape-up* locations (an old longshoreman term) are in the Outer Boroughs, but they also are found in Chinatown, the Garment District, and Washington Heights. Other common places for those seeking work include Westchester Square and Fordham in the Bronx; Bensonhurst, Sunset Park, and Bushwick in Brooklyn; Port Richmond and Tompkinsville in Staten Island; and Astoria, Jackson Heights, Woodside, Forest Hills, and Flushing in Queens.

Workers are sometimes abused and occasionally are short-changed or completely stiffed on wage payment. Complaints to government authorities are not forthcoming because most day laborers in the *shape-ups* are illegal immigrants. Some immigrant advocacy groups and church organizations monitor the system.

The New York Sun's headline on August 25, 2003 read: *Bloomberg Supports Amnesty for Illegals.* Mayor Michael Bloomberg was quoted during an appearance at the annual Pakastani Independence Day Parade as calling for a blanket amnesty to everyone presently in the United States. *I've always felt that the solution to the fact that we have a large number of undocumented people living in New York City and living in the country is to make them all citizens and then get control of the borders. We're not going to deport them, and leaving them in this limbo state isn't good for them and it isn't good for society.* In fact, following the September 11, 2001 attacks on the World Trade Center the Justice Department did deport several hundred illegal aliens mostly from the Middle East.

In 2006 the United States Census Bureau released data from their 2005 American Community Survey that showed a continuation of fast-paced immigration from Mexico and Latin America, China, and India. More immigrants came to the United States from Mexico than from any other country. Immigration from Europe dropped sharply. Changes in American demographics were mirrored in New York City.

The same report also revealed that New Yorkers have become increasingly well educated. Thirty-two percent have college degrees though it varies greatly from borough to borough with Manhattan boasting a fifty-seven percent college education rate, Queens twenty-eight percent, Brooklyn and Staten Island twenty-seven percent each, and the Bronx sixteen percent. The city has been attracting well-educated, affluent people from across the United States and abroad. New York City shares this distinction with San Francisco and Seattle and a number of smaller college towns.

The present surge of immigration, larger and more sustained than the German and Irish wave in the early 19th century or the large immigration from Eastern and Southern Europe at the turn of the last century, has once again altered the relative numbers of New Yorkers. It has also pushed the population to 8,400,000 in 2014, its highest point ever. The population of the U.S., which was 76,000,000 in 1900 and 151,000,000 in 1950, reached 300,000,000 in 2006 and is projected by the U.S. Census Bureau to arrive at 400,000,000 in 2040.

With so many immigrants arriving in New York City each year, how does the population remain relatively stable? New Yorkers, like most Americans, move frequently. As local people leave the city for greener pastures, usually in the suburbs, the South, the Southwest, or the West Coast, newcomers from other states or countries take their places. The process never stops.

New York City has been changed continually since shortly after the American Revolution by successive waves of immigration and spurts of economic growth. Those changes have been accelerated at the close of the 20th and beginning of the 21st centuries. Sixty percent of New Yorkers in 2005 were immigrants and children of immigrants. In the suburbs it was twenty percent, an all-time high.

As people move into the city others leave. From 2000 to 2005 the number of whites in New York City fell by 100,000, but increased in Manhattan and Brooklyn. The black population also fell by 100,000 but in all five boroughs. The Hispanic population increased by 100,000 and the Asian population rose by 136,000.

Each year the New York City Department of Transportation publishes a list of days when alternate-side of the street cleaning parking rules are suspended. That means automobile-owners do not need to move their cars. Originally intended to help observant Jews on holidays when Jewish law prohibits operating machinery, it has come to include a wide array of Christian, Muslim, and Hindu holidays --- religions where there are no prohibitions about driving cars. So alongside Passover (four days), Rosh Ha-Shanah (2 days), and Yom Kippur, are Ash Wednesday, Eastern Orthodox Holy Thursday and Good Friday, All Saints' Day, Solemnity of the Ascension, Feast of the Assumption, Feast of the Immaculate Conception, Asian Lunar New Year, Diwali, Id al-Adha (3 days), and Id al-Fitr (3 days). There are thirty-seven holidays blocking out forty-three days of traffic rules. No one objects. Immigration and pluralism are accepted facts of life in New York City.

CHAPTER 125
Architecture of the 20th Century

Most buildings in New York City were built in the 20th century, so much of the architecture we see is less than one hundred years old. Aging buildings are demolished and new ones built. The goal is always the same: to squeeze in more office or residential space into the fixed dimensions of a lot.

Great spatial changes occurred in 20th century New York City. First, in 1898 the city was expanded to encompass five counties. (No other American city takes up more than one county.) Second, the relatively prosperous period after the First World War, the Roaring 20s, saw hundreds of thousands move from cramped apartments in crowded Manhattan neighborhoods to fill up the outer boroughs. The Bronx and Brooklyn filled first, then Queens, and finally, after completion of the Verrazano Narrows Bridge (1964), Staten Island was packed with houses and people. By the end of the century the five boroughs had truly become one enormous city.

Grand avenues like Eastern Parkway and Ocean Parkway in Brooklyn and the Grand Concourse in the Bronx drew people out of Manhattan with large, spacious apartments on tree-lined boulevards. Popular apartment designs included Art Deco, Egyptian Revival, and Tutor Revival. The six-story buildings had elevators. Lobbies were the outer manifestation of luxury. They were large marble-paneled spaces with tiled floors that sometimes included overstuffed chairs. (Tenements had no lobbies and no elevators, just narrow hallways and stairwells.)

Individual houses or two-family houses appeared everywhere in the outer boroughs as the quest for more space became an important feature of 20th century housing. Though not always obtained, a premium was put on providing a separate bedroom for each child.

The 20th century had many construction fads, especially in commercial buildings, but housing for families was truly eclectic.

Every form of architecture was used and often mingled together: Colonial Revival (Dutch, English, French), Neo-Classical, Italian Renaissance, Romanesque Revival, Gothic Revival, Tudor Revival, Beaux Arts, Spanish Mission, Prairie, Bungalow, Cape Cod, Ranch House, and Split-level House. When several housing styles were placed randomly on one block the look was odd, but as the trees and shrubs grew, the stylistic discordance was softened.

In the first half of the century, office buildings were generally built of granite like the Woolworth Building (1913), Chrysler Building (1930), Empire State Building (1931), and Rockefeller Center (1940). The Bauhaus style, often called the International style, became dominant for office buildings after the Second World War. The principles of the style pioneered by German architect Walter Gropius in the 1920s were dominated by the quest for open space, natural light, sleek lines, and inexpensive, simple building materials: glass, steel, concrete. The construction materials were inexpensive and could be partially prefabricated. Glass, the most eye-catching building material of the International style, was made of melted sand. The inexpensive nature and feeling of modernism caught on in New York City and all around the world.

Whimsical buildings like Frank Lloyd Wright's circular Guggenheim Museum (1959) on 5th Avenue were a welcome change. But most International style buildings were predictable. What had started as innovative became dull. Three new structures set the post-war pace: the Secretariat Building of the United Nations (1950) at Turtle Bay, and the 24-story *glass cage* Lever House (1952) and the Seagram Building (1958), both on Park Avenue. They offered a taste of what was to come in the next thirty years. Canyons of glass and steel (6th Avenue from 42nd Street to 59th Street) and clusters of glass and steel (Financial District) began to appear boring. The ultimate in overdone International style was the monstrous Twin Towers of the World Trade Center finished in 1976. While basic International style principles continued to be used, they were sometimes softened by color, and the angles were often rounded or given surprising shapes to avoid the *big glass box* look.

Well known examples were Citicorp Center (1978) with its sharply sloping roof, the gently sloping slightly concave 9 West 57th Street Building (1983), SONY Building (originally AT&T headquarters, 1984) with a roof pediment like an 18th century Chippendale chair back or cabinet top, the red, brown, and pink 885 Third Avenue Building (1986) dubbed the *Lipstick Building* because of its rounded shape and telescoping tiers, Zeckendorf Towers (1987) at Union Square, World Financial Center in Battery Park City (1988), Citicorp Office Building in Long Island City, Queens (1989), and the Condé Nast Building (1999) and Reuters Building (2001) both at Times Square. The change in basic contour, color, and roof style was often called Post-Modern.

Preservation became a conscious goal in the late 20th century. New York never stops its building-demolishing-rebuilding cycle as developers compete to pack more space onto a small lot. Poorly constructed buildings deserve to be torn down and commonplace structures are not missed. But some jewels have been lost in the process; the destruction of Ebbetts Field (1960) and Pennsylvania Station (1963) were monumental acts of sanctioned vandalism.

Most often the preservation movement has been focused on preserving or restoring old houses and churches such as the Pieter Claesen Wyckoff House (1652), Dyckman House (1661), John Bowne House (1661), Friends (Quaker) Meeting House (1694), Van Cortlandt House (1749), Lefferts Homestead (1783), Kingsland Homestead (1785), St. Paul's Chapel (1764-1796), and the John Street Methodist Church (1841).

More recently there has been an appreciation for preserving modern buildings, even ugly structures, so monuments to all architectural styles survive. Examples of buildings in this category are the Lever House on Park Avenue, Pan Am Building (known now as Met Life Building) on top of Grand Central Station and Holy Trinity Chapel (Roman Catholic Center) at New York University.

Some people tried unsuccessfully to preserve Two Columbus Circle (which has housed the New York City Department of Cultural Affairs and the Gallery of Modern Art), and the Trans World Airlines Flight Center at Kennedy Airport, both modern structures. They were remodeled in the early 21st century. The TWA Flight Center was a terminal built to look like a bird. Its dynamic, sculpted form of molded concrete and glass curves blended walls and ceiling in a form suggesting flight. Air travel was new when it was built and it was an appealing icon of aviation. The main problem was that it became obsolete. It needed to be enlarged so it could move thousands of people a day to and from their gates.

With modern buildings the guiding principle was the triumph of lines. The buildings were free of the burden of history and could concentrate on technology: modern facilities for living and working.